Adobe Photoshop CS4
for Photographers

Adobe Photoshop CS4 for Photographers

A professional image editor's guide to the creative use of Photoshop for the Macintosh and PC

Martin Evening

ELSEVIER

AMSTERDAM • BOSTON • HEIDELBERG • LONDON • NEW YORK • OXFORD
PARIS • SAN DIEGO • SAN FRANCISCO • SINGAPORE • SYDNEY • TOKYO
Focal Press is an imprint of Elsevier

Focal
Press

Focal Press is an imprint of Elsevier
Linacre House, Jordan Hill, Oxford OX2 8DP, UK
30 Corporate Drive, Suite 400, Burlington, MA 01803, USA

First published 2009

British Library Cataloguing in Publication Data
Evening Martin
    Adobe Photoshop CS4 for Photographers : learn photoshop the Martin Evening way!
    1. Adobe Photoshop   2. Photography – Digital techniques   I. Title
    775'.02856686

Library of Congress Control Number: 2008938834

ISBN: 978-0-240-52125-1

For information on all Focal Press publications visit our website at:
 www.focalpress.com

Trademarks/Registered Trademarks
Brand names mentioned in this book are protected by their respective trademarks and
are acknowledged

Printed and bound in Canada

09 10 11 12 12 11 10 9 8 7 6 5 4 3 2 1

Working together to grow
libraries in developing countries

www.elsevier.com | www.bookaid.org | www.sabre.org

ELSEVIER   BOOK AID
            International   Sabre Foundation

Chapter 1: Photoshop Fundamentals   1

Chapter 2: Configuring Photoshop   79

Chapter 4: Sharpening and Noise Reduction   231

Contents

Chapter 9: Layers, Selections and Masking   415

Chapter 10: Essential Filters for Photo Editing   487

Chapter 11: Image Management   507

Chapter 12: Color Management   561

Chapter 13: Print Output   611

Chapter 14: Output for the Web   629

Chapter 15: Automating Photoshop   645

Index   660

Foreword

by John Nack

Is Photoshop for photographers? And do photographers really need Photoshop? A couple of years ago, these questions might have seemed a little silly. No professional photographer would seriously consider foregoing Photoshop's image-manipulation power, whether to apply subtle color corrections or to make radical image alterations. Now, however, new workflow-centric applications like Adobe Lightroom have come into the market. With these tools focusing purely on photographers' needs, how relevant does Photoshop remain?

To me the situation is a bit like what I've found with photography: yes, you can start out and sometimes get by with a limited set of equipment but, the more you know, the more you value specialized tools that can make the difference in critical scenarios. It's quite true that many photographers will spend more time in Bridge/Camera Raw, Lightroom, and the like, and less in Photoshop proper but, for many demanding shots, only the full power of Photoshop will do.

Martin is in a unique position to explain the new balance of power – when to use a raw converter/image manager, and when to use the imaging tools in Photoshop itself. Throughout his long and intimate relationship with both the Photoshop and Lightroom development teams, he's helped shape today's digital imaging world.

You know the old cliché 'Those who can't do, teach,' right? No one says that about Martin Evening. He earns his knowledge the hard way, making a living as a highly regarded fashion photographer. His workflow advice comes not from theory, but from the practice of keeping a business in motion.

I came to work on Photoshop only after logging many years earning a living with the product day in and day out, and I greatly value the insights that come only from those who really practice their craft. Martin is one of the best examples of those teacher-practitioners. I could not have been more honored than to have stood beside him as we were both inducted into the Photoshop Hall of Fame in 2008.

When it's all said and done, tools – whether hardware or software – are just tools, and it's your ideas and images that matter. You'll find that Martin knows both sides of the equation and never lets the techniques distract from the vision. I think you'll find his perspective and experience invaluable.

John Nack
Principal Product Manager, Adobe Photoshop
Adobe Systems

Introduction

When I first started using Photoshop, it was a much simpler program to get to grips with compared to what we see today. Adobe Photoshop CS4 has evolved to provide photographers with all the tools they need, and my aim is to provide you with a working photographer's perspective of what Photoshop CS4 can do and how you can make the most effective use of the program.

One of the biggest problems writing a book about Photoshop is that while new features are added, Adobe rarely remove anything from the program. Hence, Photoshop has got bigger and more detailed over the last 12 years I have been writing this series of books. When it has come to updating each edition, this has left the question, should I make the book bigger, or should I take things out? For this particular edition I decided to have a complete rethink about the way the book's subject matter was tackled. This edition of the book is the same size as the previous versions, but it is now completely focused on all the essential information you need to know about Photoshop, Camera Raw and Bridge, plus all that's new in Photoshop CS4 for photographers. Consequently, if you have bought a previous edition of this book, you'll find a lot of the content here is new and goes into greater detail than before on subjects such as Camera Raw editing and high dynamic range imaging.

As a result of this editing process, a lot of the older favorite techniques had to be removed. To make up for this I decided to get together with Jeff Schewe to co-write a new Photoshop for Photographers book, which we are calling *The Ultimate Workshop*. This is a book in which Jeff and I hammer out a series of techniques designed for professional Photoshop users which, as the title suggests, will be like attending the ultimate training workshop on Photoshop techniques.

One of the main selling points of this book is that I work mostly as a professional studio photographer, running a busy photographic business close to the heart of London. On the days when I am not shooting or working on a production I use that time to study Photoshop, write articles and present seminars, which may be one of the reasons why this series of Photoshop books has become so successful. This is because like you, I too had to learn all this stuff from scratch! I make no grandiose claims to have written the best book ever on the subject. I simply write from personal experience and aim to offer a detailed manual on the subject of digital photography and Photoshop, written by somebody who has first-hand professional experience and a close involvement with the people in San Jose who make the Adobe Photoshop program.

This book was initially aimed at intermediate to advanced users, but it soon became apparent that all sorts of people were enjoying the book. Over the years I have adapted the content to satisfy the requirements of a broad readership. I still provide good solid professional-level advice, but at the same time I try not to assume too much prior knowledge and ensure that everything is explained as clearly and simply as possible.

This latest edition has been thoroughly revised to ensure that you are provided with an updated account of everything that is new in Photoshop CS4. As the program has evolved over the years, the book content has had to undergo regular changes in order to reflect the new ways of working. The techniques shown here are based on the knowledge I have gained from working alongside some of the greatest Photoshop experts in the industry – people such as Jeff Schewe and the late Bruce Fraser, who I have regarded as true Photoshop masters. I have drawn on this information to provide you with the latest thinking on how to use Photoshop to its full advantage. So rather than me just tell you 'this is what you should do, because that's the way I do it', you will find frequent references to how the program works. These discussions are often accompanied by diagrams that will help improve your understanding of the Photoshop CS4 program.

We have recently seen the greatest changes ever in the history of photography and, for many photographers, it has been a real challenge to keep up with all the latest developments. My philosophy is to find out which tools in Photoshop allow you to work as efficiently and as non-destructively as possible, plus take into account the changing factors that require us to use Photoshop differently. Hopefully, the key points you will learn from this book are that Camera Raw is the ideal, initial editing environment for all raw (and sometimes non-raw) images. Once an image has been optimized in Camera Raw you can use Photoshop to carry out fine-tuned corrections, or more complex retouching. Although there are lots of ways to approach using Photoshop, you'll generally find with Photoshop CS4 that the best tools for the job are often the simplest to use! There is much to cover in this book, but you should find that the chapter order plus the accompanying content on the DVD will help enlighten you to the joys of working with Photoshop CS4.

Book and DVD contents

The DVD contents are presented in the form of a Photoshop CS4 Help Guide. Load the DVD into your computer and for improved performance copy the contents across to your hard drive. Double-click on the start.htm file to launch the DVD contents into your web browser. The Photoshop Help Guide contains movie versions of many of the step-by-step techniques shown in this book, is designed to run on Macintosh and PC systems, and only requires you to install Flash and QuickTime on your computer in order to view them. If you should experience any problems running the disk, please always refer to the FAQ section on the disk or on the website for guidance on how to configure your computer for optimum viewing. Educators may also be interested to know that the images used in the movies are provided on the DVD, along with the relevant extracts from the book in PDF format.

About the images on the disk

You can access most of the images shown in this book, but not all of them. The reason for this is that some of the photographs, especially where models are featured in the picture, do have restricted usages that do not permit me to simply give them away. And some of the other images were kindly released by fellow photographers for use in the book only. So although there are quite a few pictures you can play with, you won't be able to access every photograph you see in this book.

Book website

There is also a website set up to promote this book where you can find many active links (including those mentioned in the book) and Help pages should you encounter problems running the movies from the DVD:

www.photoshopforphotographers.com

Rod Wynne-Powell

Over the several editions of this series of books, I have been able to elicit the technical help of Rod Wynne-Powell to check the accuracy of what I have written, and double-check, and sometimes modify, the techniques I have discussed. His enthusiasm and dedication to this task continues to be invaluable – if I am puzzled by some aspect and ask his advice, he will diligently seek out the answer, either through his contacts or via the Web, and provide me with a comprehensive reply accompanied by his own evaluation.

I put his name forward to my publishers, Focal Press, when they were considering their forthcoming Workflow series, and he was accepted, so he is now to join their team of authors by writing about the other aspect of many photographers' lives – the operating system that underpins the Mac user's platform for Photoshop, Bridge and Lightroom – Mac OS X. The book, *Mac OS X for Photographers* was published in 2008 and I wish it every success.

Rod offers training, consultancy and retouching under the banner 'SOLUTIONS photographic' and is able to boast having trained photographers in both France and Italy as well as those from all over the UK, mostly on a one-to-one basis. Rod can be contacted via email, Skype and telephone:

Email: rod@solphoto.co.uk
Skype: rodders63
T: +44(0)1582-725065
M: +44(0)7836-248126

Acknowledgments

I must first thank Andrea Bruno of Adobe Europe for her suggestion that I write a book about Photoshop aimed at photographers and thank you to all at Focal Press: David Albon, Ben Denne and Hayley Salter. None of this would have got started without the founding work of Adam Woolfitt and Mike Laye who helped form the Digital Imaging Group (DIG) forum for UK digital photographers. The production of this book was done with the help of Rod Wynne-Powell, who reviewed the final manuscript and provided help with technical advice and assistance, David Field who provided PC tech edit advice, Matt Wreford who helped with the separations, Soo Hamilton for the proof reading and Jason Simmons, who came up with the book layout template. I must give a special mention to fellow Photoshop alpha tester Jeff Schewe for all his guidance and help over the years (and wife Becky), not to mention the other members of the 'pixel mafia': Katrin Eismann, Seth Resnick, Andrew Rodney and Bruce Fraser, who sadly passed away in December of 2006.

Thank you also to the following clients, companies and individuals: Adobe Systems Inc., Neil Barstow, Russell Brown, Steve Caplin, Ansell Cizic, Kevin Connor, Harriet Cotterill, Chris Cox, Eylure, Claire Garner, Greg Gorman, Mark Hamburg, Peter Hince, Thomas Holm, Ed Horwich, Carol Johnson, Julieanne Kost, Peter Krogh, John Nack, Imacon, Thomas Knoll, Bob Marchant, Marc Pawliger, Pixl, Herb Paynter, Red or Dead Ltd, Eric Richmond, Addy Roff, Martin Soan, Tresemme, Gwyn Weisberg, Russell Williams, *What Digital Camera* and X-Rite. Thank you to the models, Courtney Hooper, Natasha De Ruyter and Alex Kordek, who featured in this book, plus my assistant Harry Dutton (who also stars as a model in a few shots!).

Lastly, thanks to all my friends and family, my wife Camilla who has been so supportive over the last year, and especially my late mother for all her love and encouragement.

Martin Evening

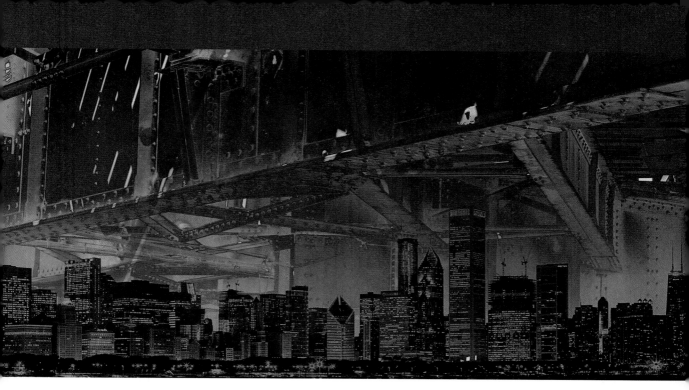

Chapter 1

Photoshop Fundamentals

et's begin by looking at some of the essentials of working with Photoshop, such as how to install the program, the Photoshop interface and what all the different tools and panels do, as well as introducing the Bridge and Camera Raw interfaces.

There have been a lot of big changes made to the Photoshop CS4 interface, so even if you are already quite familiar with how Photoshop works, or have read previous editions of this book, I would still recommend you begin reading here to learn about some of the things that are new in this latest version of Photoshop. You can also use this chapter as a reference as you work through the remainder of the book.

An overview of the book chapters

Chapter 1: Photoshop fundamentals

The chapter you are reading now introduces the Photoshop interface and its main features such as the tools, panels, layers, and Bridge image browsing. This is a general introduction to how Photoshop works.

Chapter 2: Configuring Photoshop

This provides a guide to all the Photoshop preference panels, plus how to optimize your computer system, how much RAM is required, and what sort of accessories you need.

Chapter 3: Camera Raw image processing

If you shoot digitally, you will most likely want to shoot in raw mode and this chapter is essential reading on how to prepare digital raw images before opening them in Photoshop and includes information on all the new Camera Raw 5.0 features.

Chapter 4: Sharpening and noise reduction

This chapter is all about how to use the sharpening sliders in Camera Raw to apply capture sharpening to your photographs, before they are edited in Photoshop, plus how to reduce noise.

Chapter 5: Image editing essentials

This is where we start looking at the general Photoshop image editing controls such as how to adjust the levels to improve the tone contrast, and how to adjust the colors. The foundation skills taught in this chapter are all essential learning whether or not you process your photos in Camera Raw.

Chapter 6: Black and white

This chapter shows you how to create optimum black and white conversions from a color original, how to produce the 'cross process' look, fake an infrared effect as well as how to produce other traditional darkroom techniques.

Chapter 7: Extending the dynamic range

This is a new chapter, in which I discuss high dynamic range image editing and other techniques for extending the dynamic range of images that have been captured digitally.

Chapter 8: Image retouching

This chapter shows various retouching techniques and strategies for removing blemishes and larger objects from a picture, as well as how to retouch in perspective using Vanishing Point.

Chapter 9: Layers, selections and masking

This chapter focuses on the use of channels, layers, layer masks and layer styles and how these can be used to seamlessly mask different image elements.

Chapter 10: Essential filters for Photoshop editing

This chapter explores some of the filters in Photoshop that are useful for photographic retouching work, such as 'Liquify'.

Chapter 11: Image management

These days, photographers can end up with hundreds of images to process from a day's shoot. Good image management can help you keep track of your work easily and quickly, and help avoid problems when hardware devices fail.

Chapter 12: Color management

Everyone needs to know a little about color management. It should be a simple matter of calibrating the monitor and selecting the correct color settings in Photoshop, but somehow life is never that easy! This chapter provides an intermediate level guide to managing colors successfully.

Chapter 13: Print output

This chapter follows on from the previous one in showing you how to make a perfect print that matches what you see on the screen and the importance of tailored output sharpening.

Chapter 14: Output for the Web

Alternatively, you may be interested in outputting your images for screen display. This chapter covers preparing images for email or websites.

Chapter 15: Automating Photoshop

This chapter shows you some of the ways you can work more efficiently in Photoshop and simplify the handling of repetitive tasks.

Task-based workflow

In all the talk about what's new in CS4 you will most probably hear the term task-based workflow, which partly refers to the way the new Photoshop interface can be customized to suit the different ways individual users work with Photoshop, as well as offering easier and more direct access to image adjustments and adjustment preset settings. For example, if you are mainly interested in doing video editing work, you can select the Video workspace setting, which will provide access to those panels that are most important for video editing work. For general photographic retouching work you are better off selecting the Essentials or Color and Tone workspaces as these layouts display the more commonly used panels for Photoshop image editing. The other interesting new feature is the way both the Mac and PC layouts are now contained in an application window giving the added benefit of making the workspace layout choices more robust. This is because as you resize the application window, the panel positions will adjust to suit. Adjustment layers are now applied via a new Adjustments panel. This makes the adjustment editing process more direct. You can select an image adjustment to work with and quickly switch back and forth between editing the adjustment settings and working on the image. You also have direct access to all the different adjustment presets that ship with Photoshop and can quickly experiment to see what happens when you choose different adjustment effects.

How to use this book

In writing this book I have tried not to assume too much prior Photoshop knowledge and have structured the chapter order so that it follows a typical Photoshop workflow, starting with an introduction to the Photoshop interface through to image management and print output. This is in many ways a personal guide and one that highlights the areas of Photoshop that I find most interesting, or those which I feel would be of interest to other photographers. It is not a complete comprehensive guide about everything that's in the program, but it is one of the most thorough and established books out there – especially designed for photographers.

The guiding philosophy throughout this book is to offer you the most up-to-date advice on how to use the photographic tools in Photoshop. Over the years I have been writing this series Photoshop has changed quite a lot, as has digital camera technology. Therefore with each new edition I have had to re-evaluate what each new version of the program has to offer and as a result revised the techniques and workflow steps described in the book.

It is inevitable in a book like this for the author to put forward their own personal views on how you should or shouldn't do things. In some ways I am perhaps just as guilty of doing this myself, but I would point out that the advice I give is based on over 15 years of experience in which I have worked intensively with the Photoshop engineering team at all stages of the program's development, as well as working closely with some of the leading Photoshop gurus such as Katrin Eismann, the late Bruce Fraser, Andrew Rodney, Seth Resnick, Jeff Schewe and Rod Wynne-Powell. The techniques described here have therefore evolved over time and the methods taught in this book reflect the most current expert thinking about Photoshop. What you will read in this book is a condensed version of that accumulated knowledge and for the benefit of my readers I have aimed to keep the explanations simple and relevant to the kind of work most photographers do.

My approach to digital imaging is to preserve all of the information that was captured in the original and (wherever possible) work non-destructively, so that my options are always kept open. In this book I recommend that you shoot in raw mode where it is appropriate to do so and make full use of the tools in Camera Raw to prepare an image, before you open it up in Photoshop. For example, the sharpening tools added to Camera Raw mean that this is the only place where you should need to pre-sharpen an image. I recommend using the wide gamut ProPhoto RGB work space because this can help preserve more color detail through to print and I also suggest editing your images in 16-bits per channel so that you can preserve the maximum number of levels of tone information and keep your options open for whatever you might want to do to an image in the future. Later in this book I will also be showing you how to use adjustment layers and Smart Object layers to keep your pixel image edits reversible.

This particular version of the book has been re-edited to put most of its emphasis on the essential Photoshop tools as well as what's new in Photoshop CS4 that is of interest to photographers. There is also a *Photoshop for Photographers Help Guide* on the DVD that accompanies the book, where you will find a lot of extra material with descriptions of all the tools and Photoshop panels. Just load the DVD into your computer, or for improved performance copy the contents across to your hard drive. Then double-click on the start.htm file to launch the DVD contents into your web browser.

In Figure 1.1 you can see how the Help Guide should appear in a web browser window. From there you can then visit the various sub-sections. For example, in the Tool Panels section you can click on a tool icon to be taken to a page that has a complete, illustrated description of what each tool does. In the other sections, you can find complete descriptions of the Photoshop panels, image adjustments and a guide to all the keyboard shortcuts in Photoshop. Plus of course, there are also the movie tutorials, which have always been a popular feature.

Macintosh and PC keys

Throughout this book I refer to the keyboard modifier keys used on the Macintosh and PC computers. Where the keys used are the same, such as the *Shift* key, these will be printed in gray. Where the keys used are different on each system, I use the Macintosh key first in magenta followed by the PC equivalent in blue. So, if the shortcut used is Command (Mac) and Control (PC) this appears abbreviated in the text as: ⌘ and *ctrl*. Other keys will be explained as you progress through this and subsequent chapters.

Chapters on the DVD

Also on the DVD is a whole chapter on digital capture and how digital cameras work, a summary of Photoshop, Bridge and Camera Raw shortcuts, a chapter on sharpening scanned images in Photoshop, plus a copy of Chapter 12 on color management. These are available as PDF documents which can be read and printed out using Adobe Acrobat or Adobe Reader programs.

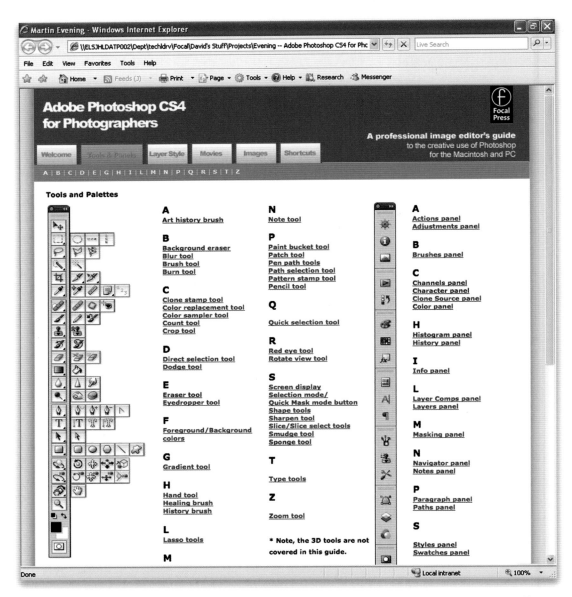

Figure 1.1 The *Photoshop for Photographers Help Guide* can be accessed from the Help Guide on the DVD and launched via a web browser. Click to select a topic such as the Tools and Panels section shown here and navigate to the subject of interest to learn more about a particular tool or panel.

Photoshop installation

Installing Photoshop is as easy as installing any other application on your computer. But make sure that your web browser and any other Adobe programs are closed prior to running the installation setup. After completing your user information and serial number details, you will be faced with a Product Activation option. This has to be selected in order to activate Photoshop. And the reason it is there is to limit unauthorized distribution of the program. The standard license entitles you to use Photoshop on up to two computers, but not both at once.

Adobe Photoshop activation

You can load Photoshop on any number of computers, but only a maximum of two installations can be active at any one time. To use any two different machines will involve deactivation and reactivation only, but not a complete install.

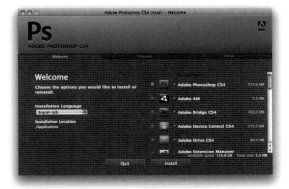

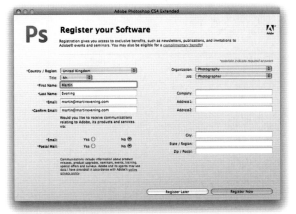

Figure 1.2 The Photoshop installer procedure will be more or less identical on both Mac and PC systems. As you complete the installation process and are about to start using the program you will be requested to complete a registration form like the one shown here.

Macintosh default workspace

The Macintosh default workspace setting uses a classic layout where the panels are floating on the desktop. If you go to the Window menu and select 'Application Frame', you can switch to the Application window layout shown in Figure 1.3.

The Photoshop interface

The new Photoshop CS4 interface allows you to work with the Photoshop program as an application window on both the Mac and PC platforms (Figures 1.3 and 1.4). This default arrangement is more in keeping with the interface conventions for Windows and is also more similar to the interface used by Lightroom. The Photoshop panels are held in placement zones with the Tools panel on the left, the Options bar and Application bar running across the top and other panels arranged on the right-hand side, where they can be docked in various ways to economize on the amount of screen space used yet still remain easily accessible.

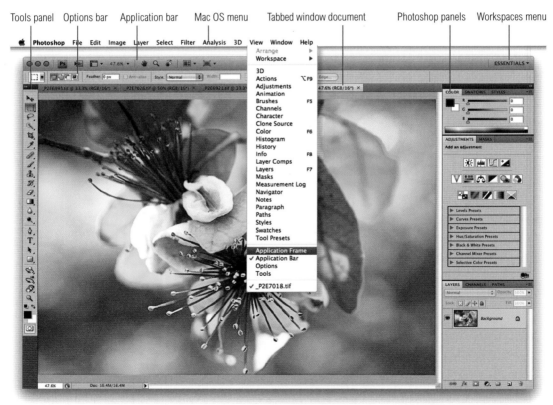

Figure 1.3 The new Photoshop CS4 Application window program workspace for the Mac OS showing the Window menu that allows you to switch between the classic mode workspace and Application Frame workspace shown here.

Tools panel   Options bar   Application bar & Windows OS menu   Tabbed window document   Photoshop panels   Workspace settings

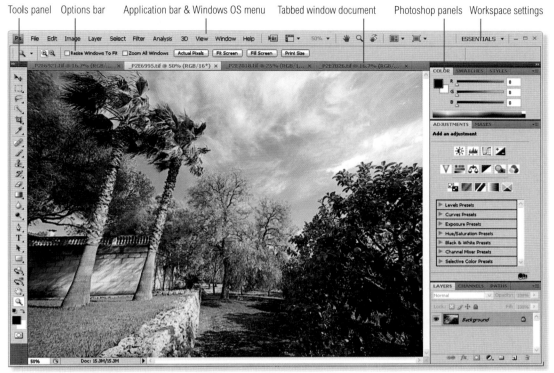

Figure 1.4 The Photoshop CS4 interface for the Windows OS showing the default program workspace.

This arrangement presents the panels in a docked mode and over the following few pages we shall look at ways to customize the layout of the interface. For example, you can reduce the amount of space taken up by the panels by collapsing them into compact panel icons (see Figure 1.19). You can also use the Workspace settings menu to quickly access alternative panel layouts, tailored for different types of Photoshop work. Apart from the redesign of the interface elements, the main difference with the CS4 interface layout is that it can now be contained in a single application window and we now have the ability to open and work with Photoshop image documents as tabbed windows.

The CS4 interface design

The Photoshop CS4 interface shares the same design features with all the other CS4 creative suite programs. By having a greater level of consistency in the interface design, this can make it easier to migrate from using one CS4 program to another.

9

OpenGL display performance

If the video card in your computer has OpenGL and you have 'Enable OpenGL drawing' selected in the Photoshop Performance preferences, you can take advantage of the new OpenGL features supported by Photoshop CS4. For example, when OpenGL is enabled you will now see smoother-looking images at all zoom display levels, plus you can use the new rotate view tool to rotate the on-screen image display (see page 52).

Tabbed windows in a classic layout

With Mac OS X you can mix having tabbed document windows with a classic panel layout. Switch off the Application Frame (see Figure 1.3) and use the Open as Tabs preference (Figure 1.6), or the Consolidate All to Here contextual menu command (Figure 1.7), or the drag and drop method (Figure 1.8) to have the open windows arranged as tabbed documents. You can then also use the N-up display options (Figure 1.10) to manage the windows.

Tabbed document windows

Let's start by looking at the way document windows are managed in Photoshop CS4. The default preference setting causes all new documents to open as tabbed windows and, in this mode, all new image document windows will appear nested in the tabbed document zone, just below the Options bar. In Figure 1.5 I have highlighted the tabbed document zone, where you can see four image documents are currently open. This approach to managing image documents makes it easier to locate a specific image when you have several images open at once, because you can now select an open image by clicking on the relevant tab. Previously you often had to click and drag on the document title bars to move image windows out the way until you had located the image you were after.

Of course, not everyone will immediately take to the new tabbed document opening. So if you find this proves annoying you can always deselect the 'Open Documents as Tabs' option in the Interface preferences (Figure 1.6). Do this and all images will open by default in floating windows. On the other hand you can have the best of both worlds by simply clicking on a tab and dragging it out from the docked zone. This action will convert the tabbed document to a floating window (as shown in Figure 1.7). Alternatively, you can right mouse-click on a tab to access the contextual menu where you can choose from various window command options such as 'Move to a New Window', or 'Consolidate All to Here', which will gather all floating windows and convert them into tabbed documents.

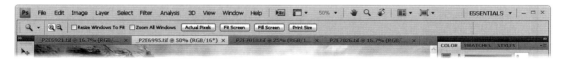

Figure 1.5 The default behavior for Photoshop CS4 is for image documents to open as tabbed windows, docked to the area highlighted here, just below the Options bar. Click on a tab to make a window active and click on the 'X' to close a particular window.

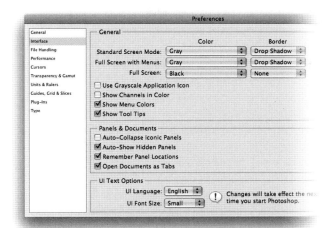

Switching between windows

The ⌘ 🔲 ctrl 🔲 shortcut can now be used to toggle between open window documents (⌘ Shift 🔲 ctrl Shift 🔲 is used to reverse the order). Note: the 🔲 key is also referred to as the ~ (tilde) key. In addition to this you can still use the old ⌘ → ctrl → shortcut to cycle through open documents and use ⌘ Shift → ctrl Shift → to reverse the cycle.

Figure 1.6 The Photoshop Interface preferences.

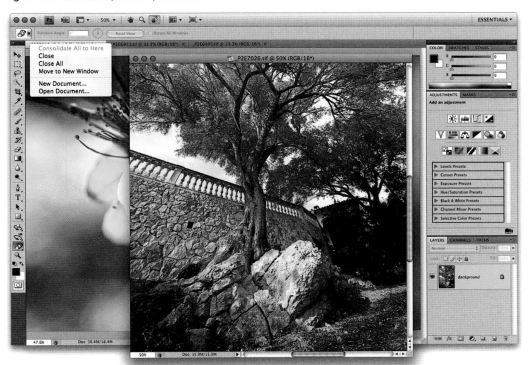

Figure 1.7 This screen shot shows two ways you can convert a tabbed document to a floating window. Either by dragging a tab out from the tabbed windows zone, or by using the contextual menu.

Synchronized scroll and zoom

In the N-up display menu (Figure 1.10) and Window ⇨ Arrange submenu you will come across controls that allow you to match the zoom, location (and rotation) of all open images, based on the current foreground image window. The Match Zoom command will match the zoom percentage based on the current selected image, while the Match Location command matches the scroll position. You can also synchronize the scrolling or magnification by depressing the *Shift* key as you scroll or zoom in and out on any window view.

Multiple window views

Multiple window views can prove useful if you wish to compare different soft proof views of the same image to get an impression on screen of how the colors in your image might appear in print. See Chapter 12 on Color Management for more about soft proofing in Photoshop.

Managing document windows

Documents can also be tabbed into grouped document windows by dragging one window document across to another (see Figure 1.8). It is also possible to create a second window view of the image you are working on, where the open image is duplicated in a second window. For example, you can have one window with the image at a Fit to Screen view and the other zoomed in close-up on a detailed area. Any changes you make can then be viewed simultaneously in both windows (Figure 1.9). You can also vary the way multiple document windows are displayed on the screen. For floating windows you can choose Window ⇨ Arrange ⇨ Cascade to have all cascading down from the upper left corner of the screen, or choose Window ⇨ Arrange ⇨ Tile to have them tiled edge to edge. For Tabbed document windows you can use the Document Layout menu to choose any of the 'N-up' options shown in Figure 1.10. This document layout method offers a much greater degree of control. It lets you choose from one of the many different layout options shown in Figure 1.10 and gives you access to the Match Zoom and Match Location controls discussed in the accompanying sidebar.

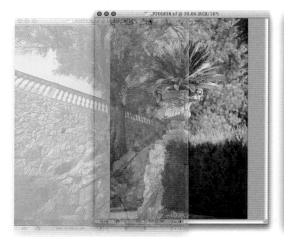 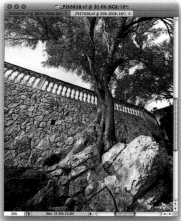

Figure 1.8 Floating windows can be grouped as tabbed document windows by dragging the title bar of one document across to another, till a blue line appears as shown above. You can also click on the empty gray area (circled in red) to drag a group of tagged document windows to the tabbed windows zone (see Figure 1.7).

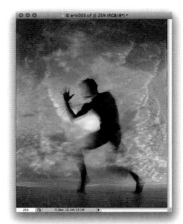
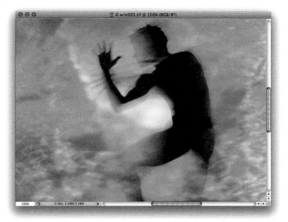

Figure 1.9 To open a second window view of a Photoshop document choose Window ⇨ Arrange ⇨ New Window for (document name). Changes applied to the close-up view are automatically updated in the second window view.

Photograph: Eric Richmond.

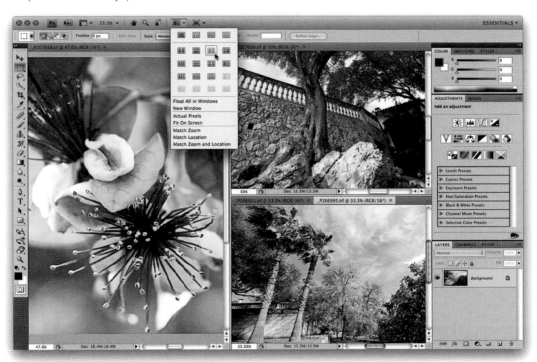

Figure 1.10 This shows the 'N-up' display options for tabbed document windows.

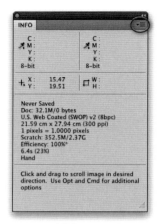

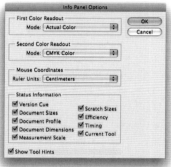

Figure 1.11 If you go to the Info panel menu (circled), you can open the Info panel options shown here, where you can choose which status items you would like to see displayed in the Status Information section of the Info panel.

Image document window details

The document window displays extra information about the image in the two boxes located in the bottom left corner of the image window (Figure 1.12). The left-hand box displays the zoom scaling percentage, showing the current zoom factor, where you can type in a new percentage of any value you like from 0.2% to 1600% up to two decimal places and set this as the new viewing resolution. In the middle is a Work Group Server button that can be used to check in or check out a document that is being shared over a WebDAV server. To the right of this is the Status Information box, which can display an information status item. If you mouse down on the arrow to the right of the box, you will see a list of all the items you can choose to display here, which are described on the page opposite. As I say, this box can only display a single item (at a time). However, if you open the Info panel options shown in Figure 1.11, you can check several or all of the Status Information items shown here. The items that are ticked will then appear in the middle section of the Info panel. In addition to this, you can also choose to enable Show Tool Hints. These appear at the bottom of the Info panel and will change according to any modifier keys you have held down at the time, to indicate extra available options.

If you mouse down in the Status Information box, this will display the width and height dimensions of the image, along with the number of channels and image resolution (Figure 1.13). If you hold down the ⌘ ctrl key as you mouse down on the Status Information box, this shows the image tiling information.

Dynamic zoom views

You can also use a scrubby slider in the Zoom Status box shown below (the box on the left with the percentage), to dynamically zoom in an out of an image. Just hold down the ⌘ ctrl key as you drag left or right.

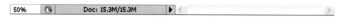

Figure 1.12 The document status is shown in the two boxes highlighted here.

Title bar proxy icons (Macintosh)

Macintosh users will see a proxy image icon in the title bar of floating windows. This is dimmed when the document is in an unsaved state and is reliant on there being a preview icon saved with the image. For example, many JPEGs will not have an icon until they are saved as something else.

To relocate the existing source file and move it to a new location, *ctrl* drag on the proxy icon and drag to a new destination. If you hold down the ⌥ key as you do this you can create a copy of the file (or if you move it to a new disk volume, it will also make a copy). To view the file's folder hierarchy and jump to a specific folder location, ⌘ click on the proxy icon.

⌘ click to display the title bar proxy icons (Mac only)

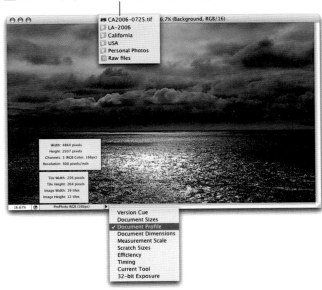

Figure 1.13 Here is the window layout of a Photoshop document as it appears on the Macintosh. If you mouse down on the arrow icon next to the Status Information box, you can select the type of information you wish to see displayed there. The status display information can be changed by mousing down on the arrow next to the Status Information box (the status items are described on the right). Mouse down in the Status Information box to display a scaled preview showing the size and position the image will print with the current page setup. Hold down ⌥ *alt* key to display the file size and resolution information and hold down ⌘ *ctrl* key to display the image tiling information.

Version Cue

Current Version Cue status.

Document Sizes

The first figure represents the file size of a flattened version of the image. The second, the size if saved including all layers.

Document Profile

The profile assigned to the document.

Document Dimensions

This displays the physical image dimensions, as would be shown in the Image Size dialog box.

Measurement Scale

Measurement units (extended version only).

Scratch Sizes

The first figure displays the amount of RAM memory used. The second shows the total RAM memory available to Photoshop after taking into account the system and application overhead.

Efficiency

This summarizes how efficiently Photoshop is working. Basically it provides a simplified report on the amount of scratch disk usage.

Timing

Displays the time taken to accomplish a Photoshop step or the accumulated timing of a series of steps. Every time you change tools or execute a new operation, the timer resets itself.

Current Tool

This displays the name of the tool you currently have selected. This is a useful aide-mémoire for users who like to work with most of the panels hidden.

32-bit Exposure

This Exposure slider control is only available for 32-bit mode images.

View menu options

The View Extras items can also be selected via the View menu. Choose View ➾ Rulers (⌘ R / ctrl R) to turn ruler visibility on or off and use the View ➾ Show submenu to toggle making the Guides (⌘ ; ctrl ;) or Grid (⌘ ' ctrl ') visible or invisible.

Is it on or off?

If a tick mark appears next to an item in the View ➾ Show menu, it means it is switched on. If you then select the item in the menu and release the mouse, you can switch it off.

Altering the ruler units

If the ruler units need altering, just ctrl right mouse-click on one of the rulers and select a new unit of measurement. If the rulers are visible but the guides are hidden, dragging out a new guide will make the other hidden guides reappear.

Precise guide placement

You can also position a guide using View ➾ New Guide... Then enter the exact measurement coordinate for the horizontal or vertical axis in the dialog box that appears.

Figure 1.14 This shows an image displaying the rulers and guides. To place a new guide, select Show Rulers from the menu list shown here or choose View ➾ Rulers. You can then drag from either the horizontal or vertical ruler to place a new guide. If you hold down the *Shift* key as you drag, this will make the guide snap to a ruler tick mark (providing View ➾ Snap is checked). If you hold down the ⌥ *alt* key as you drag, this allows you to switch dragging a horizontal guide to dragging it as a vertical (and vice versa). Lastly, you can use ⌘ H ctrl H to toggle hiding/showing Extras like Guides.

Rulers, Guides & Grid

If you mouse down on the View Extras menu in the Application bar (circled in Figure 1.14), you can switch on the following view items: Guides, Grids and Rulers. Guides can be flexibly positioned anywhere in the image area and used for the precise positioning and alignment of image elements. Guides can be added at any time (providing the Rulers are displayed). To add a new guide, you just mouse down on the ruler bar and drag a new guide out and release the mouse to drop the guide in place. If you are not happy with the positioning, you can select the move tool and drag the guide into the exact required position. But once positioned, it is sometimes a good idea to lock the guides (View ➾ Lock Guides) to avoid accidentally moving them again. The Grid (Figure 1.15) provides a means for aligning image elements to the horizontal and vertical axis (to alter the grid spacing, open the Photoshop preferences and select Guides & Grid).

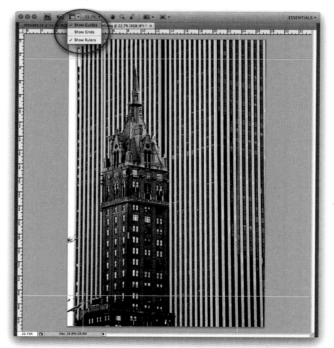

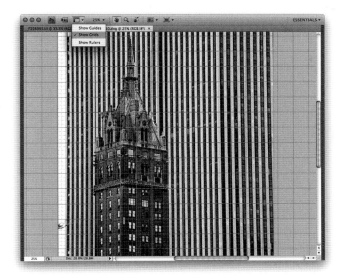

Figure 1.15 This shows an image displaying the Grid view, which can be used to help align objects to a horizontal and vertical axis. The Grid view can be enabled via the Display options in the Application bar or by choosing View ⇨ Show ⇨ Grid. ⌘ H ctrl H will toggle hiding/showing Extras like the Grid.

Smart Guides

When Smart Guides are switched on in the View ⇨ Show menu these can help you align layers as you drag them with the move tool (see page 114).

'Snap to' behavior

The Snap option in the View menu allows you to toggle the 'Snap to' behavior for the Guides, Grid, Slices, Document bounds and Layer bounds. The shortcut for toggling the 'Snap to' behavior is ⌘ Shift ; ctrl Shift ;. When the 'Snap to' is active and you reposition an image, type or shape layer, or use a crop or marquee selection tool, these will snap to one or more of the above. It is also the case that when Snap is active, and new guides are added with the Shift key held down, the guide will snap to the nearest tick mark on the ruler or, if the Grid is active, to the closest grid line. Objects on layers will snap to position when placed within close proximity of a guide edge. The reverse is also true: when dragging a guide, it will snap to the edge of an object on a layer at the point where the opacity is greater than 50%.

Pixel Grid view

The Pixel Gird view described in Figure 1.16 is useful when editing things like screen shots and can, for example, aid the precise placement of the crop tool. Although this will only be seen if you have OpenGL enabled (see page 103).

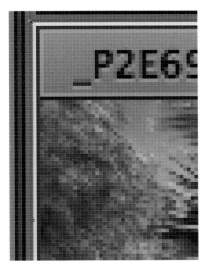

Figure 1.16 The Pixel Grid view can be enabled by going to the View ⇨ Show menu and selecting 'Pixel Grid'. When enabled, Photoshop displays pixels in a grid (like the example shown here) when an image is inspected at a 500% magnification or greater.

Application bar

The Application bar is new to CS4 and lets you quickly access some essential controls such as the 'N-up document layout' options and the View extras for showing/hiding rulers, grid or guides that I just mentioned. Those I haven't mentioned yet include the Launch Bridge button that will take you directly to the Bridge program (see pages 72–77) from where you can double-click on an image in the Content panel to open it up in Photoshop. The Zoom Scale box shows the current zoom setting and you can use this menu to quickly select a 25%, 50%, 100% or 200% zoom view setting. The Hand, Zoom and Rotate controls duplicate those also found in the Tools panel and the 'Screen display mode' options (discussed on page 54) have also been moved here from the Tools panel. The Workspace settings menu isn't exactly new, but is now more prominently displayed. The main difference between the Mac and PC versions of Photoshop CS4 is that with the Macintosh interface (Figure 1.17), the Photoshop menu remains static at the top of the screen, whereas on the Windows platform (Figure 1.18) the application menu items are incorporated into the Application bar itself.

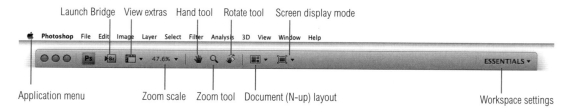

Figure 1.17 The Photoshop CS4 Application bar (Mac OS).

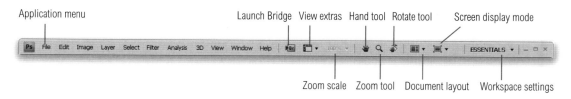

Figure 1.18 The Photoshop CS4 Application bar (Windows OS).

The Photoshop panels

The default workspace layout settings will place the panels in a docked layout where the panels are grouped into column zone areas on the right. But the panels can also be placed anywhere on the desktop and repositioned by mousing down on the panel title bar (or panel icon) and dragging to a new location. A single-click on the empty panel tab area (circled red in Figure 1.19) will compact the panel upwards and clicking on the tab area will unfurl the panel. A single-click on the darker gray panel header bar (circled blue in Figure 1.19) will collapse the panel into the compact icon view mode and clicking on the panel header will expand the panel again. Some expanded panels, such as the Info panel are of a fixed size, while others, such as the Layers panel have a Resize tab in the bottom right corner that allows you to adjust the height and width of the panel.

Panels can be organized into groups by mousing down on the Panel tab and dragging it across to another panel (Figure 1.20). When panels are grouped in this way they look a bit like folders in a file cabinet. Just click on a tab to bring that panel to the front of the group and to separate a panel from a group, mouse down on the panel tab and drag it outside the panel group again.

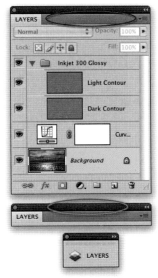

Figure 1.19 Photoshop panels can be collapsed with a single-click in the empty panel tab area (circled in red), while a single-click on the dark gray panel header (circled in blue) will shrink the panel to the compact panel size shown here.

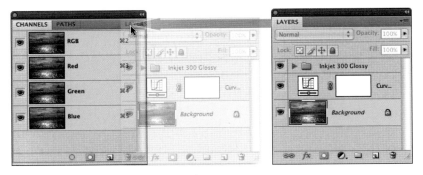

Figure 1.20 To group panels together, mouse down on the tab (or anywhere on the panel header) and, with the mouse held down, drag the tab across to another panel (or group of panels) and release the mouse once it is inside the other panels. To remove a panel from a group, mouse down on the panel tab and drag it outside the panel group.

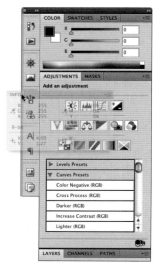

Figure 1.21 As you reposition a panel and prepare to dock it inside or to the edges of the other panels a thick blue line will indicate that when you release the mouse, this is where the panel will attach itself.

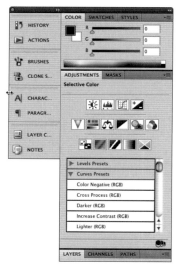

Figure 1.22 When panels are docked you can adjust the width of all the panels at once by dragging anywhere along the side edge of the panels.

Panel arrangements and docking

The default 'Essentials' workspace will arrange the panels using the panel layout shown in Figures 1.3 and 1.4 at the beginning of this chapter, but there are quite a few other different workspace settings to choose from as well (see Workspace settings on page 22) and you easily create custom workspace settings by arranging the panels to suit your own preferred way of working. Panels can be docked together by dragging a panel to the bottom or side edge of another panel and in Figure 1.21 you can see how an example of the thick blue line that will appear as a panel is made to hover close to the edge of another panel. Release the mouse at this point and the panels will become docked to the side or the bottom of the other panels.

When panels are compressed (as shown in the middle and bottom examples in Figure 1.19), you can drag on either side of the panel to adjust the panel's width. At the most compact size, only the panel's icon is displayed, but as you increase the width of a panel (or column of panels), the panel contents will expand and you get to see the names of the panels appear alongside their icons (see Figure 1.22).

Just remember that if you are searching for a particular panel and can't find it, then it may just be hidden. If this happens, go to the Window menu, select the panel name from the menu and it will then reappear again. It is worth remembering that the **Tab** key shortcut (also indicated as ⇥ on some keyboards) toggles hiding and showing all the panels, while **Tab** **Shift** toggles hiding/showing all the currently visible panels except for the Tools panel and Options bar. These are useful shortcuts to bear in mind. So, if you are working in Photoshop and all your panels seem to have disappeared, just try pressing **Tab** and they'll all be made visible again.

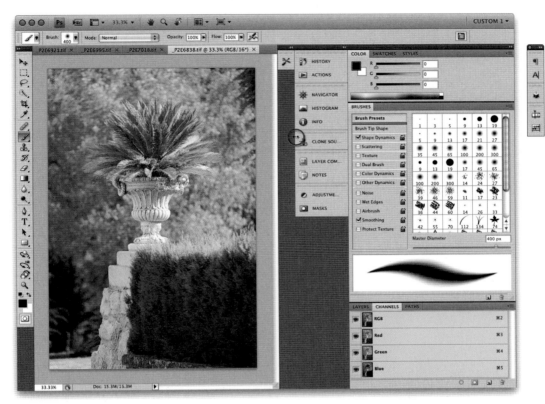

Figure 1.23 This shows a multi column workspace layout with some of the panels grouped in a docked, compact icon layout, outside the main application window.

In the Figure 1.23 example shown above, the tabbed image documents fill the horizontal space between the Tools panel on the left and the three panel columns on the right. I have also shown here how you can mouse down on the column edge to adjust the column width (see the double-arrow icon circled in red). Photoshop panels can be grouped into as many columns as you like within the application window or positioned separately outside the application window, such as on a separate monitor (see Figure 1.29).

Closing panels

To close a panel, click on the Close button in the top right corner (or choose 'Close' from the panel options fly-out menu).

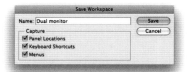

Figure 1.24 The Save Workspace menu in Photoshop can be used to save custom panel workspace setups. These can be recalled by revisiting the menu and highlighting the workspace name. To remove a workspace, choose Delete Workspace... from the menu.

Workspace settings

If at any time you wish to restore the panel positions, go to the Workspace menu in the Application bar and choose one of the standard workspace settings such as: Essentials or Basic. You can also save the current panel arrangement as a custom workspace via the Workspace menu in the Application bar or by going to the Window menu and choosing Workspace ➪ Save Workspace... The dialog box shown in Figure 1.24 appears and asks you to select the items you want to save as part of the workspace. Name the workspace and save it (note how the Workspace settings can also be used to save specific keyboard shortcuts and menu settings). You will then see the saved workspace appear in the Application bar Workspace menu listing (Figure 1.25).

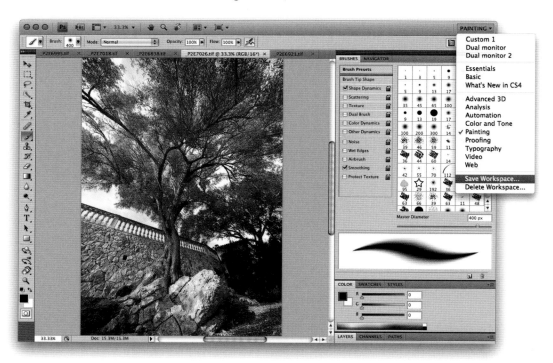

Figure 1.25 The Workspace settings can be accessed via the Application bar list shown here, or via the Window ➪ Workspace submenu.

Customizing the menu options

As the number of features in Photoshop has grown over the years, the menu choices have become quite overwhelming and this is especially true if you are new to Photoshop. However, if you go to the Edit menu and choose Menus... this will open the Keyboard Shortcuts and Menus dialog shown in Figure 1.27, where you can customize the menu options and decide which menu items will remain visible. This Customize menu feature is like a 'make simpler' command. You can hide those menu options you never use and apply color codings to the menu items you use most often, to make them appear more prominent. For example, if you select the 'Basic' workspace, this setting abbreviates the menu lists in Photoshop and hides the more advanced features. This is therefore a useful workspace for someone who is just beginning to learn Photoshop since they will find it easier to locate the menu commands they need when starting out. The philosophy behind this feature is: 'everything you do want with nothing you don't want'! Another example is the 'What's New in CS4' workspace (Figure 1.26). This doesn't alter the layout of the panels or hide any menu items, but instead applies a blue color coding to all new Photoshop CS4 menu items.

In Basic mode, a Show All Menu Items command will appear at the bottom of each menu list. You can select this menu item to restore the menus so that they show a full list of options.

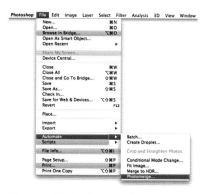

Figure 1.26 The Custom workspace menu options, which are shown here using the 'What's New in CS4' setting that color codes all the new menu items in blue.

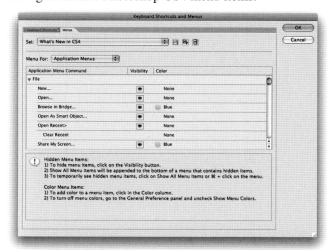

Figure 1.27 The Keyboard Shortcuts and Menus dialog.

Creating workspace shortcuts

If you scroll down to the Window section in the Keyboard Shortcuts for Application menus, you will see a list of all the currently saved Workspace presets. You can then assign a keyboard shortcut for each workspace. This will allow you to jump quickly from one workspace setting to another (see Figure 1.25).

Customizing the keyboard shortcuts

While you are in the Keyboard shortcuts and Menus dialog, you can click on the Keyboard Shortcuts tab to reveal the Keyboard shortcut options shown below in Figure 1.28 (or you can go to the Edit menu and choose Keyboard Shortcuts...). In this dialog you first select an area to create shortcuts for, such as Application Menus, Panel Menus or Tools. You can then navigate the menu list below, click in the Shortcut column next to a particular menu item and hold down the combination of keys that you wish to assign as a shortcut for that particular tool or menu item. Now the thing to be aware of here is that Photoshop has already used up nearly every key combination there is, so you are going to be faced with the choice of reassigning an existing shortcut, or using multiple modifier keys such as ⌘ ⌥ Shift or ctrl alt Shift plus a letter or Function key, when creating a new shortcut.

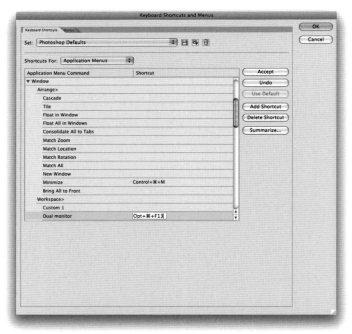

Figure 1.28 The Keyboard Shortcuts and Menus dialog showing the Keyboard Shortcuts options for the Application menus.

Working with a dual monitor setup

If you have a second monitor display, you can arrange things so that the panels are all placed on the second screen, leaving the main monitor clear to display the application window as a floating window or in one of the full screen modes. Figure 1.29 shows a screen shot of a Dual Monitor panel layout workspace that I use with the computer setup in the office. In this example I have ensured that only the panels I use regularly are made visible and that I can easily see and access all the essential panel options I need at once. The important thing to remember is to save such a panel layout as a workspace setting so that you can easily revert to it when switching workspace settings.

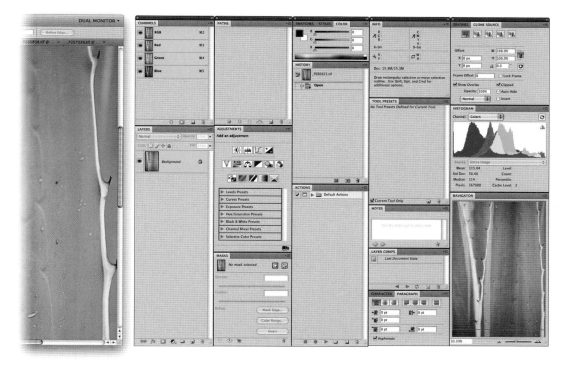

Figure 1.29 This shows an example of how you might like to arrange the Photoshop panels on a second monitor placed to the right of the primary screen (which contains the main Photoshop application window).

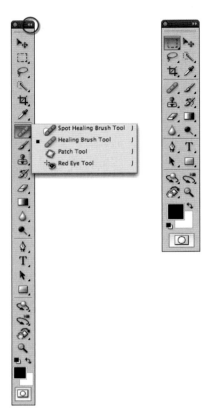

Figure 1.30 On the left you can see the default single column panel view. You can click on the double arrow (circled) to toggle between this and the double column view shown on the right. Where tools are marked with a triangle in the bottom right corner, you can mouse down on the tool to see all the other tools that are nested in that particular group.

Spring-loaded keys

You can use the keyboard shortcuts shown in Figure 1.31 to switch tools. However, if you hold the key down instead, you can temporarily switch to using the tool associated with that keyboard shortcut. Release the key and you will revert to working with the previously selected tool.

Photoshop CS4 Tools panel

The Tools panel contains 70 separate tools. Clicking any tool will automatically display the Tool options panel (if it happens to be hidden) and from there you can select the individual options for that tool (see page 28). Most of the tools in the Tools panel have a triangle in the bottom right corner of the tool icon, indicating there are extra tools nested in a tool group. If you mouse down on a tool icon, this will reveal the additional tool choices (see Figure 1.30) and you can click on any of the tools in this list to make it the selected tool for that group.

You will notice that most of the tools (or sets of tools) have keyboard shortcuts associated with them. These are displayed whenever you mouse down to reveal the nested tools or hover with the cursor to reveal the tool tip info (if this is set in Photoshop's preferences); you can use these shortcuts to quickly select a tool without having to go via the Tools panel. For example, pressing **V** on the keyboard will select the move tool and pressing **J** will select one of the healing brush group of tools (whichever is currently selected in the Tools panel). Photoshop CS4 also features spring-loaded tool selection behavior, which you can read about in the sidebar panel. Where more than one tool shares the same keyboard shortcut, you can cycle through these other tools by holding down the **Shift** key as you press the keyboard shortcut. If on the other hand you prefer to restore the old behavior whereby repeated pressing of the key would cycle the tool selection, go to the Photoshop menu, select Preferences ⇨ General and deselect the Use Shift Key for Tool Switch option (personally, I prefer using the Shift key method). You can also **⌥** **alt**-click the tool icon in the Tools panel to cycle through the grouped tools.

There are specific situations when Photoshop will not allow you to use certain tools and instead displays a prohibit sign (⊘). For example, you might be editing an image in 32-bit mode where only some tools can be used to edit the image. Clicking once in the image document window will call up a dialog explaining the exact reason why you cannot access or use a particular tool.

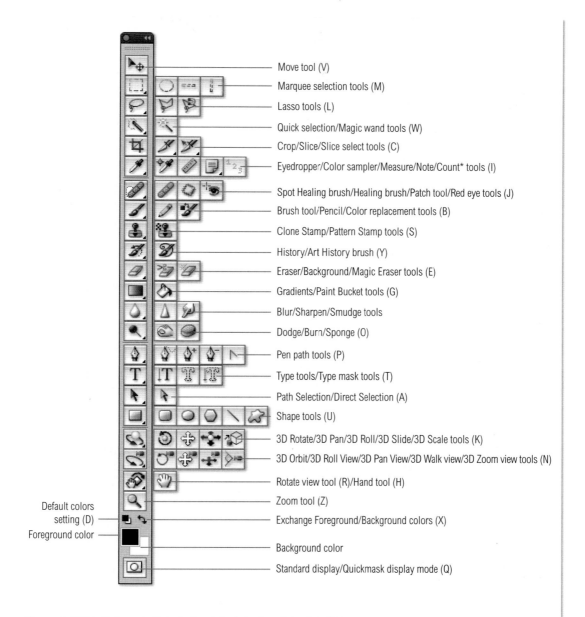

Move tool (V)
Marquee selection tools (M)
Lasso tools (L)
Quick selection/Magic wand tools (W)
Crop/Slice/Slice select tools (C)
Eyedropper/Color sampler/Measure/Note/Count* tools (I)
Spot Healing brush/Healing brush/Patch tool/Red eye tools (J)
Brush tool/Pencil/Color replacement tools (B)
Clone Stamp/Pattern Stamp tools (S)
History/Art History brush (Y)
Eraser/Background/Magic Eraser tools (E)
Gradients/Paint Bucket tools (G)
Blur/Sharpen/Smudge tools
Dodge/Burn/Sponge (O)
Pen path tools (P)
Type tools/Type mask tools (T)
Path Selection/Direct Selection (A)
Shape tools (U)
3D Rotate/3D Pan/3D Roll/3D Slide/3D Scale tools (K)
3D Orbit/3D Roll View/3D Pan View/3D Walk view/3D Zoom view tools (N)
Rotate view tool (R)/Hand tool (H)
Zoom tool (Z)
Exchange Foreground/Background colors (X)

Default colors setting (D)
Foreground color

Background color
Standard display/Quickmask display mode (Q)

Figure 1.31 The Tools panel with the keyboard shortcuts shown in brackets. Note that the count tool is only available in the extended version of Photoshop CS4.

Hovering tool tips

In order to help familiarize yourself with the Photoshop tools and panel functions, a Help dialog box will normally appear after a few seconds whenever you leave a cursor hovering over any one of the Photoshop buttons or tool icons (see Show Tool Tips in the General Preferences).

Options bar

The Options bar (Figure 1.32) will normally appear at the top of the screen, just below the Application bar, and you will soon appreciate the ease with which you can use it to make changes to any of the tool options. However, it can be removed from its standard location and placed anywhere on the screen by dragging the gripper bar (on the left edge).

The Options bar contents will vary according to the tool you have currently selected and there are a few more examples of the individual Options bar settings to be found in the rest of this chapter (a complete list of the Options bar views can be seen in the Help Guide for Photoshop tools on the DVD). Quite often you will see 'tick' and 'cancel' icons on the right-hand side of the Options bar and these are there so that you can OK or cancel a tool that is in a modal state. For example, if you were using the crop tool to define a crop boundary you could use these buttons to accept or cancel the crop, although you may find it easier to use the **Enter** key to OK or the **esc** key to cancel such tool operations. To reset a tool or all tools, **ctrl** right mouse down on the tool icon in the Options bar and choose 'Reset Tool' or 'Reset All Tools'. And as I mentioned earlier on page 20, you can use the **Shift Tab** shortcut to toggle hiding the panels only and keep just the Tools panel and Options bar visible.

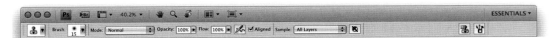

Figure 1.32 The Options panel.

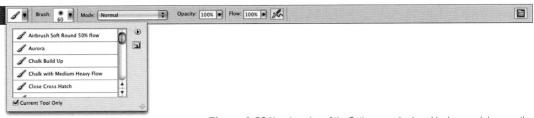

Figure 1.33 Here is a view of the Options panel, where I had moused down on the arrow next to the Brush tool icon to reveal the Tool Presets menu.

Tool Presets panel

Many of the Photoshop tools will offer a wide range of possible tool options. In order to manage these settings more effectively, the Tool Presets panel can be used to store multiple saved tool settings, which can then be accessed via the Options bar (shown in Figure 1.33), or the Tool Presets panel (shown in Figure 1.34).

With Tool Presets you can access any number of tool options very quickly and this will save you the bother of having to reconfigure the Options bar settings each time you choose a particular tool. For example, you might find it useful to save crop tool presets for the different image dimensions and pixel resolutions you typically use. Likewise, you might like to store pre-configured brush preset settings, rather than have to keep adjusting the brush shape and attributes. To save a new tool preset, click on the New Preset button at the bottom of the Tool Presets panel and to remove a preset, click on the Delete button next to it.

If you mouse down on the 'Tool Presets' options, you can use the menu shown in Figure 1.35 to manage the various Tools Presets. In Figure 1.34 the 'Current Tool Only' option was deselected which meant that all the tool presets could be accessed at once. This can be useful, because clicking on a preset will simultaneously select the tool and the preset at the same time. But most people will find the Tool Presets panel is easier to manage when the 'Current Tool Only' option is checked.

You can use the Tool Presets panel to save or load pre-saved tool preset settings. For example, if you create a set of custom presets, you can share these with other Photoshop users by choosing Save Tool Presets... to create a saved set of settings for a particular tool. Another thing that may not be immediately apparent is the fact that you can also use Tool Presets to save type tool settings. This again can be useful, because you can save the font type, font size, type attributes and font color settings all within a single tool preset. This feature can also be really handy if you are working on a web or book design project.

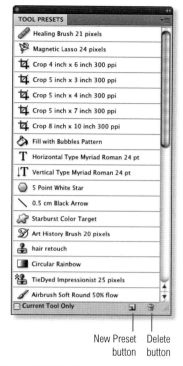

New Preset   Delete
button   button

Figure 1.34 The Tool Presets panel.

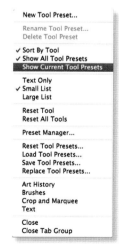

Figure 1.35 The Tool Presets options.

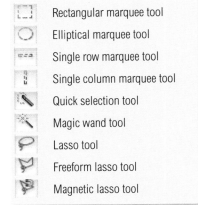

Rectangular marquee tool

Elliptical marquee tool

Single row marquee tool

Single column marquee tool

Quick selection tool

Magic wand tool

Lasso tool

Freeform lasso tool

Magnetic lasso tool

Selection tools

In Photoshop the usual editing conventions apply: pixels can be cut, copied and pasted just as you would when working with text in a word processing document and mistakes can be undone by using the Edit ⇨ Undo command (⌘ Z ctrl Z) or by selecting a previous history state via the History panel.

The Photoshop selection tools can mainly be used to define a specific area of the image that you wish to modify, or have copied. The use of the selection tools in Photoshop is therefore just like highlighting text in a word processor program in preparation to do something with the selected content. In the case of Photoshop, you might want to make a selection to define a specific area of the image, so that when you apply an image adjustment or a fill, only the selected area will be modified. Alternatively, you might use a selection to define an area you wish to copy and paste, or define an area of an image that you want to copy across to another image document as a new layer.

The marquee selection tool options include the rectangular, elliptical and single row/single column selection tools. The lasso tool can be used to draw freehand selection outlines and has two other modes: the polygon lasso tool, which can draw both straight line *and* freehand selections, plus the magnetic lasso tool, which is like an automatic freehand lasso tool that is able to auto-detect an edge you are trying to trace.

The quick selection tool is a bit like the magic wand tool. It can be used to make selections based on pixel color values; however the quick selection tool is a little more sophisticated than the standard magic wand and hence it has been made the default tool in this particular tool group. For full descriptions of these and other tools mentioned here don't forget to install the *Photoshop CS4 for Photographers Help Guide* that is available on the DVD.

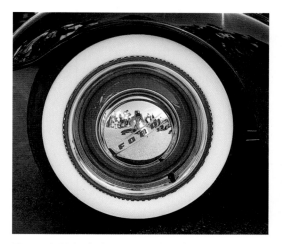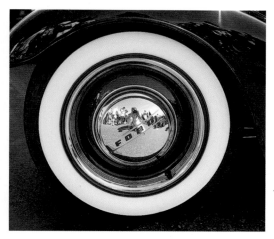

Figure 1.36 A selection can be used to define a specific area of an image that you wish to work on. In this example, I made an elliptical marquee selection of the inner tire wheel and followed this with an image adjustment to desaturate the red color.

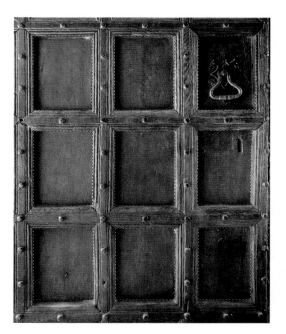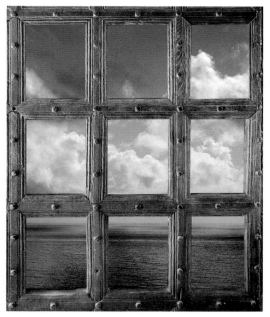

Figure 1.37 In this example I used the rectangle marquee tool to marquee one of the inner panels and followed this by holding down the *Shift* key to select more panels with the rectangular marquee. I deleted the selected areas and placed the cut-out image as a layer above a seascape image (see Figure 1.56 for an example of how Photoshop layers work).

Color Range tip

A Color Range selection tool can only be used to make discontiguous selections. But it is possible to make a selection first of the area you wish to focus on and then choose Color Range to make a color range selection within the selection area.

Out-of-gamut selections

Among other things, you can use the Color Range command to make a selection based on out-of-gamut colors. This means you can use Color Range to make a selection of all those 'illegal' RGB colors outside the CMYK gamut and apply corrections to these pixels only. This task is made easier if you feather the selection slightly and hide the selection edges (View ⇨ Hide Extras). Then choose View ⇨ Gamut Warning. Adjustments can be made using the Selective Color or Hue/Saturation commands. Local areas may also be corrected with the sponge tool set to Desaturate.

More on Color Range selections

I have provided here just a brief introduction to the Color Range. There is a further example of Color Range in use coming up later in Chapter 9.

Color Range

In the Photoshop Select menu you will see an item called Color Range, which is a color-based selection tool. While the quick selection and magic wand tools create selections based on luminosity, Color Range can be used to create selections that are based on similar color values. Some important new functionality has been added to Color Range in this version of Photoshop, so it deserves to be given a little more of a mention in this edition of the book.

To make a Color Range selection, go to the Select menu, choose Color Range... and click anywhere in the image window (or Color Range preview area) to define an initial selection. To add colors to the selection, select the Add to Sample eyedropper and keep clicking to make the selection grow. To subtract from a selection, click on the Subtract from Sample eyedropper and click in the image to select the colors you want to see removed from the selection. You can then adjust the Fuzziness slider to adjust the tolerance of the selection, which will increase or decrease the number of pixels that are selected based on how similar pixels are in color to the already sampled pixels, while the Range slider determines which pixels are included based on how far in distance they are from the already selected pixels. If the Localized Color Clusters box is checked, Color Range can now process and merge data from multiple clusters of color samples. As you switch between sampling colors to add to the selection and selecting colors to remove, Photoshop calculates these clusters of color samples within a three-dimensional color space. As you add and subtract more colors, Photoshop can now produce a much more accurate color range selection mask based on the color sample data.

The selection preview options for the document window can be set to None (the default), Grayscale, a Matte color such as the White Matte example shown in Figure 1.39, or as a Quick Mask. Overall I find that Grayscale is a really useful preview mode if you want to get a nice large view in the document window of what a Color Range selection will look like and is especially useful if you find the small Color Range dialog preview too small to judge from.

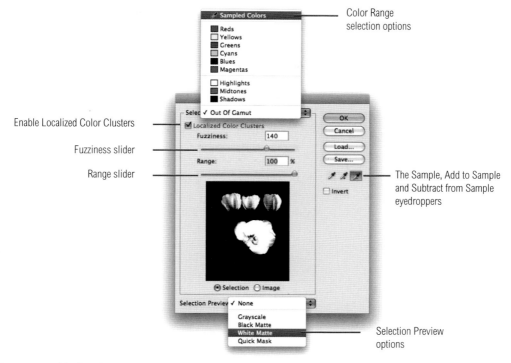

Color Range
selection options

Enable Localized Color Clusters

Fuzziness slider

Range slider

The Sample, Add to Sample
and Subtract from Sample
eyedroppers

Selection Preview
options

Figure 1.38 The Color Range dialog with expanded menus showing the full range
of options for the Color Range selection dialog.

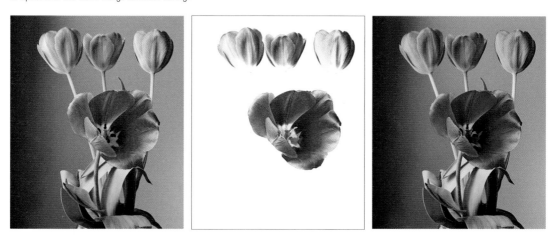

Figure 1.39 This shows a before image (left), Color Range White Matte preview
(middle) and a color adjusted image (right), made using the Color Range selection.

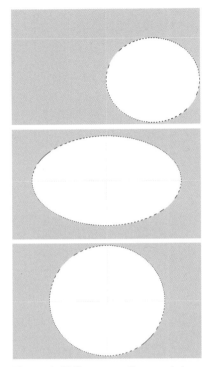

Figure 1.40 These composite screen shots show Quick Mask views of selections created by dragging out from the center with *Shift* held down (top), with ⌥ *alt* held down (middle) and *Shift* ⌥ *Shift* *alt* (bottom).

Modifier keys

Macintosh and Windows keyboards have slightly different key arrangements, hence the double sets of instructions throughout the book, where the ⌘ key on the Macintosh is equivalent to the *ctrl* key on a Windows keyboard and the Macintosh ⌥ key is equivalent to the *alt* key in Windows. Although on most Macintosh keyboards the Option key is labeled 'Alt' anyway (see Figure 1.41).

Windows users (and Mac users with a 'Mighty Mouse' or equivalent) can use the right mouse button to access the contextual menus (Mac users can also use the *ctrl* key to access these menus) and, finally, the *Shift* key which operates the same on both Mac and PC computers.

These keys are referred to as 'modifier' keys, because they modify tool behaviors. In Figure 1.40 you can see how if you hold down the *Shift* key when drawing a marquee selection this will constrain the selection to a square or circle. If you hold down ⌥ *alt* when drawing a marquee selection it will center the selection around the point where you clicked on the image. And if you hold down *Shift* ⌥ *Shift* *alt* when drawing a marquee selection, this will constrain the selection to a square or circle and center the selection around the point where you first clicked. The Spacebar is also a modifier key, in that it allows you to reposition your selection midstream.

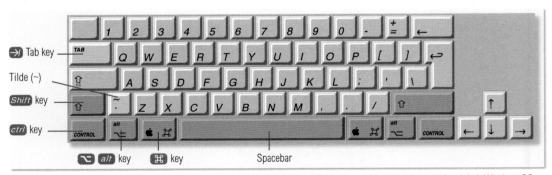

Tab key

Tilde (~)

Shift key

ctrl key

⌥ *alt* key   ⌘ key   Spacebar

Figure 1.41 The modifier keys on a Macintosh keyboard and their Windows PC equivalents are indicated in brown. The other keys commonly used in Photoshop are the Tab and Tilde keys, shown here in blue.

After you have created an initial selection, the modifier keys will behave differently. In Figure 1.42 you can see how if you hold down the *Shift* key as you drag with the marquee or lasso tool, this will add to the selection (holding down the *Shift* key and clicking with the magic wand tool also adds to an existing magic wand selection). If you hold down the *⌥* *alt* key as you drag with the marquee or lasso tool, this will subtract from the selection (holding down the *⌥* *alt* key and clicking with the magic wand tool also subtracts from the existing selection). And the combination of holding down the *Shift* *⌥* *Shift* *alt* keys together whilst dragging with a selection tool (or clicking with the magic wand) will create an intersection of the two selections. As well as using the above shortcuts, you will find there are also equivalent selection mode options on the Options bar for the marque and lasso selection tools (see Figure 1.43).

Modifier keys can also be used to modify the options that are available elsewhere in Photoshop. For example, if you hold down the *⌥* *alt* key as you click on the marquee tool in the Tools panel you will notice how this allows you to cycle through the tools available in this group. And whenever you are in a Photoshop dialog box it is also worth exploring what happens to the dialog buttons when you hold down the *⌥* *alt* key. You will often see the button names change to reveal more options.

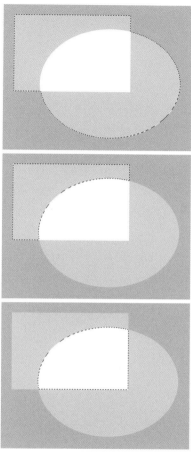

Figure 1.42 These composite screen shots show Quick Mask views of selections that have been modified after the initial selection stage. The top view shows an elliptical selection combined with a rectangular selection with *Shift* held down, adding to a selection. The middle view shows an elliptical selection combined with a rectangular selection with *⌥* *alt* held down, which will subtract from the original selection. The bottom view shows an elliptical selection combined with a rectangular selection with *Shift* *⌥* *Shift* *alt* held down, which will result in an intersected selection.

Normal   Subtract from Selection

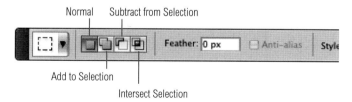

Add to Selection

Intersect Selection

Figure 1.43 The Options bar has four modes of operation for each of the selection tools: Normal; Add to Selection; Subtract from Selection; and Intersect Selection. These are equivalent to using the modifier modes described in the main text when the tool is in Normal mode.

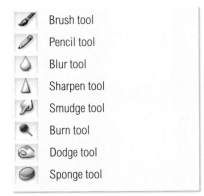

Brush tool	
Pencil tool	
Blur tool	
Sharpen tool	
Smudge tool	
Burn tool	
Dodge tool	
Sponge tool	

Brush size limits

The standard brush presets in Photoshop range from a single pixel to a 2500 pixel-wide brush, with varying degrees of softness.

Painting tools

The next set of tools I want to focus on are the painting tools. These include the brush, pencil, blur, sharpen, smudge, burn, dodge and sponge tools, which can all be used to add to or edit the pixel information in an image. If you want to keep your options open you will usually find it preferable to do your paint work on a separate new layer, and you can do this with all of the above tools except for the eraser. But in the case of the clone stamp and pattern stamp you can adjust the sample options so that you are able to sample from either all the layers in an image or just the layers below.

When you select any of the painting tools, the first thing you will want to do is to choose a brush size, which you can do by going to the Brush Preset Picker (the second item from the left in the Options bar) and selecting a brush from the drop-down list shown in Figure 1.44. Normally you can choose from many different shapes and sizes of brushes but you can also use the Master Diameter and Hardness sliders to modify the brush size/shape characteristics of a selected brush preset.

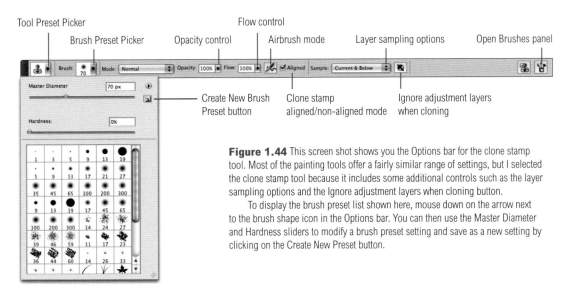

Figure 1.44 This screen shot shows you the Options bar for the clone stamp tool. Most of the painting tools offer a fairly similar range of settings, but I selected the clone stamp tool because it includes some additional controls such as the layer sampling options and the Ignore adjustment layers when cloning button.

To display the brush preset list shown here, mouse down on the arrow next to the brush shape icon in the Options bar. You can then use the Master Diameter and Hardness sliders to modify a brush preset setting and save as a new setting by clicking on the Create New Preset button.

On-the-fly brush changes

Instead of visiting the Brush Picker every time you want
to adjust the size or hardness of a brush, you will find it is
often quicker to use the square bracket keys as described
in Figures 1.45 and 1.46 to make such on-the-fly changes.
Also, if you *ctrl* right mouse-click in the image you are
working on this will open up the Brush Preset menu,
directly next to the cursor. Click on the brush preset you
wish to select and once you start painting, the Brush Preset
menu will close (or alternatively, use the *esc* key). Note
that if you are painting with a Wacom stylus you can close
this pop-up dialog by lifting the stylus off the tablet and
squeezing the double-click button. If you then *ctrl* *Shift*-
click right mouse *Shift*-click in the image while using a
brush tool, this will open the blending mode list shown
in Figure 1.47. These blend modes are like rules which
govern how the painted pixels are applied to the pixels in
the image below. For example, if you paint using the Color
mode, you'll alter the color values only in the pixels you
are painting.

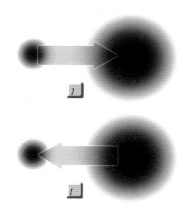

Figure 1.45 There is no need to visit the
Brush or Tool presets each time you want to
change the size of a brush. Use the right square
bracket key *]* to make a brush bigger and the
left square bracket key *[* to make it smaller.

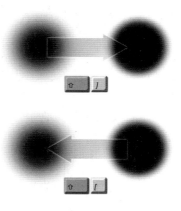

Figure 1.46 Combine the square bracket keys
with the Shift key on your keyboard and you can
use the *Shift* *]* to make a brush edge harder
and *Shift* *[* to make a brush edge softer.

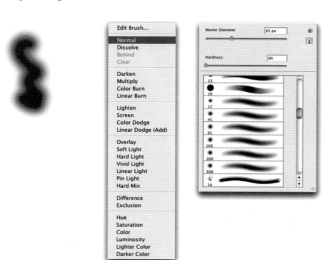

Figure 1.47 When using any of the paint tools in Photoshop, a *ctrl* *Shift*-click
or right mouse *Shift*-click will reveal the Brush blending modes list shown here,
while a *ctrl* right mouse-click will open the Brush Preset menu shown on the right.

Brush preview overlay color

If you go to the Photoshop Cursors preferences you can customize the overlay color used for the brush preview.

Dodge and burn tools

Photoshop CS4 features new improved dodge and burn tools. Although these perform much better than before, they are still limited to working directly on the pixel data. This means they may prove useful when working on copied pixel layers used for retouching, rather than for general use. If your aim is to apply general dodging and burning, you will be better off using the new Camera Raw adjustment tools, or adjustment layers, as described in Chapter 5.

Photoshop CS4 now offers on-screen brush adjustments. If you hold down the *ctrl* ⌥ keys (Mac), or the *alt* key and right-click (PC), dragging to the left will make the cursor size smaller, while dragging to the right will make it bigger. If you hold down the ⌘ *ctrl* ⌥ keys (Mac), or the *alt* *Shift* keys and right-click (PC), dragging to the left will make the brush shape softer and dragging to the right, harder. Figure 1.48 shows an example of how the paint tool cursor looks when you do this. Note how the brush hardness is represented with a Quick Mask type overlay.

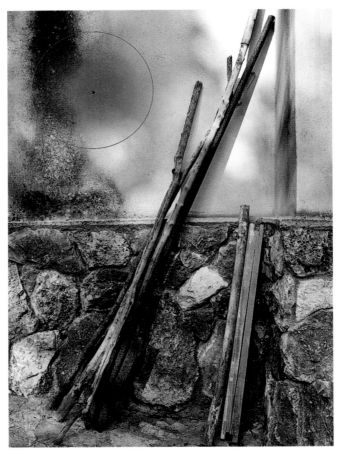

Figure 1.48 You can now dynamically adjust the size and hardness of the painting tool cursors on screen using the modifier keys described in the main text.

Brushes panel

If you click on 'Brush Presets' (circled in Figure 1.50), this will reveal the same list of brush presets that was shown in Figure 1.44. You can then append or replace this list of brush presets by going to the panel fly-out menu shown below and select a new brush settings group from the list.

So far we have looked at the Brush options that are used to determine the brush shape and size, but if you click on any of the brush attribute settings highlighted in Figure 1.50, the brush presets list will be replaced to reveal the individual brush attribute options (see Figure 1.51). The brush attributes include things like how the opacity of the brush is applied when painting, or the smoothness of a brush. You can therefore start by selecting an existing brush preset, modify it, as in the example shown in Figure 1.49, and then click on the Create New Brush button at the bottom to define as a new custom brush preset setting.

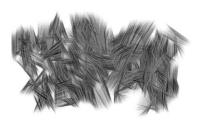

Figure 1.49 In this example I selected the Aurora brush preset and experimented with the pen tilt settings for things such as the size and angle in the Shape Dynamics settings. I then set turquoise as the foreground color and purple for the background and used a pen pressure setting to vary the paint color from the foreground to the background. I created the doodle shown in this image by twisting the pen angles as I applied the brush strokes.

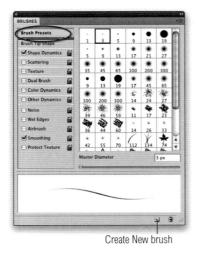

Create New brush

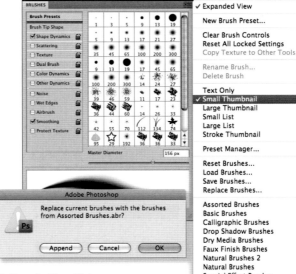

Figure 1.50 If you open the Brushes panel, the default panel setting will show an Expanded View and list the various brush presets in the right-hand section of the panel. If you click on any of the brush attributes in the list on the left, the right-hand section will change to reveal the various options settings (see Figure 1.51). If you go to the Brushes panel menu you can select any of the brush settings listed here, which will then ask if you want to Append or Replace the current list of presets.

Airbrush mode

Photoshop no longer has a separate airbrush tool. Instead, the brush tools have an Airbrush mode button in the Options bar.

Brushes panel options

The following notes and tips on working with the Brushes panel will apply to most, but not all, of the painting tools. To create your own custom brush preset settings, you need to first click on any of the brush attribute items listed on the left-hand side of the panel.

The Jitter controls introduce randomness into the brush dynamics behavior. Increasing the Opacity Jitter means that the opacity will still respond according to how much pen pressure is applied, but there is a built-in random fluctuation to the opacity that will vary even more as the jitter value is increased. The Flow Jitter setting governs the speed at which the paint is applied. To understand how the brush flow dynamics work, try selecting a brush and quickly paint a series of brush strokes at a low and then a high flow rate. When the flow rate is low, less paint is applied, whereas more paint is applied if you increase the flow setting, apply more pressure, or paint more slowly. Other tools like the dodge and burn toning tools use the terms Exposure and Strength. But essentially these have the same meaning as the opacity controls.

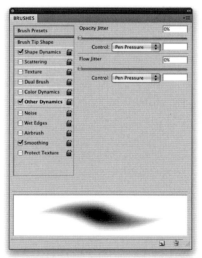

Figure 1.51 Click on a brush attribute settings shown in the list on the left and the right-hand side of the panel switches to display the options associated with each attribute. Specific brush panel settings can be locked by clicking on the Lock buttons.

The Shape Dynamics can be adjusted to introduce jitter into the size, angle and roundness of the brush and the scattering controls will enable you to produce broad, sweeping brush strokes with a random scatter. The Color Dynamics let you introduce random color variation to the paint color and the Foreground/Background color control that's included in this section can be useful as this will let you vary the paint color between the foreground and background color, according to how much pressure is applied (see Figure 1.49). The Dual Brush and Texture Dynamics can introduce texture and more interactive complexity to the brush texture (it is worth experimenting with the Scale control in the Dual Brush options) and the Texture Dynamics utilize a choice of blending modes for different effects, where of course you can add a custom texture of your own design, direct from the Pattern presets.

Pressure sensitive control

If you are using a pressure sensitive pen stylus, you will see additional options in the Brushes panel that enable you to link the pen pressure of the stylus to how the effects are applied. You can therefore use these options to determine things like how the paint opacity and flow will be controlled by the pen pressure or by the angle of tilt or rotation of the pen stylus.

Brush tool presets

When you have finished adjusting the Brushes panel dynamics and other settings, you can save a combination of the brush preset shape/size setting, the Brushes panel attribute settings plus the Brush blending mode (and brush color even) as a new Brush tool preset. To do this, go to the Tool Presets panel and click on the New Preset button at the bottom (see Figure 1.52). Or, you can mouse down on the Tool Preset Picker in the Options bar and click on the New Brush Setting button. Give the brush shape a name and click OK to append it to the current list. Once you have saved a brush tool preset, you can access it at any time via the Tool Presets panel or the Tool Preset menu in the Options bar.

Wacom™ tablets

The Wacom™ Intuos range includes some pens that have a thumb wheel control and in Photoshop you can exploit all of these responsive built-in Wacom features to the full via the brush dynamics settings. You will notice that as you alter the brush dynamics settings, the brush stroke preview below will change to reflect what the expected outcome would be if you had drawn a squiggly line that faded from zero to full pen pressure (likewise with the tilt and thumb wheel). This visual feedback is extremely useful as it allows you to experiment with the brush dynamics settings in the Brushes panel and learn how these will affect the brush dynamics behavior.

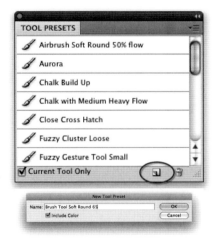

Figure 1.52 The Tool Presets panel. When you click on the New Preset button (circled) this opens the New Tool Preset dialog, where you can name it as a new tool preset.

▭	Rectangle tool
▭	Rounded rectangle tool
◯	Elliptical tool
⬡	Polygon tool
✿	Custom shape tool
╲	Line tool
◊	Paint bucket tool
▬	Gradient tool

Tools for filling

The various shape tools and line tool are of more use to graphic designers for creating things like buttons or adding vector shapes to a design layout. In Figure 1.53 you can see an example of how a custom, filled vector shape layer has been added above a gradient fill layer.

The paint bucket tool is like a combination of a magic wand selection combined with an Edit ⇨ Fill with foreground color command. As much as I try to ignore the paint bucket, people keep coming up with ways to prove me wrong. Recently, photographer Stuart Weston showed me how he used the paint bucket tool to add small filled patches of color to a large composite fashion image. The final image really did look quite good!

The gradient tool should be of more interest to photographers. You can also use the Adjustment layer menu to add a solid or Gradient Fill layer to an image, and Gradient Fill layers can be applied in this way to create gradient filter type effects, but you will also find that the gradient tool comes in use when you want to edit the contents of a layer mask. For example, you can add a black to white gradient to a layer mask to apply a graduated fade to the layer opacity.

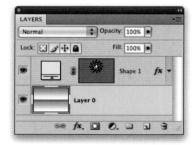

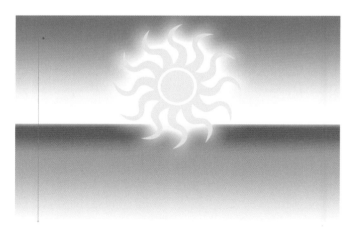

Figure 1.53 In this example I filled the background using a linear gradient tool and the sun was added as a custom shape layer filled with a solid color.

Tools for drawing

If you want to become a good retoucher, then you are at
some stage going to have to bite the bullet and learn how
to use the pen tools. The marquee, lasso and magic wand
selection tools are fine for making approximate selections,
but the pen tools are essential for all those other times
where you need to create precision selections and masks.

The pen tool group includes the main pen tool, a
freeform pen tool (which in essence is not much better than
the lasso or magnetic lasso tools) and modifier tools to add,
delete or modify path points. There are several examples
coming up in Chapter 9 where I will show you how to use
the pen tools to draw a path.

✎	Pen tool
✎⁺	Add anchor point tool
✎⁻	Delete anchor point tool
✎	Freeform pen tool
⌐	Convert point tool
▶	Path selection tool
▷	Direct selection tool

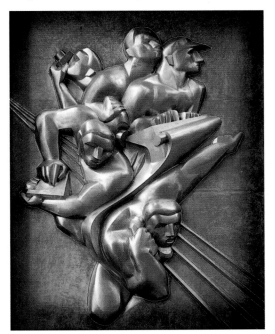
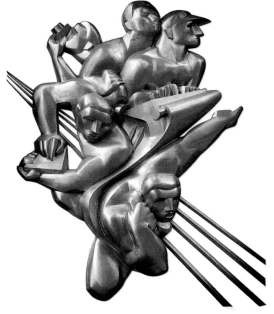

Figure 1.54 If you need to isolate an object or create a cut-out like the one shown
here, the only way to do so is to use the pen and pen modifier tools to draw a path
outline. You see, with a photograph like this, there is very little color differentiation
between the object and the background, and it would be very difficult for an auto
masking tool to accurately predict the edges in this image. I timed myself and it took
me just over 8 minutes to draw the path outline that was used to create the cut-out
shown on the right.

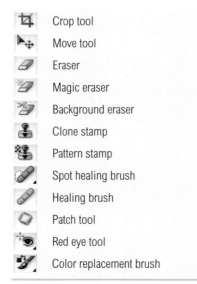

Crop tool

Move tool

Eraser

Magic eraser

Background eraser

Clone stamp

Pattern stamp

Spot healing brush

Healing brush

Patch tool

Red eye tool

Color replacement brush

Image editing tools

The editing tools line-up has changed quite a bit from the early days of Photoshop. You have the crop tool that can be used to trim pictures or enlarge the canvas area. The eraser tools are still there should you wish to erase the pixels directly, although these days it is more common to use layer masks to selectively hide or show the contents of a layer. The background eraser and magic eraser tools do offer some degree of automated erasing ability, but I would be more inclined to use the quick selection tool combined with a layer mask for this type of masking.

The clone stamp tool has been around since the beginning of Photoshop and this is definitely an essential tool for all types of retouching work. You can use the clone stamp to sample pixels from one part of the image and paint with them in another (as shown in Figure 1.55). The clone stamp tools were joined a few years back by the healing brush and patch tool. The healing brush can be used almost exactly the same way as the clone stamp, except it cleverly blends the pixels around the edges where the healing brush retouching is applied, to produce almost flawless results. The patch tool functions exactly like the healing brush except it uses a selection to define the area to be healed. The spot healing brush is rather clever because you don't even need to set a sample point: you simply click and paint over the blemishes you wish to see removed.

Providing you use the right flash settings on your camera it should be possible to avoid red eye occurring in your portrait photographs. But for all those times when the camera flash leaves your subjects looking like beasts of the night, the red eye tool provides a fairly basic and easy way to auto-correct such photographs. The color replacement brush is kind of like a semi-smart color blend mode painting tool which analyzes the area you are painting over and replaces it with the current foreground color, using either a Hue, Color, Saturation or Luminosity blend mode. It is useful for making quick and easy color changes without needing to create a Color Range selection mask first.

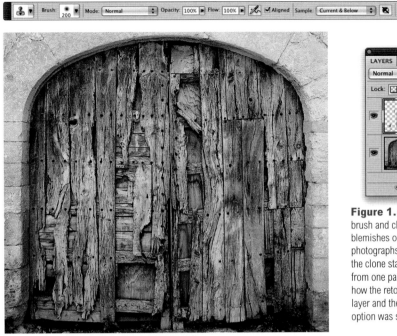

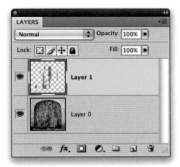

Figure 1.55 I mostly use the healing brush and clone stamp tools to retouch small blemishes or to remove sensor dust marks from photographs. In this example I have shown how the clone stamp tool can be used to paint detail from one part of an image onto another. Note how the retouching is applied to an empty new layer and the Sample: 'Current & Below' layers option was selected in the Options bar.

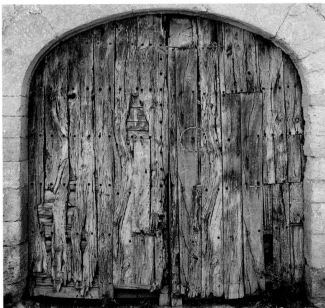

Blending modes

Photoshop image layers can be made to blend with the layers below them using any of the 25 different blending modes. Layer effects/styles allow you to add effects such as drop shadows, gradient/pattern fills or glows to any layer. Custom styles can be loaded from and saved to the Styles panel.

Working with Layers

Photoshop layers allow you to edit an image by building up the retouching and added bits in multiple layered sections, such as in the example shown in Figure 1.56. A layer can be an image element, such as a duplicated background layer, a copied selection made into a layer, or content that has been copied from another image. Or, it can be text or a vector shape layer. Or lastly, these are adjustment layers which are like image adjustment instructions applied in a layered form.

Layers can be placed together in groups, which makes the layer organization easier to manage, and you can apply masking to the contents of a layer with either a pixel layer mask or a vector mask. You will find plenty of examples throughout this book where I show you how to work with layers and layer masks.

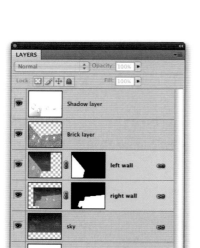

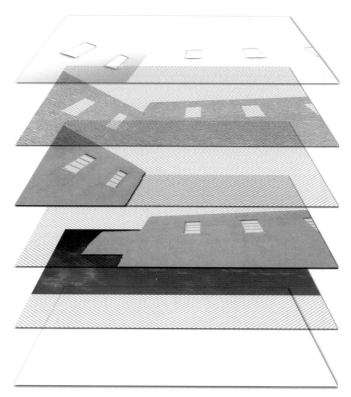

Figure 1.56 The above Layers panel shows the layer contents of a multi-layered Photoshop image. The diagram on the right shows the image that this Layers panel view refers to, where the layers have been pulled apart.

Automating Photoshop

Why spend more time than you have to performing repetitive tasks when Photoshop is able to automate many of these processes for you? For example, the Actions panel will let you load and save Photoshop actions, which are basically recordable Photoshop scripts. In Figure 1.57 you can see a screen shot of the Actions panel displaying an expanded view of the Default Actions set. As you can see from the action descriptions, these will perform automated tasks such as adding a vignette or creating a wood frame edge effect. OK, these are not exactly the sort of actions you would use every day, but if you go to the panel fly-out menu and select Load Actions... you will be taken to the Photoshop CS4/Presets/Photoshop Actions folder. Here you will find lots of useful actions that are worth installing. If someone sends you a Photoshop action, such as via email, all you have to do is to double-click it and this will automatically install the action in the Actions folder and, if Photoshop is not running at the time, launch the program at the same time.

To run an action, you will usually need to have a document already open in Photoshop and then press the Play button. It is also quite easy to record your own custom actions and once you get the hang of how to do this you can progress to using the File ➪ Automate ➪ Batch... function to apply a recorded action to a batch of images, as well as converting actions into droplets, which are like self-contained batch action operations (Figure 1.58). In Chapter 15 I will explain in more detail how to automate Photoshop using these methods.

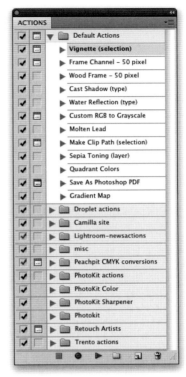

Figure 1.57 The Actions panel.

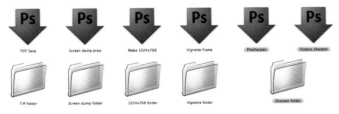

Figure 1.58 With Photoshop droplets you can apply a batch action operation by simply dragging and dropping an image file or a folder of images onto a droplet.

Nudging layers and selections

The keyboard arrow keys can be used to nudge a layer or selection in 1 pixel (10 pixels with the *Shift* key also held down) increments. A series of nudges count as a single Photoshop step in history and is undone with a single undo or step back in history.

Move tool alignment options

The move tool Options panel now also integrates the alignment options that were previously only listed in the Layer menu. To find out more about layer alignment and distribution refer to page 472.

Move tool

The move tool can perform many functions such as moving layer contents, directly moving layers from one document to another, copying layers, applying transforms, plus selecting and aligning multiple layers. In this respect the move tool might be more accurately described as a move/ transform/alignment tool. The move tool can also be activated any time another tool is selected by holding down the ⌘ *ctrl* key (except for the slice, slice select, hand, pen tool or path selection tools). Holding down the ⌥ *alt* key while the move tool is selected will then let you copy a layer or selection contents. It is therefore useful to know that using the ⌥ *alt* key plus ⌘ *ctrl* (the move tool shortcut) will let you make a copy of a layer or selection contents when any other tool is selected (apart from those I just listed). If the Show Transform Controls box is checked a bounding box will appear around the bounds of the selected layer and, when you mouse down on the bounding box handles to transform the layer, the Options bar will change to display the numeric transform controls.

Layer selection using the move tool

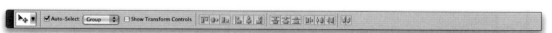

Figure 1.59 The move tool Options bar.

Group or layer

There is a menu item in the move tool Options panel that will allow you to choose between Group or Layer auto-selection. When Layer is selected, Photoshop only auto-selects individual layers. But when Group is selected, Photoshop will auto-select whole layer groups.

When the move tool is selected, dragging with the move tool will move a layer or image selection contents (the cursor does not have to be centered on the object or selection, it can be anywhere in the image window). However, when the Auto-Select Layer option is switched on, the move tool will auto-select the uppermost layer containing the most opaque image data below the cursor; this can be useful when you have a large numbers of image layers stacked up. The move tool also makes multiple layer selection possible, because when the move tool is in the Auto-Select Layer mode you can marquee drag with the move tool from outside the canvas area to select multiple layers, the same way as you make a marquee selection using the mouse cursor to select multiple folders or documents in the Finder/Explorer (see Figure 1.60). It is also worth noting that if you have the move tool selected and the Auto-Select Layer option is currently unchecked, holding down ⌘ ctrl will temporarily invert the state of the move tool to Auto-Select Layer mode.

Where you have many layers that overlap, remember there is a Contextual mode for the move tool that will help you target specific layers (use ctrl right mouse-click to access the Contextual layer menu). Any layer with an opacity greater than 50% will then show up in the contextual menu, allowing you to select a specific layer beneath the cursor point with greater precision.

Align/Distribute layers

When several layers are linked together, you can click on the Align and Distribute buttons in the Options bar as an alternative to navigating via the Layer ⇨ Align Linked and Distribute Linked menus (see Chapter 9 for more about the Align and Distribute commands).

Layer selection shortcuts

You can at any time use the ⌘ ⌥ A ctrl ⌥ A shortcut to select all layers. But note that the move tool layer selection method will not select layers that are locked. So if you use the Auto-Select layer mode to marquee drag across the image to make a layer selection, the background layer will not be included in the selection.

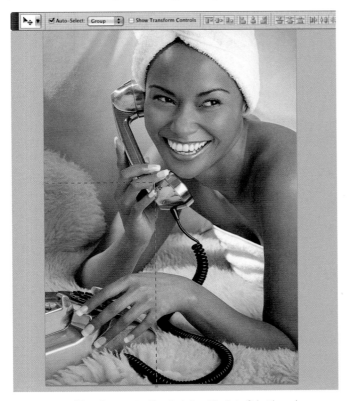

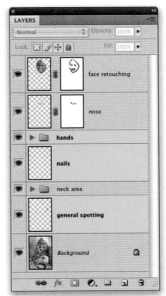

Figure 1.60 When the move tool is selected and the Auto-Select Layer box is checked, you can marquee drag with the move tool from outside of the canvas area inwards to select specific multiple layers. If the 'Auto-Select Layer' option is deselected, you can also hold down ⌘ ctrl to temporarily switch the move tool to the Auto-Select Layer mode.

Client: ET Nail Art
Model: Susannah @ Storm
Makeup: Camilla Pascucci

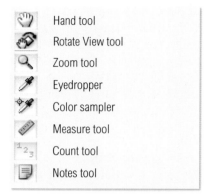

Hand tool

Rotate View tool

Zoom tool

Eyedropper

Color sampler

Measure tool

Count tool

Notes tool

Figure 1.61 The Info panel showing an eyedropper color reading, a measurement readout, plus two color sampler readouts below.

Zoom resize shortcuts

As well as double-clicking the tools panel icons (as described in the main text), you will also find some button options in the hand and zoom tool Options bar. These buttons will let you resize the image screen display to: Actual Pixels, Fit Screen, Fill Screen and Print Size.

Eyedropper sampling

The eyedropper tool options now allow you to sample colors based on the 'Current Layer' or 'All Layers'.

Navigation and information tools

To zoom in on an image you can either click with the zoom tool to magnify or drag with the zoom tool, marqueeing the area you wish to inspect in close-up. This combines a zoom and scroll function in one (in Normal mode, a plus icon appears inside the magnifying glass icon). To zoom out, hold down the ⌥ *alt* key and click (the plus sign is replaced with a minus sign). You can also zoom in by holding down the Spacebar + ⌘ key (Mac) or Spacebar + *ctrl* key (PC). This keyboard shortcut calls up the zoom tool and you can then click to zoom in. You can also zoom out by holding down the Spacebar + ⌥ key (Mac) or Spacebar + *alt* key (PC). This keyboard shortcut calls up the zoom tool in zoom out mode and you can then click to zoom out. Note that these shortcuts cannot be used if the type tool is selected.

When you are viewing an image in close-up, you can select the hand tool from the Tools panel or Application bar and drag to scroll the image on the screen, plus you can also hold down the Spacebar at any time to temporarily access the hand tool (except when the type tool is selected). The hand and zoom tools also have another navigational function. You can double-click the hand tool icon in the Tools panel to make an image fit to screen and double-click the zoom tool icon to magnify an image to 100%.

The eyedropper tool can be used to measure pixel values directly from a Photoshop document – these values will be displayed in the Info panel, as shown in Figure 1.61. The color sampler tools can be used to place up to four color samplers in an image to provide persistent readouts of the pixel values. This is useful for those times when you need to closely monitor the pixel values as you make adjustments to an image. The measure tool can be used to measure distance and angles in an image and, again, this data is displayed in the Info panel. The count tool is only available in the extended version and is perhaps more useful to those working in areas like medical research, where you can use the count tool to count the number of cells in a microscope image.

Flick panning

With OpenGL enabled in the Photoshop Performance preferences, you can also check the Enable Flick Panning option in the General preferences (see page 95). When this option is activated, Photoshop will respond to a flick of the mouse pan gesture by continuing to scroll the image in the direction you first scrolled, taking into account the acceleration of the flick movement. When you have located the area of interest just click again with the mouse to stop the image from scrolling any further.

Bird's-eye view

Another OpenGL option is the Bird's-eye view feature. If you are viewing an image in a close-up view and hold down the **H** key as you click with the mouse and hold, the image view will swiftly zoom out to fit to the screen and at the same time show an outline of the close-up view screen area (a bit like the way the Navigator panel view works). With the **H** key and mouse key still held down, you can then click and drag to reposition the close-up view outline, release the mouse, and the close-up view will recenter to the newly selected area in the image.

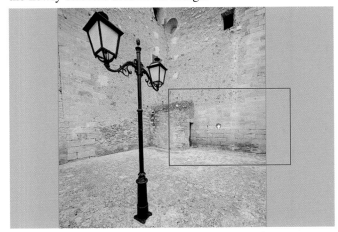

Figure 1.62 If a window document is in OpenGL mode and in a close-up view, you can hold down the **H** key and click with the mouse to access a bird's-eye view of the whole image. You can then drag the rectangle outline shown here to scroll the image and release to return to a close-up of the image centered around this new view.

More zoom keyboard shortcuts

Traditionally, the **⌘ ⌥ 0** **ctrl alt 0** shortcut can be used to zoom in to a 100% pixels view and the **⌘ 0** **ctrl 0** shortcut is used to zoom out to provide a fit to screen zoom view. Photoshop CS4 now also uses the **⌘ 1** **ctrl 1** shortcut to zoom to 100%. This has been implemented in order to unify the window document zoom controls across all of the Creative Suite applications. As a consequence of this, the channel selection shortcuts have been shifted along two numbers. **⌘ 2** **ctrl 2** selects the composite channel and you now need to use **⌘ 3** **ctrl 3** to select the red channel, **⌘ 4** **ctrl 4** to select the green channel and so on. The Tilde key has also changed use. Prior to CS4 **⌘ ~** **ctrl ~** was used to select the composite color channels (after selecting a red, green or blue channel) but is now used to toggle between open window documents.

Another handy zoom shortcut is **⌘ +** **ctrl +** to zoom in and **⌘ —** **ctrl —** to zoom out (note that the **+** key is really the **=** key and the **—** key is the one just to the left of the **=** key). If your mouse has a wheel, you can use it with the **⌥** **alt** key held down to zoom in or out. If you have OpenGL enabled you can carry out a continuous zoom by simply holding down the zoom tool (and use the **⌥** **alt** key + zoom tool to zoom out). Also, if you have a MacBook Air or later MacBook Pro Laptop, CS4 supports two-fingered zoom gestures such as drawing two fingers together to zoom in and spreading two fingers apart to zoom out.

Rotate view shortcut

The rotate view tool uses the R keyboard shortcut, which was previously assigned to the blur/sharpen/sponge tool set. I reckon this will be generally accepted as a positive move, but you can, if desired, use the Keyboard Shortcuts menu described on page 24 to reassign the keyboard shortcuts to whatever scheme you prefer.

Rotate view tool

If OpenGL is enabled in the Photoshop preferences (Performance section), you can use the new rotate view tool to rotate the Photoshop image canvas (as shown below in Figure 1.63). Having the ability to quickly rotate the image view can sometimes make it easier to carry out certain types of retouching work, rather than be forced to draw or paint at an uncomfortable angle. To use the rotate view tool, select it from the Tools panel and click and drag in a window to rotate the image around the center axis. As you do this, you will see a compass overlay that indicates the image position relative to the default view angle (indicated in red), which can be useful when you are zoomed in close on an image. If you hit esc or click on the Reset View button in the Options bar, this resets the view angle to 'Normal' again.

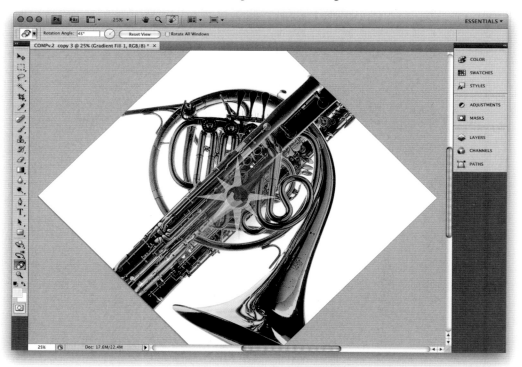

Photograph: Eric Richmond

Figure 1.63 The rotate view tool shown here in action.

Notes tool

The notes tool is handy for adding sticky notes to an open image in Photoshop. Photoshop CS4 has done away with open note windows and uses instead a Notes panel (Figure 1.64) to store the recorded note messages. This new method makes the notes display and management easier to control.

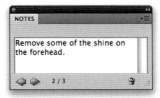

Figure 1.64 The new Notes panel.

I use this tool quite a lot at work because when a client calls me to discuss a retouching job, I can open the image, click on the area that needs to be worked on and use the Notes panel to type in the instructions for whatever further retouching needs to be done (usually with the receiver in one hand and typing with the other!) However, if the client you are working with has Photoshop, they can use the notes feature to mark up images, which when opened in Photoshop can be inspected as shown in Figure 1.65 below.

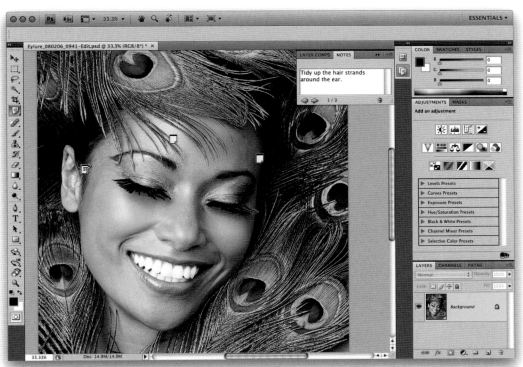

Figure 1.65 This shows an example of the notes tool in action.

Full screen view mode

The Full screen view mode is usually the best view mode for concentrated retouching work as it allows full movement of the image, not limited by the edges of the document bounds. In other words, you can scroll the image to have a corner centered in the screen and edit things like path points outside the bounds of the document. Also note that the **F** key can be used to cycle between screen modes and **Shift F** to cycle backwards.

Screen view modes

In Figure 1.66 I have highlighted the screen view mode options in the Application bar, where you can switch between the three main screen view modes. The standard screen view displays the application window the way it has been shown in all the previous screen shots and allows you to view the document windows as floating windows or tabbed to the dock area. In Full screen mode, the frontmost document fills the screen, while allowing you to see the menus and panels. Lastly, the Absolute full screen view mode displays a full screen view without showing the menus and panels.

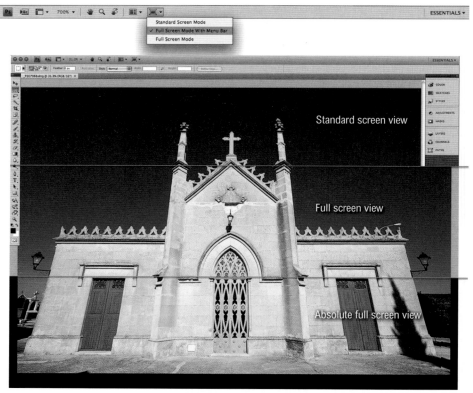

Figure 1.66 This illustration highlights the Screen mode options in the Application bar and you can see an example here of the three screen view modes in the Photoshop interface, showing the standard document window view (top), Full screen view (middle) and the Absolute full screen view (bottom).

Preset Manager

The Preset Manager lets you manage all your presets from within the one dialog. It keeps track of brushes, swatches, gradients, styles, patterns, layer effect contours and custom shapes. For example, Figure 1.67 shows how you can use the Preset Manager to edit a current set of Custom Shapes. You can append or replace an existing set of presets via the Preset Manager options and the Preset Manager can also be customized to display the preset information in different ways, such as in Figure 1.68 where I used a Large List to display thumbnails of the Gradient presets.

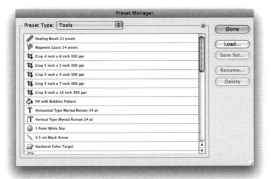

Figure 1.67 You can use the Photoshop Preset Manager to load custom settings or replace them with one of the pre-supplied defaults. Presets include: Brushes, Swatches, Gradients, Styles, Patterns, Contours, Custom Shapes and Tools.

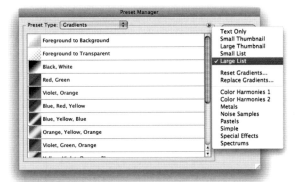

Figure 1.68 Apart from being able to load and replace presets, you are able to choose how the presets are displayed. In the case of Gradients, it is immensely useful to be able to see a thumbnail preview alongside the name of the gradient.

Saving presets as Sets

As you create and add your own custom preset settings, you can manage these via the Preset Manager. This means, for example, that you can select a group of presets and click on the Save Set... button to save these as a new group of presets. These can then be recalled, offloaded and even swapped to avoid losing items that have been appended to existing default sets. The thing to be aware of here is that tool preset settings can easily get deleted when you update or reinstall Photoshop. When you save brush or tool settings, it is easy to reload these again later.

Loading presets

If you double-click any Photoshop setting that is outside the Photoshop folder, it will automatically load the Photoshop program and append the preset to the relevant list in the Preset Manager.

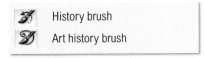

History brush

Art history brush

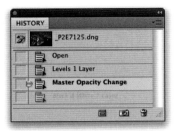

Figure 1.69 A previous history state can be selected by clicking on the history state name in the History panel. When the History panel is set to its default configuration, you will notice how when you go back in history like this, the history states that appear after the one that is selected will now appear dimmed. If you have moved back in history, and then you make further edits to the image, the history states after the selected history state will become deleted. However, you can change this behavior by selecting Allow Non-linear History in the History panel options (see history settings pages 57–58).

History

The History feature was introduced in Photoshop 5.0 and back then it was considered a real breakthrough feature, because for the first time Photoshop was able to offer multiple undos during a single Photoshop editing session. History can play a really important role in the way you use Photoshop. I thought here would be a good opportunity for me to describe this feature in more detail and explain how history can help you use Photoshop more efficiently.

As you work on an individual image, Photoshop will record a history of image states as steps which can be viewed in the History panel (Figure 1.69). If you want to reverse a step you can still use the conventional Edit ⇨ Undo command (⌘ Z ctrl Z), but if you visit the History panel you can go back as many stages in the edit process as you have saved history steps. The history steps can also be saved as Snapshots, which will temporarily prevent them from 'slipping off the radar' and becoming deleted as more history steps are created. One can therefore look at the history as a multiple undo feature in which you can reverse through up to 1000 image states. But it is actually a far more sophisticated tool than just that. For example, there is a non-linear history option for multiple history path recording and a history source column that allows you to select a history state to sample from when working with the history brush. Painting from history can save you from tedious workarounds like having to duplicate a portion of the image to another layer, retouching this layer and merging back down to the underlying layer again.

The History panel

The History panel displays the sequence of Photoshop states recorded during a Photoshop session and its main purpose is to let you manage and access the history states recorded by Photoshop. To revert to a previous state, drag the slider up the list of history states or, alternatively, you can click directly on a specific history state. In Figure 1.69 I carried out a simple one-step undo by clicking on the one but last history step.

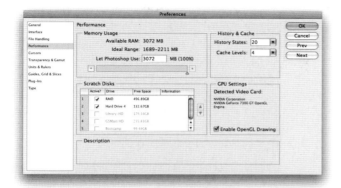

Figure 1.70 The number of history states is set via the Performance section of the Photoshop preferences dialog.

History settings and memory usage

The number of recorded histories can be set in the Photoshop Performance preferences (Figure 1.70). When the maximum number of history states has been reached, the earliest history state at the top of the list will be discarded. Note that if you reduce the number of history states allowed, via the preferences, any subsequent action will immediately cause all earlier states beyond this new limit to be discarded. To set the options for the History panel, mouse down on the fly-out menu and select History Options... (Figure 1.71) I'll come on to the snapshot settings shortly, but at this stage you may want to consider enabling non-linear history. This will allow you to select a previous history state, but instead of undoing those steps between the earlier state and the latest, and deleting them, non-linear history will allow you to shoot off in a new direction and still preserve all the original history states. 'Make Layer Visibility Changes Undoable' makes switching layer visibility on or off a recordable step in history, although this can be annoying when you are mixing layer visibility on or off with an undo/redo of the last Photoshop step.

History cleverly makes use of the image tiling to limit any unnecessary drain on memory usage. Conventional wisdom would suggest that any multiple undo feature is bound to tie up vast amounts of scratch

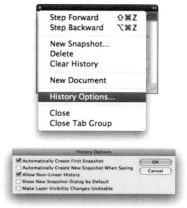

Figure 1.71 The History Options are accessed via the History panel fly-out menu. These will allow you to decide the snapshot settings. I usually prefer to check the Allow Non-Linear History option because this enables me to use the History feature to its full potential (see page 61).

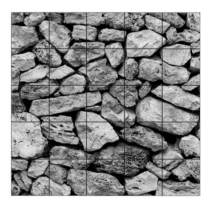

Figure 1.72 This picture shows the underlying tiled structure of a Photoshop image. In this example we have a width and height of five tiles. This is the clue to how history works as economically as possible. The history stores the minimum amount of data necessary at each step in Photoshop's memory. So if only one or two tile areas are altered by a Photoshop action, only the data change for those tiles is recorded.

History stages	Scratch disk
Open file	461 MB
Levels adjustment	721 MB
16 bit to 8 bit	945 MB
Healing brush	986 MB
Healing brush	998 MB
Healing brush	1010 MB
Marquee selection	982 MB
Feather selection	1011 MB
Inverse selection	1010 MB
Add adjustment layer	1140 MB
Flatten image	1110 MB
Unsharp Mask filter	1190 MB

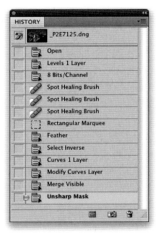

Figure 1.73 The accompanying table shows how the scratch disk usage will fluctuate during a typical Photoshop session. The opened image was 95 MB in size and 3 GB of memory was allocated to Photoshop. The scratch disk overhead is always quite big at the beginning of each Photoshop session, but notice how there is little proportional increase in scratch disk size with each added history state.

disk space to store all the previous image states. However, proper testing of history indicates that this is not really the case. It is true that a series of global Photoshop steps may cause the scratch disk usage to rise, but localized changes will not. (You can observe this for yourself by monitoring the scratch disk usage over a number of Photoshop steps.) This is because every Photoshop image is made up of tiled sections. When a large image is in the process of redrawing you may see these tiles rendering across the screen and Photoshop's history memorizes the changes that take place in each tile only. If a brush stroke takes place across two image tiles, only the changes taking place in those tiles are updated (Figure 1.72). When a global change takes place such as a filter effect, the whole of the image area is updated and the scratch disk usage will rise accordingly.

A savvy Photoshop user will want to customize the History feature to record a reasonable number of histories, while at the same time being aware of the need to change this setting if the history usage is likely to place too heavy a burden on the scratch disk. Figure 1.73 demonstrates that successive histories need not consume an escalating amount of memory. After the first adjustment layer, successive adjustment layers have little impact on the scratch disk usage (only the screen preview is being changed). Clone stamp tool cloning and brush work affect changes in small tiled sections. Only the Flatten Image and Unsharp Mask filter, which are applied at the end, add a noticeable amount to the scratch disk usage.

Even so, the Purge History command in the Edit ⇨ Purge menu provides a useful way to keep the amount of scratch disk memory used under control. If the picture you are working with is exceptionally large, then having more than one undo can be both wasteful and unnecessary, so you should perhaps consider restricting the number of recordable history states. On the other hand, if multiple history undos are well within the scratch disk memory limits of your system, then make the most of them. And remember, history is not just there as a mistake correcting tool – it has great potential for mixing composites from previous image states.

History brush

The history brush can be used to paint from a previous history state. To do this you don't change the current history state, but instead you set a source history state for the history brush by clicking a box in the column next to the history state you wish to sample from. In Figure 1.74 you can see how I set the Levels history state as the history source. The small history brush icon indicates which history state (or snapshot) is currently being used as the source and I was then able to paint with the history brush from this previous history state. The history brush therefore allows you to selectively restore the previously held image information as desired. In Figure 1.74 I was using the history brush to paint over the areas where I had applied the healing brush, in order to restore those parts of the picture to the Levels adjusted history state.

Use of history versus undo

As you will have seen so far, the History feature is capable of being a lot more than a repeat Edit ⇨ Undo command. Although the History feature is sometimes described as a multiple undo, it is important not to confuse Photoshop History with the role of the Undo command. For example, there are a number of Photoshop procedures that are only undoable with the Edit ⇨ Undo command – like intermediate changes made when setting the shadows and highlights in the Levels dialog. Plus there are things which can be undone using Edit ⇨ Undo that have nothing to do with the history. For example, if you delete an action or delete a history, these are also only recoverable using Edit ⇨ Undo. The Undo command is also a toggled action and this is because the majority of Photoshop users like to switch quickly back and forth to see a before and after version of the image. The current combination of Undo commands and history has been carefully planned to provide the most flexible and logical approach. History is not just an 'oh I messed up. Let's go back a few stages' feature, the way some other programs work; it is a tool designed to ease the workflow and provide you with extra creative options in Photoshop.

Art history brush

The art history brush is something of an oddity. It is a history brush that allows you to paint from history but does so via a brush which distorts the sampled data and can be used to create impressionist type painting effects. You can learn more about this tool from the *Photoshop CS4 for Photographers Help Guide* that can be installed from the DVD.

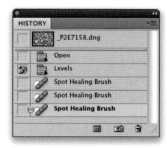

Figure 1.74 A previous history state can be selected as the source for the history brush by going to the History panel and clicking in the empty space to the left of the history state you want to paint from using the history brush.

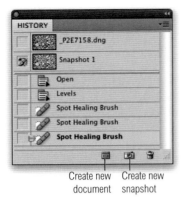

Create new document   Create new snapshot

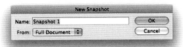

Figure 1.75 To record a new snapshot, click on the New Snapshot button at the bottom of the History panel. This will record a snapshot of the history at this stage. If you ⌥ *alt*-click the button, there are three options: Full Document, which stores all layers intact; Merged Layers, which stores a composite; and Current Layer, which stores just the currently active layer. Note that if you have the Show New Snapshot dialog by Default turned on in the History panel options the New Snapshot dialog will appear directly, without you having to ⌥ *alt*-click the New Snapshot button. The adjacent New Document button will create a duplicate image of the active image in its current history state.

Snapshots

Snapshots are stored above the divider and used to record the image in its current state so as to prevent this version of the image from being overwritten (for as long as the document is open and being edited in Photoshop). The default settings for the History panel will store a snapshot of the image in its opened state and you can create further snapshots by clicking on the Snapshot button at the bottom of the panel (Figure 1.75). This feature is particularly useful if you have an image state that you wish to store temporarily and don't wish to lose it as you make further adjustments to the image. There is no real constraint on the number of snapshots that can be added, and in the History panel options (Figure 1.71) you can choose to automatically generate a new snapshot every time you save the image (which will also be time-stamped). The Create New Document button (next to the Snapshot button) can be used to create a duplicate image state in a new document window, which can then be saved as a separate image.

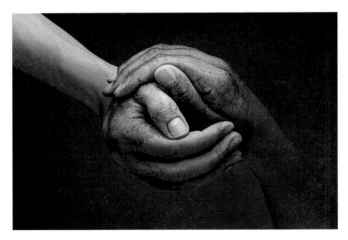

Figure 1.76 Photographer Jeff Schewe has had a long standing connection with the Adobe Photoshop program and its development. The origins of the History feature can perhaps be traced back to a seminar where he used the Globe Hands image shown here to demonstrate his use of the Snapshot feature in Photoshop 1.5. Jeff was able to save multiple snapshots of different image states in Photoshop and then selectively paint back from them. This was all way before layers and history were introduced in Photoshop. Chief Photoshop Engineer Mark Hamburg was suitably impressed by Jeff's technique, and the ability to paint from snapshots became an important part of the History feature. Everyone had been crying out for a multiple undo in Photoshop, but when history was first introduced in Photoshop 5.0 it came as quite a surprise to discover just how much the History feature would allow you to do.

Non-linear history

The non-linear history option lets you branch off in several directions and experiment with different effects without needing to add lots of new layers. Non-linear history is not an easy concept to grasp, so the best way to approach it is to imagine a series of history states as having more than one 'linear' progression, allowing the user to branch off in different directions instead of in a single chain of events in Photoshop (Figure 1.77). You can therefore take an image down several different routes, while you are working on it in a Photoshop session, and a history step from one branch can be blended with a history step from another branch without having to save duplicate files.

Non-linear history requires a little more thinking on your part in order to monitor and recall image states, but ultimately makes for a more efficient use of the available scratch disk space. Overall, I find it useful to have non-linear history switched on all the time, regardless of whether I need to push this feature to its limits or not.

Non-linear history in use

In Chapter 8 you can see a practical example of how to use this and other History features in a typical Photoshop retouching session.

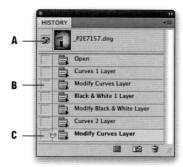

Figure 1.77 The Non-linear history option allows you to branch off in different directions and simultaneously maintain a record of each history path up to the maximum number of history states that can be allowed. Shown here are three history states selected from the History panel: The initial opened image state (A); another with a Curves adjustment layer (B); and thirdly, an alternative version where I added a Black and White adjustment layer followed by a Curves adjustment layer to add a sepia tone color effect.

Corrupt files

There are various reasons why a file may have become corrupted and refuses to open. This will often happen to images that have been sent as attachments and is most likely due to a break during transmission somewhere, resulting in missing data.

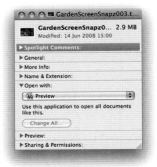

Figure 1.78 The header information in some files may contain information that tells the operating system to open the image in a program other than Photoshop. On a Macintosh go to the File menu and choose File ⇨ Get Info and under the 'Open with' item, change the default application to Photoshop. On a PC you can do the same thing via the File Registry.

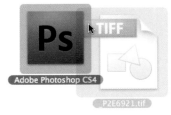

Figure 1.79 When files won't open up directly in Photoshop the way you expect them to, then it may be because the header is telling the computer to open them up in some other program instead. To force open an image in Photoshop, drag the file icon on top of the Photoshop application icon or an alias or shortcut thereof, such as an icon placed in the dock or on the desktop.

When files won't open

You can open image files up using Bridge (which is described on pages 72–75), or from anywhere on your computer. As long as the file you are opening is in a file format that Photoshop recognizes, it will open in Photoshop when you double-click it and, if the program is not running at the time, this action launches Photoshop too.

However, every document file on your computer will contain a header section, which among other things tells the computer which application should be used to open it. For example, Microsoft Word documents will (naturally enough) default to opening in Microsoft Word. Photoshop can recognize nearly all types of image documents regardless of the application they may have originated from, but sometimes you will see an image file with an icon for another specific program, like Macintosh Preview, or Internet Explorer. If you simply double-click these files, they will open in these respective programs. To get around this, you can follow the instructions described in Figure 1.78. Alternatively, you can use the File ⇨ Open command from within Photoshop, or you can drag a selected file (or files) to the Photoshop program icon or a shortcut/alias of the program icon (Figure 1.79). In each of these cases you can override the computer operating system which normally reads the file header to determine which program the file should be opened in. If you use Bridge as the main interface for opening image files in Photoshop, then open the File Type Association preferences (described in Chapter 11) to check that the file formats for the files you are opening are all set to open via Photoshop.

Yet there are times when even these methods will fail too and this points to one of two things. Either you have a corrupt file, in which case the damage is most likely permanent. Or, the file extension has been wrongly changed. It says .psd, but is it really a PSD? Is it possible that someone has accidentally renamed the file with an incorrect extension? In these situations, the only way to open it will be to use the Photoshop File ⇨ Open command and navigate to locate the mis-saved image (which should then be resaved to register it in the correct file format).

Save often

Do you remember the bit at the end of the movie *Stand by Me* where the author shuts down the computer at the end of writing his book? Every computer literate person in the theater wanted to shout 'No, don't. Save first!' It goes without saying that you must always remember to save, often while working in Photoshop. Thankfully you won't come across many crashes when working with the latest operating systems for Macintosh and PC. But that doesn't mean you should relax too much. Saving a file is easy to do, but there are still some pitfalls to be aware of.

Choosing File ⇨ Save will always create a safe backup of your image but, as with everything else you do on a computer, make sure you are not overwriting the original with an inferior modified version. There is always the danger that you might make permanent changes, such as a drastic reduction in the image size, by accidentally hitting Save, and lose the original in the process. But before you close a file you can always go back a step or two in the History panel and resave the image in the state it was in before it was modified.

When you save an image in Photoshop, you are either resaving the file (which will overwrite the original) or forced to save a new version using the Photoshop file format. The determining factor will be the type of file format the image was in when you opened it and how it has been modified in Photoshop. Some of the different file formats are discussed over the next few pages, but the main thing to be aware of is that some file formats will restrict you from being able to save things like layers, pen paths or extra channels. If, for example, you open a JPEG format file in Photoshop and modify it by adding a pen path, you can choose File ⇨ Save and overwrite the original without any problem. But if you open the same file and add a layer or an extra alpha channel, you won't be able to save it as a JPEG any more. This is because although a JPEG file can contain pen paths it cannot contain layers or additional channels, so it has to be saved using a file format that is capable of containing these extra items.

History saves

Alas, it is not possible to save a history of everything you did to an image, but if you go to the Photoshop preferences you can choose to save the history log information of everything that was done to the image. This can record a log of everything that was done during a Photoshop session and be saved to a central log file or saved to the file's metadata.

The other thing you can do is go to the Actions panel and click to record an action of everything that is done to the image. The major downfall here is that Actions cannot record everything. For example, you cannot record brush strokes within an action.

Version Cue

Version Cue was first introduced as a component of the original Adobe Creative Suite and is included when you buy a complete Creative Suite set of applications. Version Cue is not installed by default when you select the easy install option and must otherwise be installed separately. Once you have done this you can enable it by choosing Preferences ⇨ File Handling and select the checkbox next to Enable Version Cue Workgroup Management. Do this and you will have a choice between using the OS Save or the Adobe Save dialogs. The latter will allow you to make use of the Version Cue features where you can share files with other users over a network and prevent others from overwriting an image file that is already open and in the process of being edited by another user.

The 'save everything' file formats

There are four main file formats that can be used to save everything you might add to an image such as image layers, type layers, channels and also support 16-bits per channel. These are: TIFF, Photoshop PDF (the large document format) PSB and lastly the native Photoshop file format, PSD. I mostly favor using the PSD format when saving master RGB images.

Quick saving

As with all other programs, the keyboard shortcut for saving a file is: ⌘ S ctrl S. If you are editing an image that has never been saved before or the image state has changed (so that what started out as a flattened JPEG now has layers added), this action will pop the Save dialog. Subsequent saves may not show the save dialog. But if you do wish to force the Save dialog to appear to save a copy version, then use: ⌘ ⌥ S ctrl alt S.

Figure 1.80 If the file format you choose to save in won't support all the components in the image, such as layers, then a warning triangle will alert you to this when you save this document, and the layers will not be included. Note that the Mac OS dialog shown here can be collapsed or expanded by clicking on the downward pointing disclosure triangle to toggle the expanded folder view.

I won't go into lengthy detail about what can and can't be saved using each format. But, basically, if you modify a file and the modifications can be saved using the same file format that the original started out in, then Photoshop will have no problem saving and overwriting the original. If the modifications applied to an image mean that it can't be saved using the original file format then it will default to using the PSD (Photoshop document) format and save the image as a new document via the dialog shown in Figure 1.80. You could choose to save such documents using TIFF or PDF, but in my view PSD is a good format with which to save any master image, since the PSD format is able to contain anything that's been added in Photoshop and also offers good, lossless file compression, which can ultimately help you save valuable disk space.

Using Save As... to save images

Following on from that, if the image you are about to save has started out as, say, a flattened JPEG, but now has layers, this will force the Save As dialog shown in Figure 1.80 to appear as you save. But you can also choose File ⇨ Save As any time you wish to save an image using a different file format or, if you want, you can save a layered

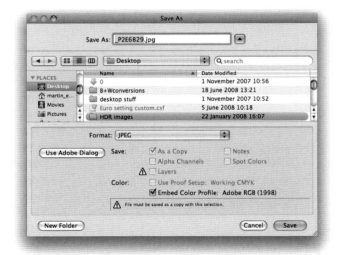

image as a flattened duplicate. In the Save As dialog you have access to various save options and in Figure 1.80 I was able to select the JPEG format when saving a layered, edited image. But as you can see, a warning triangle will appear to alert you if layers (or other non-compatible items) can't be stored when choosing JPEG. In these circumstances, incompatible features like this are automatically highlighted and grayed out in the Save As dialog, and the image is saved as a flattened version.

File formats

Photoshop supports nearly all the current, well-known image file formats. And for those that are not supported, you will find that certain specialized file format plug-ins are supplied as extras on the Photoshop application DVD, which when installed in the Plug-ins folder will allow you to extend the range of file formats that can be chosen when saving. Your choice of format when saving images should be mainly determined by what you want to do with a particular file and how important it is to preserve all the features (such as layers and channels) that may have been added while editing the image in Photoshop. Some formats such as PSD and PSB are best suited for archiving master image files, while others, such as TIFF, are ideally suited for prepress work.

Photoshop native file format

The Photoshop file format is a universal file format and therefore a logical choice when saving and archiving your master files, since the Photoshop (PSD) format will recognize and contain all known Photoshop features. But so too will the TIFF and PDF file formats. However, there are several reasons why I find it preferable to save the master images using the PSD format. Firstly, it helps me to distinguish the master, layered files from the flattened output files (which I usually save as TIFFs). But more importantly, when saving layered images, I find the PSD format is faster and more efficient compared to using TIFF.

Maximum compatibility

Only the Photoshop, PDF, PSB and TIFF formats are capable of supporting all the Photoshop features such as vector masks and image adjustment layers. But for Photoshop format documents to be completely compatible with other programs (especially Photoshop Lightroom), you must ensure you have 'Maximize PSD and PSB Compatibility' checked in the Photoshop File Handling preferences. The reason for this is because Lightroom is unable to read layered PSD files that don't include a saved composite saved within the file. If PSD images fail to be imported into Lightroom, it is most likely because they were saved with this preference switched off.

Smart PSD files

Adobe InDesign and Adobe Dreamweaver will let you share Photoshop format files between these separate applications so that any changes made to a Photoshop file will automatically be updated in the other program. This modular approach means that most Adobe graphics programs are able to seamlessly integrate with each other.

PSD lossless compression

The native Photoshop format is usually the most efficient format to save in because large areas of contiguous color such as a white background are recorded using an LZW type of compression that can make the file size more compact, but without degrading the image quality.

TIFF image compression options

An uncompressed TIFF is usually about the same size as the figure you'll see displayed in the Image Size dialog box. But the TIFF format in Photoshop offers several compression options. LZW is a lossless compression option, where data is compacted and the file size reduced without any image detail being lost. Saving and opening will take longer when LZW is utilized, so some clients request that you do not use it. ZIP is another lossless compression encoding that like LZW is most effective where you have images that contain large areas of a single color. JPEG image compression offers a lossy method, which can offer even greater levels of file compression. But, again, be warned that this option can cause problems downstream with the printer RIP if it is used when saving output files for print.

Save Image Pyramid

The 'Save Image Pyramid' option will save a pyramid structure of scaled-down versions of the full resolution image. TIFF pyramid-savvy DTP applications (there are none I know of yet) will then be able to display a good quality TIFF preview, but without having to load the whole file.

PSB (Large Document Format)

The PSB file format is provided as a special format that can be used when saving master layered files that are in 32-bits per channel mode and/or when you need to save files that exceed the normal 30,000 × 30,000 pixel dimensions limit in Photoshop. The PSB format has instead an upper limit of 300,000 × 300,000 pixels. This implies that you can create huge-sized files. But the only photographic application I can think of where you might need such a large file would be if you were creating a long panoramic image. Even so, a lot of applications and printer RIPs cannot handle files greater than 2 GB anyway. But there are exceptions, such as ColorByte's ImagePrint and Onyx's PosterShop. For this reason the 30,000 × 30,000 limit has been retained for all existing file formats in Photoshop, where the TIFF specification is limited to 4 GB and the native Photoshop PSD format limit is 2 GB maximum size. You also have to bear in mind that only Photoshop CS or later is capable of reading the PSB format.

TIFF (Tagged Image File Format)

The main formats used for publishing work are TIFF and EPS. Of these, TIFF is the most universally recognized industry-standard image format, but this does not necessarily imply that it is better, because the PDF file format is also gaining popularity for DTP (desktop publishing) work. TIFF files can readily be placed in QuarkXpress, InDesign and any other DTP or word processing document. The TIFF format is more open though and, unlike the EPS format, you can make adjustments within the DTP program as to the way a TIFF image will appear in print.

Labs and output bureaux generally request that you save your output images as TIFFs, as this file format can be read by most other imaging computer systems. If you are distributing a file for output as a print or transparency, or for someone else to continue editing your master file, it will usually be safer to supply the image using the TIFF format.

TIFFs saved using Photoshop 7.0 or later will support alpha channels, paths, image transparency and all the extras that can normally be saved using the native PSD and PDF formats. Labs or service bureaux that receive TIFF files for direct output will normally request that a TIFF file is flattened and saved with the alpha channels, and other extra items removed. For example, earlier versions of Quark Xpress had a nasty habit of interpreting any path that was present in the image file as a clipping path.

Flattened TIFFs

If an open image contains alpha channels or layers, the Save dialog in Figure 1.80 will indicate this and you can keep these items checked when saving as a TIFF. If you have 'Ask Before Saving Layered TIFF Files' switched on in the File Saving preferences, a further alert dialog will warn you that Including Layers will increase the file size after clicking OK, the first time you save an image as a layered TIFF.

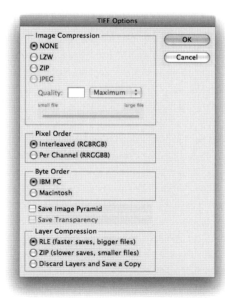

Figure 1.81 This dialog shows the save options that are available when you save an image as a TIFF.

Pixel order

The Photoshop TIFF format has traditionally saved the pixel values in an interleaved order. So if you were saving an RGB image, the pixel values would be saved as clusters of RGB values using the following sequence: RGBRGBRGB. All TIFF readers are able to interpret this pixel order. The Per channel pixel order option will save the pixel values in channel order, where all the red pixel values are saved first, followed by the green, then the blue. So the sequence is more like: RRRGGGBBB. Using the Per channel order can provide faster read/write speeds and better compression. Most third-party TIFF readers should support Per channel pixel ordering, but there is a very slim chance that some TIFF readers won't.

Byte order

The byte order can be made to match the computer system platform the file is being read on. But there is no need to worry about this since I know of no examples where this can cause compatibility problems.

Layer compression

If there are layers present in the image, compression options can be applied separately to the layers. RLE stands for Run Length Encoding and provides the same type of lossless compression as LZW. The ZIP compression is another form of lossless compression. Or alternatively you can choose Discard Layers and Save a Copy, which will save a copy version as a flattened TIFF.

PDF versatility

The PDF format in Photoshop is particularly useful for sending Photoshop images to people who don't have Photoshop, but do have Adobe Reader™ on their computer. If they have a full version of Adobe Acrobat they will even be able to conduct a limited amount of editing, such as the ability to edit the contents of a text layer. Photoshop is also able to import or append annotations added in Adobe Acrobat.

Photoshop PDF

The PDF (Portable Document Format) is a cross-platform file format that was initially designed to provide an electronic publishing medium for distributing documents without requiring the recipient to have a copy of the program that originated the document. Acrobat enables others to view documents the way they are meant to be seen, even though they may not have the exact same fonts that were used to compile that document. All they need is the free Adobe Reader program.

Adobe PDF has now gained far wider acceptance as a reliable and compact method of supplying pages to printers, due to its color management features and its ability to embed fonts, and compress images. It is now becoming the native format for Illustrator and other desktop publishing programs. But it is also gaining popularity for saving Photoshop files, because it can preserve everything that a Photoshop (PSD) file can. Adobe Reader™ and its predecessor Acrobat Reader™ are free, and can easily be downloaded from the Adobe website. But the full Adobe Acrobat™ program is required if you want to distill page documents into the PDF format and edit them on your computer.

But best of all, Acrobat documents are small in size and can be printed at high resolution. I can create a document in InDesign and export it as an Acrobat PDF using the Export command. Anyone who has installed the Adobe Reader program can open a PDF document I have created and see the layout just as I intended it to be seen, with the pictures in full color plus text displayed using the correct fonts. The Photoshop PDF file format can be used to save all Photoshop features such as Layers, with either JPEG or lossless ZIP compression and is backwards compatible in as much as it will save a flattened composite for viewing within programs that are unable to fully interpret the Photoshop CS4 layer information. I have shown and described all the PDF Save dialog options on pages 70–71.

PDF security

The PDF security options allow you to restrict file access to authorized users only. This means that a password will have to be entered before an image can be opened in either Adobe Reader, Acrobat or Photoshop. And you can also introduce a secondary password for permission to print or modify the PDF file in Acrobat. Note: this level of security only applies when reading a file in a PDF reader program and you can only password protect the opening of a PDF file in a program like Photoshop. Once opened, it will then be fully editable. Even so, this is still a useful feature to have, since PDF security allows you to prevent some unauthorized, first level access to your images. There are two security options: 40-bit RC4 for lower-level security and compatibility with versions 3 and 4 of Acrobat and 128-bit RC4, for higher security using Acrobat versions 5–8. However, because the PDF specification is an open-source standard, some other PDF readers are able to by pass these security features and can quite easily open a password-protected image! So the security features are not totally infallible, but marginally better than using no security at all.

Placing PDF files

The Photoshop Parser plug-in enables Photoshop to import any Adobe Illustrator, EPS or generic single/multi-page PDF file. Using File ⇨ Place, you can select individual pages or ranges of pages from a generic PDF file, rasterize them and save to a destination folder. Use File ⇨ Place to extract all or individual image/ vector graphic files contained within a PDF document as separate image files (see Figure 1.82 below).

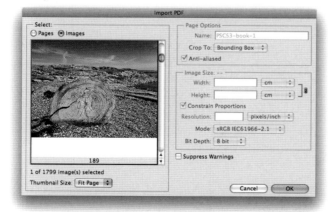

Figure 1.82 If you try to open a generic Acrobat PDF from within Photoshop by choosing File ⇨ Open, or File ⇨ Place, you will see the Import PDF or Place PDF dialog shown here. This will allow you to select individual or multiple pages or selected images only and open these in Photoshop or place them within a new Photoshop document.

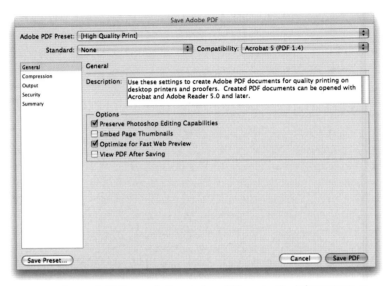

Figure 1.83 You can start by selecting a PDF preset setting before you save, or configure the settings, starting with the General options. In most situations you will want to preserve the ability to edit the saved PDF image again in Photoshop and improve the performance of PDFs on web servers. If you want to preview the PDF in Adobe Acrobat afterwards, then check 'View PDF After Saving'.

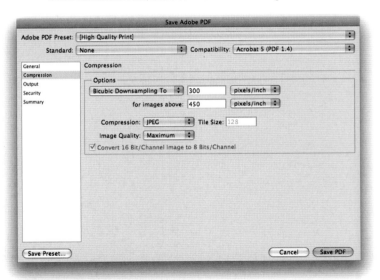

Figure 1.84 The Compression options allow you to decide which compression method (if any) should be used.

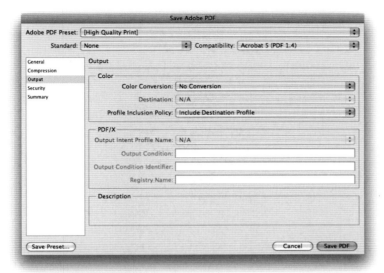

Figure 1.85 The Output options allow you to set document level color management policies. So, for example, you could save an RGB file with a Convert to Destination policy and set the destination space below.

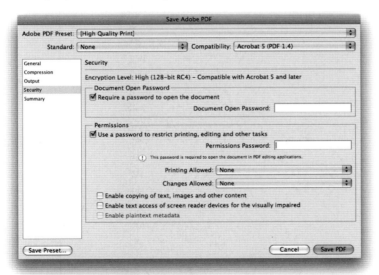

Figure 1.86 The Security options will be linked to the version compatibility you have selected, but essentially these allow you to restrict access by requiring a password to open the document and have a separate password to restrict edit changes or document printing.

Adobe Bridge CS4

Bridge is designed to provide you with an integrated way to navigate through the folders on your computer and provide complete compatibility with all the other Creative Suite applications. The Bridge interface will allow you to inspect images in a folder, make decisions about which ones you like best, rearrange them in the Content panel, hide the ones you don't like and so on.

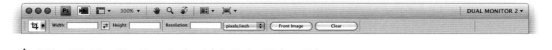

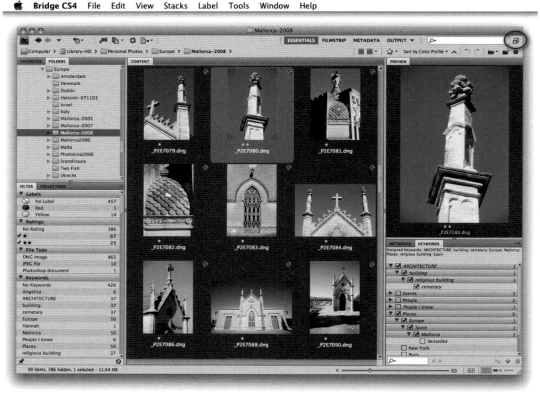

Figure 1.87 The Bridge CS4 interface consists of three column zones which are used to contain the Bridge panel components. This will allow you to customize the Bridge layout in any number of ways. For a complete overview of the components that make up the Bridge interface please refer to Chapter 11.

You can use Bridge to quickly review the images in a folder and open them up in Photoshop, while at a more advanced level you can perform batch operations, share properties between files by synchronizing the metadata information, apply Camera Raw settings to a selection of images and use the Filter panel to fine-tune your image selections. It is very easy to switch back and forth between Photoshop and Bridge and one of the key benefits of having Bridge operate as a separate program is that Photoshop isn't fighting with the processor whenever you use Bridge to perform image browsing tasks.

The Bridge interface

Bridge can be accessed from Photoshop by choosing File ⇨ Browse... or clicking on the Launch Bridge button which is circled in the Application bar in Figure 1.87 (you can also set the Photoshop preferences so that Bridge launches automatically as you launch Photoshop). Bridge initially opens a new window pointing to the last visited folder of files. You can also have multiple Bridge windows open at once and this is useful if you want to manage files better by being able to drag them from one folder to another more easily. It also saves having to navigate back and forth between different folders. To make multiple Bridge windows more manageable, you can click on the Compact mode button in the top right corner to toggle shrinking/expanding the Bridge windows (Figure 1.88).

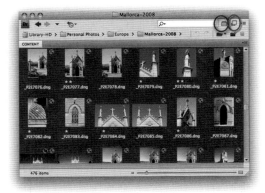

Most of the time you will probably click on the Launch Bridge button in Photoshop to go to Bridge and, when you have selected an image to open, this will take you back to Photoshop again of course. But you can also toggle between the two programs by using ⌘ ⌥ O _ctrl_ _alt_ O to go from Photoshop to Bridge. Once in Bridge you can use the same keyboard shortcut to return to Photoshop again, although to be more precise this shortcut always returns you to the last used application. So if you had just gone to Bridge via Illustrator, the ⌘ ⌥ O _ctrl_ _alt_ O shortcut will in this instance take you from Bridge back to Illustrator again.

Figure 1.88 If you click on the Switch to Compact mode button (circled in Figure 1.87), this will shrink the Bridge window to a compact Content panel only view like the one shown here, and if you click on the Ultra Compact mode button (circled here), this will compact the window further to display the title and Application bars only. To return to a full window view, click on the Switch to Full mode button (circled in blue). Note that compact Bridge windows are always displayed in front of all other windows on the display, even when you are working in another program.

The new Bridge output modes

Up until now, Bridge has always had to rely on Photoshop to use the Contact Sheet and Web Photo Gallery automate functions. These have now been done away with in Photoshop and are provided directly within Bridge. On the plus side, this makes the contact sheet and web gallery generation easier to access. This much is certainly an improvement over what went on before but, as Adobe have not yet done anything really to speed up the output process, it's still as dog slow as ever.

The Lightroom alternative

If you regularly need to prepare a lot of contact sheets or web galleries, there is no doubt that Lightroom is the better program to use. The tools in Lightroom are much better suited for these kinds of tasks, and the contact sheet generation in Lightroom in draft mode is roughly 100 times faster than Bridge CS4! What can take 10 minutes to process in Bridge can be done in a matter of a few seconds using Lightroom.

It makes sense to resize the Bridge window to fill the screen and if you have a dual monitor setup you can always have the Photoshop application window on the main screen and the Bridge window (or windows) on the other. Image folders can be selected via the Folders or Favorites panels and the folder contents viewed in the Content panel area as thumbnail images. When you click on a thumbnail, an enlarged view of the individually selected images can be seen in the Preview panel and images can be opened by double-clicking on the thumbnail. The main thing to be aware of is that you can have Bridge running alongside Photoshop without compromising Photoshop's performance; it has been considered good practice to use Bridge in place of the Finder/Explorer as your main tool for navigating the folders on your computer system and opening documents. This can include opening photos directly into Photoshop, but of course you can use Bridge as a browser to open up any kind of document: not just those that are linked to the Adobe Creative Suite programs but others such as Word documents can be made to open directly in their host applications.

Custom workspaces in Bridge

The Bridge panels can be grouped together in different ways and the panel dividers dragged so, for example, the preview panel can be made to fill the Bridge interface more fully and there are already a number of workspace presets which are available from the Application bar. In Figure 1.89 you can see Bridge being used with the Output workspace setting, where it offers a special Output Preview panel for previewing print or web gallery outputs directly from Bridge

Slideshows

You can also use Bridge to generate instant slideshows. Just go to the View menu and choose Slideshow, or use the ⌘ L ctrl L keyboard shortcut. Figure 1.90 shows an example of a Slideshow and instructions on how to access the Help menu that's shown here.

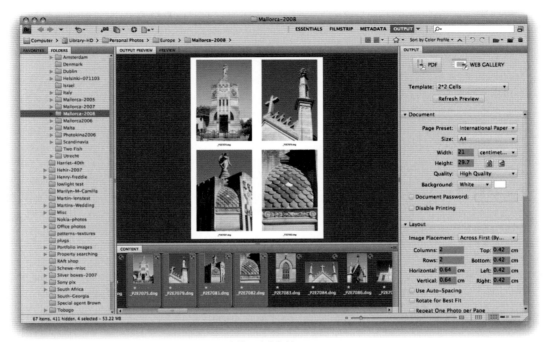

Figure 1.89 You can use the different workspaces to quickly switch Bridge layouts. This example shows the Output workspace in use, where one can edit print or Web output layouts for creating direct outputs via Bridge.

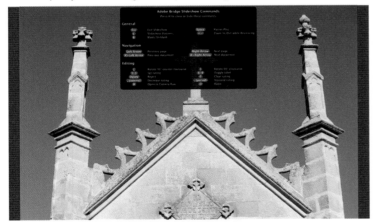

Figure 1.90 You can use the Bridge application View ⇨ Slideshow mode to display all selected images in a slideshow form, where you can make all your essential review and edit decisions with this easy-to-use interface. Press the **H** key to call up the Slideshow shortcuts shown here.

Saving from raw files

If you save an image opened up from a raw file original, Photoshop will by default suggest you save it using the Photoshop native file format. You are always forced to save it as something else and never to overwrite the original raw image. Most raw formats have unique extensions anyway like .crw or .nef. But Canon did once decide to use a .tif extension for some of their raw file formats (so that the thumbnail would show up in their browser program). The danger here was that if you overrode the Photoshop default behavior and tried saving an opened Canon raw image as a TIFF, and you also ignored the warning you were about to overwrite the original image, you did run the risk of degrading the original raw file!

New Auto logic

The Auto setting in Camera Raw has been improved so that selecting 'Auto' will most of the time give you better and more consistent results than could be achieved with previous versions of Camera Raw.

Opening photos via Camera Raw

There are a lot of things you can do in Bridge by way of managing and filtering images and other files on your computer and you will find a more detailed analysis of Bridge in Chapter 11. For now, all that you really need to familiarize yourself with are the Favorites and Folders panels and how you can use these to navigate the folder hierarchy. The Content panel is then used to inspect the folder contents and you can use the Preview panel to see an enlarged preview of the image (or images) you are about to open. Once photos have been selected, just double-click the images within the Content panel (not the Preview panel) to open them directly into Photoshop.

However, if you are opening a raw or DNG image, it will automatically open via the Camera Raw dialog shown in Figure 1.91, and if you are opening multiple raw images from Bridge you will see a filmstrip of thumbnails down the left-hand side of the Camera Raw dialog. But there is also a preference setting in Bridge CS4 that will allow you to open up JPEG and TIFF images via Camera Raw too. All of Chapter 3 is devoted to looking at the Camera Raw controls and I would say that the main benefit of using Camera Raw is that any edits you apply in Camera Raw are non-permanent. This latest version in CS4 offers yet further major advances in raw processing capability.

If you are still a little intimidated by the Camera Raw dialog interface, you can for now just click on the Auto button in Camera Raw (circled in Figure 1.91) and then click on the Open Image button without concerning yourself too much just yet with what all the controls do. When the default settings in Camera Raw are set to Auto, these will automatically optimize the image settings for you. This should give you a good image to start working with in Photoshop, and the beauty of working with Camera Raw is that you will never overwrite the original master raw file (but do heed the warning in the sidebar about saving raw TIFF files). If you don't like the auto settings Camera Raw is giving you, then it is relatively easy to adjust the tone and color sliders to improve upon the auto adjustment settings.

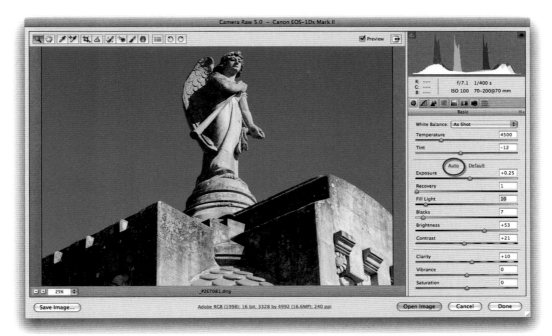

Figure 1.91 When you select a single raw image in Bridge, and double-click to open, you will be faced with the Camera Raw dialog. The Basic panel controls (shown here) are a good place to get started but, as was mentioned in the text, the Auto button can often provide you with an ideal setting for most types of images. Once you are happy, click on the Open Image button at the bottom to open in Photoshop.

Full screen mode

If you click on the Full screen mode button in Camera Raw, you can quickly switch the Camera Raw view to Full screen mode.

What's new in Camera Raw 5.0

There are quite a few notable additions here. The most significant is the fact that you can use the adjustment brush and Gradient filter to apply localized edits to a raw image. The Clarity slider can be used to apply a negative clarity amount, which can be used to produce a nice 'diffusion printing' look or used in conjunction with the adjustment brush soften areas of a picture, such as the skin tones. There is the ability to apply vignetting to post-cropped images and, of course, the improved Sharpening and Noise Reduction which were both introduced with the Camera Raw 4.1 update. With all these new features, there is even more you can achieve now at the Camera Raw stage before taking an image into Photoshop.

ATWs

Being a member of the team that makes Photoshop has many rewards. But one of the perks is having the opportunity to add little office in-jokes in a secret spot on the Photoshop splash screen. It's a sign of what spending long hours building a new version of Photoshop will do to you! The instructions for how to access these are described in the main text.

Photoshop code names

Nearly every version of the Photoshop beta program has traditionally been named after a music track or a movie. Past honored music artists have included: Adrian Belew, William Orbit and Lou Reed.

Adobe On-line

Adobe On-line... is available from the Help menu and lets you access any late-breaking information along with on-line help and professional Photoshop tips.

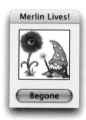

Figure 1.92 Can you find Merlin?

Easter eggs

We'll round off this chapter with some of the hidden fun items in Photoshop. If you drag down from the system or Apple menu to select About Photoshop... the splash screen reopens and after about 5 seconds the text starts to scroll telling you lots of stuff about the Adobe team who wrote the program, etc. Hold down ⎇ _alt_ and the text will scroll faster. And last, but not least, a special mention to the most important Photoshop user of all... . Now hold down ⌘ _ctrl_ _alt_ and choose About Photoshop... and you will see the Stonehenge beta test version of the splash screen (Figure 1.93). This could be because of the Photoshop team's new found interest in archeology, or it might just be another tribute to the movie _Spinal Tap_. I somehow suspect the latter. When the credits have finished scrolling, carefully ⎇ _alt_-click in the white space above the credits, but below the image, to see what are known as Adobe Transient Witticisms appearing one at a time above the credits. If you want to see another Easter egg, go to the Layers panel, hold down ⎇ _alt_ and choose Panel Options from the panel submenu (see Figure 1.92).

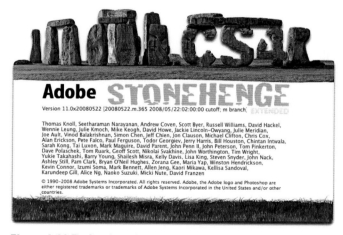

Figure 1.93 The Stonehenge beta splash screen.

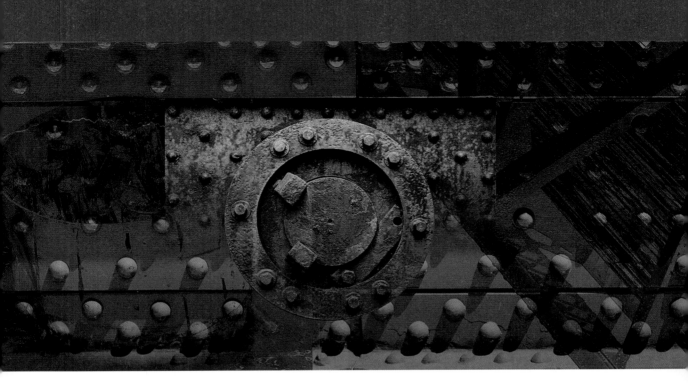

Chapter 2

Configuring Photoshop

I n order to get the best performance out of Photoshop, you need to ensure that your computer system has been optimized for image editing work. When I first began writing the 'Photoshop for Photographers' series of books, it was always necessary to guide readers on how to buy the most suitable computer for Photoshop work and what hardware specifications to look for. These days I would suggest that almost any computer you can buy is capable of running Photoshop and can be upgraded later to run the program faster. As always, I try to avoid making distinctions between the superiority of the Macintosh or PC systems. If you are an experienced computer user, you know what works best for you and I see no reason to evangelize my preference for using a Mac. Throughout my computer career, it's what I have grown

64-bit processing support

It is well worth installing as much RAM memory as possible in your computer, as the RAM figures quoted here are the minimum recommended amounts. Personally, I would advise installing at least 2 GB RAM if you can. With the 32-bit version of the program, Photoshop is able to make use of up to 4 GB of RAM memory. However, 64-bit processing is now the new standard for the latest computer hardware and if you are running a Windows 64-bit operating system you can install a 64-bit version of Photoshop CS4, which offers the key benefit of letting you take advantage of having more than 4GB of RAM memory installed in your computer. This has the potential to boost the speed for some operations (like the time it takes to open large documents).

If you are a Macintosh user you can only install a 32-bit version of Photoshop CS4 and allocate up to 4 GB (less whatever the operating system frameworks take up, so effectively up to 3.5 GB). This lack of support for 64-bit processing is down to the fact that Apple decided in June 2007 to switch from Carbon to Cocoa for its 64-bit requirements and, as Photoshop has previously been written for Carbon, this announcement came too late for Adobe (or other software companies) to update their code for Cocoa. For more information on this subject, check out Scott Byer's Adobe blog: http://blogs.adobe.com/scottbyer/2006/12/64_bitswhen.html, as well as John Nack's coverage of this topic at: http://blogs.adobe.com/jnack/2008/04/photoshop_lr_64.html

up with and it feels like home. The same arguments apply if you're a Windows PC user. Apart from anything else, once you have bought a bunch of programs, you are kind of locked into using that particular system, and if you switch you face the prospect of buying most of your favorite software packages all over again.

What you will need

Today's entry level computers will contain everything you need, but here is a guide to the minimum system requirements for Macintosh and Windows machines:

Macintosh

Photoshop CS4 will run on a Power PC G4, G5 or any of the latest Intel-based Macs running Mac OS 10.3 or later including Leopard (10.5). The minimum RAM requirement is 320 MB (but 384 MB is recommended) and Photoshop CS4 requires an estimated 1.5 GB of hard disk space. You will also need a monitor with at least 1024 x 768 pixel resolution driven by a 16-bit graphics card with at least 64 MB video RAM and a CD/DVD drive. All the current range of Apple Macintosh computers are capable of meeting these requirements, although with some of the older G4 and G5 computers you may need to upgrade the RAM memory and graphics card.

Windows

Photoshop CS4 will run on Pentium 4, Centrinos, Intel Xeon and Xeon Dual processors running Windows XP with Service Pack 2 or higher, as well as Vista. Minimum RAM requirement is 320 MB (384 MB is recommended) and requires an estimated 650 MB of hard disk space. You will also need a monitor with at least 1024 x 768 pixel resolution driven by a 16-bit graphics card with at least 64 MB video RAM and a CD/DVD drive. Almost any new PC system you buy should have no trouble meeting these requirements. But if you have an older computer system, do check that you have enough RAM memory and a powerful enough graphics card.

The ideal computer setup

Your computer working environment is important. Even if space is limited there is much you can do to make your work area an efficient place to work in. Figure 2.1 shows a general view of the office area from where I run my photography business and do all my Photoshop work and, as you can see, it allows three operators to work simultaneously. The desk unit was custom built to provide a large continuous worktop area with good cable management in order to minimize the number of stray leads hanging all over the place. The walls are painted neutral gray with paint I was able to get from a local hardware store, which, when measured with a spectrophotometer, is almost a perfect neutral color. The under shelf lighting uses cool fluorescent strips that bounce off behind the

Chip acceleration

Upgrading the processor chip is the most dramatic way you can boost a computer's performance. But not all computers will allow you to do this. If you have either a daughter card slot or some other processor upgrade slot then you will be able to upgrade your old computer and give it a new lease of life. The upgrade card may also include an increase of backside cache memory to further enhance performance. The cache memory stores frequently used system commands and thereby takes the strain away from the processor chip allowing faster performance on application tasks.

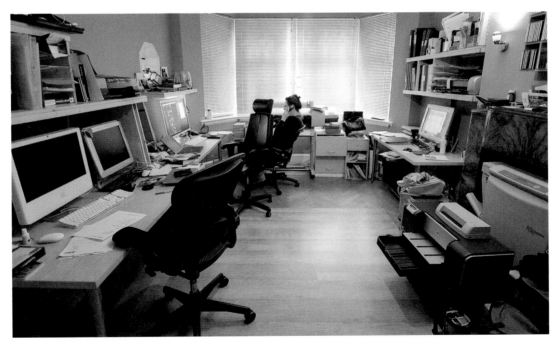

Figure 2.1 This is the office area where I carry out all my Photoshop work. It has been custom built so that the desk area remains as clear as possible. The walls are painted neutral gray to absorb light and reduce the risk of color casts affecting what you see on the monitor screens. The lighting comes from daylight balanced tubes which backlights the monitor screens. I usually have the light level turned down quite low, in order to maximize the monitor viewing contrast.

Chip speed

Microchip processing speed is expressed in megahertz, but performance speed also depends on the chip type. A 2 GHz Pentium class 4 chip is not as fast as a 2 GHz Intel Core Duo processor. Speed comparisons in terms of the number of megahertz are only valid between chips of the same series. Many of the latest computers are also enabled with twin processing. Another crucial factor is the bus speed, which refers to the speed of data transfer from RAM memory to the CPU (the central processing unit, i.e. the chip). CPU performance can be restricted by slow system bus speeds so faster is definitely better, especially for Photoshop work where large chunks of data are always being processed.

Eizo ColorEdge

Eizo have established themselves as offering the finest quality LCD displays for graphics use. The ColorEdge CG301 is the flagship model in the range. A 30" wide screen, it is capable of providing uniform screen display from edge to edge, encompasses the Adobe RGB gamut and comes with ColorNavigator calibration software that can be used with X-Rite calibration devices. This display is more expensive than most, but is highly prized for its color fidelity.

displays to avoid any light hitting the screens directly. The window is north east facing, so I never have too many problems with direct sunlight entering the room and what daylight does enter the office can be controlled with the venetian blinds. It is also important to choose chairs that are comfortable, ideally one with arm rests and adjustable seating positions so that your wrists can rest comfortably on the table top, and the monitor should be level with your line of view or slightly lower.

Once you start building an imaging workstation, you will soon end up with lots of electrical devices. While these in themselves may not consume a huge amount of power, do take precautions against too many power leads trailing from a single power point. To prevent damage or loss of data from a sudden power cut, place an uninterruptible power supply unit (UPS) between your computer and the mains source. These devices will also smooth out any voltage spikes or surges in the electricity supply.

Choosing a display

The display is one of the most important components in your entire kit. It is what you will spend all your time looking at as you work in Photoshop and you really do not want to economize by buying a cheap screen that is unsuited for graphics use. The only displays you can buy new these days are liquid crystal displays (LCDs), which range in size from the small screens used on laptop computers to the big 30" desktop displays. An LCD display contains a translucent film of fixed-size liquid crystal elements that individually filter the color of a backlit, fluorescent light source. Therefore, the only hardware adjustment you can usually make is to adjust the brightness of the backlit screen. You can calibrate according to the brightness of the LCD hardware, but that is about all you can do. The contrast of an LCD is fixed, but it is usually more contrasty than CRT monitors ever were, which is not a bad thing when doing Photoshop work for print output.

Because LCDs are digital devices they tend to produce a more consistent color output. They do still need to be calibrated and profiled of course, but the display's performance should remain fairly consistent over longer periods of time. On the other hand, with some screens there may be some variance in the image appearance depending on the angle from which you view the display, which means that the color output of an LCD may only appear correct when the screen is viewed front on. This very much depends on the design of the LCD display and the worst examples of this can be seen on ultra-thin laptop screens. But the evenness of output from an Apple Cinema display and other desktop LCD screens is certainly a lot more consistent. The higher grade LCD screens do feature relatively good viewing angle consistency, are not too far off from providing a neutral color at a D65 white balance and won't fluctuate much in performance. As with everything else in life, you get what you pay for.

Wide dynamic range displays

It is interesting to speculate what displays will be like in the future. Dolby recently acquired BrightSide Technologies (http://www.dolby.com/promo/hdr/technology.html) who developed an LCD display which uses a matrix of LED lights instead of a fluorescent light source to pass light through the LCD film (Figure 2.2). These screens have an incredible dynamic range and are capable of displaying a 16-bit per channel image with an illumination range that makes an ordinary 8-bit display look dull and flat by comparison. We may one day even see display technologies that can get closer to simulating the dynamic range of natural light. These will be great for viewing computer games and video, but for Photoshop print work we want the display we are looking at to match our expectations of what can be reproduced on a print.

Video cards

The graphics card in your computer is what drives the display. It processes all the pixel information and converts it to draw a color image on the screen. An accelerated graphics card will enable your screen to do several things.

NEC LCD3090

NEC have recently released a 30" display called the LCD3090, which has similar specifications to the Eizo ColorEdge range. This professional quality display has also won a lot of praise from industry color gurus.

Adding a second display

To run a second display you may need to buy an additional PCI card that provides a second video port. You can then get a second screen and have this located beside the main monitor to display the Photoshop panels and keep the main screen area clear of clutter.

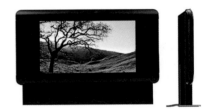

Figure 2.2 This shows the Dolby DR37-P 37" wide extended dynamic range screen.

Which video card is best?

The main point to make here is that nothing will be lost in performance capability (relative to Photoshop CS3) by not upgrading your video card. But if you do want to take advantage of what OpenGL can offer in CS4, then it might just be necessary to purchase a new one. At the time of writing, there is a long list of the video cards that are capable of providing OpenGL support in Photoshop CS4 for Mac OS X 10.4.11 (or later), Windows Vista and limited support for Windows XP. It is difficult though to point to any one group of cards and say that 'these are best'. This is because the OpenGL performance in Photoshop will be down to not just the card, but also the computer platform and operating system used. As a general rule you can assume that more on-board memory will indicate better graphics processing power. But you might also want to check out anecdotal evidence of what other Photoshop CS4 users find works best for them with their particular computers and operating systems. Until someone finds the time to test a dozen or so high-end graphic cards with a variety of different operating systems, it will be impossible to offer precise guidance here. What I do know is that the basic MacBook computer is unable to offer OpenGL support because the MacBook utilizes 64MB of the computer's on-board RAM memory to power the display, and this limits it from offering OpenGL support.

It will allow you to run your screen display at higher screen resolutions, hold more image screen view data in memory and it will use the monitor profile information to finely adjust the color appearance. When more of the off-screen image data remains in memory, the image scrolling is enhanced and this generally provides faster screen refreshes. In the old days, computers would be sold with a limited amount of video memory and if you were lucky you could just about manage to run a small screen in millions of colors. If you buy a computer today the chances are that it will already be equipped with a good, high performance graphics card that is easily capable of meeting all your needs. A video card will probably have at least 128 MB of dedicated memory, which is enough to satisfy the minimum requirements for Photoshop CS4. However, with the advent of the latest OpenGL features, it is now worth considering video cards that were previously considered only necessary for gaming and 3D work. Check the Adobe Help site to find out which cards are designated as being compatible for Photoshop CS4 and OpenGL.

Display calibration and profiling

We now need to focus on what is the most important aspect of any Photoshop system: getting the monitor to correctly display your images in Photoshop at the right brightness and ensure that the screen colors can be relied upon to match the print output. This basic setup advice should be self-evident, because we all want our images in Photoshop to be consistent from session to session and match in appearance when they are viewed on another user's system. The initial calibration process should get your display close to an idealized state, and the next step is to build a monitor profile that describes how well the display actually performs after it has been calibrated, which at a minimum describes the white point and chosen gamma. The more advanced LCD displays such as the Eizo ColorEdge and NEC LCD3090 do provide hardware calibration for a more consistent and standardized output, but the only adjustment you can make on most LCD monitors is to adjust the brightness.

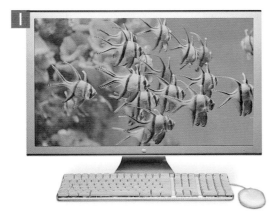

1 An uncalibrated and unprofiled monitor cannot be relied on to provide an accurate indication of how colors should look.

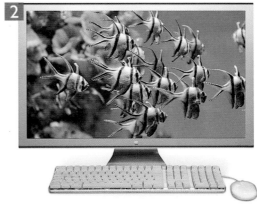

2 The calibration process simply aims to optimize the display for brightness and get the luminance within a desired range.

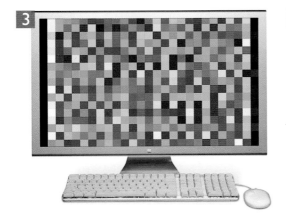

3 The profiling process takes into account the target white balance and gamma. The profiling process will also measure how a broad range of colors is displayed. Recording this extra color information is the only way you can truly produce an accurate profile.

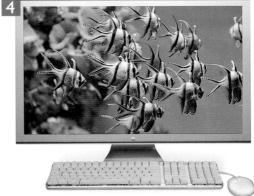

4 To create a profile of this kind you need a colorimeter device. A calibrator such as the X-Rite i1Display 2 or i1Photo with the i1Match or Profile Maker Professional software will produce the most accurate results. Once calibrated and profiled, you will have a computer display that can be relied upon when assessing how colors will reproduce in print.

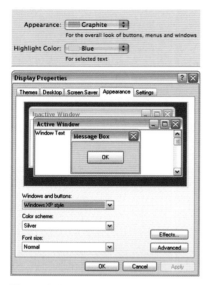

Figure 2.3 This shows the operating system Appearance options for Macintosh (top) and Windows XP (bottom).

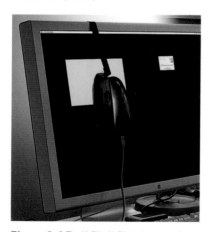

Figure 2.4 The X-Rite i1 Photo is a popular spectrophotometer that can be used with the accompanying software to calibrate and build an ICC profile for your display.

Calibration hardware

Let's now look at the practical steps for calibrating your computer. First, get rid of any distracting background colors or patterns on the computer desktop. And consider choosing a neutral color theme for your operating system (the Mac OS X system has a graphite appearance setting especially there for Photoshop users!) If you are using a PC, go to Control Panels ⇨ Appearance ⇨ Themes, choose Display and click the Appearance tab (Figure 2.3). Click on the active and inactive window samples and choose a gray color for both. If you are using Windows XP, try choosing the silver color scheme. This is all very subjective of course, but personally I think these adjustments will improve the look of both operating systems.

The only reliable way to calibrate and profile your display is by using a hardware calibration system. Some displays, such as the LaCie range, can be bought with a bundled hardware calibrator, but there are many other types of stand-alone calibration packages to consider. The ColorVision Monitor Spyder and Spyder2Pro Studio are affordable, and are sold either with PhotoCal or the more advanced OptiCal software, although the Monitor Spyders are just colorimeter devices and can therefore only be used to measure the output from a monitor display.

The X-Rite product range includes the i1 system, which is available in several different packages. The i1 Photo (Figure 2.4) is an emissive spectrophotometer that can measure all types of displays and build printer profiles too when used in conjunction with the ProfileMaker 5 or i1 Match software, while the EZ Color is a low cost colorimeter device bundled with the i1 Display 2 software. The newest product in their range is the ColorMunki Photo which is an integrated calibration/profiling device that can work with everything, including LCD beamer projectors.

If all you are interested in is calibrating and profiling a computer display, there is no great advantage in choosing a spectrophotometer over the more economically priced colorimeter devices. But whatever you do, I certainly advise you to include a calibrator/software package with any display purchase.

The calibration/profiling procedure

Over the next few pages I want to show you how to use the i1Match 3.6.2 software with an X-Rite monitor calibration device. You will be asked to start by selecting the type of device you want to calibrate (in this instance, a display) and then select the Basic or Advanced options. Shown here are the steps that would be used for an Advanced calibration.

White point

The white point information tells the video card how to display a pure white on the screen so that it matches a specified color temperature. Unlike the old CRT displays, it is not possible to physically adjust the white point of an LCD screen. For this reason, it is better to select the native white point option when calibrating an LCD display (as shown below in Figure 2.5), rather than calibrate to a prescribed white point value. Remember that all colors are seen relative to what is perceived to be the whitest white in a scene, and the eye will compensate naturally from the white point seen on the display to the white point used by an alternative viewing light source (see accompanying side-bar on the white point setup).

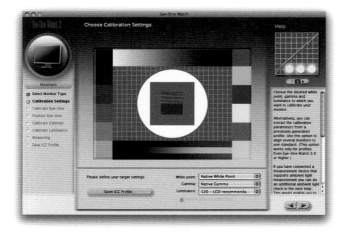

Figure 2.5 I like using the i1Match software because it is easy to set up and use. In this case, I wanted to calibrate and profile an LCD display and set the white point and gamma to 'Native' and the luminance to 120 candelas m², which is the recommended target setting for desktop LCD displays.

White point setup

There is a lot of seemingly conflicting advice out there on how to set the white point in a calibration setup. In the days of CRT monitors there was a choice to be made between a 5000 K and a 6500 K white point for print work. My advice then was to use 6500 K, since most CRT displays would run naturally at a white point of 6500 K. Some people did regard 5000 K as being the correct value to use for CMYK proofing work but in reality the whites on your display would appear far too yellow at this setting. 6500 K may have been cooler than the assumed 5000 K standard, but 6500 K provided much better viewing. These days, most LCD displays have a native color temperature of around 6000–7000 K and it is now considered best to choose the native white point when calibrating and profiling an LCD display.

The main thing to remember in all this is that your eyes will adjust quite naturally to the white point color of any display, in the same way as your eyes constantly adjust to the fluctuations in color temperature of everyday lighting conditions. Therefore, your eyes will judge all colors relative to the color of the whitest white, so the apparent disparity of using a white point for the display that is not exactly the same as that of a calibrated viewing lightbox is not something you should worry about. When it comes to comparing colors, your eyes will naturally adapt as they move from the screen to the viewing lightbox.

Monitor gamma and display brightness

Note that the gamma you choose when creating a monitor profile does not affect how light or dark an image will be displayed in Photoshop. This is because the monitor profile gamma only affects how the midtone levels are distributed. Whether you use a Mac or PC computer, you should choose the Native Gamma option (for an LCD display) or a gamma of 2.2.

The Macintosh 1.8 gamma option

The link between 1.8 gamma and the Macintosh system dates back to the early days of Macintosh computing when the only printer you could use with the Mac was an Apple black and white laser printer. At the time, it was suggested that the best way to match the screen appearance to the printer was to set the monitor gamma to 1.8 . I once asked an engineer who designs monitor calibration software why they still included 1.8 gamma as an option and he replied that it's only there to comfort Mac users who have traditionally been taught to use 1.8. So now you know.

Gamma

The gamma setting tells the video card how much to adjust the midtone levels compensation. You will typically have three options to choose from here: 1.8, 2.2 or Native Gamma. Now quite often you are told that PC users should use a 2.2 gamma and Macintosh users should use a 1.8 gamma. But 2.2 can be considered the ideal gamma setting to use regardless of whether you are on a Mac or a PC. You can build a correct monitor profile using a 1.8 gamma option, but 2.2 is closer to the native gamma of most displays. However, in Figure 2.5 you can see that I actually selected the Native Gamma option. Most LCD screens have a native gamma that is fairly close to 2.2 and if you choose 'Native' rather than 2.2, you can create a satisfactory display profile without forcing the video card to stretch the display levels any more than is necessary.

Luminance

You need to make sure that the brightness of the LCD display is within an acceptable luminance range. The target luminance will vary according to which type of display you are using A typical modern LCD display will have a luminance of 250 candelas m^2 or more at its maximum luminance setting, which is way too bright for image editing work in subdued office lighting conditions. A target of around 120–40 candelas m^2 is ideal for a desktop LCD monitor display, and for laptops the ideal luminance to aim for is around 100–110 CD m^2.

It is important to note that as displays get older they do tend to lose their brightness, which is one of the reasons why you will need to use a calibration device like the X-Rite i1 Photo, shown in Figure 2.4, to recalibrate from time to time. There may also come a point where the display becomes so dim that it can no longer be successfully calibrated or considered reliable enough for Photoshop image editing.

Device calibration and measurement

With the i1Match software you will be asked to calibrate the device (Figure 2.6) before proceeding to measure the brightness of the display (Figure 2.7). It is at this stage that the Luminance indicator appears and you can tweak the display brightness until the target luminance is reached.

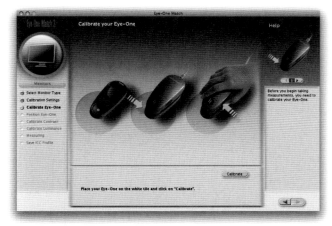

Figure 2.6 i1Match will ask you to calibrate the device, by placing it on the base unit to measure the white tile, before hanging the device over the screen.

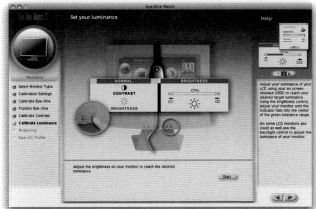

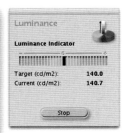

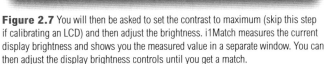

Figure 2.7 You will then be asked to set the contrast to maximum (skip this step if calibrating an LCD) and then adjust the brightness. i1Match measures the current display brightness and shows you the measured value in a separate window. You can then adjust the display brightness controls until you get a match.

Old monitor profiles

Do you really need to hang on to old monitor profiles? I recommend that you purge the Colorsync Profiles folder on your system of older monitor profiles to avoid confusion. All you really need is one good up-to-date profile for each display.

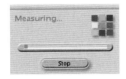

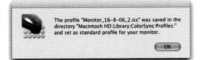

The profiling process

When you click on the forward-arrow button in Figure 2.7, i1Match will start flashing a series of colors on the screen while the calibration device measures them. Once it has completed doing this, it generates a monitor profile named with today's date. All you have to do is click OK to establish this as the new monitor profile to use, replacing any previous monitor profile. You might also want to set a reminder for when the next monitor profile should be made. If you are using an LCD, once every 4 weeks should be just fine.

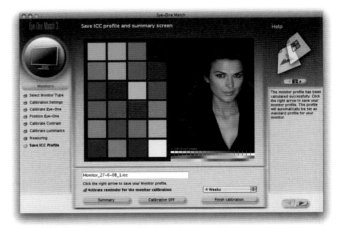

Figure 2.8 In this last step, the i1Match software starts measuring a sequence of colors that are flashed up on the display and from this builds an ICC profile of the display, which is automatically saved to the correct system folder where it will be picked up by the system and referenced by Photoshop's color management system.

Do you want good color or just OK color?

Let me summarize in a few paragraphs why you should pay special attention to how your images are displayed in Photoshop and why good color management is essential.

The choice of an LCD or CRT display used to be a matter of individual choice, but these days the only real option is to buy a good quality LCD display that is designed for graphic use. Once you have chosen a good display you need to consider how you are going to calibrate and profile the display. This is crucial and if done right it means you can trust the colors you see on the screen when determining what the print output will look like. In the long run you are going to save yourself an awful lot of time and frustration if you calibrate and profile the screen properly from the start. Not so long ago, the price of a large screen, plus a decent video card, would have cost a small fortune and monitor display calibrators were considered specialist items. These days, a basic monitor calibration and profiling device can cost about the same as a medium sized external hard drive, so I would urge anyone setting up a computer system for Photoshop to put a monitor display calibrator high on their spending list. A standard colorimeter like the i1 EZ Color from X-Rite is simple to operate and is bundled with the Display2 software, which can make it easy for you to calibrate and build a profile for your monitor.

All the monitor display calibrator products I have tested will automatically place the monitor profile that is generated in the correct system folder so that you are then ready to start working straight away in Photoshop with your display properly calibrated and with the knowledge that Photoshop automatically knows to read the profile you have just created.

Once you are in Photoshop you need to make sure you are using the right color settings for your workflow: see pages 577–578 for instructions on how to check if you are using the right settings for a photography setup. Once this is done, the Color Settings will remain set until you change them. And after that, all you need to worry about is making sure that the calibration and profiling for your display is kept up to date. With LCD displays, regular calibration will not be quite so critical and it will probably be enough for you to check just once a month.

Color management does not have to be intimidatingly complex and nor does it have to be expensive. So the question is, do you want good color or simply OK color? Or, to put it another way, can you afford not to?

Using canned profiles

If you are not going to invest in a calibration/measuring device, your only other option is to load a canned profile for your monitor and keep your fingers crossed. This approach is better than doing nothing. But it is rarely all that successful, so I would still urge you to consider buying a proper calibration device and software package.

Eyeball calibration

The other option is to use a non-device calibration method, such as the Display Calibration Assistant that is part of the Mac OS X operating system. Again, this is better than doing nothing, but still not a proper substitute for hardware calibration and profiling.

Color managing the print output

This leaves the question of how to profile the print output? Getting custom profiles built for your printer is a good idea, and it is a topic that I'll be covering in some detail in Chapter 12. However, calibrating and building a profile for your display is by far the most important first step in the whole color management process. Get this right and the canned profiles that came with your printer should work just fine. Follow these instructions and you should get a much closer match between what you see on the display and what you see coming out of your printer. But without doubt, a custom print profile will help you get even better results.

Synchronizing the Color Settings

If you are using other programs that are part of the Adobe Creative Suite, such as Illustrator and InDesign, it is a good idea to keep the Color Settings synchronized across all of these programs (see Figure 2.9). Once you have selected a desired color setting in Photoshop, I suggest you open Bridge and synchronize the Color Settings there. This will ensure that the same color settings are used throughout all the other programs in the Creative Suite. Finding this out later can be a real problem, and is so easy to avoid.

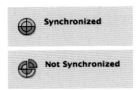

Figure 2.9 The pie chart icon in the Color Settings dialog tells you if the Color Settings have been synchronized across the Creative Suite or not.

Turn off 'Ask when Opening'

One tweak I do recommend at this stage is to turn off the 'Ask When Opening' option in the Profile Mismatches section. Doing this will minimize the number of times you are shown the profile mismatch warning dialog when working with image files that are in different color spaces. When you customize the color settings presets in this way, the preset menu will say 'Custom'. I suggest that you save and name this preset, as it is therefore available elsewhere, and you do not need to set the individual parameters at a later date, but simply choose this preset.

Color management settings

One of the very first things you should do after installing Photoshop is to adjust the color management settings. The default Photoshop color settings are configured using a general setting for the region you live in, which will be: North America, Europe or Japan. If you are using Photoshop for design work or photography, you will want to change this to a regional 'prepress' setting. Go to the Edit menu and select Color Settings... This will open the dialog shown in Figure 2.10. Next, go to the Settings menu and select one of the prepress settings. The individual prepress settings only differ in the default RGB to CMYK conversions that are used, and these will depend on the geographical area you are working in. So if you live and work in the USA, choose North America Prepress 2 and you will be fine with that setting. Please note that choosing a prepress setting will change the RGB working space from sRGB to Adobe RGB. This is a good thing to do if you intend editing RGB photographs in Photoshop (although I would personally recommend using ProPhoto RGB).

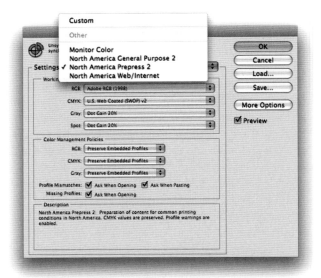

Figure 2.10 The Photoshop Color Settings. All the Photoshop color settings can be managed from within this single dialog (⌘ Shift K ctrl Shift K).

The prepress settings will also adjust the policy settings to preserve embedded profiles and alert you when there are profile mismatch warnings.

You don't need to worry too much more about the ins and outs of Photoshop color management just yet, but as your Photoshop knowledge increases you will definitely want to read in more detail about the color management system in Chapter 12 as well as Chapter 13 on print output.

Extras

An internal 16× or faster DVD/CD drive is usually fitted as standard in most computers. But you will also need to buy extra hard drives so that you can back up your main computer hard drive as well as have additional storage to store your image documents. It is tempting to accumulate lots of image files on the computer hard drive, but you have to ask yourself what would happen if your computer got stolen or one of the hard drives failed? By keeping your important data on separate hard drives, this will make it easier to store them somewhere safe when the computer is not in use.

USB 2 and FireWire 800 (IEEE 1394) are the latest connection standards for peripheral devices. You can have up to 127 USB devices linked to a single computer and you can plug and unplug a USB device while the machine is switched on. USB 2 is the latest standard and has many advantages for those in a PC working environment. USB 1.0 is slow, but it's fine for connecting control devices such as the mouse, Wacom tablet or printer. FireWire has the potential to provide fast data transfer rates of 49 MB per second (faster still with FireWire 800) and is popular with Macintosh users, but USB 2 is more universal and almost as fast. Although having said that, I discovered an alarming discrepancy between the download speeds on a Mac and those on a PC when using my Canon EOS 1Ds MkIII camera. The USB 2 data transfer speed is actually around five times faster when operating via Windows XP, compared with Macintosh OS X 10.5.

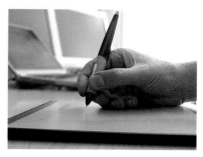

Figure 2.11 Wacom™ pad and pen.

Graphics tablets

I highly recommend you get a digitizing graphics tablet like the one shown in Figure 2.11. This is pressure responsive and is easier to draw with, and can be used alongside the mouse as an input device. But bigger is not necessarily better. Some people like using the A4 sized tablets, while others find it easier to work with an A5 or A6 tablet from the Wacom Intuos™ range, which now features a cordless mouse and switchable pens. You don't have to move the pen around so much with smaller pads and these are therefore easier to use for painting and drawing. Once you have experienced working with a pen, using the mouse is like trying to draw while wearing boxing gloves! The Wacom Cintiq™ device is a combination of LCD monitor and digitizing pen pad, and this radical new design will potentially introduce a whole new concept to the way we interact with the on-screen image. I don't know if it is going to be generally seen as the ideal way of working with photographs, but there are those who reckon it makes painting and drawing a more fluid experience.

Backup strategies

For a more detailed look at how to back up your files, please refer to Chapter 11 on image management.

Backing up image data

The solution I use here is to archive important data on primary and backup hard drives and maintain a further backup archive using DVD disks. These days the cost of hard disk storage space is so cheap that this is now an easily affordable solution. It means I can access important files more easily while I am working on the computer, and I am using the one method of disk storage which has so far remained relatively unchanged over the years and therefore has more chance of continuing to be supported in the future. For a basic studio setup I would recommend storing all your archive images and 'work in progress' images on an external drive and carrying out scheduled backups to a secondary hard drive of matching size that can be stored off-site or kept in a fireproof safe.

For extra backup, I like to archive my files on removable media. In the lifetime of the Photoshop program we have seen many different systems come and go. Floppies, Syquests, Magneto Opticals... the list goes on. And although you can still obtain devices capable of reading these media formats, the question is for how long? And what will you do in the future if a specific hardware device fails to work? The introduction of recordable CD/ DVD media has provided a reasonably consistent means of storage since for at least 12 years now nearly all computers have been able to read CD and DVD disks, and DVD drives have evolved to provide much faster read/write speeds. DVD media may be able to offer increased storage space in the future, and we are already seeing bigger disk media storage systems such as Blu-ray Disk and HD-DVD. So how long will CD and DVD media remain popular and be supported by future computer hardware devices? More to the point, how long will the media disks themselves last? It is estimated that aluminium and gold CD disks could last up to 30 years, or longer, if stored carefully in the right conditions, such as at the right temperature and away from direct sunlight, while DVD disks that use vegetable dyes may have a shorter lifespan. Even so, it is worth keeping extra backups of your data on DVD media as this at least protects your data from the prospect of virus attacks.

Photoshop preferences

The Photoshop preferences let you customize the various Photoshop functions and are located in the Edit menu in Windows and the Photoshop menu in OS X. A new preference file is generated each time you exit Photoshop and deleting or removing this file will always force Photoshop to reset all of its preference settings. The preference file is stored along with other program settings in the system level Preferences folder (Mac) or Registry folder (PC): C:/Documents and Settings/Current User/ Application Data/Adobe/Photoshop/11.0/Adobe Photoshop CS4 Settings.

General preferences

When you open the preferences you will first be shown the General preferences (Figure 2.12). I suggest you leave the Color Picker set to Adobe (unless you have a strong attachment to the system Color Picker), and leave the Image Interpolation set to Bicubic. If you need to override this particular setting then you can do so in the Image ⇨ Image Size dialog.

The 'Auto-Update Open Documents' can be used if you know you are likely to share files that are open in

Resetting the preferences

If you hold down ⌘ ⌥ Shift ctrl alt Shift during the startup cycle, this will pop a dialog box that allows you to delete the current Photoshop preference file.

Back up the preference file

After setting up the preferences, always make a duplicate of the Photoshop preference file and store it somewhere safe. Having ready access to a clean preference file can speed resetting the Photoshop settings should the working preference file become corrupted.

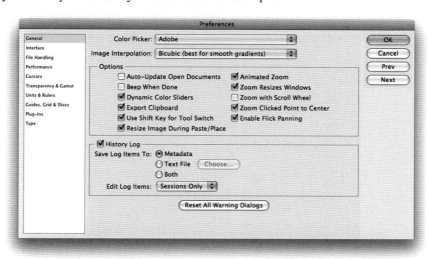

Figure 2.12 The General preferences dialog.

Resetting dialog warnings

You will often come across warning dialogs in Photoshop that contain a Don't Warn Me Again checkbox. If you have in the past clicked on these boxes to prevent seeing the warning dialog appear again, you can undo this by clicking on the Reset All Warning Dialogs button in the General preferences.

Photoshop but have been updated by another application. It used to be important when ImageReady was provided as a separate web editing program to accompany Photoshop, but has less relevance now for photography users and can be left switched off. Only check the Beep When Done box if you want Photoshop to signal a sound alert when tasks are complete. The Dynamic Color Sliders option ensures that the colors change in the Color panel as you drag the sliders, so keep this selected. Unchecking the Export Clipboard box can save time when you exit Photoshop to launch another program. If you really need the ability to paste clipboard contents to another program then leave it on, but otherwise I suggest you switch this off. The 'Use Shift Key for Tool Switch' option answers the needs of users who wish to disable the need for the *Shift* key modifier for switching tools in the Tools panel with repeated keyboard strokes (see page 26). The 'Resize Image During Paste/Place' is useful if you want pasted or placed items to be automatically scaled to match the size of the image you are pasting/placing them in. The Animated Zoom option is another OpenGL only option, which is intended to provide smoother transitions on screen when zooming using the ⌘ − *ctrl* − or ⌘ + *ctrl* + keys. Check the 'Zoom Resizes Windows' option if you want the image window to shrink to fit whenever you use a keyboard zoom shortcut such as ⌘ − *ctrl* − or ⌘ + *ctrl* +. And then there is the 'Zoom with Scroll Wheel' option which will enable you to zoom in and out via the scroll wheel (if you have one on your mouse). When this option is selected, holding down *Shift* will constrain the zoom to the usual percentage increments. Instead of selecting this option you can also hold down the ⌥ *alt* key to temporarily access this zoom wheel behavior. When the 'Zoom Clicked to Center' option is checked the image will zoom in centered around the point where you click, and the best way to understand the distinction between having this option on or off is to see what happens when you click to zoom in on the corner of a photo. When checked, the corner point of the photo will keep recentering as you zoom in. I discussed the new Flick Panning option earlier in Chapter 1, on page 51. This is another new CS4 feature and is dependent on OpenGL being enabled for this option to take effect.

The History log is useful if you wish to keep track of everything that has been done to an image, because the History Log options will let you save the history log directly in the image file metadata or to a saved text file stored in a pre-configured folder location, or both. The edit log items can be recorded in three modes. Sessions will record which files are opened and closed and when. The Concise mode will record an abbreviated list of which tools or commands were applied, again with times. Both these modes can provide basic feedback that could be useful in a studio environment to monitor time spent on a particular project and calculate billing. The Detailed mode records everything, such as the coordinates used to make a crop. This mode can be useful, for example, in forensic work.

Interface

If you refer to the screen view modes shown on page 54, you will see an example of the three main screen modes that are available in Photoshop. The outer canvas areas can now be customized by selecting alternative colors via

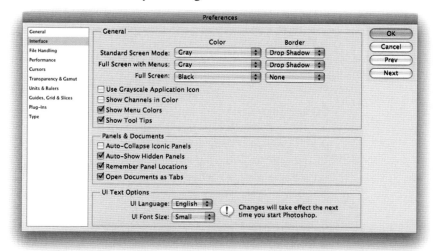

Figure 2.13 Interface preferences.

Canvas color and the paint bucket

An alterative way to alter the color of the outer canvas area is to select the paint bucket tool, choose a new foreground color and hold down the *Shift* key as you click with the paint bucket in the canvas area. This replaces the existing canvas color with the current foreground color.

Customizing the UI Font Size

LCD computer displays are getting bigger all the time and are only really designed to operate at their best when using the finest resolution setting. This can be great for viewing photographs, but the downside is that the application menu items are getting smaller and smaller. The UI (user interface) Font Size option allows you to customize the size of the smaller font menu items in Photoshop so that you don't have to strain your eyes too hard to read them. For example, when using a large LCD screen, the Medium font size option may make it easier to read the smaller font menu items from a distance. But to be honest, the new 'all caps' panel headers are dominating enough as it is, so I would personally keep the UI small in size at all times.

the Interface preferences (Figure 2.13) as can the borders, which can be shown as a drop shadow, thin black line, or with the border style set to 'None'. There is also another way you can set the canvas color, which has been around for a while (see sidebar). The useful thing to know here is you can use these Interface preference items as a way to quickly reset everything to the default canvas and borders.

Regarding what I said earlier about removing distracting colors from the interface, the 'Use Grayscale Toolbar Icon' option will remove the blue color from the Photoshop icon in the Application bar and turn it gray instead. The 'Display Color Channels in Color' option is a somewhat redundant feature as this does not really help you visualize the channels any better. If anything it is a distraction and best left unchecked.

Photoshop allows you to create custom menu settings and use colors to highlight favorite items, but this feature aspect can be disabled by unchecking the 'Show Menu Colors' option. When 'Show Tool Tips' is checked you will see tool tips displayed a few seconds after you roll over most items in the Photoshop interface. Tool tips are an excellent learning tool, but can become irritating after a while, so you can use this checkbox to turn them on or off as desired. The 'Auto-Collapse Icon Panels' option will allow you to open panels from icon mode and auto-collapse them back to icon mode again as soon as you start editing an image. And if you would like Photoshop to always remember the last used panel layout, check the Remember Panel Locations box. Should you need to reset the panel positions, you can use the default Workspace settings mentioned earlier on pages 20–22 to reset the panel positions to one of the default workspace layout positions.

The UI in the 'UI text options' stands for 'user interface' and these options allow you to choose an alternative UI language (if available) and UI text size. The default setting is 'Small' which most users will find plenty big enough (especially now the panel headers are kind of screaming at you with the all caps lettering). If you prefer though, the UI text size can be made bigger.

File Handling

In the File Handling preferences (Figure 2.14) you will normally want to include image previews when you save a file. It is certainly useful to have image thumbnail previews that are viewable in the system dialog boxes although the Bridge program is capable of generating large thumbnails regardless of whether a preview is present or not. You can also choose to save a Windows and Macintosh thumbnail with your file, to enable better cross-platform compatibility. Appending a file with a file extension is handy for knowing which format a document was saved in and is also very necessary when saving JPEG and GIF web graphics that need to be recognized in an HTML page. If you are exporting for the Web, you may want to check the 'Use Lower Case' option for appending files. But the instances of where servers trip up on upper case naming are fairly rare these days.

File compatibility

Photoshop CS3 allowed JPEG and TIFF images to open up via Camera Raw for the first time, as if they were raw files. A number of people had misgivings about this new development, partly because of the potential confusion

Economical web saves

There are times though when you don't need previews. Web graphic files should be uploaded as small as possible without a thumbnail or platform-specific header information. If you use Save for Web & Devices, this removes the previews and keeps the output files compact in size. But as well as this I usually upload files to my server in a raw binary format, which strips out the previews and other file resource information anyway.

Restart to activate preferences

Some of the Photoshop preferences will only take effect after you quit and restart the program. For example, the Scratch Disk preference settings will only come into effect after a restart, while the OpenGL preferences will only come into effect after you open or create a new window in Photoshop.

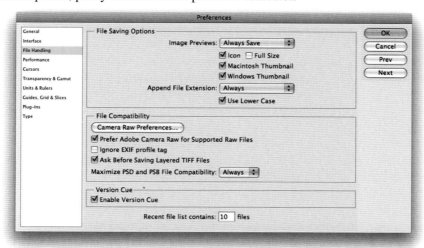

Figure 2.14 The File Handling preferences.

Version Cue

The Enable Version Cue Workgroup File Management relates to the use of Adobe Version Cue. This option caters for those working in a networked environment and where they are sharing working on image files with other Photoshop users. When a user 'checks out' a file, only he or she can edit it. The other users who are sharing your files will only be able to make edit changes after the file has been checked back in. This precautionary file management system means that other users cannot overwrite your work while it is being edited.

Why open JPEGs in ACR?

This is useful if you shoot in JPEG mode and wish to use Camera Raw to process the JPEG masters (as you would a raw capture image) without actually editing the master files. This is because Camera Raw records all the edits as separate instructions.

Why open TIFFs in ACR?

The same argument applies to opening TIFF files via Camera Raw, but the important thing to note here is that Camera Raw can only open flattened TIFFs and will not open TIFFs with saved layers (regardless of whether a composite image has been saved or not). The main reason why it is useful to use Camera Raw to open TIFF is if you want to process TIFF scan images via Camera Raw so that you can take advantage of things like the capture sharpening controls that are in Camera Raw.

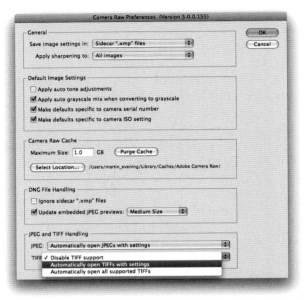

Figure 2.15 This shows the Camera Raw preferences dialog with the JPEG and TIFF handling options at the bottom.

this might cause, but also because of the way it was implemented in Photoshop CS3. For example, you had the Photoshop File Handling preferences plus another setting in the Bridge preferences, and there was no simple way to summarize how these should be configured in order to get JPEG or TIFF images to open up via Camera Raw in the way you would expect. In fact, even fellow Photoshop experts were just as confused as everyone else as to how to manage the preference settings in these two different locations. To be honest, it was a bit of a mess.

Things have been improved somewhat with Photoshop CS4. In the File Saving preferences you can click on the Camera Raw Preferences... button to open the dialog shown in Figure 2.15. At the bottom are the JPEG and TIFF Handling preferences where you have three options with which to decide how JPEG and TIFF images should be opened in Photoshop CS4 and, unlike CS3, these are fairly easy to understand and more predictable in their behavior (see sidebar 'JPEG/TIFF Camera Raw policies' on page 101).

The 'Prefer Adobe Camera Raw for Supported Raw Files' option will always launch Adobe Camera Raw as your favored raw processor when opening a proprietary raw file. Some cameras may embed an sRGB profile tag in the EXIF metadata of a JPEG capture file (where the profile used isn't a correct sRGB profile anyway). If you check the 'Ignore EXIF profile tag' option, Photoshop will ignore this particular part of the metadata and read from the (correct) embedded profile data instead.

A TIFF format file saved in Photoshop 6.0 or later can contain all types of Photoshop layer information and a flattened composite is always saved in a TIFF. If you then place a layered TIFF image in a page layout, only the flattened composite will be read by the program when the page is finally converted to print. Some people argue that there are specific instances where a layered TIFF might trip up a print production workflow, so it might be safer to never save layers in a TIFF. But you know, there are a large number of Photoshop users who successfully use layered TIFFs when saving master images, so my advice is not to be put off including layers. When the 'Ask Before Saving Layered TIFF Files' option is checked, Photoshop presents you with an option to either flatten or preserve the layers when saving a layered image as a TIFF. If this is unchecked, then the layer information is saved regardless and there will be no warning dialog.

However, standard Photoshop PSD files created in Photoshop CS4 are never going to be 100% compatible if they are likely to be read by someone using an earlier version of Photoshop and this has always been the case with each upgrade of the program. Setting the Maximize PSD and PSB Compatibility to 'Always' will allow you to do the same thing as when saving a flattened composite with a TIFF. This option ensures that a flattened version of the image is included with the saved Photoshop file and the safe option is to always keep this checked. For example, if you include a Smart Object layer, the Photoshop file will not be interpreted correctly when read by Photoshop CS or earlier, unless you maximize the compatibility of the

JPEG/TIFF Camera Raw policies

If 'Disable JPEG (or TIFF) support' is selected, this safely takes you back to the way things were before – where all JPEG or TIFF files will always open in Photoshop directly. If 'Automatically open all supported JPEGs (or TIFFs)' is selected, this will cause all supported JPEGs and TIFFs to always open via Camera Raw. However, if 'Automatically open JPEGs (or TIFFs) with settings' is selected, Photoshop CS4 will only open a JPEG or TIFF via Camera Raw if it has previously been edited via Camera Raw. When this option is selected you have the option in Bridge to use a double-click to open a JPEG directly into Photoshop, or use ⌘ R ctrl R to force JPEGs to open via Camera Raw. But note that when you edit the Camera Raw settings for that JPEG, the next time you use a double-click to open, it will default to opening via Camera Raw.

Recent File list

The Recent File list refers to the number of image document locations remembered in the Photoshop File ⇨ Open Recent submenu. I usually like to set this number to remember the last 10 opened images. But you may wish to set this higher.

Layered files in a DTP layout

Adobe InDesign allows you to place Photoshop format (PSD) files in a page layout but, if you do so, the Maximize Backwards Compatibility option must be checked in the General preferences (to generate a flattened composite). If you use layered TIFF, PSD (or Photoshop PDF) format files in your page layout workflow, you can modify the layers in Photoshop and the page design image preview will immediately be updated. This way you don't run the risk of losing synchronization between the master image that is used to make the Photoshop edits and a flattened version of the same image that is used solely for placing in the layout. If you want to 'round trip' your images this way, TIFF is the more universally recognized file format. The downside is that you may end up with bloated files and these can significantly increase the file transmission times.

It so happens that a lot of the image files used in the production of this book have been placed as layered TIFF RGB files, which allows me to edit them easily in Photoshop. Keeping the files as layered RGBs is perfect at the text editing stage, but the final TIFF files that are used to go to press with are all flattened CMYK TIFFs.

saved PSD. In these circumstances, if Photoshop is unable to interpret an image, it will present an alert dialog. This will warn that certain elements cannot be read and offer the option to discard these and continue, or to read the composite image data. Discarding the unreadable data will allow another user to open your image but, when opened, it will be missing all the elements you added and most likely look very different from the file you intended that person to receive. But if they click the Read Composite Data button, and a composite was saved, the image will open using a flattened composite layer which does look the same as the image you created and saved. If no composite was created, they will just see a white picture and a multi-language message saying that no composite data was available.

Maximizing PSD compatibility will let images load quicker in Bridge. Another crucial point is that Adobe Photoshop Lightroom is only able to read layered PSD files that have this option turned on. If there is no saved composite, Lightroom won't be able to import it.

Performance

The Performance preferences section (Figure 2.16) lets you configure all the things in Photoshop that influence how efficiently Photoshop is able to run on your computer. The memory usage can be set using a sliding percentage scale and you will notice how Photoshop provides a hint as to what the ideal range should be for your particular computer. In the History & Cache preferences section the default number of history states is 20 and you can set this to any number you like from 1–1000, but remember that the number of histories you choose will have a bearing on the scratch disk usage. The Cache Level settings affect the speed of screen redraws and setting a higher number can help if you often work with very large images in Photoshop (see page 110). In the Scratch Disks section you can nominate up to four hard drives as scratch disks. Note how you get to see information about each disk used and can drag to rearrange them in order of priority (I'll be discussing memory and scratch disk usage over the next few pages).

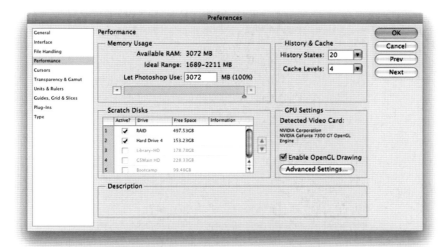

Figure 2.16 The Performance preferences, where you can configure the Memory usage, History, Cache, Scratch Disks and GPU settings.

GPU settings

Photoshop is able to detect the graphics card used by your computer and if it has a built-in Graphics Processor Unit (GPU) capability, you can then check the 'Enable OpenGL Drawing' option and make full use of the graphics processor memory on GPU enabled graphics cards. As was explained earlier, in Chapter 1, this preference setting will affect images opened in Photoshop on a per-window document basis.

The advantages of enabling OpenGL were described mostly in Chapter 1, but to summarize these are: smooth views when using odd number viewing percentages, image rotation, flick panning, smooth animated zooms, the bird's-eye view zoom-out feature plus pixel grid display at view magnifications greater than 500%. Note that OpenGL is only available if you are running Mac OS X 10.4.11 (or later), Windows Vista or Windows XP.

If you click on the Advanced Settings... button this will take you to the dialog shown in Figure 2.17 where you can fine-tune the OpenGL performance, but these controls apply mainly to 3D design work rather than photography.

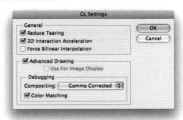

Figure 2.17 The OpenGL Advanced settings dialog.

OpenGL availability

Computers dealing with graphics are now trying to offload processor-intensive activity from the CPU to a Video card's GPU (Graphics Processing Unit) as this lessens the burden of the CPU. The CPU simply issues commands and awaits the response from the GPU, so the CPU is always able to avoid distractions, which the dedicated GPU is able to handle immediately. This is because of its speed and its own on-board RAM; it knows exactly what it has to do, and drives the monitor accordingly.

RAM memory upgrades

Most PCs and Macs use DIMMs (Dual In-line Memory Modules). The specific RAM memory chips may vary for each type of computer, so check carefully with the vendor that you are buying the right type for your machine. RAM memory used to cost a small fortune, but these days the price of RAM is almost inconsequential. If you have four RAM slots on your machine, you should easily be able to install 4 ×1 GB RAM or 4 ×2 GB RAM memory chips, which will give you 4 or 8 GB of installed RAM.

Move don't copy

To copy selections and layers between documents, use the drag and drop method with the move tool. This saves on memory usage and also preserves the current clipboard contents.

Virtual memory tricks

The Apple Macintosh and Windows operating systems are able to make efficient use of memory using their own virtual memory management systems. The Windows VM file should be set to at least 1.5 times your physical memory size. There are some software utilities that claim to double your RAM, but these will conflict with Photoshop's virtual memory and should not be used.

RAM memory and scratch disks

The amount of RAM memory you have installed will determine how efficiently you can work in Photoshop. Adobe recommend that you allocate a minimum of 320 MB RAM memory, which means that if you allow an additional 128–256 MB of RAM for the operating system, you will need to have at least 512 MB of RAM installed. If you also take into account the requirements of other programs and the likelihood of newer operating systems needing even more memory, it is safer to suggest you will need a minimum of 1GB RAM memory in total.

Each time you launch Photoshop a certain amount of RAM memory will be set aside for use by the application, and this will depend on the amount set in the Performance preferences as a percentage of the total amount of RAM that is available to Photoshop. The figure you see in the Performance preferences is the RAM reserved for Photoshop imaging use (although the RAM you set aside for Photoshop will be shared by other applications when it is not actively being used by Photoshop), but don't forget that you will need to allow some RAM memory to run Adobe Bridge at the same time as Photoshop.

How much RAM is available to Photoshop will depend on the total amount of RAM memory installed. If you run Photoshop on a 64-bit Macintosh computer that has 4 GB or more of RAM installed, a maximum of 3 GB is allocated to Photoshop for handling image data. If you have a 64-bit PC computer (and appropriate operating system), you have the option to install a 64-bit version of the program, in which case there is no RAM limit and Photoshop CS4 can take advantage of all the RAM that is installed.

When you go to the Performance preferences, the total available RAM is displayed in the Memory Usage section and below this you will see the recommended percentage of memory to allocate to Photoshop. On a Windows system the default setting is 50% and on a Mac it will be 70%. If the memory is set too high Photoshop may end up competing with the operating system for memory and this will slow performance, although the memory assigned to Photoshop is freed up whenever Photoshop is not running.

Enhancing memory and performance

The Performance preferences provide a guide for the ideal RAM setting for your computer and what the upper limit should be, but you can always try allocating 5% above the recommended amount of memory, then relaunch Photoshop and closely observe the Efficiency readout in the status bar or Info panel. Monitor the Efficiency readout: anything less than 100% will indicate that Photoshop is running short of RAM memory and having to make use of extra scratch disk space. But if you allocate too high a percentage, this will also compromise efficiency. The trick is to find the optimum percentage before you see a drop in performance. You might also find the speed test described in the sidebar is a useful tool for gauging Photoshop performance.

Even if you are hit by the 4GB RAM limit on a Macintosh, if you have more than 4 GB memory installed (up to 8 GB on Mac OS X) the RAM above 4 GB can also be used by the operating system as a cache for the Photoshop scratch data. So although you can't allocate this extra memory directly, installing extra memory can still help boost Photoshop's performance.

Photoshop stores data such as recent history states and clipboard data in its memory on the scratch disk. Copying a large selection to the clipboard also uses up a lot of the scratch disk memory. Should you experience a temporary slowdown in performance you might want to purge Photoshop of any excess temporarily held data in the memory. To do this, choose Edit ⇨ Purge ⇨ Undo, Clipboard, Histories or All.

Scratch disks

Photoshop utilizes free hard disk space as an extension of RAM memory and makes use of all the available free hard disk as specified in the Scratch Disks section as 'virtual memory'. When you launch Photoshop it will check to see how much hard disk space is free for scratch disk usage and it is worth noting here that should you for any reason have less scratch disk space than RAM memory space, the RAM memory will be restricted by the amount of scratch disk space that is available.

Speed and efficiency test

To help evaluate the performance efficiency of your computer setup, there is a really useful weblink to a site hosted by a company called Retouchartists.com: retouchartists.com/pages/speedtest.html From there you can download a test file which contains a sample image and a Photoshop action that was created by Alex Godden. All you have to do is time how long it takes for the action to complete, to gauge and compare how fast your computer is running. And then you can compare your speed test results with others.

Scratch disk usage and history

The scratch disk usage will vary according to how many history states you have set in the History and Cache section and also how you use Photoshop. Generally speaking, Photoshop will store a version of each history state, but it does not always store a complete version of the image for each history state. As was explained in Chapter 1, the History feature only needs to save the changes made in each image tile. So if you carry out a series of brush strokes, the history only stores changes made to the altered image tiles. For this reason, although the scratch disk usage will increase as you add more history states, in practice the usage does not increase in large chunks, unless you were to perform a series of global filter changes.

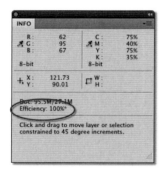

Figure 2.18 You can monitor how efficiently Photoshop is running by adjusting the Info panel options to display an Efficiency readout. If the efficiency reading drops below 100% this means that Photoshop is having to rely on the designated scratch disk as a virtual memory source.

The primary scratch disk should ideally be one that is separate to the disk running the operating system and Photoshop. If you partition the main disk volume and designate an empty partition as the scratch disk, this serves no useful purpose because the disk drive head will simply be switching back and forth between different sectors of the same disk as it tries to do the job of running the computer system and providing scratch disk space. For optimal image editing, at least 4 GB of free hard disk space is recommended, but ideally you want a scratch disk with a minimum of 20–40 GB of free space, and the disk used should be as free as possible of fragmentation.

Photoshop always makes the most efficient use of real RAM memory and tries to keep as much RAM as possible free for memory-intensive calculations. Low-level data like the 'last saved' version of the image is stored in the scratch disk memory giving priority to the current version and last undo versions being held in RAM. Normally, Photoshop uses all the available free RAM as buffer memory in which to perform real-time calculations and mirrors the RAM memory contents on the scratch disk. Photoshop does this whenever there is a convenient opportunity to do so. For example, after you open a new image you may notice some disk activity as Photoshop writes from the RAM memory buffer to the scratch disk. Photoshop then continually looks for ways to economize the use of RAM memory, writing to the hard disk in the background whenever there are periods of inactivity. Scratch disk data is also compressed when it is not in use (unless the optional plug-in extension that prevents this has been loaded at startup).

When Photoshop exhausts its reserves of RAM memory, it is forced to use the extra space on the scratch disk as a source of virtual memory and this is where you will start to see a major slowdown in efficiency. When the Efficiency indicator (Figure 2.18) drops below 100% this means that the RAM buffer is full and Photoshop is now relying exclusively on the hard disk scratch disk space as a memory reserve.

Scratch disk performance

With all this reliance on the scratch disk (or multiple scratch disks) to read/write data from the RAM memory buffer, the hard disk performance of the scratch disk plays an important role in maintaining Photoshop efficiency. There is provision in Photoshop for as many as four scratch disks. Each individual scratch file created by Photoshop can be a maximum of 2 GB and Photoshop can keep writing scratch files to a scratch disk volume until it becomes full. When the primary scratch disk runs out of room to accommodate all the scratch files during a Photoshop session, it will then start writing scratch files to the secondary scratch disk and so on. This makes for more efficient and faster disk usage.

Interface connections

Most modern Macs and PCs have IDE, ATA or SATA drives as standard. A fast internal hard disk is adequate for getting started. But for better performance results, you should really install a second internal or external hard drive and have this dedicated as the primary scratch disk (make this the number one scratch disk in the Performance preferences). Your computer will most likely have the choice of a USB or FireWire connector for linking external devices. USB 2 offers a much faster connection speed than the old USB 1, while FireWire (IEEE 1394) has many advantages over the older SCSI interface. Firstly, FireWire is a lot faster and secondly, it will often allow you to hot swap a drive between one computer and another. This is particularly useful when you wish to shuttle very large files around quickly. With the advent of FireWire 800 we are now seeing an appreciable improvement in data transfer speeds. FireWire drives are basically IDE drives with a Bridge Chipset to provide the FireWire connection and, since the Oxford Chipset came out, they have been able to enhance the throughput closer to the theoretical limit. Note that it is the data transfer and not the data access time that is the measure of disk speed to look out for.

Assigning scratch disks at startup

If you hold down the ⌘ ⌥ *ctrl* *alt* keys as you launch Photoshop, this will pop the Disk options on the screen and allow you to add or change the Scratch Disk settings. If you hold down the ⌘ *Shift* ⌥ *ctrl* *Shift* *alt* keys during startup, this will allow you to delete the current Photoshop preferences.

Hard drive spindle speeds

Most desktop computers use internal drives which run at 7200 rpm and you can easily find spare internal drives that run at this speed or faster. For example, there are drives that even run at 15,000 rpm, but these are hard to come by and expensive. Laptop computers usually have slower hard drives fitted as standard (typically 5400 rpm). It may therefore be worth checking if you can select a faster speed hard drive as a build-to-order option.

eSATA drives

External SATA drives (eSATA) are now regarded as faster than Firewire 800 and are sometimes available as multiport drives like the LaCie d2 series. In theory they are better, but I experienced nothing but trouble with the two eSATA drives I used (see page 109). But I might just have been unlucky of course!

RAID speed versus reliability

A RAID 0 setup will offer faster speed but be less reliable, since if one drive fails the stored data will be lost across the whole combined volume. A RAID 1 setup offers greater security but the downside is that RAID 1 read/write speeds are slower because the RAID 1 system has to back up data between one drive and the other.

Internal RAID issues

An internal RAID setup will definitely speed up the time it takes Photoshop to read and write data to the scratch disk. However, if you have more hard drives running simultaneously this will mean more power consumption, which in turn can generate extra heat and possibly more noise too. Be warned that this heat may cause problems for the cooling system in your computer and put extra strain on the internal power supply unit.

RAID setups

RAID stands for Redundant Array of Independent Disks. A simple way to explain RAID is that it allows you to treat multiple drives as a single drive volume to provide either increased data integrity, capacity, transfer rates or fault-tolerance compared to a single volume. How it does this depends on the RAID level you choose. You will need a minimum of two disks to configure a RAID system and most off-the-shelf RAID solutions are sold as a bay dock that can accommodate two or more drives with a built-in RAID controller. A RAID disk can usually be connected via internal SCSI or an external FireWire 400/800 connection.

RAID 0 (striping)

A RAID 0 setup is an ideal choice for use as a Photoshop scratch disk. With a RAID 0 setup, two or more drives are striped together to create a single large volume drive. For example, if two 400 GB drives are striped using a RAID 0 setup you will end up with a single 800 MB volume. RAID 0 is useful where you require fast hard drive access speeds because the drive access speed will increase proportionally to the number of drives that are added. So if you have a 2 x 400 GB drive RAID 0 system, the hard drive access speed should be two times that of a single 800 GB drive.

RAID 1 (mirroring)

A RAID 1 setup stores duplicate data across two drives. This means that if you have, say, two 400 GB drives configured in a RAID 1 setup, the data on one drive will be mirrored on the other and the total drive capacity will be equal to that of a single drive (in this case 400 GB). RAID 1 systems are used as a way to protect against sudden drive failure, since if one drive fails a mirror copy of that data can immediately be accessed from the other drive, and if you replace the defunct drive with a new one the RAID 1 system will rebuild a copy of the data on the new drive.

Internal RAID

You can fit an internal RAID system with a do-it-yourself kit consisting of two internally mounted drives and a RAID controller card. This should not be too challenging to install yourself, but if you are in any doubt about whether you are capable of doing this then you should get a qualified computer specialist to install such a system in your computer. The advantage of an internal RAID is that it is always there whenever you turn the computer on and is an economical solution compared to buying an external RAID drive setup. Most PC tower computer systems should have plenty of free hard drive bays, which will make it fairly easy for you to install internal RAID. Note that some of the older G5 desktops only have room to fit one extra drive. So a Quad G5 computer will only suit one internal mirrored RAID 1 or striped RAID 0 setup, which is not much use for Photoshop work. But if you get one of the WiebeTECH G5 Jam Plus kits, this will allow you to install up to four extra drives and includes a RAID controller card.

External RAID

External RAID hard drive units (Figure 2.19) are not overly expensive and you can easily buy a ready assembled bay dock with a couple of drives and a built-in RAID controller hardware that can be configured for RAID 0. The speed will be governed not just by the number of drives making up the RAID but also by the speed of the cable connection. Most RAID systems these days they will connect to the computer via a FireWire 400/800 or SATA connection, which may again require a special card in order to connect to the computer (for now). At the time of writing it seems that computers in the future are more likely to support SATA as standard. My own personal experience has led me to be rather wary of relying on SATA. I have had two SATA RAID units fail or cause problems maintaining a connection to the computer. For this reason I have chosen to stick with FireWire 800, and even this I find isn't completely dependable on the Mac OS X system.

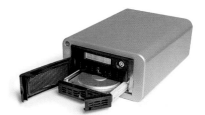

Figure 2.19 A RAID system drive setup contains two or more drives linked together that can provide either faster disk access or more secure data backup.

Software RAIDs

It used to be the case that software-created RAIDs, such as the one included with the Mac OS X Disk Utilities program, were a lot slower than a dedicated system. True, the read/write speeds from a software RAID will still be somewhat slower than a true dedicated RAID system, since a software RAID will be stealing some of your computer processor cycles, but these days the speed loss is not so bad as it used to be. For example, a software-driven internal striped RAID 0 can bring about a 45% increase in disk access speed. Overall I recommend that if you do choose to go down the internal RAID route, you include a RAID controller.

Image Cache

The image cache settings (see Figure 2.16) affect the speed of screen redraws. Whenever you are working with a large image, Photoshop uses a pyramid type structure of lower resolution cached versions of the full resolution picture. Each cached image is a quarter scale version of the previous cache level and is temporarily stored in memory to provide speedier screen previews. Basically, if you are viewing a large image on screen in 'Fit to screen' display mode, Photoshop will use a cache level that is closest to the fit to screen resolution to provide a screen refresh view of any edit changes you make at this viewing scale. The cached screen previews can therefore provide you with faster screen redraws and larger images will benefit from using a higher cache level, since a higher setting will provide a faster screen redraw, but at the expense of sacrificing the quality of the preview. This is because a lower resolution cache preview is not as accurate as choosing to view the image at Actual Pixels.

Cache pyramid structure

If you have OpenGL switched off, or your video card does not support OpenGL, you may sometimes notice how layered Photoshop images are not always displayed with complete accuracy at anything other than the 100% magnification. For example, if you have added a pixel layer that has a sharp edge, you might see a line appear along the edges when viewed at smaller viewing percentages. This is simply the image cache at work and nothing to worry about – it is speeding up the display preview at the expense of accuracy. If you have to work on an image (without OpenGL) at a less than 100% magnification, then do make sure the magnification is a wholly divisible number of 100%. In other words, it is better to work at 50%, 25% or 12.5% magnification rather than at 66% or 33%. Note also that the number of cache levels chosen here will affect the structure of a TIFF file when the 'Save Image Pyramid' option is selected (see Figure 1.81 on page 67).

Cursors

The painting cursor can be displayed as a painting tool icon, a precise crosshair or with the default setting, which is an outline of the brush shape at its 'most opaque' size in relation to the image magnification (Figure 2.20). You can also choose to display a Full Size brush tip, representing the entire outer edge reach of a soft edged brush, although it is debatable whether this improves the appearance of the painting cursors or not (Figure 2.21). The Show Crosshair in Brush Tip option will allow you to additionally display a crosshair inside the brush size cursor. In the Other Cursors section, the Standard option will represent other tools using the tool icon. I suggest you change this to the Precise setting, because this will make it easier for you to target the placement of these tools.

The *Caps Lock* key can be used to toggle the cursor display. When the standard paint cursor is selected, *Caps Lock* will toggle between standard and precise. When the precise or brush size paint cursor option is selected, *Caps Lock* will toggle between precise and brush size. When standard cursor mode is selected for all other cursors, *Caps Lock* will toggle between the standard and the precise cursor.

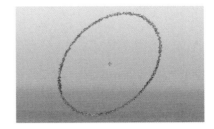

Figure 2.21 This is an example of the brush cursor using the Full Size Brush Tip mode with Show Crosshair in Brush Tip.

Brush opacity and cursor size

When the Normal brush tip is selected, the brush cursor size will represent the boundary of the brush shape up to where the brush opacity is 50% or denser in opacity, whereas the full size cursor will represent the complete brush area size.

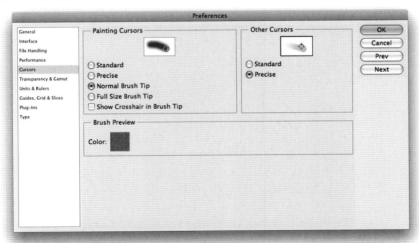

Figure 2.20 The Display & Cursors preferences.

Removing the checkerboard

If you go to the preferences shown here you can select different grid sizes and colors, but you can also select 'None'. When 'None' is selected the transparent areas will be displayed as solid white.

Color Picker gamut warning

The Gamut warning can also be invoked independently of the image in Photoshop's Color Picker dialog. The default overlay color is a neutral gray at 100% opacity, but I suggest reducing the opacity to make the gamut warning appear as a semi-transparent overlay.

Transparency & Gamut

The Transparency settings (Figure 2.22) determine how the transparent areas in an image are represented on the screen. If a layer contains transparency and is viewed on its own with the background layer visibility switched off, the transparent areas are normally shown using a checkerboard pattern. The display preferences let you decide how the checkerboard grid size and colors are shown on the screen.

The Gamut Warning will alert you in advance to any colors that will be out of gamut after a conversion is made from, say, the RGB Color mode to whichever color space is currently loaded in the View ⇨ Proof Setup menu. So, if you are working on an image in RGB mode and you choose View ⇨ Gamut Warning, Photoshop will highlight these out-of-gamut colors with a color overlay. The gamut warning is, in my view, a rather crude instrument for determining whether colors are in gamut or not, since a color that is only slightly out of gamut will be highlighted as strongly as a color that is hugely out of gamut. A good quality graphics monitor coupled with a custom proof setup view mode is a much more reliable guide.

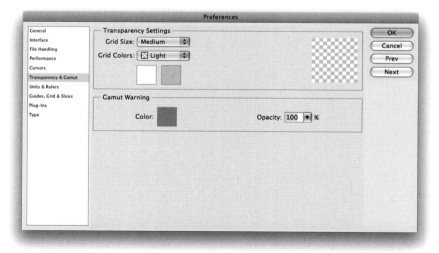

Figure 2.22 The Transparency display settings are editable. You have a choice of Transparency display settings: None, Small, Medium or Large grid pattern, and a choice of different grid colors.

Units & Rulers

You can use this preference section to set the Ruler measurements (inches or centimeters, etc.) and the units used. But as well as using the preferences, the measurement units can be changed via the Info panel submenu or by `ctrl` right mouse-clicking on a ruler to open the contextual menu (you can also double-click the ruler bar as a shortcut for opening the preference window shown in Figure 2.23).

The New Document Preset Resolution options allow you to decide what the default pixel resolution should be for screen display or print output work when you select a preset from the File ⇨ New Document dialog (Figure 2.24). The Screen Resolution has typically always been 72 ppi. But there is no real significance to whatever resolution is set here for an image that is destined to appear in a web page design. Web browser programs are only concerned with the physical number of pixels an image has and the resolution setting actually has no relevance. The Print Resolution setting is more useful as this has an important bearing on the size that an image will print.

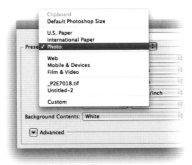

Figure 2.24 The New Document Preset Resolution settings will have a bearing on the resolution used when selecting a new document preset from the File ⇨ New Document dialog. In this example, if I were to select the U.S. Paper, International Paper or Photo preset the file resolution would be set to whatever the Print resolution is in the Units & Rulers preferences.

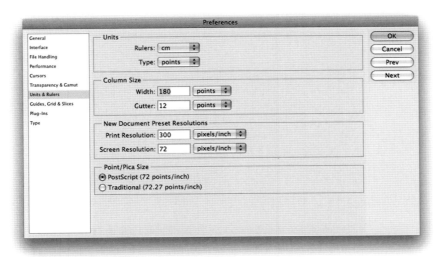

Figure 2.23 Ruler units can be set in pixels, inches, cm, mm, points, picas or as a percentage. The percentage setting is ideal for recording actions that you wish to apply proportionally at any image size.

Ensuring preferences are saved

Once you have configured your preferences and got everything set up just the way you want, it is a good idea to Quit and restart Photoshop, as this will then force Photoshop to save these preferences as it updates the preference file.

Guides, Grid & Slices

These preferences let you choose the colors for the Guides, Smart Guides and Grid (Figure 2.25). Both Grid and Guides can be displayed as solid or dashed lines, with the added option of dotted lines for the Grid. The number of Grid subdivisions can be adjusted to suit whatever project you are working on and the Slice options include Line Color style and whether the Slice numbers are displayed or not.

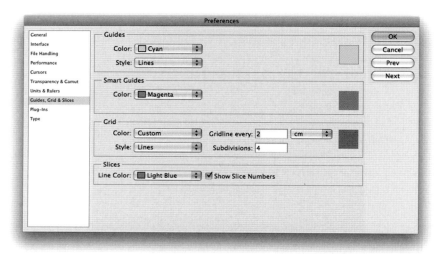

Figure 2.25 The Guides, Grid & Slices preferences.

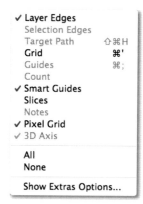

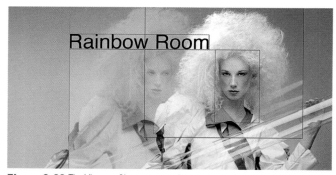

Figure 2.26 The View ⇒ Show menu options include Layer Edges. When this is selected the currently selected layer or layers will be indicated with a rectangular color edge border. The Smart Guides option is useful as a visual aid for aligning layer elements. The Smart Guides (shown here in pink) will flash on and off to indicate when a layer element is aligned to other layers in the image.

Plug-ins

The Plug-ins folder will automatically be recognized by Photoshop so long as it resides in the same application folder. Figure 2.27 shows how you can also choose an Additional Plug-ins Folder that may be located in another application folder such as Adobe Bridge (see sidebar on the JPEG 2000 file format), so these plug-ins can in effect be shared with Photoshop. To do this click on the Choose... button to locate the additional folder. If you install any third-party plug-ins that pre-date Photoshop CS4, they may possibly incorporate a hidden installation process that looks for a valid Photoshop serial number that was linked to a previously installed version of Photoshop. So, if you experience this type of problem, where certain plug-ins fail to launch, just remember that you can enter your old Photoshop serial number in the Legacy Serial Number box.

Note: if you keep the ⌘ ⌥ ctrl alt keys held down at the beginning of the Photoshop startup cycle, this will pop a Navigation dialog that will let you point to the location of the Additional Plug-ins Folder (Figure 2.28).

Accessing older plug-ins

For various reasons, a number of plug-ins and extensions have been removed from the standard Photoshop CS4 install. However, these 'missing' plug-ins, such as Contact Sheet, Picture Package, Extract, Pattern Maker and Photomerge can still be accessed and installed from the Photoshop installer DVD. All you need to do is locate the 'Extras' folder (or search on-line) and install these separately.

JPEG 2000

The same thing applies to the JPEG 2000 file format plug-in, but this plug-in will be installed in the Bridge Plug-ins folder. So if you click the Additional Plug-ins Folder checkbox, click on the Choose button and navigate to the Bridge Plug-ins folder, you will be able to save images out of Photoshop using the JPEG 2000 file format after you relaunch Photoshop.

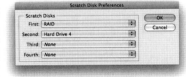

Figure 2.28 This Scratch Disk Preferences will show if you hold down the ⌘ ⌥ ctrl alt keys during the startup cycle as you launch Photoshop.

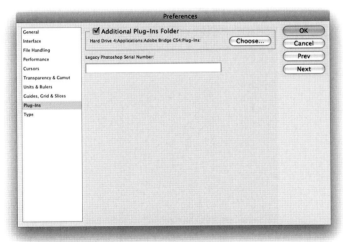

Figure 2.27 The Plug-ins preferences.

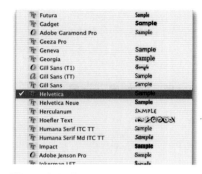

Figure 2.29 Photoshop presents the font lists using a WYSIWYG menu listing.

Type tool initialization

When you select the type tool for the first time during a Photoshop session, there will be a brief pause in which Photoshop initializes the type tool engine. You may notice that if the type tool was selected when you last closed Photoshop, the initialization process happens during the startup cycle.

Type preferences

Lastly, we come to the Type preferences (Figure 2.30), which are mainly of importance to graphics users rather than photographers. We could all do with smart quotes I guess, but the smart quotes referred to here are a preference for whether the text tool uses vertical quotation marks or rounded ones that are inverted at the beginning and end of a sentence. The 'Show Asian Text Options' is there for Asian users, to enable the Chinese, Japanese and Korean text options in the Character panel. The 'Show Font Names in English' option will be of more significance to non-English language users, as it will allow them the option to display the font names in English, as an alternative to their own native language. The 'Enable Missing Glyph Protection' option will switch on automatic font substitution for any missing glyph fonts (those swirly graphic font characters).

The Type tool Options panel also provides a WYSIWYG menu listing of all the available fonts when you mouse down on the Font Family menu (see Figure 2.29). The Font Preview Size menu will determine the font sizes used when displaying this list; this menu item should not be confused with the UI Font Size preference that is in the General preferences section.

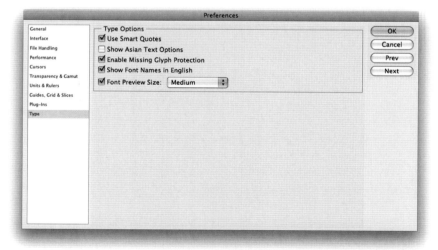

Figure 2.30 The Type preferences.

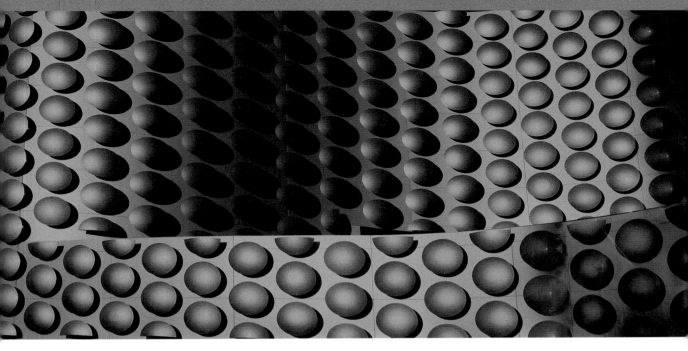

Chapter 3

Camera Raw Image Processing

I n the 12 years that I have been writing this series of books, the photography industry has changed out of all recognition. When I first began writing about Photoshop, most photographers were shooting with film cameras, getting their pictures scanned, and only a few professionals were shooting with high-end digital cameras. In the last few years the number of photographers who shoot digitally has grown to the point where the photographers who shoot film are now in the minority. I therefore reckon that the vast majority of photographers reading this book will be working with pictures that have been shot using a digital SLR or high-end digital camera that is capable of capturing files in a raw format that can be read by the Adobe Camera Raw plug-in. This is why I have devoted a whole chapter (and more) to discussing Camera Raw image editing.

Camera Raw 4.1

In 2008 Adobe did something rather unusual: they released the Camera Raw 4.1 update for Photoshop's Camera Raw plug-in shortly after the launch of Photoshop CS3. This was remarkable for two reasons. Adobe don't usually update the feature spec for Photoshop in between new versions of the program coming out, but also because it marked a new turning point in the way digital photographers were able to work with Photoshop. With the 4.1 update, Adobe refined the sharpening and noise reduction processing so that it now makes even more sense to carry out all your pre-image edit adjustments using Camera Raw.

Camera Raw advantages

Although Camera Raw started out as an image processor exclusively for raw files, it has, since version 4.0, been capable of processing any RGB image that is in a JPEG or TIFF file format. This means that you can use Camera Raw to process any image that has been captured by a digital camera, or any photograph that has been scanned by a film scanner and saved as an RGB TIFF or JPEG. Camera Raw allows you to work non-destructively, and anything you do to process an image in Camera Raw is saved as an instruction edit and the pixels in the original file are never altered. In this respect, Camera Raw treats your master files as if they were your negatives and you can use Camera Raw to process an image in any way that you like without ever altering the original.

The new Camera Raw workflow

When Camera Raw first came out it was regarded as a convenient tool for processing raw format images, without having to leave Photoshop. The early versions of Camera Raw had excellent controls for applying basic tone and color adjustments, but Camera Raw could never on its own match the sophistication of Photoshop. Because of this, photographers would typically follow the Camera Raw workflow steps described below in Figure 3.1. They would use Camera Raw to do all the 'heavy lifting' work such as

⇨ Set the White point
⇨ Set the highlight and shadow clipping points
⇨ Adjust the Brightness and Contrast
⇨ Adjust the color saturation
⇨ Compensate for chromatic aberrations and vignetting
⇨ Apply basic Sharpening and Noise Reduction
⇨ Apply a Camera Calibration fine-tuned adjustment
⇨ Apply a crop
⇨ Open images in Photoshop for further image editing

Figure 3.1 Camera Raw 1 offered a limited but useful range of image adjustments, and this list remained unchanged through to version 3.0 of the plug-in.

adjusting the White point, Exposure and Contrast and from there output the picture to Photoshop, which is where they would to carry out the remaining image editing.

Camera Raw 5 in Photoshop CS4 offers much more extensive image editing capabilities (such as localized adjustments) and it is now possible to replicate in Camera Raw the things that would normally have been done only in Photoshop. The net result of all this is that you can (and should) use Camera Raw as your first port of call when preparing any photographic image for editing in Photoshop. Let's be clear, Camera Raw does not replace Photoshop. It simply enhances the workflow and offers a better set of tools to work with in the early stages of an image editing workflow. Add to this what I mentioned earlier about being able to work with JPEG and TIFF images, and you can see that Camera Raw is a logical place for any image to begin its journey through Photoshop.

If you look at the suggested workflow listed in Figure 3.2 you will see that Camera Raw 5 now has all the tools you need to optimize and enhance a photograph.

⇨ Set the White point
⇨ Set the highlight and shadow clipping points
⇨ Compensate for missing highlight detail using Recovery
⇨ Compensate for hidden shadow detail using Fill Light
⇨ Make basic Brightness and Contrast adjustments
⇨ Boost the midtone contrast (Clarity)
⇨ Fine-tune the tone curve contrast
⇨ Fine-tune the color saturation/vibrance plus HSL color
⇨ Compensate for chromatic aberrations and vignetting
⇨ Retouch spots using a clone or heal brush
⇨ Make localized adjustments (brush or graduated filter)
⇨ Full capture Sharpening and Noise Reduction
⇨ Apply a Camera Calibration fine-tuned adjustment
⇨ Apply a crop
⇨ Open images in Photoshop for further image editing

Figure 3.2 Camera Raw 5 has now extended the list of things that can be done to an image at the Camera Raw editing stage.

Adobe Photoshop Lightroom

The Adobe Photoshop Lightroom program is designed as a raw processor and image management program for photographers. As mentioned in the text, it uses the exact same Adobe Camera Raw color engine that is used in Photoshop CS4, which means that raw files that have been adjusted in Lightroom can also be read and opened via Photoshop. However, Lightroom has the advantage of offering a full range of workflow modules designed to let you edit and manage raw images all the way from the camera import stage through to print and web output.

There is no differentiation made between a raw or non-raw file other than how the default settings are applied when a photo is first imported. When you choose to open a Lightroom imported, non-raw file (a JPEG, TIFF or maximum compatibility PSD) into Photoshop, Lightroom offers you the choice to apply or not apply Lightroom edited image adjustments.

Raw is the negative

You can liken capturing in raw mode to shooting with negative film, and the great thing about negative film is that it doesn't matter if someone makes a bad print, because you can always make an improved print from the original negative. When you shoot raw, you are recording a master file that contains all the color information that was captured at the time of shooting. To carry the analogy further, shooting in JPEG mode is like taking your film to a high street photo lab, throwing away the negatives and then making scans from the prints. If you shoot using JPEG, the camera is deciding automatically at the time of shooting how to set the white balance and the tonal corrections, often clipping the highlights and shadow detail in the process.

Camera Raw support

Camera Raw has kept pace with nearly all the latest raw camera formats in the compact range and digital SLR market, but only supports a few of the higher-end cameras such as the Leaf systems and latest Hasselblad H2 and H3 cameras (which also support the DNG format).

It can also be argued that if you use Camera Raw to edit your photographs, this will replace the need for Photoshop adjustments such as Levels, Curves and Hue/Saturation. To some extent this is true but, as you will read later in Chapter 5, these Photoshop adjustment tools are still relevant for fine-tuning images that have been output from Camera Raw, especially when you want to edit your photos directly or apply certain kinds of image effects that require the use of adjustment layers or additional image layers.

Does the order matter?

When you edit an image in Camera Raw it does not matter which order you apply the adjustments in. The lists shown in Figures 3.1 and 3.2 are presented as just one possible Camera Raw workflow. So for example you could refer to the list of steps in Figure 3.2, start by applying the crop and work your way through the remainder of the list backwards. However, you are normally advised to start with the major adjustments, such as setting the White point and Exposure in the Basic panel first before going on to fine-tune the image using the other controls.

Raw capture

If you are shooting with a professional back, digital SLR, or an advanced compact digital camera, you will almost certainly have the capability to shoot using the camera's raw format mode. The advantages of shooting in raw as opposed to JPEG mode are not always well understood. If you shoot using JPEG, the files are compressed by varying amounts and this file compression will enable you to fit more captures on a single card. Some photographers assume that shooting in raw mode simply provides you with uncompressed images without JPEG artifacts, but there are some more important reasons why capturing in raw mode is better than shooting with JPEG. The main benefit is the flexibility this gives you. The raw file is like a digital negative, waiting to be interpreted any way you like. It does not matter about the color space or white balance setting that was used at the time of capture, since these can all be set later in the raw processing. The only thing you have to concern yourself with is the ISO setting and camera exposure. But this advantage can also be seen by some as its biggest drawback since the Camera Raw stage will add to the overall image processing, meaning more time spent working on the images and an increase in the capture file size and download times. For these reasons, news photographers and others will find that JPEG capture is preferable for them.

JPEG capture

When you shoot in JPEG mode, your options are more limited since the camera's on-board computer makes its own automated decisions about how to optimize for tone, color, noise and sharpness. This means that you have to make sure that the camera settings are absolutely correct for things like the white balance and exposure. There is some room for manoeuvre when editing JPEGs, but not as much as you get when editing raw files. In JPEG mode, your camera will be able to fit more captures onto a card, and this will depend obviously on the capture file size and compression settings used. But it is worth noting that at the highest quality setting, JPEG capture files are sometimes not that much smaller than those stored using the native raw format. What you will find is that the length of the burst capture rate is greater when shooting in JPEG mode and for some photographers, such as those who cover sports events, speed is everything.

Editing JPEGs and TIFFs in Camera Raw

Not everyone has been keen on using Camera Raw to open non-raw images. However, the Camera Raw processing tools are so powerful and intuitive to use that why shouldn't they be available to work on images other than raw files? The idea of applying further Camera Raw processing may seem redundant in the case of JPEGs but, despite these concerns, Camera Raw does happen to be a good JPEG image editor. So from one point of view Camera Raw can be seen as offering the best of all worlds,

Discarded image data

When you shoot using JPEG or TIFF, the camera is immediately discarding up to 88% of the image information captured by the sensor. This is not as alarming as it sounds because, as you know from experience, you don't always get a bad photograph from a JPEG capture. But consider the alternative of what happens if you shoot using a raw mode capture. The raw file is saved to the memory card without being altered by the camera. This allows you to work with all 100% of the image data captured by the sensor.

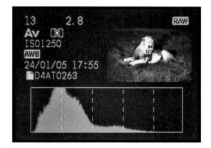

Figure 3.3 The camera's on-board processor is used to generate the low resolution JPEG preview image that appears in the LCD screen. The histogram is also based on the JPEG preview and is therefore a poor indicator of the true exposure potential of a raw capture image.

From light to digital

The CCD or CMOS chip in your camera converts the light hitting the sensor into a digital image. In order to digitize the information, the signal must be processed through an analog-to-digital converter (ADC). The ADC measures the amount of light hitting the sensor at each photosite and converts the analog signal into a binary form. At this point, the raw data simply consists of image brightness information coming from the camera sensor. The raw data must then be converted somehow and the raw conversion method used can make a huge difference to the quality of the final image output. Most cameras will have an on-board microprocessor that is able to convert the raw data into a readable image file, which in most cases will be in a JPEG type format. The quality of a digital image is primarily dependent on the lens optics used to take the photograph, the recording capabilities of the CCD or CMOS chip, and the analog-to-digital converter. But it is the raw conversion process that matters most. If you choose to process the raw data on your computer instead, you have much greater control than is the case if you had let your camera automatically guess which are the best raw conversion settings to use.

Third-party raw converters

The other software programs that can read and convert the raw camera data include: Bibble: www.bibblelabs.com, FotoStation: www.fotostation.com, Apple's Aperture, Capture One from Phase One and of course now, Adobe Photoshop Lightroom.

but it can also be seen as a major source of confusion (is it a raw editor or what?)

Perhaps the biggest problem so far has been the implementation rather than the principle of non-raw Camera Raw editing. Earlier in Chapter 2, I made the point that opening JPEGs and TIFFs via Camera Raw was made unnecessarily complex in Photoshop CS3, but this issue has now been resolved in CS4 and the Camera Raw file opening behavior for non-raw files is much easier to configure and anticipate (see page 101 for the full details).

On the other hand, if you look at the Lightroom program I think you will find that the use of Camera Raw processing on non-raw images works very well. I'll be explaining the Lightroom approach to non-raw editing a little later but it has to be said that the process of editing non-raw files in Lightroom is much easier to get to grips with, since Lightroom manages to process JPEGs quite seamlessly (see sidebar on page 119).

Alternative Raw processors

While I may personally take the view that Camera Raw is a powerful raw processor, there are now a lot of other alternative raw processing programs photographers can choose from. Some camera manufacturers supply their own brand of raw processing programs which either come free with the camera or you are encouraged to buy separately. Other notable programs include Capture One which is favored by a lot of professional shooters and Apple's Aperture which can be seen as a rival for Adobe's own Lightroom program. If you are using some other program to process your raw images and are happy with the results you are getting then that's fine. Even so, I would say that the core message of this chapter still applies, which is to use the raw processing stage to optimize an image so that you can rely less on using Photoshop's own adjustment tools to process the photograph afterwards. Overall it makes good sense to take advantage of the non-destructive processing in Camera Raw to freely interpret the raw capture data in ways that you can't using Photoshop alone.

A basic Camera Raw/Photoshop workflow

The standard Camera Raw workflow should be kept quite simple. Select the photo you wish to edit and double-click the thumbnail in Bridge to open it in Camera Raw. Or, you can use the ⌘R ctrl R shortcut to open in Camera Raw via Bridge (this is discussed later on page 144). In the example that's shown over the next few pages, I mainly used the Basic panel controls to adjust the white balance, the shadow and highlight clipping, and the tone contrast. These adjustments can be used to produce a well-balanced color master image that can then be edited in Photoshop, where layers and filters can be added as necessary. Any special effects or black and white conversions are best applied at the end in the form of an undoable adjustment layer, as shown in Step 5.

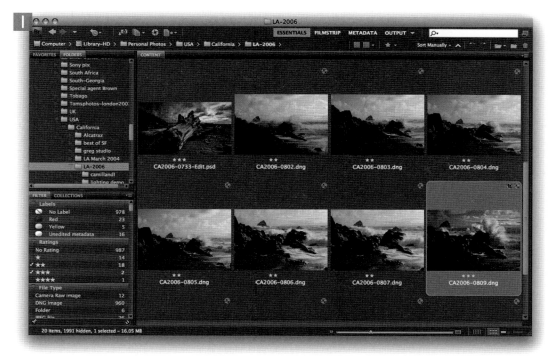

1 In this first step I opened a window in Bridge, selected a raw photo that I wished to edit and double-clicked on the highlighted thumbnail to open it via Camera Raw in Photoshop.

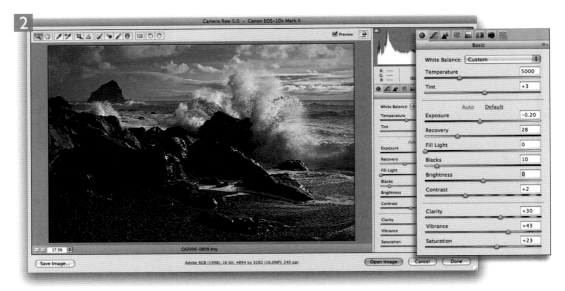

2 This shows the photograph opened up via the Camera Raw dialog hosted by Photoshop using just the Camera Raw Auto settings.

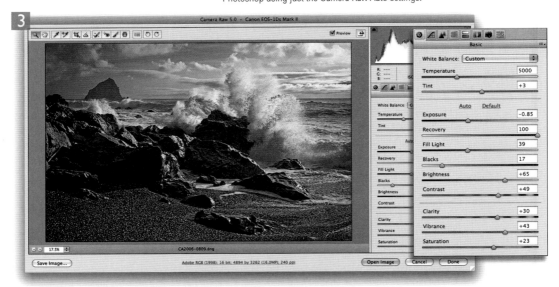

3 You can use the panel controls on the right to optimize the tone color and contrast, and improve the look of the photograph. Once you are happy with the way the image is looking, click the Open Image button to continue editing in Photoshop.

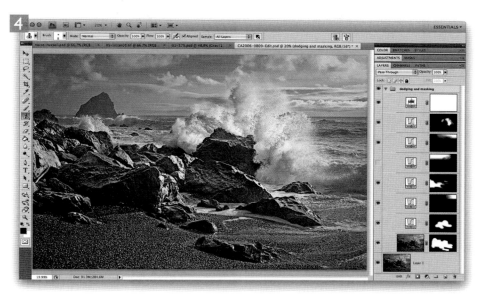

4 The Open Image button renders a pixel image version of the raw file that can then be edited in Photoshop using all the tools that Photoshop has to offer.

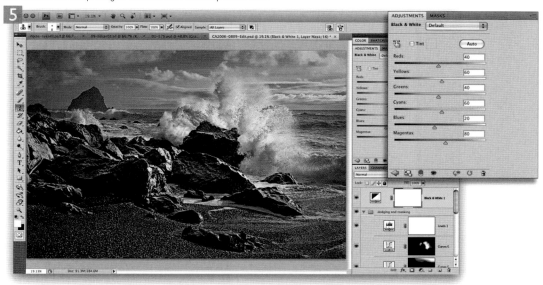

5 In this step I added a black and white adjustment layer to the top of the layer stack. This allowed me to preserve the color data in the retouched image and retain the ability to switch the conversion on or off.

The Photoshop sandwich

I like to describe this particular workflow as using Photoshop as a 'sandwich filler' for Lightroom. This is because the Develop controls in Lightroom are used at the beginning, Photoshop is then used to edit an Edit-copy pixel version of the master, and the Develop controls in Lightroom are used again at the end to add the finishing touches.

A Lightroom/Photoshop workflow

This workflow applies to Lightroom users only and I have included it here in order to illustrate an alternative approach to including Camera Raw style processing in a Photoshop workflow. In this example you can see how Camera Raw adjustments are applied at the beginning stage to optimize the master image. An Edit copy is opened in Photoshop and when the retouching is complete you can use the Develop controls in Lightroom to further edit the image, such as the grayscale conversion that was applied here.

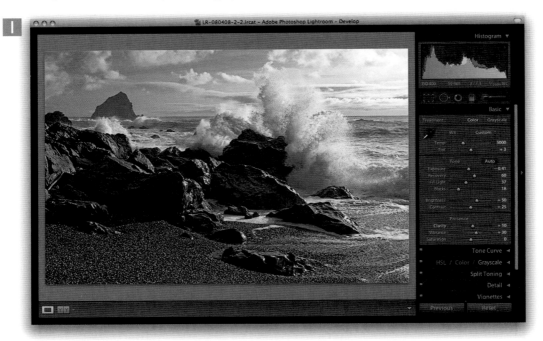

1 The Lightroom/Photoshop workflow starts off more or less the same as the Camera Raw/Photoshop workflow. Select a photo from the Lightroom Catalog, go to the Develop module (shown here) and apply some basic image adjustments to optimize the tones and colors. When you want to take the photo into Photoshop, go to the Photo menu and choose Edit in ⇨ Edit in Adobe Photoshop CS4 (⌘ E ctrl E). This will open the selected master photo in Photoshop as a pixel image copy of the original master, ready for you to edit. When you save the image, this will add the copy photo to the catalog (in the same folder location) and add an '-Edit' suffix to the file name.

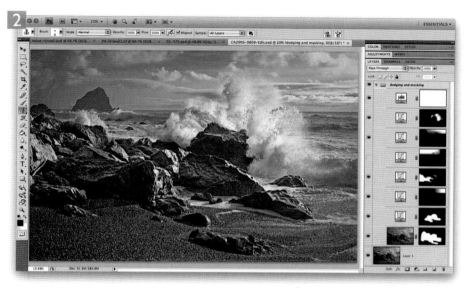

2 As before, you can use Photoshop to edit the Edit-copy pixel image, working here on the Edit-copy version that was rendered from Lightroom.

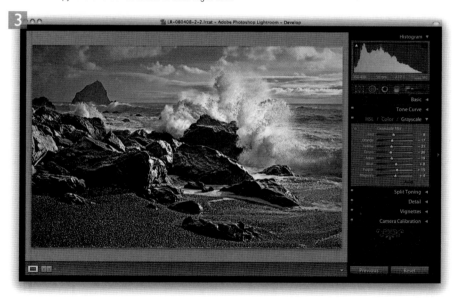

3 As the image is edited in Photoshop and saved, the Lightroom preview is updated. In Lightroom, you can apply post-Photoshop edit adjustments in the Develop module. One can therefore use Lightroom to colorize an image or convert to black and white, rather than add an extra adjustment layer in Photoshop.

Forward compatibility for raw files

Adobe's policy is to provide ongoing Camera Raw support throughout the life of a particular Photoshop product. This means if you bought Photoshop CS3, you would have been provided with free Camera Raw updates, up until version 4.5. Once a new Photoshop program comes out, Camera Raw support is continued for those new customers only. Consequently, you are obliged to upgrade your version of Photoshop if you wish to take advantage of the support offered for new cameras. However, you won't be completely blocked off from doing so. If you refer to the end of this chapter you can read about the free DNG Converter program that is always released at the same time as any Camera Raw updates. What you can do is to use DNG Converter to convert any supported raw camera format file to DNG. When you do this, the DNG file can then be read by any previous version of Camera Raw.

Camera Raw support

Camera Raw won't 'officially' interpret the raw files from every digital camera, but over 175 different raw formats are now supported, and Adobe is committed to providing intermittent free Camera Raw updates that will always include any new camera file interpreters as they become available. This generally happens about once every three months and sometimes sooner if a significant new camera is released. It is probably no coincidence that Thomas Knoll, who is a Canon EOS 1Ds user, always happens to have a new Camera Raw update for the 1Ds soon after a new model comes out! Camera Raw updates don't usually include new features, although the Camera Raw 4.1 update for Photoshop CS3 was unique in that it offered a whole new refined approach to image sharpening. There is always a chance this might happen again with CS4 but, for the most part, Camera Raw updates are provided to offer additional camera support and/or improved integration with Lightroom. For example, the Camera Raw 4.5 update was released so that Photoshop CS3 users could read raw files that have been edited in Lightroom 2.

Now understand that while not all raw camera file formats are supported, this is in no way the fault of Adobe. Certain camera manufacturers have in the past done things like encrypt the white balance data, which makes it difficult for anyone but themselves to decode the raw image data.

DNG compatibility

The DNG file format is an open standard file format for raw camera files. DNG is a file format that was devised by Adobe and there are already a few cameras (most noticeably the Hasselblad H3) that can shoot directly to DNG; plus there are now quite a few raw processor programs that can read DNG; including Camera Raw and Lightroom of course. Basically, DNG files can be read and edited just like any other proprietary raw file format and it is generally regarded as a safer file format to use for archiving your digital master files. For more about the DNG format refer to pages 228–230 at the end of this chapter.

Getting raw images into Photoshop

There was a time, not so long ago, when one would simply scan a few photographs, put them in a folder and double-click to open them up in Photoshop. These days most photographers are working with large numbers of images and it is therefore important to be able to import and manage those images efficiently. When Photoshop 7 came along Adobe introduced the File Browser, which was like an alternative open dialog interface incorporated within Photoshop that offered a superior way to manage your images, allowing you to preview and manage multiple images at once. The File Browser was superseded by the Bridge program in Photoshop CS2. As image browser programs go, Bridge's main advantage is that you have ready access to Photoshop to open up single or multiple images and apply batch operations directly from within the program. If you compare Bridge with other browser programs, it has enough basic functionality to suit most photographers' needs, although it has to be said that Bridge has yet to provide the full functionality that professional photographers have come to rely on in other programs, such as those dedicated to the task of managing large numbers of photographs (like Lightroom or Aperture).

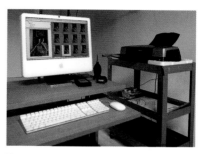

Figure 3.4 Here is a typical studio setup where I have an iMac computer stationed close to the actual shooting area, ready to process the captured images from the shoot. With the setup shown here I can either import camera card images via a Firewire card reader or shoot tethered.

Image ingestion

The first thing we should look at is how to get images from the camera and on to the computer ready to be worked on. This process is sometimes referred to as 'image ingestion', which is not a particularly elegant phrase but is how some like to describe the process.

Bridge features a Photo Downloader utility program that makes the downloading process much easier to carry out than was the case in earlier versions of Bridge, and over the next few pages I have outlined all the steps that are required when working with the Photo Downloader. For comparison purposes I have followed this up with an example of how to use the Adobe Photoshop Lightroom program, because this is the method I normally use when bringing photographs into the computer for Photoshop editing.

Importing images via Photo Downloader

EOS_DIGITAL

1 The process begins by inserting a camera card into the computer via a Firewire or USB 2.0 card reader. The card should then mount on the desktop or appear in the My Computer window as a new mounted volume.

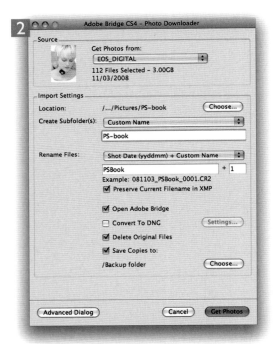

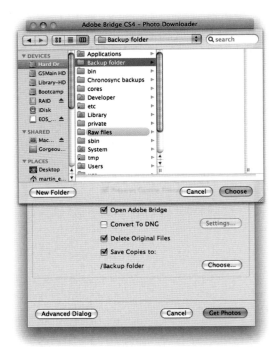

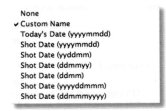

None
✓ Custom Name
Today's Date (yyyymmdd)
Shot Date (yyyymmdd)
Shot Date (yyddmm)
Shot Date (ddmmyy)
Shot Date (ddmm)
Shot Date (yyyyddmmm)
Shot Date (ddmmmyyyy)

Figure 3.5 The subfolder naming options.

2 Now launch Bridge CS4 and choose File ➡ Get Photos from Camera... This will open the Photo Downloader dialog shown here, where you can start by selecting where to download the files from (in this instance, the EOS_Digital camera card). Next, choose a location to download the photos to. Here, I selected the Pictures folder. I then selected 'Custom Name' from the Create Subfolder(s) menu (see Figure 3.5) and typed in a name for the shoot import (this name is appended to the Location setting to complete the file path). If the 'Delete Original Files' option is checked, Photo Downloader will give you the option to delete the files from the camera card once they have been successfully downloaded to the computer. I then checked the Save Copies to: option and clicked on the Choose... button to locate a backup folder to save the files to.

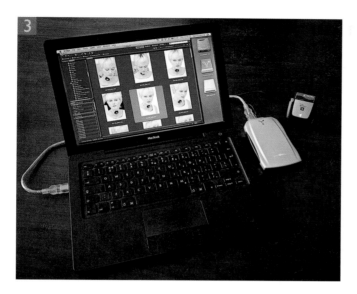

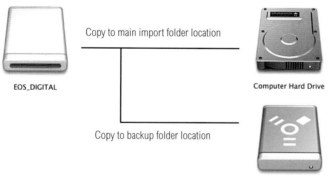

EOS_DIGITAL

Copy to main import folder location

Copy to backup folder location

Computer Hard Drive

Backup Hard Drive

Backup insurance

Your camera files are vulnerable to loss for as long as they remain in one location only, especially if they only exist on the camera card, which can easily get lost or the data might be corrupted. This is why it is always a good idea to get the camera files off the card and safely stored on a computer hard drive as soon as possible. Not only that, it is also a good idea to make a backup of the camera files as you do so. Note that Bridge will apply the settings setup in the Photo Downloader to the files that are copied to the main folder location. But, the files copied to the backup location will be plain clone copies of the original camera files. The backup copy files will not be renamed (as are the main import files). This is a good thing because should you make a mistake during the rename process you always retain a backup version of the files just as they were named when captured by the camera. Basically, backup files are like an insurance policy against both a drive failure as well as any file renaming mix-ups.

3 Lets review the Photo Downloader settings that have been applied so far. The camera card contained the images I wished to import and the Photo Downloader settings have so far been configured to copy these files to the primary disk location (which in this instance would be the computer hard drive), and at the same time make a backup copy of all the images to a secondary location (in this case, a backup hard drive). With the setup shown here, I was able to use Photo Downloader to make renamed copies of the files to the principal drive/folder location and, if desired, convert the files to DNG as I did so. With this type of configuration I will end up with two copies of each image imported and stored on the computer system.

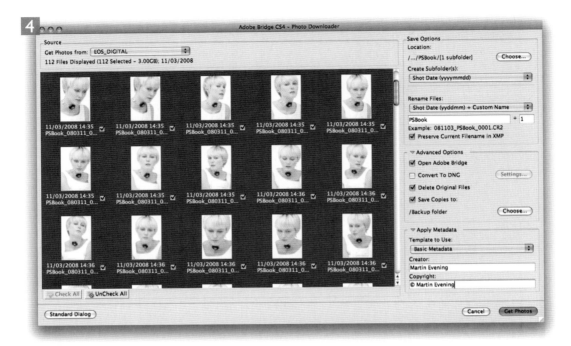

Do not rename files
Today's Date (yyyymmdd)
Shot Date (yyyymmdd)
Shot Date (yyddmm)
Shot Date (ddmmyy)
Shot Date (ddmm)
Shot Date (yyyyddmmm)
Shot Date (ddmmmyyyy)
Custom Name
Shot Date (yyyymmdd) + Custom Name
✓ Shot Date (yyddmm) + Custom Name
Shot Date (ddmmyy) + Custom Name
Shot Date (ddmm) + Custom Name
Shot Date (yyyyddmmm) + Custom Name
Shot Date (ddmmmyyyy) + Custom Name
Custom Name + Shot Date (yyyymmdd)
Custom Name + Shot Date (yyddmm)
Custom Name + Shot Date (ddmmyy)
Custom Name + Shot Date (ddmm)
Custom Name + Shot Date (yyyyddmmm)
Custom Name + Shot Date (ddmmmyyyy)
Same as Subfolder Name

Figure 3.6 Here are the options for the Rename Files menu, highlighted in the dialog above.

4 If you click on the Advanced dialog button in the bottom left corner (see Step 2) you will show an expanded version of the Photo Downloader dialog. This will allow you to see a grid preview of the images on the card you are about to import from. You can now decide which images will be imported by clicking on the thumbnail checkboxes to select or deselect individual photos. You can also use the Check All and Uncheck All buttons in the bottom left of the dialog to select or deselect all the thumbnails at once.

The Rename Files section lets you choose a renaming scheme from the list of options shown in Figure 3.6. Which you should choose will depend on what works best for you, and this is a topic I will explore in greater detail in the Image Management chapter. In this example I chose to rename using the shoot date followed by a custom shoot name. You can see how the renaming will work by inspecting the Example filename above, where you will note that the imported files are automatically renumbered starting from the start number entered here. If you check 'Preserve Current Filename in XMP', this will give you the option to use the Batch Rename feature in Bridge to recover the original filename at a later date.

The Advanced Options will let you decide what happens to the imported images after they have been renamed. You will most likely want to check the Open Adobe Bridge option so that Bridge displays the image download folder contents as the images are being imported.

In the Apply Metadata section you can choose a pre-saved metadata template (see Chapter 11) and enter your author name and copyright information. This data will then be automatically embedded as metadata in the files as they are imported.

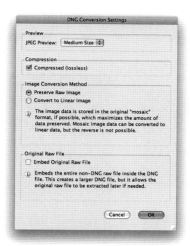

Converting to DNG

To read more about converting proprietary raw files to DNG and the conversion settings shown here, please refer to pages 228–230 at the end of this chapter.

5 If the Convert to DNG option is selected, this can be used to convert raw images to the DNG file format as they are imported. For some people it can be useful to carry out the conversion straight away, but be warned that this will add to the time it takes to import all the photos. If you click on the Settings... button (next to the Convert to DNG option in Photo Downloader) this will open the DNG Conversion Settings dialog shown here. If you select the Medium size JPEG Preview option, this will generate a standard size preview for the imported pictures – there is no point in generating a full size preview just yet since you may well be changing the camera raw settings soon anyway, so to get reasonably fast imports it is better to choose 'Medium Size'. Check the Compressed option if you would like smaller file sizes (note that this uses lossless compression and does not risk degrading the image quality). In the Image Conversion Method section I suggest you don't choose 'Convert to Linear Image', but choose 'Preserve Raw Image' as this will keep the raw data in the DNG in its original state. And lastly, you can choose to embed the original raw data (along with the DNG data) in the DNG file, but I would advise against this unless you really need to preserve the proprietary raw file.

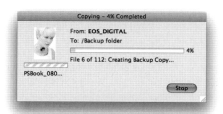

6 After I clicked on the Get Photos button in the Photo Downloader dialog, the images started to download from the card to the disk location specified in the Save Options. The Progress dialog shows you how the download process is proceeding.

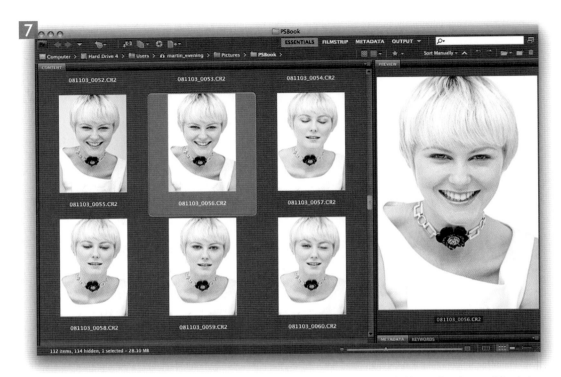

Deleting camera card files

It isn't actually necessary to delete the files from the camera card first, because formatting a card in the camera will delete everything that is on the card anyway. Formatting the card is good housekeeping practice as this will help guard against future file corruptions occurring with the card. However, I find that if I am in the midst of a busy shoot it is preferable to get into a routine of deleting the files before you put the card back in the camera. Otherwise I am always left with the nagging doubt: 'have I downloaded all the files on this card yet? Is it really safe to delete everything on this card?'

7 Because the 'Open Adobe Bridge' option had been selected, once all the photos were downloaded Bridge opened a new window to display the imported photos that were now in the main download images folder.

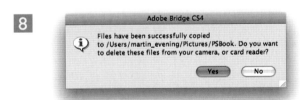

8 Also, because the 'Delete Original Files' option was selected, the above warning dialog appeared once the downloads to the primary destination folder (and backup folder) were complete. This step conveniently clears the camera card of all the images that were stored on it and prepares it for reuse in the camera. Be warned that this step bypasses any opportunity to confirm if you really want to delete these files. Once you click 'Yes', the files will be permanently deleted from the card. When I put a card back in the camera I usually reformat it anyway before shooting a fresh batch of photos to that card (see sidebar 'Deleting camera card files').

Tethered shoot imports

There is no direct support for tethered shooting in Bridge CS4, but if Bridge were able to do so it would have to offer tethered support for all the cameras that Camera Raw already supports. Enabling full tethered shoot functionality is difficult enough to do for one camera let alone several hundred, which is why some software programs, such as Capture One and Bibble, that do offer tethered shooting, only do so with a range of popular digital SLR cameras. For some people this is justification enough for spending the extra money to shoot tethered.

However, it is possible to shoot in tethered mode with Bridge, but it all depends on the capabilities of your camera and whether it has a suitable connection socket and software that will allow you to download files directly to a computer. Many cameras (especially digital SLR cameras) will most likely come with some kind of software that allows you to hook your camera up to the computer via a Firewire or USB 2 cable (Figure 3.7). If you are able to download files directly to the computer then Bridge can monitor that folder, and this will give you a next best solution to a dedicated software program that is designed to operate in tethered mode.

The only drawback to shooting tethered is that the camera must be wired up to the computer and you don't have the complete freedom to wander around with the camera. If you have a wireless communication device then it may be possible to shoot in a direct import mode to the computer, without the hassle of a cable but, at the time of writing, wireless shooting isn't particularly speedy when shooting raw files with a typical digital SLR.

Over the next few pages I have described a method for shooting in tethered mode with a Canon EOS camera, using the Canon EOS Utility program that ships with most of the Canon EOS digital cameras. This program lets you download camera files as they are captured, to a designated watched folder. Nikon owners will find that Nikon Capture includes a Camera Control component that allows you to do the same thing as the Canon software and establishes

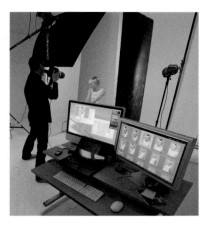

Figure 3.7 Here is a photograph of me at work in the studio, shooting in tethered mode.

Which utility?

One of the problems with the Canon system is the way the utility programs have been named and updated with succeeding generations of cameras. First of all there was EOS Viewer Utility, and now EOS Utility, which have both interacted with a program called EOS Capture. On top of this you also have to make sure that you are using the correct version of 'utility' software for the camera type you are using. It would help if there were just one program that was updated to work with all Canon cameras.

Which transfer protocol?

Nikon and Canon systems both offer FTP and PTP transfer protocols. Make sure you select the right one, as failure to do so can result in an inability to get tethered shooting to work.

a watched folder to download the images to. The latest version of Nikon Capture supports all the D Series cameras as well as the Nikon Coolpix 8700. Alternatively, you might want to consider buying Bibble Pro 4.10 software from Bibble Labs (www.bibblelabs.com). Bibble Pro costs a lot less than Nikon Capture. It enables tethered shooting with a wide variety of digital cameras and, again, allows you to establish a watched folder for the downloaded images, which you can monitor using Bridge CS4.

EOS Utility

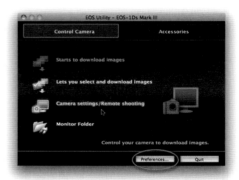

1 To begin with, make sure the camera is tethered to the computer correctly and is switched on, then launch EOS utility and click the Preferences button (circled) to open the preferences shown in Step 2 below.

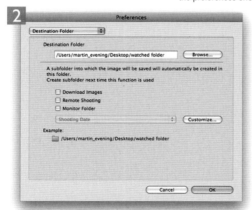
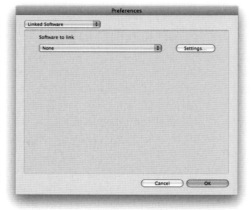

2 In the Destination Folder section, click on the Browse... button and select a destination folder that the camera captures will be downloaded to. This could be an existing folder, or a new folder, such as the 'Watched folder' selected here. Meanwhile, in the Linked Software section, set the 'Software to link to' as 'None'.

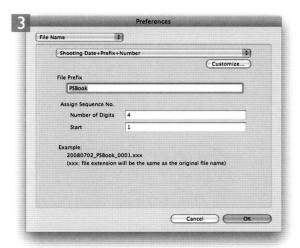

3 You will also need to set up a file renaming scheme. You could carry out the file renaming in Bridge afterwards, but establishing this beforehand will save time and help reduce the risk of error when it's applied automatically as the files are captured. In this example, I selected the Shooting Date+Prefix+Number file naming scheme and set the start count number to '1'.

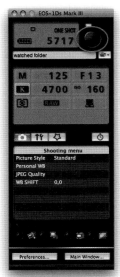

4 I clicked OK to the Camera Settings in Step 3 and then clicked on the Camera Settings/Remote shooting option that the cursor is pointing to in Step 1. This will open the Camera control window shown here, where you can configure the camera settings remotely. As soon as this window appears you are ready to start shooting.

Lightroom conflicts

If you are also running Lightroom, the one thing to watch out for here is that the Watched folder you select in Step 2 does not conflict with any Watched folder that might currently be monitored by Lightroom. If this is the case, then you will need to disable the auto-import feature in Lightroom first before using it to import photos that can be viewed via Bridge.

Auto-renumbering

When you select a numbering option in the File Name section, the numbering will keep on auto-updating until such time as you change the file prefix name. This is useful to know because it means that if you were to lose a camera connection or switch the camera off between shoots, the EOS Utility program will know to continue the file renaming of the import files from the last number used.

Remote shooting controls

As soon as the Camera control window appears you know that you have succeeded in establishing a tethered connection and are ready to start shooting. This can be done by pressing the shutter on the camera or, alternatively, you can use the EOS Capture utility to capture the photos remotely from the computer by clicking on the large round button (circled). You can also use this window to adjust the camera settings by selecting any of the status items in the window and use the left or right keyboard arrow keys to cycle between the various mode options or decrease or increase the settings.

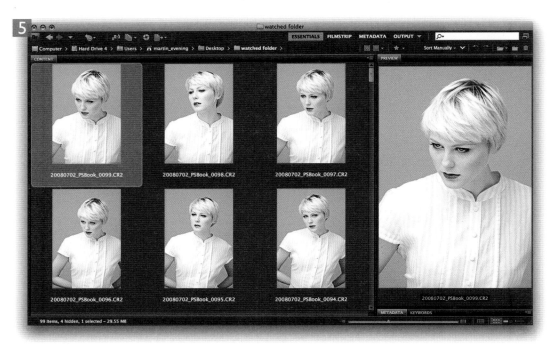

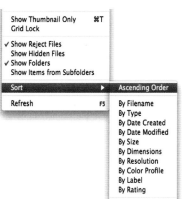

5 As you start shooting, the EOS utility will enable the import of the camera files directly into the Watched folder you selected in Step 1 and rename them (as configured in Step 2). All you need to do now is point Bridge at the same Watched folder as was configured in the EOS Utility preferences and you'll see the pictures appear in Bridge directly. Of course, if you are shooting continuously in the studio or location with such a setup, then you will most likely wish to see the newest pictures appear first at the top of the content area in the Bridge window. To do this, go to the View menu and check if the Ascending Order item in the Sort menu is deselected (as shown in the screen shot on the left). Do this and the files will now be sorted in reverse order with the most recent appearing first.

When you have finished shooting in tethered mode, you will either need to move the files out of the watched folder or give it a new name. The main thing to be aware of here is that every time you start a new shoot, you will either want to choose a new job folder to download the photos to, or move the files from this folder to a new location and make sure that the Watched folder you are linking to has been emptied.

Importing images via other programs

Figure 3.8 highlights some of the various methods that can be used for importing images. There is no one program that can do everything perfectly, but of these I would say that Capture One is the only program capable of ticking all the essential boxes (as long as your camera is supported). ImageIngester is a great little utility that can provide a fast and robust import workflow, and the standard version for Mac and PC is currently available to download for free.

Ever since Adobe Photoshop Lightroom made its first appearance as a beta product, I have been using Lightroom in the studio and on location and now use it all the time to import images from cards as well as when shooting in tethered mode. I have now stopped using Bridge completely at the import stage. Although Lightroom is a separate program that would need to be bought separately, I thought I should at least show you the workflow I now prefer using when I wish to import new photos into the computer.

ImageIngester™ program

The ImageIngester™ program designed by Marc Rochkind is aimed at photographers who shoot digitally, use a raw workflow, and need to ingest hundreds of images from a typical shoot. You can download the basic ImageIngester program for free from the following link: www.basepath.com/ImageIngester/

An ImageIngester Pro version is on the cards, but at the time of writing I cannot confirm if this will be sold as a product.

	Direct integration with Bridge	File renaming	Full auto renumbering	Secondary backup of data	Convert to DNG	Import settings saved for concurrent imports	Tethered shooting	Preview and pre-selection of import files
Photo Downloader	✗	✗	✗	✗	✗	✗		✗
Tethered shooting via Bridge	✗						✗*	
DNG Converter		✗	✗		✗	✗		
Lightroom Import Photos		✗	✗	✗	✗	✗		✗
Lightroom Auto Import		✗	✗			✗	✗*	
Image Ingester Standard		✗	✗	✗	✗	✗		
Capture One		✗	✗	✗	✗	✗	✗	

Figure 3.8 In this table I have compared the features available using some of the various methods that are available when importing camera images into the computer. As you can see, there is no one perfect solution out there that will let you do everything.

* In these instances, tethered shooting is only possible if done in conjunction with a camera manufacturer's import software.

Bridge versus Lightroom

In earlier editions of this book, I suggested how you could use the File Browser (which then became Bridge) as one way to bring your photos into Photoshop. Unfortunately, Bridge CS3 didn't really manage to offer much in the way of additional benefits, while Lightroom 1.0 steamed ahead in offering a much improved workflow for photographers. The good news is that Bridge CS4 has now regained some of its focus and managed to overcome a few of the pitfalls that were initially there in CS3. For example, the Bridge 2.1 update managed to resolve the auto-renumbering problem, which means that the Photo Downloader is now up to the task of importing photos without you having to constantly monitor the import settings as you do so.

The main thing to note here is that Bridge is a File Browser, while Lightroom is a dedicated cataloging program. The times that I find Bridge most useful are when I am working on a project like this book and have hundreds of files to manage that are stored in specific book folders. The times when I find Lightroom useful is when I wish to source the master original files. The Lightroom cataloging features allow me to search and navigate these much quicker.

Lightroom imports

One of the main reasons I have adopted Lightroom as my program of choice for importing and managing the photos in my image library is because I need a program that is dedicated to the management of images. With Lightroom, photos have to be explicitly imported into the Lightroom catalog before you can work on them but, once they are there, they are easier to manage and recall. With Bridge you do have immediate access to browse the entire contents of your computer, but the trade-off here is that because you can browse everything this doesn't always make it so easy to locate the photos you are specifically looking for.

In the Import Photos dialog you have similar options to those found in Photo Downloader, such as the ability to make backups, rename the files and apply basic metadata information. But in addition to this you have the option to apply develop settings and add custom keywords on import. You can also use Import Photos to report suspected duplicate files and prevent these from being reimported. This can be useful if you happen to reuse a card and forgot to delete the photos that were downloaded previously.

After the files have been imported into Lightroom, the imported images will appear listed in the Folders panel of the Library module, which displays all the images that have been imported so far into Lightroom using the same disk volume and hierarchy structure as the folders that are found in the system folder organization (see Step 4 on page 143). Moving files or folders in Lightroom is like moving files or folders at the system level or via Bridge, except you must use Lightroom to do the moving otherwise you'll end up with broken links. One of the main features of Lightroom is that master files are always preserved as the original files, and Develop module edits in Lightroom are applied in the form of metadata instructions (just like Camera Raw). To open pictures from Lightroom into Photoshop, you need to create an Edit copy of the master either with or without Lightroom adjustments and edit it in Photoshop, just as you would when opening a file from Bridge. The Edit-copy files are then saved back to the folder they came from and added to the Lightroom catalog.

Importing photos via Lightroom 2

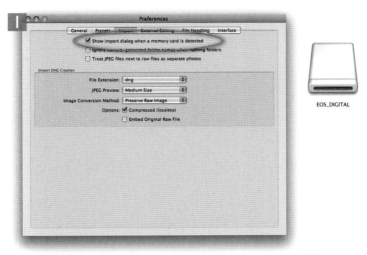

1 The Lightroom 2 preferences are accessed via the Lightroom menu (Mac) or Edit menu (PC). If you check the 'Show import dialog' option for when a memory card is detected, Lightroom will automatically launch the Import Photos dialog each time a memory card is inserted.

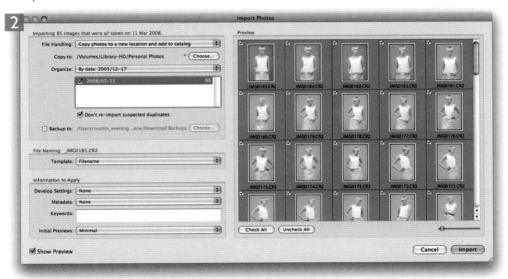

2 This shows the Import Photos dialog. If the Show Preview option is checked you can quickly scroll through the thumbnails of the images you are about to import and choose which ones to include in the import process.

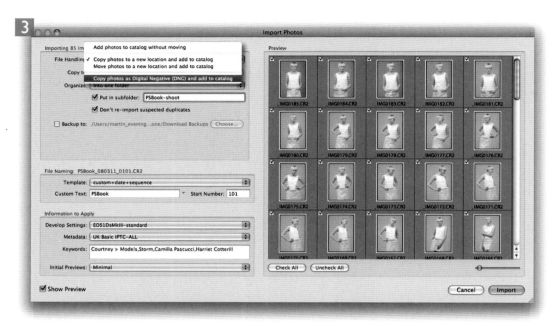

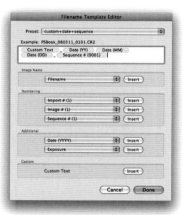

Figure 3.9 The Filename Template Editor offers far more versatile options for creating file renaming templates. And, more importantly, Lightroom keeps track of files as they are imported and will auto-update the renumbering until you next change the Import Photos settings.

3 If importing from a camera card, the quickest option is to select the 'Copy photos to a new location and add to catalog' option. Alternatively you can select the 'Copy Photos as Digital Negative (DNG) and add to catalog' option. This will make a duplicate copy of all the images on the memory card and convert them to the DNG format. At this stage I sometimes prefer to organize the imported images into a single named folder and ignore any suspected duplicates. You can also check the 'Backup To' option and choose a folder to store backups of the files as they are imported.

The File Renaming section makes use of file renaming templates such as the one shown in Figure 3.9. Below that you can enter a custom text for use in the file renaming plus a start number for the numbering sequence.

In the Information to Apply section you can apply a pre-created Develop setting (a Lightroom Camera Raw image adjustment) at the import stage. Information that might be considered important, such as your copyright and contact information, can be added by selecting a pre-created metadata template from the Metadata menu, and information that relates specifically to the image collection you are about to import can be entered using custom keywords. As you type in the first few letters of a keyword, Lightroom will try to auto-complete a name for you and pop a menu of possible keywords. This will help you avoid spelling mistakes and be consistent in your keywording.

And lastly, we have the Initial Previews options. Choosing 'Render Standard-Sized Previews' will slow down the import process since it forces Lightroom to render previews of the images using the selected Develop setting before displaying them in Lightroom. 'Minimal' is a much faster option. Once you have configured all the import settings, you can click 'Import' to start copying the images to the computer.

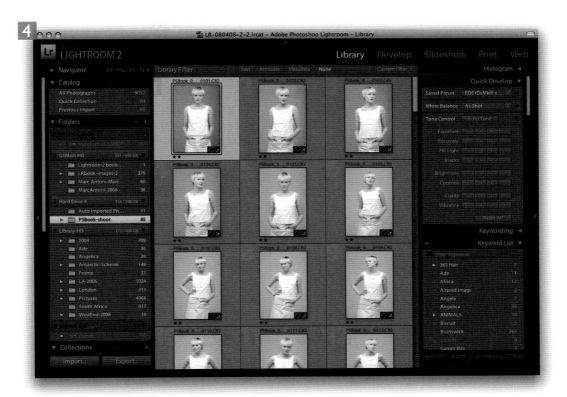

4 As the images are imported the thumbnails will start to appear one by one in the content area. You will also see the import progress shown in the Status indicator in the top left corner and this progress bar will give you an indication of how long it will take to complete the import process. You should not normally encounter any problems when importing files from a camera card, but if you choose the Copy Photos as DNG option you will be alerted to any corruptions in the files as they are imported. Once you have successfully imported all the images across to the computer and backup drive (if applicable), you can now safely delete the images on the card, eject the camera card and prepare it for reuse.

The Adobe Photoshop Lightroom 2 book

If you want to find out more about Lightroom, I have written a complete guide about this new program called simply *The Adobe Photoshop Lightroom 2 Book*, published by Adobe Press. ISBN: 0-321-55561-9

Closing Bridge as you open

If you hold down the [⌥] [alt] key as you double-click to open a raw image, this will close the Bridge window as you open the Camera Raw dialog hosted by Photoshop.

JPEG and TIFF handling

Please refer to the sidebar on page 161 for a summary of the JPEG and TIFF handling behavior.

Basic Camera Raw image editing

Working with Bridge and Camera Raw

The mechanics of how Photoshop and Bridge work together are designed to be as simple as possible so that you can open single or multiple images or batch process images quickly and efficiently. Figure 3.10 summarizes how the linking between Bridge, Photoshop and Camera Raw works. Central to everything is the Bridge window interface, where you can browse, preview and make selections of which images you want to process. The way most people are accustomed to opening images is to select the desired thumbnail icon (or icons) and either double-click, use the File ⇨ Open command, or the [⌘][O] [ctrl][O] shortcut. The way things are set up in Bridge, all of the above methods will open a selected raw image (or images) via the Camera Raw dialog hosted by Photoshop (if the image is not a raw file, it will open in Photoshop directly). Alternatively, you can use File ⇨ Open in Camera Raw... or use the [⌘][R] [ctrl][R] shortcut to open images via the Camera Raw dialog hosted by Bridge, which will allow you to perform batch processing operations in the background without compromising Photoshop's performance. If the 'Double-click edits Camera Raw Settings in Bridge' option is deselected in the General Bridge preferences, [Shift] double-clicking will allow you to open an image or multiple selection of images in Photoshop directly, bypassing the Camera Raw dialog.

Opening single raw images via Photoshop is quicker than opening them via Bridge and opening multiple images via Photoshop will take about the same time, but Photoshop will consequently be tied up managing the Camera Raw processing. The advantage of opening via Bridge is that Bridge can process large numbers of raw files, while freeing up Photoshop to perform other tasks. And you can toggle between the two programs. So for example, you can be processing an image in Camera Raw while you switch to viewing another image in Photoshop for comparison with the one you are editing in Camera Raw.

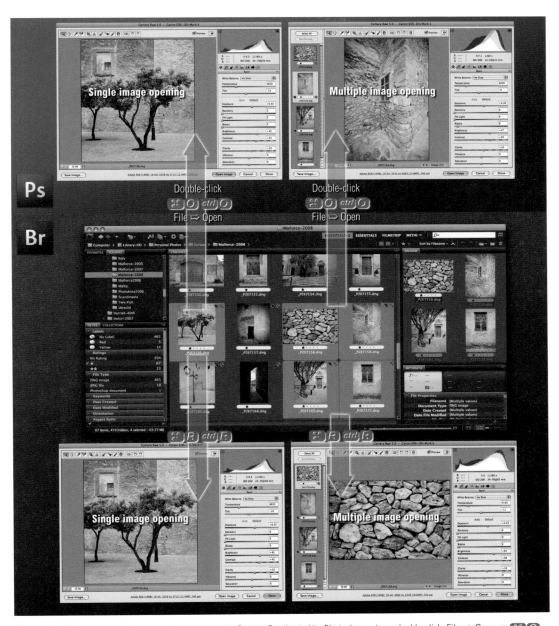

Figure 3.10 You can open single or multiple images via Camera Raw hosted by Photoshop using a double-click, File ⇨ Open, or ⌘ O / ctrl O. Photoshop is ideal for processing small numbers of images. If you use ⌘ R / ctrl R, Bridge will host the single or multiple Camera Raw dialog. Opening via Bridge is better suited for processing large batches of images in the background.

Camera Raw tools

🔍 Zoom tool (Z)

Use as you would with the normal zoom tool to zoom in or out the preview image.

✋ Hand tool (H)

Use as you would with the normal hand tool to scroll an enlarged preview image.

✐ White balance tool (I)

The white balance tool is used to set the White Balance in the Basic panel.

✐ Color sampler tool (S)

This allows you to place up to nine color sampler points in the preview window.

🔲 Crop tool (C)

The crop tool can apply a crop setting to the raw image which will only be applied when the file is opened in Photoshop.

📐 Straighten tool (A)

Use this tool to drag across a horizontal or vertical line to apply a 'best fit', straightened crop.

✐ Spot removal (B)

Use to remove sensor dust spots and blemishes from a picture.

👁 Red eye removal tool (E)

For removing red eye from portraits shot using on-camera direct flash.

✐ Adjustment brush (K)

Use this brush tool to paint in localized adjustments.

◣ Graduated filter (G)

Use the Graduated filter to apply graduated localized adjustments.

☰ ACR preferences (⌘ ctrl–K)

Opens the Adobe Camera Raw preferences dialog.

↺ Rotate counterclockwise (L)

Rotates the image 90° counter clockwise.

↻ Rotate clockwise (R)

Rotates the image 90° clockwise.

General controls for single file opening

When you open a single image, you will see the Camera Raw dialog shown in Figure 3.11 (which in this case, shows Camera Raw hosted via Bridge). The status bar shows which version of Camera Raw you are using and the make of camera for the file you are currently editing. In the top left section you have the Camera Raw tools, which I have listed on the left, and below that is the image preview area where the zoom setting can be adjusted via the pop-up menu at the bottom. The initial Camera Raw dialog displays the Basic panel control settings and in this mode the Preview checkbox will allow you to toggle previewing any global adjustments made in Camera Raw. Once you start selecting any of the other panels, the Preview will toggle showing only the changes that have taken place within a particular panel.

The histogram represents the output histogram of an image and is calculated based on the RGB output space selected in the Workflow options. As you carry out the Basic panel Exposure and Blacks adjustments, the shadow and highlight triangles in the histogram display will help indicate the shadow and highlight clipping. As either of these get clipped, the triangles will light up with the color of the channel or channels that are about to be clipped and, if you click on them, they will display a color overlay (blue for the shadows, red for the highlights) to indicate which areas in the image are being clipped.

At the bottom are the Show Workflow Options, which when clicked will open the Workflow Options shown in Figure 3.12. The destination color space should ideally match the RGB workspace setting used in the Photoshop color settings, and I would suggest setting the bit depth to 16-bits per channel as this will ensure that the image bit depth integrity is maintained when the image is opened up in Photoshop. The file size setting will let you open the image using smaller or larger pixel dimensions than the default capture file size (these size options are indicated by + or − signs), and the Resolution field lets you set the file resolution in pixels per inch or per centimeter, but note that the value selected has no impact on the pixel dimensions.

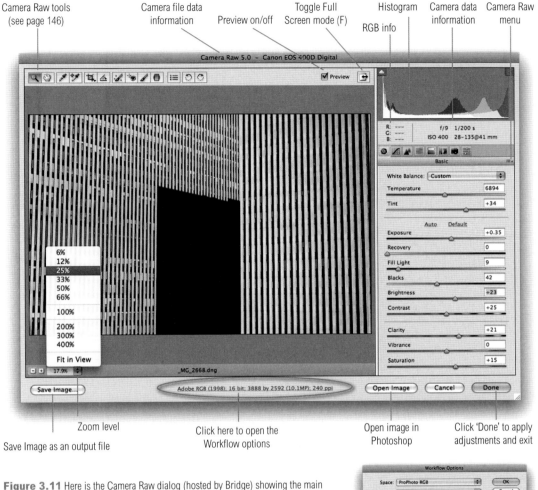

Camera Raw tools
(see page 146)

Camera file data
information

Preview on/off

Toggle Full
Screen mode (F)

Histogram

RGB info

Camera data
information

Camera Raw
menu

Save Image as an output file

Zoom level

Click here to open the
Workflow options

Open image in
Photoshop

Click 'Done' to apply
adjustments and exit

Figure 3.11 Here is the Camera Raw dialog (hosted by Bridge) showing the main controls and shortcuts for the single file open mode. You can tell if Camera Raw has been opened via Bridge because the Done button is highlighted. This is an 'update' button, which you click when you are done making Camera Raw edits and wish to save these settings, but without opening the image.

If you click on the Workflow options (circled) this will open the Workflow Options dialog shown in Figure 3.12, where you can adjust the settings that determine the color space the image will open in, the bit-depth, cropped image pixel dimensions plus resolution (i.e. how many pixels per inch).

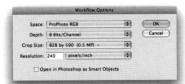

Figure 3.12 The workflow options let you set the color space and pixel dimensions. Plus, there is an option to open in Photoshop as a Smart Object (see page 150).

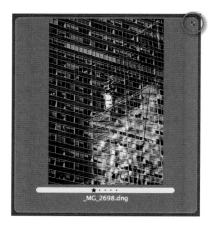

Figure 3.13 After opening or applying 'Done' to an image via the Camera Raw dialog, you will see a settings badge appear in the top right corner of the image thumbnail (circled), which indicates that the image has been edited in Camera Raw.

Full size window view

The Toggle Full screen mode button (**F**) can be used to expand the Camera Raw dialog to fill the whole screen, which can make Camera Raw editing easier when you have a bigger preview area to work with, and clicked again to restore the normal Camera Raw window size view.

General controls for multiple file opening

If you have more than one photo selected in Bridge, you can open them all up via Camera raw at once. If you refer back to Figure 3.10, you can see a summary of the file opening behavior, which is basically as follows. If you double-click or use File ⇨ Open (**⌘**_O_ _ctrl_ _O_) this will open the multiple image Camera Raw dialog hosted via Photoshop (as shown in Figure 3.14) and if you choose File ⇨ Open in Camera Raw... or **⌘**_R_ _ctrl_ _R_ this will open the multiple image Camera Raw dialog via Bridge.

The multiple image dialog contains a filmstrip of the selected images running down the left-hand side of the dialog and you can select individual images by clicking on the thumbnails in the filmstrip, or use the Select All button to select all the photos at once. You can also make custom selections of images via the Filmstrip by using the _Shift_ key to make continuous selections, or the **⌘** _ctrl_ key to make discontinuous selections of images. Once you have made a selection you can then navigate the photos that are displayed in the preview area, by using the navigation buttons to progress through them one by one, and apply Camera Raw adjustments to individual selected images. The Synchronize... button will then allow you to synchronize the Camera Raw settings adjustments across all the images that are selected, based on the current 'most selected' image, which will be the thumbnail highlighted with a blue border. When you click on the Synchronize... button, the Synchronize dialog (Figure 3.15) lets you choose which of the Camera Raw settings you want to synchronize. You can learn more about this and how to synchronize Camera Raw settings on page 227, as well as how to copy and paste Camera Raw settings via Bridge.

Select all images

Synchronize settings

Mark for deletion (X)

Preview on/off

Warning triangle warns that the image preview has not refreshed completely yet

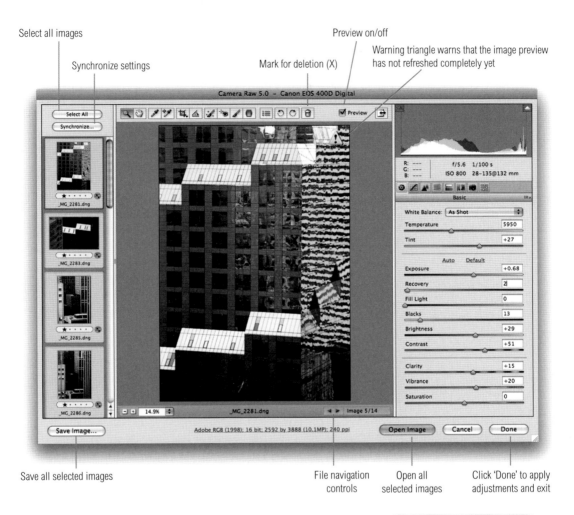

Save all selected images

File navigation controls

Open all selected images

Click 'Done' to apply adjustments and exit

Figure 3.14 Here is a view of the Camera Raw dialog, in the multiple file open mode, hosted in Photoshop (you can tell because the Open Image button is highlighted). This screen shot shows the filmstrip of opened images on the left where 5 of the 14 opened images are currently selected and the top image (highlighted with the blue border) is the one that is 'most selected' and displayed in the preview area. Camera Raw adjustments can be applied to the selected photos one at a time, or synchronized with each other by clicking on the Synchronize settings button, which will open the Synchronize dialog shown in Figure 3.15. Note that if you hold down the ⌥ *alt* key as you do so, this will bypass the Synchronize dialog and synchronize everything.

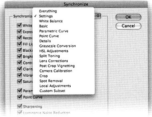

Figure 3.15 The Synchronize dialog.

Opening raw files as Smart Objects

One of the top requests we hear for Photoshop is to have Camera Raw style adjustment layers. It's a nice idea, but limited by the fact that some of the Camera Raw adjustments rely on masking methods and therefore can't be applied as layers, in the same way as filters can't be applied as adjustment layers (although, having said that, there is now a Vibrance adjustment control for Photoshop). But what we can do is to use the Smart Objects feature in Photoshop that can be used to convert raw images or layers into Smart Objects, which are like independent images within an image and can be processed non-destructively.

In the case of Camera Raw, Smart Object opening is almost like a hidden feature but, once discovered, can lead to all sorts of exciting possibilities. There are two ways to go about this. You can click on the Workflow options link highlighted in Figure 3.16 to open the Workflow Options dialog and select the 'Open in Photoshop as Smart Objects' option. If checked, this will make *all* Camera Raw processed images open as Smart Object layers in Photoshop when you click on the Open Image button. The other option is to simply hold down the *Shift* key as you click on 'Open Image'.

Let's now look at a practical example of opening two raw images as Smart Object layers and merging them in Photoshop.

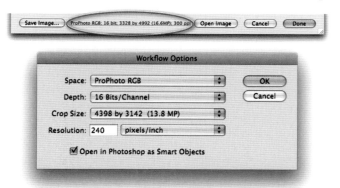

Figure 3.16 If you click on the Workflow options link (circled above) this will open the Workflow Options dialog, where you can check the 'Open in Photoshop as Smart Objects' option.

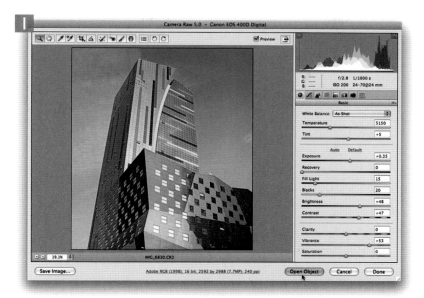

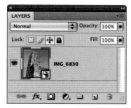

1 In this first step, I opened a raw image of the building shown here and held down the *Shift* key as I clicked on the Open Image button to open it as a Smart Object layer in Photoshop.

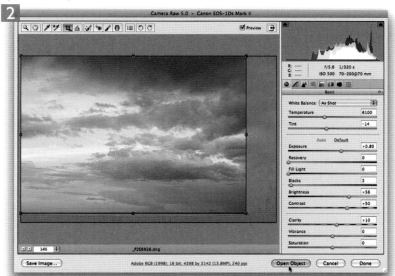

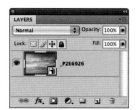

2 In this next step I selected a new image, this time a photo of a sky and, again held the *Shift* key as I clicked on the Open Image button to open it as a Smart Object layer.

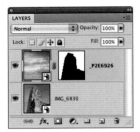

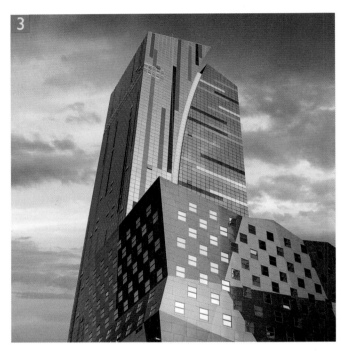

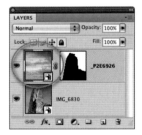

3 In Photoshop I dragged the Smart Object layer of the sky across to the Smart Object layer image of the building to add it as a new layer. I then created a mask of the sky outline and applied this as a layer mask to create the merged photo shown here.

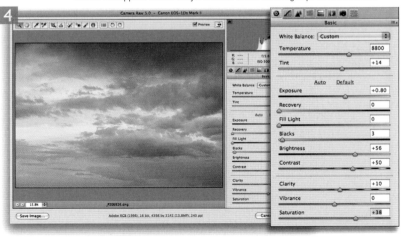

4 Because both of these layers were raw image Smart Objects, I was able to double-click the top layer thumbnail (circled) to open the Camera Raw dialog and edit the settings. In this example I decided to emphasize the sunset colors in the sky.

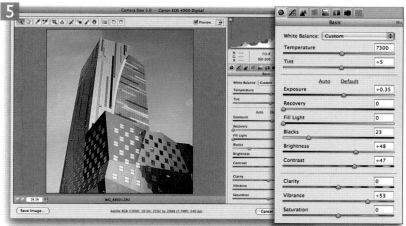

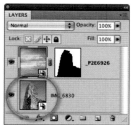

5 The same thing happened when I double-clicked the lower layer (circled). This too opened the raw image Smart Object layer via Camera Raw and allowed me to warm the colors and add more contrast to the building.

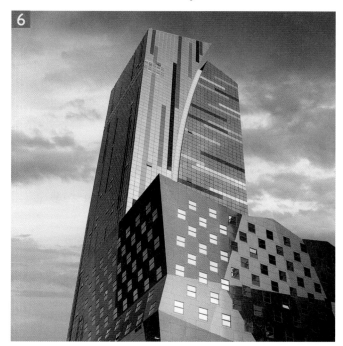

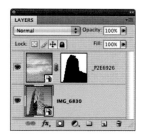

6 This shows how the revised Smart Object layers looked in the Photoshop image. The beauty of this technique is that any edits made to the Smart Object layers are all completely non-destructive.

Saving images via Camera Raw

If you hold down the ⌥ [alt] key as you click on the Save... button, this will bypass the Save dialog box and save the image (or images) with the last used Save Options settings, which is handy if you want to add file saves to a queue and continue making more edit changes in this or the single view Camera Raw dialog.

Saving a JPEG as DNG

Although it is possible to save a JPEG or TIFF original as a DNG via Camera Raw, it is important to realize that this step does not actually allow you to convert a JPEG or TIFF file into a raw image. Once an image has been rendered as a JPEG or TIFF it cannot be converted back into a raw format. Saving to DNG merely allows you to use DNG as a container format for a JPEG or TIFF and it brings no special advantage.

Resolving naming conflicts

A Save operation from Camera Raw will auto-resolve any naming conflicts so as to avoid overwriting any existing files in the same Save destination. This is important if you wish to save multiple versions of the same image as separate files and avoid overwriting the originals.

Saving photos from Camera Raw

When you click on the Save Image... button you have the option of choosing a folder destination for saving the images to and a File Naming section for customized file naming. In the Format section you can choose which file format to use, which includes PSD, TIFF, or JPEG for rendering pixel images. If you have used the crop tool to crop the image in Camera Raw, the PSD options will allow you to preserve the cropped pixels by saving the image with a non-background layer (in Photoshop you can then use Image ⇨ Reveal All if you wish to revert to an uncropped state). The JPEG and TIFF format saves provide the usual compression options and if you save using the DNG format you can convert any raw original to DNG, but see the sidebar about saving JPEGs and TIFFs as DNG.

The file save processing is then carried out in the background, allowing you to carry on working in Bridge or Photoshop (dependent on which program is hosting Camera Raw at the time) and you will see a progress indicator (circled in Figure 3.17) as to how many photos there are left to save.

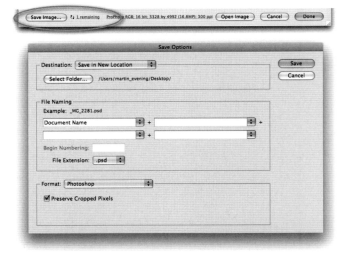

Figure 3.17 Clicking on the Save Image... button opens the Save Options dialog shown here. After configuring the options and clicking on the Save button, you will see a status report next to the Save Image button that shows how many images remain to be processed.

The histogram display

The Camera Raw Histogram provides a preview of how the Camera Raw output image histogram will look after the image data has been processed and output as a pixel image (such as a TIFF, PSD or JPEG). The histogram appearance is affected by the tone and color settings that have been applied in Camera Raw but, more importantly, it is also influenced by the RGB space selected in the Workflow options (see Figure 3.18). It can therefore be interesting to compare the effect of different output spaces when editing a raw capture image. For example, if you edit a photo in an RGB space like ProPhoto or Adobe RGB and then switch the RGB output setting to sRGB, you will most likely see some color channel clipping in the shadow region of the histogram. Such clipping can then be addressed by readjusting the Camera Raw settings to suit the smaller gamut RGB space, but I think you will find that this exercise is useful in demonstrating why it is better to output your Camera Raw processed images in the ProPhoto or Adobe RGB color spaces.

Some digital cameras provide a histogram display that enables you to check the quality of what you have just shot. This too can be used as an indication of the levels captured in a scene. However, the histogram you see displayed is usually based on a JPEG capture only. If you are shooting in JPEG mode, that's what you are going to get. But if you prefer to shoot using raw mode, the histogram you see here does not provide an accurate guide to the true potential of the image you have captured.

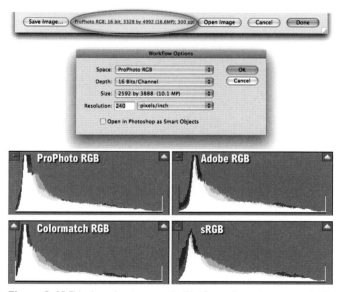

Figure 3.18 This shows how to access the Workflow options, plus an example of how the Camera Raw histogram varies depending on which color space is selected.

Deleting images

As you use Camera Raw to edit your shots, the *Delete* key can be used to mark images that are to be sent to the trash. This places a big red X in the thumbnail and can be undone by hitting *Delete* again.

Image browsing with Camera Raw

In multiple view mode, the Camera Raw dialog can also be used as a magnified view image browser. You can match the magnification and location across all selected images to check and compare details, inspect them in a sequence and apply ratings to selected images.

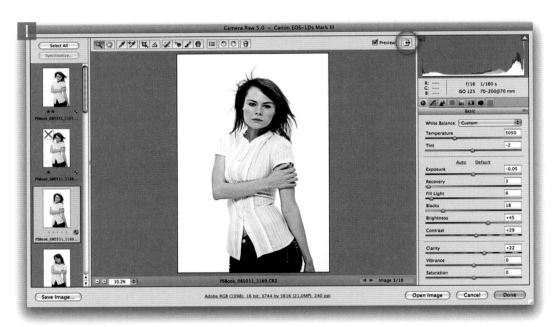

Selecting rated images only

If you ⌘ *ctrl*-click on the Select All button, it selects the rated images only. This means that you can use star ratings to mark the images you are interested in during a 'first pass' edit and then use the above shortcut to make a quick selection of just the rated images only.

1 If you have a large folder of images to review, the Camera Raw dialog can be used to provide a synchronized, magnified view of the selected pictures. The dialog is shown here in a normal window view, but you can click on the Full Screen mode button (circled) to expand the dialog to a Full screen view mode.

2 Here, I selected the first image in the sequence and clicked on the Select All button. I then used the zoom tool to magnify the preview. This action synchronized the zoom view display for all selected images in the Camera Raw dialog, plus I was able to use the hand tool to synchronize the scroll location for the selected photos.

3 Once this has been done you can deselect the thumbnail selection and start inspecting the photographs. This can be done by clicking on the file navigation controls (circled) or by using the ⟵ ⟶ keyboard arrow keys to progress through the images one by one. You can then mark your favorite pictures by using the usual Bridge shortcuts: ⌘ > *ctrl* > will progressively add more stars to a selected image; ⌘ < *ctrl* < will progressively decrease the number of stars.

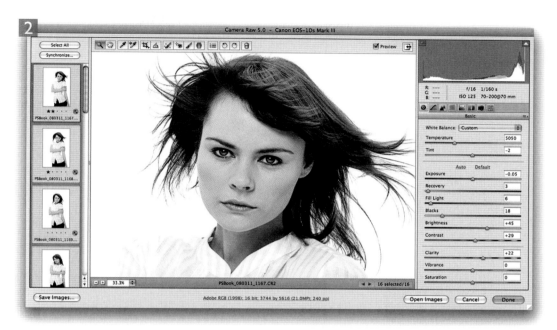

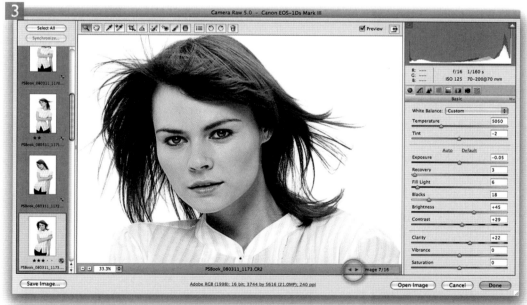

Model: Natasha De Ruyter @ Take 2.

XMP sidecar files

Camera Raw edit settings are written as XMP metadata and this data can be stored in the central Camera Raw database on the computer and can also be written to the files directly. In the case of JPEG, TIFF and DNG files, these file formats allow the XMP metadata to be written to the XMP space in the file header. But in the case of proprietary raw file formats such as CR2 and NEF, it would be unsafe to write XMP metadata to an undocumented file format. To get around this, Camera Raw writes the XMP metadata to XMP sidecar files that accompany the image in the same folder and stay with the file when you move it from one location to another via Bridge.

Camera Raw preferences

The Camera Raw preferences (Figure 3.19) can be opened by clicking on the Open Preferences button in the Camera Raw dialog, the ⌘ K ctrl K shortcut while in the Camera Raw dialog, or by choosing Bridge CS4 ⇨ Camera Raw Preferences... (Mac), or Edit ⇨ Camera Raw Preferences... (PC).

Let's look at the General section first. In the 'Save image settings' section I suggest you choose 'Sidecar ".xmp" files'. If the XMP data cannot be stored internally within the file itself (such as is the case with a DNG file), this will force the image settings to be stored locally in XMP sidecar files that accompany the image files. Should you wish to preview your adjustments with the sharpening turned on, but without actually sharpening the output the 'Apply sharpening to' option can be set to 'Preview images only'. This is because you might want to use a third-party sharpening program in preference to Camera

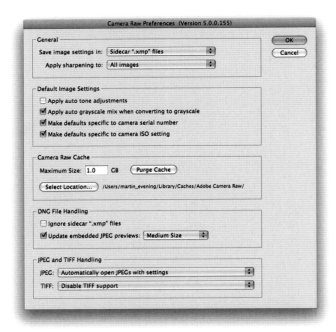

Figure 3.19 Camera Raw preferences dialog.

Raw. However, with the advent of Camera Raw's improved sharpening controls, you will now want to leave this set to 'All images' if you wish to make full use of Adobe Camera Raw sharpening.

Auto corrections

Camera Raw has the useful ability to apply auto tone corrections, where if you click on 'Auto' in the Camera Raw dialog (circled in Figure 3.21) you can quickly auto correct an individual image (you can also use the ⌘ Ⓤ *ctrl* Ⓤ shortcut).

In the Default Image Settings section, you can set 'Apply auto tone adjustments' as a Camera Raw default. When this is switched on, Camera Raw will automatically apply an auto tone adjustment to new images it encounters that have not been processed in Camera Raw yet, while any images you have edited previously via Camera Raw will remain as they are. Auto tone adjustments work really well on most images, such as outdoor scenes and natural lit portraits (note the auto algorithm has been updated and improved for Camera Raw 5), but works less well on photographs that have been shot in the studio under controlled lighting conditions. In these instances it can be something of a nuisance and is best left switched off.

The 'Apply auto grayscale mix when converting to grayscale' option refers to the HSL/Grayscale controls, where Camera Raw will apply an auto slider grayscale mix adjustment when converting a color photograph to black and white.

Camera-specific default settings

The next two options in the Default Image Settings section allow you to make any default settings camera-specific. Basically, if you go to the Camera Raw options shown in Figure 3.20, there is a menu option that will allow you to 'Save New Camera Raw Defaults' as the new default setting to be used every time Bridge or Camera Raw encounters a new image. On its own, this menu item allows you to create a default setting based on the current Camera

Auto grayscale and white balance

The auto slider settings are in fact determined by the white balance setting. If you adjust the Temp and Tint White Balance controls in the Basic panel (Figure 3.21) and then deselect and reselect the Convert to Grayscale box in the HSL/Grayscale panel shown in Figure 3.41 on page 188 (with Auto enabled), you will see the Grayscale sliders readjust according to how the White Balance sliders have been adjusted.

Default settings examples

You have to be careful how you go about using the 'Save New Camera Defaults' option. When used correctly you can cleverly set up Camera Raw to apply appropriate default settings for any camera and ISO setting. But it is all too easy to make a mistake or, worse still, select the 'Reset Camera Defaults' option and undo all your hard work!

The main thing to watch out for is that you don't include too many Camera Raw adjustments (such as the HSL/ Grayscale panel settings) as part of a default setting. One approach would be to open a previously untouched image, apply a Camera Calibration panel adjustment plus a Detail panel sharpening setting and save this as a camera-specific default. Alternatively, you might find it useful to adjust the Detail panel noise reduction settings for an image shot at a specific ISO setting and save this as a 'Make defaults specific to camera ISO setting'. Or, you might like to combine both Camera Raw preference options and set up defaults for different ISO settings with specific cameras.

Raw settings and apply this to all photos (except where you have already overridden the default settings). However, if the 'Make defaults specific to the camera serial number' option is selected in the Camera Raw preferences, selecting 'Save New Camera Raw Defaults' will only make apply this setting as a default to files that match the same camera serial number. Similarly, if the 'Make defaults specific to camera ISO setting' option is checked, this will allow you to save default settings for specific ISO values. And when both this and the previous option are checked, you can effectively have in Camera Raw multiple default settings that will take into account the combination of the camera model and ISO setting.

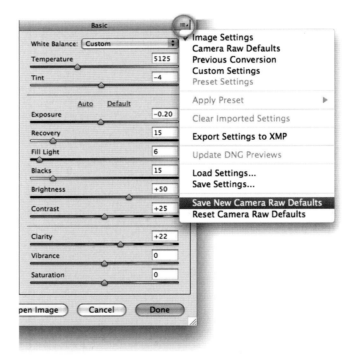

Figure 3.20 This shows the Camera Raw dialog menu options that you can access by clicking on the small icon (circled) in the Camera Raw panels header.

Camera Raw cache size

The Preview cache is used to store all the thumbnail and preview data as compressed images in a central location. Bridge and Camera Raw use this data to populate the previews. If you have enough free hard disk space available, you may want to increase the size limit for the cache, or choose a new location to store the central preview cache data.

DNG file handling

Camera Raw and Lightroom will embed the XMP metadata in the XMP header space of a DNG file. There should therefore be no need to use sidecar files to read and write XMP metadata when sharing files between these two programs. However, some third-party programs may create sidecar files for DNG files. If 'Ignore sidecar "xmp" files' is checked, Camera Raw will not be sidetracked by the sidecar files that might in these instances accompany a DNG file. But there are times where it may be useful to read XMP metadata from a sidecar file. DNG files contain embedded previews that will represent how an image will look with the current applied Camera Raw settings. When the Update embedded JPEG preview is checked, this will force the previews in all DNG files to be rebuilt based on the current Camera Raw settings, overriding previously embedded previews. However, it is important to point out that DNG previews created by Camera Raw can only be considered 100% accurate when viewed by other Adobe programs such as Lightroom or Bridge and, even then, they must be using the same version of Camera Raw.

While DNG is a safe format for archiving raw data, other DNG compatible programs (that are not made by Adobe, or that use an earlier version of Camera Raw), will not always be able to read the Camera Raw settings that have been applied using the latest version of Camera Raw or Lightroom.

The following information relates to the JPEG and TIFF handling section of the Camera Raw preferences that can be accessed via the Bridge menu (Mac) or Edit menu (PC).

If 'Disable JPEG (or TIFF) support' is selected, all JPEG or TIFF files will always open in Photoshop directly. If 'Automatically open all supported JPEGs (or TIFFs)' is selected, this will cause all supported JPEGs and TIFFs to always open via Camera Raw. However, if 'Automatically open JPEGs (or TIFFs) with settings' is selected, Photoshop CS4 will only open a JPEG or TIFF via Camera Raw if it has previously been edited via Camera Raw. When this option is selected you have the option in Bridge to use a double-click to open a JPEG directly into Photoshop, or use ⌘ R ctrl R to force JPEGs to open via Camera Raw. But note that when you edit the Camera Raw settings for that JPEG, the next time you use a double-click to open, it will default to opening via Camera Raw.

Sharing XMP metadata

While I may prefer to archive files in DNG, I am wary of converting to DNG too soon. This is especially true when working with Bridge. I find if I keep my raw capture files unconverted, I can easily swap the XMP sidecar files from one computer to another as a way of quickly transferring and updating the image edit information such as settings and ratings. Once the initial edits are complete, I can then safely convert to DNG.

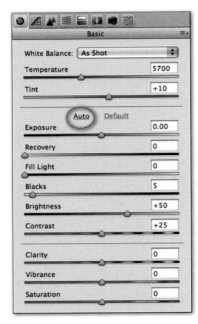

Figure 3.21 The Camera Raw Basic panel controls. Clicking Auto will apply an auto adjustment and clicking Default will apply the default Camera Raw settings (which will differ according to whether you are editing a raw or non-raw image). ⌘ U ctrl U can also be used to apply an Auto setting.

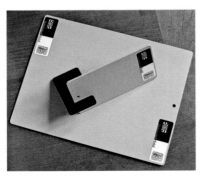

Figure 3.22 WhiBal™ cards come in different sizes and are available for order from RawWorkflow.com.

Basic panel controls

The Basic controls are best approached and adjusted in the order you find them. Start with the white balance adjustments and Exposure and work your way down.

White balance

The white balance refers to the color temperature of the lighting conditions at the time a photograph was taken and essentially describes the warmth or coolness of the light. Quartz-halogen lighting has a warmer color and a low color temperature value of around 3400 K, while daylight has a bluer color (and a higher color temperature value of around 6500 K). If you choose to shoot in raw mode it does not matter how you set the white point settings at the time of shooting, because you can decide later what is the best white balance setting to use.

Camera Raw was first designed by Thomas Knoll, one of the original creators of the Photoshop program. Thomas has cleverly used two profile measurements, one made under tungsten lighting conditions and another done using daylight balanced lighting. From this data, Camera Raw is able to extrapolate and calculate the white balance adjustment for any color temperature value that falls between these two white balance measurements, as well as calculating the more extreme values that go beyond either side of these measured values.

The default white balance setting will normally use the 'As Shot' white balance setting that was embedded in the raw file metadata at the time the image was taken. This might be a fixed white balance setting that was used on your camera or it could be an auto white balance that was calculated at the time the picture was shot. If this is not correct, you can try mousing down on the White Balance pop-up menu and select a preset setting that correctly describes the white balance that should be used. Alternatively, you can simply adjust the Temperature slider to make the image appear warmer or cooler, and adjust the Tint slider to balance the white balance green/magenta tint bias.

Using the white balance tool

The easiest way to set the white balance manually is to select the white balance tool and click on an area that is meant to be light gray color. Don't select an area of pure white as this may contain some channel clipping and produce a skewed result, which is why it is better to sample a light gray color instead. You will also notice that as you move the white balance tool across the image, the sampled RGB values are displayed just below the histogram; when you click to set the white balance, these numbers should appear even.

There are also calibration charts that you can use such as the X-Rite ColorChecker chart, which can be used in carrying out a custom calibration, although the light gray patch on this chart has been regarded as being a little on the warm side. For this reason, you may like to look into a using a WhiBal™ card (Figure 3.22). These cards have been specially designed for obtaining accurate white point readings under varying lighting conditions.

In the days of color film we basically had just two choices of film emulsion: daylight and tungsten. Daylight film was rated at 6500 degrees Kelvin and was used for outdoor photography and studio flash, while tungsten film was rated at 3400 degrees Kelvin and used for photography with artificial tungsten lighting. These absolute values would rarely match the lighting conditions you were shooting with, but they would enable you to get roughly close to the appropriate color temperature of the light you were using in either a daylight/strobe lighting or indoor/tungsten light setting. One could then fine-tune the color temperature by using filters over the camera lens or color gel filters over the lights themselves.

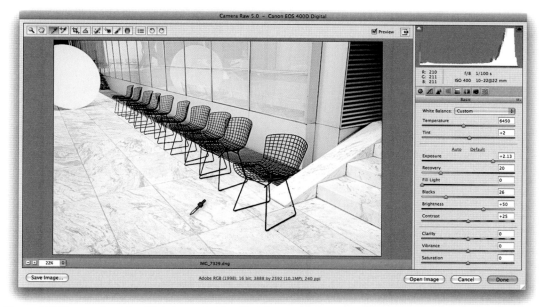

Figure 3.23 To manually set the white balance, select the white balance tool and find what should be a light gray neutral area and click to update the white balance.

How Camera Raw calculates

Camera sensors have a linear response to light and the unprocessed raw files therefore exist in a 'linear gamma space'. Human vision on the other hand interprets light in a non-linear fashion, so one of the main things a raw conversion has to do is to apply a gamma correction to the original image data to make the correctly exposed raw image look the way our eyes would expect such a scene to look (see Digital exposure on pages 174–175). So the preview image you see in the Camera Raw dialog presents a gamma corrected preview of the raw data, while the adjustments you apply in Camera Raw are in fact being applied directly to the raw linear data. The reason I mention this is to illustrate one aspect of the subtle but important differences between the tonal edits that can be made in Camera Raw to raw files and those that are applied in Photoshop where the images have already been 'gamma corrected'. Note that in the case of non-raw files, Camera Raw has to temporarily convert the image to a linear RGB space to carry out the calculations.

The tone adjustment controls

The tone adjustment controls allow you to make further adjustments to the highlight and shadow clipping points as well as the overall tone, balance and brightness.

Exposure

The Exposure slider is used to set the overall brightness, so that the photograph looks 'correctly exposed'. You can use the Exposure slider to visually assess how brightly exposed you want the picture to be and use this as your primary tool for adjusting the image brightness. You can if you like hold down the ⌥ *alt* key as you drag the Exposure slider to see a threshold preview that indicates where there might be highlight clipping, or you can rely on the highlight clipping indicator shown in Figure 3.25 to tell you which highlights are about to be clipped.

Recovery

You don't have to worry too much about setting the Exposure too bright or clipping the highlights, because the Recovery slider can be used to restore some of the detail which at first may appear lost. The Recovery slider cleverly utilizes the highlight detail in whichever channels contain the best recorded highlight detail and uses this to boost the detail in the weakest highlight channel. There are limits as to how far you can push a Recovery adjustment, but you may be able to recover as much as a stop or more of overexposure. Plus Camera Raw can sometimes use extra tricks such as ignoring digital gain values used to create higher ISO captures. If you hold down the ⌥ *alt* key as you drag the Recovery slider you will get to see a Threshold mode preview, which can often make it easier to determine the optimum setting.

Blacks

The Blacks slider is a little less critical, but again I find it useful to hold down the ⌥ *alt* key to obtain a Threshold mode preview to help determine the point where the shadows just start to clip.

Fill Light

The Fill Light kind of matches the behavior of the Shadow amount slider in the Shadow/Highlight image adjustment. If you drag the Fill Light slider to the right this adds more lightness to the dark tone areas and lightens the darkest shadow areas. If you overdo this adjustment, it may knock back the contrast too much and you'll end up with an artificial looking result such as the Figure 3.24 example.

Suggested order for the basic adjustments

The first step should be to set the Exposure to get the overall image brightness looking right, taking care not to introduce too much highlight clipping. If necessary, use the Recovery slider to restore any important detail that may be clipped in the highlight areas (see page 169). Next, use the Blacks slider to set the shadow clipping, followed by the Fill Light slider should you need to reveal more detail in the shadow areas. The Brightness and Contrast sliders should be used last to fine-tune the image after you have adjusted these four sliders first.

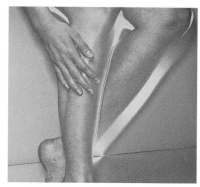

Figure 3.24 Be careful when setting the Fill Light. Shown here is an extreme example of a solarization type effect that can occur with some photos if you apply too much Fill Light.

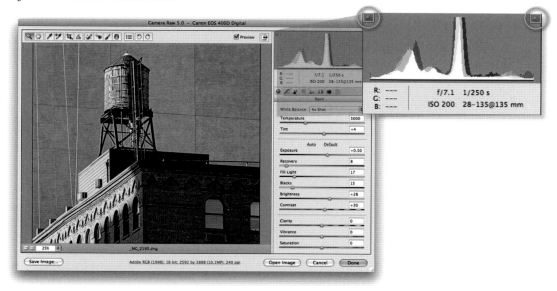

Figure 3.25 If you click on the clipping indicators in the Histogram panel you will see a colored overlay in the preview image that indicates any shadow and highlight clipping.

Basic image adjustment procedure

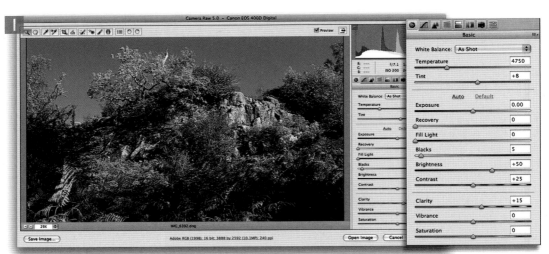

1 This shows a raw image as viewed in the Camera Raw dialog, using the default settings in the Basic panel. One way to quickly optimize an image is to click on the Auto button. If you then want to reset all the settings you can do so by double-clicking on the individual sliders, or by clicking on the Default button.

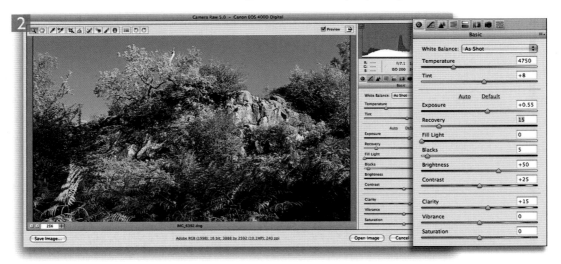

2 In this example I adjusted the Exposure to make the photograph look lighter and achieve what looked like the best visual brightness. You don't have to worry about blowing out the highlight detail because you can use the Recovery slider to restore any highlight detail that may be clipped (but without destroying the exposure effect).

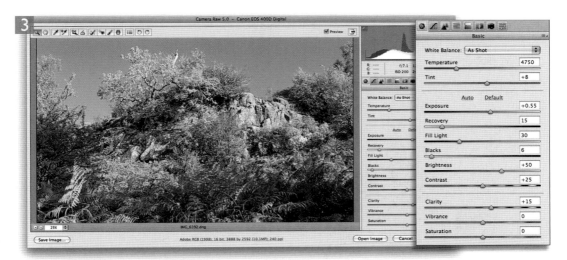

3 The next step was to optimize the shadows. I used the Blacks slider to set the clipping point for the shadow detail and after that I used the Fill Light slider to lighten the darker areas of the photograph such as the bracken in the foreground. Note that as you adjust the Recovery and Blacks sliders, you can hold down the ⌥ *alt* key as you drag to see a threshold view of the image, which can help you determine how far to drag to set the correct amount of clipping.

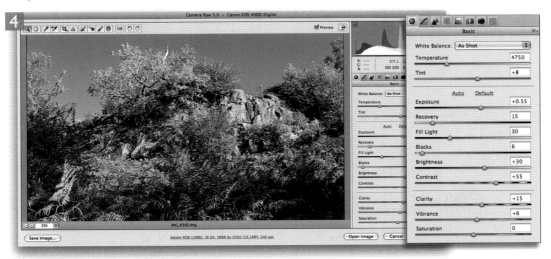

4 And last of all, I used the Brightness and Contrast sliders to fine-tune the tonal balance of the photograph. It is important that you use the Basic adjustment controls in the order suggested here, instead of adjusting the Brightness first and then tweaking the Exposure afterwards.

Preserving the highlight detail

As you apply basic adjustments in Camera Raw, you want to make the brightest parts of the photo go to white so the highlights are not too dull. But at the same time you want to ensure that important highlight detail is always preserved, which means not clipping the highlights too much as this might otherwise result in important highlight detail being lost when you come to make a print from the processed image. How you clip the highlights is therefore very much a subjective decision and one that can be arrived at by referring to the following guidelines.

Where you set the clipping point is really dependent on the nature of the image. In most cases you can adjust the Exposure and Recovery sliders so that the highlights just begin to clip and not worry about losing any important highlight detail. But if the picture you are editing contains a lot of delicate highlight information then you will want to be careful when setting the highlights so that the brightest whites in the photo are not too close to the point where the highlights get clipped. The reason for this is all down to what happens when you ultimately send a photo to a printer or convert an image to CMYK and send it to the press to be printed. Most photo inkjet printers are generally very good at reproducing highlight detail at the top end of the print scale, but at some point you will find that the highest pixel values will not equate to a printable tone on paper. Basically, the printer may be unable to produce a dot that is light enough to print successfully.

Some inkjet printers use light colored inks such as a light gray, light magenta and light cyan to complement the regular black, gray, cyan, magenta, yellow ink set, and these printers are better at reproducing feint highlight detail. CMYK press printing is a whole other matter. Presses will vary of course, but there is a similar problem where a halftone dot will be too small for any ink to adhere to the paper. In each of the above cases there is an upper threshold limit where the highlight values won't print. So when you are adjusting the Exposure and Recovery sliders, it is important to examine the image and ask yourself if certain highlight detail matters

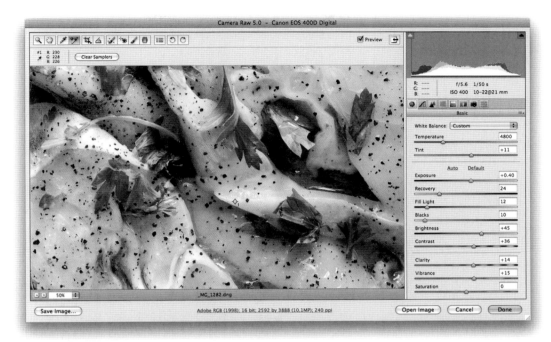

Figure 3.26 In this example it was important to preserve the delicate highlight tones in the fish steaks. To be absolutely sure that I didn't risk making the highlight detail areas too bright, I placed a color sampler over an area that contained important highlight detail. This allowed me to check that the RGB highlight value did not go too high. In this case I knew that with a pixel reading of 230, 228, 226, the highlight tones in this part of the picture would print fine using almost any print device.

or not. Some pictures will contain subtle highlight detail (such as in Figure 3.26), while others may look like the example over the page in Figure 3.27 where the highlights are referred to as 'specular highlights', such as the light reflecting off a shiny metal surface. In these cases the last thing you need to concern yourself with is preserving the detail. You can safely clip such highlights and thereby force these specular highlights to print as pure white. Because there is no actual detail in such highlights there is nothing worth preserving anyway, and by forcing the specular highlights to a maximum white you are safely enhancing the image contrast.

When to clip the highlights

You have to be careful when judging where to set the highlight point. If you clip too much then you risk losing important highlight detail. But what if the image contains bright specular highlights, such as highlight reflections on shiny metal objects? Specular highlights such as those shown in Figure 3.27 contain no detail. It is safe to clip these, because if you clip them too conservatively you will end up with dull highlights in your prints. In this case the aim is for the shiny reflections to print to paper white. So when adjusting the Exposure slider for a subject like this, use the Exposure slider first to visually decide how bright to make the photo and don't be afraid to let the specular highlights blow out to white.

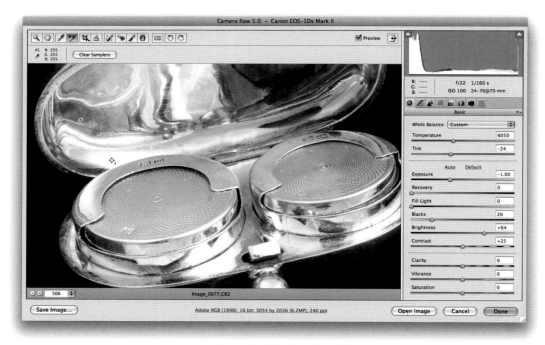

Figure 3.27 The highlights in this photograph contain no detail, so there is no point in trying to preserve detail in the shiny areas as this will only limit the contrast. One can safely afford to clip the highlights in this image without losing important image detail and, as you can see here, the color sampler over the shiny reflection measures a highlight value of 255, 255, 255. Images like this will usually need no Recovery adjustment.

How to clip the shadows

Setting the Black clipping point is by comparison a much easier thing to decide. Put aside for now any concerns you might have about matching the black clipping point to the printing device – I'll explain how that works over the next two pages. Blacks slider adjustments are simply about deciding where you want the shadows to clip. The default setting is 5 and this will usually be about right for most images. You may want to ease the clipping off to around 2 or 3 on some images, but it is inadvisable to take the setting all the way down to zero. Some photos such as the one shown below in Figure 3.28 can actually benefit from heavy black clipping so that the dark areas all print to black.

Hiding shadow noise

Introducing shadow point clipping will add depth and contrast to your photo, but it will also help to hide some of the shadow noise in an image with noisy shadows.

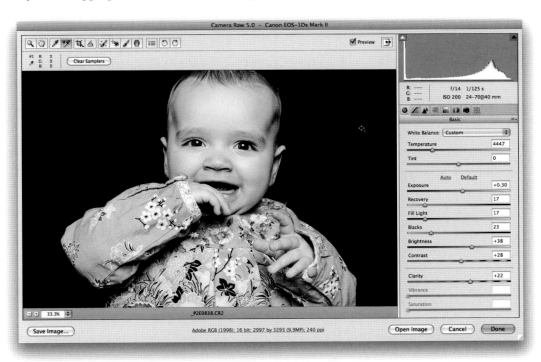

Figure 3.28 In this picture of my daughter, Angelica, you can see that the blacks in this photo are well and truly clipped. This is because I deliberately wanted to force any shadow detail in the backdrop go to make it a solid black and as you can see, the color sampler over the backdrop in this picture shows an RGB reading of 0,0,0.

Is it wrong to set levels manually?

All I am suggesting here is that it is an unnecessary extra step to use Photoshop to set the black output levels to anything higher than the zero black after you have already set the black clipping to the desired setting at the Camera Raw editing stage (or done so in Photoshop). If you do set the black output levels manually to a setting that is higher than zero you won't necessarily get inferior print outputs, providing that is you set the black levels accurately and don't set them any higher than is needed. And there's the rub: how do you know how much to set the output levels, and what if you want to output a photo to more than one type of print paper? You see, it's easier to let Photoshop work this out for you.

Some picture libraries are quite specific about how you set the output levels, but their suggested settings are usually very conservative and unlikely to result in weak shadows when printed to most devices. It is therefore probably better to oblige the libraries with what they ask for, rather than fight them over the logic of their arguments.

The only time when you may need to give special consideration to setting the shadows to anything other than zero is when you are required to edit an already converted CMYK or grayscale file that is destined to go to a printing press, where the black output levels have been set incorrectly. But as I say, if you use Photoshop color management properly you are not likely to encounter such problems.

Shadow levels after a conversion

You will sometimes come across advice that the output levels for the black point in an RGB image should be set to something like 20, 20, 20 (for the Red, Green, Blue RGB values). The usual reason given for this is because anything darker than, say, a 20, 20, 20 shadow value will reproduce in print as a solid black. Just to add to the confusion, different numbers are suggested for the output levels: one person suggests using 10, 10, 10 while another advises you to use 25, 25, 25. In all this you are probably left wondering how to set the Blacks in Camera Raw, since you can only use the Blacks slider to clip the Black input levels and are offered no means to set a black levels output value using any of the above suggested output settings.

This is one of those areas where the advice given is more complex than it needs to be. It is well known that because of factors such as dot gain it has always been necessary to make the blacks in a digital image slightly lighter than the blackest black (0, 0, 0) before outputting it to print. As a result of this, in the early days of digital imaging the only way to get a digital image to print correctly was to manually adjust the output levels so that the black clipping point matched the print device. Back then, if you set the levels to 0, 0, 0 RGB, the blacks would print too dark and you would lose detail in the shadows. Therefore the solution was to set the output levels point to a value higher than this (such as 20, 20, 20 RGB), so that the blacks in the image matched the blackest black for the print device. These are the background reasons for such advice, because the black levels had to be adjusted differently for each type of print output including CMYK prepress files.

For the last 10 years or so, Photoshop has had a built-in automated color management systems that is designed to take care of the black clipping at the print stage. The advice these days is therefore quite simple: you decide where you want the blackest blacks to be in the picture and clip them to 0, 0, 0 RGB (as discussed on the previous page). When you save the image out to Photoshop as a pixel image and send the image data to the printer, the Photoshop or print

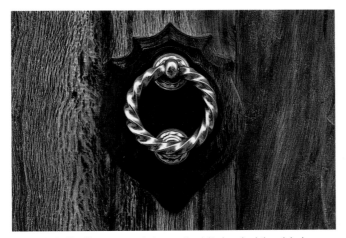

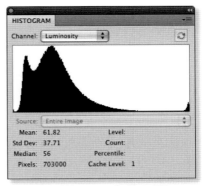

Original histogram – ProPhoto RGB

Figure 3.29 The Histogram panel views on the right show (top) the original histogram for this ProPhoto RGB image. The middle histogram shows a comparison of the image histogram after converting the ProPhoto RGB data to a print profile space for Innova Fibraprint glossy paper printed to an Epson 4800 printer. The print output histogram is overlaid here in green and you can see that the black levels clipping point has been automatically indented. The bottom example shows the print profile for a Somerset Velvet matte paper printed to an Epson 9600 printer, again colored green so that you can compare it more easily with the before Histogram. The black clipping point is moved inwards even more here because the matte paper needs a higher black clipping point to avoid clogging up the shadow detail. The same thing also happens when you make a CMYK conversion, but the black point will possibly shift inwards even more. Please note that the histograms shown here were all using the Luminosity mode since this mode accurately portrays the composite luminance levels in each version of the image.

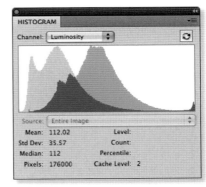

Innova Fibraprint glossy paper

driver software will automatically calculate the precise amount of black clipping adjustment that is required for each and every print/paper combination. In Figure 3.29 you can see how the black clipping point for different print papers is automatically compensated when converting the data from the edited image to the profile space for the printing paper. But don't just take my word, it is easy to prove this for yourself. Open an image, set the Channel display in the Histogram panel to Luminosity and refresh the histogram to show the most up-to-date histogram view. Then go to the Edit menu, choose Convert to Profile, select a CMYK or RGB print space and compare the before and after histograms.

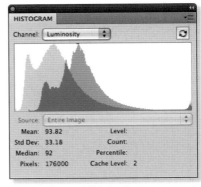

Somerset Velvet matte paper

173

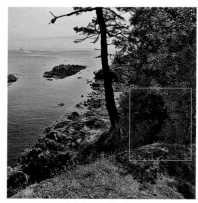

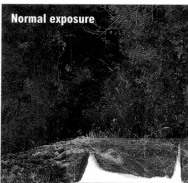

Normal exposure

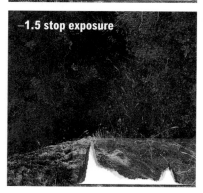

−1.5 stop exposure

Figure 3.30 This shows the difference the exposure can make in retaining shadow information. The darker the exposure, the fewer discreet levels the CCD chip can capture and this can result in poorly recorded shadow detail.

Digital exposure

Shooting with a digital camera requires a whole new approach when determining the optimum exposure setting compared to shooting with film. Most digital cameras such as digital SLRs and even the raw enabled compacts are capable of capturing 12 bits of data, which is equivalent to 4096 recordable levels per color channel. As you halve the amount of light that falls on the chip sensor, you potentially halve the number of levels that are available to record an exposure (see Figure 3.31).

Let us suppose that the optimum exposure for a particular photograph at a given shutter speed is f16. This exposure will make full use of the chip sensor's dynamic range and consequently the potential is there to record up to 4096 levels of information. If one were then to halve the exposure to f22, you would only have the ability to record up to 2048 levels per channel. It would still be possible to lighten the image in Camera Raw or Photoshop to create an image that appears to have similar contrast and brightness. But (and it's a big but) that one stop exposure difference has immediately lost half the number of levels that could potentially be captured by using a one stop brighter exposure. The image is now effectively using only 11 bits of data per channel instead of 12. This is true of digital scanners as well. Perhaps you may have already observed how difficult it can be to rescue detail from the very darkest shadows, and how these can end up looking very posterized. Also, have you also noticed how much easier it is to rescue highlight detail compared to shadow detail when using the Shadow/Highlight adjustment? This is because far fewer levels are available to define the information recorded in the darkest areas of the picture and these levels are easily stretched further apart as you try to lighten the shadows. This is why posterization is always much more noticeable in the shadows (see Figure 3.30). It also explains why it is important to target your digital exposures as carefully as possible so that you make the brightest exposures possible, but without the risk of blowing out the highlight detail.

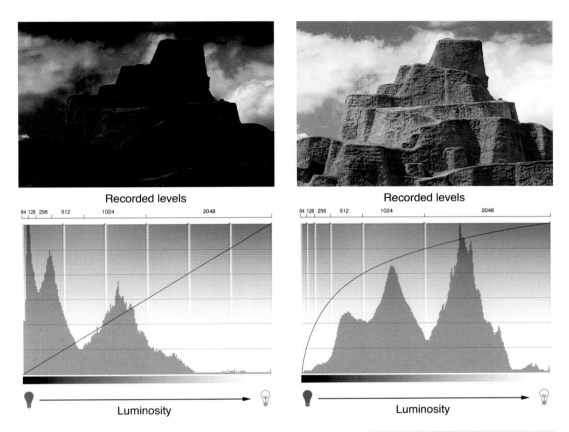

Recorded levels

Luminosity

Recorded levels

Luminosity

Figure 3.31 If you could inspect a raw capture image in its native linear gamma state, it would look something like the image shown top left. Notice that the picture is very dark, it is lacking in contrast and the levels (representing the tonal information) in the histogram appear to be mostly bunched up to the left. During the raw conversion process, a gamma curve correction is applied when converting the linear data so that the processed image matches the way we are used to viewing the relative brightness in a scene. The picture top right shows the same image after a basic raw conversion.

As a consequence of this, the more brightly exposed areas will preserve the most tonal information and the shadow areas will end up with fewer levels. A typical CCD sensor can capture up to 4096 levels of tonal information. Half these levels will be recorded in the brightest stop exposure range and the recorded levels are effectively halved with every stop decrease in exposure. The digital camera exposure is therefore quite critical. Ideally, you want the exposure to be as bright as possible so that you make full use of the Levels histogram, but at the same time be careful to make sure the highlights don't get clipped.

Camera histograms

The histogram that appears on a compact camera or digital SLR screen is unreliable for anything other than JPEG capture. This is because the histogram you see there is usually based on the camera-processed JPEG and is not representative of the true raw capture. The only way to check the histogram for a raw capture file is to open the image via a raw processing program such as Camera Raw.

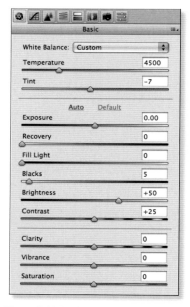

Figure 3.32 The Camera Raw Basic controls.

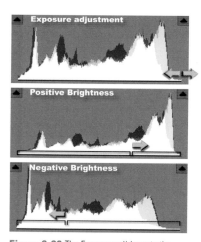

Figure 3.33 The Exposure slider sets the highlight clipping, and the midtones and shadows adjust smoothly relative to this point. The Brightness slider adjusts the brightness by shifting the levels between the set shadow and highlight points.

Brightness

There is sometimes confusion between when to use Brightness and when to use Exposure to adjust an image, because to the newcomer they both appear to be doing the same thing. There is, however, an important difference between the way these two sliders work.

The Exposure slider is essentially a white clipping point tool that is used to set the highlight clipping point. As you move the slider the image will appear to get brighter or darker, but what the Exposure slider adjustment is actually doing is deciding where to set the highlight clipping and smoothly mapping all the other tones from the midtones down to the shadows relative to this point. Another trick you can do with the Exposure slider is to set a negative highlight adjustment which can help recover highlight detail that would otherwise have been clipped.

The Brightness slider is a midtone correction tool that behaves much like the gamma (middle input levels) slider in the Photoshop Levels dialog and can be used to make a photo appear relatively lighter or darker. The difference here is that the Brightness slider adjusts the image tones by compressing one end of the tonal scale as it expands the other. In this respect, the Brightness control should be regarded as a more brutal image adjustment than the Exposure slider, which is why you are advised always to use Exposure first to get the brightness right, use Recovery to compensate for any undesirable clipping and then use the Brightness slider to fine-tune the photo's brightness.

Figure 3.33 illustrates how these adjustments affect the histogram. In the top histogram view, the Exposure adjustment will set the highlight clipping point and evenly expand or compress all the tones that are darker than this. The middle histogram shows how if you make a Brightness adjustment the brighter tone levels get compressed and the darker tones tone levels are expanded. Conversely, if you apply a darkening Brightness adjustment the highlight levels get expanded and the shadow tones become more compressed. Figure 3.34 clearly illustrates the practical consequences of a Brightness adjustment versus Exposure.

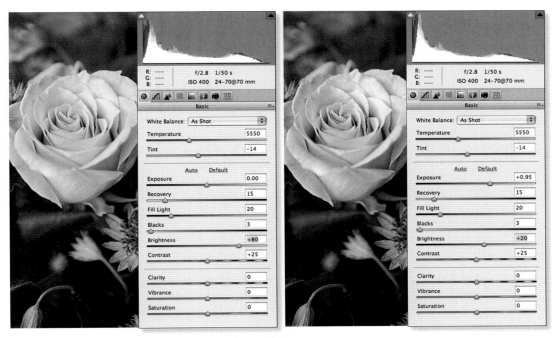

Figure 3.34 Superficially these two close-up views look the same. In the one on the left, I used the Brightness slider only to adjust the image brightness. In the other I used the Exposure slider to set the highlight clipping point and brightness, and then used the Brightness slider to fine-tune the brightness. You should be able to see more highlight contrast and detail in the petals in the version on the right.

In the left-hand image you will notice that there is less contrast in the highlights and therefore less detail. This is because the highlight levels have been compressed and this has resulted in a flatter contrast. None of this is to suggest that you shouldn't use Brightness. Far from it. Although compressing and expanding the levels is a destructive process, it is just an inevitable part of the digital image editing process. The main point to learn from all this is to use Exposure first to expose for the best brightness and use the Brightness slider second to fine-tune the brightness.

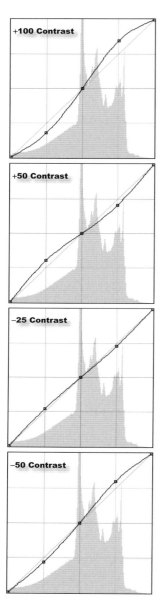

Figure 3.35 These curve shapes shown here approximate the curve shape that is applied by Camera Raw when you adjust the Contrast in the Basic panel.

Contrast

The Contrast slider applies a non-linear contrast type adjustment. In Photoshop terms it is equivalent to applying an 'S' shape curve to the image. But unlike the Contrast slider in the legacy version of Photoshop's Brightness/ Contrast image adjustment, this adjustment never forces the levels to clip at either end of the tonal scale and is completely safe to use. A positive contrast adjustment creates a steeper 'S' shape type curve that increases the image contrast, while a negative Contrast adjustment will flatten the curve to create an inverse 'S' shaped curve that flattens the contrast. Figure 3.35 shows a simulation of how the Contrast adjustment would look if applied as a Curve adjustment to an image in Photoshop. Note that the curve shape is also affected by the Brightness amount and the curves shown here represent the contrast curve shape when Brightness is at its default (+50) setting.

One of the things that confuses some people is the fact that there is a Contrast adjustment in the Basic panel as well as a separate Tone Curve panel and that these appear to perform the same function. But think of it this way: it is already quite common for people to apply a Contrast adjustment when they initially edit an image and then add a second Contrast adjustment later to fine-tune the first Contrast adjustment. There are basically three ways you can edit the contrast in Camera Raw and all of them are equally valid. You might decide the Basic panel Contrast slider is all that you need: make a simple slider move and you are done. You might choose not to use the Contrast slider at all and use just the Tone Curve to adjust the contrast. Or alternatively, you might use the Contrast slider when applying an initial set of basic panel adjustments to get the contrast looking close to what looks right and then use the Tone Curve panel to tweak the contrast because you like the fine-tune control you get with the Tone Curve sliders. The important thing to understand here is that when you work with Camera Raw, it does not matter that you are applying a Contrast adjustment on top of a Contrast adjustment. When the image is finally output as a JPEG, TIFF or PSD, everything is applied as a single adjustment.

Clarity

The Clarity slider is the first of three 'presence' controls in Camera Raw. Adding Clarity to a photo can be thought of as adding sharpness, but it is more accurate to say that Clarity is adding localized, midtone contrast. What does this mean? Well, the Clarity slider can be used to build up the contrast in the midtone areas by effectively applying a soft, wide radius unsharp mask to the midtones only. When you add a positive Clarity adjustment, you will notice increased tonal separation in the midtones while the shadows and highlights remain unaffected. A small positive Clarity adjustment will therefore increase the local contrast across narrow areas of detail, and a bigger positive Clarity adjustment will increase the midtone contrast over broader regions of the photo.

How much Clarity should you add?

All photos will benefit from having a small amount of Clarity added. I would say a default of +10 would work well for most pictures. But you can safely add a maximum Clarity adjustment if you think a picture needs it (such as in the Figure 3.36 example below).

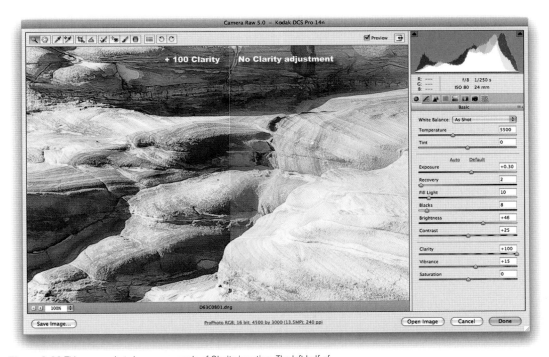

Figure 3.36 This screen shot shows an example of Clarity in action. The left half of the Camera Raw preview shows Clarity being applied at +100 and the right half of the preview shows how the photo looked before Clarity was added.

179

Negative clarity

Just as you can use a positive clarity adjustment to boost
the midtone contrast, you can now apply a negative clarity
adjustment to soften the midtones. There are two uses
that come to mind here. Clicio Barroso and Ettore Causa
(who helped beta test the Lightroom program) suggested
that a negative clarity adjustment could be useful for
softening the skin tones in portrait and beauty shots (as
shown in Figure 3.37). This works great if you use the
adjustment brush tool (discussed on pages 207–216) to
apply a negative clarity in combination with a Sharpening
adjustment. The other idea I had was to use negative clarity
to simulate a diffusion printing technique that used to
be popular with a lot of traditional darkroom printers. In
Figure 3.38 you can see examples of a before and after
image where I used a maximum negative clarity to soften
the midtone contrast to produce a kind of soft focus look.
You will find that this technique works particularly well
with photos that have been converted to black and white.

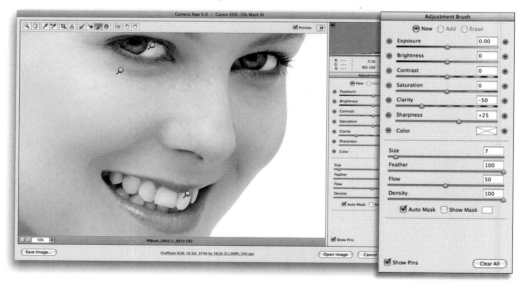

Model: Courtney @ Storm

Figure 3.37 This shows the results of an adjustment brush applied using the
combination of a −50 Clarity effect with a +25 Sharpness effect to produce the skin
softening look achieved here. I have applied this stronger than I would do normally,
just to emphasize the type of effect this can produce.

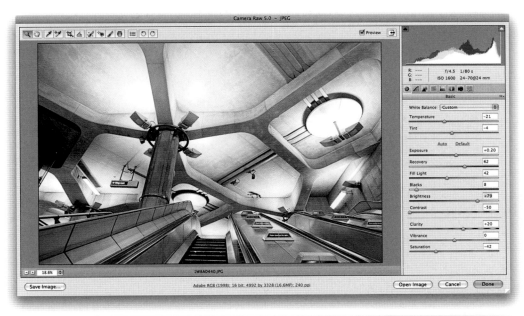

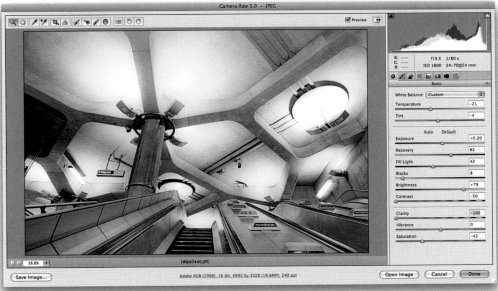

Figure 3.38 This shows the before version (top) and an after version (below), where
I applied a −100 Clarity adjustment.

Negative vibrance and saturation

Not all of us want to turn our photographs into super-colored versions of reality. You can use the Vibrance and Saturation sliders to apply negative adjustments too. If you take the Saturation down to −100 this will convert an image to monochrome, but lesser negative Saturation and Vibrance adjustments can also be used to produce interesting pastel-colored effects.

Vibrance and Saturation

The Saturation slider can be used to boost color saturation, but extreme saturation adjustments will soon cause the brighter colors to clip. However, the Vibrance slider can be used to apply what is described as a non-linear color saturation adjustment, which means colors that are already brightly saturated in color remain relatively protected as you boost the vibrance, whereas the colors that are not so saturated will receive a greater saturation boost. The net result is a saturation control that allows you to make an image look more colorful, but without the attendant risk of clipping those colors that are saturated enough already. Try opening a photograph of some brightly colored flowers and compare the difference between a Vibrance and a Saturation adjustment. The other thing that is rather neat about the Vibrance control is that it has a built-in skin tone protection filter which does rather a good job of not letting the skin tones increase in saturation as you move the slider to the right. In Figure 3.39 I boosted the Vibrance to +40, which boosted the colors in the dress without giving the model an unnaturally 'vibrant' suntan.

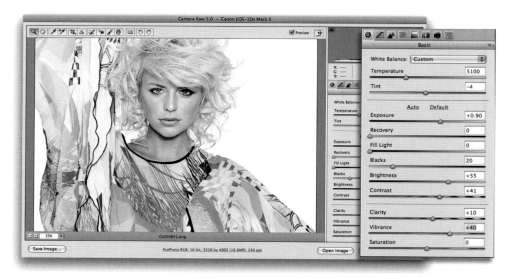

Client: Clipso. Model: Carina @ FM

Figure 3.39 Boosting colors using the Vibrance control in the Basic panel.

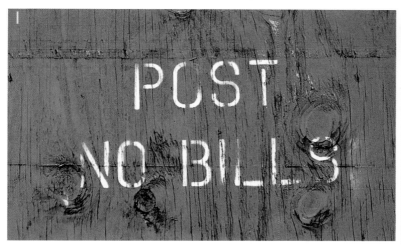
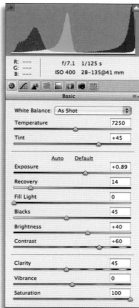

1 In this example you can see what happens if you choose to boost the saturation in a photo using the Saturation slider only to enrich the blue colors. If you look at the histogram you will notice how the blue channel is clipped. This is what we would expect, because the Saturation slider in Camera Raw applies a linear adjustment that will push the already saturated blues off the histogram scale.

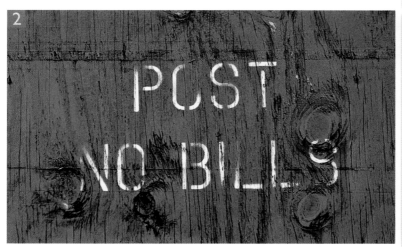
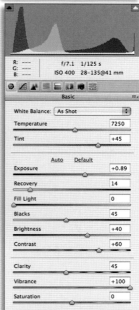

2 Compare what happens when you use the Vibrance slider instead. In this example you will notice how none of the blue channel colors are clipped. This is because the Vibrance slider boosts the saturation of the least saturated colors most, tapering off to no saturation boost for the already saturated colors. Hence, no clipping.

183

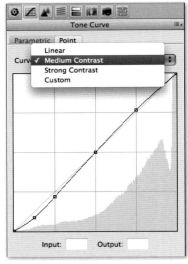

Figure 3.40 The Tone Curve panel, shown here in Point Curve editor mode displaying the default Medium Contrast tone curve setting.

Tone Curve panel

The Tone Curve panel offers a fine-tuning contrast control that can be applied in addition to the Tone and Contrast adjustments made in the Basic panel. There are two modes for the Tone Curve panel. In the Point Curve editor mode, you can manipulate the shape of the tone curve as you would with the Curves adjustment in Photoshop. The default setting used here applies a Medium Contrast curve, which kind of matches the default contrast used by most cameras when producing a JPEG image, and will probably produce the 'snappiest' looking results. However, it is just a default and you can turn it off by simply setting the curve to 'Linear'. The Parametric Curve editor mode provides a new mechanism for editing the tone curve shape where, instead of clicking to add points and dragging them, you use the slider controls to control the curve shape; judging from responses so far, photographers generally find this method more intuitive to work with. Here is an example of how to edit the Tone Curve in the Parametric editor mode.

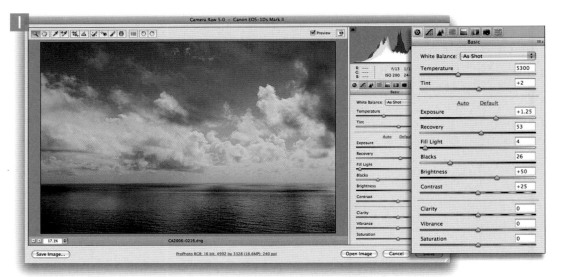

1 In this first example the image tones were adjusted using the Basic panel controls to produce an optimized range of tones that were ready to be enhanced further. I could have used the Brightness and Contrast sliders next, but the Tone Curve panel provides a simple yet effective interface for manipulating the contrast and brightness.

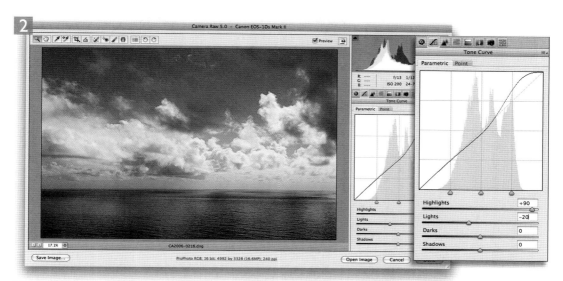

2 Over in the Tone Curve panel I selected the Parametric curve option and by dragging the Highlights slider to the right and lowering the amount for the Lights slider I was able to increase the contrast in the sky.

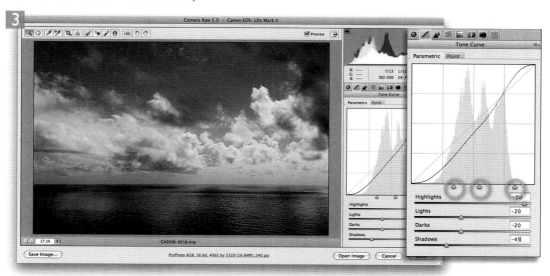

3 I then adjusted the Darks and Shadows sliders to add more contrast in the dark regions of the photograph. But in addition to this I fine-tuned the scope of adjustment for the Tone Curve sliders by adjusting the positions of the three tone range split points (circled).

Correcting a high contrast image

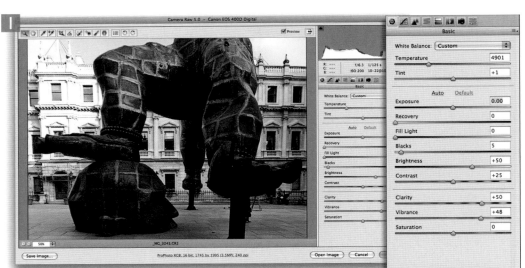

1 Here is a photograph that was taken in bright daylight with a wide subject brightness range, as viewed in Camera Raw using the default settings.

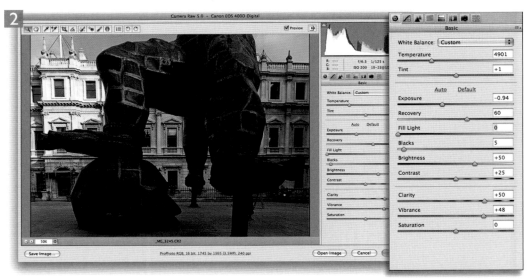

2 The first step was to take care of the highlights. I adjusted the Exposure slider to apply a negative exposure adjustment, followed by a Recovery adjustment to hold more of the detail in the highlights.

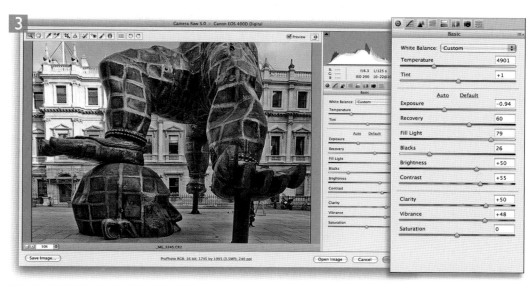

3 I then tackled the Shadow detail by raising the Fill Light setting. When you are required to push the Fill Light adjustment to such extremes, it is not uncommon to have to raise the Blacks (as I did here). The picture is not yet perfect, but we can now see detail at both ends of the tonal scale.

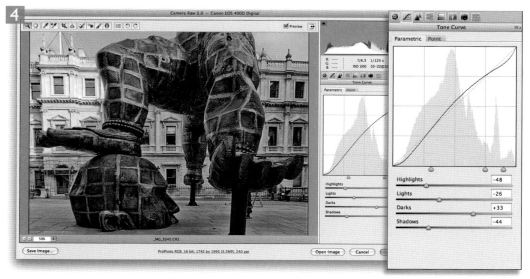

4 Lastly, I went to the Tone Curve panel and used the slider settings shown here to carefully add contrast to the photograph where it was needed most.

Detail panel information

In case you are wondering, there is a whole section on working with the Detail panel coming up in the following chapter.

HSL color controls

The choice of color ranges for the HSL sliders is really quite logical when you think about it. We may often want to adjust skin tone colors, but skin tones aren't red or yellow – they are more of an orange color. And the sea is often not blue but more of an aqua color. Basically, the hue ranges in the HSL controls are designed to provide a more applicable range of colors for photographers to work with.

HSL/Grayscale panel

The HSL controls provide eight color sliders with which to control the Hue, Saturation and Luminance. These work in a similar way to the Hue/Saturation adjustment in Photoshop, but are in many ways better; from my experience I find that these controls are more predictable in their response. In Figure 3.41 I used the Luminance controls to darken the blue sky and add more contrast in the clouds, plus I lightened the grass and trees slightly. Do this using Hue/Saturation in Photoshop and you will find that the blue colors will tend to lose saturation as you darken the luminosity. You will also notice that instead of using the traditional additive and subtractive primary colors of red, green, blue, plus cyan, magenta and yellow, the color slider controls in the HSL panel are based on colors that are of more actual relevance when editing photographic images. For example, the Oranges slider is useful for adjusting skin tones and Aquas can target the color of a swimming pool, but without affecting the color of a sky.

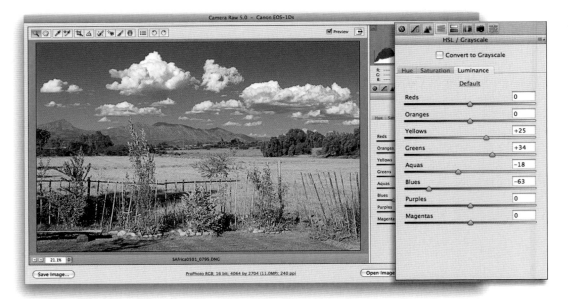

Figure 3.41 In this example, the HSL/Grayscale panel was used to add more cloud contrast to the sky by going to the Luminance section and darkening the Aquas and Blues sliders.

Recovering out-of-gamut colors

Figure 3.42 highlights the problem of how the camera you are shooting with is almost certainly capable of capturing a greater range of colors than can be displayed on the monitor or seen in print. Just because you can't see them doesn't mean they're not there! Although a typical monitor can't give a true indication of how colors will print, it is all you have to rely on when assessing the colors in a photo. The HSL Luminance and Saturation sliders can sometimes be used to reveal hidden color detail (Figure 3.43).

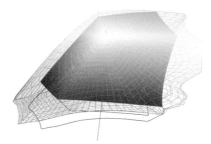

Figure 3.42 This diagram shows a plot of the color gamut of an LCD monitor (the solid shape in the center) compared to the actual color gamut of a digital camera. Assuming you are using a wide gamut RGB space such as Adobe RGB or better still ProPhoto RGB, the colors you are able to edit will almost certainly extend beyond what can be seen on the screen.

Tech note

The previews shown here are not simple screen grabs, but mocked up using fully processed ProPhoto RGB images. You can judge the effectiveness of this adjustment by how they are printed in the book.

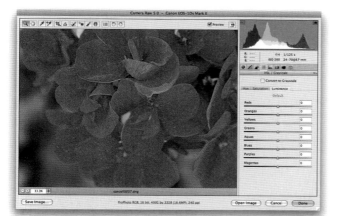

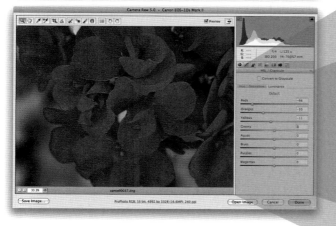

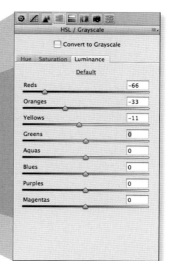

Figure 3.43 These two screen shots show a dramatic improvement between the before version where the reds in the flowers appeared flat (top) and after applying a negative luminance adjustment to darken the red, orange and yellow colors (bottom).

Grayscale conversions

To find out about how to apply grayscale conversions in Camera Raw, please refer to pages 358–359 in the Black and White chapter.

Emulating Hue/Saturation behavior

In Photoshop's Hue/Saturation dialog there is a Hue slider that can be used to apply global hue shifts, which can be useful if you are interested in shifting all of the hue values in one go. With Camera Raw you can create preset HSL settings where all the Hue sliders are shifted equally in each direction. Using such presets you can quickly shift all the hues in positive or negative steps, without having to drag each slider in turn.

Adjusting the hue and saturation

The Hue sliders in the HSL/Grayscale panel can be used to fine-tune the hue color bias for each of the eight color sliders. In Figure 3.44 I adjusted the Reds hue slider to make the reds look less magenta and more orange. In other words, this is a useful HSL/Grayscale panel tip for improving the look of snapshot pictures taken with a compact digital camera, where the skin tones can sometimes look too pink.

The Saturation sliders allow you to decrease or increase the saturation of specific colors. In Figure 3.45 you can see how I was able to use these to knock back specific colors so that everything in the photograph ended up in monochrome, except for the red guitar in the foreground. I could have used the new adjustment brush to do this, but adjusting the Saturation sliders offers a very quick method for selectively editing the colors in this way.

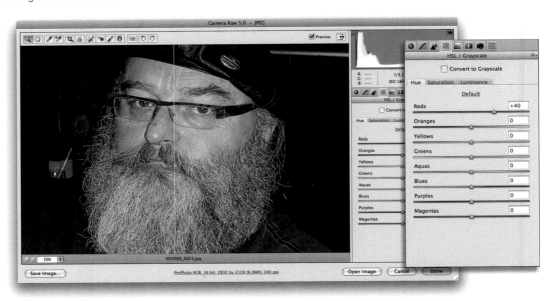

Figure 3.44 This snap shot was taken of my friend Jeff Schewe at a party in New York. Here, I used a positive Reds Hue adjustment to take some of the redness out of the picture to make the skin tones look more natural, but I may have needed to increase the amount used here as extra glasses of wine were consumed.

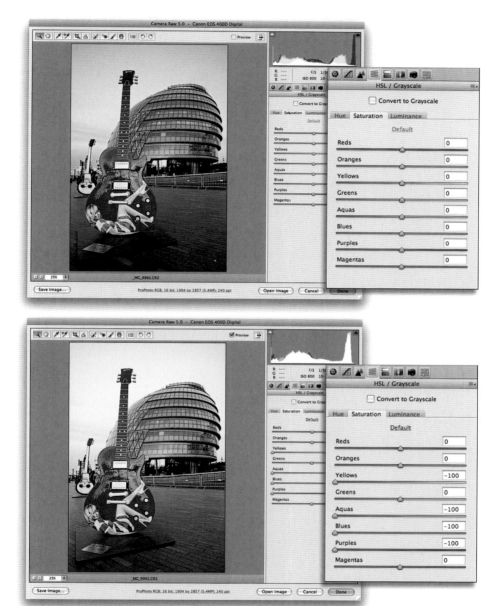

Figure 3.45 In this example I have shown the before version (top) and a modified version (below), where I used the HSL/Grayscale panel Saturation sliders to selectively desaturate some of the colors in this scene.

Lens Correction filter

The Chromatic Aberration controls discussed here are also available in the Photoshop Lens Correction filter.

Lens Corrections panel

The Lens Corrections controls can help correct some of the optical problems that are associated with digital capture. If you inspect an image closely towards the edge of the frame area you may notice some color fringing, which will be most apparent around areas of high contrast (Figure 3.46). This is mainly a problem you get with cheaper lens optics, but it can even occur with a good lens when photographing

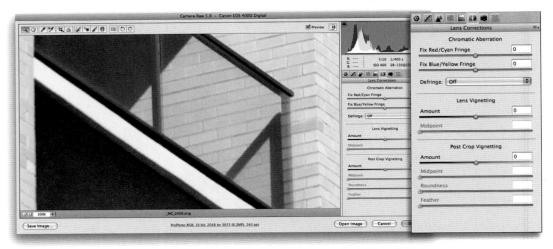

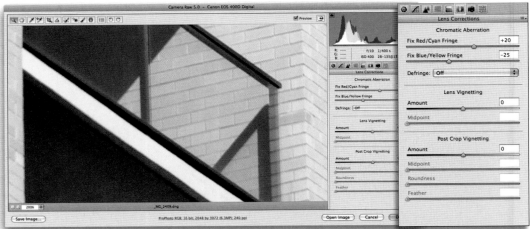

Figure 3.46 The top screen shot shows a 200% close-up view of an image where you can see strong color fringing around the strong contrast edges. In the lower version I used a Chromatic Aberration correction to remove the color fringes.

brightly colored subjects. The Chromatic Aberration controls in the Lens Corrections panel can be used to help remove any visible color fringing.

To correct for chromatic aberrations you do need to be viewing the photo at a magnification of 100% or higher. The Red/Cyan Fringe adjustment works by adjusting the scale size of the Red channel relative to the Green channel, and the Blue/Yellow Fringe slider will adjust the scale size of the Blue channel relative to the Green channel. The net result is that with careful manipulation of both these sliders you should be able to remove all signs of chromatic aberration across the whole image, even though you are only analyzing one small section of the photo.

Defringe

The Defringe options provide an extra level of defringing in addition to the manual slider adjustments. To be honest, the Highlight Edges and All Edges settings usually have a very subtle effect, but if you are going to use this I would suggest choosing the All Edges option (Figure 3.48). It can also sometimes help clean up any remaining color fringes.

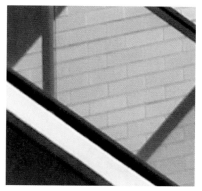

Figure 3.47 If you hold down the 🔲 *alt* key as you make adjustments to the Blue/Yellow Chromatic aberration controls you can hide the Red/Cyan color fringing (but you must be viewing at 100% magnification or higher). Do the same with the Red/Cyan Chromatic aberration controls to hide the Blue/Yellow color fringing.

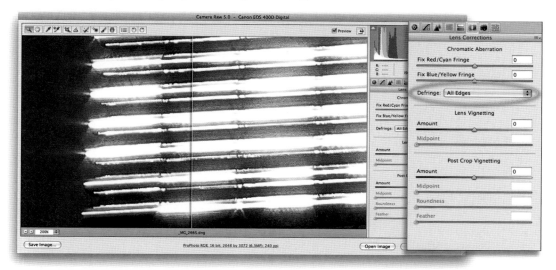

Figure 3.48 The left half of this Camera Raw preview shows the before version and the right half view shows the same image with the All Edges Defringe option selected.

UV filters and edge detail

Fixing a UV filter over the lens is generally considered a good way to filter out the UV light when photographing outdoors, plus it can also offer a first line of defence against the lens getting damaged. However, this not such a good idea for wide-angle or wide-angle zoom lenses as the light entering the lens from the extreme edges is forced to go through the UV filter at an angle and this can cause the image to degrade more at the edges of the frame since the light passes through the filter glass at an oblique angle.

Lens Vignetting control

With certain camera/lens combinations you may see some brightness fall-off occur towards the edges of the picture frame. This is a problem you are more likely to encounter with wide-angle lenses, and you may only notice this particular lens deficiency if the subject contains a plain, evenly-lit background. The Lens Vignetting Amount slider can be used to correct for this by lightening the corners relative to the center of the photograph, while the Midpoint slider can be used to offset the rate of fall-off. As you increase the Midpoint value, the exposure compensation will be accentuated more towards the outer edges.

Vignetting is not always a result of the lens used. In the studio I am fond of shooting with extreme wide-angle lenses and the problem here is that it's often difficult to get the backdrop evenly lit for the area of coverage that is required. In these kinds of situations I find it helps to use the Lens Vignetting slider to compensate for the fall-off in light towards the corners of the frame by lightening the edges (as shown in Figure 3.49 below).

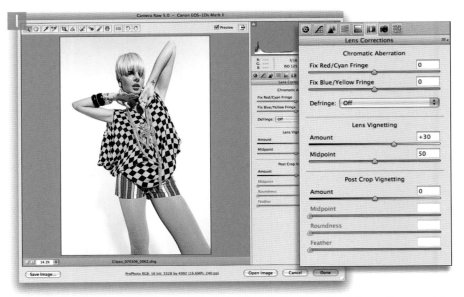

Client: Clipso.
Model: Lucy Edwards @ Bookings.

Figure 3.49 An example of the Lens Vignetting sliders being used to compensate for the light fall-off on a studio backdrop, to produce a more even-balanced white.

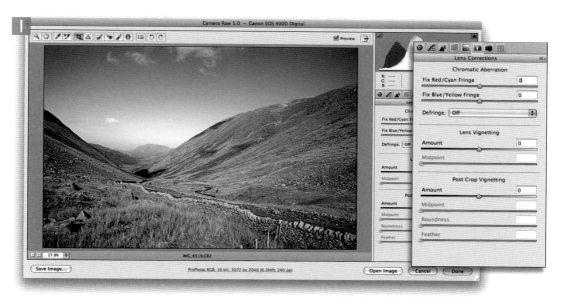

1 Here is an example of a photograph shot with a wide-angle lens, where lens vignetting can be seen in the corners of the frame.

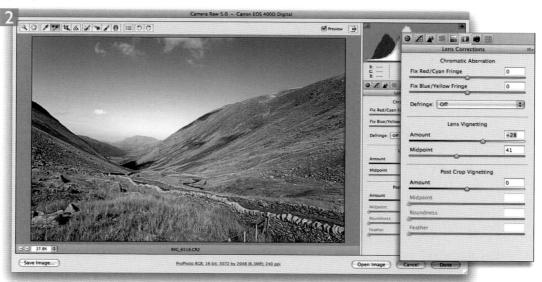

2 In this example I used the Lens Corrections panel to compensate for the Vignetting. I set the Amount slider to +28, and adjusted the Midpoint to fine-tune the correction. The aim here was to obtain an even exposure at the corners.

Combined effects

Now that we have post crop vignette controls as well as the standard Lens correction vignette sliders, you can achieve even more varied results by combining different combinations of slider settings, whether a photo is cropped or not.

Post Crop vignetting control

A lot of photographers have got into using the Lens Vignetting controls as a creative tool for darkening or lightening the corners of their pictures. The only problem with this is that the lens vignetting can only be applied to the whole of the image frame area. But with Camera Raw 5 you can now use the Post Crop Vignette sliders to apply a vignette relative to any cropped image area. This means that you can use the Lens Vignetting controls for the purpose they were intended (to counter any fall-off that occurs towards the edges of the frame) and use the Post Crop Vignette sliders as a creative tool for those times when you deliberately wish to lighten or darken the edges of a photo via Camera Raw.

The Post Crop Vignetting Amount and Midpoint sliders work identically to the Lens Vignetting controls, except in addition to this you can adjust the Roundness and the Feathering of the vignette adjustment.

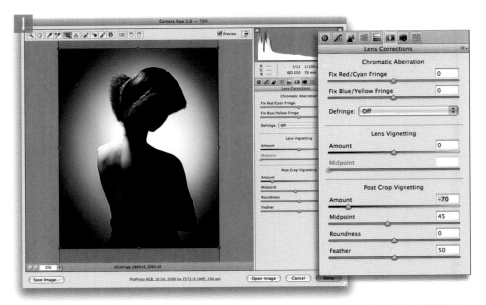

Client: Andrew Collinge Hair & Beauty. Hair by Andrew Collinge artistic team. Make-up: Liz Collinge.

1 In this first example I applied a –70, darkening vignette offset with a +45 Midpoint setting. This adjustment was not too different from a normal Lens Vignetting adjustment, except it was applied to the cropped area of an image.

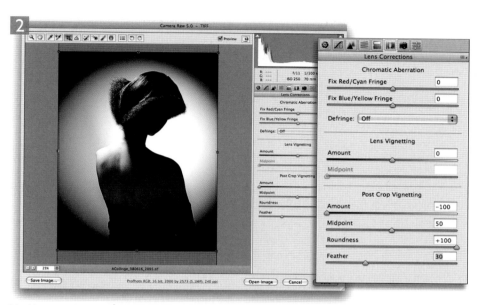

2 In this next version I adjusted the Roundness slider to make the vignette shape less elliptical and adjusted the Feather slider to make the vignette edge harder.

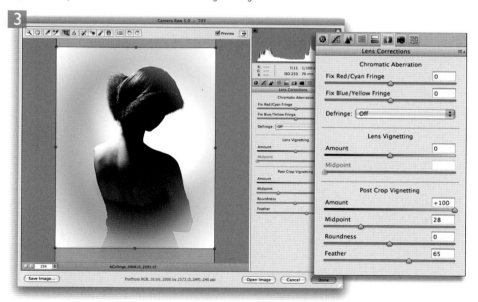

3 For this final version I applied a +100 vignette Amount to lighten the corners of the cropped image, combined with a narrow Midpoint and a softer Feather setting.

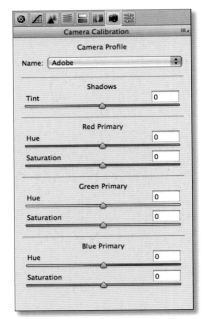

Figure 3.50 The Camera Calibration panel controls can be used to fine-tune the Camera Raw color interpretation. The Camera Profile setting at the top can offer a choice of camera profile settings, depending on whether there is more than one Camera Calibration profile to choose from.

ACR compatible cameras

The list of cameras compatible with the latest version of Camera Raw can be found at the Adobe website by following this link: www.adobe.com/products/photoshop/cameraraw.html

Camera Calibration panel

Everyone wants or expects their camera to be capable of capturing perfect colors, whether they really need to or not. For a start, what is perfect color? Some photographers will look at the results they get when looking at a JPEG version of an image and judge everything according to that, while others, who shoot raw, may prefer the default look they get from a particular raw processing program. Apart from anything else, is the display you are using capable of showing all the colors that your camera can capture?

Camera Raw is the product of much camera testing and raw file analysis carried out by Thomas Knoll at Adobe. Test cameras were used to build a two-part profile of each camera sensor's spectral response under standardized tungsten and daylight balanced lighting conditions. From this, Camera Raw is able to calculate a pretty good color interpretation under these lighting conditions, and beyond, across a wide range of color temperatures. This method may not be as accurate as having a proper profile built for your camera, but to be honest profiling a camera is something that can only really be done where the light source conditions are always the same, because you would otherwise need to reprofile the camera every time the lighting was changed.

The Camera Calibration panel controls (Figure 3.50) provide a mechanism for fine-tuning the color adjustments in Camera Raw so that you can address any slight differences between your camera and the ones Thomas used to test with, and customize the Camera Raw output to produce a custom calibration for each individual camera body. This system of calibration does require a little extra effort to set up, but it is worth doing if you want to fine-tune the color calibration for each individual camera you shoot with.

You also have to bear in mind that many of the default Camera Raw settings were achieved through testing a limited number of cameras. It has been reported that there can be a discernible variation in color response between individual cameras. So it was as a result of testing a wider pool of cameras that Thomas Knoll decided to update the default settings for certain makes of camera and in some cases provide later version default camera profiles (in addition to keeping the legacy profile available for use). This is why you will sometimes see extra profiles listed that refer to earlier builds of Camera Raw, such as ACR 2.4 or ACR 3.6, etc. (see sidebar on choosing the right profile). In addition to this, Adobe have also provided a range of new profiles for Camera Raw where the Adobe profile should now be the new default profile for Camera Raw 5.

Some writers have tended to gloss over the Camera Calibration panel and suggest that you 'tweak the sliders until the photograph kind of looks right'. Well, there is a more scientific approach to using this panel and although it may look complicated, it is in fact quite easy to carry out and only needs to be done once for each camera.

The ACR Calibrator script

In the early days of Camera Raw I used to shoot an X-Rite ColorChecker chart and use a visual color comparison technique with a synthetic ColorChecker chart to adjust the Calibrate settings. It was all very complex! But fortunately there is now an easier way to calibrate your camera equipment. First of all, you still need to buy an X-Rite ColorChecker chart (either the standard or Mini size will do). One of these can be ordered on-line and will cost you around $100 (Figure 3.52). You will then need to photograph the chart with your camera in raw mode. It is important that the chart is evenly lit and exposed correctly, and the best way to do this is to use two studio lights in a copy light setup or, failing that, use a diffuse light source. Apart from that it does not matter what other camera settings are used, although I would recommend you shoot at a low ISO rating.

The next thing you will need is the ACR Calibrator script which will work for Mac or PC with Photoshop CS, CS2, CS3 or CS4. This is free and can be downloaded from Tom Fors Chromaholics website: http://fors.net/chromoholics/ Once installed, the ACR Calibrator script will be available for use via the File ⇨ Scripts menu in Photoshop.

Choosing the right profile

When a profile is updated for a particular camera, it is necessary for Camera Raw to preserve the older profiles since these need to be kept in order to satisfy customers who have relied on the previous profile setting. It wouldn't do to find that all your existing Camera Raw processed images suddenly looked different because the profile had been updated. So in order to maintain backward compatibility, Adobe leave you a choice of which profiles to use.

Accurate white balance measurement

An X-Rite ColorChecker chart is essential for measuring the color response of your camera, but it is generally felt that the white and gray patches on these cards are a tad warm. If you want to get a really accurate white balance measurement for individual shots I can recommend you use a WhiBal™ card as sold by RawWorkflow. com. These are available in various sizes and offer one of the most accurate ways you can measure the white balance in any lighting setup (see Figure 3.22).

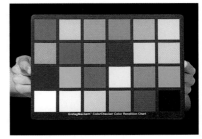

Figure 3.51 X-Rite ColorChecker charts can be bought as a mini chart or the full-size chart you see here.

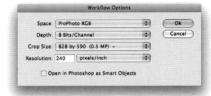

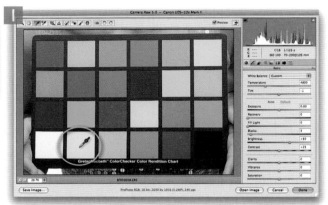

1 To use the script, you will need to open a raw image that was taken of the X-Rite ColorChecker chart and open it in Photoshop via the Adobe Camera Raw dialog. Use the white balance tool to measure the patch next to the white patch (circled). Crop the image tightly around the ColorChecker chart. Go to the Workflow options, set the crop size to the smallest pixel size possible and set the bit depth to 8-bits per channel. There are no other settings you need concern yourself with. It does not matter if auto settings have been applied and it does not matter which RGB output color space is selected. Now click 'Open' to open the image in Photoshop.

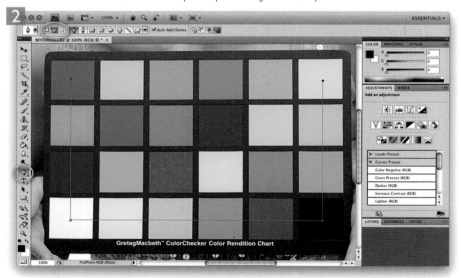

2 With the image open in Photoshop, select the pen tool with the Paths mode option selected in the Options panel (circled). Click with the pen tool on the brown patch. Now hold down the *Shift* key and click on the white patch, the black patch and lastly the blue-green patch. Now go to the File ⇨ Scripts menu and select the ACR Calibrator script that you installed earlier.

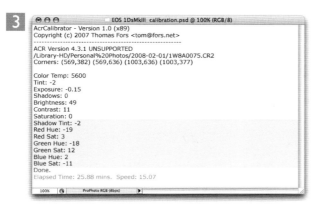

Skin tone calibration settings

Going back to what I said earlier about 'what is proper color'... it is all very well creating a perfect calibration, but sometimes the most accurate color doesn't always quite match expectations. For example, proper camera calibrations tend to produce Caucasian skin tones that look slightly too magenta for most people's liking. You may therefore want to tweak the settings slightly. Try adding 10 units to the red hue measurement and save this modified setting as a camera calibration for use with Caucasian skin tone subjects.

3 The ACR Calibrator script will automatically open the raw file many times over and gradually build a status report in a new Photoshop document. This process can take a long time to complete, which is why it is important to keep the bit depth at 8-bits per channel and the image size small. It will also help if you hide all the Photoshop panels first before you run the script. Shown here is the ACR Calibrator status window after the script had run its full course; I have highlighted the calibration settings in yellow.

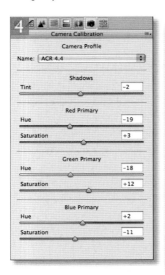

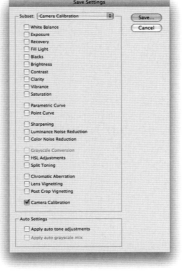

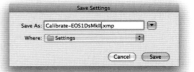

4 You'll need to make a note of the figures highlighted in Step 3 and enter them in the Camera Calibration panel in Camera Raw and save this as a custom calibration setting for your camera. When you save the Camera Raw settings, check only the Camera Calibration checkbox. You can now apply this setting to all photos that have been shot using this camera and expect to see more accurate color results.

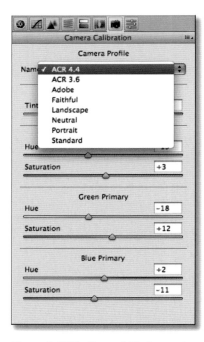

Figure 3.52 The Camera Calibration panel showing the new Camera Profile options.

DNG Profile editor

The DNG Profile editor is a separate program that you can download free from the Adobe website. If you are feeling up to the task, this utility program will allow you to edit your own 'profile look settings' and add these to the ones offered here in Camera Raw 5.

New Camera Profile availability

Not all the Camera Raw supported cameras have new profiles so you may not see the full list of profile options for every Camera Raw compatible camera, just the newer and most popular camera models.

New Camera Raw profiles

I mentioned earlier the ACR profiles and how these were updated as Thomas chose to revise the earlier Camera Raw profiles and provide newer ones based on improved testing. More recently, Eric Chan on the Camera Raw team has worked to improve many of the standard ACR profiles as well as extending the range of profiles that can be applied via Camera Raw (Figure 3.52). Older profiles such as ACR 3.6 and ACR 4.4 will still be honored and made available where appropriate. But for Camera Raw 5, the 'Adobe' profile is now the new default and this and the other profiles you see listed in the Profile menu options are the result of improved analysis as well as an effort to match some of the camera vendor 'look settings'.

If you are happy to trust the new 'Adobe' profile, then I suggest you leave this as the default setting. The differences you will see with this profile are going to be slight, but I think you will find these still represent an improvement and are worth keeping as the default. The 'Standard' profile is rather clever because Eric has managed to match the default camera vendor settings for most of the main cameras supported by Camera Raw. So, if you choose the Standard profile you can get the Camera Raw interpretation to match the default color renderings applied by the camera manufacturer software. This means that if you apply the Standard profile as the default, Camera Raw will apply the exact same kind of default color rendering as the camera vendor's software and it will also match the default camera JPEG renderings. When you next bring your photos into Camera Raw, you won't see any jumps in color as the Camera Raw processing kicks in because Camera Raw is now able to match the JPEG rendering for many of the supported cameras.

The other profiles you may see listed are designed to let you match some of the camera vendor 'look settings'. These profiles include: Faithful, Landscape, Neutral and Portrait. In Figure 3.53 you can see an example of how these can compare with the standard ACR and Adobe profiles.

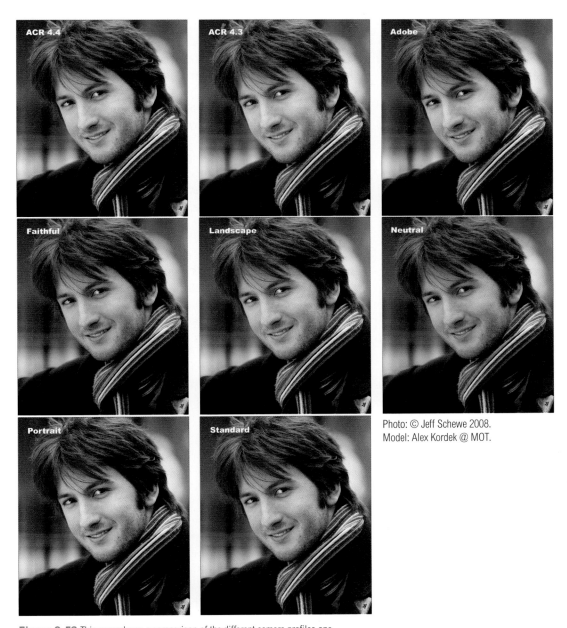

Photo: © Jeff Schewe 2008.
Model: Alex Kordek @ MOT.

Figure 3.53 This page shows a comparison of the different camera profiles one can now choose from and the effect these will have on the appearance of an image shot using a Canon EOS 1Ds MkIII camera that has been processed via Camera Raw.

Clearing the retouching work

You can remove individual retouch circles by selecting them and hitting the `Delete` key. Or, you can click on the Clear All button to delete all retouch circles.

Turning off the preview

In Camera Raw 5, you can now use the Preview option to toggle showing/hiding the spot removal retouching.

Spot removal tool

You can use the spot removal tool (B) to retouch spots and blemishes. Whenever the spot removal tool is active you will see the Spot Removal options appear in the panel section on the right, where you can choose between Heal and Clone type retouching (Figure 3.54) and, ideally, you should work on the image at a 100% magnification. In Clone mode, the tool behaves like a cross between the spot healing brush and clone stamp in Photoshop. It will carry out a straightforward clone of the image with a soft feathered edge circle and automatically select the area to sample from. In Heal mode, the tool behaves like a cross between the spot healing and normal healing brush in Photoshop, where it auto-selects an area to sample from and blends the sampled data with the surrounding data outside the spotting circle. In either case, you can click to select an applied clone circle and use the Type menu to switch from one mode to the other. With both the Clone and Heal modes you have the option to adjust the radius of

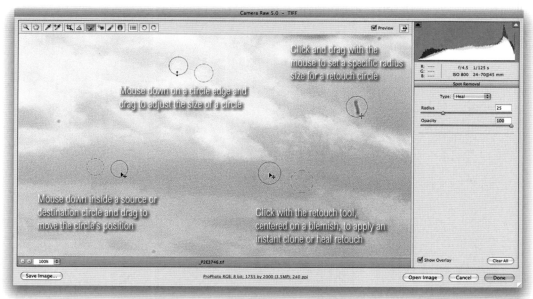

Figure 3.54 This screen shot shows the retouch tool in action, with explanations of how to apply and modify the retouch spot circles.

the spot removal tool as well as the opacity. You can use the **[ ]** keys to tweak the radius, but it is usually simpler to follow the instructions in Figure 3.54 and drag with the cursor instead. The opacity slider is new and this allows you to lower the opacity setting should you wish. You can also click on the Show Overlay box or use the **H** key to toggle showing and hiding the circles so that you can view the retouched image without seeing the retouch circles.

Synchronized spotting with Camera Raw

You can also synchronize the spot removal as you apply it! Make a selection of images in Bridge and open them up via Camera Raw (as shown in Figure 3.55). Now click on the Select All button. This will select all the photos and if you now use the spot removal tool you can retouch the most selected photo (the one shown in the main preview), and the spotting work will automatically be updated to all the other selected images.

Keeping the sensor clean

Dust marks are the bane of digital photography and ideally you want to do as much as you can to avoid dust or dirt getting onto the camera sensor. I have experimented with various products and find that the Sensor Swabs used with the Eclipse cleaning solution from Photographic Solutions Inc (www. photosol.com) are reliable products. I use these from time to time to keep the sensors in my cameras free from marks.

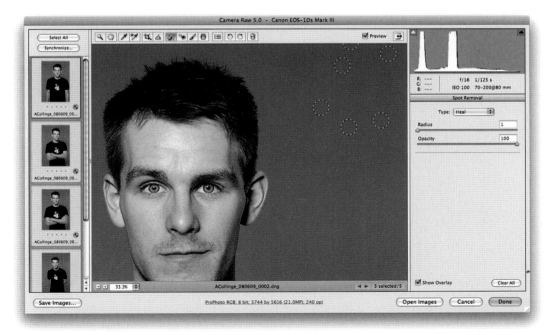

Figure 3.55 Here is an example of the Camera Raw dialog being used to carry out synchronized spotting.

Hiding the red eye rectangles

As with the spot removal tool, you can click on the Show Overlay box to toggle showing and hiding the rectangle overlays (or use the **H** key).

Red eye removal

The remove red eye tool is useful for correcting photos taken of people where the direct camera flash has caused the pupils to appear bright red. To apply a red eye correction, select the red eye removal tool and mouse drag over the eyes that need to be adjusted. In Figure 3.56 I dragged with the mouse to roughly select one of the eyes. As I did this, Camera Raw was able to detect the area that needed to be corrected and automatically adjusted the marquee size to fit. The Pupil Size and Darken sliders can then be used to fine-tune the Pupil Size area that you want to correct as well as the amount you want to darken the pupil by. You can also revise the red eye removal settings by clicking on a rectangle to reactivate it, or use the *Delete* key to remove individual red eye corrections. If you don't like the results you are getting, you can always click on the Clear All button to delete the red eye retouching and start over again.

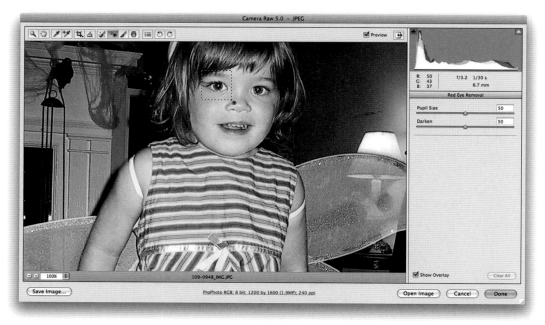

Figure 3.56 Here is an example of the red eye tool in action.

Localized adjustments

We now come to the adjustment brush and graduated filter tools, which can be used to apply localized edits to photos in Camera Raw. Although localized editing made an appearance in Aperture 2.1, the Camera Raw tools are quite different as they truly do allow non-destructive editing. Just like the spot removal and red eye removal tools you can revise the edits as many times as you like, without having to render an interim pixel version of the raw master. Not only that, these are more than just dodge and burn tools. There are a total of seven adjustment effects to choose from, not to mention an Auto Mask option.

Adjustment brush

When you select the adjustment brush tool (**K**) the tool options shown in Figure 3.57 will appear in the panel section on the right with the New button selected, and below that a set of sliders you can use to configure the brush adjustment before you apply it.

Camera Raw versus Aperture

It is worth making the point here that Camera Raw 5 and Aperture 2.1 have adopted completely different approaches to localized editing. Aperture creates a rendered pixel image that can be manipulated via what is essentially a basic pixel image editing program, and to be honest, if you are going to render a pixel image, you might as well edit in Photoshop. Camera Raw on the other hand offers true non-destructive raw image editing.

Toggle the main panel controls

Hit the **K** key to revert to toggle between the main edit panel mode and the Adjustment Brush panel.

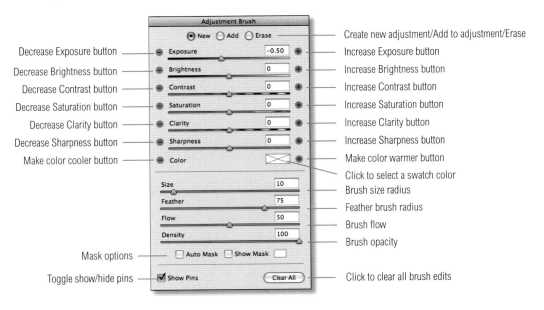

Figure 3.57 The Adjustment brush options.

Return to the main panels

Click **K** to toggle between the Adjustment Brush tool mode and other panel modes.

Hiding and showing brush edits

Use the Preview button in the Camera Raw dialog to toggle showing and hiding all Adjustment brush edits.

On-screen brush resizing

If you hold down the **ctrl** key (Mac) or use a right-mouse click (Mac and PC), you can drag to resize the cursor before you start using it to retouch the image.

Initial Adjustment brush options

To apply a brush adjustment, click on the New Brush button at the top of the panel and then select the effect options you wish to apply by using either the plus or minus buttons or the sliders. For example, clicking on the Exposure plus button will increase the exposure setting to +0.50 and clicking on the negative button will set it to −0.50 (these are your basic dodge and burn settings). The effect buttons therefore make it fairly easy for you to quickly create the kind of effect you are after. You can only select one effect setting at a time using the buttons, but if you use the slider controls you can fine-tune the adjustment brush effect settings and combine multiple types of effects.

Brush settings

Below this are the brush settings. The Size slider adjusts the brush radius, plus you can also use the **[ ]** keys to make the brush smaller or larger. The Feather slider adjusts the softness of the brush and you can also use the **Shift]** keys to make the brush edge softer and **Shift [** to make the brush harder. Note that these settings will be reflected in the cursor shape shown in Figure 3.58.

The Flow slider is a bit like an airbrush control. If you select a low Flow setting, you can apply a series of brush strokes that successively build to create a stronger effect. As you brush back and forth with the brush, you will notice how the paint effect gains opacity and, if you are using a pressure-sensitive tablet such as a Wacom™, the Flow of the brush strokes is automatically linked to the pen pressure that you apply.

The Density slider determines the maximum opacity for the brush. This means that if you have the brush set to 100% Density, the flow of the brush strokes can build to a maximum density of 100%. If on the other hand you reduce the Density, this will limit the maximum brush opacity to a lower opacity value. For example, if you lower the Density and paint over an area that was previously painted at a density of 100% you can paint with the adjustment brush to reduce the opacity in these areas and, if you reduce the Density to 0%, the adjustment brush will act like an eraser.

Adding a new brush effect

You are now ready to start painting. When you click on the image, a pin marker is added and the Adjustment Brush panel will show that it is now in Add mode (Figure 3.59). As you start adding successive brush strokes these will be collectively associated with this marker and will continue to do so until you click on the New button and click to add a new set of brush strokes.

The pin markers therefore provide a tag for identifying groups of brush strokes and you can click on a pin marker whenever you need to add or remove brush strokes or re-edit the brush settings that were used previously. If you want to hide the markers you can do so by clicking on the Show Pins box to toggle showing/hiding, or use the H key shortcut.

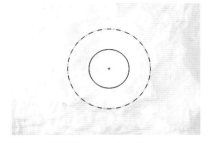

Figure 3.58 The outer edge of the adjustment brush cursor represents the overall size of the brush, while the inner circle represents the softness (feathering) of the brush relative to the overall brush size.

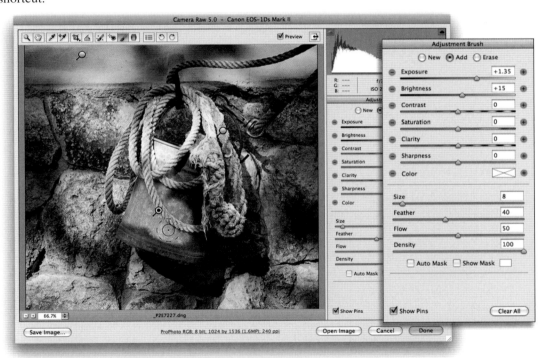

Figure 3.59 In this example I added several pin markers representing groups of brush strokes. The one at the top was used to darken and the one that is currently active was used to lighten the bucket with a positive Exposure value.

Undoing and erasing brush strokes

As you work with the Adjustment brush, you can undo a brush stroke or series of strokes using the Undo command (⌘ Z ctrl Z).

Previewing the mask more clearly

Sometimes it is useful to initially adjust the settings to apply a stronger effect than is desired. This will let you judge the effectiveness of your masking more clearly. You can then reduce the effect settings to reach the desired strength for the brush strokes.

Resetting the sliders

Double-clicking a slider name will reset to zero, or to its default value.

Editing brush adjustments

To edit a series of brush strokes, just click on an existing pin marker to select it (a black dot will appear in the center of the pin). This takes you into the Add mode, where you can add more brush strokes or edit the current brush settings. For example, in Step 2 (opposite) I might have wanted to drag the Exposure slider to lighten the selected brush group more. You might also want to erase portions of a brush group, which you can do by clicking on the Erase button at the top of the Adjustment Brush panel where you can independently edit the brush settings for the eraser mode (except for the Density slider which is locked at zero). Alternatively, you can hold down the ⌥ alt key to temporarily access the adjustment brush in eraser mode. When you are done editing, click on the New button to return to the New adjustment mode where you can now click on the image and add a new set of brush strokes.

Previewing the brush stroke areas

If you click on the Show Mask option, you'll see a temporary overlay view of the painted regions (Figure 3.60). The color overlay represents the areas that have been painted and can also be seen as you roll the cursor over a pin marker.

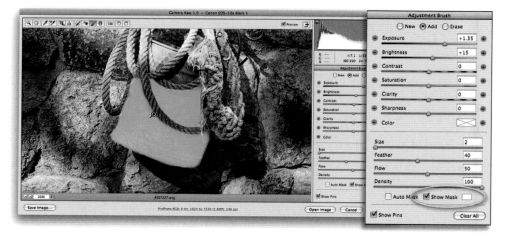

Figure 3.60 In this screen view, the 'Show Mask' option is checked and you can see an overlay mask for the selected brush group. Click on the swatch next to it if you wish to choose a different color for the overlay display.

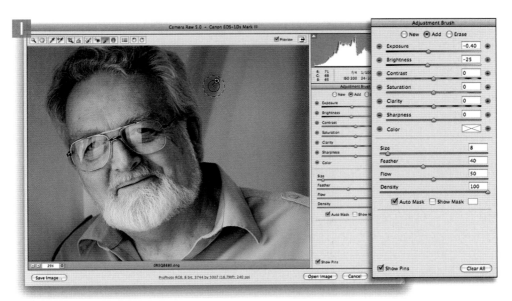

1 Here is a portrait of Rod Wynne-Powell who tech-edited the book for me. To add a new adjustment brush group, I adjusted the effect sliders, clicked on the image and started painting. In this first step I applied a darkening effect to the background.

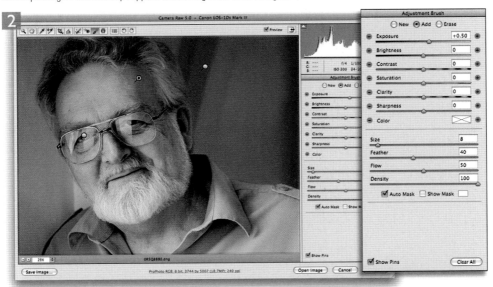

2 I then added further brush groups. In this step I added a new brush group to lighten the eyes and a third brush group (highlighted here) to lighten Rod's forehead.

Photograph: © Jeff Schewe 2008

211

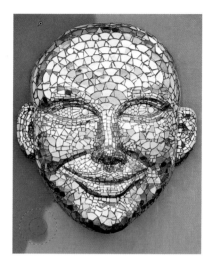

Figure 3.61 Quite often all you need to do is to click on an area of a picture with the color you wish to target and drag the adjustment brush in auto mask mode to quickly adjust areas of the picture that share the same tone and color.

Auto masking

The Auto Mask option is at the bottom of the Adjustment Brush panel and when switched on will cleverly mask the image at the same time as you paint. It does this by analyzing the colors in the image where you first click and then proceeds to apply the effect to only those areas with the same matching tone and color (Figure 3.61). It does this on a contiguous selection basis. For example, in the steps shown here I dragged with the adjustment brush in auto mask mode around the outside of the basket handle to darken the outer area and then dragged separately on the inside of the basket handle to include this in the auto mask brush group. While the Auto Mask can do a great job at auto-selecting the areas you want to paint, at extremes it can lead to ugly 'dissolved pixel' edges. This doesn't happen with every photo, but it's something to be aware of. The other thing to watch out for is a slow-down in brush performance. As you add more brush strokes, the Camera Raw processing takes a knock anyway, but it gets even worse when you apply lots of auto mask brushing.

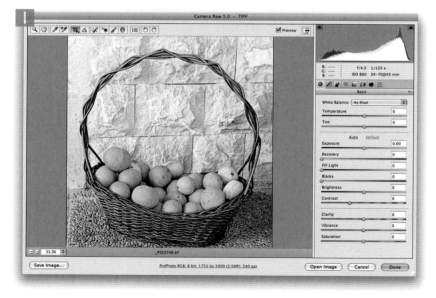

1 This shows the original photograph of a basket of oranges against a stone wall, so far with just the Basic panel corrections applied.

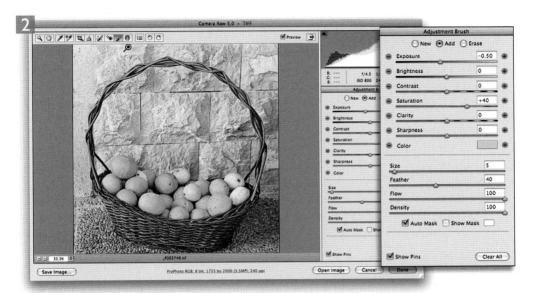

2 I selected the adjustment brush and clicked on the minus Exposure button to set this to −0.50, dragged the Saturation slider to +50, and started painting the wall. Because Auto Mask was checked, the brush effect only adjusted the stone wall area.

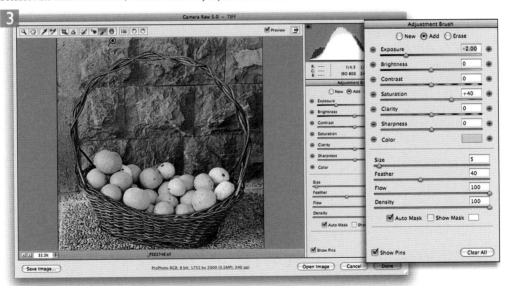

3 To demonstrate how effective the auto masking was in this image I lowered the Exposure slider to −2.00, which darkened the wall even further. You can see how the basket handle and fruit stood out more as I did this.

Adjustment brush speed

The fact that you can apply non-destructive localized adjustments to a raw image is a clever innovation, but this type of editing can never be as fast as editing a pixel image in Photoshop. The example shown here demonstrates how far you could take localized edits with the adjustment brush tool, but in reality it can be extremely slow to carry out complex retouching with the adjustment brush. Even on a fast computer.

Hand-coloring in Color mode

The adjustment brush tool can also be used to tint black and white images and is a technique that works well with any raw photograph, or JPEG/TIFF image that is in color to start with. This is because the auto mask feature can be used to help guide the adjustment brush to colorize regional areas that share the same tone and color and, if the underlying image is in color, then the auto mask has more information to work with. To convert the image to black and white you can take the Saturation slider in the Basic panel all the way to the left, or you can go to the HSL panel and drag all the Saturation sliders to the left. The advantage of this approach is that you then have the option to adjust the luminance sliders to vary the black and white mix (see Chapter 6). Once you have done this you can select the adjustment brush and click on the color swatch to open the Color Picker dialog and choose a color to paint with. In the following steps you can see how I went about coloring a photo that had been converted to black and white.

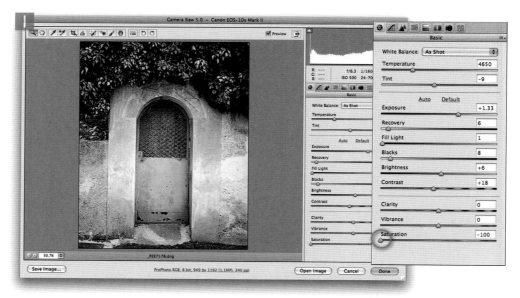

1 The first step was to go to the Basic panel and desaturate the colors in the image by dragging the Saturation slider all the way to the left.

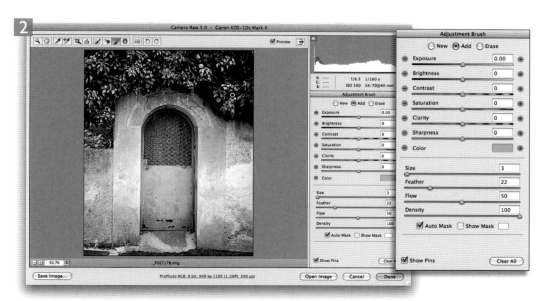

2 Once I had done this I selected the adjustment brush and edited the brush settings. In this instance I clicked on the swatch to choose a green color and, with Auto Mask selected, started coloring the leaves.

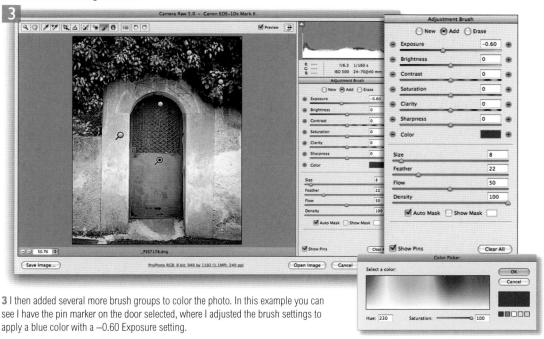

3 I then added several more brush groups to color the photo. In this example you can see I have the pin marker on the door selected, where I adjusted the brush settings to apply a blue color with a −0.60 Exposure setting.

Two Smart Object sharpening layers

As I have mentioned in the accompanying text, the Sharpness slider is rather limited compared to the full range of sharpening controls now offered in the Detail panel. An alternative approach would be to use the 'Opening raw files as Smart Objects' technique described on page 150 to open an image twice. You could apply one set of Detail panel settings for one layer and a stronger sharpening effect on the other. You could then use a layer mask (as described in Chapters 5 and 8) to blend these two layers so that you manage to combine two methods of sharpening in the one image.

Sharpness slider

The Sharpness effect can be adjusted in either direction. A positive value can be used to add sharpness, which is using a cross between the old Camera Raw and new Camera Raw (Camera Raw 4.1 or later) sharpening logic. Basically, a positive slider adjustment is equivalent to an Amount slider adjustment in the Detail panel, but without the additional sliders to provide radius control or edge masking (see Chapter 4). From this point of view the Sharpness effect can be used to 'paint in' extra sharpness (see Figure 3.62), but without the subtlety offered by the Detail panel controls for global sharpening. Even so, the Sharpness effect can be used in moderation to retouch a raw photo and enhance areas that could do with a touch more sharpening than the rest of the photo. You will also note in Figure 3.37 (on page 180) how I used a +25 Sharpness effect in conjunction with a −50 Clarity adjustment to produce a skin retouching brush effect.

Negative sharpness undoes the sharpening and at its maximum strength gives you only a slightly blurred version of the original and is therefore nothing quite as dramatic as a Gaussian Blur tool for Camera Raw.

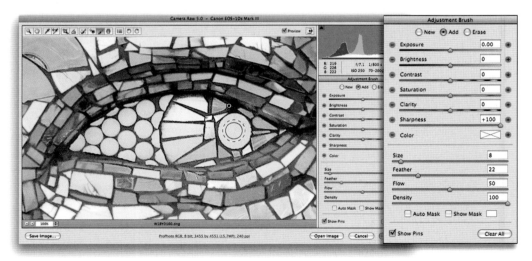

Figure 3.62 This shows a positive sharpness effect being applied to the eye area in this photo at +100%. You would normally want to reduce the overall amount to something less aggressive than this, since heavy sharpening can enhance artifacts.

Graduated filter tool

Everything that has been described so far about working with the adjustment brush more or less applies to working with the Graduated filter, which allows you to add linear graduated adjustments (Figure 3.63). To use the tool, just click in the picture to set the start point (the point with the maximum effect strength), drag the mouse to define the spread of the Graduated filter, and release to set the point of minimum effect strength. There is no midtone control with which you can offset a Graduated Filter effect, and there are no Graduated Filter options other than 'linear'.

Graduated filter effects are indicated by two pin markers with a dashed line between these two points. This indicates the spread of the filter; you can change the width by dragging the outer pins further apart, and move the position of the gradient by clicking and dragging the central line. When a gradient is selected, the green dashed line represents the maximum effect strength and the red dashed line represents the minimum effect strength.

Toggle the main panel controls

Hit the **G** key to revert to toggle between the main edit panel mode and the Graduated Filter panel.

Resetting the sliders

As with the adjustment brush options, double-clicking a slider name will reset to zero, or to its default value.

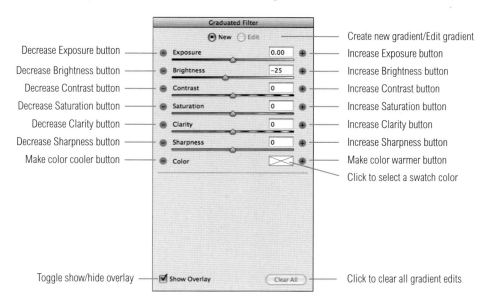

Figure 3.63 The Graduated filter tool options.

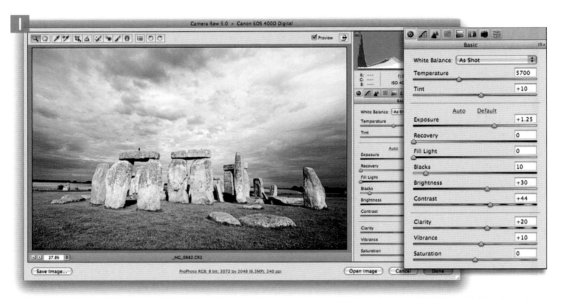

1 This shows how the original photograph looked after I had applied just the main Basic panel adjustments to optimize the highlights, shadows, and contrast.

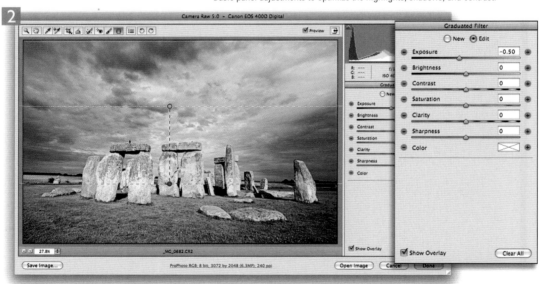

2 I selected the Graduated filter tool, which revealed the Graduated Filter panel. I selected a negative Exposure as the effect to use, and dragged the Graduated filter tool from the middle of the sky downward.

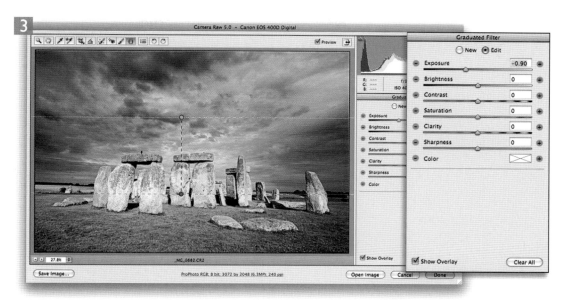

3 I then decided to strengthen the darkening Graduated filter effect by decreasing the Exposure setting to −0.90.

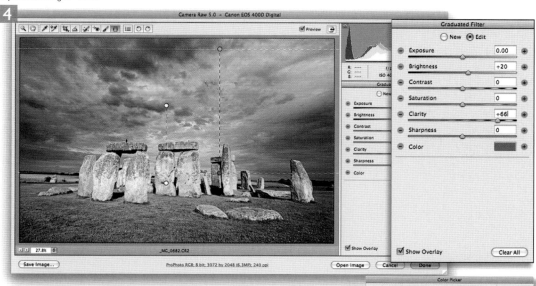

4 After that, I clicked on the color swatch to open the Color Picker shown here, selected a blue color and added a new Graduated filter adjustment by dragging from the top of the photograph downward to the horizon.

Angled gradients

As you drag with the Graduated filter you can do so at any angle and also edit the angle afterwards. For example, if you click on a pin marker to select it (as shown in Figure 3.64) you can drag the marker, rotating it around the other marker point and, if you hold down the *Shift* key, you can constrain the angle of rotation to 45° increments.

Adding clarity and contrast

In this last example, I wanted to show another series of steps using the graduated filter, but this time to demonstrate how to add contrast and clarity to an image. I took this particular shot early one morning in Chicago at sunrise, but I never really managed to get the dramatic colors that I was after. This was mainly because of the early morning misty sky. I realized this picture would benefit from some added contrast in the softer parts of the image, so I experimented with the localized adjustment tools to see if these could be used to modify the original raw image.

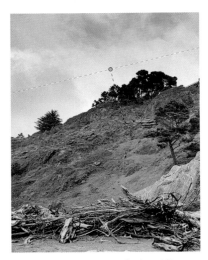

Figure 3.64 This shows a Graduated filter being rotated, where the red pin marker is being dragged and rotates around the green marker.

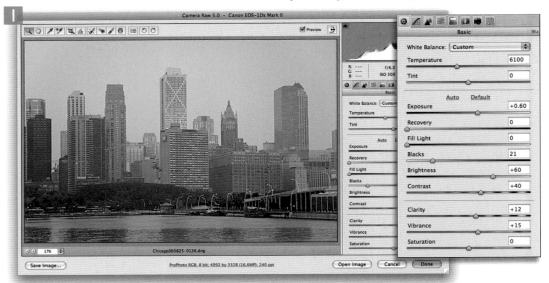

1 Here is the original version which I had optimized for the highlights, shadows and contrast, plus I added a little Clarity and Vibrance to bring out more definition and color in the buildings.

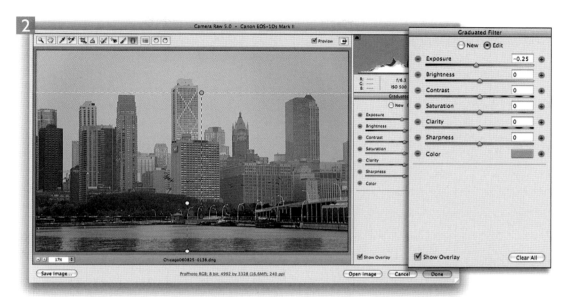

2 I then selected the Graduated filter tool and added two color effect gradients: a light
blue gradient over the water and a warm colored gradient to add warmth to the sky.

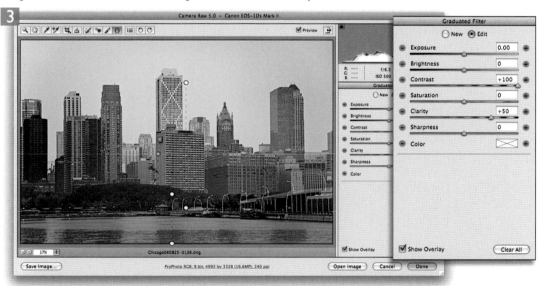

3 But still the buildings in this photograph lacked presence, so I added a further
gradient in which I combined a +100 Contrast effect with +50 clarity and dragged
from the middle of the picture down to the water line.

Removing a crop

To remove a crop, open the image in the Camera Raw dialog again, select the crop tool and choose 'Clear Crop' from the menu. Alternatively, you can hit _Delete_ or simply click outside of the crop in the gray canvas area.

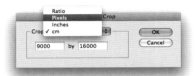

Figure 3.65 This shows the Custom Crop settings, available from the Crop tool menu (Figure 3.66). In this example I set a custom pixel size to set both the proportions of the crop size and enable the file to open at a larger pixel size than the maximum currently allowed.

Camera Raw cropping and straightening

You can crop an image in Camera Raw before it is opened in Photoshop. Note that the cropping is limited to the bounds of the image area only. The crop you apply in Camera Raw will be updated in the Bridge thumbnail and preview, and applied when the image is opened. If you save a file out of Camera Raw using the Photoshop format, there will also be an option to preserve the cropped pixels so you can recover the hidden pixels later. Meanwhile, the Camera Raw straighten tool can initially be used to measure a vertical or horizontal angle and apply a minimum crop to the image, which you can then resize accordingly.

One of the useful tips I learnt from Bruce Fraser was how you can use the Custom Crop settings (Figure 3.65) to create a crop size using the pixels units and create a custom size output that matches the size required for a specific layout, or one that exceeds even the standard output sizes available in the Workflow Options.

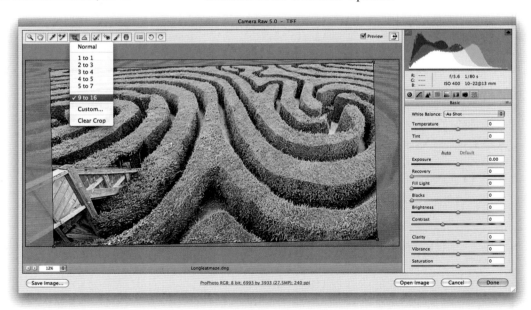

Figure 3.66 The Camera Raw crop tool sub options include a range of preset crop proportions where you can add your own custom presets by clicking on the Custom... item in the menu shown here. The crop units can be adjusted to crop according to the aspect ratio (the default) or by pixels, inches or centimeters.

Camera Raw settings menu

If you mouse down on the Camera Raw menu (circled in Figure 3.67) the menu includes several settings options. 'Image Settings' will be whatever the current Camera Raw settings are for the image. This might be the default settings or it might be a custom setting that you created when you last edited the image in Camera Raw. 'Camera Raw Defaults' will reset the default settings in all the panels and apply whatever the white balance setting was at the time the picture was captured, while 'Previous Conversion' will apply the Camera Raw settings that were applied to the previous saved image. If you proceed to make any custom changes while the Camera Raw dialog is open, then the settings will change to display 'Custom Settings'. The currently applied setting is usually shown with a check mark next to it and below that there is the Apply Preset menu where you can readily access presaved presets (just as you can via the Presets panel discussed on page 225).

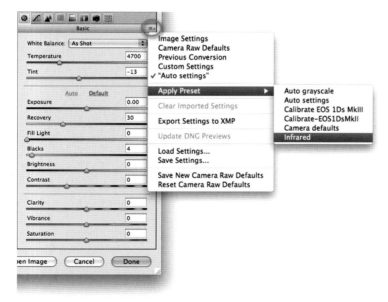

Figure 3.67 The Camera Raw menu options can be accessed via any of the main panels by clicking on the small icon circled here.

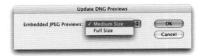

Figure 3.68 When 'Update DNG Previews' is selected you can update the JPEG previews in a DNG file, choosing either a Medium Size or Full Size preview.

Export settings to XMP

If you refer to the Camera Raw preferences shown in Figure 3.19 on page 158, there is an option to 'Save image settings' in sidecar ".xmp" files, or to the 'Camera Raw database'. In the case of most file formats (including DNG), when the 'Sidecar ".xmp" files' option is selected, the image settings information is automatically written to the XMP space in the file header. However, in the case of proprietary raw files, it would be unsafe for Camera Raw to edit an unknown file format, so the information is stored using XMP sidecar files which accompany the image whenever you use Bridge (or Lightroom) to move the raw files from one location to another. If 'Save image settings in Camera Raw database' is selected you can use the Export Settings to XMP option to manually export the XMP data with selected images. Of course, if the 'Save image settings in sidecar ".xmp" files' option is selected, Camera Raw will export the XMP data anyway and the Export Settings to XMP command becomes identical to clicking the Done button (which confirms saving the XMP settings data to the file's XMP space). However, if you are editing a filmstrip selection of images and want to save the XMP data for some images, but not all, you can use the Export Settings to XMP command to do this.

Update DNG previews

DNG files can store a JPEG preview of how a processed image will look based on the last saved Camera Raw settings. If you refer again to the Camera Raw preferences (Figure 3.19), there is an option to 'Update embedded JPEG previews'. When this is checked, DNG JPEG previews are automatically updated. But if this option is disabled in the Camera Raw preferences, you can manually update the JPEG previews by selecting 'Update DNG Previews' from the Camera Raw menu (Figure 3.68).

Load/Save Settings

These menu options allow you to load and save pre-created XMP settings. Overall, I find it preferable to click on the

New Preset button in the Preset panel (discussed on this page) when saving a new Camera Raw preset.

Camera Raw defaults

The 'Save New Camera Raw Defaults' option will create a new default setting based on the current selected image. But note that these defaults will be affected by the 'Default Image Settings' selected in the Camera Raw preferences (see 'Camera-specific default settings' on pages 159–160).

Presets panel

In the Presets panel, you can click on the New Preset button (circled in Figure 3.69) to save the current Camera Raw settings as a new custom preset using the dialog shown in Figure 3.70.

New Camera Raw defaults

The Save New Camera Raw Defaults option will make the current Camera Raw settings stick every time from now on when Camera Raw encounters a new file. This includes images processed by Bridge. So for example, if you were working in the studio and had achieved a perfect Camera Raw setting for the day's shoot, you could make this the new Camera Raw default setting and all subsequent imported images will use this setting by default. At the end of the day you can select Reset Camera Raw defaults to clear this behavior and restore the default Camera Raw settings.

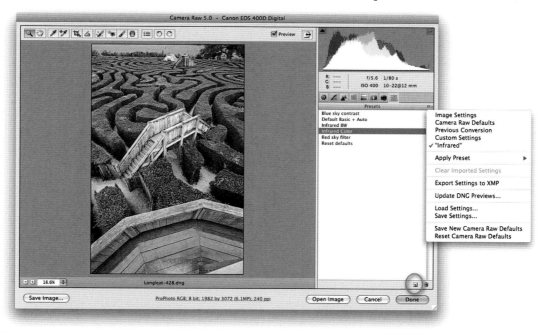

Figure 3.69 When the Presets panel is selected, you can click on the button at the bottom (circled) to add Camera Raw settings as a new preset. In this example I saved an Infrared Color preset using the New Preset settings shown in Figure 3.67. You can also use the Load/Save Settings menu options to load or save new presets.

Camera Raw preset wisdom

Before you save a Camera Raw preset, it is important to think carefully about which items you need to include in a preset. The trick when saving presets is to save just the bare minimum number of options. In other words, if you are saving a grayscale conversion preset, you should save the grayscale conversion option only. If you are saving a camera body and ISO-specific camera default, you might want to save just the Camera Calibration, Sharpening, Luminance Noise Reduction and Color Noise Reduction settings. The problem with saving too many attributes is that although the global settings may have worked great for one image, there is no knowing if they will work as effectively on all other images. It is therefore a good idea to break your presets down into smaller chunks.

Saving and applying presets

To save a preset, you can go to the Camera Raw fly-out menu and choose Save Settings... or you can click on the Add Preset button in the Presets panel to create a new Camera Raw preset. A preset can be one that is defined by all Camera Raw settings, or it can be one that is made up of a subset of settings (as shown in Figure 3.70). Either way, a saved preset will next appear listed in the Presets panel as well as in the Apply Preset menu (Figure 3.67). Just click on a setting to apply it to an image. To remove a preset setting, go to the Presets panel (Figure 3.69), select it and click the Trash button at the bottom.

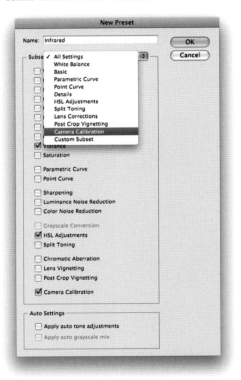

Figure 3.70 The New Preset dialog can be accessed by clicking on the New Preset button (circled in Figure 3.69). You can choose to save All Settings to record all the current Camera Raw settings as a preset. You can select a sub setting selection such as: Basic, or HSL Adjustments, or manually check the items that you want to include in the subset selection that will make up a saved Camera Raw preset.

Copying and synchronizing settings

If you have a multiple selection of photos in the Camera
Raw dialog, you can make a selection of images from
the filmstrip or click on the Select All button to select all
images, then any adjustments you make to the selected
photo will be simultaneously updated in all the other
pictures as well. Alternatively, if you make adjustments to
a single image then include other images in the filmstrip
selection and click on the Synchronize... button, this will
pop the Synchronize dialog shown in Figure 3.71. Select
the specific settings you wish to synchronize and click
OK. The Camera Raw settings will now synchronize to
the currently selected image. You can also copy and paste
the Camera Raw settings via Bridge. Select an image
and choose Edit ⇨ Apply Camera Raw Settings ⇨ Copy
(⌘ ⌥ C ctrl alt C). Select the image or images you
wish to paste the settings to and choose Edit ⇨ Apply
Camera Raw Settings ⇨ Paste (⌘ ⌥ V ctrl alt V).

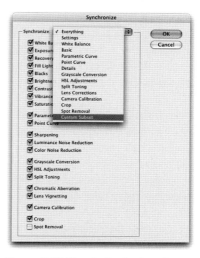

Figure 3.71 When the Synchronize options
dialog box appears you can select a preset range
of settings to synchronize or make your own
custom selection of settings to synchronize the
currently selected images.

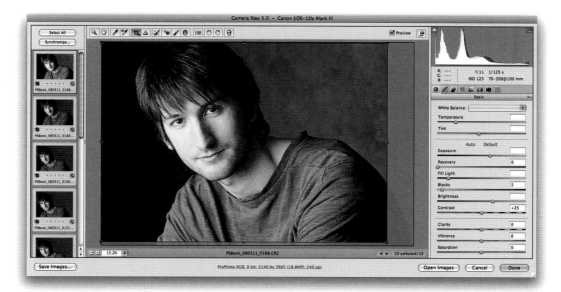

Figure 3.72 In this example I made a selection of images via the Filmstrip and
clicked on the Synchronize button, which opened the dialog shown in Figure 3.71.

Photograph: © Jeff Schewe 2008

Whose data is it anyway?

If photographers think it is a good thing for the industry to move towards a standardized raw file format, then the DNG format deserves to succeed. It will also encourage other software manufacturers to support DNG and give the camera user even more choice. The only sticking point appears to be those camera manufacturers who have adopted a protective stance about the raw file processing. One gets the impression that there is a certain amount of irritation within some camera companies whenever outsiders have managed to 'crack the code' and successfully reverse engineered their proprietary raw file formats. One manufacturer once went so far as to devise a method of encryption that would defeat any attempts to make the file format more widely accessible. Photographer and Photoshop expert Jeff Schewe raised an important point here: 'After I have taken a photograph and captured an image as a raw file, whose data is it? It's my damn data, and not anyone else's!' Which neatly brings us back to the whole raison d'être of the DNG file format, which is to make raw shooting more accessible for all. The opportunity is there for everyone to gain. Photographers have a file format that will enable them to archive their raw captures with confidence for the future. If the camera manufacturers support the new DNG format they will make their customers happy too. But the real choice will be down to the consumer. They will decide which camera choice to make and support for DNG should be regarded as an important decision when making future purchases of camera equipment.

DNG file format

In the slipstream of every new technology there follows the inevitable chaos of lots of different new standards competing for supremacy. Nowhere is this more evident that in the world of digital imaging. In the last 12 years or so, we have seen many hundreds of digital cameras come and go along with other computer technologies such as Syquest disks and SCSI cables, and in that time I have probably encountered well over a hundred different raw format specifications. It would not be so bad if each camera manufacturer had adopted a raw format specification that could be applied to all the cameras they produced. Instead we have seen raw formats evolve and change with each new model that has been released and those changes have not always been for the better.

The biggest problem is that with so many types of raw format being developed, how reliable will a raw format be for archiving your images? Ten years ago Adam Woolfitt and myself conducted a test report on a range of professional and semi-professional digital cameras. Wherever possible, we shot using raw mode. I still have the CD of master files and, if I want to access those images today, in some cases I am going to have to track down a computer running Mac OS 8.6 in order to load the camera manufacturer software required to read the data! If that is a problem now, what will the situation be like in 60 years' time?

It is the proprietary nature of all these formats that is the central issue here. At the moment, all the camera manufacturers appear to want to devise their own brand of raw format and therefore if you need to access the data from a raw file, you are forced to use *their* brand of software to do so. Now while the camera manufacturers are excellent at designing fantastic hardware, the raw processing software supplied by the manufacturers has mostly been quite basic. Just because a company builds excellent digital cameras, it does not follow that they are going to be good at designing the graphics software to read and process the raw data.

The DNG solution

Fortunately there are third-party companies who have devised ways of processing some of these raw formats. So you are not always limited to using the software that came with the camera. Adobe is the most obvious example here of a company who offers a superior alternative. At the time of writing, Camera Raw will recognize raw formats from over 175 different cameras. The DNG (digital negative) file format specification came about partly as a means of making Adobe's life easier for the future development of Camera Raw and making Adobe Photoshop compatible with as many cameras as possible. DNG is a well thought out file format that is designed to accommodate the many specification requirements of all today's cameras and is also flexible enough to adapt to future technologies. Because it is an open standard, the specification is freely available for anyone to develop and to incorporate into their software or camera system. It is therefore hoped that the camera manufacturers will continue to adopt the DNG file format more widely and that the DNG format will be offered as the main raw file format, or at least offered as an alternative choice on the camera. This brings several advantages. Where DNG has been adopted there is less risk of your raw image files becoming obsolete, as there will be ongoing support for the DNG standard despite whatever computer operating system or platform changes take place in the future. Whenever a new camera is released, the DNG format will allow the raw files to be immediately accessible, assuming the camera is enabled to provide DNG raw files.

DNG adoption

Over the last few years DNG has been adopted by many of the mainstream software programs such as iView (now Microsoft Expression), Capture One, Portfolio and Photo Mechanic. And at the time of writing, Hasselblad, Leica, Samsung and Ricoh cameras all support a DNG raw capture format option.

Support the petition!

If you agree that a common raw format standard would be beneficial to the photographic industry and would like to let the manufacturers know this, then you can register your feelings by going to www.rawformat.com and signing the DNG petition.

OpenRAW.org

You might also like to visit the www.openraw.org site where you can join the Open Raw discussion group and read the results of their raw survey.

Should you keep the original raws?

It all depends on whether you feel comfortable discarding the originals and keeping just the DNGs. Some proprietary software such as Canon DPP is able to recognize and process dust spots from the sensor using a proprietary method that relies on reading private XMP metadata information. If you delete the original CR2 files you won't be able to process the DNG versions in DPP unless you chose to embed the original raw file data, in which case you can extract the raw originals.

Maintaining ACR compatibility

If you refer back to page 128, you can read how it is possible to use the DNG Converter program to convert new camera files to DNG and thereby maintain Camera Raw support with older versions of Photoshop and Camera Raw.

DNG Converter

Adobe have made the DNG converter program (Figure 3.73) available for free and it can be downloaded from their website: www.adobe.co.uk/products/dng/main.html The DNG converter is able to convert raw files from any camera currently supported by Camera Raw for Photoshop into DNG files. The advantage of doing this is that you can start making backups of your raw files in a file format that will preserve all the data in your raw captures and archive them now in a format that has a greater likelihood of support in the future.

I personally feel quite comfortable converting my raw files to DNG and then deleting the original camera raw files, and I don't see the need to embed the original raw file data in the DNG file since this unnecessarily increases the file size. However, if you do feel it is essential to preserve complete compatibility, then embedding the original raw file data will allow you to extract the original native raw file from the DNG at some later date. The advantage of this is complete compatibility with the camera manufacturer software. The downside is that you will more than double the size of your DNG files.

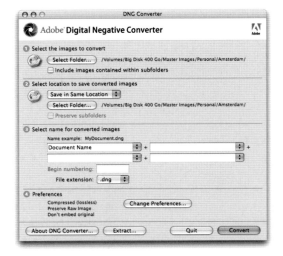

Figure 3.73 The DNG Converter program

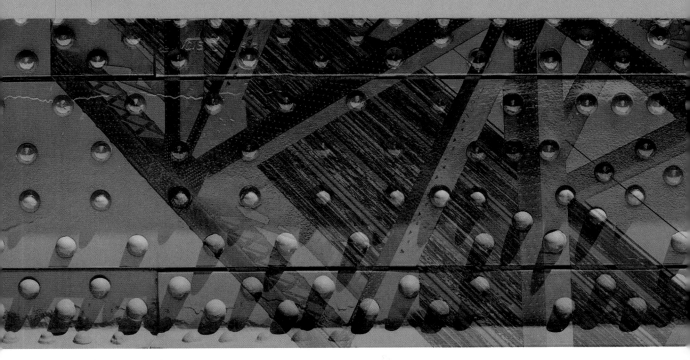

Chapter 4

Sharpening and Noise Reduction

This chapter is all about how to pre-sharpen your photographs in Photoshop and reduce different types of image noise. Here, I will be discussing which types of images need pre-sharpening, which don't and what are the best methods to use for camera captured or scanned image files.

In previous editions of this book I felt it necessary to go into a lot of detail about the Unsharp Mask filter and the sharpen refinement techniques that could be used to improve the smoothness of such sharpening. Now that capture sharpening is built into Camera Raw I feel that this is the best place to carry out the capture sharpening stage for both raw and scanned TIFF images. The first part of this chapter is therefore devoted entirely to Camera Raw sharpening.

Real World Image sharpening

If you want to learn more about image sharpening in Photoshop then I can recommend Bruce Fraser's book: *Real World image sharpening with Adobe Photoshop CS2* which is available from Peachpit Press. ISBN: 978-0321449917.

One-step sharpening

It may seem like a neat idea to use a single-step sharpening that will take care of the capture sharpening and print sharpening in a single step, but it's just not possible to arrive at a formula that will work for all source images and all output devices. There are simply too many variables that have to be taken into account. By splitting the sharpening into two stages: capture sharpening and output sharpening, this actually makes it a lot simpler to get the initial image sharpening right and then apply the right amount of output sharpening dependent on the type of print you are making and the size of the print output.

Print output sharpening

This chapter will focus just on the capture and creative sharpening techniques for raw and non-raw images. Print output sharpening is covered later in Chapter 13.

When to sharpen

All digital images will require sharpening at one or more stages in the digital capture and editing process. Even if you use the finest camera and lens, it is inevitable that some image sharpness will get lost along the way from capture through to print. At the capture end, image sharpness can be lost due to the quality of the optics and the image resolving ability of the camera sensor, which in turn can also be affected by the anti-aliasing filter that covers the sensor (and blurs the camera focused image very slightly). With scanned images you have a similar problem: the resolving power of the scanner sensor and the scanner lens optics can lead to scans that are slightly lacking in sharpness. These main factors can all lead to capture images that are less sharp than they should be.

When we come to make a print, all print processes will lose sharpness, so it is always necessary to add extra sharpening at the end, just before sending the photograph to the printer. Also, between the capture and print stages you may find that some photographs can do with a little localized sharpening to make certain areas of the picture appear that extra bit sharper. This briefly summarizes what we call a multi-pass sharpening workflow: capture sharpening followed by an optional creative sharpen, followed by a final sharpening for print.

Capture sharpening

The majority of this chapter focuses on the capture sharpening stage, which is also referred to as 'pre-sharpening'. It is critical that you get this part right because capture sharpening is one of the first things you do to an image before you start doing the retouching. The question then is, which images need sharpening and, of those that do need sharpening, how much sharpening should you apply?

Let's deal with JPEG capture images first. If you shoot using the JPEG mode your camera will have already sharpened the capture data, so no further pre-sharpening is necessary. I suppose you could argue that since some cameras allow you to disable the sharpening in JPEG mode you could do this separately in Camera Raw, but I think this runs counter to the very reason why some photographers prefer to shoot JPEG in the first place. They do so because they want their pictures to be fully processed and ready to proceed to the retouching stage. So if you are exclusively shooting in JPEG mode, capture sharpening isn't something you really need to worry about and you can skip to the section on localized sharpening techniques.

If you shoot in raw mode it won't matter what sharpen settings you have set on your camera; these will have no effect on the raw file, since it's an unprocessed image. Any capture sharpening must be done either in the raw processing program or afterwards in Photoshop. Up until recently most experts (myself included) were suggesting that you disable the sharpening in Camera Raw and use Photoshop to apply the capture sharpening. Well, all that changed with the Camera Raw 4.1 update. The new Camera Raw sharpening controls rewrote the rules completely and it now makes sense to carry out the capture sharpening at the raw processing stage before you open your images in Photoshop.

Capture sharpening for scanned images

Scanned images may have already been pre-sharpened by the scanning software, as some scanners do this automatically without you even realizing it. If you prefer to take control of the capture sharpening you can do so by disabling the scanner sharpening and using whatever other method you prefer. For example, you could use a third-party plug-in like PhotoKit Sharpener™, or follow the Unsharp Mask filter techniques I describe in the image sharpening PDF on the DVD. Providing you export your scanned images using the TIFF format, you can open a scanned image via Camera Raw and use the same raw image sharpening methods that are described here when working with scanned TIFFs.

So what about all those techniques that rely on Lab mode sharpening or luminosity fades? Well, if you analyze the way new Camera Raw works within Photoshop, these

Camera Raw JPEG settings

If you are opening a JPEG or TIFF image via Camera Raw it is usually safe to assume that the image has already been pre-sharpened and it is for this reason that the default sharpening for non-raw files is set at 0%. You should only apply sharpening to JPEGs or TIFF images if you know for sure that the image has not already been sharpened.

PhotoKit™ Sharpener

Bruce Fraser devised the PhotoKit Sharpener plug-in from Pixel Genius, which can be used to apply capture, creative and output sharpening via Photoshop. The work Bruce did on Photokit capture sharpening inspired the improvements made to the Sharpening controls in Camera Raw. It can therefore be argued that if you use Camera Raw you won't need to use the capture sharpening in Photokit Sharpener. Also, if you are using Lightroom 2 you will find the Photokit Sharpener print sharpening routines have now been included in the Lightroom 2 Print module. However, if you have Photoshop CS4 and Lightroom 2, Photokit Sharpener can still be useful for the creative sharpening and halftone sharpening routines it offers.

How to use the Unsharp Mask filter

The main book no longer covers the manual pre-sharpening techniques that use the Unsharp Mask filter. But you will find a 20-page PDF document on the DVD that fully describes the Unsharp Mask filter sliders and outlines some of the advanced ways you can use the Unsharp Mask filter to achieve better capture sharpening results.

sharpening controls have almost completely replaced the need for the Unsharp Mask filter. In fact, I would say that the Unsharp mask filter has, for some time now, been a fairly blunt instrument for sharpening images, plus I don't think it is advisable to convert from RGB to Lab mode and back again if you don't really need to. Compare the old ways of sharpening (including those I described in my previous books) with the Camera Raw method and I think you'll find that this is now the most effective, if not the only way, to capture sharpen your photographs.

Sample sharpening image

To help explain how the Camera Raw sharpening tools work, I have prepared a sample test image that you can access from the DVD. The Figure 4.1 image has been especially designed to highlight the way the various slider controls work when viewed at 100%. Although this is a TIFF image, it's one where the image has been left unsharpened and the lessons you learn here can equally be applied when sharpening raw photos.

Figure 4.1 The sample image used on the following pages can be accessed on the DVD. To open this photo via Camera Raw use Bridge to locate the test image and use File ⇨ Open in Camera Raw, or use the ⌘ R ctrl R keyboard shortcut.

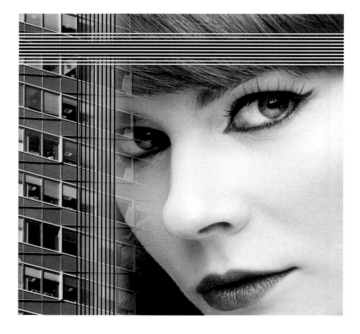

Detail panel

To sharpen an image, start off by going to Bridge, select the photo you want to process and choose File ⇨ Open in Camera Raw or use the ⌘ R ctrl R keyboard shortcut. The Sharpening controls are all located in the Detail panel in the Camera Raw dialog (Figure 4.2) and these consist of four slider controls: Amount, Radius, Detail and Masking. The Noise Reduction sliders can be used to remove image noise and we'll come onto these later, but for now I just want to guide you through what the sharpening sliders do.

The sharpening effect sliders

Let's start by looking at the sharpening effect controls: Amount and Radius. These two sliders control how much sharpening is applied and how the sharpening gets distributed.

If you want to follow the steps shown over the next few pages, I suggest you make a copy the Figure 4.1 image from the DVD, use Bridge to open it via the Camera Raw dialog, and then go to the Detail panel section (Figure 4.2). If you are viewing a photo at a fit to view preview size you will see a warning message that says: 'Zoom preview to 100% or larger to see the effects of the controls in this panel', which means you should follow the advice given here and set the image view magnification in the Camera Raw dialog to 1:1 or higher. The test image I created is actually quite small and will probably display at 100% or higher anyway. But the main thing to remember is that when you are sharpening normal images, the preview display must always be set to a 100% view or higher before you can judge the sharpening accurately. In addition to this I should also point out that the screen shots over the next few pages were all captured as grayscale sharpening previews, where I held down the ⌥ alt key as I dragged the sliders. Once again, you will only get to see these grayscale previews if you are viewing the image at a 100% view or higher.

When you open a raw image via Camera Raw, you will see the default settings shown in Figure 4.2. But as I mentioned on the previous page, if you open a non-raw image up via Camera Raw, such as a JPEG or TIFF, the Amount setting defaults to 0%.

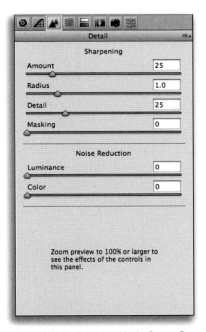

Figure 4.2 The Detail panel in the Camera Raw dialog.

235

Amount slider

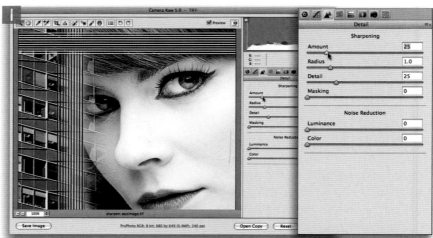

Displaying the grayscale preview

As was mentioned in the main text, you access the grayscale previews by holding down the ⌥ alt key as you drag the sliders.

1 The Amount slider is like a volume control. As you increase the Amount, the overall sharpening is increased. A default setting of 25% is applied to all raw or raw DNG images but, if you open a TIFF or JPEG image, Camera Raw assumes the image has already been pre-sharpened and applies a 0% Amount setting. So if you are editing the image that came on the DVD you will need to set this to 25% to simulate the default setting shown here.

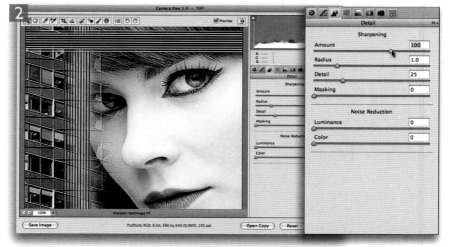

2 As you increase the Amount setting to 100% you will notice how the image gets sharper. 100% is plenty strong enough but you can take the Amount even higher. Camera Raw allows this extra headroom because it can sometimes be necessary when you start dampening the sharpening effect with the Detail and Masking sliders.

Radius slider

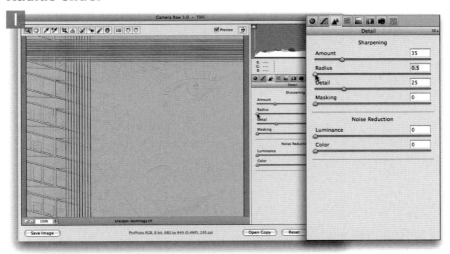

1 The Radius slider is identical to the one found in the Unsharp Mask filter. The Radius determines the width of the halos generated around the edges in the photo. A small radius setting can be used to pick out fine detail in a picture, but will have a minimal effect on the soft, wider edges in a picture.

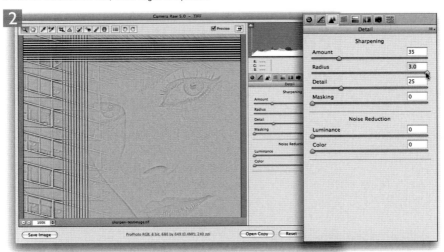

2 A high radius setting will overemphasize the fine edges, but do more to enhance the soft edges such as the facial features in a portrait. I have shown here the two extremes that can be used, but for most sharpening adjustments you will want to stick close to a 1.0 Radius and make small adjustments around this setting.

Detail slider settings

Where I describe the Detail panel as acting like a suppression control it is important to understand that when Detail is set to 100 this matches the old Camera Raw sharpening, where no additional edge halo suppression was employed, and any setting that is less than 100 effectively suppresses the Camera Raw sharpening. Therefore a low Detail setting has a maximum effect and a high Detail setting has a minimum effect.

The suppression controls

The Amount and Radius sliders are used to create the sharpening effect, while the next two sliders are what I refer to as the 'suppression' controls; these are used to constrain the sharpening and target the sharpening effect where it is most needed.

Detail slider

The Detail slider suppresses the halo effects in a picture. It allows you to increase the Amount sharpening but without generating noticeable halo edges in the picture. There has always been a certain amount of halo suppression built into the Camera Raw Sharpening, but you can now use the Detail slider to fine-tune the Amount and Radius effects by setting Detail to a low value. The following screen shots were again captured with the ⌥ *alt* key held down as I dragged the Detail slider. Note that these previews show an isolated preview of the sharpening effect (see 'Interpreting the grayscale previews' on page 240).

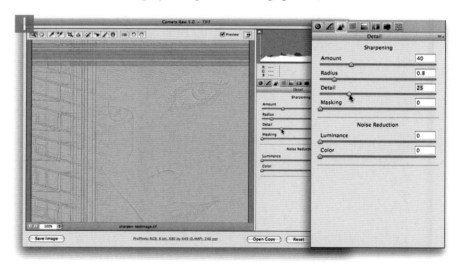

1 In this first example the Detail slider is at its default setting of 25, and captured here with the ⌥ *alt* key held down. This displays an isolated grayscale preview of the sharpening effect. At this setting the Detail slider is gently suppressing the halo effects to produce a strong image sharpening effect but without over-emphasizing the fine detail or noisy areas of the picture.

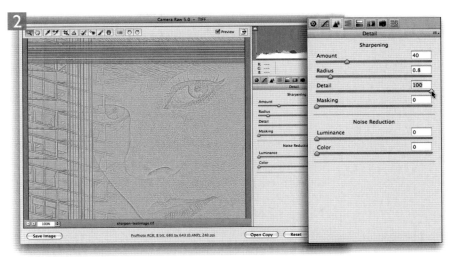

2 If you take the Detail slider all the way to 100, the capture sharpening will be almost identical to a standard Unsharp Mask filter effect applied in Photoshop at a zero Threshold setting.

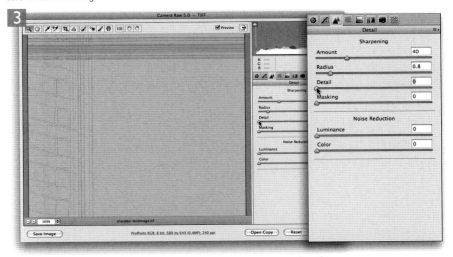

3 If on the other hand you take the Detail slider down to zero, you can see how the picture looks with maximum halo suppression. What we learn from this is how to set the Detail slider between these two extremes. For portraits and other subjects that have soft edges I would recommend a lowish Detail setting of around 20–30 so that you prevent the flat tone areas from becoming too noisy, and for images that have lots of fine detail I would mostly suggest using a higher value of 30–50, because you don't want to suppress the halo edges quite so much. With these types of photos you will probably want to add more emphasis to the fine edges.

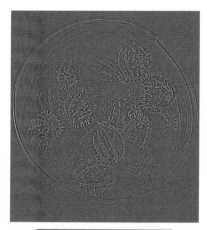

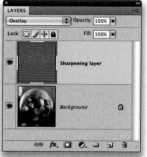

Figure 4.3 This is a Photoshop simulation of what the grayscale Radius and Detail previews in Camera Raw are showing you. Imagine the sharpening effect being carried out on a separate layer above the background layer with the blend mode set to 'Overlay'. A 50% gray would have no effect on the layer below. A gray darker than this would darken the layer below and a lighter gray than 50% would lighten. If you analyze the grayscale preview in this context you will understand better that the low contrast preview image represents an isolated preview of the sharpening effect.

Interpreting the grayscale previews

In all the screen shots you have seen so far, I captured these with the ⌥ *alt* key held down as I dragged on the sliders. In the case of the Amount and Radius adjustments, holding down the ⌥ *alt* key will allow you to preview the effect these two adjustments have on the full color image by displaying a grayscale image which shows the sharpening effect as if applied to the luminance information only.

One of the things that has been well known about the conventional Photoshop Unsharp Masking method is that a 'normal mode' Unsharp Mask filter effect will sharpen all the color channels equally. In the past, people have strived to sharpen the image luminance, without sharpening the color information. This is what the 'convert to Lab mode, sharpen the Lightness channel, convert back to RGB mode' technique is doing. The same thing applies when using an Edit ⇨ Fade Unsharp Mask ⇨ Luminosity mode fade. However, with Camera Raw, the sharpening is always applied to the luminance of the image, so you won't see any color artifacts generated when you apply a sharpening effect. This explains the purpose of the grayscale preview for the Amount slider, which is to show you exactly how the sharpening is applied to the luminance of the photo – hiding the color information so that you can judge the sharpening effect more easily.

Radius and Detail grayscale preview

With the Radius and Detail sliders you are seeing a slightly different kind of preview when you hold down the ⌥ *alt* key as you adjust these sliders. The grayscale preview you see here displays the sharpening effect in isolation as if it were an effect applied via a separate layer. For those who know Photoshop well, imagine a layer in Photoshop that is filled with 50% gray and where the blend mode is set to 'Overlay'. This layer would have no effect on the layers below until you start darkening or lightening parts of the layer. In Figure 4.3 you can see a mock up of what the Detail grayscale preview is actually showing you. It displays the sharpening effect in isolation.

Masking slider

If you take the Masking slider all the way to zero, no mask
is generated and the sharpening effect is applied without
any masking. As you increase the Masking, more areas
are protected. The mask is generated based on the image
content, so that areas of the picture where there are high
contrast edges will remain white (the sharpening effect is
unmasked) and the flatter areas of the picture where there is
smoother tone detail will turn black (the sharpening effect
is masked). I like to think of this effect as being like a layer
mask that's masking the layer applying the sharpening
effect (see Figure 4.4). The calculations required to
generate the mask are quite intensive, so if you are using
an older computer it may seem slow as the preview takes
its time to process, but on a modern fast computer you will
hardly notice any time delays.

The Masking slider was inspired by a Photoshop
edge masking technique that was originally devised by
Bruce Fraser. You can read all about Bruce's Photoshop
techniques for Input and Output sharpening in his book
*Real World image sharpening with Adobe Photoshop
CS2*, which includes instructions for applying the edge
masking technique. As I said earlier, the way this and other
improved sharpening methods have been incorporated into
Camera Raw now mean that the Detail panel slider controls
provide a better capture sharpening workflow solution.
For example, the original edge masking technique offered
a method for producing a fixed width mask. While you
could vary some of the settings to refine the look of the
final mask, it was rather tricky and cumbersome to do so.
With Camera Raw it is now much easier to vary the mask
because you have a single slider control to do this.

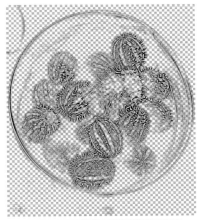

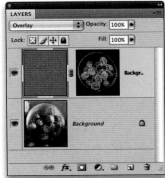

Figure 4.4 Here is another simulation of
what the Camera Raw Masking slider grayscale
preview is showing you. As you hold down the
⌥ *alt* key and drag the Masking slider you
are effectively previewing a layer mask that is
masking the sharpening layer effect.

Masking slider example

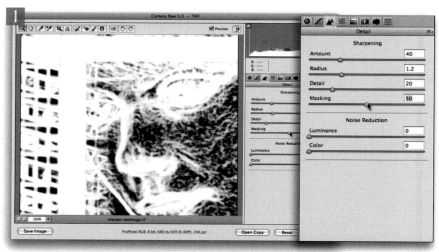

1 When the Masking slider is at the default zero setting, no masking is applied to the sharpening effect. If you hold down the ⌥ *alt* key as you drag the Masking slider, you can see a grayscale preview of the mask that is being generated. At the 50% setting shown here, the mask is just starting to protect the areas of flat tone from being sharpened.

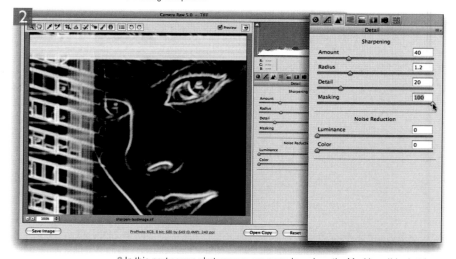

2 In this next screen shot you can see a preview where the Masking slider is taken to the maximum 100% setting. In this example the masking is a lot stronger and protects all the flat tone areas, leaving only the strongest edges unmasked. The sharpening effect is now only applied to the white areas.

Some real world sharpening examples

Now that I have given you a run down on what the individual sharpening sliders do, let's look at how you would use them in practice to sharpen an image.

Sharpening a portrait

Figure 4.5 shows a 1:1 close-up view of a male portrait where I used the following settings: *Amount:35, Radius: 1.2, Detail: 20, Masking: 70.* This combination of Sharpening slider settings is most appropriate for use with male or female portraits, or any photo where you wish to sharpen the important areas of detail such as the eyes and lips, but protect the smooth areas (like the skin) from being sharpened.

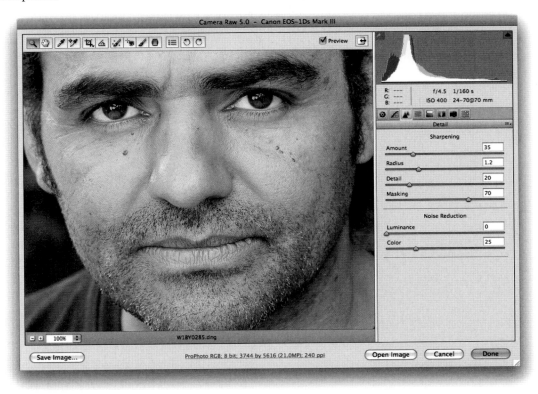

Figure 4.5 An example of the sharpening settings used to pre-sharpen a portrait.

Sharpening a landscape

Figure 4.6 shows the settings that would be used to sharpen a landscape image. The settings used here were: *Amount: 40, Radius: 0.8, Detail: 50, Masking: 0.* This combination of Sharpening slider settings is most appropriate for subjects such as the seascape scene shown in this photograph. You could include quite a wide range of subject types in this category and basically you would use this particular combination of slider settings whenever you needed to sharpen photographs that contained a lot of narrow edge detail.

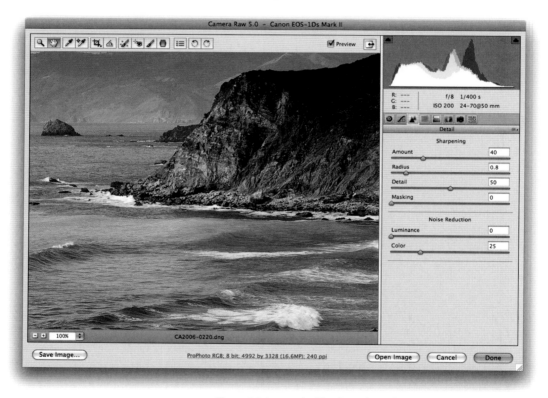

Figure 4.6 An example of the sharpening settings used to pre-sharpen a landscape.

Sharpening a fine-detailed subject

Figure 4.7 shows an example of a photograph that contains a lot of fine-edge detail, where the Sharpening sliders in the Detail panel needed be taken to extremes. In order to sharpen the fine edges in this picture I had to take the Radius down to a setting of 0.5 or 0.6. I also wanted to emphasize the detail and therefore ended up setting the Detail slider to +80. This is a lot higher than one would want to use normally, but I have included this here to show an example of a photograph that required a unique treatment. As with the previous example, I didn't need to add any masking because there were no areas in the photograph where I needed to hide the sharpening.

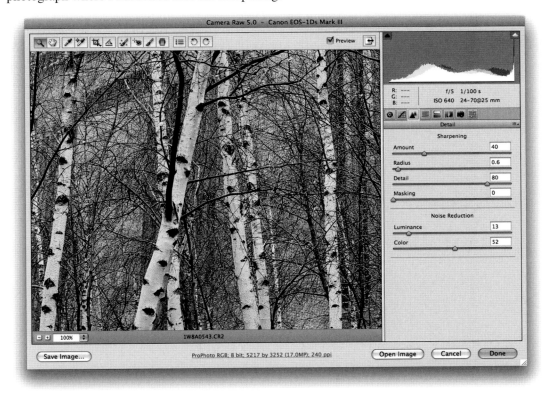

Figure 4.7 An example of the sharpening settings used to pre-sharpen a fine-detailed subject.

Default sharpening settings

The standard default sharpening setting for raw images uses the settings shown earlier in Figure 4.2. This isn't a bad starting point but, based on what you have learned in the last few examples, you might like to modify this and set a new default. For example, if most of the work you shoot is portraiture, you might like to use the settings shown in Figure 4.5 and set these as a default making this specific to your camera (see pages 159–160).

How to save sharpening settings as presets

You can save the sharpening settings as ACR presets and load them as required, depending on what type of photograph you are editing. You could try using the settings in Figure 4.5 and 4.6 as a starting point and stick reasonably close to the settings suggested here.

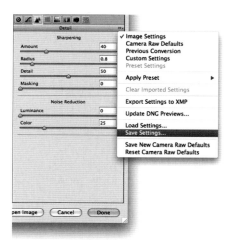

1 After configuring the Detail panel settings, go to the fly-out menu and choose 'Save Settings...'.

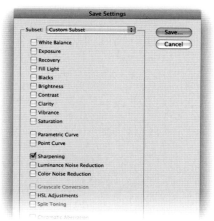

2 This will open the Save Settings dialog shown here. Check the Sharpening box only and click the Save... button.

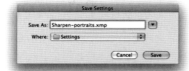

3 Now name the setting and leave the Save location as is. Don't try to change the location you are saving the setting to, as it should be saved to the folder shown here (Settings).

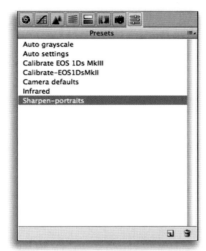

4 When you need to access the saved setting, go to the Settings panel in the Camera Raw dialog and click on a saved setting to apply it to an image. Since the setting here has been saved with the Sharpening adjustments only, when you select this preset it will only adjust the sharpening sliders when you apply it to another image.

Capture sharpening roundup

Hopefully this section will give you the confidence to now carry out all your capture sharpening in Camera Raw. Remember, the only images that should need presharpening are normally camera shot raws or scanned TIFFs, although you can process any image in Camera Raw providing it is in a JPEG, TIFF, raw or DNG format and in an RGB or Lab mode color space. Camera Raw processed images can then be saved as RGB mode, 8-bit or 16-bit files using the sRGB, Adobe RGB, Colormatch RGB or ProPhoto RGB color space.

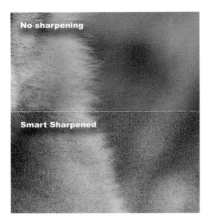

Figure 4.8 Take care when using the Smart Sharpen filter. Applying an excessive amount of Smart Sharpen can lead to ugly artifacts like those seen in the bottom half of this screen grab.

Smart Filter layers

In the example on the page opposite I went to the Filter menu and chose 'Convert for Smart Filters', which converted the Background layer to a Smart Object layer. I was then able to apply the Smart Sharpen filter as a 'smart filter'. The advantage of doing this was that it allowed me to edit the coverage of the filter by painting on the layer mask. An alternative option would be to duplicate the Background layer and apply the Smart Sharpen filter to that layer, but the advantage of using a smart filter layer is that the Smart Sharpen filter settings remain editable. You simply double-click the Smart Sharpen layer to reopen the Filter dialog shown in Step 1. For more about Smart Filters, please refer to Chapter 9.

Selective sharpening

As was explained in the previous section, you use the Camera Raw Sharpening controls to tailor the capture sharpening adjustment to suit the image content. Soft-edged subjects such as portraits will suit a higher than 1.0 Radius, low Detail and high Masking, while fine detailed subjects such as the Figure 4.6 example will suit a small Radius, high Detail and low Masking approach. The aim is always to apply enough sharpening to make the subject look visually sharp on the screen, but without over-sharpening to the point where you see edge artifacts or halos in the picture. If you overdo the capture sharpening you are storing up trouble for later when you come to retouch the photograph. This next section is about how to apply localized sharpening where it is needed most.

Smart Sharpen filter

One way to apply localized sharpening is to use the Smart Sharpen filter. Don't be too taken in by the fact that it's called a 'Smart' Sharpen filter. Some people figure this is a kind of 'Super Unsharp Mask' filter and therefore a better tool to use for general sharpening. If used correctly, it can compensate for areas where there is a distinct lack of sharpness, but if used badly it can soon introduce ugly artifacts (see Figure 4.8). The Smart Sharpen filter also runs very slowly compared to the Unsharp Mask filter and Camera Raw sharpening. Therefore, I generally consider Smart Sharpen to be more useful as a tool for 'corrective' rather than general sharpening.

Basic Smart Sharpen mode

The Smart Sharpen filter has three blur removal modes. Gaussian Blur is more or less the same as the Unsharp Mask filter, but the Lens Blur method is the most useful as it enables you to counteract optical lens blurring. Lastly, there is Motion Blur removal, which can sometimes be effective at removing small amounts of Motion Blur from an image. After you have selected a blur removal method, you can use the Amount and Radius slider controls to adjust the sharpening effect.

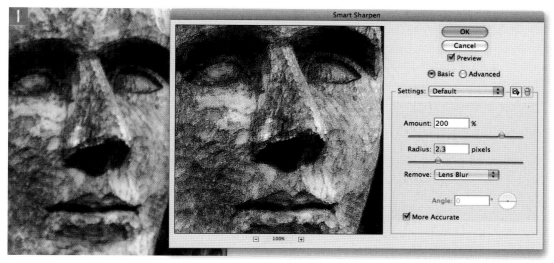

1 This shows a close-up view of a photograph where the main subject was slightly out of focus. I didn't want to apply any further global sharpening as this would have created artifacts in the background, so I converted the Background image layer to a Smart Object and applied the Smart Sharpen filter using the settings shown here.

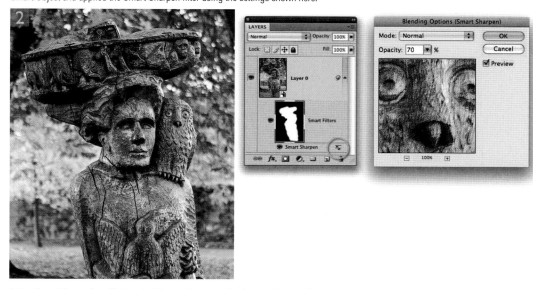

2 The Smart Sharpening effect worked fine on the statue, but increased the artifacts in the background (see Figure 4.8), so I clicked on the Smart Object mask layer, filled with black and painted on this layer with white so that the smart filtering was revealed on the statue only. I then double-clicked the Smart Object layer options (circled) to open the Blending Options dialog and reduced the filter opacity to 70%.

Saving the Smart Sharpen settings

You can save Smart Sharpen settings as you work by clicking on the save settings icon circled below in Figure 4.9 and calling these up via the Settings menu in the Smart Sharpen filter dialog.

Advanced Smart Sharpen mode

In Advanced mode you will get to see two additional tabbed sections marked Shadow and Highlight. The controls in these sections act like a dampener on the main smart sharpening effect. The Fade Amount slider selectively reduces the amount of sharpening in either the shadow or highlight areas. This is the main control to play with as it will have the most initial impact in reducing the amount of artifacting that may occur in the shadow or highlight areas. Below that is the Tonal Width slider which operates in the same way as the one in the Shadow/Highlight image adjustment: you use this to determine the tonal range width that the fade is applied to. These two main sliders allow you to subtly control the smart sharpening effect. The Radius also works in a similar way to the Radius slider in the Shadow/Highlight adjustment and is used to control the area width of the smart sharpening.

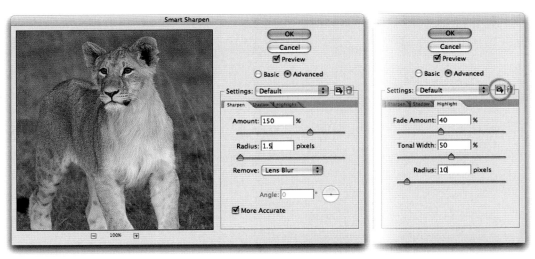

Figure 4.9 In this photograph I set the Smart Sharpen filter to Advanced mode and applied an Amount of 150% at a Radius of 1.5 using the Lens Blur mode with the More Accurate box checked. Once I had chosen suitable settings for the main Smart Sharpen, I clicked on the Shadow and Highlight tabs and used the settings in these sections to decide how to limit the main sharpening effect. A high Fade Amount setting will fade the sharpening more, while the Tonal Width determines the range of tones that are to be faded. And lastly, there is the Radius slider where you can enter a Radius value to determine the scale size for the corrections.

Removing Motion Blur

The Motion Blur mode can be used to correct for mild camera shake or small amounts of subject movement in a photograph. When Remove Motion Blur is selected, the trick here is to get the angle in the dialog to match the angle of the Motion Blur in the picture and adjust the Radius and Amount settings to optimize the Motion Blur correction. If you want to achieve optimum results with any of these sharpening modes, then do check the 'More Accurate' option below. This will increase the time it takes the filter to process the image, but if you want to get the very best results I suggest you leave it checked.

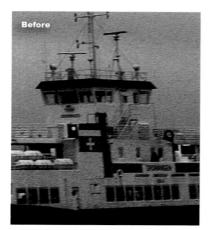

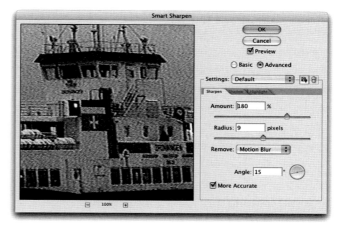

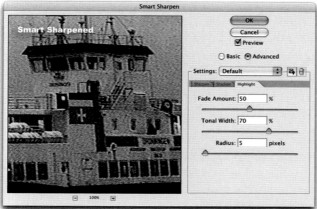

Figure 4.10 The Motion Blur method of smart sharpening is reasonably good at improving sharpness where there is just a slight amount of camera shake or subject movement. In this example I initially set the Amount, Radius and Angle to achieve the most effective sharpening, and in Advanced mode went to the Highlight tab to adjust the Fade Amount and Tonal Width settings so as to dampen the sharpening effect in the highlights. This helped achieve a slightly smoother-looking result.

No to Smart Filter layers

On page 248 I described why it was advantageous to use Smart Filter layers when applying a localized filter effect, mainly because with a Smart Object layer you can go back and revise the filter settings. But you won't be able to apply the technique described here using Smart Object layers, because there are no options to set the layer blending (as shown in Step 2). There is also no way to get the two filter effects applied in Step 3 to merge as one when setting the blend mode to 'Overlay'. Basically, Smart Filter layers might be a great idea, but they are still quite limited in their application to tasks such as this.

Adjusting the Depth of field settings

The Unsharp Mask and High Pass filter settings used here were designed to add sharpness to areas that contained a lot of narrow edge detail (such as the edges in a landscape). You will want to vary these settings when treating other types of photographs where you perhaps have wider edges that need sharpening. For example, Bruce's original formula suggests using a Radius of 4 pixels in the Unsharp Mask filter combined with a 40 pixel Radius High Pass filter.

Creating a depth of field brush

On page 248 I showed how you could use the Smart Sharpen filter to remove some of the blurriness from an image and selectively apply the filter effect through a layer mask. There is also another way you can reduce blur in a photograph and this technique is closely based on a technique described by Bruce Fraser in his book *Real World image sharpening with Photoshop CS2*. The only thing I have done here is to change some of the settings used, in order to produce a narrower edge sharpening brush. Basically, you can adapt these settings to produce sharpness layers that suit different types of focus correction.

Of course, you can't really make out-of-focus elements in a picture come back into focus, but you can make the blurred image detail appear to look sharper by adding a blended mixture of sharp and soft halos which create an illusion of apparent sharpness. The following technique requires you to first create a duplicate of the Background layer and adjust the Layer Style options, so that the filter effects you are about to apply are limited to affecting the midtone areas only and the extreme shadows and highlights are protected. Changing the blend mode to 'Overlay' will initially make the image appear more contrasty but, after you have applied the Unsharp Mask and High Pass filters, this increase in contrast will be limited to the soft edge areas only, which is the main feature of this technique.

In Step 3 you will notice I apply the Unsharp Mask filter at a maximum strength of 500%, with a Radius of 1.0 pixel and the Threshold set to zero. The purpose of this step is to aggressively build sharp, narrow halos around all the edge detail areas, and in particular the soft edges, while the High Pass filter step is designed to add wider, overlapping, soft edged halos that increase the midtone contrast. When these two filters are combined you end up with a layer that improves the apparent sharpness in the areas that were out of focus, but the downside is that the previously sharp areas become degraded. By adding a layer mask filled with black, you can use the brush tool to 'paint in' the adjustment to just those areas where it is needed most.

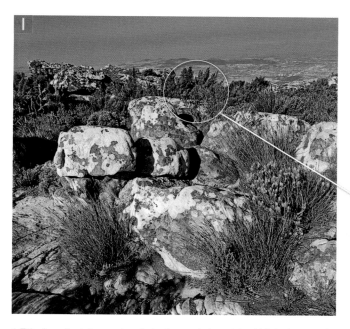

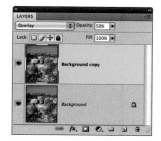

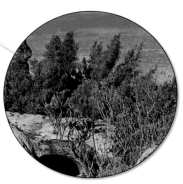

1 This shows the before version of a landscape photograph in which the foreground was perfectly sharp, but there was a fall-off in focus towards the middle distance. In this first step, I simply made a duplicate of the Background layer.

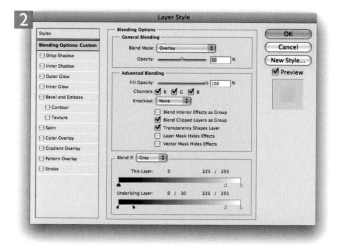

2 I then double-clicked the Background layer to open the Layer Style options and adjusted the settings as follows. The blend mode was set to 'Overlay' and the layer Opacity reduced to 50%. The layer 'Blend If' sliders were adjusted as shown above to provide more protection for the extreme shadows and highlights.

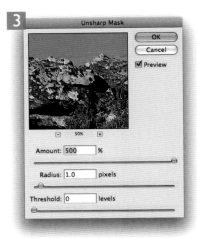

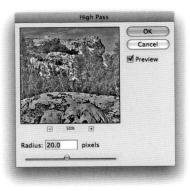

3 I clicked OK to the Layer Style changes and applied an Unsharp Mask filter to the Background copy layer, using an amount of 500% and a Radius of 1.0 pixel. This was followed by a High Pass filter (Filter ➩ Other ➩ High Pass), with a Radius of 20 pixels.

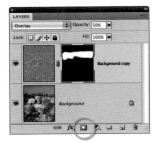

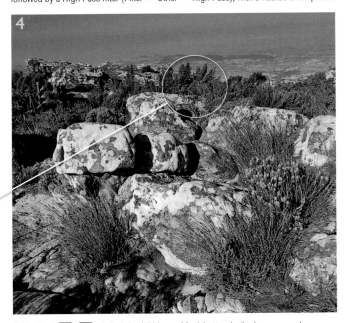

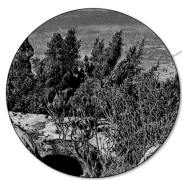

4 Finally, I ⌥ alt clicked the Add Layer Mask button in the Layers panel (circled). This added a layer mask filled with black, which hid the layer contents. I was then able to select a normal brush and paint on the layer mask with white to reveal the depth of field sharpening layer and thereby add more apparent sharpness to the middle distance.

Removing noise

All images are likely to suffer from some degree of noise, but the amount of noise present will vary according to a number of factors. The noise we see in scans made from film originals will mainly be down to the actual film grain in the film emulsion (especially if the image originated from a 35mm film emulsion), whether it came from a color negative or chrome original, and what particular film emulsion was used. It can also be due to noise generated by the scanning process itself.

With digital photographs the noise will vary depending on the quality of the camera sensor and what ISO setting the photograph was shot at. Some sensors definitely perform better than others when used at higher ISO speeds and with the most recent digital SLR cameras we have seen a remarkable improvement in high ISO image capture quality. Another factor is exposure. Earlier, in Chapter 3, I showed on page 174 how deliberately underexposing a digital photograph can lead to problems with shadow noise as you try to adjust the overall brightness. In fact, it is always the shadow areas that are going to be the problem, and you should always check the shadows first to determine how successful your camera (or scanner) is as at handling image noise.

Photoshop offers several strategies for reducing noise. If you process your images via Camera Raw, you can use the Luminance and Color Noise Reduction sliders, while in Photoshop itself there is the Reduce Noise filter. The tools available in Camera Raw and Photoshop work well enough for the majority of images where there isn't a huge amount of noise to conquer. Whenever you are required to apply major noise reduction, this inevitably leads to some softening of the image detail, unless you incorporate counter steps to preserve the all-important edges in the picture. Let's look at the two main noise reduction techniques that are available in Photoshop, starting with a noise removal method for scanned images where film grain is the problem.

Third-party noise reduction

If you are dissatisfied with the noise reduction in Camera Raw and Photoshop, there are third-party noise reduction programs you can buy such as Noise Ninja™ from Picturecode or Noiseware™ from Imagenomic. These are just two of the more popular products favored by photographers. Noise Ninja is highly regarded by many photographers, but I am personally more familiar with Noiseware and have been very impressed by the way it is capable of removing noise from even the most tricky subjects, particularly grainy film scans.

Reducing film grain noise

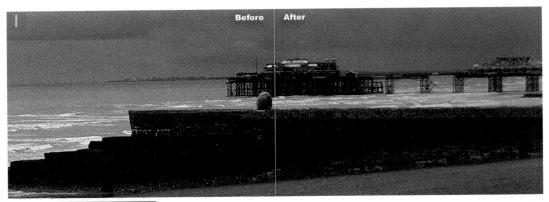

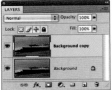

1 This shows a close-up detail of a 35mm film scan, with a before and after version of the image. The left half shows the unsharpened image before noise reduction was applied and the right half shows the image after noise reduction. Rather than run the noise reduction on the original image, it is best to make a copy of the Background layer first and then run the noise reduction steps on this layer only.

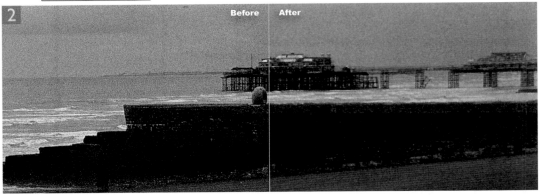

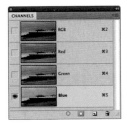

2 Here is how the noise reduction was done. The technique involved selecting each of the RGB color channels and applying multiple passes of the Despeckle filter, which is located in the Filter ⇨ Noise submenu. In this example, I applied two passes of Despeckle to the Red and the Green channel, and four passes to the Blue channel (because the Blue channel is usually the noisiest). Although the noise reduction softens the photo, you can now flatten the image and proceed to sharpen the picture using the sharpening techniques described earlier, but without further enhancing the noise in the original scan. Remember, because the noise reduction is applied to a copy layer you have the ability to fade the opacity of the layer or mask the layer contents to restore more of the original version of the image.

Noise removal in Camera Raw

Whenever you shoot using a high ISO setting on the camera, you will almost certainly encounter noise and the Noise Reduction sliders in the Camera Raw Detail panel can help improve the appearance of images that suffer from such noise artifacts. The Luminance slider can be used to smooth out the physical lumpiness of the noise artifacts while the Color Noise slider can get rid of the colored speckles. Noise will vary a lot from camera to camera so it is hard to give out any specific settings advice, but Figure 4.11 shows the settings that were used on a fairly noisy capture which was shot using the camera's maximum ISO setting. For the most part you can safely set the Color Noise Reduction to maximum, unless the photograph you are editing contains a lot of blue color detail such as an underwater photograph. The problem here is that too much color noise reduction can significantly soften the blue edge detail in a photograph.

Better Camera Raw noise reduction

The noise reduction underwent some changes in Camera Raw 4.1. The demosaicing algorithm was improved and an algorithm added to analyze the image for extreme high frequency noise and calculate how to remove this without degrading the high frequency image texture. As a result of this, Camera Raw noise reduction is now better at removing the outlying pixels – those additional random light or dark pixels that are generated when an image is captured at a high ISO setting.

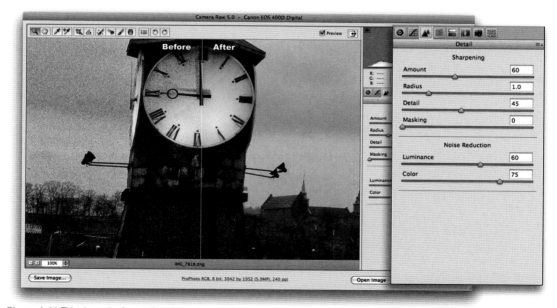

Figure 4.11 This shows the Camera Raw Detail panel controls for noise reduction. The preview is shown here divided in two. The left half shows the before image and the right half shows the preview with the Luminance Smoothing and Color Noise Reduction applied.

Reduce Noise filter

The other alternative to noise reduction in Camera Raw is to use the Reduce Noise filter, which is found in the Filter ⇨ Noise menu in Photoshop. This filter uses a method of smart noise reduction that can remove noise from an image, but without destroying the edge detail in the picture. Overall, the Reduce Noise filter is a useful one shot filter that is better at reducing the noise in images that originated as digital captures, rather than reducing film grain noise from scanned 35mm images. This filter is mainly designed to target the twin problems of digital luminance noise, which is like a very fine speckly grain, and color noise,

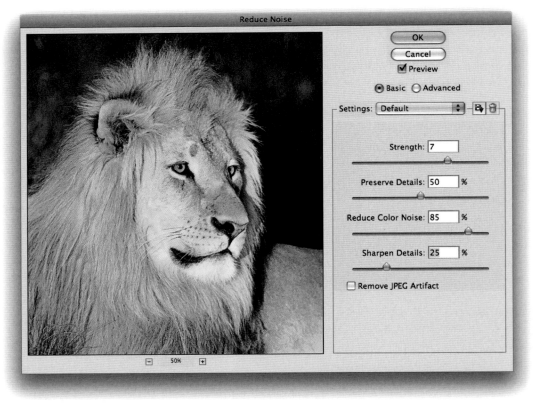

Figure 4.12 Here is the Reduce Noise filter being used to help remove the noise from a digital capture which was shot at 1250 ISO, where the Reduce Noise filter helped get rid of most of the noise artifacts.

which is commonplace with digital captures shot at high ISO settings. The only problem with this filter is that it is quite memory-intensive, so be prepared for a wait while it performs its calculations. Although it can appear quite effective at removing heavy noise, if you do have to apply extreme settings you can sometimes end up with an enhanced noise pattern instead.

In Basic mode you can simply adjust the strength of the noise reduction and then use the controls below that to modify the noise filtering; these should be adjusted in the order they are displayed. The Strength slider adjusts the amount of noise reduction that is applied, while the Preserve Details slider helps preserve the edge luminance information. The luminance noise reduction will appear strongest when you set Preserve Details to zero %, but as you increase Preserve Details more edge detail (and often more noise) will become visible. Below that is the Reduce Color Noise slider, which allows you to separately control the color noise suppression.

After you have adjusted all of the above settings, it is very likely that the image will have suffered some loss in sharpness. The Sharpen Details slider allows you to dial back in some detail sharpness. But I would urge caution here, because adding too much sharpening can simply introduce more artifacts.

Advanced mode noise reduction

In Basic mode you are only able to adjust the Reduce Noise settings so that they affect the overall strength and preservation of image detail. When the Advanced mode button is checked you can apply the noise reduction adjustments on a per channel basis. This can be useful if you wish to apply differential noise reduction to individual channels. Whether you are treating a digital capture or scanned film emulsion the Blue channel is usually the noisiest, so it can therefore be a good idea to apply more reduction to this channel and less to the Red and Green channels where the noise is usually not such a major problem.

Color bleed caution

There are times when you may want to crank up the Color Noise Reduction to 100% in order to remove as much of the noise artifacts as possible, but be aware that adding too much Color Noise Reduction can sometimes cause colors to bleed badly and cause too much softening of the image.

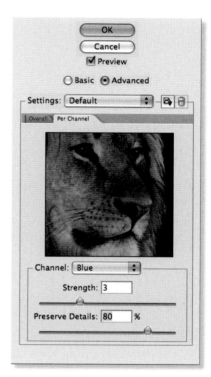

Figure 4.13 A close-up view of the Reduce Noise filter settings in Advanced mode.

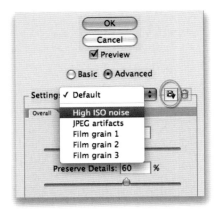

Figure 4.14 Accessing Reduce Noise settings.

JPEG noise removal

You can also use the Reduce Noise filter to smooth out JPEG artifacts. If you have a heavily compressed JPEG image, the Reduce Noise filter can certainly help improve the image smoothness. But I reckon you can also use the Reduce Noise filter in this mode to improve the appearance of GIF images as well. Of course you will need to convert the GIF image from Indexed Color to RGB mode first. But once you have done this you can use the Reduce Noise filter adjustments to help get rid of the banding by taking the Preserve Details slider down to zero % and raising the Sharpen Details to a higher amount than you would be advised to use normally.

Saving the Reduce Noise settings

Favorite Reduce Noise settings can be saved by clicking on the Save Changes to Current Settings button. And Reduce Noise settings can be deleted by clicking on the trash icon next to it.

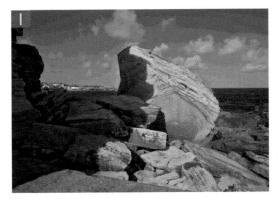

1 The Reduce Noise filter has a Remove JPEG Artifact option that can be useful if you wish to improve the appearance of an image that has suffered from over-heavy JPEG compression. But it can also help rescue a GIF image where a lot of the color levels information has been lost in the conversion to Indexed Color mode.

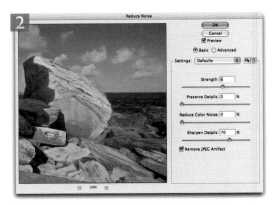

2 A GIF image will have to be converted to RGB mode first. You can then apply the Reduce Noise filter. In this example I checked the Remove JPEG Artifact box. To remove the color banding, the Preserve Details had to be set to 0%, and to make the image sharp again I increased the Sharpen Details to 70%.

260

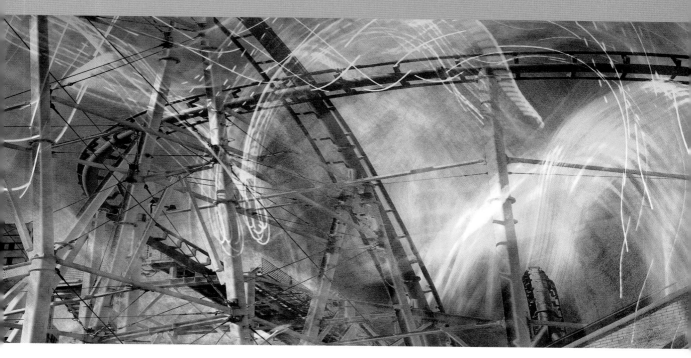

Chapter 5

Image Editing Essentials

So far I have shown you just how much can be done when editing a photo in Camera Raw, before you bring it into Photoshop. Some of the techniques described in this chapter will appear to overlap with Camera Raw, but image adjustments such as Levels and Curves play an important role in everyday Photoshop work, plus this chapter also explains how to work with images that have never been near Camera Raw, such as images that are supplied directly as TIFFs or JPEGs. I'll start off by outlining a few of the fundamental principles of pixel image editing such as bit depth and the relationship between resolution and image size. After that we'll look at the main image editing adjustments and how they can be used to fine-tune the tones and colors in a photograph.

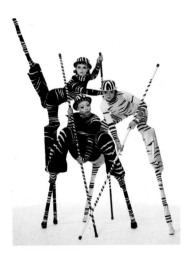

Pixels versus vectors

Digital images are constructed of pixels and as such are resolution-dependent. You can scale a pixel image up in size but, as you do so, the finite information in a pixel image can only be stretched so far before the underlying pixel structure becomes apparent. Objects created in programs like Adobe Illustrator are defined mathematically so if you draw a rectangle, the proportions of the rectangle edges, the relative placement on the page and fill color can all be described using mathematical expressions. An object defined using vectors can be output at any resolution; it does not matter if the image is displayed on a computer screen or as a huge poster, it will always be rendered with the same amount of detail (see Figure 5.1).

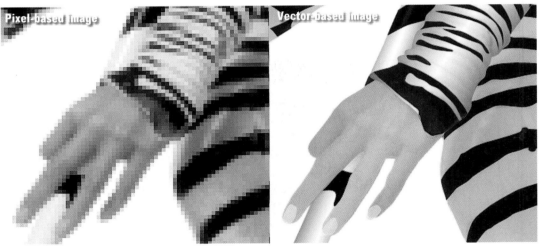

'Stalkers' by The Wrong Size.
Photograph: © Eric Richmond.

Figure 5.1 Digital images are made up of a mosaic of pixels. This means that a pixel-based digital image will always have a fixed resolution and is said to be 'resolution-dependent'. If you enlarge such an image beyond the size at which it is meant to be printed, the pixel structure will soon become apparent, as can be seen here in the left-hand close-up view. But suppose the picture shown above originated not as a photograph, but was drawn as an illustration using a program like Adobe Illustrator. If the picture is drawn using vector paths, the image will be resolution-independent. The mathematical numbers used to describe the path outlines shown in the bottom right example can then be scaled to reproduce at any size: from a postage stamp to a billboard poster. As you can see in the comparison shown here, the pixel image starts to break up as soon as it is magnified, whereas the outlines in the vector-drawn image will reproduce perfectly smoothly.

Terminology

Before proceeding further let me help clarify a few of the confusing terms used and their correct usage when describing resolution.

ppi: pixels per inch

This describes the digital, pixel resolution of an image. But you will notice the term 'dpi' is often inappropriately used to describe the digital resolution of images as well. This is an incorrect use of the term 'dpi' because input devices like scanners and cameras don't produce dots, they produce pixels. Only printers can produce dots! However, it's become quite common now for scanner manufacturers and other software programs to use the term 'dpi' when what they really mean is 'ppi'. Unfortunately this has only added to the confusion, because you often hear people describing the resolution of an image as having so many 'dpi'. But if you look carefully, Photoshop always refers to the input resolution as being in pixels per inch or pixels per centimeter. So if you have an image that has been captured on a digital camera scanned from a photograph, or displayed in Photoshop, it is always made up of pixels and the pixel resolution (ppi) is the number of pixels per inch in the input digital image.

lpi: lines per inch

This is the number of halftone lines or 'cells' in an inch (also described as the screen ruling). The origins of this term go back way before the days of digital desktop publishing. To produce a halftone plate, the film exposure was made through a finely etched criss-cross screen of evenly spaced lines on a glass plate. When a continuous tone photographic image was exposed this way dark areas formed heavy halftone dots and the light areas formed smaller dots, which when viewed from a normal distance gave the impression of a continuous tone image on the page. The line screen resolution (lpi) is therefore the frequency of halftone dots or cells per inch.

Photoshop as a vector program

Photoshop is mainly regarded as a pixel-based graphics program, but it has the capability to be a combined pixel and vector editor because it does also contain a number of vector-based features that can be used to generate things, such as custom shapes and layer clipping paths. This raises some interesting possibilities because you can create various graphical elements like type, shape layers and layer clipping paths in Photoshop and these are all resolution-independent. These 'vector' elements can be scaled up in size in Photoshop without any loss of detail, just as with an Illustrator graphic.

Confusing terminology

You can see from this description where the term 'lines per inch' originated. In today's digital world of imagesetters, the definition is somewhat archaic, but is nonetheless commonly used. You may hear people refer to the halftone output as 'dpi' instead of 'lpi', as in the number of 'halftone' dots per inch, and the imagesetter resolution referred to as having so many 'spi' or 'spots per inch'. Whatever the terminology I think we can all logically agree on the correct use of the term 'pixels per inch', but I am afraid there is no clear definitive answer to the mixed use of the terms 'dpi', 'lpi' and 'spi'. It is an example of how the two separate disciplines of traditional repro and those who developed the digital technology chose to apply different meanings to these same terms.

dpi: dots per inch

This refers to the resolution of printing devices. An output device such as an imagesetter is able to produce tiny 100% black dots at a specified resolution. Let's say we have an imagesetter capable of printing at a resolution of 2450 dots per inch and the printer wished to use a screen ruling of 150 lines per inch. If you divide the dpi of 2450 by the lpi of 150, you get a figure of 16. Within a matrix of 16 × 16 printer dots, an imagesetter can generate a halftone dot varying in size from 0 to 255, which is 256 print dots. It is this variation in halftone cell size (constructed from the combined smaller dots) which gives the impression of tonal shading when viewed from a distance.

Desktop printer resolution

In the case of desktop inkjet printers the term 'dpi' is used to describe the resolution of the printer head, and the dpi output of a typical inkjet can range from 360 to 2880 dpi. Although this is a correct usage of dpi, in this context the dpi means something else yet again. Most inkjet printers lay down a scattered pattern of tiny dots of ink that accumulate to give the impression of different shades of tone, depending on either the number of dots, the varied size of the dots, or both. The principle is roughly similar to the halftone process, but not quite the same. But as you might expect, if you select a finer print resolution such as 1440 or 2880 dpi, you should expect to see smoother print outputs when these are viewed close up.

While a correlation can be made between the pixel size of an image and the 'dpi' setting for the printer, it is important to realize that the number of pixels per inch is not the same as the number of dots per inch created by the printer. When you send a Photoshop image to an inkjet printer, the pixel image data is processed by the print driver and converted into a form that the printer uses to map the individual ink dots that make the printed image. The 'dpi' used by the printer refers to the fineness of the dots. Therefore a print resolution of 360 dpi can be used for speedy, low quality printing, while a dpi resolution of 2880 can be used to produce higher quality print outputs.

Choosing the right pixel resolution for print

There have been theories about choosing the appropriate pixel (ppi) resolution to match the dpi resolution of the printer. For example, it has in the past been suggested that the optimal pixel resolution should ideally be the printer dpi divisible by a whole number. Therefore, if you intended printing at 2880 dpi, the following pixel resolutions could be used: 144, 160, 180, 240, 288, 320, 360. More recently, this theory has been displaced as it has been shown that there isn't really a need to make the pixel resolution match any particular formula in relation to the dpi setting used on the printer.

Image resolution

What are the minimum number of pixels required to print at a particular size? Plus, what is the relationship between the pixel dimensions and image resolution? These questions crop up time and time again. Digital cameras are usually classed according to the number of pixels they can capture. If a CCD chip contains 3000×4500 pixel elements, it can be said to capture a total of 13.5 million pixels, and therefore be described as a 13.5 megapixel camera. When we talk about the resolution of an image we are principally referring to the number of pixels that are contained in the picture. Basically, every digital image contains a finite number of pixels and the more pixels you have, the greater potential there is to capture more detail.

The pixel dimensions of an image are an absolute value. Therefore, a 2400×1800 pixel image will contain 4.32 megapixels and this is an absolute measurement of how much information is contained in the image. But a digital image of this size could be printed at 12" × 9" at 200 pixels per inch, or it could be printed at 8" × 6" at 300 pixels per inch. So if you want to know how big an image can be printed, you simply divide the number of pixels along either dimension of the picture by the pixel resolution you wish to print at (see Figure 5.2). This can be expressed clearly in the following formula: the number of pixels = physical dimension × (ppi) resolution. In other words, there

Megapixels to megabytes

If you multiply the 'megapixel' size by three you will get a rough idea of the megabyte size of the RGB image output. In other words, a 12 megapixel camera can produce a 36 MB RGB, 8-bit per channel image. Quoting megabyte sizes is a less reliable method of describing things because document file sizes can also be affected by the number of layers and alpha channels present and whether the file has been compressed or not. Nevertheless, referring to image sizes in megabytes has become a convenient shorthand when describing a standard uncompressed, 8-bit per channel flattened TIFF image.

is a reciprocal relationship between pixel size, the physical dimensions and resolution. If you quote the resolution of an image as being so many pixels by so many pixels, there can be no ambiguity about what you mean.

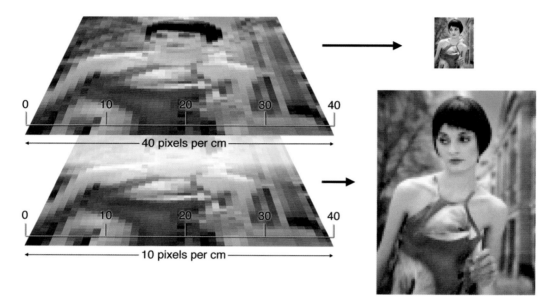

Figure 5.2 In this diagram you can see how a digital image comprised of a fixed number of pixels can have its output resolution interpreted in different ways. For illustration purposes let's assume that the image is 40 pixels wide. The file can be printed small at a resolution of 40 pixels per cm, or printed big (and more pixelated) at a resolution of 10 pixels per cm.

Repro considerations

The structure of the final CMYK print output bears no relationship to the pixel structure of a digital image, since a pixel in a digital image does not equal a cell of halftone dots on the page. To explain this, if we analyze a CMYK cell or rosette, each color plate prints the screen of dots at a slightly different angle, typically: Yellow at 0 or 90 degrees, Black: 45 degrees, Cyan: 105 degrees and Magenta: 75 degrees. If the Black screen is at a 45 degree angle (which is normally the case), the (narrowest) horizontal width of the black dot is 1.41 (square root of 2)

The relationship between ppi and lpi

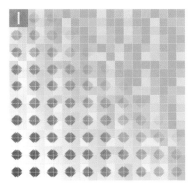

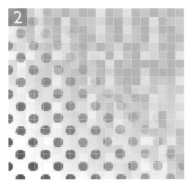

1 The halftone screen shown here is angled at zero degrees. If the pixel resolution were calculated at x2 the line screen resolution, the RIP would use four pixels to calculate each halftone dot.

2 To reproduce a CMYK print output four plates are used, of which only the yellow plate is actually angled at zero degrees. The black plate is normally angled at 45 degrees and the cyan and magenta plates at less sharp angles. Overlay the same pixel resolution of x2 the line screen and you will notice that there is no direct relationship between the pixel and line screen resolutions.

3 There is no single empirical formula that can be used to determine the ideal 'half toning factor'. Should it be x2 or x1.5? The black plate is the widest at 45 degrees and the black plate information is usually more prominent than the three color plates. If a half toning factor of x1.41 (the square root of 2) were used, the pixel resolution will be more synchronized with this angled halftone screen. There is no right or wrong half toning factor – the RIP will process pixel data at any resolution. If there are too few pixels, print quality will be poor. But having more than the optimum number does not necessarily equate to better output, it just means more pixels.

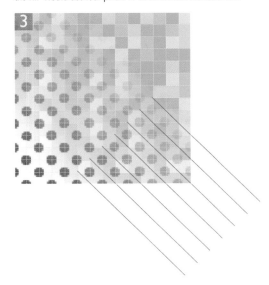

4 Each halftone dot is rendered by a PostScript RIP from the pixel data and output to a device called an imagesetter. The halftone dot illustrated here is plotted using a 16 x 16 dot matrix. This matrix can therefore reproduce a total of 256 shades of gray. The dpi resolution of the imagesetter, divided by 16, will equal the line screen resolution. 2400 dpi divided by 16 = 150 lpi screen resolution.

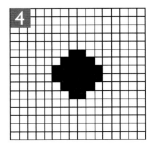

Determining output image size

Image size is determined by the final output requirements and at the beginning of a digital job the most important information you need to know is:

- How large will the picture appear on the page, poster, etc.?
- What is the screen frequency being used by the printer – how many lpi?
- What is the preferred halftone factor used to determine the output resolution?
- Will the designer need to allow for page bleed, or want to crop your image?

But we always use 300 ppi!

There is a common misconception in the design industry that everything must be supplied at 300 pixels per inch. This crops up all the time when you are contacting clients to ask what resolution you should supply your image files at. Somehow the idea has got around the industry that everything from a picture in a newspaper to a 48-sheet poster must be reproduced from a 300 ppi file. It does not always hurt to supply your files at a higher resolution than is necessary, but it can get quite ridiculous when you are asked to supply a 370 MB file in order to produce a 30" x 36" print!

times shorter than the width of the Yellow screen (widest). If we want the frequency of the number of pixels to match the frequency of the halftone cells, then we can multiply the line screen frequency by a factor of 1.41 to work out the ideal pixel resolution to use. This is because using a multiplication factor of 1.41 for the pixel resolution will match the spacing of the 45 degree rotated black plate.

For this reason, you will find that the image output resolution asked for by printers is usually at least 1.41 times the halftone screen frequency used. This multiplication is also known as the 'halftone factor', but you will also find that multiples of ×1.41, ×1.5 or ×2 are commonly used, so which is best? Ask the printer what they prefer you to supply them with and some will say that the 1.41:1 or 1.5:1 multiplication produces the sharpest detail, while others may request a ratio of 2:1. I usually reckon that a halftone factor of 1.5:1 should be fine for general image reproduction, but photographic subjects with fine image detail will benefit from a higher halftone factor. You also have to take into account the screening method used. It is claimed that Stochastic or FM screening permits a more flexible choice of ratios ranging from 1:1 to 2:1.

Let me give you a practical example here. If the line screen used by the printer is, say, 175 lpi, the pixel resolution will therefore need to be around at least 260 pixels per inch (if you use the ×1.5 multiplying factor), but probably no more than 350 pixels per inch (if you use the ×2 multiplying factor).

If a print job does not require the images to be larger than 10 MB, then you may want to know this in advance rather than waste time and space working on unnecessarily large files. On the other hand, designers like to have the freedom to take a supplied image and scale it in the design layout program to suit their requirements. It may seem contrary for me to state that I normally supply clients with files using a ×2 halftone factor. However, the reason I do this is because I know there will always be enough data in the supplied file to crop or scale up in size without adversely compromising the final print quality.

Creating a new document

If you want to create a new document in Photoshop with a blank canvas, go to the File menu and choose New... . This will open the dialog shown in Figure 5.3, where you can select a preset setting type from the Preset pop-up menu followed by a preset size option from the Size menu. When you choose a preset setting, the resolution will adjust automatically depending on whether it is a preset used for print or computer screen type work (you can change the default resolution settings for print and screen in the Units & Rulers Photoshop preferences). Alternatively, you can manually enter new document dimensions and resolution in the fields below.

The Advanced section lets you do extra things like choose a specific profiled color space and after you have entered custom settings in the New Document dialog these can be saved by clicking on the Save Preset... button. In the New Document Preset dialog that's shown below you will notice that there are options that will allow you to select which attributes are to be included in the saved preset.

Pixel Aspect Ratio

The Pixel Aspect Ratio is there to aid multimedia designers who work in stretched screen formats. So, if a 'non-square' pixel setting is selected, Photoshop will create a scaled document which previews how a normal 'square' pixel Photoshop document will actually display on a stretched wide screen. The title bar will then add [scaled] to the end of the file name to remind you that you are working in this special preview mode. When you create a non-square pixel document the scaled preview can be switched on or off by selecting the Pixel Aspect Correction item in the View menu.

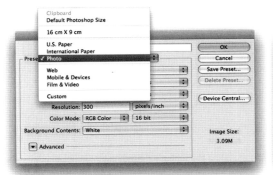

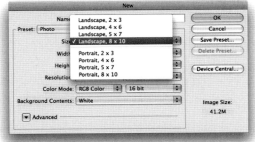

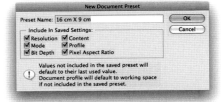

Figure 5.3 When you choose File ⇨ New, this will open the New document dialog shown here (top left). Initially, you can go to the Preset menu and choose a preset type such as: Photo, Web or Film & Video. Depending on the choice you make here, this will affect the size options available in the Size menu (top right). If you use the New document dialog to configure a custom setting, you can click on the Save Preset... button to save this as a New Document preset (right). When you save a New Document preset this will appear listed in the main Preset menu (see top left).

Resolution and viewing distance

In theory the larger a picture is printed, the further away it is meant to be viewed, and the pixel resolution should not have to be scaled up in size in order to achieve the same perception of sharpness. There are limits though, below which the quality will never be sharp enough at normal viewing distance (except at the smallest of print sizes). It also depends on the image subject matter – a picture containing a lot of intricate detail will need more pixels to do the subject justice and be reproduced successfully. If you have a picture of a softly lit, cloudy landscape you can quite easily get away with enlarging a small image through interpolation, beyond the normal constraints.

Altering the image size

The image size dimensions and resolution can be adjusted using the Image Size dialog. The Image Size dialog will normally open with the Resample Image box checked, which means that as you enter new pixel dimension values, measurement values or alter the resolution, the overall image size adjusts accordingly. As you alter one set of units you'll see the others adjust simultaneously. When Resample Image is unchecked, the pixel dimensions will be grayed out and any adjustment made to the image will not alter the total pixel dimensions (only the relationship between the measurement units and the resolution). Remember the rule I mentioned earlier: the number of pixels = physical dimension × (ppi) resolution. You can put that to test here and use the Image Size dialog as a training tool to better understand the relationship between the number of pixels, the dimensions and the resolution. The Constrain Proportions checkbox links the horizontal and vertical dimensions, so that any adjustment is automatically scaled to both axis. Only uncheck this box if you wish to squash or stretch the image when adjusting the image size.

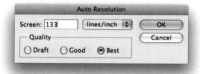

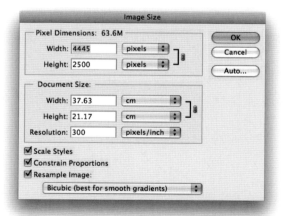

Figure 5.4 To change the image output dimensions but retain the resolution, leave the Resample box checked. To change the image output dimensions with a corresponding change in resolution, leave the Resample box unchecked. Click on the Auto button to open the Auto Resolution dialog. This will help you pick the ideal pixel resolution for repro work based on the line screen resolution.

Image interpolation

Image resampling is also known as interpolation and Photoshop can use one of five methods when calculating how to resize an image. These interpolation options are all located in a menu just below the Resample Image checkbox (see Figure 5.5).

I generally consider 'interpolating up' an image in Photoshop is preferable to the interpolation methods found in basic scanner software. Digital files captured from a scanning back or multishot digital camera are extremely clean and, because there is no grain present, it is usually possible to magnify a digitally captured image more successfully than you can a scanned image of equivalent size. There are other third-party programs that claim to offer improved interpolation, but there appears to be little evidence that you will actually gain any major improvements in image quality over and above what you can achieve using Photoshop. Here is a guide to how each of the interpolation methods works and which are the best ones to use and when.

Nearest Neighbor is the simplest interpolation method yet I use this quite a lot, such as when I want to enlarge screen grabs of dialog boxes by 200% for use in this book. This is because I don't want the sharp edges of the dialog boxes to appear fuzzy in print.

Bilinear interpolation calculates new pixels by reading the horizontal and vertical neighboring pixels. It is fast, and perhaps that was an important consideration in the early days of Photoshop, but I don't see much reason to use this now.

Bicubic interpolation provides better image quality when resampling continuous tone images. Photoshop reads the values of neighboring pixels vertically, horizontally and diagonally, to calculate a weighted approximation of each new pixel value. Photoshop intelligently guesses the new pixel values, by referencing the surrounding pixels.

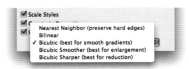

Figure 5.5 This is a close-up view of the Image Resize dialog, showing the five interpolation options.

Planning ahead

Once an image has been scanned at a particular resolution and manipulated, there is no going back. A digital file prepared for advertising usage may never be used to produce anything bigger than a 35 MB CMYK separation, but you never know. It is safer to err on the side of caution and better to sample down than have to interpolate up. It also depends on how much manipulation you intend doing. Some styles of retouching work are best done at a magnified size and then reduced. Suppose you wanted to blend a small element into a detailed scene. To do such work convincingly, you need to have enough pixels to work with to be able to see what you are doing. For this reason some professional retouchers will edit a master file that is around 100 MB RGB or bigger even.

Another advantage of working with large file sizes is that you can always guarantee being able to meet clients' constantly changing demands, although the actual resolution required to illustrate a glossy magazine double-page full-bleed spread is probably only around 40–60 MB RGB or 55–80 MB CMYK. Some advertising posters may even require smaller files than this, because the print screen on a billboard poster is that much coarser. When you are trying to calculate the optimum resolution you cannot rely on being fully provided with the right advice from every printer. Sometimes it will be necessary to anticipate the required resolution by referring to the table in Figure 5.6. This shows some sample file size guides for different types of print job.

Bicubic interpolation methods

The Photoshop bicubic interpolations are improved and more accurate than before, especially with regard to the downsampling of images. If you need to apply an extreme image resampling, either up or down in size, I suggest that you consider using the Bicubic Sharper or Bicubic Smoother interpolation methods.

Bicubic Smoother is the ideal choice for making pictures bigger, as this will result in smoother interpolated enlargements. It has been suggested that you can also get good results using Bicubic sharper when interpolating up and then go directly to print. However, this ignores the fact that the sharpening should really be applied as a separate step *after* interpolating the image, and the sharpening should be tailored to the final output size (see Chapter 13). It is therefore better to use Bicubic smoother followed by a separate print sharpening step. This is because the smooth interpolation prevents any artifacts in the image from being enhanced too much and the sharpening can be applied at the exact right amount for whatever size of print you are making.

Bicubic Sharper should be used when you want to reduce an image in size more accurately. If you have a high resolution digital capture of a detailed subject and want to make a duplicate copy but at a much lower pixel resolution, the scaled down image will retain more detail and sharpness if you use Bicubic Sharper. This will help avoid the stair-step aliasing that can occur when using other interpolation methods.

Step interpolation

Some people might be familiar with the step interpolation technique, where you gradually increase or decrease the image size by small percentages. This is not really necessary now because you can use Bicubic Sharper or Bicubic Smoother to increase or decrease the image size in a single step. Some people argue that for really extreme image size changes they still prefer the 10% step method.

Pixel size	Megapixels	MB (RGB)	MB (CMYK)	Inches 200 ppi	Centimeters 80 ppc	Inches 300 ppi	Centimeters 120 ppc
1600 x 1200	2	6	7.5	8 x 6	20 x 15	5.5 x 4	13.5 x 10
2400 x 1800	4.3	12.5	16.5	12 x 9	30 x 22.5	8 x 6	20 x 15
3000 x 2000	6	17.5	23.5	15 x 10	37.5 x 25	10 x 6.5	25 x 17
3500 x 2500	8.75	25	33.5	17.5 x 12.5	44 x 31	11.5 x 8.5	29 x 21
4000 x 2850	11.4	32.5	43.5	20 x 14	50 x 36	13.5 x 9.5	33.5 x 24
4500 x 3200	14.4	41	54.5	22.5 x 16	56 x 40	15 x 10.5	37.5 x 27
5000 x 4000	20	57	76	25 x 20	62.5 x 50	16.5 x 13.5	42 x 33.5

Figure 5.6 The above table shows a comparison of pixel resolution, megapixels, megabyte file size and output dimensions at different resolutions, both in inches and in centimeters.

Output use	Screen ruling	x1.5 Output resolution	MB Grayscale	MB CMYK	x2 Output resolution	MB Grayscale	MB CMYK
A3 Newspaper single page	85 lpi	130 ppi	3	12.5	170 ppi	5.5	21.5
A3 Newspaper single page	120 lpi	180 ppi	6	24	240 ppi	10.5	42.5
A4 Magazine mono single page	120 lpi	180 ppi	3	NA	240 ppi	5.3	NA
A4 Magazine mono double page	120 lpi	180 ppi	6	NA	240 ppi	10.6	NA
A4 Magazine single page	133 lpi	200 ppi	3.7	14.8	266 ppi	6.5	26.1
A4 Magazine double page	133 lpi	200 ppi	8	29.6	266 ppi	13	52.2
A4 Magazine single page	150 lpi	225 ppi	4.7	18.7	300 ppi	8.3	33.2
A4 Magazine double page	150 lpi	225 ppi	9.4	37.4	300 ppi	17	66.4

Figure 5.7 Here is a rough guide to the sort of file sizes required to reproduce either a mono or CMYK file for printed use. The table contains file size information for output at multiples of x1.5 the screen ruling and x2 the screen ruling.

273

Raw to pixel image conversions

Once a raw image has been rendered as a pixel image you cannot revert to the raw data version because the raw to pixel image conversion is a one-way process. Once you have done this, the only way you can undo something in the raw processing is to revert to the original raw image and generate a new pixel image copy. Although the goal of this book is to show you how to work as non-destructively as possible, this is the one step in the process where there is no going back and you therefore need to be sure that the photograph you start editing in Photoshop is as fully optimized as possible. In the case of JPEG images, you can edit these in Camera Raw if you like, or you can cut out Camera Raw completely and use the examples shown in this chapter and use Photoshop to carry out the image optimization.

WYSIWYG image editing

If you want true WYSIWYG editing (what you see is what you get), it is important that you follow the instructions laid out in the Chapter 2 on how to calibrate the display and configure the color settings. Do this and you will now be ready to start editing your photographs with confidence.

Basic pixel editing

In Chapter 3 we explored the use of adjustments and other tools in Camera Raw to optimize a photo before it is opened in Photoshop as a rendered pixel image. The following section is all about the main image adjustment controls in Photoshop and how you can use these to fine-tune your images, or use them as an alternative to Camera Raw such as when editing camera shot JPEGs or scanned TIFFs. The techniques discussed here should be regarded as essential foundation skills for Photoshop image editing because however you bring your images into Photoshop, you will at some point need to know how to work with the basic image editing tools such as Levels and Curves.

If you intend bringing your images in via Camera Raw, it can be argued that Photoshop image adjustments are unnecessary since Camera Raw provides you with everything you need to produce perfectly optimized photos. Even so, you will still find the information in this chapter is important, since these are the techniques every Photoshop user needs to be aware of and use when applying things like localized corrections. So, for now, let's look at some basic pixel image editing principles and techniques.

The image histogram

The histogram is a bar chart that graphically represents the relative distribution of the various tones (referred to as Levels) that make up a digital photograph. An 8-bit per channel grayscale image has a single channel and uses 256 shades of gray to describe all the levels of tone from black to white. Black has a levels value of 0 (zero), white has a levels value of 255 and all the numbers in between represent the shades of gray going from black to white. The histogram is like a graph with 256 increments, each representing how often a particular levels number (a specific gray color) occurs in the image. Figure 5.8 shows a typical histogram such as you'll see in the Histogram, Levels and Curves panels. This diagram also shows how the appearance of the graph relates to the tonal structure of a photographic image.

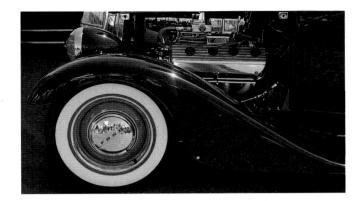

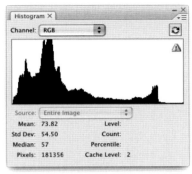

Figure 5.9 The warning triangle in the Histogram panel indicates that you need to click on the Refresh button above to update it.

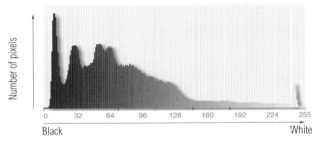

Figure 5.8 Here is an image histogram that represents the distribution of tones from the shadows to the highlights. Because this photograph mostly contains dark shades of gray you will notice that the levels are predominantly located to the left end of the histogram. The height of each bar in the histogram indicates the frequency of pixels that occur at each levels point.

The Histogram panel

There has always been a histogram in the Levels dialog and there is also a Histogram panel, which when working in Photoshop gives you even more feedback. With the Histogram panel, you can continuously observe the effect your image editing has on the image levels and you can also check the histogram while making any type of image adjustment. The Histogram panel only provides an approximate representation of the image levels. So, to ensure that the Histogram panel is giving an accurate representation of the image levels it is advisable to force Photoshop to update the histogram view, by clicking on the Refresh button at the top of the panel.

Now let's look at what that information can tell us about a digital image. The histogram graphically shows the distribution of tones in an image. A low-key photograph (such as the one shown in Figure 5.8) will show most of the peaks on the left. Most importantly, it shows the positioning of the shadow and highlight points. When you apply a tonal correction using Levels or Curves, the histogram provides a visual clue that helps you judge where the brightest highlights and deepest shadows should be. The histogram also tells you something about the condition of the image you are editing. If there are peaks jammed up at either ends of the histogram, this suggests that the highlights or shadows are most likely clipped and that when the original photograph was scanned or captured it was effectively under- or overexposed. Unfortunately, if

Interpreting an image

A digital image is nothing more than a lot of numbers and it is how those numbers are interpreted in Photoshop that creates the image you see on the display. We can use our eyes to make subjective judgements about how the picture looks, but we can also use the number information to provide useful and usable feedback. The Info panel is your friend. If you understand the numbers, it can help you see the fine detail that your eyes are not sharp enough to discern. And we also have the Histogram panel, which is a godsend to geeks who just love all that statistical analysis stuff but it is also an excellent teaching tool. The Histogram panel makes everything that follows much easier to understand.

the levels are clipped at either end of the scale you can't restore the detail that has been lost here. If there are gaps in the histogram, this will most likely indicate a poor quality scan or that the image had previously been heavily manipulated.

Throughout this book I will try to guide you to work as efficiently and as non-destructively as possible. But even so, anything we do to adjust the levels to make an image look better will result in some data loss. This is quite normal and an inevitable consequence of the image editing process. The steps on the page opposite illustrate what happens when you edit a photograph. As you adjust the input levels, moving the Input sliders further apart, you will stretch the levels and gaps will start appearing in the histogram. But more importantly, stretching the levels further apart can result in less well-defined tonal separation and therefore less detail in these regions of the image. This is particularly a problem at the shadow end of the scale because there are fewer levels of usable tone information in the shadows compared with the highlights (see the section on Digital exposure on page 174).

As you move the Input sliders closer together you will compress the tones in the image and these can appear as spikes in the histogram. This too can cause data loss, sometimes resulting in flatter tone separation (there is also an example of this in the section on Camera Raw Brightness adjustments on page 177).

The histogram can therefore be used to provide visual feedback on the levels information in an image and to show whether there is clipping at either end of the scale. But does it really matter whether we obtain a smooth histogram or not? If you are preparing a photograph to go to a print press, you would be lucky to detect more than 50 levels of tonal separation from any single ink plate. So the loss of a few levels at the completed edit stage does not necessarily imply that you have too little digital tonal information from which to reproduce a full-tonal range image in print. However, if you begin with a bad-looking histogram, the image is only going to be in a worse state after it has been retouched. For this reason it is best to start out with the best quality scan or capture you can get.

Basic Levels editing and the histogram

This example was carried out on an 8-bit RGB image, so it should come as no surprise that the histogram broke down as soon as I applied a simple Levels adjustment (in the following section we are going to look at the advantages of editing in 16-bits per channel mode).

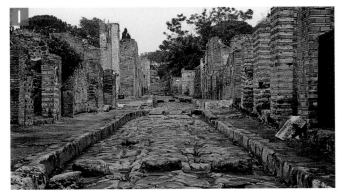

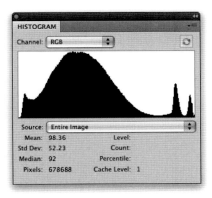

1 Here is an image that displays an evenly distributed range of tones in the accompanying Histogram panel.

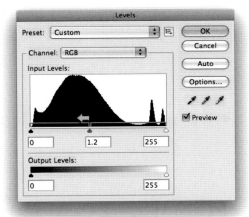

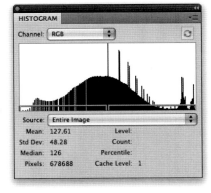

2 If I apply a Levels image adjustment and drag the middle (Gamma) Input slider to the left, this will lighten the image. The Histogram panel on the right shows the histogram display after the adjustment has been applied. To understand what has happened here, this histogram represents the newly mapped levels. The levels that were in the section of the histogram to the left of the Gamma slider have been stretched and the levels that were to the right of the Gamma slider have now been compressed.

277

Understanding bit depth

To understand what the bit depth numbers mean it is best to begin with a grayscale image where there is just luminosity. A 1-bit or bitmapped image contains black or white pixels only. A 2-bit image contains 4 levels (2^2), 3-bit 8 levels (2^3) and so on, up to 8-bit (2^8) with 256 levels of gray. Therefore, a 24-bit RGB color image is made up of 3 x 8-bit channels where each grayscale channel represents a red, green or blue color and, because the channels overlap, each pixel is capable of defining up to 16.7 million possible colors (2^8 x 3).

Bit depth

Bit depth refers to the maximum number of levels per channel that can be contained in a photograph. For example, a 24-bit RGB color image is made up of three 8-bit image channels, where each 8-bit channel can contain up to 256 levels of tone, while a 16-bit per channel image can have up to 32,768 data points per color channel (because in truth, Photoshop's 16-bit depth is 15 bits +1). So although Photoshop's 16-bits per channel mode is actually 15-bits, this shouldn't really matter since 15-bits is plenty enough levels to contain the levels data that can be captured by any camera or scanner device. JPEG images are always limited to 8-bits, but TIFF and PSD files can be in 8-bits or 16-bits per channel. Photoshop only offers 8-bits or 16-bits per channel modes for standard integer channel images (32-bit support uses floating point

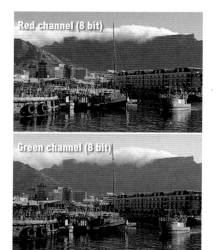

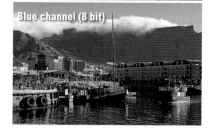

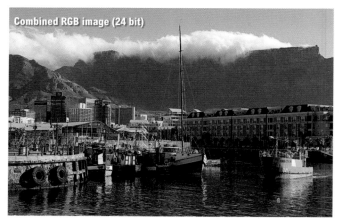

Figure 5.10 The bit depth of an image is a mathematical description of the maximum levels of tone that are possible, expressed as a power of 2. A bitmap image contains 2 to the power of 1 (2 levels of tone), in other words, either black or white tone only. A normal Photoshop 8-bit grayscale image or individual color channel in a composite color image will contain 2 to the power of 8 (up to 256 levels of tonal information). When three RGB 8-bit color channels are combined together to form a composite color image, the result is a 24-bit color image that can contain up to 16.7 million shades of color.

channels). Therefore, any source image with more than 8-bits per channel has to be in the 16-bits per channel mode. Most scanners are capable of capturing 12-bits per channel data, which means that scanned images have to be saved using 16-bits per channel in order to preserve all of the 12-bits per channel data. Once the image is opened in Photoshop you'll then have access to all the levels data that was captured in the original scanned image.

In the case of raw files, a raw image contains all the original levels data, which is usually captured at a bit depth of 12-bits or even 14-bits per channel. Camera Raw image adjustments are calculated using 16-bits per channel so, once again, all the levels information that was in the original can be preserved when you save a Camera Raw processed raw image using 16-bits per channel.

8-bit versus 16-bit image editing

There are those who have argued that 16-bit editing is a futile exercise because no one can tell the difference between an image that has been edited in 16-bit and one that has been edited in 8-bit. Personally I believe this to be a foolish argument. If a scanner or camera is capable of capturing more than 8-bits per channel, why not make full use of the extra tonal information? In the case of film scans, you might as well save the freshly scanned images using the 16-bits per channel mode and apply the initial Photoshop edits using Levels or Curves in 16-bits. If you preserve all the levels in the original through these early stages of the edit process, you'll have more headroom to work with and avoid dropping useful image data. It may only take a second or two longer to edit an image in 16-bits per channel compared with when it is in 8-bit, but even if you only carry out the initial edits in 16-bit and then convert to 8-bit you'll retain significantly more image detail.

The second point is you never know what the future has in store. On pages 310–313 we shall be looking at Shadows/Highlights adjustments. This feature can be used to emphasize detail that might otherwise remain hidden in the shadows or highlights. This feature exploits the fact that a deep-bit image can contain lots of hidden levels data that

Bit depth precision

A higher bit depth doesn't add more pixels to an image. Instead, it offers a greater level of precision to the way tone information is recorded by the camera or scanner sensor. One way to think about bit-depth is to consider the difference between having the ability to measure something with a ruler that is accurate to the nearest inch, compared with one that can measure to the nearest millimeter.

Why is 16-bits really 15-bits?

If you have a keen knowledge of math, you will notice that Photoshop's 16-bits per channel mode is actually 15-bit as it uses only 32,768 levels out of a possible 65,536 levels when describing a 16-bit mode image. This is because having a tonal range that goes from 0 to 32,767 is more than adequate to describe the data coming off any digital device. And also because from an engineering point of view, 15-bit math calculations give you an exact midpoint value, which can be important for precise blending.

Bit depth status

You can check the bit depth of an image quite easily by looking at the document window title bar, where it will indicate the bit-depth as being 8, 16 or 32-bit.

Comparing 8-bit with 16-bit editing

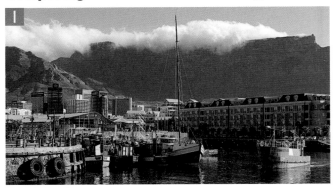

1 Here, I started out with a full color image that was in 16-bits per channel mode and created a duplicate that was converted to 8-bits per channel mode.

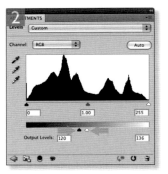 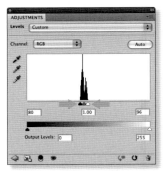

2 With each version I applied two sequential Levels adjustments. The first (shown here on the left) compressed the output levels to an output range of 120–136. I then applied a second Levels adjustment in which I expanded these levels to 0–255 again.

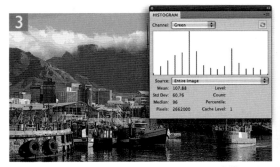 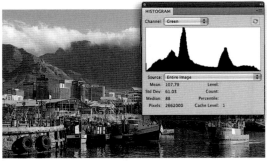

3 The outcome of this can be clearly seen when examining the individual color channels. On the left you can see the image histogram for the 8-bit file green channel and on the right you can see a much smoother histogram with the original 16-bit file.

can be manipulated to reveal more detail in the shadows or highlight areas. The Shadows/Highlights adjustment works fine with 8-bit images of course, but you'll get better results if you scan or capture in 16-bit per channel mode first.

Photoshop also offers extensive support for 16-bit mode editing. You can crop, rotate, make all the usual image adjustments, use all the Photoshop tools and work with layers in 16-bit mode, in grayscale, RGB, CMYK and Lab color modes, but only a few filters are available such as the Lens Correction and Liquify filter. You may not feel the need to use 16-bits per channel all the time for every job, but I would say that for critical jobs where you don't want to lose an ounce of detail, it is essential to make at least all your preliminary edits in 16-bits.

In the tutorial shown opposite, I started with an image that was in 16-bits mode and created a duplicate that was converted to 8-bits. I then proceeded to compress the levels and expand them again in order to demonstrate how keeping an image in 16-bits per channel mode provides a more robust image mode for major tone and color edits. Admittedly this is an extreme example, but preserving an image in 16-bits offers a significant extra margin of safety when making everyday image adjustments.

16-bit and color space selection

For a long time now Photoshop experts such as myself have advocated editing in RGB using a conservative gamut color space such as Adobe RGB (if you want to find out more about RGB color spaces then you will need to read Chapter 12 on color management). Although 16-bit editing is not new to Photoshop, it is only since the advent of Photoshop CS that it has been possible to edit more extensively in 16-bit. One of the advantages this brings is that we are no longer limited to editing in a relatively small gamut RGB workspace. It is perfectly safe to use a large gamut space such as ProPhoto RGB when you are editing in 16-bits per channel mode because you'll have so many more data points in each color channel to work with compared to when you edit in a standard RGB space such as ColorMatch or Adobe RGB (see the following section on RGB edit spaces).

Camera Raw and bit depth output

Bearing in mind what I have said about the importance of carrying out all the major tone edits in 16-bit, Camera Raw does just that. If you use Camera Raw to process a raw camera file or a 16-bit TIFF, the initial image edits will all be done in 16-bits. If you are satisfied that the result of the Camera Raw processing is a perfectly optimized image, it can be argued there is less harm in converting such a file to an 8-bits per channel mode image in Photoshop. But as I mentioned in the main text, you never know when you might be required to adjust an image further. Keeping a photo in 16-bits can give you peace of mind, knowing that you've preserved as many levels as possible from the original.

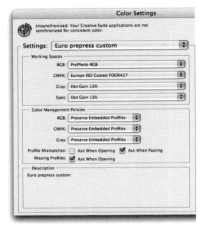

Figure 5.11 The Color Settings dialog.

The RGB edit space and color gamut

No Photoshop book for photographers would be complete without a discussion about which RGB working space to choose from the RGB Working Spaces menu in the Edit ➪ Color Settings dialog (Figure 5.11).

For photo editing work, the choice really boils down to Adobe RGB or ProPhoto RGB. The best way to illustrate the differences between these two RGB color spaces is to consider how colors captured by the camera or scanner are best preserved when they are converted to print. Figure 5.12 shows (on the left) top and side views of a 3D plot for the color gamut of a digital camera, seen relative to a wire frame of the Adobe RGB working space. Next to this you can see top and side views of a glossy inkjet print space relative to Adobe RGB. You will notice here that Adobe RGB does clip both the input and output color

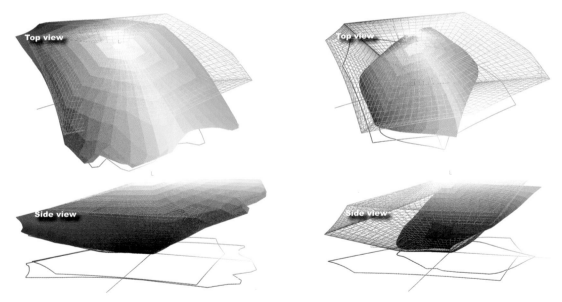

Figure 5.12 This diagram shows on the left, a top and side view of the gamut of a digital camera source space plotted as a solid shape within a wire frame shape representing the color gamut of the Adobe RGB edit space. On the right is a top and side view of the gamut of a glossy inkjet printer color space plotted as a solid shape within a wire frame of the same Adobe RGB space.

spaces. This can be considered disadvantageous because all these potential colors will be clipped when editing an image. Meanwhile, Figure 5.13 offers a direct comparison showing what happens when you use the ProPhoto RGB space. The ProPhoto RGB color gamut is so large it will barely clip the input color space and is certainly big enough to preserve all the other colors through to the print output stage. In my view, ProPhoto RGB is the best space to use if you really want to preserve all the color detail that was captured in the original photo and see those colors preserved through to print.

The other choice I should mention is the sRGB color space, but this is only really suited for Web output work (or when sending pictures to clients via email).

Is ProPhoto RGB too wide a space?

In the past there have been concerns that the ProPhoto RGB space is so large that the large gaps between one levels data point and the next could lead to posterization. This might have been a valid argument when images were edited in 8-bits per channel throughout. These days you can use Camera Raw to optimize an image prior to outputting as a ProPhoto RGB pixel image. In practice, you can edit a ProPhoto RGB image in 16-bits or 8-bits per channel mode, but 16-bits is safer.

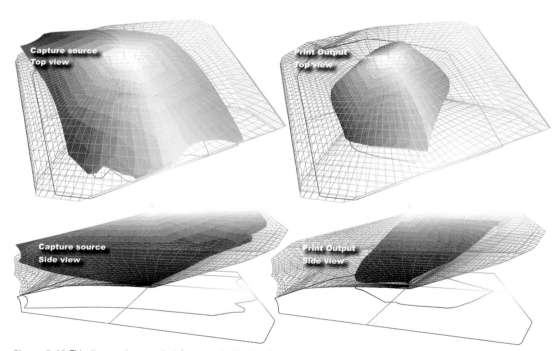

Figure 5.13 This diagram shows on the left, a top and side view of the gamut of a digital camera source space plotted as a solid shape within a wire frame shape representing the color gamut of the ProPhoto RGB edit space. On the right is a top and side view of the gamut of a glossy inkjet printer color space plotted as a solid shape within a wire frame of the same ProPhoto RGB space.

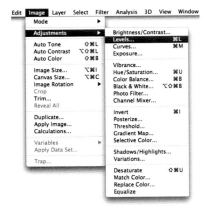

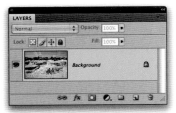

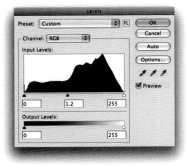

Figure 5.14 This shows the basic workflow for applying a normal image adjustment. Go to the Image ⇨ Adjustments menu and choose an adjustment type. In this example I selected Levels..., adjusted the settings and clicked OK to permanently apply the adjustment to the image.

Direct image adjustments

Most Photoshop image adjustments can be applied in one of two ways. There is the traditional direct adjustment method where image adjustments can be accessed via the Image ⇨ Adjustments menu and applied to the whole image (or image layer) directly. Figure 5.14 shows an example of how one might apply a basic Levels adjustment. Here, I had an image open with a Background layer, then went to the Image Adjustments menu and selected 'Levels...'. This opened the Levels dialog where I was able to apply a permanent tone adjustment to the photograph.

Direct image adjustments are appropriate for those times where you don't need the editability that adjustment layers have to offer. They are also applicable when editing an alpha channel or layer mask, since you can't use adjustment layers when editing Photoshop channels. Lastly, the Shadows/Highlights command can only be applied directly to an image and not as an adjustment layer. Although, having said that, you can apply a Shadows/Highlights adjustment as a Smart Filter to a Smart Object layer (see page 496).

Adjustment layers and Adjustments panel

There is also the adjustment layer method where an image adjustment can be applied in the form of an editable layer adjustment. Adjustment layers can be added to an image in several ways. You can go to the Layer ⇨ New Adjustment layer submenu, or you can click on the Add new adjustment layer button in the Layers panel to select an adjustment type. But in Photoshop CS4, you can now use the new Adjustments panel to add adjustment layers and update the adjustment settings. In the Figure 5.15 workflow example I again started out with an image with a Background layer. I went to the Adjustments panel (shown top) and clicked on one of the icons to select an adjustment type, such as Levels (circled). This added a new Levels adjustment layer above the Background layer and the Adjustments panel switched to display the Levels adjustment controls.

There are several advantages to the Adjustment layer approach, especially with the way the options are now presented in Photoshop CS4. First of all, adjustment layers are not permanent. If you decide to undo an adjustment or readjust the settings, you can do so at any time. Adjustment layers offer the ability to apply multiple image adjustments and/or fills to an image and for the adjustments to remain 'dynamic'. In other words, an adjustment layer is an image adjustment that can be revised at any time and enables the image adjustment processing to be deferred until the time when an image is flattened. The adjustments you apply can also be masked when you edit the associated layer mask and the mask can also be refined using the Masking panel (which I'll be describing later). Best of all, adjustment layers are no longer restricted to a modal state where you had to double-click the layer first in order to access the adjustment controls. Now that we have an Adjustments panel, you have the potential to quickly access the adjustment layer settings any time you need to. In addition to this you can switch between tasks. So, if you click on an adjustment layer to select it, you can paint on the layer mask, adjust the layer opacity and blending options and have full access to the adjustment layer controls throughout.

Adding an adjustment layer procedure

Here's how you would go about adding a new adjustment layer. First of all, go to the Adjustments panel shown in Figure 5.15 and select an adjustment type by clicking on one of the buttons (you'll see a list of all the buttons over the page and a brief summary of what each one does). Once you have selected an adjustment, the panel switches to display the adjustment controls (which I have shaded yellow in Figure 5.17) plus there are additional controls top and bottom for managing the adjustment layer, such as toggling the preview on or off. If you deselect the adjustment layer or click on the 'Return to list' button, this takes you back to the Adjustments panel list view where you can add a new adjustment layer. As you click on adjustment layers the Adjustments panel will refresh the controls view to show the controls and settings for that particular layer.

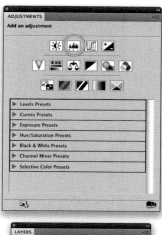

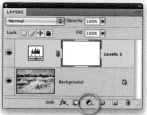

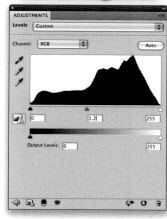

Figure 5.15 This shows the Adjustment layer workflow. Go to the Adjustments panel and choose an adjustment type (in this example Levels) and make the adjustment, which will then be added as a new adjustment layer. You can also mouse down on the Add Adjustment layer button in the Layers panel (circled) to add a new adjustment layer.

Adjustment panel options

☼ Brightness Contrast

A basic brightness and contrast tone adjustment.

Levels

Used for setting the black and white clipping points and adjusting the gamma.

Curves

Used for more accurate tone adjustments.

Exposure

Primarily for adjusting the brightness of 32-bit images.

▽ Vibrance

A new, tamer saturation adjustment control.

Hue/Saturation

A color adjustment for editing both hue color and saturation.

Color Balance

Basic color adjustments.

Black & White

Used for simple black and white conversions.

Photo Filter

Adds a coloring filter adjustment.

Channel Mixer

For adjusting the balance of the individual color channels that make up a color image.

Invert

Converts the image to a negative.

Posterize

Used to reduce the number of levels in an image.

Threshold

Reduces the number of levels to 2 and allows you to set the midpoint threshold.

Gradient map

Uses gradients to map the output colors.

Selective Color

Applies CMYK selective color adjustments based on RGB or CMYK colors.

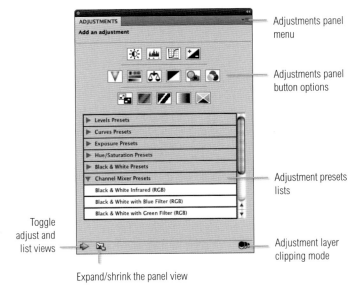

Toggle adjust and list views

Expand/shrink the panel view

Figure 5.16 The Adjustments panel adjustment list options.

Adjustments panel menu

Adjustments panel button options

Adjustment presets lists

Adjustment layer clipping mode

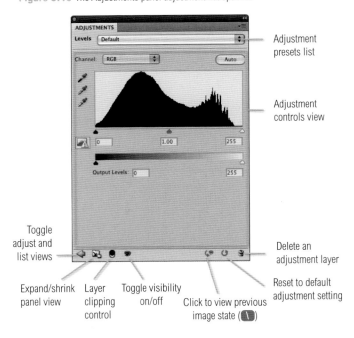

Adjustment presets list

Adjustment controls view

Toggle adjust and list views

Delete an adjustment layer

Expand/shrink panel view

Layer clipping control

Toggle visibility on/off

Click to view previous image state (■)

Reset to default adjustment setting

Figure 5.17 The Adjustments panel adjustment mode options.

Adjustment panel controls

Figure 5.16 shows the default Adjustments panel list view, where you can click on any of the buttons to add an adjustment. The button icons may take a little getting used to at first, but you can use the summary list on the page opposite to help guide you here or mouse down on the Adjustments panel menu to access a named list of adjustments. You can also use the Presets list to quickly access supplied, or your own, preset settings for the various image adjustments. Just click on a preset name and this will add a new adjustment layer with the preset settings. It is easy to get carried away with this feature as you can soon end up with a dozen or more adjustment layers. One way to avoid this is to use the Undo command before you select a new adjustment preset. So the routine would be: select an adjustment and see if you like the result. If not, use ⌘ Z *ctrl* Z to undo the adjustment layer and select another preset instead and so on. The adjustment layer clipping mode determines whether new adjustments are applied to all the layers below where you add the adjustment layer, or are just clipped to the layer below (see Figure 5.18).

When you are in the Adjustments panel controls mode you can access the adjustment presets from the list at the top. The difference here is that you can run through the list of presets selecting each in turn, seeing what each effect does, but without adding new layers. Note that in controls mode, the Adjustments panel menu will allow you to save and load presets, so you can add your own custom settings to this list. The middle section contains the main adjustment controls and at the bottom you again have the clipping control to switch between adjusting all the layers below or the layer immediately below. Next to this, there is an eyeball icon for turning the adjustment layer visibility on or off. Further along there is a button for switching between the previous state and the current edited state where, if you click and hold the mouse down (or hold down the ❶ key), you can see what the image looked like before the last series of image adjustments were applied. Lastly, there is a Reset button for cancelling the most recent adjustments and a Delete button to remove the current adjustment layer.

Images that contain adjustment layers are savable in the Photoshop native, TIFF and PDF formats. Adjustment layers add very little to the overall file size and, best of all, provide limitless opportunities to edit and revise any of the adjustments that have been made to the image.

Use Tool Tips

If you have the 'Show Tool Tips' option selected in the Photoshop Interface preferences, this will display the name of an adjustment as you roll the cursor over the button icons.

Undoing adjustment steps

There is a Reset button at the bottom of the controls mode Adjustments panel, but you can also use the Undo command ⌘ Z *ctrl* Z to toggle undoing and redoing the last adjustment and use the ⌘ ⌥ Z *ctrl* *alt* Z shortcut to progressively undo a series of adjustment panel edits.

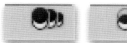

Figure 5.18 This shows the two clipping layer modes for adding a new adjustment layer. The one on the left is for applying an adjustment to all layers below the adjustment layer. The one on the right is for clipping adjustments to the layer below only.

Auto image adjustments

The Auto button will set the clipping points automatically (the Auto settings are covered later in this chapter).

Levels adjustments

There was a time when every Photoshop edit session would begin with a Levels adjustment to optimize the image. But these days, if you use Camera Raw to process your raw or JPEG photos, there shouldn't be so much need to use Levels for this particular purpose since you should already have optimized the shadows and highlights during the Camera Raw editing. However, it is still useful to understand the basic principles of how to use Levels since there are times when it is more convenient to apply a quick Levels adjustment to a scanned or supplied image rather than take it through Camera Raw. Levels adjustments can also be used to apply dodge and burn layers as well as when editing channels and layer masks (pages 330–335).

Levels adjustments can be applied directly or as Adjustment layers (see Figure 5.19), and if you are optimizing an RGB image for output the same principles apply here as with Camera Raw. All you need to worry about is making sure that the blacks go to black and the whites go to white (see pages 168–173).

Figure 5.19 This shows a view of the Adjustments panel for adding Levels adjustments. The Input sliders are just below the histogram display and you can use these to adjust the input shadows, highlights and gamma (the relative image brightness between the shadows and highlights). Below these are the Output sliders and you use these to set the output shadows and highlights. It is best not to adjust the output sliders unless you are retouching a prepress file in grayscale or CMYK, or for some reason you deliberately wish to reduce the output contrast.

Input shadows slider   Gamma slider   Input highlights slider

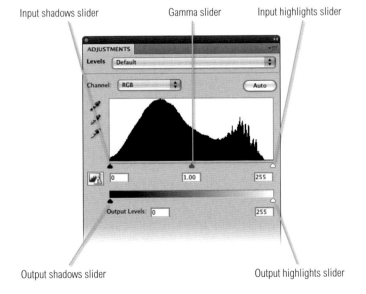

Output shadows slider   Output highlights slider

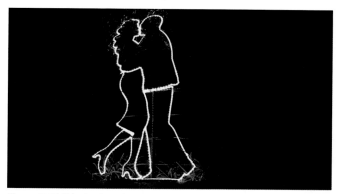

Figure 5.20 If the levels are bunched up towards the left, this is a sign of shadow clipping. But in this example we would probably want the shadows to be clipped in order to produce a rich black background.

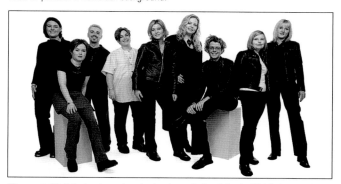

Figure 5.21 If the levels are bunched up towards the right, the highlights may be clipped. But in this image I wanted the white background to burn out to white.

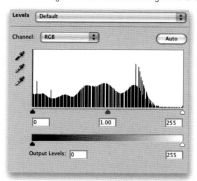

Figure 5.22 A histogram with a comb-like appearance indicates that either the image has already been heavily manipulated or an insufficient number of levels were captured in the original scan.

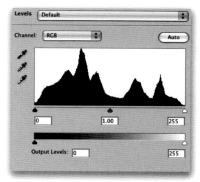

Figure 5.23 This histogram shows that the image contains a full range of tones, without any shadow or highlight clipping and no gaps between the levels.

Using Levels to improve the contrast

1 I chose to use a monochrome photograph here because it would make the following contrast enhancing Levels adjustment clearer to see. The Histogram panel below displays a histogram of the image's levels and, as you can see, the tonal contrast could be improved by expanding the levels. To do this we need to apply a Levels adjustment.

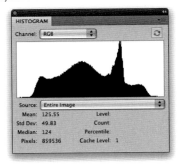

2 One way to improve the tonal contrast using Levels is to simply look at the histogram in the Levels adjustment and drag the Input sliders inwards until they meet either end of the histogram. However, you can get a better idea of where to set the endpoints by enabling the Threshold display mode. To do this, hold down the ⌥ *alt* key as you drag the Input shadow levels slider inwards. The preview will now show a threshold view that enables you to discern more easily where the darkest shadows are in the picture. The Threshold view you see here is rather extreme so you would want to back off from this setting, otherwise the shadows would become too clipped. But you should get the general idea here that the black clipping in the threshold mode preview indicates the points at which the blacks will get clipped.

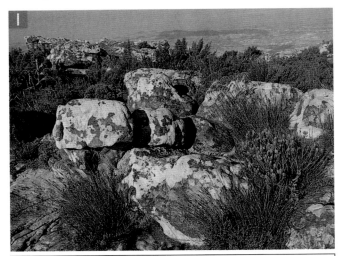

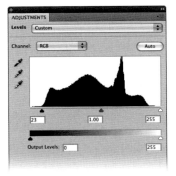

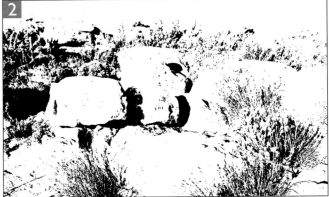

290

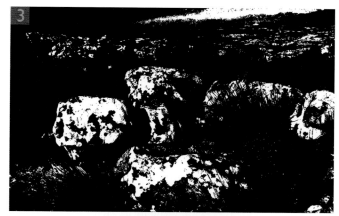

3 Let's now turn to the highlights. The same technique can be applied here too. If you hold down the ⌥ *alt* key as you drag the Highlight slider inwards the Threshold display mode will start off completely black and the lightest points in the image (where you might want to clip the highlights) will appear first as you drag the Highlight input levels slider inwards. As in the previous example, this preview shows an extreme adjustment so you would want to ease off a bit and search for the lightest highlight point and then maybe reduce the clipping slightly since you don't want to risk clipping any of the important (non-specular) highlight detail (see pages 168–170 for more about what to watch out for when clipping the highlights).

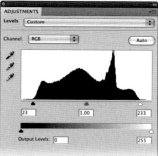

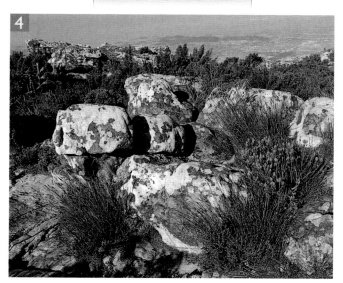

4 Here is the final image, showing what the version in Step 1 looked like after applying the Levels adjustment described here. The levels in the photograph have been expanded to reveal a fuller range of tones in the histogram and, as you can see, the photograph now has more tonal contrast.

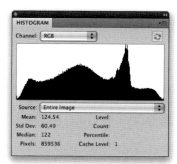

Are Curves all you need?

I have become a firm believer in trying to make Photoshop as simple as possible. There are 22 different items listed in the Image Adjustments menu and of these I reckon that you can achieve almost all the image adjustments you need by using just Curves and Hue/Saturation. Although Curves can replace the need for Levels, I do still like to use the Levels dialog because it is nice and simple to work with. Plus there are also a lot of tutorials out there that rely on the use of Levels.

As if Photoshop were not complicated enough already, you are likely to come across lots of suggestions on ways to tonally adjust images by different means. And you know what, in most cases these techniques can often be summarized with a simple single Curves adjustment. It's just that it can sometimes actually work out quicker (and feel a lot more intuitive) to use a slightly more convoluted route. In Photoshop there is always more than one way to achieve a particular effect. But to quote Fred Bunting: there are always those techniques that are 'more interesting than relevant.'

Ink percentages display

The Pigment/Ink curves display that is used when editing CMYK images is preferable for repro users who prefer to see the output values expressed as ink percentages.

Curves adjustment layers

Any image adjustment that can be done with Levels can also be done using Curves, except with Curves you can accurately control the tonal balance and contrast of the master composite image as well as the individual color channels. You can also target specific points on the tone curve and remap the pixel values to make them lighter or darker and adjust the contrast in that tonal area only.

As with all the other image adjustments, there are two ways you can work with Curves. There is the direct route (via the Image ⇨ Adjustments menu) and the Adjustments panel method described here. In the case of Curves, the two layouts are quite different and I have chosen to concentrate on the Adjustments panel first because I believe this method is the more useful for general image editing, while the direct Curves dialog offers some unique legacy features that are still worth mentioning.

Figure 5.24 shows the Adjustments panel displaying the Curves controls, where the default RGB units are measured in brightness levels from 0 to 255 and the linear curve line represents the output tonal range plotted against the input tonal range, going from 0 in the bottom left corner to 255 levels top right. The vertical axis represents the output and the horizontal axis the input values (and these numbers correspond to the levels scale for an 8-bit per channel image). When you edit a CMYK image, the input and output axis is reversed and the units measured in ink percentages instead of levels. The Curves grid normally uses 25% increments for RGB images and 10% increments for CMYK images, but you can toggle the Curves grid display mode by ⟍ *alt*-clicking anywhere in the grid.

Let's now look at the Curves control options. At the top of the controls section you have a channel selection menu. This defaults to RGB or CMYK meaning that all channels are equally affected by the adjustments you make, but you can use this menu to select specific color channels, which can be useful for carrying out color corrections (see Figure 5.25). The Auto button in Curves is the same as the one in Levels. When you click on this button, it

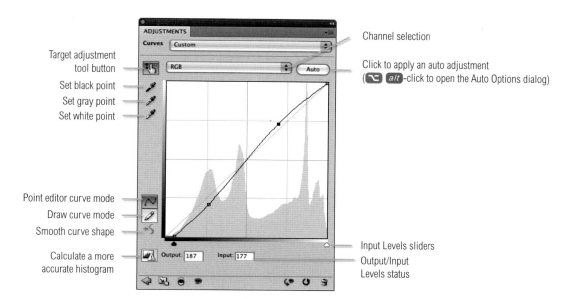

Target adjustment tool button

Set black point
Set gray point
Set white point

Point editor curve mode
Draw curve mode
Smooth curve shape

Calculate a more accurate histogram

Channel selection

Click to apply an auto adjustment
(⌥ *alt*-click to open the Auto Options dialog)

Input Levels sliders
Output/Input
Levels status

Figure 5.24 The Curves dialog is an alternative way of representing the input and output levels, in which the levels' relationship is plotted as a graph. In this example, the shadow end of the curve has been dragged inwards (as you would in Levels), in order to set the optimum shadow point. You can control both the lightness and the contrast of the image by clicking on the curve line to add curve points and adjust the shape of the curve.

applies an auto adjustment based on how the auto settings are configured (see Auto Corrections on pages 316–317). The Input levels sliders work the same way as the ones in Levels and you can drag these with the ⌥ *alt* key held down to access the Threshold view modes as described on the previous two pages. The Output and Input boxes provide numeric feedback for the current selected curve point so that you can also adjust the curve points precisely. There is a histogram warning button that may sometimes appear to warn you that the histogram displayed in the grid area is not an accurate reflection of what the true histogram should be and, if you click on this, it will force an update. The Curves dialog uses the Point curve editor mode by default, but there is also a Pencil button for switching to a draw curve mode which allows you to draw the curve shape directly. Plus there is a 'Smooth curve shape'

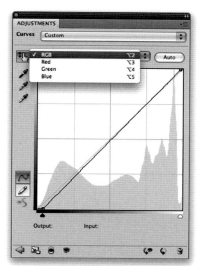

Figure 5.25 When you choose Levels or Curves, the default setting will simultaneously correct all the color channels that make up the composite color image. If you mouse down on the Channel menu, you can select an individual color channel to edit. This is how you can use Curves to make color adjustments.

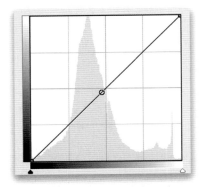

Figure 5.26 When the cursor is dragged over the image, a hollow circle will indicate where the tone value is on the curve.

Adding curve point tip

In non-target adjustment tool mode, if you select the eyedropper tool from the tools panel you can ⌘ *ctrl*-click to add a point to the curve.

Choose a large sample size

With both the eyedropper and the target adjustment tool methods, the pixel sampling behavior is determined by the sample options for the eyedropper tool (see Figure 5.27). If a small sample size is used, curve point placement can become tricky because the hollow circle will dance up and down the curve as you move the cursor over the image. But if you select a large sample size, this will average out the readings and make the cursor placement and on-image editing a much smoother experience.

button that allows you to smooth out drawn curve shapes. Overall, you're not likely to use the draw curve mode much. If you double-click the eyedroppers, you can edit the desired black point, gray point and white point colors and then use these eyedroppers to click in the image to set the appropriate black, gray and white point. There was a time in the early days of Photoshop where the eyedropper controls were important, but there are two reasons why this is less the case now. Firstly, you can accurately set the black and white clipping points in Camera Raw (as described on pages 168–173) and, secondly, the color management system in Photoshop will automatically map the black point for you when you convert to CMYK or use the Photoshop print dialog to make a color managed print. However, the Gray eyedropper can still prove useful for auto color balancing a photo (as described on page 316).

On-image Curves editing

If you click on the target adjustment tool button to activate it and move the cursor over the document window, you will notice a hollow circle that hovers along the curve line. This indicates where any part of the image appears on the curve and if you simply click on the image a new curve point will be added to the curve (Figure 5.26). However, if you click to add a curve point and at the same time drag the mouse up or down in the image window, this will simultaneously move the newly added curve point up and down on the curve. This means that when the target adjustment tool mode is active, you can click and drag directly on the image to make specific tone areas lighter or darker (see the tutorial opposite). Note that if you can get the cursor to hover over an existing curve point you can ⌘ *ctrl*-click to delete it from the curve line.

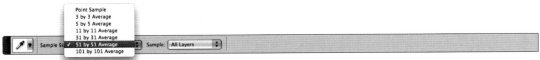

Figure 5.27 The eyedropper tool Options bar showing the Sample size options. For on-image selections it can be useful to choose a large sample size.

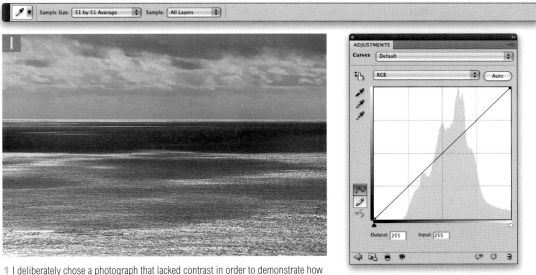

1 I deliberately chose a photograph that lacked contrast in order to demonstrate how the on-image curves editing works. To begin with I added a new Curves adjustment layer and made sure that I had a large sample size set for the eyedropper tool options.

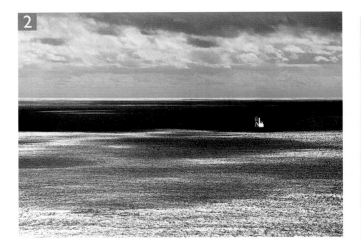

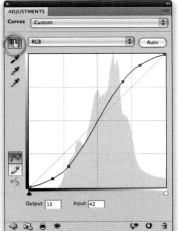

2 I then clicked on the target adjustment tool button (circled) and moved the cursor over the image. I was then able to click with the mouse on the image to add new points to the curve. As I dragged the cursor upwards, this raised the curve upward and lightened the tones beneath where I had clicked in the image. Likewise, as I dragged downwards I was able to darken these tones in the image.

When to use direct curves

The same principles apply here as with the Levels adjustments. Adjustment Curves is the way to go for most image editing work, but if you wish to edit individual Photoshop channels or layer masks the only way to do this is by using direct Curves adjustments. Having said that, it can be argued that the ability to see overlapping channel curve lines and use CMYK percentage units when editing RGB images can be seen as extra features which are lacking in the Adjustments Curves panel.

Direct Curves dialog

Many of the options in the direct Curves dialog are the same as those found in the Adjustments panel (including the new target adjustment mode option). However, in addition to this, there is a Show Clipping option for turning on the shadow and highlight clipping threshold preview when dragging the black point or white point Input sliders. Plus there is also a Curve Display Options section at the bottom. Here you can get to choose between the Light Curves mode (showing levels from 0–255) or the Pigment/Ink Curves mode where the curves values are expressed in percentages. So in the Direct Curves dialog you aren't as restricted as you are in the Adjustments panel and can use the Pigment/Ink Curves mode when working in RGB mode, or the Light Curves mode when working on a CMYK image. There are also button options to switch between showing 25% or 10% increments in the graph display. Or, you can toggle this by ⌥ *alt* -clicking in the graph area.

Checking the Color Overlays option will allow you to simultaneously see the individual color channel curves as you edit the main composite channel curve (Figure 5.28). If you check the Histogram box, you will get to see a 'cached' histogram appear in the curves grid area, which is just like the one you find in Levels. Checking the Baseline option will display a standard reference line to compare your curve movements against. The Intersection Line option will temporarily display intersection lines as you mouse down on a curves point. The reason this is there is so that you can more easily reference a curve point against the outline of the histogram.

Saving and loading curves

Curve settings can be saved by going to the Curves options menu (circled in Figure 5.29) and selecting the Save Preset... option. Once you have named and saved a setting, the preset will then be accessible via the Presets list that appears at the top of both types of Curves dialogs. To delete an existing preset make it active, go to the Adjustments panel options and select 'Delete Current Preset'.

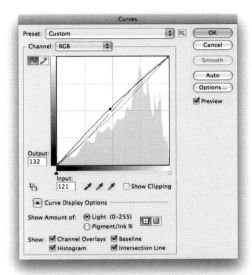
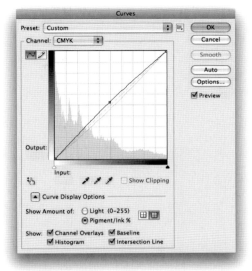

Figure 5.28 If you ⌥ *alt*-click anywhere inside the grid area the grid units will switch from 25% to 10% increments.

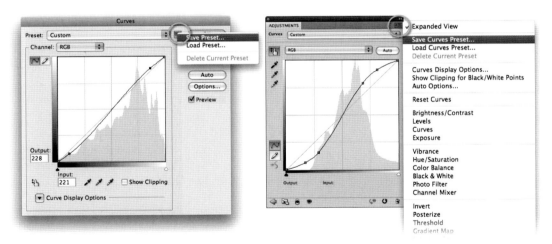

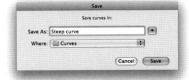

Figure 5.29 You can save any image adjustment as a reusable setting by choosing Save Preset... from the Curves menu (circled). This will pop the Save dialog shown here. Once a curves setting has been saved, it will appear listed in the Curves preset file list (you can save a curve setting wherever you like, but it will only remain in the Presets list if you keep it stored in the default Curves folder). Pre-existing curve settings can be added by going to the same menu and choosing Load Preset... . Note that a curve setting must by identified with the .acv extension; you can only load a curves setting if it has the .acv extension.

Threshold mode preview

The Curves input sliders work exactly like the ones in Levels. You can preview the shadow and highlight clipping by holding down the ⌥ *alt* key as you drag on the Shadow and Highlight sliders circled in the Curves dialog shown in Figures 5.30 and 5.31.

Using Curves in place of Levels

You can adjust the shadow and highlight levels in Curves in exactly the same way as you would using Levels. For example, in the Curves adjustment dialogs you have Input shadows and Input highlights sliders and you can drag these sliders inwards to clip the shadow and highlight levels. If you select a shadow or highlight curves point and move it up or down, you can adjust the Output levels for the shadows or highlights. In Levels you adjust the relative brightness of the image using the Gamma slider, while in the Curves adjustment you can add a single curve point and move it left to lighten or right to darken. The added advantage of this is that you can add more curve points and this will allow you to make more fine-tuned tone adjustments.

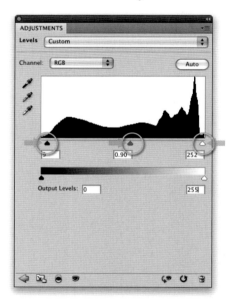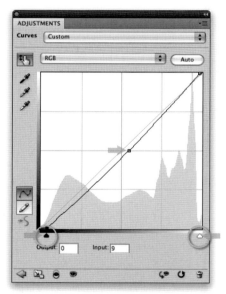

Figure 5.30 The Levels and Curves panel settings shown here will both apply identical adjustments to an image. In the Levels adjustment I moved the Shadows and Highlight input levels sliders inwards. You will notice that the Curves adjustment has an identical pair of sliders with which you can map the shadow and highlight input levels. In the Levels adjustment I moved the Gamma slider to the right to darken the midtones. In the Curves adjustment one can add a point midway along the curve and drag this to the right to achieve an identical kind of 'gamma' midtone adjustment.

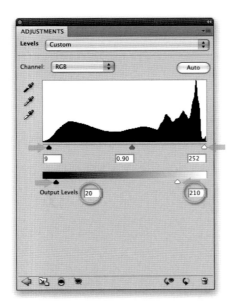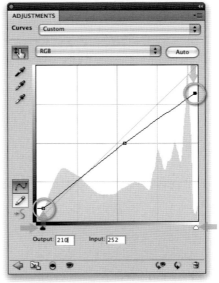

Figure 5.31 The Levels and Curves settings shown here will also apply identical adjustments. In the Levels adjustment I kept the input levels the same and adjusted the output levels to produce an image where the optimized levels were mapped to a levels range of 20–210. In the Curves dialog you can see the highlight point is selected and the curve point has been moved downwards to show a corresponding output value of 210 (the same value as the one entered in the Levels Output Levels).

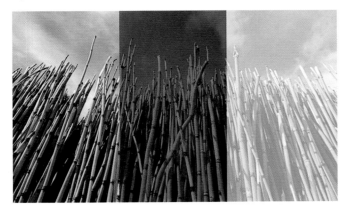

Figure 5.32 Setting the output levels to something other than zero is not something you would normally want to do, except for those times where you specifically want to dull down the tonal range of an image. In the example shown here, the left section shows standard optimized levels, the middle section shows the same image with reduced highlight output levels and the right section shows the image with reduced shadow output levels.

Using Curves to improve contrast

So far I have shown how a Levels or Curves adjustment can be use to expand the levels in order to achieve an image in which the tones have been fully optimized. But there are also times where you may wish to modify the contrast, but without clipping the levels at either end of the histogram. This is where Curves adjustments come into their own.

Figures 5.33–5.35 show three examples of how you can use a Curves adjustment to manipulate the contrast. In Figure 5.33, the shadows and highlights have been optimized, but the curve has been left as a straight line between these two points. In Figure 5.34, two curve points have been added to create a steep 'S' shape curve. By steepening the curve you increase the contrast in the tones that reside in that portion of the curve. In this example, more contrast was added to the midtones. In Figure 5.35, two curve points were added to create a shallow 'S' shape curve. In this example you will notice that there is a decrease in contrast in the midtone areas, because this is where the curve is at its shallowest.

When you first start working Curves you should aim to add just a few points at a time. As you develop your Photoshop skills you can try adding more points, but as you do so, take care to maintain a nice smooth curve shape. Adding more points (especially if they are set too close together) can cause sharp kinks in the curve which can produce an unwanted solarized look.

Curves luminance and saturation

A Normal mode Levels or Curves adjustment will always adjust both the luminance and the color. Which means that as you steepen the curve to increase the contrast, you will be increasing both the luminance and color contrast at the same time. It can therefore be handy to filter a curves adjustment so that it applies either a luminance or color adjustment only (see pages 302–303).

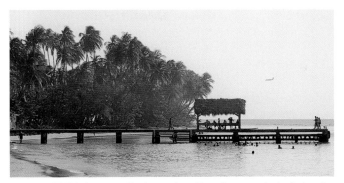

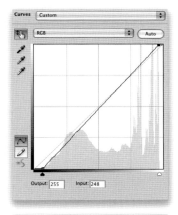

Figure 5.33 This is a normal landscape view with no Curves contrast adjustment.

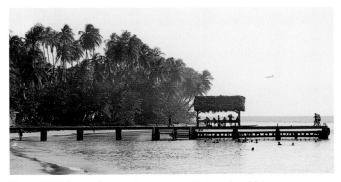

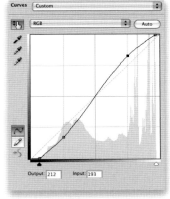

Figure 5.34 You can increase the contrast in this image by adding two or more curve points to create an 'S'-shaped curve as shown in the accompanying Curves adjustment.

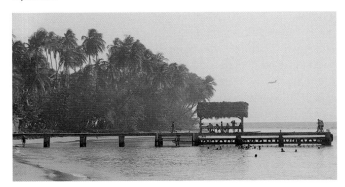

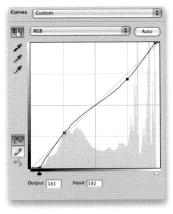

Figure 5.35 You can also decrease the contrast in the same image by adding two or more curve points and creating an 'S'-shaped curve in the opposite direction as shown in the accompanying Curves adjustment.

Easier blend mode access

One of the main benefits of the Adjustment panel approach is that you can switch easily between editing the adjustment controls and adjusting the layer opacity and blend mode settings.

Edit Fade command

If you happen to prefer the direct adjustment method, you can always go to the Edit menu after applying a Curves (or any other adjustment such as a brush stroke or a filter) and choose Fade Curves... (⌘ Shift F ctrl Shift F). This will open the Fade dialog shown in Figure 5.36 where you can fade the opacity of the adjustment as well as change the blend mode.

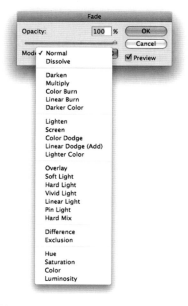

Figure 5.36 The Edit ⇨ Fade dialog.

Luminosity and Color blending modes

The problem with using Normal mode tone adjustments is that as you use Levels or Curves to adjust the tonal balance of a picture, the adjustments you make will simultaneously affect the color saturation as well. In some instances this might be desirable. For example, whenever you start off with a flat image that requires a major Levels adjustment, the process of optimizing the shadows and highlights will leave you with a nice bright-looking picture with increased contrast and colors that are more saturated. This can be considered to be a good thing, but if you are carrying out a careful tone adjustment and want to manipulate the contrast or brightness *without* affecting the saturation, changing the blend mode to Luminosity can isolate an adjustment so that it targets the luminosity values only.

This is where using adjustment layers can come in useful, because you can easily switch the blend modes for any adjustment layer. In the example shown opposite, a Curves adjustment was used to add more contrast to this sunset view of the mountain. When this adjustment is applied in the Normal mode (as shown in Step 1), there is an increase in the color saturation. However, if the curve is applied using a Luminosity blend mode, we get the increase in contrast but without increasing the saturation. Incidentally, I quite often use the Luminosity blend mode whenever I add a Levels or Curves adjustment layer to an image, especially if the tones and colors have already been optimized for contrast and color. This is because whenever I add localized corrections I usually don't want these adjustments to further affect the saturation of the photograph. Similarly, if you are applying an image adjustment (such as Curves) to alter the colors in a photograph, you will want the adjustment to target the color only and leave the luminance values as they are. So whenever you make a color correction using, say, Levels, Curves, Hue/Saturation or any other method, it is often a good idea to change the adjustment layer blend mode to Color.

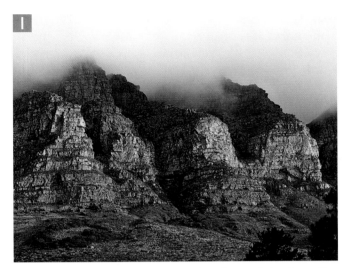

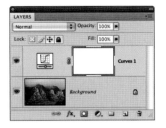

1 When you increase the contrast in an image using a Curves adjustment, you will also end up increasing the color saturation. Sometimes this can produce a desirable result because some photographs are improved when you boost the saturation.

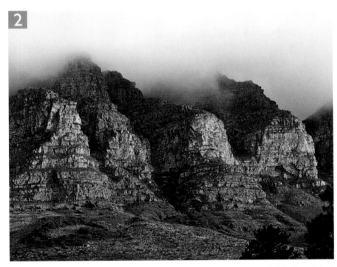

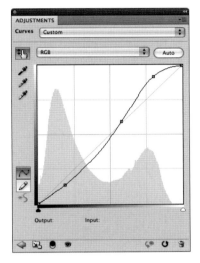

2 In this example I applied the same Curves adjustment as was applied in Step 1, but I changed the layer blend mode to Luminosity. This effectively allowed me to increase the contrast in the original scene, but without increasing the color saturation.

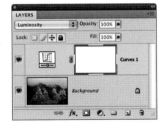

303

Curve presets

At the top of the Curves dialog you will see a Preset menu (Figure 5.37). This contains a number of custom curve presets that shipped with the program plus any curves presets that you have saved recently. The standard curves presets offer some fairly straightforward settings: you can make an image lighter or darker, or apply different contrast curves. These presets might be useful as starting point settings and you can run through the Presets menu selecting the various curve settings just to see how they will affect the look of an image. Some of the other curve settings ambitiously aim to apply a cross process style effect or convert a color negative scan to make a positive image. In my opinion, these are a bit hit or miss. If you want to take a color negative scan and make it into a positive, you would need to create special custom curve setting for each different type of color negative emulsion (see page 305). In all honesty, if you are going to scan color negatives then you are probably going to be better off using the scanner software settings to do the conversion for you.

Figure 5.37 Here is a view of the Curves dialog, showing the Custom curves menu. Note that if you create a manual curves setting and then select a preset, the applied setting will overwrite the previous curve setting, but you can always use the undo command (⌘ Z ctrl Z) to revert to a previous curves setting.

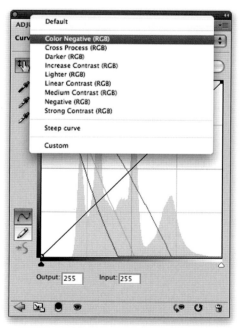

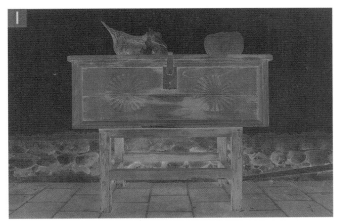

1 If you use Photoshop to convert a color negative to make a positive you could try selecting the Color Negative preset shown in Figure 5.37, but it is unlikely to produce a successful conversion.

2 In most instances it will be necessary to adapt the shape of the curve in the composite channel and individual color channels to achieve an optimum negative to positive conversion.

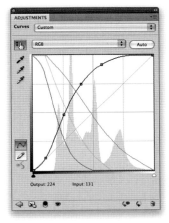

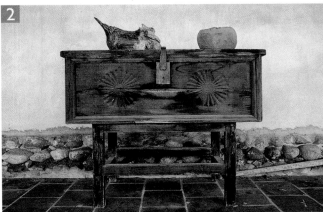

3 In the bottom example I added a saturation boost to the image. Because of the extreme nature of such adjustments, it is better to work on an image that has been scanned in 16-bits per channel.

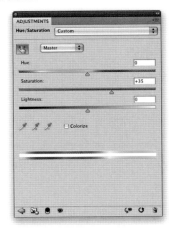

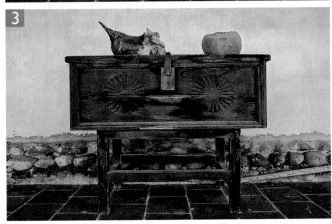

Locking down portions of the curve

Once you get beyond the stage of adding one or two points to a curve, you need to be careful to keep the curve shape under control. Once you start adding more than one point to the curve, adjusting a point on one part of the curve will cause the curve shape to move, pivoting around the adjacent points. One solution is to sometimes lay down 'locking' points on the curve, as shown in Figure 5.38.

Figure 5.38 In this example I wanted to make the dark tones darker, but without affecting the mid to highlight tones so much. Here is what I did. I placed one curve point on the middle intersection point of the curve and another on the 75% intersection point. I then added a third curve point towards the toe of the curve and dragged downwards to darken the shadows and steepen the curve in the shadow to midtone areas. You will notice that because I had added the other two curve points first, adjusting the third curve point had very little effect on the upper portion of the curve.

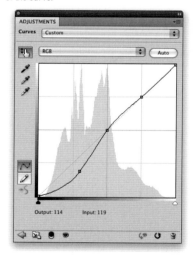

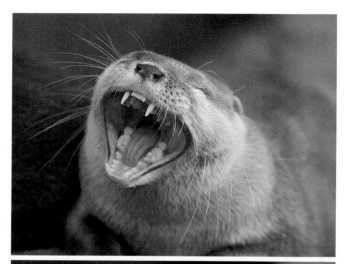

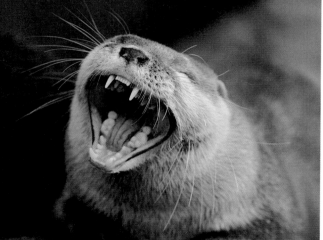

Creating a dual contrast curve

Now let's look at adding even more curve points. There are times where you may want to manipulate the contrast in two sections of the curve at once. For this you will need to place three or more points on the curve such as in Figure 5.39 below. You are now entering dangerous territory, because if you are not careful you can end up either making some of the tones look solarized or flattening them and losing a significant amount of tonal detail.

Figure 5.39 In this example I wanted to boost the contrast in the shadows and the highlights separately. To do this, I applied the curve shape shown here where you will see that by using five curve points I was able to lock down the middle portion of the curve and independently steepen the shadow/midtone and highlight portions of the curve. Note that in order prevent the curve from boosting the color saturation, I set the curve blend mode to Luminosity.

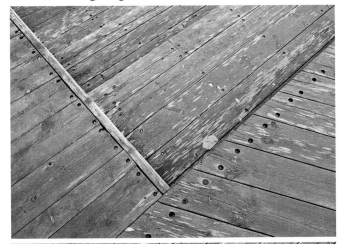

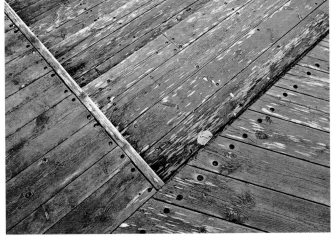

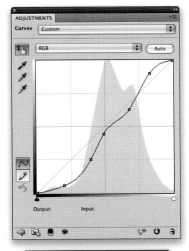

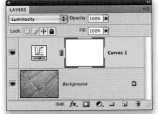

Mask adjustments

The one time when you may find it useful to use the legacy style Brightness/Contrast image adjustment is when you want to edit the contents of an image layer mask. The crudeness of the Brightness and Contrast adjustments can actually be beneficial when you want to force the mask highlight areas to go to white or black.

Brightness and Contrast

For as long as Photoshop has been around, there has been an adjustment control called Brightness/Contrast. For years now many authors and experts have done their best to discourage people from using this adjustment control. This was because of the potential harm it could do to your pictures. Yet so many people continued to use it, oblivious to the fact that it was never intended for photographic use.

However, since Photoshop CS3 the default behavior has been changed to match the Brightness and Contrast sliders found in Camera Raw (see Chapter 3), where the shadow and highlight endpoints are preserved and the image adjustments are constrained to operate between these two points. However, the old legacy behavior is still available as an extra option (Figure 5.40). The main reason for retaining this old style behavior is to maintain compatibility with legacy images where the old style Brightness/Contrast adjustment was recorded as part of a Photoshop action.

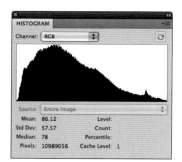
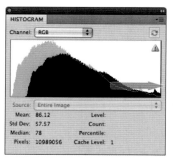
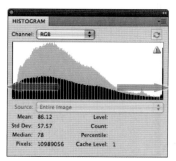
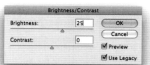
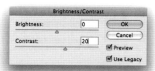

Figure 5.40 The Histogram panel can be used to demonstrate why the legacy Brightness/Contrast image adjustment setting is unsuited for photographic tonal corrections. The histogram on the left shows the normal histogram. If you use the Brightness slider to increase the Brightness, all you are doing is shifting all the tones lighter and, as a consequence of this, the highlight detail will become clipped. If you increase the Contrast, the tones are stretched in both directions so that both the shadows and highlights become clipped.

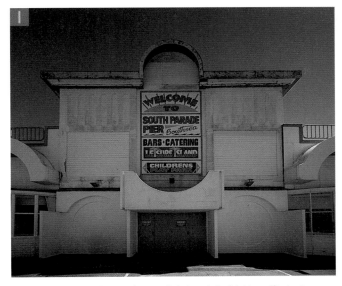

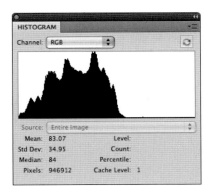

1 This before version shows a photograph that needed a Brightness/Contrast adjustment to brighten the picture.

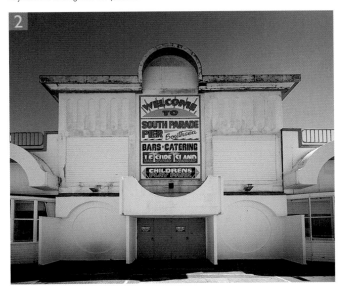

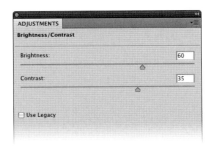

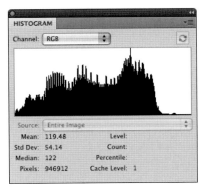

2 Here is the same photograph after I had applied a Brightness/Contrast adjustment (with the Use Legacy box unchecked). Notice how the histogram in the corrected version preserves the full tonal range from the shadows to the highlights.

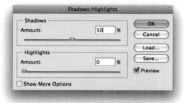

Figure 5.41 The Shadows/Highlights adjustment dialog is shown here in Basic mode. Checking the Show More Options box will reveal the Advanced mode dialog shown in Figure 5.42.

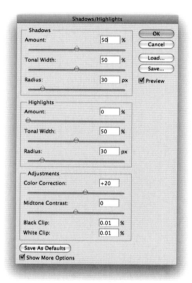

Figure 5.42 The Show More Options mode Shadows/Highlights dialog contains a comprehensive range of controls. I would advise you to always leave the Show More Options box checked so that you open using this as the default mode for Shadows/Highlights adjustments.

Correcting shadow and highlight detail

The Shadows/Highlights image adjustment (Figure 5.41) can be used to reveal more detail in either the shadow or highlight areas of a picture. Shadows/Highlights is a great image adjustment tool to use whenever you have useful tonal information but it is just too compressed to be seen properly. It can be used to perform wonders on most images, not just those where you desperately need to recover detail in the shadows and highlights.

The Shadows/Highlights image adjustment tool makes adaptive adjustments to an image; it works much in the same way as our eyes do when they automatically compensate and adjust to the amount of light illuminating a subject. The Shadows/Highlights adjustment works by looking at the neighboring pixels in an image and making a compensating adjustment based on the average pixel values within a given radius. In Advanced mode, the Shadows/Highlights dialog has various controls which allow you to make the following fine-tuning adjustments.

Amount

This is an easy one to get to get to grips with. The default Amount setting is 50%. Increase or decrease this to achieve the desired amount of highlight or shadow correction. I find this default setting does tend to be rather annoying, so I usually try setting the slider to a lower amount or zero and click on the 'Save As Defaults' button to set this as the new default setting for every time I open Shadows/Highlights.

Tonal Width

The Tonal Width determines the tonal range of pixel values that will be affected by the Amount set. A low Tonal Width setting will narrow the adjustment to the darkest or lightest pixels only. As the Tonal Width is increased the adjustment will spread to affect more of the midtone pixels as well (see Figure 5.43).

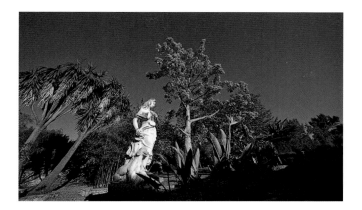

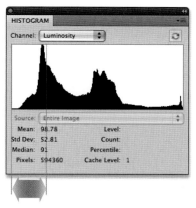

Radius

The Radius setting basically governs the pixel width of the area that is analyzed when making an adaptive correction. Let's concentrate on what would happen when making a shadow correction. If the Shadow Radius is set to zero, the result will be a very flat-looking image. You can increase the Amount to lighten the shadows and restrict the Tonal Width, but if the Radius is low or is set to zero Photoshop will have very little 'neighbor pixel' information to work with when trying to calculate the average luminance of the neighboring pixels. So if the sample Radius is too small, the midtones will also become lightened. If the Radius setting is set too high, this will have the effect of averaging all of the pixels in the image and likewise the lightening effect will be distributed such that all the pixels will get the lightening treatment, not just the dark pixels. The optimum setting is always dependent on the image content and the area size of the dark or light pixels. The optimum pixel Radius width should be about half that amount or less. In practice you don't have to measure the pixel width of the light and dark in every image to work this out. Just be aware that after you have established the Amount and Tonal Width settings you should adjust the Radius setting, making it larger or smaller according to how large the dark or light areas are. There will be a 'sweet spot' where the Shadows/Highlights correction is just right.

Figure 5.43 The Tonal Width slider determines the range of levels the Shadows/Highlights adjustment is applied to. So, for example, if the Shadow adjustment Tonal Range is set to 50, then the pixels which fall within the darkest range from level 0 to level 50 will be adjusted (such as the deep shadows in this photograph).

Radius halos

As you make an adjustment to the Radius setting you will sometimes notice a soft halo appear around sharp areas of contrast between dark and light areas. This is a natural consequence of the Radius function and is most noticeable if you apply large Amount corrections. Aim for a Radius setting where the halo is least noticeable or apply a Fade... adjustment after applying the Shadows/Highlights adjustment. If I am really concerned about reducing halos I sometimes use the history brush to selectively paint in a Shadows/Highlights adjustment.

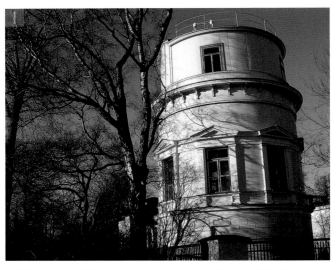

1 In this photograph there are a lot of dark shadows in the trees. With a little help from the Shadows/Highlights adjustment I can bring out more detail in this picture, but without degrading the overall contrast.

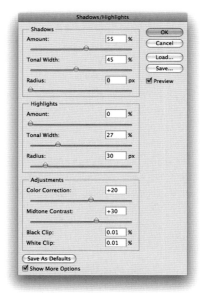

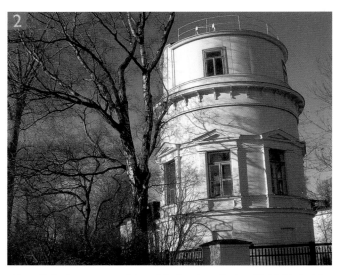

2 I went to the Image menu and chose Adjustments ⇨ Shadows/Highlights. I set the Amount to 55% and raised the Tonal Width to 45%. The Radius adjustment is now crucial because this determines the distribution width of the Shadows/Highlights adjustment. As you can see in this step, if I set the Radius to zero the result will appear flat in contrast.

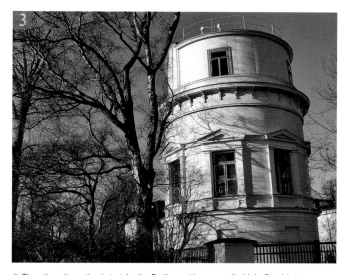

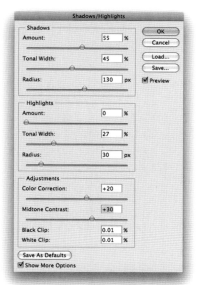

3 The other alternative is to take the Radius setting up really high. But this too can diminish the Shadows/Highlights adjustment effect. It is useful to remember here that the optimum Radius setting is 'area size' related and will fall somewhere midway between these two extremes. In the end, I went for a Radius setting of 130 pixels for the shadows. This was because I was correcting large shadow areas and this setting appeared to provide the optimum correction for this particular photograph. I also increased the Midtone Contrast to +30. This final tweak helped prevent the contrast reduction in the shadows from making the midtones look too flat.

Color Correction

As you correct the highlights and the shadows, the color saturation may change unexpectedly. This can be a consequence of using the Shadows/Highlights to make extreme adjustments. The Color Correction slider will let you compensate for any undesired color shifts.

Midtone Contrast

Even though you may have paid careful attention to getting all the above settings optimized just right so that you target only the shadows or highlights (or both), the midtone areas may still get affected and you can lose some contrast. The Midtone Contrast slider control lets you restore or add more contrast to the midtone areas.

CMYK Shadows/Highlights adjustments

You can use Shadows/Highlights on CMYK files as well as RGB images.

Adobe Camera Raw adjustments

Shadows/Highlights adjustments can work great on a lot of images but now that Camera Raw can be used to edit JPEG and TIFF images as well as raw files, you may like to explore using the Recovery and Fill Light adjustments described on pages 164–165. In many cases you'll find that Recovery and Fill Light work better than using Shadows/Highlights.

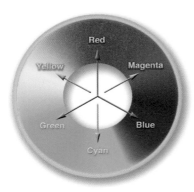

Figure 5.44 The Variations dialog displays color balance variations based on the color wheel model. Here you see the additive primaries (red, green, and blue) and the subtractive primaries (cyan, magenta, and yellow) placed in their complementary positions on the color wheel. Red is the opposite of cyan; green is the opposite of magenta; and blue is the opposite of yellow. Use these basic rules to gain an understanding of how to correct color.

Color corrections

We shall now look at using the image adjustment controls to adjust the colors in an image. Again, almost everything you want to do to edit the color in a flattened pixel image can be achieved using just Levels, Curves and Hue/ Saturation. But before we get into how these should be used, we should take a quick look at the Variations adjustment (Figure 5.45). This image adjustment is a good learning tool for beginners because all the basic image editing tools are combined in a single interface (you can also see how Variations adjustments relate to the color wheel diagram shown in Figure 5.44). Having said that, I would not advise using Variations as a general tool for color correction because it does nothing more than provide a Levels style Gamma slider control to adjust the individual color channels or overall brightness. Anything you do using Variations can be done more simply using Levels (or more accurately using Curves), plus Variations can only be applied to 8-bit images. While Variations does have a Saturation control, the Hue/Saturation adjustment offers more versatile controls. The same goes for the Color Balance image adjustment. This too is simply offering you another way to apply Levels style adjustments.

Figure 5.45 The Variations interface will let you modify the color of the shadows, highlights or midtones separately. For example, clicking on the More Red thumbnail image will cause the red variant to shift to the center and readjust the surrounding thumbnail previews accordingly. Clicking on the More Cyan thumbnail will restore the central preview to its original color balance. In this respect, Variations is just like the Color Balance adjustment, but you also have built in the saturation adjustments and a lighter or darker option. And you can save or load a previous Variations adjustment setting. Variations may be a crude color correcting tool, but it is nonetheless a useful means by which to learn color theory.

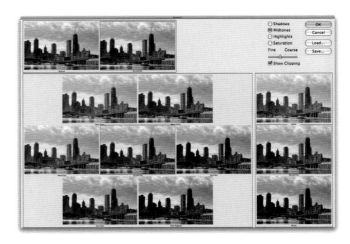

Basic color balancing with Levels

You can correct color casts in an image by using the
Input and Output sliders in the Levels dialog to adjust the
individual color channels. To edit an individual channel,
go to the pop-up menu next to where it says 'Channel',
mouse down here and choose a color channel to edit.
Let's say you have a picture which looks too blue and you
want to add more yellow (such as in Figure 5.46 below).
If you select the Blue channel in the Levels adjustment
and drag the Gamma slider to the right, this will make the
image more yellow. Another way to neutralize midtones
in the Levels or Curves dialog box is to select the gray
eyedropper and click on an area in the image that should
be a neutral gray. With a Levels adjustment, this action
will automatically adjust the gamma setting in each color
channel to remove the cast. Levels may be adequate
enough to carry out basic image corrections, but doesn't
provide you with too much control beyond reassigning the
highlights, shadows and midpoint color values. The best
tool to use for color correction is Curves, because with
Curves you can change the color balance and contrast with
a degree of precision that is simply not available with other
image adjustments.

Color corrections in RGB

You will note that the instructions for all
the color corrections described in this
chapter are done using the RGB color
mode. This is because RGB is a more
versatile color mode for photographers to
work in. There are further reasons why I
recommend this particular workflow, which
I will discuss in more detail in Chapter 12.

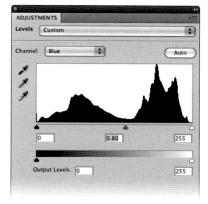

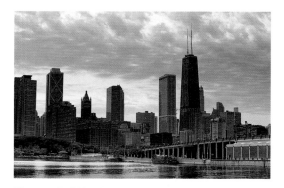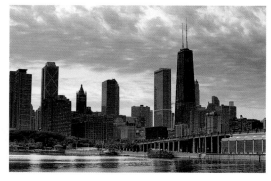

Figure 5.46 With a photograph like the one shown on the left it is not necessarily
a bad thing to have a color cast, but let's say I wanted to apply a basic color
correction to make it more yellow. If I add a Levels adjustment, I can select the Blue
channel from the Channel menu and move the Input gamma slider to the right. This
adjustment will decrease the gamma in the Blue channel and make the midtones in
the image more yellow.

PhotoKit Color gray balancing

I was the project manager for a Pixel Genius plug-in called PhotoKit Color 2. PhotoKit Color 2 contains a set of gray balancing effects which provide effective automatic color balancing with most images. The RSA Neutralize is especially good at the automatic removal of heavy color casts. www.pixelgenius.com/color/

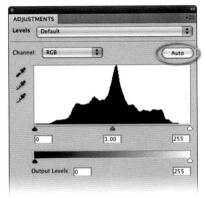

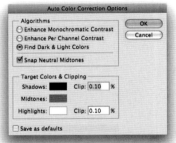

Figure 5.47 The Auto image adjustments can also be accessed when you click on the Options... button in the direct Levels or Curves dialogs, or ⌥ *alt*-click the Auto button (circled) in the Adjustment Layer dialogs. If Snap Neutral Midtones is selected, Auto Color will neutralize these too. You can also customize the clipping values to determine how much the highlights and shadow tones are clipped by the image adjustment.

Auto image adjustments

The Image ⇨ Adjustments menu contains three auto image adjustment tools that are designed to provide automated tone and color correction: Auto Tone, Auto Contrast and Auto Color (see Figure 5.48).

The Auto Tone adjustment works by expanding the levels in each of the individual color channels. This per-channel levels contrast expansion will always result in an image that has fuller tonal contrast, but it may also change the color balance of the image as well. The Auto Tone can produce improved results, but sometimes not. If you want to improve the tonal contrast, but without affecting the color balance of the photograph then try using the Auto Contrast adjustment instead. This carries out a similar type of auto image adjustment as Auto Tone, except it optimizes the contrast by applying an identical Levels adjustment to each of the color channels.

Lastly, there is the Auto Color adjustment. This provides a combination of Auto Contrast to enhance the tonal contrast, combined with an auto color correction that maps the darkest colors to black and the lightest colors to white.

If you open the direct Levels or Curves dialogs you will see an Options... button just below the Auto button. Click on this and you will see the Auto Color Correction Options shown in Figure 5.47. If you are using a Levels or Curves adjustment layer, ⌥ *alt*-click the Auto button to open the Auto Color Correction Options dialog. The algorithms listed here match the auto adjustments. Enhance Per Channel Contrast is the same as Auto Tone. Enhance Monochromatic Contrast is equivalent to Auto Contrast and Find Dark & Light Colors is the same as Auto Color. But notice there is also a Snap Neutral Midtones option. When this is checked, a gamma adjustment is applied in each color channel which aims to correct the neutral midtones as well as the light and dark colors. A clipping value can also be set for the highlights and shadows and this will determine by what percentage the endpoints get automatically clipped.

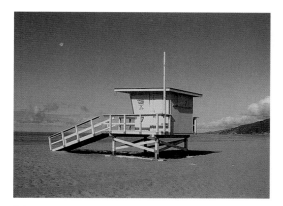

Before

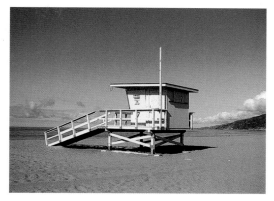

Auto Tone (Enhance Per Channel Contrast)

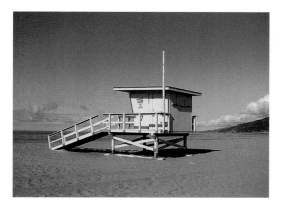

Auto Contrast (Enhance Monochromatic Contrast)

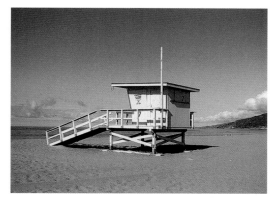

Auto Color (Find Dark & Light Colors + Snap Neutral Midtones)

Figure 5.48 This shows the three auto adjustment methods (with equivalent descriptions for how they are described in the Levels and Curves 'Auto Color Correction Options' dialogs). Auto Tone optimizes the shadow and highlight points in all three color channels. This will generally improve the contrast and color balance of the image. Auto Contrast applies an adjustment across all three channels that will increase the contrast, but without altering the color balance. The Auto Color option maps the darkest and lightest colors to a neutral color (if the swatch colors shown in Figure 5.47 have been altered, you may see a different result). Lastly, I have shown an example of an Auto Contrast adjustment followed by a PhotoKit Color RSA Neutralize effect.

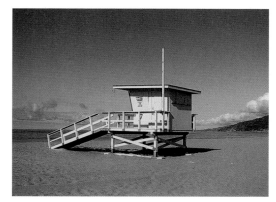

Auto Contrast + PhotoKit Color RSA Neutralize

Channel selection shortcuts

Along with other changes to channel selection shortcuts, those for selecting the color groups in Curves have changed. Use [⌥] [2] [alt] [2] to select the composite curve channel, use [⌥] [3] [alt] [3] to select the Red channel and so on. Likewise, you can use [⌘] [⌥] [2] [ctrl] [alt] [2] to load the composite (luminosity) channel as a selection, [⌘] [⌥] [3] [ctrl] [alt] [3] to load the Red channel as a selection, etc.

For what it is worth, Adobe are making available a plug-in which, when enabled, will allow users to restore the old channel selection behavior. This does of course override the new shortcuts described in the book. Personally, I think it is better to adapt to the new 'universal' shortcuts as these are here to stay, they resolve some of the international keyboard conflicts and help unify the user experience between the other Creative Suite programs.

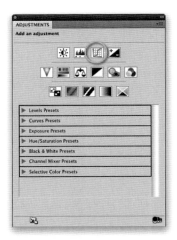

Color correction with Levels or Curves

Of all the color correction methods described so far, Auto Color provides the best automatic one-step tone and color correction method. If you prefer to carry out your color corrections manually, then I would suggest you forget Variations and Color Balance and explore using Levels or Curves color channel adjustments. Earlier I showed how to set the highlight and shadow points in Levels and how to use a gamma adjustment to lighten or darken the image. To keep things simple I used a monochrome photograph. But let's now take things one stage further and use this technique to optimize the individual color channels in an RGB color image.

On these pages I show how you can use the Threshold mode analysis technique to discover where the shadow and highlight endpoints are in each of the three color channels and use this feedback information to set the endpoints. This is a really good way to locate the shadows and highlights and set the endpoints at the same time because, once you have corrected the highlight and shadow colors, all the other colors will usually fall into place and the photograph won't require any further color correction.

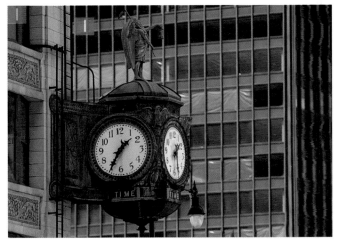

1 This photograph has a blue cast in the shadows and a magenta cast in the highlights. The first step was to go to the Adjustments panel and click on the Curves button (circled) to add a new Curves adjustment layer.

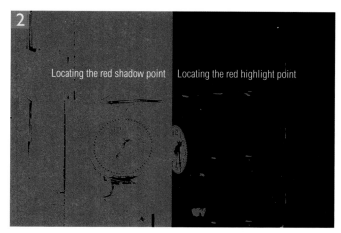

Locating the red shadow point · Locating the red highlight point

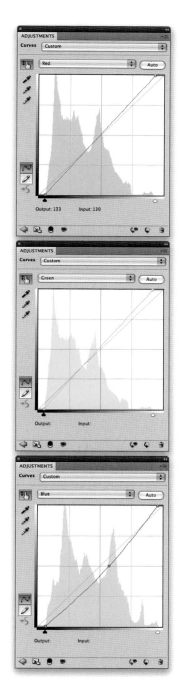

2 I went to the Channel menu, selected the Red channel and adjusted the Shadow and Highlight input sliders until the red shadow and highlight points were set just to the point where they started to clip. If you hold down the ⌥ *alt* key as you do this you will see the Threshold display mode (shown above) which will help you locate the shadow and highlight points more easily. I then repeated these steps with the Green and Blue channels until I had individually adjusted the shadow and highlight points in all three color channels.

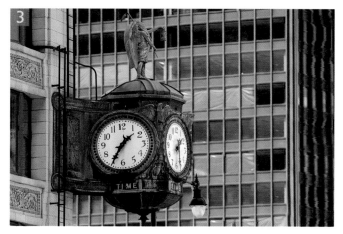

3 This technique of adjusting the color channels one by one will help you remove color casts from the shadows and highlights with greater precision. The trick is to use the Threshold display mode as a reference tool to indicate where the levels start to clip in each channel and consider backing off slightly, so that you leave some headroom in the composite/master channel to make general refinements to the Curves adjustment, ensuring that the highlights do not blow out. Finally, I added a midpoint in the Blue channel and dragged it to the right to add more yellow.

Finding a neutral RGB value

If you are editing an image in RGB mode and using one of the standard RGB color spaces such as Adobe RGB, sRGB, ColorMatch RGB or ProPhoto RGB you can use the eyedropper or color sampler tools to match the RGB values (see Figure 5.49).

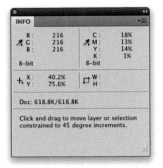

Figure 5.49 The Info panel can be used to read color information which helps determine whether the colors are neutral or not regardless of any monitor inaccuracies. Equal Red, Green and Blue values will always mean a color is neutral.

Direct Curves shortcuts

The Adjustment curves panel shortcuts have been adapted to take into account the fact that these Curves adjustments are non-modal. As a consequence of this, some of the previous Curves dialog shortcuts have had to be revised, which is why you now need to use the ➕ and ➖ keys in both the Adjustments panel and direct Curves dialogs to select next and previous curve points.

Precise color correction using Curves

The Levels adjustment technique can be quite effective at correcting the color at the shadows, highlights and midtones. It therefore follows that you can carry out more precise color corrections by using Curves to adjust the individual channels. As a general rule, once you have corrected for a cast in the highlights and shadows then all the other colors should more or less fall into place, and a further tweak to the midtones may be all you need. However, there are still plenty of situations where you may wish to exploit the full potential of a Curves adjustment to improve the color appearance. In the steps shown opposite, instead of adjusting the end points, I found that I needed to use two midpoint Curves adjustments in the Red and Blue channels to correct a blue/cyan cast.

Let's look at how to make Curves adjustments based on pixel color measurements. If you ⌘ *ctrl*-click anywhere on an image, this will add a new control point on the corresponding portion of the curve. This is useful when making basic tone edits, as you can determine where to add Curve control points by simply ⌘ *ctrl*-clicking on the image. Now let's take this one stage further. You can use the Info panel shown in Figure 5.49 to determine whether a gray color is actually neutral or not. Based on this readout information, you can hold down the ⌘ *Shift* *ctrl* *Shift* keys and click in the document window to add control points to all three color channels at once (but not to the main composite curve). So, when adding control points to color correct the white dress image example that follows on pages 322–323, I ⌘ *Shift* *ctrl* *Shift*-clicked on top of each of the color sampler points to add these as control points in all three color channels in the Curves dialog. When you are editing the points in the Curves dialog, you can *Shift*-click additional points on the curve to select multiple points. Then, as you adjust one control point the others will move in unison (to deselect all the points use ⌘ *D* *ctrl* *D*). When a single point is selected you can select the next point using the ➕ key, and you can select the previous point by using the ➖ key (see sidebar on working in the Direct Curves dialog).

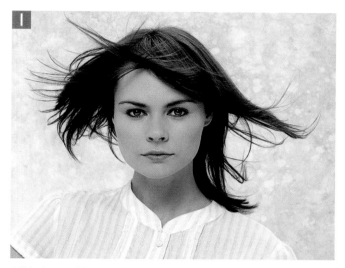

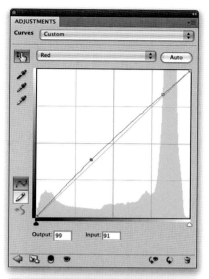

1 This photograph has a cold blue cast that is particularly noticeable in the backdrop, which should be a neutral gray. I went to the Adjustments panel and chose Curves...

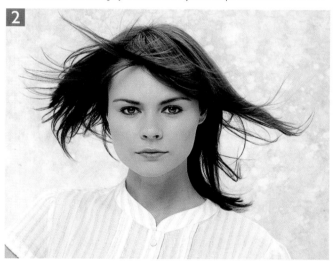

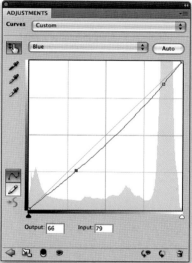

2 This step shows the curves corrected version, where I was able to get rid of the cast in stages by adjusting the shape of the curve in the individual color channels. I first selected the Red color channel from the Channel menu and added a couple of control points to the curve to adjust the color balance for the midtones and highlights. I then went to the Blue channel and added two points to the curve, this time to correct the color for the shadows and highlights in the Blue channel. I simply applied these corrections based on appearance and what made the image look right.

1 Whenever you have something white or gray photographed against a neutral background, any color cast will be extremely noticeable. In this example I selected the color sampler tool and clicked on the image in three different places on the model's white dress, plus once on the backdrop. Each click positioned a new persistent color sampler readout and the readout values were displayed in the Info panel. The intention here was to measure the color at different points of lightness so that these measurements could be used to calculate a precise Curves adjustment.

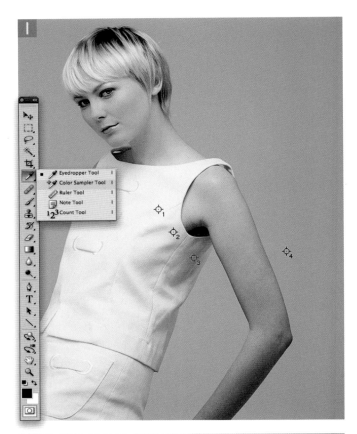

2 The color sample points can be repositioned as necessary by dragging on them with the color sampler (you can access the tool while in an Image Adjustment dialog by holding down the Shift key). Once the color sampler readouts were in place, it was time to add a Curves adjustment layer. With the Curves dialog open, I zoomed in to get a close-up view of the dress where the points had been placed and ⌘ Shift ctrl Shift -clicked on top of each of the sampler points. This added a corresponding curve control point to the individual RGB channel curves. When I inspected the Red, Green and Blue channels in the Curves dialog I could see three points had been added in each channel.

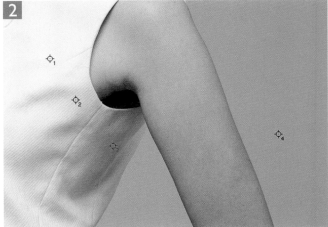

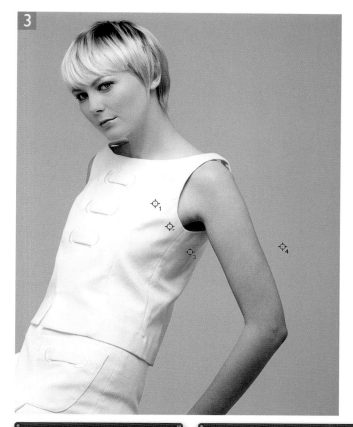

3 Here is an example of the Curves adjustment that was made to the three channels based on the Info panel information. The first RGB readout figure indicates the original input value. At each point I looked at the three numbers to see which of these represented the median value. I then adjusted the points in the other two channels so that these other two output values matched the median value (you can manually drag the point or use the keyboard arrows to balance the output value to match those of the other two channels). Note that *Shift* +arrow key moves the control points in multiples of 10.

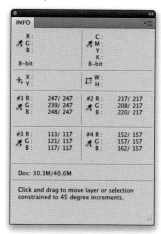

INFO

R: C:
G: M:
B: Y:
                K:
8-bit   8-bit

X: W:
Y: H:

#1 R: 247/ 247   #2 R: 217/ 217
   G: 239/ 247   G: 208/ 217
   B: 248/ 247   B: 220/ 217

#3 R: 113/ 117   #4 R: 152/ 157
   G: 121/ 117   G: 157/ 157
   B: 117/ 117   B: 162/ 157

Doc: 30.3M/40.6M

Click and drag to move layer or selection constrained to 45 degree increments.

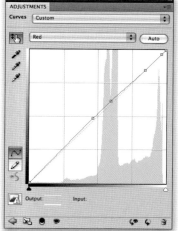
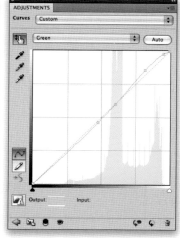
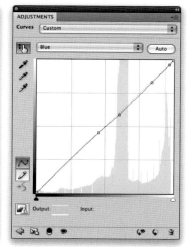

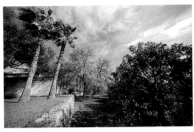

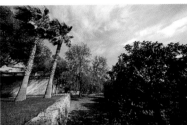

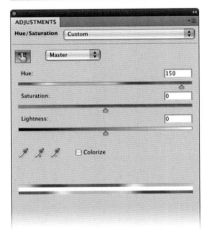

Figure 5.50 This shows an extreme example of
how a Hue/Saturation adjustment can be used to
radically alter the appearance of a photograph. As
you move the Hue slider left or right the colors in
the image will be mapped to new values. You get
an indication of this transformation by looking at
the two color ramps at the bottom of the dialog.
The top one represents the original 'input' color
spectrum and the lower ramp represents how
those colors are translated as output colors.

Hue/Saturation

The Hue/Saturation dialog controls are based around the
HSB (Hue, Saturation, Brightness) color model, which is
basically an intuitive form of the Lab Color model. When
you select the Hue/Saturation image adjustment you can
adjust the image colors globally. Or, you can selectively
apply an adjustment to a narrower range of colors. The
two color spectrum ramps at the bottom of the Hue/
Saturation dialog box provide a visual clue as to how the
colors are being mapped from one color to another. The
hue values are based on a 360 degree spectrum, where red
is positioned mid-slider at 0 degrees and all the other colors
are assigned numeric values in relation to this. So cyan
(the complementary color of red) can be found at either
−180 or +180 degrees. Adjusting the Hue slider only will
alter the way colors in the image are mapped to new color
values; Figure 5.50 shows an extreme example of how the
colors in a normal color image would look if they were
mapped by a Hue adjustment only. As the Hue slider is
moved you will notice how the lower color ramp position
slides left or right, relative to the upper color ramp.

Saturation adjustments are easy enough to understand.
Positive values boost saturation, while negative values
reduce the saturation. Outside the Master edit mode, you
can choose from one of six preset color ranges with which
to narrow the focus of a Hue/Saturation adjustment.
Once you have selected one of these color range
options, you can then sample a new color value from the
image window, and this will center the Hue/Saturation
adjustments around the sampled color. *Shift*-click in the
image area to add to the color selection and **⌥** *alt*-click
to subtract colors (see page 325).

Colorize mode

When the Colorize option is checked, the hue component
of the image is replaced with red (Hue value 0 degrees),
Lightness will remain the same at 0%, and Saturation
at 25%. You could use this to colorize a monochrome
image, but you would be better off using the Photo Filter
adjustment (see page 328).

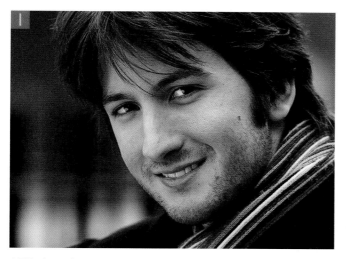

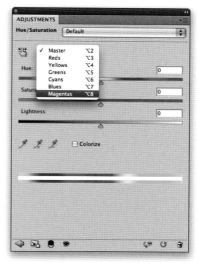

1 This picture shows a portrait photograph in which I would like to target the purple background color and make it less intense. One way to approach this is to go to the target color group menu shown here and select 'Magentas'.

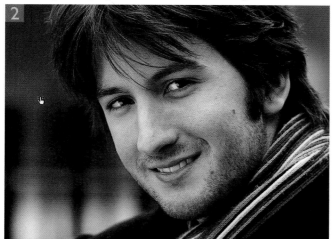

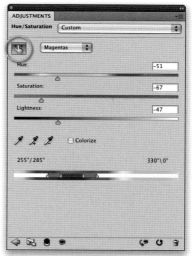

2 Another approach is to make the target mode option active (circled) and carry out an on-image adjustment by dragging on the color area you wish to modify (this will also select the target color group from the menu). You can then drag to the left or right to decrease or increase the saturation. You'll notice I also used the Hue and Lightness sliders to further modify the adjustment. The Magentas color group can also be narrowed down. In the color ramp at the bottom, the dark shaded area represents the selected color range and the lighter shaded area (defined by the outer triangular markers) represent the fuzziness drop-off either side of the color selection. You can modify the range and fuzziness of the selection by dragging the slider bars.

Color selection shortcuts

The shortcuts for selecting the color groups in Hue/Saturation have changed. Use ⌃2 alt 2 to select the Master group, ⌃3 alt 3 to select the Reds and so on.

325

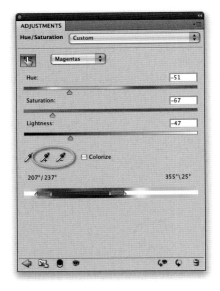

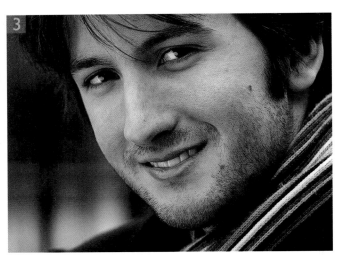

3 As well as manually dragging the sliders, you can also use the eyedroppers (circled) to add or subtract from a color range selection. For this step, I selected the plus eyedropper and clicked on the edges of hair, to add these colors to the Magentas selection and remove the purple color from the hair. However, you'll also notice that as the color ramp selection is widened, other colors were included in the selection such as the lips and the scarf.

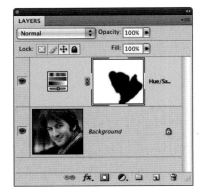

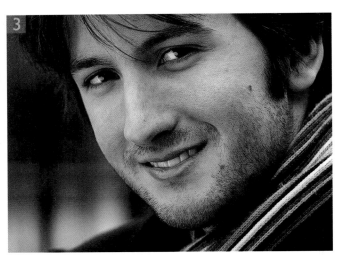

4 This brings us to the final step, which was to paint on the adjustment layer mask with black in order to hide the Hue/Saturation mask and prevent this adjustment from affecting the skin tones and the scarf. Painting with black restored the colors in these regions to how they were originally.

Photo: © Jeff Schewe 2008

Vibrance

The Vibrance adjustment is available as a direct and Adjustment panel option (Figure 5.51) and allows you to carry out Camera Raw style Vibrance and Saturation adjustments directly in Photoshop. If you refer back to Chapter 3 you will recall that Vibrance applies a non-linear style saturation adjustment in which the less saturated colors receive the biggest saturation boost, while those colors that are already brightly saturated remain relatively protected as you boost the vibrance. The net result is a saturation control that allows you to make an image look more colorful, but without the attendant risk of clipping those colors that are saturated enough already. As you can see in Figure 5.52 below, Vibrance also prevents skin tones from becoming over-saturated as you increase the amount setting. As I say, the Saturation control matches that found in Camera Raw. It is similar to the Saturation slider in Hue/Saturation, but applies a slightly gentler adjustment.

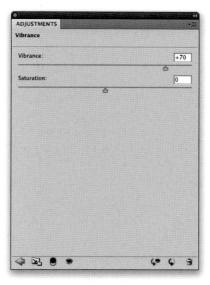

Figure 5.51 The Vibrance Adjustment panel.

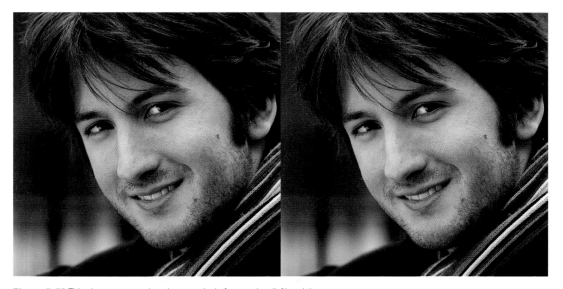

Figure 5.52 This shows a comparison between the before version (left) and the after version (right), in which I boosted the Vibrance by 70%. As you can see, this has made the purple colors in the background and on the scarf appear more saturated, but there is a more modest increase in saturation for the skin tones.

Color temperature

Color Temperature is a term that links the appearance of a black body object to its appearance at specific temperatures, measured in degrees Kelvin. Think of a piece of metal being heated in a furnace. At first it will glow red but as it gets hotter, it emits a red, then yellow and then a white glow. Indoor tungsten lighting has a low color temperature (a more orange color), while sunlight has a higher color temperature and emits a bluer light.

Photo Filter blending

The Photo Filter effectively applies a solid fill color layer with the blend mode set to 'Color', although you can achieve different results by using different layer blend modes.

Photo Filter

One of the advantages of shooting digitally is that most digital cameras will record a white balance reading at the time of capture and this information can be used to automatically process an image that is more or less color corrected. This can be done either in-camera or by using the 'As Shot' white balance setting in Camera Raw when processing a raw capture image. If you are shooting with color film, the only way to compensate for fluctuations in the color temperature of the lighting is to use the right film (daylight or tungsten balanced) and, if possible, use the appropriate color compensating filters.

However, you can also crudely adjust the color balance in Photoshop by using the Photo Filter adjustment, which is available in the Image ⇨ Adjustments menu or as an Adjustment panel option. The Photo Filter offers a preset range of filter colors, but if you click on the Color button you can select any color you like (after clicking on the color swatch) and adjust the Density to modify the filter's strength. Figure 5.53 shows a creative application for the Photo Filter adjustment.

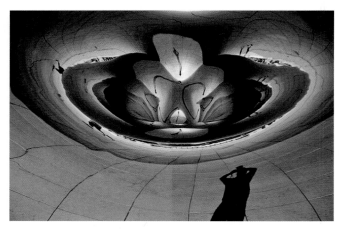

Figure 5.53 The original version (left) had a strong orange cast. To modify this photograph, I added a Photo Filter adjustment. But instead of selecting a filter from the Filter presets list I clicked on the Color swatch option (which opened the Color Picker dialog) and selected a deep blue color to filter the image with.

Multiple adjustment layers

When you add multiple adjustment layers you can preview how the image will look using various combinations of adjustment layers and readjust the settings as many times as you want before applying them permanently to the photo. For example, you might want to use multiple adjustment layers to apply different coloring treatments to a picture. Instead of producing three versions of an image, all you need to do is add three adjustment layers, each using a different coloring adjustment, and switch the adjustment layer visibility on or off to access each of the color variations (Saving Layer Comps can help here).

While it is possible to keep adding more adjustment layers to an image, you should try to avoid any unnecessary duplication of the layers. It is wrong to assume that when the image is flattened the cumulative adjustments will somehow merge to become a single image adjustment. When you merge down a series of adjustment layers, Photoshop will apply them sequentially, the same as if you had made a series of normal image adjustments. So the main thing to watch out for is any doubling up of the adjustment layers. If you find you have a Curves adjustment layer above a Levels adjustment layer, it would be better to try and combine the Levels adjustment within the Curves adjustment instead. Of course, when you use masked adjustment layers to adjust specific areas of a picture you can easily end up with lots of adjustment layers. One potential drawback of this is that it may slow down the screen preview times. This slowness is not a RAM memory issue, but to do with the extra calculations that are required to redraw the pixels on the screen. If you think this is happening then try switching off some of the adjustment layers while you are editing the photograph.

To summarize, the chief advantages of adjustment layers are: the ability to defer image adjustment processing, and the ability to edit the layers and make selective image adjustments.

Grouped adjustments

If you place your image adjustment layers inside a layer group you can use the layer group visibility to turn multiple image adjustments on or off at once (see Figure 5.54). You can also add a layer mask to a layer group and use this to hide or show all the adjustments in a group.

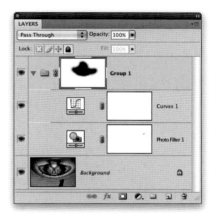

Figure 5.54 This shows an example of how adjustments can be grouped together and a single mask applied to the combined group of layers.

Repeated adjustments warning

It is important to stress here that the pixel data in an image can easily become degraded through repeated image adjustments. Pixel data information will progressively become lost through successive adjustments as the pixel values are rounded off. This is one reason why it is better to use adjustment layers, because you can keep revising these adjustments without damaging the photograph until you finally decide to flatten the image.

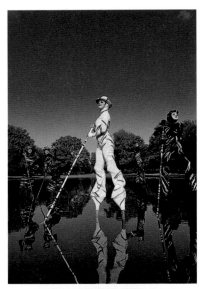

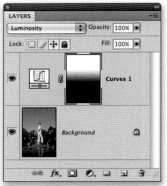

Figure 5.55 This shows an example of a darkening adjustment layer applied to an image, but with a black to white gradient applied to the layer mask to fade out the adjustment from the middle of the image downwards.

'Stalkers' by The Wrong Size.
Photograph: © Eric Richmond

Adjustment layer masks

Although there are dodge and burn tools in Photoshop, which have been improved in Photoshop CS4, they are not really suited for dodging and burning broad areas in a photograph. If you want to dodge or burn a photograph, such as darken a sky or lighten someone's face, then the best way to do this is to use a masked adjustment layer. This is not to say that the dodge and burn tools serve no use. Even though they have been improved in CS4, they are just not ideal for this type of photographic retouching. Working with adjustment layers is by far the best way to shade or lighten portions of an image, because you have the freedom to re-edit an adjustment layer to make the adjustment lighter or darker. Adjustment layers have an active layer mask, which means that whenever an adjustment layer is active, you can paint or fill using black to selectively hide an adjustment effect, and paint or fill with white to reveal again. Plus you can also keep editing the adjustment layer mask (painting with black or white) until you are happy with the quality of the mask (see Figure 5.55).

Masks panel controls

The Masks panel (Figure 5.57) is also new to Photoshop CS4 and can be used to refine the mask or masks associated with a layer. Layer masking is a topic I'll be discussing more fully in Chapter 9 but, because it is relevant to masking adjustment layers, I thought it best to briefly introduce the Masks panel features here first.

Adjustment layers are added to the layer stack with a pixel mask attached, so the default mode for the Masks panel will show the Pixel mask mode options. If you click on the Vector mask mode button next to it, you can add and edit a vector layer mask (see Step 4 on page 333). You can tell which mode is active because it will say Pixel Mask or Vector mask at the top of the panel and the relevant mode button will have a stroked border.

The Density slider can be used to adjust the density of the mask. If you apply a black mask this will normally hide all the black masked contents on a layer, but if you reduce the Density, this lightens the black mask color and therefore allows you to soften the contrast of the mask. So, when Density is set to 50%, the black mask colors will only apply a 50% opacity mask and the lighter mask colors will be proportionally reduced.

The Feather slider can be used to soften the mask edges up to a 250 pixel radius. Beneath this though is the Mask Edge... button which will open the Refine Edge dialog (Figure 5.56), where you'll find you have even greater control over the mask edges and softness.

The Color Range button allows you to make selections based on colors that are in the image you are editing. This means that you can select colors to add or subtract from a Color Range selection and see the results applied directly as a mask. Beneath that is the Invert button for reversing a masking effect and at the bottom of the panel are options for converting a mask to a selection, deleting the mask and applying it to the layer, enabling/disabling the mask and a Delete button to remove the mask.

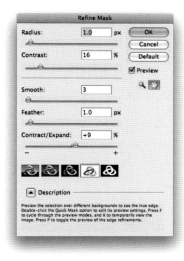

Figure 5.56 The Refine Edge dialog (see Chapter 9 for more information on using Refine Edge).

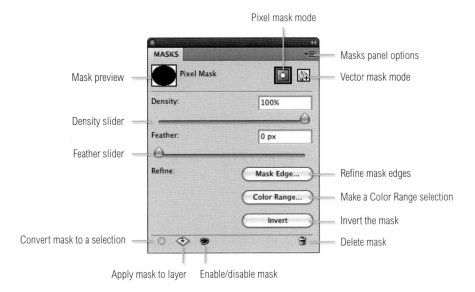

Figure 5.57 The Masks panel controls.

Masks panel editing

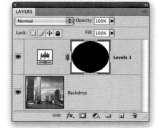

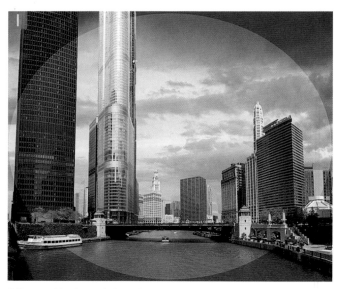

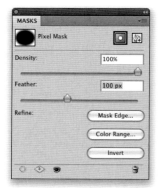

1 You can add a vignette in Photoshop by adding a darkening Levels (or Curves) adjustment, making an elliptical selection and filling the pixel mask with black.

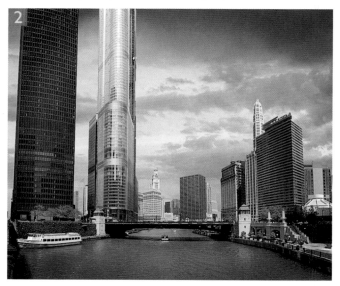

2 If you go to the Masks panel you can increase the Feather amount to make the hard mask edge softer.

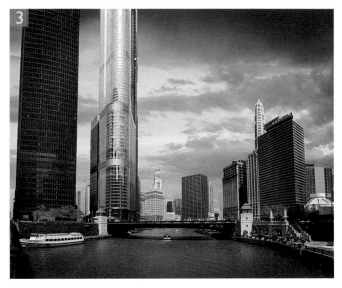

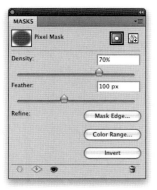

3 But let's say I wanted to soften the transition between the masked and unmasked areas. By decreasing the Density one can make the black areas of the mask lighter and thereby reveal more of the adjustment effect in the center of the image.

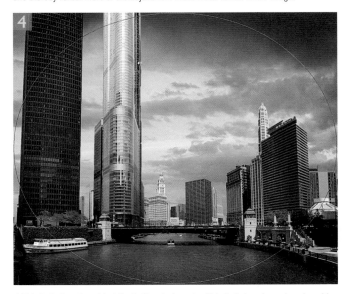

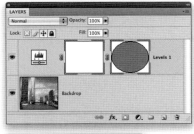

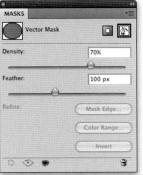

4 This technique is not just limited to pixel masks. This last step shows how I could have started with a subtractive elliptical pen path shape, applied this as a Vector mask and used the exact same Masks panel settings to soften the mask edge.

Color Range adjustment layer masking

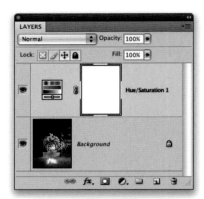

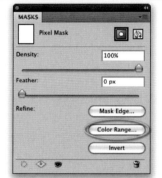

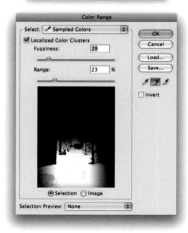

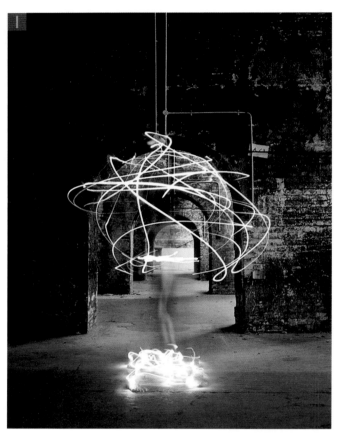

1 In this example I wanted to demonstrate how to use the Masks panel controls in conjunction with an image adjustment to modify the image shown here, so that I could simultaneously control the adjustment effect and the adjustment masking. To start with, I added a new Hue/Saturation adjustment layer. I then went to the Masks panel and clicked on the Color Range button, which opened the Color Range dialog shown here. With the Localized Color Clusters option checked, I used the plus eyedropper tool to add color samples to the selection, sampling the blues in the central area of the photograph while avoiding the walls. I then adjusted the Fuzziness and Range, till I was happy with the way the selection looked, and clicked OK to the Color Range selection.

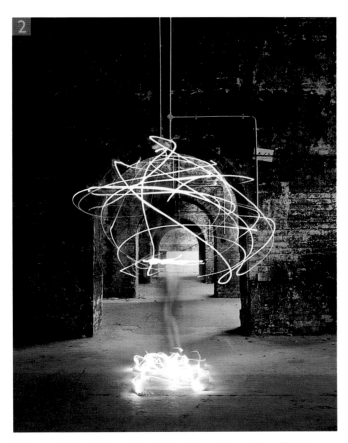

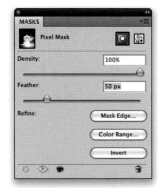

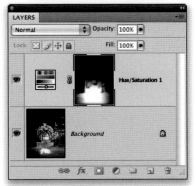

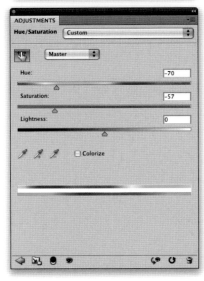

2 I then went to the Masks panel and feathered the selection, adding a 50 pixel feather. You can see a preview of the mask in both the small Masks panel preview as well as in the Layers panel. All I needed to do now was to adjust the Hue/Saturation sliders in the Adjustments panel. For this step I decided to make some of the blue colors more green and reduce the color saturation slightly.

The main thing to learn from this particular example is that you can switch back and forth between the Adjustments panel and the Masks panel to re-edit the adjustment effect and masking. When you combine the ease of adjustment editing with the power of the new Masks panel and Color Range selections, Photoshop CS4 has the potential to allow you to make selections and modify images like never before.

Photograph: © Eric Richmond

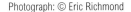

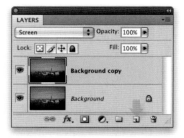

Figure 5.58 Here is the first of two examples showing how you can use blend modes to adjust an image. In this example I dragged the Background layer down to the New Layer panel button to make a duplicate layer and changed the layer blending mode from Normal to Multiply. When the image was saved, the file size doubled to 64 MB.

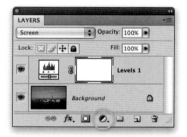

Figure 5.59 In this example I added a new Levels adjustment layer, but didn't apply any changes to the Levels settings. I then changed the adjustment layer blend mode from Normal to Multiply. Both this and the Figure 5.58 example produced identical results, but in this case the file size was only increased by 57 kilobytes.

Blend mode adjustments

You can lighten, darken or add contrast to an image by adding an adjustment layer above the Background layer (or at the top of the layer stack) and simply change the blend mode to Screen, Multiply or Overlay. You don't need to apply a specific image adjustment, just add a neutral adjustment layer (any will do) and select one of the above layer blending modes. The Screen mode can be used to lighten an image, Multiply to darken and Overlay to add more contrast. You could achieve the same type of result by duplicating the Background layer and changing the blend mode of the duplicate layer, but this is actually quite unnecessary and you'll end up with an image that is twice the file size, whereas adding an adjustment layer will normally increase the file size by just a few kilobytes.

Blend modes are in effect a shorthand for applying different, set-value Curves adjustments. For example, the late Bruce Fraser devised a semi-automated workflow in which he recorded separate Photoshop actions to apply a Screen, Multiply of Overlay neutral adjustment layer and filled the layer mask with black. All he had to do then was select a paint brush or gradient tool to paint on the layer mask and reveal the adjustment effect.

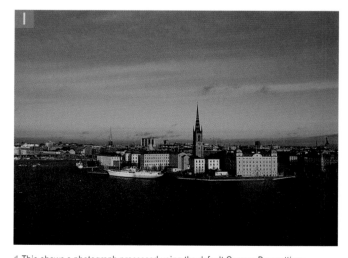

1 This shows a photograph processed using the default Camera Raw settings.

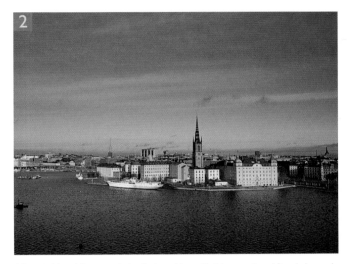

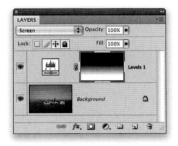

2 I started by adding a neutral adjustment layer (in this case, Levels) and changed the layer blend mode to Screen. This step lightened the whole image, but since I was mainly interested in lightening the water, I applied a linear, black to white gradient to the adjustment layer mask to fade out the adjustment from the horizon upwards.

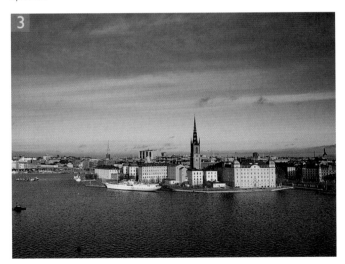

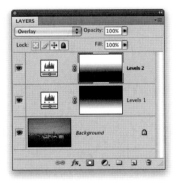

Overlay alternatives

Instead of using the Overlay blend mode, you might also like to try using the Soft Light or Hard Light blend modes for gentler or stronger contrast adjustments.

3 I then wanted to darken the sky, so I added a second neutral adjustment layer. At this stage I could have used a Multiply blend mode to darken the image, but instead, I used the Overlay blend mode to apply more contrast. Again, I used the gradient tool to add a linear, black to white gradient to fade out the adjustment, this time from the horizon downwards.

Front Image cropping

If you want a crop to match the dimensions and resolution of a document that is already open in Photoshop, click on that document to make it active. Then click on the Front Image button in the Crop Options bar. This will load the document dimensions and resolution into the Crop Options settings. Now select the image you wish to crop and, as you drag with the crop tool, the aspect ratio of the front image will be applied. When you OK the crop, the image size will be adjusted to match the front image resolution.

Cropping

The image you are editing will most likely require some kind of crop, either to remove unwanted edges or to focus more attention on the subject. Select the crop tool from the Tools panel and drag to define the area to be cropped. To zoom in on the image as you make the crop, you may sometimes find it useful to use the zoom tool shortcut: hold down the Spacebar followed by the ⌘ *ctrl* key and marquee drag over the area you want to magnify, and to zoom out use the Spacebar plus ⌥ *alt* or use ⌘ *O* *ctrl* *O* (which is the shortcut for View ⇨ Fit To Window). You can then zoom back in again to magnify another corner of the image to adjust the crop handles.

If the crop tool does not behave as expected try clicking on the Clear button in the tool Options bar and this will reset the tool. In the normal default mode the crop tool will allow you to set any rectangular-shaped crop you like and merely trim away the unwanted pixels without changing the image size or resolution. Figures 5.60 and 5.61 show and explain the normal and modal states for the crop tool options.

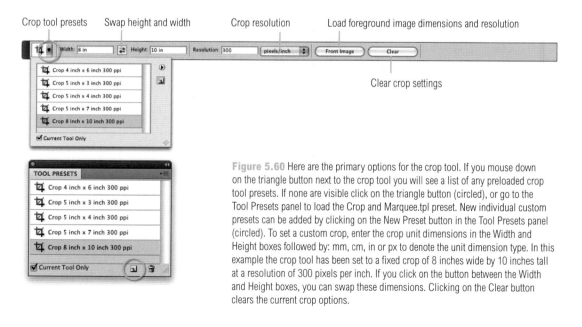

Figure 5.60 Here are the primary options for the crop tool. If you mouse down on the triangle button next to the crop tool you will see a list of any preloaded crop tool presets. If none are visible click on the triangle button (circled), or go to the Tool Presets panel to load the Crop and Marquee.tpl preset. New individual custom presets can be added by clicking on the New Preset button in the Tool Presets panel (circled). To set a custom crop, enter the crop unit dimensions in the Width and Height boxes followed by: mm, cm, in or px to denote the unit dimension type. In this example the crop tool has been set to a fixed crop of 8 inches wide by 10 inches tall at a resolution of 300 pixels per inch. If you click on the button between the Width and Height boxes, you can swap these dimensions. Clicking on the Clear button clears the current crop options.

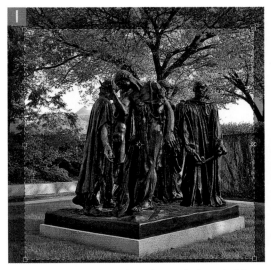

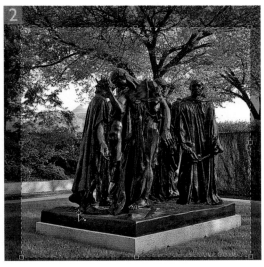

1 I selected the crop tool and dragged across the image to define the crop area. The cursor can then be placed above any of the eight handles in the bounding rectangle to readjust the crop.

2 Dragging the cursor inside the crop area will allow you to move the crop. You can also drag the crop bounding box center point to create a new central axis of rotation.

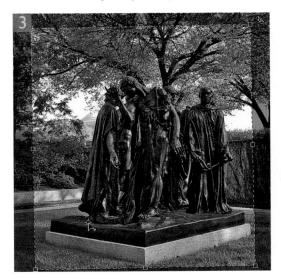

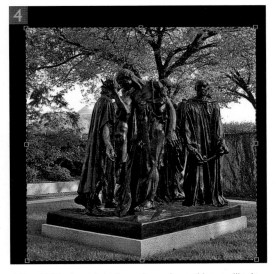

3 You can mouse down outside the crop area and drag to rotate the crop around the center point (which can even be positioned outside the crop area). You normally do this to realign an image that has been scanned slightly at an angle.

4 The shield color and shade opacity can be anything you like. In this example I increased the shading opacity to 100% to produce a completely opaque shield. You can even use ⌘ H ctrl H to hide the bounding box completely and still be able to drag the corners or sides of the crop to make adjustments.

Shade cropped area   Shade color   Enable perspective cropping   Apply crop

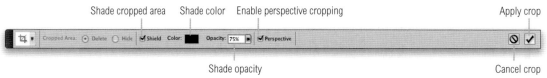

Shade opacity   Cancel crop

Figure 5.61 After you have dragged with the crop tool and before you commit to a crop, the tool Options bar will change (as shown here) to what is known as a modal state. These modal crop tool options allow you to change the color and opacity of the shield/shading of the outer crop areas. To apply a crop, you can click on the Apply Crop button in the Options bar, double-click inside the crop area or hit the *Enter* or *Return* keys. Click on the Cancel Crop button or hit the *esc* key to cancel a crop.

Fixed aspect ratio crops

One of the big advantages of using the rectangular marquee tool to make a selection crop is that you can set a fixed aspect ratio for the crop in the marquee tool options (see Figure 5.62).

Selection-based cropping

You can also make a crop that is based on an active selection by simply choosing Image ⇨ Crop. Where the selection has an irregular shape, the crop will be made to the outer limits of the selection and the selection will be retained. The practical advantages of this is that you might want to ⌘ *ctrl*-click a layer to make a selection based on a single layer and then execute a crop (as described in Figure 5.63 below).

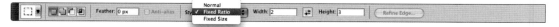

Figure 5.62 If you select the rectangular marquee tool you can use the Constrain Aspect Ratio option to make a proportional crop without altering the image resolution or dimension units. Enter the desired proportions in the Width and Height boxes, drag the marquee selection tool across the image to define the area to be cropped and then chose Image ⇨ Crop.

Figure 5.63 Sometimes it is quicker to make a crop from a selection instead of trying to precisely position the crop tool. In the example shown here, if we want to make a crop of the box containing the letter D, the quickest solution would be to ⌘ *ctrl*-click on the relevant layer in the Layers panel and then choose Image ⇨ Crop.

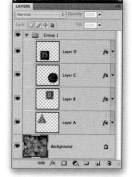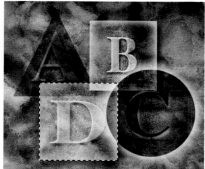

Perspective cropping

With Photoshop's crop tool you can crop and correct any converging vertical or horizontal lines in a picture with a single crop action. In Figure 5.64 we might wish to remove the converging verticals or 'keystone' effect in the photograph. If you check the Perspective box, you can accurately reposition the corner handles on the image to match the perspective of the building and then apply the crop to straighten the lines that should be vertical. A perspective crop adjustment can be made even more precisely if you hold down the *Shift* key as you drag a corner handle. This will restrict the movement to one plane only. I also find the perspective crop tool is useful when preparing photographs of flat copy artwork as it enables me to always get the copied artwork perfectly aligned.

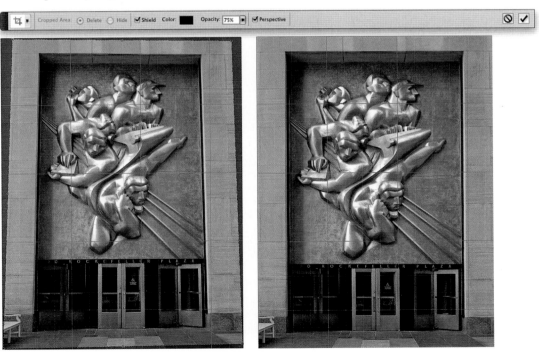

Figure 5.64 The crop tool is great for correcting the perspective in a photograph. Once the crop is defined you are then able to check the Perspective box in the Options bar and move the corner handles independently. By using this method, you will find it much easier to zoom in and gauge the alignment of the crop edges against the converging verticals in the photograph. It also helps here to switch on the Grid display. Go to the Window menu and choose Show ⇨ Grid (or use the *⌘ '* *ctrl '* keyboard shortcut).

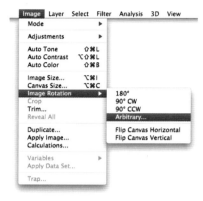

Figure 5.65 The Image ⇨ Rotate menu including the Arbitrary option which is described below in Figure 5.66.

Image rotation

If an image needs rotating you can use the Image ⇨ Rotate controls to orientate your picture the correct way up or flip it horizontally or vertically even. More likely you will want to make a precise image rotation, especially if a critical part of the picture is not perfectly straight. You can correct a wonky image by making a rotated crop with the crop tool, or by making an angle measurement with the measure tool followed by an arbitrary rotation as described in Figure 5.66.

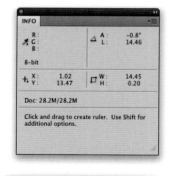

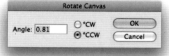

Figure 5.66 When an image is opened up in Photoshop, you may discover that it is not perfectly aligned. Although the crop tool will allow you to both crop and rotate at the same time, there is another more accurate way you can correct the alignment. Select the measure tool from the Tools panel and drag along what should be a vertical or horizontal edge in the photo. After doing this, go to the Image menu and select Rotate Canvas ⇨ Arbitrary... . You will find that the angle you have just measured is already entered in the Angle box. Choose to rotate either clockwise or counterclockwise and the image will be accurately rotated so that it appears to be perfectly level (although Photoshop usually manages to auto-select the correct direction to rotate with).

Canvas size

The Image ➪ Canvas size lets you enlarge the image canvas area, extending it in any direction. This is useful if you want to extend the image dimensions in order to place new elements. If you check the Relative box you can enter the unit dimensions you want to see added to the current image size. The pixels that are added will then be filled using the current background color but you can also choose other fill options from the Canvas Size dialog (see Figure 5.67). It is also possible to add to the canvas area without using Canvas Size. You can use the crop tool as an 'add canvas tool' by dragging beyond the document boundaries (see the instructions in Figure 5.68 below).

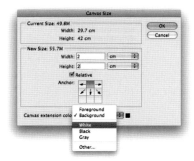

Figure 5.67 To add extra pixels beyond the current document bounds, use the Canvas Size from the Image menu. In the example shown here, the image is anchored so that pixels will be added equally left and right and to the bottom of the image only. The Relative box is checked and this allows you to enter the number of units of measurement you wish to add 'relative' to the current image size.

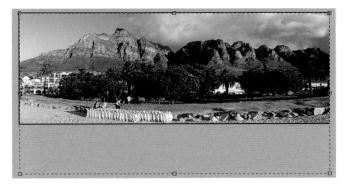

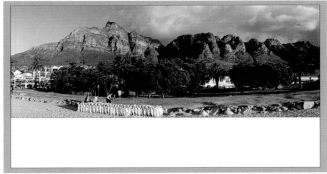

Figure 5.68 To use the crop tool as a canvas size tool, first make a full frame crop, release the mouse and then drag any one of the bounding box handles outside of the image and into the canvas area. Double-click inside the bounding box area or hit *Enter* to add to the canvas size, filling with the background color.

Edge detection success rate

The Content-Aware Scale feature is very clever at detecting which edges you would like to keep and those you would like to stretch or squash, but it won't work perfectly on every image. You can't expect miracles, but if you follow the suggestions on these pages you will pick up some of the basic tips for content-aware scaling. What I have noticed though is it does appear to do a very good job of recognizing circular objects and can preserve these without distorting them. Russell Brown has done some very cool demos on working with this feature and I can recommend you check them out on his site: www.russellbrown.com/tips_tech.html

Content-Aware Scaling

This is probably the star feature of Photoshop CS4, yet also the most controversial since it invites Photoshop users to tamper with photographs in ways that are likely to raise the hackles of photography purists. Does this spell the 'death of real photography (DORP)'? I don't know, but over the next few pages I have outlined some of the ways you can work with this new tool and suggested some practical uses. Advertising and design photographers will at least appreciate the benefits of being able to adapt a single image to multiple layout designs.

To use this feature, you need an image that's on a normal layer (not a Background layer) and you simply go to the Edit menu and choose Content-Aware Scale (or use the ⌘ ⌥ Shift C ctrl alt Shift C shortcut). You can then drag the handles that appear on the bounding box for the selected layer to scale the image, making it narrower/ wider or shorter/taller. The preview updates to show you the outcome and you can use the Options bar to access some of the extra features discussed here.

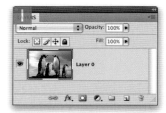

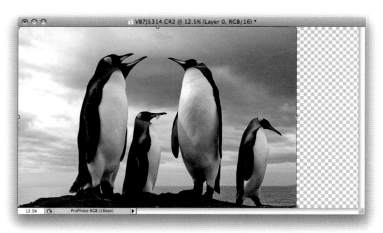

1 There is a set routine that you will want to carry out before applying any kind of 'content aware scaling'. To start with, double-click the background layer (or create a new merged copy layer, positioned at the top of the layer stack) and then add extra canvas to the image. This can be done using either of the methods shown on the previous page. You can use the Canvas Size dialog to enter a precise image size, or simply drag with the crop tool beyond the boundaries of the image. Alternatively, use Image ⇨ Reveal All after applying a scale adjustment.

Photograph: © Jeff Schewe 2008

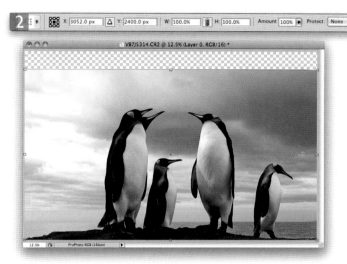

Amount slider

After you have scaled a photograph, you can use the Amount slider to determine the amount of content-aware scaling that is applied to the layer. If you set this to zero, no special scaling is applied, and the image will be stretched as if you had applied a normal transform. You will note that I left the slider setting to 100% in all the examples shown here, in order to demonstrate the full effect of the content-aware scaling.

2 This shows what the photograph looked like after I had used the Edit ⇨ Content-Aware Scale command to stretch the image width-ways. You'll notice how the penguins have not been stretched, but instead have been moved further apart, and the left side of the image has been stretched most of all.

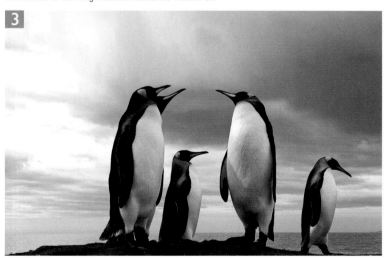

3 This shows what happened when I used the Content-Aware Scale command to make the photograph taller. Whenever you scale an image using this command, you have to watch carefully for the point where parts of the picture start to show jagged edges, or critical areas of the photo (such as the penguins) show signs they are being stretched. When this happens, you'll need to ease off and consider scaling the image in stages. In this example I stretched the photo upwards halfway, clicked OK and then applied a second scaling to complete the picture.

How to protect skin tones

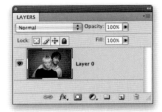

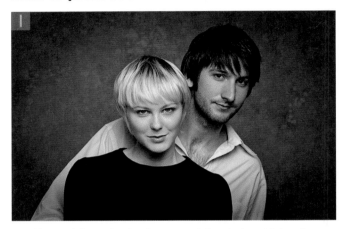

1 In this example I wanted to show how you can help protect people's faces from being squashed or stretched as you scale an image.

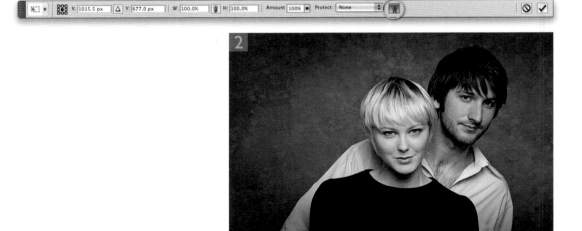

2 In general, you will find that the Content-Aware Scale feature does a pretty good job of distinguishing and preserving the important areas of a photograph and tends to scale the less busy areas of a photograph first, such as a sky, or in this case the mottled backdrop. However, if you click on the Protect Skin Tones button (circled), this will usually ensure that faces in a photograph remain protected by the scaling adjustments. As you can see here, I was able to stretch this picture so that the couple in this photograph were moved across to the right. I stretched the image quite a bit, but without distorting the faces.

Photograph: © Jeff Schewe 2008

346

How to remove objects from a scene

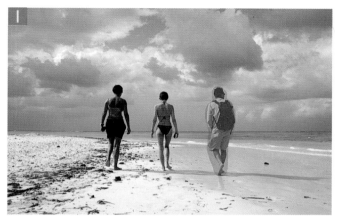

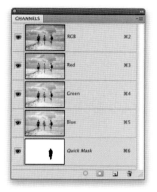

1 The Content-Aware Scale feature can also be used as a tool to selectively remove objects from a scene. The results won't be completely flawless, but it can still work pretty well where you wish to squash an image tighter and remove certain elements as you do so. For the first step, I hit the **Q** key to switch to Quick Mask mode (see Chapter 9) and painted on the image to outline the bits that I wished to remove from the scene. Remember, white protects and black indicates the areas to remove.

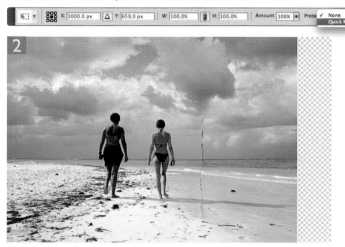

2 Next, I reselected the RGB composite channel in the Channels panel and then selected the Edit ⇨ Content-Aware Scale command. In the Protect menu in the Options bar, I selected the Quick Mask I had just created and, as I scaled the image, the masked figure started to disappear. As before, it is important to watch carefully for jagged edges and not compress the image too much. As you can see, this technique doesn't completely remove all the pixels, but this edited image could easily be tidied up using the healing brush.

Photograph: © Jo Cowler 2003

Background layers and big data

If your image contains a Background layer and you want to preserve the data on this layer after making a 'hide' crop, you must first double-click the Background layer to promote it to a normal layer. If you don't take this step you will still end up deleting everything on this layer when you crop.

Big data

The Photoshop, PDF and TIFF formats all support 'big data'. This means that if any of the layered image data extends beyond the confines of the canvas boundary, it will still be saved as part of the image when you save it, even though it is no longer visible. If you have layers in your image that extend outside the bounds of the canvas, you can expand the canvas to reveal all of the big data by choosing Image ⇨ Reveal All. But remember, you will only be able to reveal the big data again providing you have saved the image using the PSD, PDF or TIFF format. When you crop a picture using the crop tool, you can delete or hide the layered big data by selecting either of these radio buttons in the modal crop Options bar (see Figure 5.69).

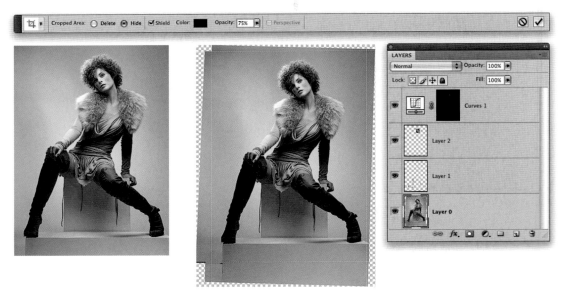

Figure 5.69 The cropped version of this picture contains several layers which, when expanded using the Image ⇨ Reveal All command, show all the hidden 'big data' that extends outside of the cropped view. The Hide option in the crop tool options allows you to preserve the pixels that fall outside the selected crop area instead of deleting them. Note also how the Background layer has been converted to a normal Photoshop layer (Layer 0). This is essential if you wish to preserve all the information on this layer as big data.

Client: Rainbow Room. Model: Nicky Felbert @ MOT.

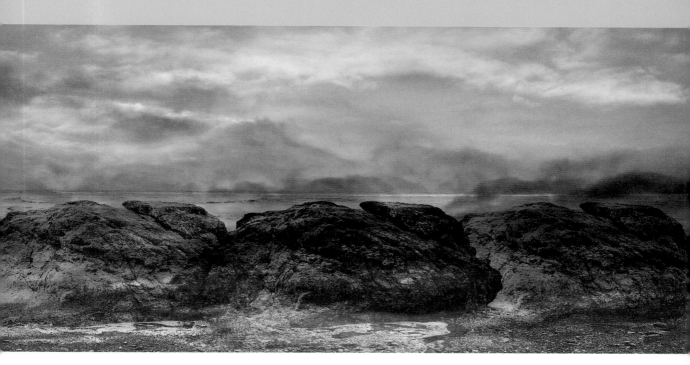

Chapter 6

Black and White

I was eleven years old when I first got into photography. My first darkroom was kept under the stairs of our house and, like most other budding amateurs, my early experiments were all done in black and white. Back then, very few amateur photographers were competent enough to know how to process color, so black and white was all that most of us could work with!

There has always been something rather special about black and white photography and digital imaging has done nothing to diminish this. If anything, I would say that the quality of capture from the latest digital cameras, coupled with the processing expertise of Photoshop and improvements in inkjet printing, have made black and white photography an even more exciting proposition.

Black and white film conversions

Traditional black and white film emulsions can all differ slightly in the way they respond to different portions of the visual spectrum (as well as the colors we can't see). This is partly what gives emulsion films their 'signature' qualities. So in a way, you could say that film also uses standard formulas for converting color to black and white and that these too are like rigid grayscale conversions. You may also be familiar with the concept of using strong colored filters over the lens when shooting with black and white film and how this technique can be used to emphasize the contrast between certain colors, such as the use of yellow, orange and red filters to add more contrast to a sky. Well, the same principles apply to the way you can use the Black & White adjustment to mix the channels to produce different kinds of black and white conversions.

Black & White slider adjustments

The Black & White slider adjustments will, for the most part, manage to preserve the image luminance range without clipping the shadows or highlights, unless you apply extreme negative or positive weightings to two or more sliders.

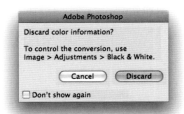

Figure 6.1 If you convert direct to Grayscale, Photoshop advises you there are better ways to convert to black and white!

Converting color to black and white

The most important tip here is to always shoot in color. Whether you shoot film or shoot digitally, you are always far better off capturing a scene in full color and using Camera Raw or Photoshop to carry out the color to mono conversion. Although having said that, you do need to use the right conversion methods to get the best black and white conversions from your color files.

The dumb black and white conversions

When you change a color image from RGB to Grayscale mode in Photoshop, the tonal values of the three RGB channels are averaged out, usually producing a smooth continuous tone grayscale. The formula for this conversion consists of blending 60% of the Green channel with 30% of the Red and 10% of the Blue. The rigidity of this color to mono conversion limits the scope for obtaining the best grayscale conversion from a scanned color original (see Figure 6.1). The same thing is true if you were to simply desaturate the image or make a Lab mode conversion, copy the Luminosity channel, convert the image back to RGB mode and choose Edit ⇨ Paste. There is nothing necessarily wrong with either of these methods, but you are not really making full use of the information contained in the image.

Smarter black and white conversions

If you capture in color, the RGB master image will contain three different grayscale versions of the original scene and these can be blended together in different ways. One of the best ways to do this is by using the Black & White image adjustment which, while not perfect, can still do a good job of providing you with most of the controls you need to make full use of the RGB channel data when applying a conversion. Black & White image adjustments can be applied to images directly, or by using the Adjustment panel, and the advantage of this is that you can quickly convert an image to black and have the option to play with the blending modes to refine the black and white conversion. Let's start by looking at the typical steps used when working with the Black & White adjustment controls.

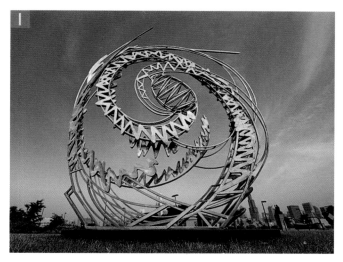

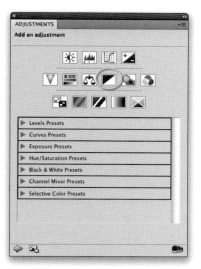

1 The following steps show the basic method for converting a full color original photograph into black and white. The Black & White image adjustment can be applied directly by going to the Image ⇨ Image Adjustments menu, or you can go to the Adjustments panel and click on the Black & White button (circled) to add a new adjustment layer.

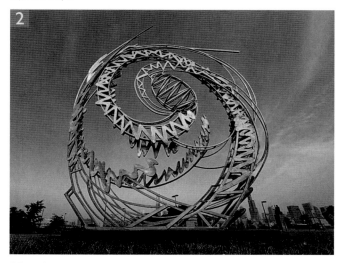

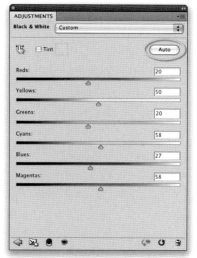

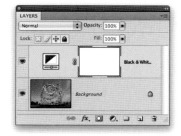

2 To begin with I clicked on the Auto button (circled). This applied an auto slider setting based on an analysis of the image color content. The auto setting usually offers a good starting point for most color to black and white conversions and won't do anything too dramatic to the image, but this is immediately a lot better than choosing Image ⇨ Mode ⇨ Grayscale.

351

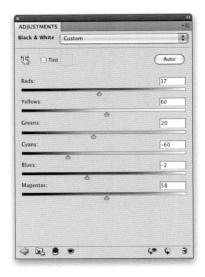

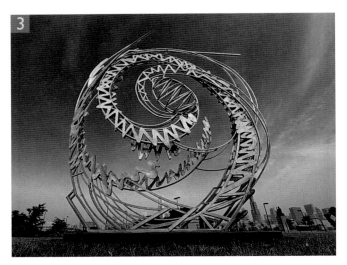

3 If you don't like the auto setting result, you can adjust the sliders manually to achieve a better conversion. In this example, I lightened the Reds and Yellows and darkened the Cyans.

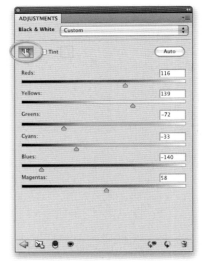

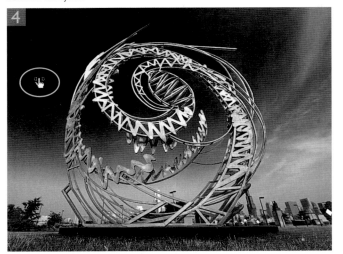

4 Lastly, I clicked on the target adjustment mode button (circled) for the Black & White adjustment. This allowed me to move the cursor over particular areas of interest (such as the sky). I then dragged directly on the image to modify the Black & White adjustment. This action selects the nearest color slider in the Black & White adjustment panel. Dragging to the left makes the black and white tones go darker and dragging to the right, lighter. The end result was a photograph in which I managed to lighten the sculpture more and increased the contrast in the sky.

Black & White adjustment presets

As with other image adjustments, the Black & White adjustment has a Presets menu at the top from which you can select from a number of shipped preset settings. Figure 6.3 shows some examples of the radically different outcomes that can be achieved through selecting different presets.

Once you have created a Black & White adjustment setting that you would like to use again, you can choose Save Preset... from the Adjustment panel options menu (Figure 6.2). For example, the slider settings used here were saved as a custom 'Red Contrast' preset.

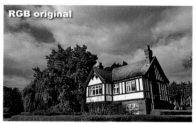

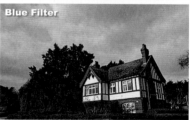

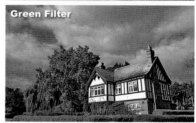

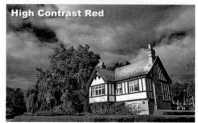

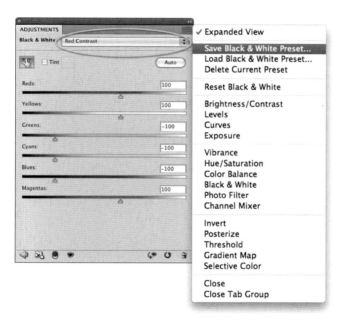

Figure 6.2 Once you have found a setting for a Black & White adjustment that you would like to use again, you can choose Save Preset... from the Adjustment panel options menu. The slider settings used here were saved as a 'Red Contrast' preset and the saved presets can be accessed by mousing down on the presets menu at the top of the adjustments panel (circled).

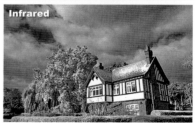

Figure 6.3 Examples of different Black & White Adjustment presets applied to a color image.

Color blend mode

You will notice that I suggest you use the Color blend mode when applying adjustment layers that are intended to color an image. The advantage of using the Color blend mode is that you are able to alter the color component of an image without affecting the luminosity. This is important if you wish to preserve more of the tone levels information.

Split color toning with Color Balance

Although the Black & White adjustment contains a Tint option for coloring images, this can only apply a single color overlay adjustment and I have never really found it that useful. It is nice to have the ability to apply a split tone coloring to a photograph and the simplest way to do this is to use the Color Balance image adjustment. The simple controls here make this an ideal adjustment tool for editing RGB images that have been converted to monochrome using the Black & White adjustment, and the Color Balance controls are really quite intuitive. If you want to colorize the shadows, click on the Shadows radio button and adjust the color settings, then go to the Midtones, make them a different color and so on. Note that it is best to apply these coloring effects with the adjustment layer set to the Color blend mode.

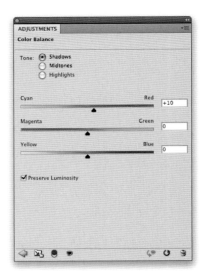

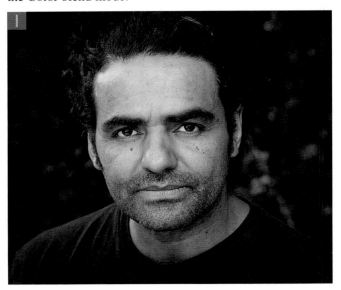

1 I started with an RGB color image and converted it to monochrome using the Black & White image adjustment. I then added a Color Balance adjustment layer to colorize this RGB/monochrome image. To do this, I went to the Adjustment panel and selected Color Balance. I first of all clicked on the Shadows button and adjusted the Red slider to apply a red cast to the shadows.

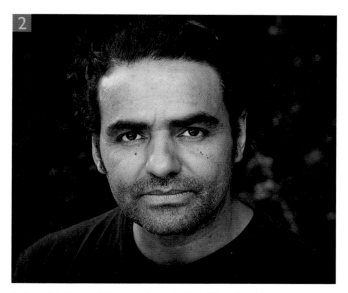

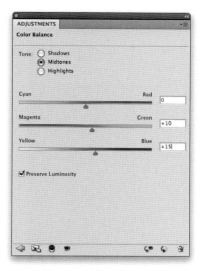

2 I then clicked on the Midtones button and adjusted the color sliders there to add a green/blue color balance to the midtones. You will notice that I had Preserve Luminosity checked. This helped prevent the image tones from becoming clipped.

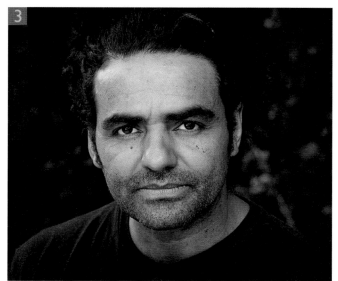

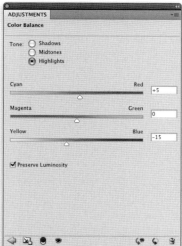

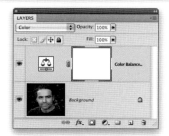

3 Finally I clicked on the Highlights button and added a yellow cast to the highlights. I also set the adjustment layer blending mode to Color, which helped to preserve the image luminance information.

Curves adjustment layer split toning

The Color Balance method is reasonably versatile, but you can also colorize a photograph by using two Curves adjustment layers and taking advantage of the Layer Style blending options to create a split tone coloring effect.

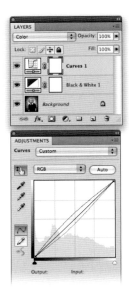

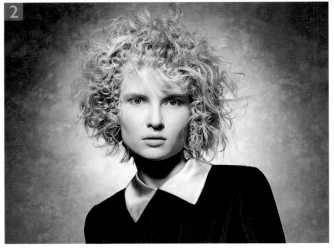

1 To tone this image, I first added a Curves adjustment above the Black & White adjustment layer and colored the photo blue.

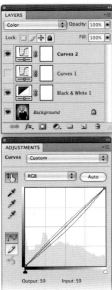

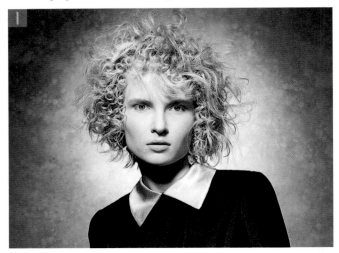

2 I then added a second Curves adjustment on top of the previous one and this time applied a sepia color adjustment.

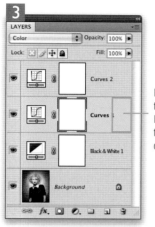

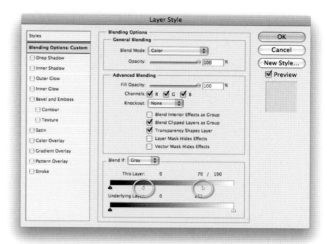

Double-click in this area of the layer to open the Layer Style dialog.

3 I made the first Curves layer active and double-clicked it to open the Layer Style dialog shown here. I then ⌥ *alt*-clicked on the divider triangle in the 'Blend If' layer options. This enabled me to separate the two dividers (circled) to split them in two, which allowed me to control where the split occurred between these two adjustments.

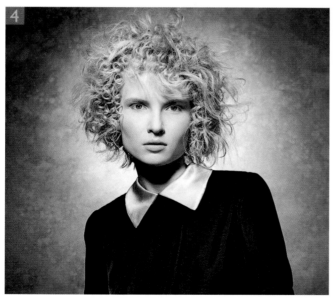

4 The advantage of this method is that you can adjust the layer opacity and Layer Style blending modes of each individual layer which offers more flexible options when it comes to coloring the shadows and highlights.

Client: Andrew Collinge Hair & Beauty.
Hair: Alfie Booth.
Makeup: Liz Collinge.
Model: Jagna Szaykowska @ Profile.

The extra color sliders

Camera Raw has more sliders than the Black & White adjustment and these allow you to adjust the in-between color ranges such as Oranges, Aquas and Purples. The Oranges slider is useful for targeting skin tones and the Aquas is useful for adjusting photographs of sunny beach scenes. Having these extra sliders provides you with extra levels of tone control.

Camera Raw black and white conversions

You may already have noticed that you can use Camera Raw to convert images to black and white. However, you are limited to only being able to process raw, JPEG, or TIFF images (providing the TIFF is flattened).

If you go to the HSL/Grayscale panel and check the Convert to Grayscale box, Camera Raw will create a black and white version of the image, which is produced by blending the color channel data to produce a monochrome rendering of the original. Clicking 'Auto' applies a custom setting that is based on the white balance setting used in the Basic panel, and if you click 'Default' this resets all the sliders to zero. You can also manually drag the sliders to make certain colors in the color original lighter or darker and the overall tone, brightness and contrast will not fluctuate much as you do so which makes it easy to experiment with different slider combinations. If you want the sky to be darker, you would do as I did in Figure 6.4 and drag the Aquas and Blues sliders to the left. I would

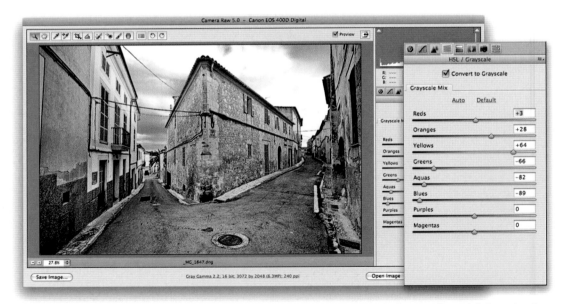

Figure 6.4 In this example, I clicked on the Convert to Grayscale button and made some custom slider adjustments to increase the tonal contrast.

also suggest sometimes switching over to the Basic and Tone Curve panels to make continued adjustments to the white balance and tone controls as these can have a strong bearing on the outcome of a black and white conversion.

Pros and cons of the Camera Raw approach

In my view, Camera Raw Grayscale has the edge over the Black & White adjustment. This is because the slider controls are better thought out and the addition of the in-between color sliders makes it possible to target certain colors more precisely (see sidebar on page 358) but, sadly, there is no target adjustment mode option in Camera Raw. The other important question is 'when is the best time to convert a photo to black and white'? If you do this at an early stage in Camera Raw, it limits what you can do to an image should you start retouching it in Photoshop. It is usually better to carry out the black and white conversion at the end, just prior to print, and have the adjustment be reversible. This is not a problem in Photoshop, because if you add a Black & White adjustment layer it is easy enough to toggle the adjustment on or off. An alternative approach is to take a Photoshop-edited image back through Camera Raw again. This can be done, but you are limited by the fact that any non-raw image you process through Camera Raw must be a JPEG or a TIFF (PSD won't work) and the TIFF must not have any layers. This means saving a flattened duplicate of the Photoshop-edited master image and then opening it up via Camera Raw. It's quite a convoluted procedure to go through just to access the Camera Raw controls, and also costly in terms of adding to the edit time and amount of hard disk space used. As I say, I do prefer the Camera Raw controls, but the only real practical way to work with Camera Raw black and white conversions is to stick to editing raw photos and retouching as much as you can in Camera Raw. There is another option though, and that is to use Lightroom. I reimport all my Photoshop-edited images back into Lightroom and use the Camera Raw processing there to carry out the conversions. Lightroom has everything I need, plus its target adjustment mode correction tool performs better than Photoshop.

Camera Raw and noisy conversions

Camera Raw Grayscale conversions have in the past been accused of being noisy. This is because the previous Camera Raw 4 version disabled any color noise adjustment that had been applied in the Detail panel. This has now been corrected in Camera Raw 5.0 and therefore you should not now see any noise problems.

HSL grayscale conversions

If you set all the Saturation sliders in the HSL panel to −100, you can then use the Luminance sliders in the HSL panel to make almost the same type of adjustments as the Grayscale mode. One of the chief advantages of this method is that you can use the Saturation and Vibrance controls in the Basic panel to fine-tune the grayscale conversion effect, which you can't do when using the ordinary Grayscale conversion mode.

Camera Raw Split Toning panel

After you have used the HSL/Grayscale panel to convert
a photograph to black and white, you can then use the
Split Toning panel to colorize the image. The controls in
this panel allow you to apply one color to the highlights,
another color to the shadows and then use the Saturation
sliders to adjust the intensity of the colors. This is how
you create a basic split tone color effect. There is also the
Balance slider, which lets you adjust the midpoint for the
split tone. For example, in Figure 6.5 the photograph I
was applying the split tone to was a high-key image and it
was therefore more appropriate to offset the Balance slider
so that the blue shadow toning would show more in the
shadows. Without such an adjustment the shadow color
would have barely registered. The HSL/Grayscale and
Split Tone controls are incredibly versatile. Bear in mind
these will work equally well with non-raw images. It is
just a shame that there isn't a Split toning panel like this in
Photoshop.

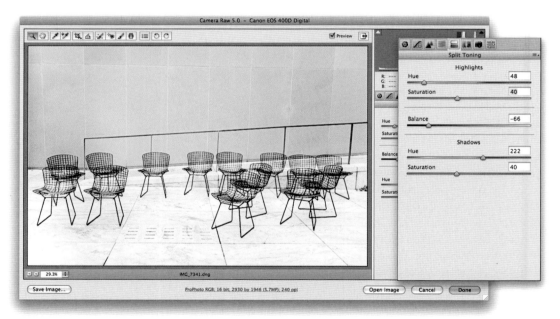

Figure 6.5 Here is an example of the Split Toning panel in action.

Camera Raw color image split toning

Although the Split Toning panel appears to be an extension
of the HSL Grayscale panel, the Split Toning controls
are just as useful for working on color images. Although
there are ways to produce a color cross-processing effect
in Photoshop, the Camera Raw Split Toning controls can
produce identical results, but with less hassle (Figure 6.6).

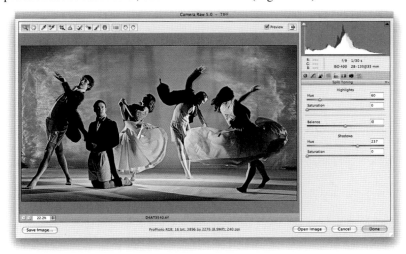

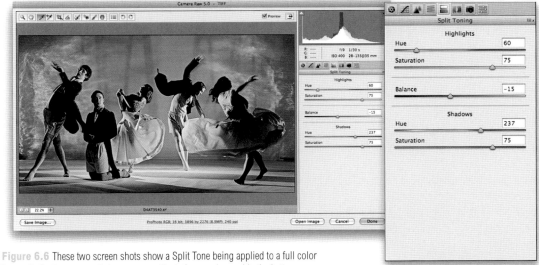

Figure 6.6 These two screen shots show a Split Tone being applied to a full color
image. In the top screen shot you can see the before version and in the bottom screen
shot you can see the result after applying a blue/sepia Split Toning effect.

Photograph: © Eric Richmond

Advanced B&W Photo tips

There are a few things you need to do in order to access and make the most of the Advanced B&W feature for Epson printers. Firstly, this is only available with certain printer models, such as the Epson 4800 that I use in my office. You can make a print using RGB or Grayscale, but the printer driver assumes the image to be in neutral RGB (ignoring any colors), or in Grayscale mode. Normally you would convert to Grayscale first, in which case the gamma of the Grayscale space you convert to should match the gamma of your RGB workspace (see page 590). In the Photoshop Print dialog you will want to select Photoshop Manages Colors and select an appropriate printer profile and rendering intent (see pages 623–624). When you click Print, this will take you to the Epson print dialog, where in the Print Settings section you will need to select an appropriate media type, such as Photo Paper > Premium Glossy Photo Paper (to match the profile selected in the Photoshop Print dialog). Note that not all paper media settings support Advanced B&W. Then select the Advanced B&W Photo from the Color menu (page 627). Having done that, click on the Advanced Color Settings to access the Print dialog options shown in Figure 6.7, where the key thing is to leave most of these sliders alone, except to choose a Color Toning method. You can choose a preset color from this menu, click on the color wheel below, or adjust the Horizontal and Vertical values. The Tone setting says 'Darker'. This is actually the default setting, but you can modify this if you wish.

Black and white output

Black and white printing should be easy, but if you are printing from RGB files you'll meet the exact same issues that affect normal color printing. Your ability to match the print to the screen will be dependent on the same factors as always: the accuracy of the monitor calibration, the type of paper you are printing to, and the effectiveness of the printer profile you are using. Mind you, with black and white printing there is perhaps more latitude for the color to be off and for you to still be pleased with the results. If you are aiming for a neutral black and white result, then the profile used must be accurate. In theory, if the measured Info panel gray values are all neutral, the print output should be neutral too. If you are using one of the more advanced Epson printers you may be interested to know that if you convert the image to grayscale you can access the Advanced B&W Photo settings shown in Figure 6.7 to apply coloring effects via the system Print dialog.

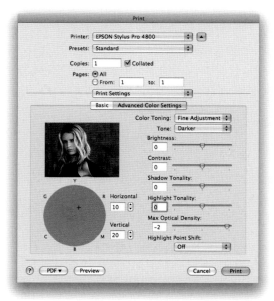

Figure 6.7 This shows the Advanced Color Settings for the Epson 4800 printer when the 'Advanced B&W Photo' option is selected in the main Print Settings section of the System print interface. This allows you to select preset black and white output toning options.

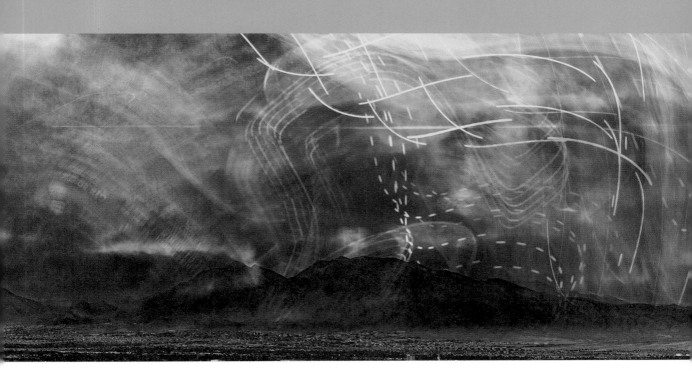

Chapter 7

Extending the Dynamic Range

For many years now, everyone has become preoccupied with counting the numbers of pixels in a digital capture as if this were the only benchmark of image quality that mattered above all else. Yet size isn't everything, because it is the quality of the pixels we should be concerned with most. Digital SLR cameras tend to have better quality sensors than compact digitals and large high-end camera backs have features such as built-in cooling mechanisms that can produce the very best in image capture quality. The one thing people haven't focused on so much is the dynamic range of a camera sensor. Dynamic range refers to the ability of a sensor to capture the greatest range of tones from the minimum recordable shadow point to the brightest highlights and this is what we are going to focus on in this chapter.

Camera Raw Smart Objects

A Smart Object can store the raw pixel data within a saved PSD or TIFF image (you'll learn more about Smart Objects in Chapter 9). This means that you can re-edit the raw data at any time. But it also means that a rendered pixel version of the Smart Object has to be stored as well and documents that include Smart Objects can therefore have quite large file sizes. The important thing to stress here is that this technique really applies to editing raw files only.

In Photoshop CS3 and CS4, you can of course use Camera Raw to edit JPEG files as well as raws. It is therefore theoretically possible to apply the technique shown here to JPEG images but it won't bring you any real benefit compared with processing proper raw images.

Multiple raw conversions

To get the most out of your raw files it can sometimes be useful to make two or more conversions using Camera Raw, combine them together as layers in a single document, then blend them to produce a composite image. One way to do this is to place a raw file as a Smart Object in Photoshop. If all you want to do is burn in the sky and dodge part of the foreground then it is probably best to use the localized correction tools in Camera Raw. But if you want to extend the dynamic range of an image capture with greater precision than this, then you need to use Photoshop, and the most flexible and non-destructive method is the one I describe here in which I show how to open a Camera Raw image as a Smart Object, process it in two different ways and blend the two versions together.

If you are able to shoot with the camera on a tripod, another alternative is to combine two separate exposures. This allows you to extend the dynamic range of your camera and blend the results using the manual method described here. This approach brings you the benefit of being able to edit the individual Camera Raw Smart Object layers.

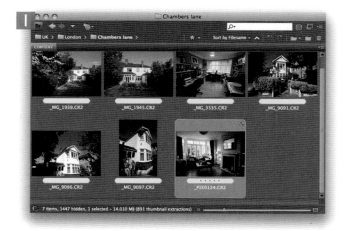

1 To begin with I went to Bridge and selected a raw image that I wanted to edit then opened this photo via Camera Raw using File ➪ Open in Camera Raw... (⌘ R / ctrl R).

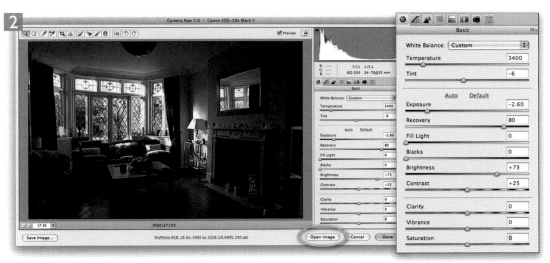

2 In the Camera Raw dialog I adjusted the Camera Raw settings to achieve the best White Balance, Exposure and Recovery adjustments to reveal the detail outside the windows. Once I was happy with these settings, I held down the *Shift* key and clicked 'Open Object', to open as a Smart Object in Photoshop.

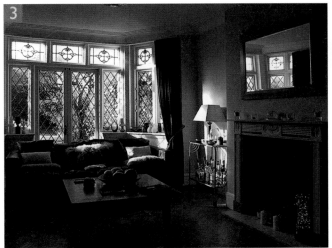

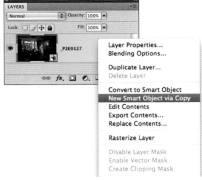

3 Here is the processed image, placed as a Smart Object layer in a new Photoshop document. I then wanted to create a new Smart Object layer of the same image where I could use new Camera Raw settings to adjust for the interior of the room. To do this, I made a right mouse-click on this first Smart Object layer to access the contextual menu and selected 'New Smart Object via Copy' (Mac users can also use the *ctrl* key to access this contextual menu).

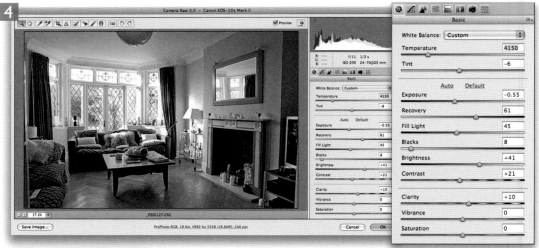

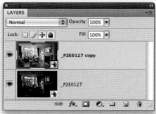

4 This duplicated the original layer and allowed me to edit the new copied Smart Object layer. The easiest way to do this was to double-click the Smart Object layer thumbnail. This opened the Camera Raw dialog again, where I was able to use the Basic panel controls to apply a lighter adjustment to bring out more detail in the room interior. When I was finished I clicked 'Done' to OK the adjustment, which then updated the Smart Object copy layer in the master image document.

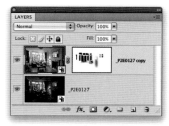

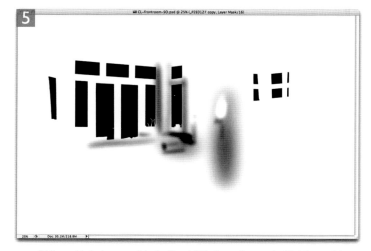

5 I then added a layer mask to the Smart Object copy layer and edited the mask to hide the windows and brush in more highlight detail in some of the brighter areas of the room interior. This screen shot shows a full image view of the layer mask that was applied to the Smart Object copy layer.

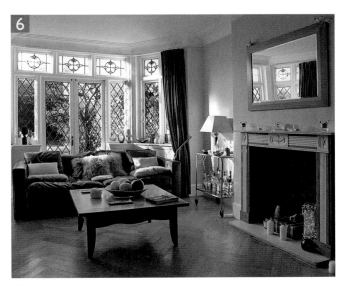

6 This final image shows the lighter processed Smart Object layer overlaying the darker processed Smart Object layer using a blend opacity of 90%. The carefully drawn mask around the window frames allowed the darker processed version to show through the windows. With this approach you can endlessly fine-tune the Camera Raw processing on each layer until you are happy with the balance achieved for the Camera Raw settings on the two layers.

Place-A-Matic script

The steps I just outlined can be carried out more easily by running Dr. Brown's Place-A-Matic script for Bridge. You can download this script for free via the Russell Brown Show website. Go to: www.russellbrown.com and then go to the Photoshop Tips & Techniques section, scroll down to the Scripts section where you can download 'Dr. Brown's Services' which, among other things, includes the Place-A-Matic script. Follow the installation instructions, and when you next launch Bridge you should see this appear as one of the new script options in the Tools menu. Basically, the Place-A-Matic script will automate almost all the steps I just described here over the last few pages and offers a quicker way to create double raw settings conversions via Smart Objects (note that you will still have to add a layer mask and decide for yourself how to blend the images).

Smart Object layer blending

This technique can be adapted in various ways. You can use the layer blending options to change the layer blend mode, but you can also double-click the Smart Object layer to open the Layer Style dialog where you can adjust the 'Blend if: This Layer' options to adjust the transition between the two Smart Object layers (see page 357 for an example of how the Layer Style 'Blend If' sliders can be controlled).

Other HDR applications

All those special effects in movies such as *Jurassic Park* were created using a 32-bit color space to render the computer-generated characters and make them interact convincingly with the real world film footage. So 32-bit image editing is useful in creating realistic animated special effects. The way this is usually done is to record what is known as a light probe image of the scene in which the main filming takes place. A light probe is an omnidirectional HDR image which can consist of a sequence of six or seven overlapping exposures shot using a 180 degree fish eye lens pointed in opposite directions. A basic light probe can be a series of photographs of a mirrored sphere taken with a normal lens. The resulting light probe image contains all the information needed to render the shading and textures on a computer-generated object with realistic-looking lighting.

32-bit rendering is applicable to the computer games industry, and the military and aeronautics industries are also particularly interested in the potential to render more realistic-looking virtual landscapes for simulation training. A wire frame landscape designed on a computer can then be made to respond dynamically to different programmed lighting environments.

Paul Debevec is a leading expert in HDR imaging. His website www.debevec.org contains much interesting information on HDR and its various applications.

High dynamic range imaging

It is interesting to see how camera sensor technology has evolved over the last few years and ponder on what the future might have in store for us a few years from now. Right now there are a lot of photographers who are interested in exploring what can be done using high dynamic range image editing. At this moment in time it is all about capturing bracketed sequences of images and blending them together to create a single high dynamic range image that captures the entire scenic tonal scale. In time we may see camera sensors become available that are able to capture high dynamic range scenes using a single exposure.

HDR cameras are not common yet but, in the meantime, Photoshop can simulate HDR capture by using the Merge to HDR feature to combine two or more images captured at different exposures with a normal digital camera and blend the selected images together to produce a 32-bit high dynamic range image. You can then convert this 32-bit HDR file into a 16-bit per channel or 8-bit per channel low dynamic range version which you can then edit further in Photoshop.

Photoshop CS3 was the first version of Photoshop to offer a 32-bit per level floating point image editing mode. Don't worry too much what that means just yet. Basically, high dynamic range image editing requires a whole new approach to the way image editing programs like Photoshop process the image data. Because of this the Photoshop team had to rewrite a lot of the Photoshop code in which some of the familiar Photoshop tools could be made to work in a 32-bit image editing environment. Photoshop now supports 32-bit image editing and offers a limited range of editing controls such as Layers and Painting to those who are using the extended version of Photoshop CS3 or CS4.

HDR essentials

Most camera sensors have traditionally been designed to record light via individual photosites. I won't complicate things with a discussion of the different sensor designs used, but essentially the goal of late has been to design sensors in which the photosites are made as small as possible and crammed together to increase the number of megapixels. Camera sensors have also been made more efficient so that they can capture images over a wide range of ISO settings without generating too much electronic noise in the shadow areas at the higher ISO settings. The problem all sensors face though is that at the low exposure extreme there comes a point where the photosites are unable to record any usable levels information against the random noise that's generated in the background. At the other extreme, when too much light hits a photosite it becomes oversaturated and is unable to record light levels beyond a certain amount. One way to look at this is to imagine photosites as being like glasses ready to be filled with water. When only a little water is added it can be hard to accurately measure how much water is in there, and if you fill the glass to the brim the water will overflow and you'll be unable to measure any extra water that is poured (see Figure 7.1).

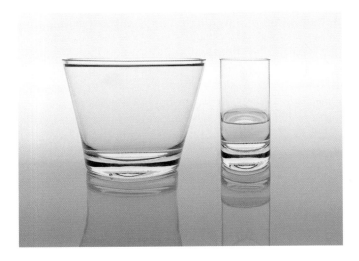

Figure 7.1 One approach to increasing the dynamic range of a camera sensor is to have two different sized photosites working together to capture the light hitting the sensor. One can liken this to having a wide rimmed glass and a narrow rimmed glass side by side. When water is poured, the wide rimmed glass is able to capture more water than the narrow rimmed glass, and can easily detect small amounts of water, but when more water is poured than the wide rimmed glass can handle, the narrow rimmed glass is able to pick up the slack and keep measuring the amount of water poured.

Fuji Super CCD

Fuji are so far the only camera company to come up with a new approach to this problem. Fuji have designed the Super CCD which comprises of two sets of photosites laid out in an octagonal pattern, where you have a standard sized photosite that can record the same dynamic range as a normal photosite and a smaller photosite next to it that is able to record detail that is brighter than the standard sized photosite is able to record. The data captured using this type of sensor can be extrapolated to create a raw capture image which represents a dynamic range wider than most other digital cameras. The latest Fuji S5 Pro camera is described as a 12 megapixel camera. Fuji classify the two photosites as a single photosite sensor, which means that the S5 camera has in fact a total of 6 million 'combined' photosites but, because of the way the photosites are laid out on the sensor chip and how the data is interpreted, the effective number of megapixels is rated as 12.1 MP. Fuji have had a problem convincing everyone that this can be regarded as a genuine megapixel rating, but wedding photographers in particular have been very impressed with the dynamic range offered by this range of cameras, which is particularly important when shooting white wedding dresses alongside dark suits under what can sometimes be less than ideal shooting conditions. Unfortunately some wedding photographers have also been sold the idea that JPEG shooting is best for them and have lost all the advantages that can be gained from high dynamic range raw capture!

Alternative approaches

Other high dynamic range sensor technologies are in the pipeline. One method relies on the ability of a sensor to quickly record a sequence of images in the time it takes to shoot a single exposure. By varying the exposure value for each of these exposures, the camera software can extract a single high dynamic range capture. The advantage of this approach is that it might be feasible to capture a high dynamic range image at fast shutter speeds, although maybe not with a high speed strobe flash unit.

Bracketed exposures

Until we have true HDR cameras, we have to rely on using bracketed exposures instead. The aim here is to capture a series of exposures that are far enough apart in exposure value so that we can extend the combined range of exposures to encompass the entire scenic tonal range as well as extending beyond the limits of the scenic tonal range. This is because by overexposing for the shadows we can capture more levels of information, which can result in cleaner, noise-free shadows. Exposing beyond the upper range of the highlights can also be useful when trying to recover information in certain tricky highlight areas. Shooting bracketed exposures is the only way most of us can realistically go about capturing all of the light levels in any given scene and merging the resulting images into a single HDR file. When this is done right, you will have the means to create some truly amazing renderings from your HDR photographs.

Displaying deep-bit color

It is hard to appreciate a significant difference between 8-bit per channel and 16-bit per channel editing when all you have to view your work with is an 8-bit per channel display. But screen display technology is rapidly improving and in the near future we will see the introduction of flat screen displays that use a combination of LEDs and LCDs, capable of displaying images at greater bit depths and over a higher dynamic range. Dolby already supply specialist high dynamic range displays and the difference is remarkable. In the future, such displays will enable you to see the images you are editing in greater tonal detail and over a much wider dynamic range, should you wish to do so.

Capturing a complete scenic tonal range

The light contrast ratio from the darkest point in a scene to the brightest will vary from subject to subject. What can be said is that in nearly every case it will always exceed the dynamic range of even the best digital camera. Our human vision can differentiate between light and dark over a contrast ratio of 1:10,000, which in photography terms is equivalent to about 14 exposure values (EV). Meanwhile, digital cameras can only capture around 6–8 EV of tonal range. Although camera sensors are unable to match the sensitivity of our eyes, we know from experience that with careful camera exposure we don't always need to record

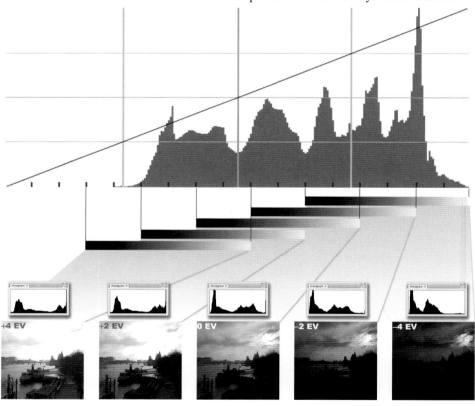

+4 EV +2 EV 0 EV –2 EV –4 EV

Figure 7.2 This diagram illustrates how individual bracketed exposures, when merged to form a single High dynamic range image, can extend the histogram scale to encompass the entire luminance of the subject scenic range.

every single tone in a scene in order to produce a good-looking photograph. We often don't need to worry about this and can deliberately allow some highlights to burn out or let the shadows go black. Figure 7.2 shows how by combining a succession of bracketed exposures we can create a single image that is capable of capturing the entire scenic range and even extend beyond that.

The objective when capturing a high dynamic range image is to make sure that you successfully capture the entire contrast range in a scene from dark to light. You can do this by taking spot meter readings and manually work out the best exposure bracketing sequence to use, plus how many brackets are required. An alternative (and simpler) approach is to use a standard method of shooting in which you first measure the best average exposure, as you would for a single exposure, and then bracket either side of that using either three-, five- or seven-bracketed exposures at 2 EV apart. This may not be so precise a method, but a five-bracketed sequence should at least double the dynamic range of your camera.

There are several benefits to capturing a high dynamic range. One is that you can potentially capture all the light that was in the original scene and edit the recorded information any way you like. The extended version of Photoshop CS3 was the first version of Photoshop that would allow you to paint and edit a high dynamic range image in 32-bits per channel. Providing you manage to capture all the individual brackets without movement, a merged HDR image will contain smoother tonal information in the shadow regions. This is because more levels are captured at the bright end of the levels histogram (see 'Digital exposure' on page 174) and, as a result, the overexposed brackets will record the shadow detail using more levels. When you successfully capture and create an HDR image, there should be little or no noise in the shadows and much more tonal information to play with, which means you have a lot more headroom to edit the shadow tones without the risk of banding that you sometimes see with normal digital images.

Trying to fool Merge to HDR

Some people have asked if it is possible to take a standard single shot image, create versions of varying darkness and merge these together as an HDR image. There are a number of reasons why this won't work. One is that you can't fool Merge to HDR since it responds to the camera time exposure EXIF metadata information in the file rather than the 'look' of the image. Secondly, you wouldn't gain more dynamic range from this approach even if it were possible to do so.

Really still, still life

The Merge to HDR dialog can automatically align the images for you, but it is essential that everything else remains static. You might just get away shooting the HDR merge images with a hand-held camera using an auto bracket setting, but if so much as just two of the pictures fail to register you won't be able to create a successful HDR merge. If you do resort to hand holding the camera, use a fast motor drive setting, raise the ISO setting at least two stops higher than you would use normally for hand-held shooting, and try to keep the camera as steady as possible (hand holding the camera should absorb some of the mirror shake movement).

HDR shooting tips

The first thing you want to do is to set up your camera to shoot auto bracketed exposures. This can usually be done via the camera controls. Some cameras only allow you to shoot just three bracketed exposures, others more. With the Canon EOS range you should find that by tethering your camera to the computer, you can use the Canon camera utilities software to set the default to five or more exposure brackets. The bracketing should be done based on varying the exposure time – the aperture must always remain fixed so that you don't vary the focus between captures. Next, you want the camera to be kept as still as possible between exposures. You can do this by shooting the pictures with a hand-held camera, but for best results you should use a sturdy tripod with a cable release. Even then you may have the problem of mirror shake to deal with. With an SLR camera, the flipping up of the mirror can set off a tiny vibration which can cause a small amount of image movement during the exposure, although this is mostly only noticeable if using a long focal length lens. If you shoot hand-held, the vibrations are usually dampened by you holding the camera, but on a tripod this can be a problem. So, apart from using a cable release, do enable the mirror up settings on your camera if you can. As a Canon user it has been frustrating going through the custom function menu options to set the camera to mirror up mode, but setting the mirror lock up has been made easier with the latest EOS 1Ds MkIII camera.

The ideal exposure bracket range will vary, but an exposure bracket of five exposures of 2 EV apart should be enough to successfully capture most scenes. You can also use just three exposures that are 2 EV apart and get good results, but you won't be recording as wide a dynamic range. As you shoot a bracketed sequence look out for any movement between exposures such as people moving through the frame, cars or wind blowing objects. Sometimes it can be hard to prevent everything in the scene from moving and there are some software programs that are capable of removing some ghosting effects. But best to avoid this if you can.

Separating your captures by two exposure values (EV) will allow you to capture a wide scenic capture range efficiently and quickly with just three to five exposures. You can consider narrowing down the exposure gap to just 1 EV between each exposure and shoot more exposures. This can make a marginal improvement to edge detail in the merged HDR image, but can also increase the risk of error if there is any unwanted movement in any of the individual exposures.

HDR File formats

True high dynamic range images can only originate from a high dynamic range capture device or be manufactured from a composite of camera exposures using the Merge to HDR option (as described over the following pages). Photoshop's 32-bit mode uses floating point math calculations (as opposed to regular whole numbers) to describe everything from the deepest shadows to the brightness of the sun and is therefore using a completely different type of image mode to describe the luminance values in an image.

If you want to save an HDR created image out of Photoshop you will be offered a choice of formats. You can use the Photoshop, Large Document format (PSB) or TIFF format to save a file that can store Photoshop layers or adjustment layers, but the downside is that the file size will be at least four times that of an ordinary 8-bit per channel image. However, there are ways to make 32-bit HDR files more compact than this. You can use the Open EXR or Radiance formats to save your HDR files more efficiently. The Open EXR format will very often be only slightly bigger than an ordinary 8-bit version of the image. The downside is that you can't save Photoshop layers using OpenEXR, but this could still be considered a good format choice for archiving flattened HDR images, despite the fact that it is utilizing less of the data than a full 32-bit per channel format such as PSB or TIFF.

Response curve

Each time you load a set of bracketed images, Merge to HDR stores a response curve in Photoshop's preferences for every camera it encounters. As you merge more images from the same camera, Merge to HDR updates the response curve to improve its accuracy. So in most cases, selecting 'Automatic' will do a good job. If consistency is important when using Merge to HDR to process files over a period of time, then you might find it useful to save a response curve and reuse this saved curve when merging images in the future.

Merge to HDR

Now that you've learnt about what a high dynamic range image is, it's time to put the experience into practice and go out and shoot some pictures! To avoid disappointment, choose an easy subject to shoot with first and follow the advice on the previous pages about bracketing and use of a tripod with a cable release. You can certainly get successful results from shooting JPEG images, so don't feel you have to use raw, but in my view raw gives you more options to apply controlled pre-sharpening and make sure the white balance is synchronized. The Merge to HDR command can be accessed via the File ⇨ Automate menu in Photoshop or via the Tools ⇨ Photoshop menu in Bridge. Opening Merge to HDR via Photoshop, selecting files and checking the alignment option is a rather laborious process. This is why I recommend using Bridge (where the image alignment is applied automatically).

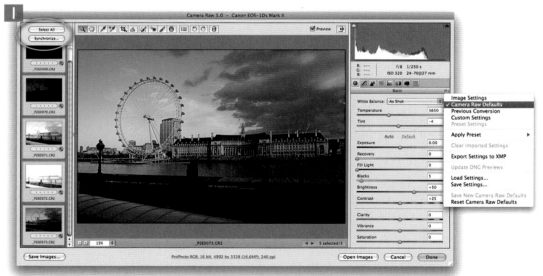

1 The original pictures were bracketed using different time exposures at two exposure values (EV) apart. I began by opening a selection of five raw digital capture images via Camera Raw. It is important that all auto adjustments are switched off. In this example, I made sure the Camera Raw Defaults were applied to the first image and synchronized this setting across all the other selected images (you may also want to sync the white balance if the camera was set to use Auto White Balance).

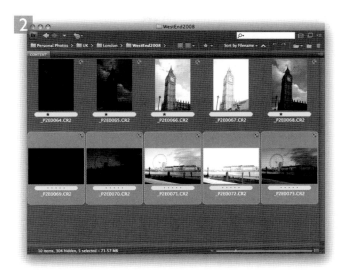

2 I kept the images selected in Bridge and went to the Tools menu and chose Photoshop ⇨ Merge to HDR.

3 This shows the Merge to HDR dialog. It is impossible to represent an HDR image on a standard monitor, so you can use the Exposure slider beneath the histogram to preview 'slices' of the final HDR image. To guide you, each red tick mark represents an exposure value (EV) on the histogram scale (I have shown here examples of how the Photoshop document preview looked at three different EV slider settings). At this stage you can also select or deselect the source image thumbnails on the left to see how this will affect the merged HDR picture. When I was done, I clicked OK to generate a 32-bit per channel HDR image.

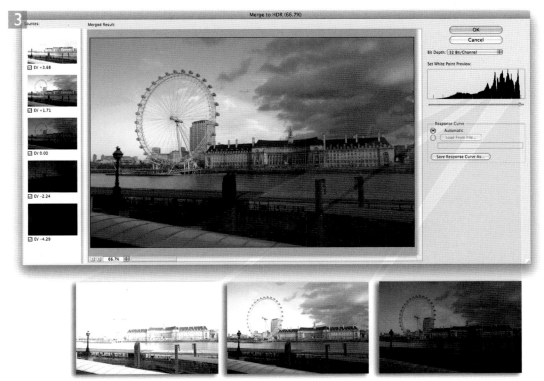

Exposure and Gamma

You can use the Exposure slider to compensate for the overall exposure brightness and the Gamma slider to (effectively) reduce or increase the contrast. These controls are rather basic, but they do allow you to create a usable conversion from the HDR image data.

Highlight Compression

The Highlight Compression simply compresses the highlights, preserving all the highlight detail. It can render good midtones and highlights at the expense of losing detail in the shadows.

Equalize Histogram

The Equalize Histogram option attempts to map the extreme highlight and shadow points to the normal contrast range of a low dynamic range Photoshop image, but this will usually make a rather blunt conversion.

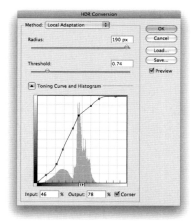

Figure 7.3 The Local Adaptation tone mapping method (displaying the Tone Curve and Histogram options).

Tone mapping HDR images

After you have created a merged 32-bit per channel HDR image, you can save the HDR master using the PSB or TIFF format to preserve maximum image detail plus layers. Or, you can use the EXR format, which as I explained earlier is the most efficient, space-saving file format for storing 32-bit images. You can if you like skip saving the merged HDR image and jump straight into the tone mapping stage by selecting the 16-bit per channel or 8-bit per channel option in the Merge to HDR dialog. I think you will find though that there are some definite advantages to preserving a master image as an HDR file. There is a real art to tone mapping an image from a high dynamic range to a normal, low dynamic range state. You won't always make the best judgement on your first try, so it makes sense to save the HDR file first and then use the Image ⇨ Mode in Photoshop to convert from 32-bits to 16-bits or 8-bits per channel. This will pop the HDR conversion dialog which offers four methods of converting an HDR image to a low dynamic range version. With each of these the aim is the same: to squeeze all of the tonal information that is contained in the high dynamic range master down into a low dynamic range version of the image, but I am mainly going to concentrate here on the Local Adaptation method.

Local Adaptation

The Local Adaptation method is designed to simulate the way our human eyes compensate for varying levels of brightness when viewing a scene. For example, when we are outdoors, our eyes will naturally adjust and compensate for the difference between the brightness of the sky and the brightness of the ground. The difference in relative brightness between these two areas accounts for the 'global contrast' in a scene. As our eyes concentrate on any one particular area, the contrast we observe in, say, the clouds in the sky, or the grass on the ground, is contrast that is perceived at a localized level. So the first two sliders in the dialog in Figure 7.3 are designed to differentiate between global and localized contrast.

According to the manual, the Radius slider determines the size of the local brightness regions, but I prefer to think of this as the 'global contrast' control. You adjust the Radius to make the global contrast less or more contrasty. Set the Radius to zero and you'll get a flat-looking picture, but you can increase the global contrast by raising the Radius slider. The Threshold slider can then be used to adjust the localized contrast. A low Threshold setting will also lead to a flat-looking result, but as you increase the Threshold you will notice how the contrast at a localized level is increased. In Figure 7.4 we have a photograph of a scene that has a high dynamic range. In this picture the Radius slider could be used to adjust the global contrast between the dark foreground and the bright background in order to simulate the way our eyes compensate when viewing such a scene, while the Threshold slider could be used to enhance the detail contrast within both areas.

The optimum settings will much depend on the image content. Just think Radius for global contrast and Threshold for local contrast and look for the best balance between the two. But take care to make sure that you don't create any ugly haloes around the high contrast edges. If you click on the disclosure triangle in the HDR Conversion dialog, this will display the Toning Curve and histogram. You can use this to create a tone enhancing contrast curve that is applied to the HDR conversion. This curve can then also be saved as a preset and applied to other HDR image conversions. Lastly, click on the OK button and Photoshop will render a low dynamic range version from the HDR master.

It has to be said that HDR to LDR converted images can sometimes look quite freaky because there is a temptation to squeeze everything into a low dynamic range. Just because you can preserve a complete tonal range does not mean you should. It is OK you know to let some highlights burn out or let the shadows remain black. The Photoshop approach will let you produce what can be a natural-looking conversion and I think you'll agree that the example on the next two pages neatly shows how the advantage of the HDR editing approach can yield some quite subtle improvements.

Photomatrix

Photoshop's tone mapping methods are designed to offer natural-looking conversions from an HDR to an LDR image. Photomatrix has proved extremely popular with photographers because it offers excellent photo merging (sometimes with more accurate image merging of hand-held shots), ghosting control and, above all, more extensive tone mapping options. Tone mapping with Photomatrix is much easier and also allows you to create those illustration-like effects that are often associated with a high dynamic range image look (which we should really call 'HDR to LDR converted images').

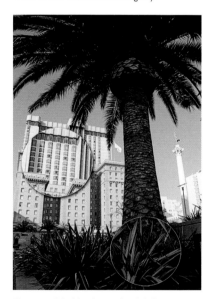

Figure 7.4 In this picture, the global contrast would be the contrast between the palm tree in silhouette against the brightly lit buildings in the background, while the localized contrast would be the detail contrast in both the bright and dark regions of the picture (magnified here).

Local Adaptation tone mapping

1 I began here with an HDR image that was produced by merging together a bracketed sequence of five photographs, shot at 2 EVs apart. To reduce any movement in the individual exposures, the camera was mounted on a tripod and the pictures were all taken using a cable release. This first screen shot shows the merged HDR file as it appeared in Photoshop in 32-bit per channel mode with the Exposure slider adjusted so that we get to see a reasonably good view here of the HDR image. In 32-bit per channel mode one can use the Exposure slider to preview the HDR image at different levels of brightness. This is a useful feature because I was able to adjust the preview exposure as I focused on retouching different parts of the picture using the clone stamp tool (from the highlights to the shadows) prior to carrying out the conversion.

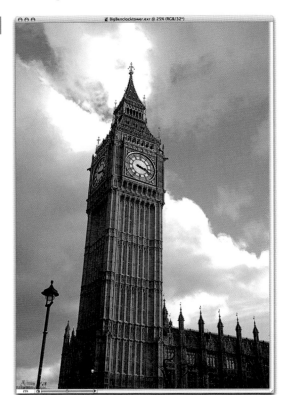

2 To convert this high dynamic range image into a low dynamic range version, I went to the Image ⇨ Mode submenu and chose the 16-bit... option, which opened the HDR Conversion dialog shown here. Of the four tone mapping options that are available in this dialog, I find that the Local Adaptation method usually works the best. For this particular conversion I set the Radius to 190 pixels. This effectively applied a soft-edge mask that masked the global contrast between the sky and the clock tower. Meanwhile I kept the Threshold low at 0.74. I then clicked on the disclosure triangle (circled) to reveal the Toning Curve and Histogram options. The hard part was getting the tone curve editing right. You normally want to maximize the tone curve across the whole of the recorded scenic tone range. Editing the HDR conversion tone curve is quite unlike using the Photoshop Curves dialog. You usually need to add lots of control points and make use of the Corner checkbox to convert some of the control points to corner points. These can anchor selected control points and preserve the tone curve shape above or below the selected point.

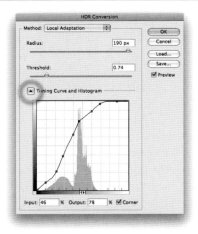

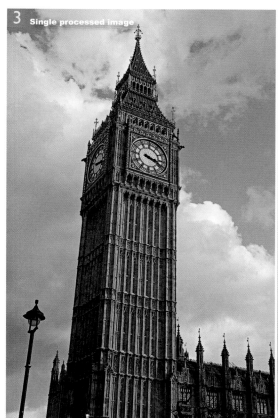

3 Single processed image

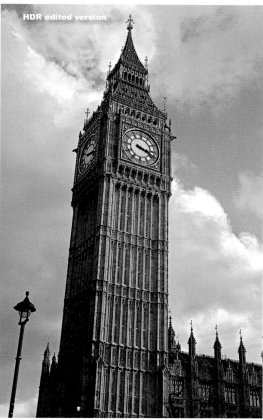

HDR edited version

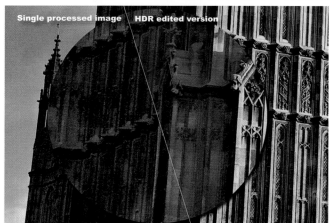

Single processed image   HDR edited version

3 On this page you can see a comparison between a single edited image (using the optimum exposed photograph processed via Camera Raw and output as a 16-bit file) and, next to it the HDR edited version after it had been converted to make a 16-bit low dynamic range image. At first glance the differences are subtle. I did after all try to get the two images to match as closely as possible, but you should notice better contrast in the clouds and the sides of the clock tower. The difference was more noticeable though when I examined the shadow areas in more detail. In this close-up section you can see there is virtually no shadow noise in the HDR converted version.

Exposure adjustments

Although you can use the Exposure adjustment directly on 16-bit or 8-bit images, it is really designed as an image adjustment for working on 32-bit images.

Work from the top downwards

When you add a new adjustment layer, it is best to add the newest layer at the bottom of the layer stack just above the Background layer, as this will reduce the length of time you see the 'Building histograms' dialog appear on the screen.

Manual tone mapping

There is yet another way to tone map an HDR image. If you have the extended version of Photoshop you can add adjustment layers to a 32-bit image and use these to edit the tone and color. In Figure 7.5 you can see a preview of an image that was in 32-bit per channel mode, where I used a combination of Exposure adjustment layers to adjust the contrast and brightness and Levels adjustment layers to adjust the color, and masked each of these individual adjustment layers to selectively apply these adjustments to specific areas of the photograph. By building up a succession of adjustment layers, I was able to accurately tone map the original HDR image just the way I wanted to without having to render it as an LDR version just yet. When saving such a file you will need to use the Photoshop, TIFF, Portable Bit Map or PSB format if you wish to preserve all the layers. Consequently, the master image file size will be increased, but direct HDR image editing does offer a lot of flexibility.

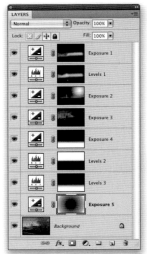

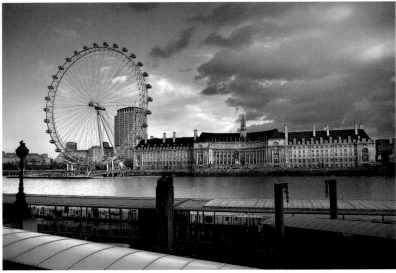

Figure 7.5 If you are using the extended version of Photoshop you can use adjustment layers to manually tone map the 32-bit data while keeping the HDR image in it's original 32-bit mode.

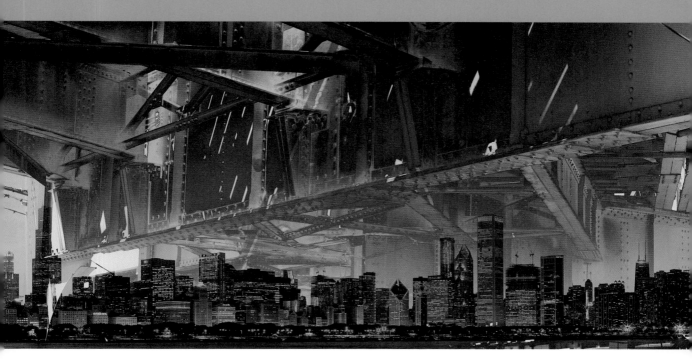

Chapter 8

Image Retouching

Photoshop has become so successful, it's very name is synonymous with digital retouching. The humble clone stamp tool has been around since the very early versions of Photoshop and used and abused in equal measure, while the new tools added since mean that you can now transform images almost any way you want. As my colleague Jeff Schewe likes to say: 'you know why Photoshop is so successful? Because reality sucks!' Well, that's Jeff's viewpoint, but then he does come from a background in advertising photography, where heavy retouching is par for the course. The techniques described in this chapter will teach you some of the basic techniques, such as how to remove artifacts like dust spots, before going on to explore some of the more advanced techniques that can be used to clean up and enhance your photographs.

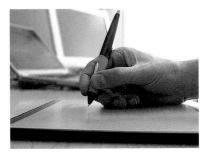

Figure 8.1 If you are carrying out any type of retouching work which relies on the use of the paint tools, a pressure-sensitive tablet and pen, such as the Wacom™ shown here, is absolutely invaluable.

Basic cloning methods

The clone stamp tool and healing brush are the most useful tools to use at the beginning of any retouching session.

Clone stamp tool

To use the clone stamp tool, hold down ⌥ alt and click to select a source point to clone from. Release the ⌥ alt key and move the cursor over to the point where you want to clone to, and click or drag with the mouse. If you have the tool set to aligned mode, this will establish a fixed relationship between the source and destination points. If the tool is set to non-aligned mode then the source point remains fixed, returning to the same spot after each each time you lift the pen or mouse. To work quickly and efficiently, I do find it helps to use something like a Wacom tablet to carry out all the retouching steps (see Figure 8.1).

Clone stamp brush settings

As with all the other painting tools, you can change the brush size, shape and opacity to suit your needs. I mostly always leave the opacity set to 100%, since cloning at less than full opacity can lead to tell-tale evidence of clone stamp retouching, although when smoothing out skin tone shadows or blemishes you might find it helpful to switch to an opacity of 50% or less. When retouching areas of soft texture you can also get away with using lower opacities for the cloning, but otherwise stick to using 100% opacity. For similar reasons, you don't want the clone stamp to have too soft an edge. For general retouching work, the clone stamp brush shape should have a slightly harder edge than you might use normally with the paint brush tools. When retouching detailed subjects such as fine textures, use an even harder edge so as to avoid creating halos. Also, if the film grain in the photograph is visible, anything other than a harder edge setting will lead to soft halos, which can make the retouched area look slightly blurred or misregistered. If you need extra subtle control, lower the Flow rate; this will allow you to build an effect more slowly, without the drawbacks of lowering the Opacity.

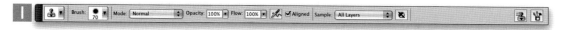

1 The best way to disguise clone stamp retouching is to use a full opacity brush with a medium hard edge at 100% opacity. It is also a good idea to add a new empty layer above the Background layer, so you can keep all the clone retouching on a separate layer. I therefore had the 'All Layers' Sample option selected so that all visible pixels were copied to this new layer.

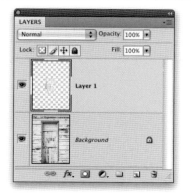

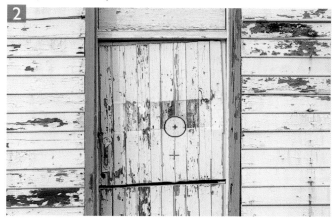

2 The Aligned box is normally checked by default in the Options bar. Here, I used the ⌥ *alt* key to set the sample point on an undamaged part of the wooden door and then clicked again further up to set the destination point. I then dragged to paint with the clone stamp. Photoshop retains this relationship for all subsequent brush strokes with the clone stamp tool until a new source and destination are created.

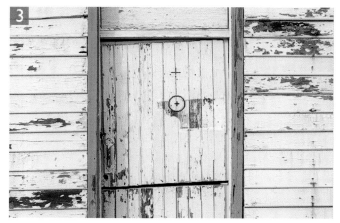

3 This screen shot shows how the door looked after I had worked on it a bit longer using the clone stamp tool to mend the weathered portions of the door. It is in situations like this that 'overlay' in the Clone Source panel can prove useful (see page 388).

All Layers option

The 'Current & Below' and 'All Layers' options are useful if you want to work with the clone stamp or healing brush and store your retouching on a separate layer. If you select the Current & Below option, Photoshop will only sample from the visible layers that are below the current layer and ignore any that are placed above it. If the 'All Layers' option is selected, Photoshop will sample from all visible layers, including those above the active layer (see also, page 395).

Healing brush

The healing brush can be used in the same way as the clone stamp tool, although it is important to stress that the healing brush is more than just a super clone stamp and has its own unique characteristics. So although it is similar to the clone stamp, you will need to take these differences into account and adapt the way you work with it. To begin with, you establish a sample point by ⌥ _alt_ -clicking on the portion of the image you wish to sample from. Release the ⌥ _alt_ key and move the cursor over to the point where you want to clone to and click or drag with the mouse to carry out the healing brush retouching.

The healing brush performs its magic by sampling the texture from the source point and blending the sampled texture with the color and luminosity of the pixels that surround the destination point. For the healing brush to work it reads the pixels within a feathered radius that is up to 10% outside the perimeter of the healing brush cursor area. By reading the pixels that are outside the brush cursor area, the healing brush is able (in most cases) to calculate a smooth transition of color and luminosity within the area that is being painted. It is for these reasons that there is no need to use a soft-edged brush since you will always get more controlled results through using a brush with a hard edge.

Once you understand the fundamental principles behind the workings of the healing brush, you will come to understand why it is the healing brush will sometimes fail to work as expected. You see, if the healing brush is applied too close to an edge where there is a sudden shift in tonal lightness, the healing brush will attempt to create a blend with what is immediately outside the healing brush area. So when you retouch with the healing brush you need to be mindful of this phenomenon, but there are things you can do to address this. For example, you can create a selection that defines the area you are about to start the retouching on and constrain the healing brush work to inside the selection area (see the example shown on page 393).

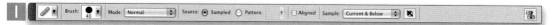

1 I selected the healing brush from the Tools panel and selected a hard-edged brush from the Options bar. The brush blending mode was set to Normal, the Source radio button selected and the Aligned box left unchecked.

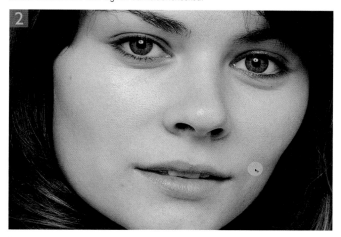

2 Before using the healing brush, I again added a new empty layer and made sure the Sample options were set to 'All Layers' or 'Current & Below'. I ⬈ *alt*-clicked to define the source point, which in this example was a clean area of skin texture, and was now ready to carry out the retouching. Here, I simply clicked on the blemishes to remove them with the healing brush. If you are using a pressure-sensitive tablet such as a Wacom tablet, the default brush dynamics will be size sensitive, so you can use light pressure to paint with a small brush and heavier pressure to apply a full-sized brush.

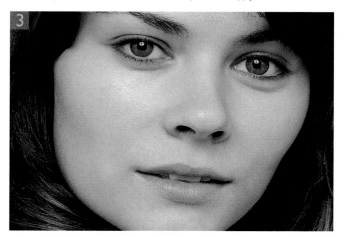

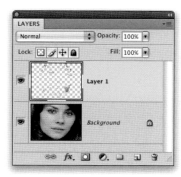

3 I continued using the healing brush to complete the skin tone retouching.

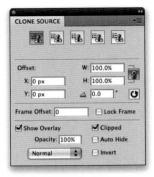

Figure 8.2 The Clone Source panel, shown here with the Show Overlay and Clipped options checked.

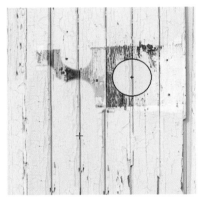

Figure 8.3 This shows how the clone stamp (or healing brush) cursor looks when using the Clone Source panel options shown in Figure 8.2.

Video edit applications

All the other features in the Clone Source panel, such as the multiple sample points, are really intended for video editing, where it may be desirable to store multiple clone sources when cloning in exact registration from one frame to another across several images in a sequence.

Choosing an appropriate alignment mode

I usually find it convenient to use the clone stamp tool in aligned mode and the healing brush in non-aligned mode. This is because when you use the clone stamp you can preserve the relationship between the source and destination points, apply a few clones, then sample a new source point and continue cloning over other parts of the photograph (Figure 8.4).

If you try to use the clone stamp over an area where there is a gentle change in tonal gradation, it will be almost impossible to disguise the retouching work, unless the point you are sampling from and the destination point match exactly in tone and color. It is in these situations that you are better off using the healing brush. For most healing brush work I suggest you use the non-aligned mode (which happens to be the default setting for the healing brush). This allows you to choose a source point that contains optimum information with which to repair a particular section of the photograph and you can keep referencing the same source point as you work with the healing brush.

Clone Source panel and clone overlays

The Clone Source panel was first introduced in Photoshop CS3, mainly as a tool for video editors. The CS4 version now offers an improved overlay cursor view where if the 'Show Overlay' and 'Clipped' options are both checked, a preview of the clone source can be seen inside the cursor area. Back on page 385 I made a reference to the Clone Source panel because this was just the kind of retouching task that would benefit from having an overlay inside the cursor to help guide you where to click when setting the destination point for the clone stamp. Figure 8.3 shows a detail view of the clone stamp in use with the settings shown in Figure 8.2, where both the 'Show Overlay' and 'Clipped' options were enabled. You might want to have the 'Show Overlay' option switched on all of the time, but there is usually a slight time delay while the cursor updates its new position and this can at times become distracting. I therefore suggest you only enable it when you need to.

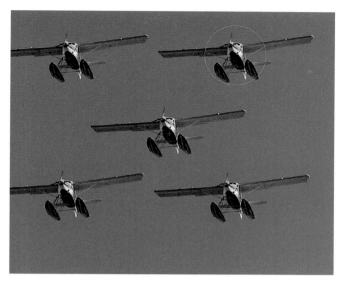

Figure 8.4 When you have the clone stamp tool selected and the Aligned box in the tool options is unchecked, the source point remains static and each application of the clone stamp will make a copy of the image data from the same original source point.

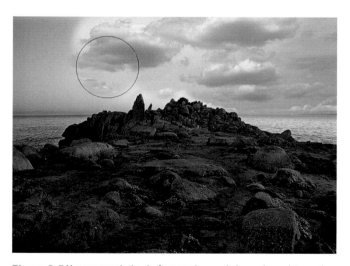

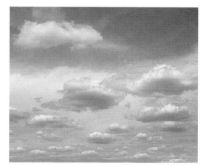

Figure 8.5 You can sample the sky from one image window and copy it to another separate image using the clone stamp. Just [⌥] [alt]-click with the clone stamp in the source (sky) image, then select the other image window and click to establish a cloning relationship between the source and destination images.

Overlay blend modes

You can adjust the opacity of the Clone Source overlay and change the blend mode. In some instances you may find it useful to work with the Difference blend mode at 100%, as the Difference blend mode will show a solid black preview when identical pixels are in register.

Upside down cloning

Here is a further example of how the Clone Source panel can help with tricky retouching jobs. In the following steps I used the Clone Source panel's ability to rotate the clone stamp or healing brush alignment through 180°. I first showed this technique in the previous edition of the book, but this has now been updated to show the improved cursor overlay display.

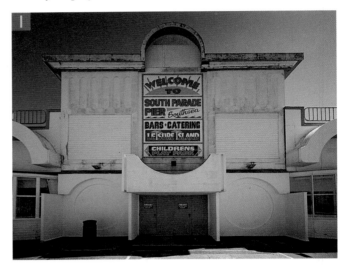

1 Here is a photograph in which there is a trash bin that I wished to remove. The tricky thing here is that the bin is just in front of a circular alcove, and this would normally make it less easy to remove. But not so when you have access to the Clone Source panel controls.

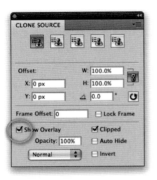

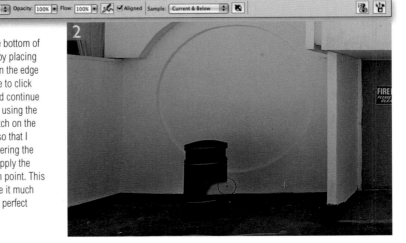

2 To start with, I wanted to remove the bottom of the bin. This could normally be done by placing the source point for the clone stamp on the edge of the black line and 'estimating' where to click with the clone stamp, so that you could continue painting along the line 'in register'. By using the Clone Source panel, I was able to switch on the 'Show Overlay' and 'Clipped' options so that I could easily align the pixels while hovering the cursor in position, before clicking to apply the cloned pixels at the correct destination point. This took away all the guesswork and made it much easier to paint with the clone stamp in perfect alignment with the underlying image.

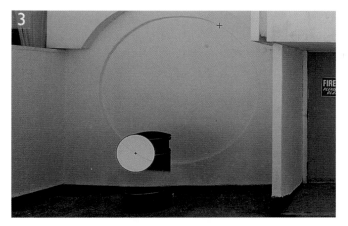

3 I now switched tools and selected the healing brush. This time I went to the Clone Source panel and set the clone source angle to be 180° relative to the destination. This meant that when I sampled using the pixels from the top right corner of the circular alcove, the preview showed a 180° rotated preview of where the pixels would be painted at the destination point. Again, the cursor overlay allowed me to precisely align the preview, so that the edge of the circle could be aligned precisely.

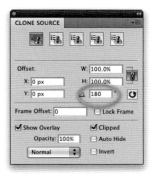

4 Here is a screen shot showing the healing brush in action. Note that it does not matter that the preview shows the cloned pixels as being a lot lighter than the ones I was painting on top of. The healing brush blended these together as soon as I finished painting.

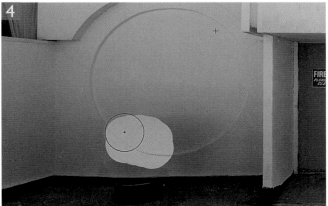

5 Here is the final result, in which I only had to carry out some minor extra retouching in order to tidy up the remaining parts of the picture.

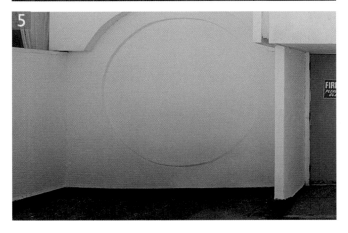

Better healing edges

Since the healing brush is blending around the outside edges, you can improve the healing effect by increasing the outer circumference. The following technique came via Russell Brown, who informs me that he was shown how to do this by an attendee at one of his seminars.

If you change the healing brush to an elliptical shape, you will tend to produce a more broken-up edge to your healing work and this will sometimes produce an improved healing blend (Figure 8.6). There are two explanations for why this works. Firstly, a narrow elliptical brush inevitably produces a longer perimeter to the painting edge. This means that more pixels are likely to be sampled when calculating the blend. The second thing you will notice is that when the healing brush is more elliptical, there is a randomness to the angle of the brush. Try changing the shape of the brush the way I describe and as you start using an elliptical-shaped brush you will see what I mean.

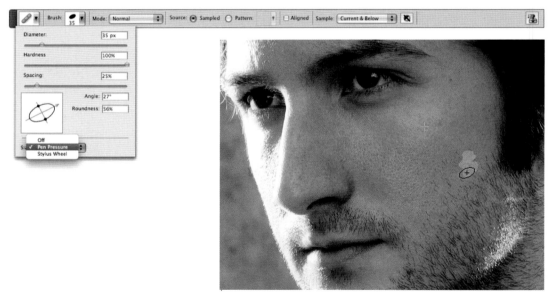

Figure 8.6 To adjust the shape and hardness of the healing brush, select the healing brush tool and mouse down on the brush options in the tool Options bar. Set the hardness to 100% and drag the elliptical handles to make the brush shape more elliptical. Notice also that if you are using a Wacom tablet or other pressure-sensitive input device, the brush size is linked by default to the amount of pen pressure applied.

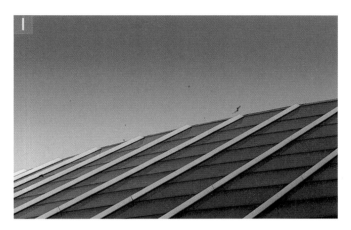

1 The healing brush is a perfect retouching tool to use when you are faced with the challenge of retouching blemishes where the sky contains gentle transitions of tone going from dark to light. It used to be extremely difficult to retouch shots like this when all you had to work with was the clone stamp tool, but not so with the healing brush.

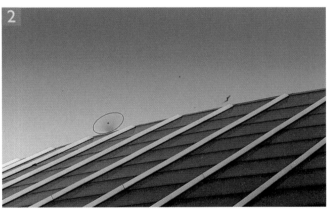

2 A potential problem arises though when you wish to retouch a blemish that is adjacent to a sudden change in lightness or color. In this picture you can see that even if you use the healing brush with a small hard-edged brush, as you brush closer to the roof the healing brush may pick up the dark edge and you will see these darker pixels bleed into the healing brush cloned area.

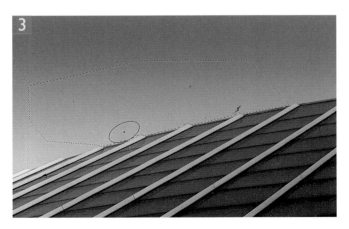

3 One answer to the problem is to make a preselection of the area you wish to heal (with maybe some minimal feathering) and thereby restrict the extent to which the healing brush tool is able to analyze the surrounding pixels. The other alternative is to switch where possible to working with the clone stamp tool when you are retouching close to edges like this.

Default healing tool

The spot healing brush is the default healing tool in Photoshop, so the first time you select it and try to use the ⎇ *alt* keys to establish a source point to sample from you will be shown a warning dialog explaining there is no need to create a sample source with this tool. This dialog will offer you the option to switch to using the normal healing brush instead.

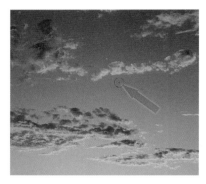

Figure 8.7 In Proximity Match mode, the spot healing brush works by searching automatically to find the best pixels to sample from to carry out a repair, but if you drag with the spot healing brush it will use the direction of the drag as the source for the most suitable texture to sample from. By dragging with the tool you can give the spot healing brush a better clue as to where to sample from.

Spot healing brush

The spot healing brush may not be quite so versatile as the healing brush, but it is in many ways a lot easier to use. All you have to do is select the spot healing brush from the Tools panel and click on the marks or blemishes you wish to remove. The spot healing brush will automatically sample the replacement pixel data from around the area you are trying to heal.

The spot healing brush tool has two basic modes of operation (Figure 8.8). The Proximity Match mode analyzes the data, around the area where you are painting, to identify the best area to sample the pixel information from. It then uses the pixel data that has been sampled in this way to replace the defective pixels beneath where you are painting. You can use the spot healing brush to click away and zap small blemishes, but when you are repairing larger areas in a picture you will usually obtain better results if the brush size used is slightly smaller than the area you are trying to repair. If you come across a problem like the one outlined on page 393, it is usually best to apply brush strokes that drag inwards from the side where the best source data exists (see Figure 8.7). This is because the spot healing brush intelligently looks around for the good pixel data to sample from, but if you drag with the brush it will look first in the direction from where you dragged.

The Create Texture mode works in a slightly different fashion. The spot healing tool reads in the data surrounding the area you are attempting to repair. As you do this it generates a texture pattern from the sampled data. So the main difference is that Proximity Match is repairing and blending with actual pixels, while Create Texture is repairing and blending with a texture pattern that has been generated on-the-fly.

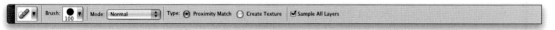

Figure 8.8 The spot healing brush Options bar.

Clone and healing sample options

The clone sample options (Figure 8.9) allow you to choose how the pixels are sampled when you use the clone stamp or healing brushes. 'Current Layer' samples the contents of the current layer only, ignoring all other layers. The 'Current & Below' option samples the current layer and visible layers below (ignoring the layers above it), while the 'All Layers' option samples all visible layers in the layer stack, including those above the current layer. If the Ignore Adjustment Layers button (circled) is turned on, Photoshop ignores the effect adjustment layers are having on the image (see sidebar). However, the spot healing brush has just the 'Sample All Layers' option in the tool Options bar to check or uncheck.

Ignore adjustment layers

When 'Ignore Adjustment Layers' is switched on, it won't matter that there may be adjustment layers active, as Photoshop now ignores the effect these have when cloning the visible pixels. This is mainly used to prevent adjustment layers above the layer you are working on from affecting the retouching done on a layer below when the 'All Layers' sample option has been selected. Prior to this you would have had to temporarily hide such adjustment layers before doing any retouching.

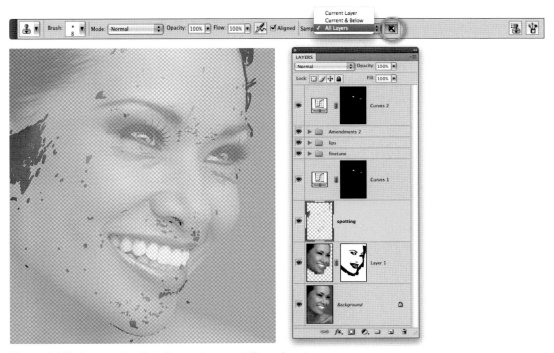

Figure 8.9 The layer sample options allow you to carry out all your clone stamp and healing brush work on an empty new layer. The advantage of this is that you can keep all your retouching work separate and leave the original Background layer untouched. In this example, the 'All Layers' option allowed me to sample from layers above and below, but because the 'Ignore Adjustment Layers' option was checked Photoshop ignored the effect any adjustment layers had on the sampled pixels.

Client: Eylure
Model: Susannah @ Storm

Source and Destination modes

In Source mode you can drag the patch tool selection area to a new destination point and preview the pixels that will replace those in the original source selection area. In Destination mode you can drag the patch tool selection area to a new destination point and Photoshop will perform a healing blend calculation, copying and blending the sampled patch area with a new area in the image.

Use Pattern option

The Use Pattern button in the Options bar will let you fill a selected area with a preset pattern using a healing type blend.

Patch tool

The patch tool uses the same complex algorithm as the healing brush to carry out its blend calculations, except the patch tool uses selection-defined areas instead of a brush. When the patch tool is selected, it initially operates in a lasso selection mode that can be used to define the area to 'patch from' or 'patch to' (for example, you can hold down the ⌥ alt key to temporarily convert the tool to become a polygonal lasso tool with which to draw straight line selection edges). You don't actually need the patch tool to define the selection; any selection tool or selection method can be used when preparing a patch selection. Then, once you have made the selection, select the patch tool to proceed to the next stage. Unlike the healing brushes, the patch tool has to work with either the Background layer or a copied pixel layer, but the selection area will preview the image as you drag to define the patch selection (the Clone Source panel settings aren't required).

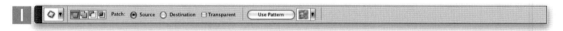

1 The patch tool works in a way that is similar to the healing brush. Using the picture opposite, I can show you how the patch tool can be used in Source mode to cover up the tattoo on this model's body. When you select the patch tool you can use it just like the lasso tool to draw around the outline of the area you wish to 'patch', and loosely define a selection area. As was mentioned in the main text, you can use any selection tool method you like to define the selection as you prepare an image for patching.

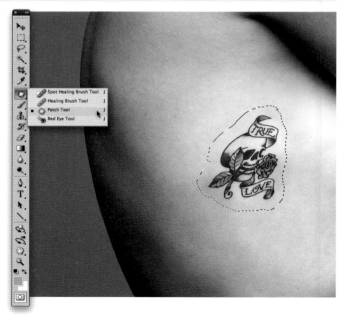

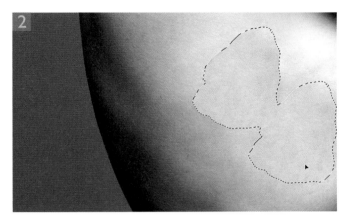

2 Having defined the area I wanted to patch, I made sure that the patch tool was now selected in the Tools panel and dragged inside the selection to locate an area of the image that could be used to 'patch over' the original area (i.e. remove the tattoo). As I dragged the patch selection this created a second selection area and I could see a live preview in the original patch selection, indicating which pixels would be cloned here.

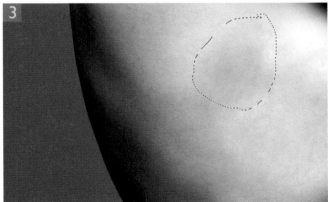

3 As I released the mouse, Photoshop began to calculate a healing blend, analyzing the pixels from the source area (that I had just defined) and using these to merge seamlessly with the pixels in the original selection area. The result of this patch transformation was pretty impressive, as it managed to remove the tattoo, but you'll notice that a dark shadow remained in the middle of the patch area.

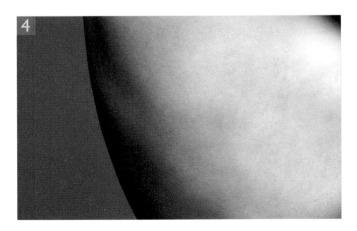

4 This is something to be expected and simply means that the patch tool action wasn't completely successful at removing the tattoo in one single step. Remember, the original patch tool selection was still active and all I had to do was carry out a further patch tool action by repeating Step 2. This screen shot shows what the model's body looked like after applying the patch tool twice. As you can see, all traces of the tattoo are now gone.

Layer blending with Auto-Align layers

Although it is not possible to use the patch tool to copy between documents, you can use the following steps to achieve a patch blend result by using the Auto-Blend Layers feature, which has now been improved in CS4.

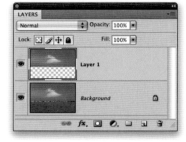

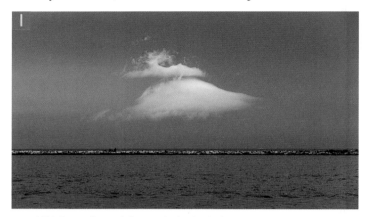

1 This is one of several photographs that I took of some intriguing clouds over Lake Michigan. I began by making a copy layer of the sky portion of the image before dragging this across to the photograph shown in Step 2, to add it as a new layer.

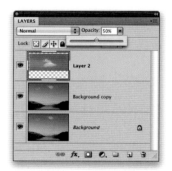

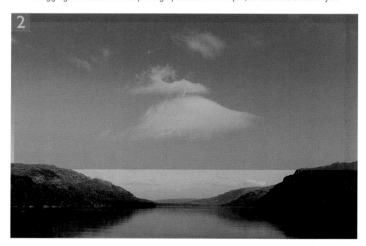

2 This shows the newly added layer, where I temporarily set the layer opacity to 50% so that I could gauge where to position the cloud relative to the other clouds in the sky. When I was happy with the position, I returned the opacity to 100%. I also created a duplicate copy of the Background layer. This was important because the blend that's coming up will modify the pixels on this layer too.

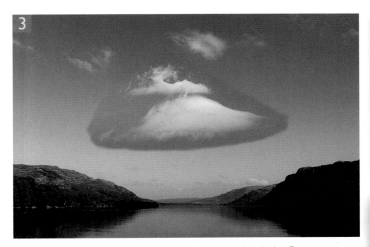

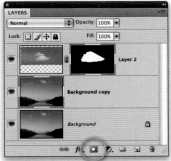

3 Now the tricky part, because the results here can be a bit hit and miss. To start with, I 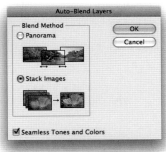 *alt*-clicked on the Add Layer Mask button in the Layers panel (circled), which added a layer mask to the cloud layer that hid the contents. I then selected the paint brush, and with white as the foreground color painted on the layer mask to reveal the cloud. In the Layers panel, I used the *Shift* key to select both this layer and the Background Copy layer and then went to the Edit menu to select Auto-Blend Layers... . In the dialog shown here, I selected 'Stack Images' and made sure the 'Seamless Tones and Colors' option was checked.

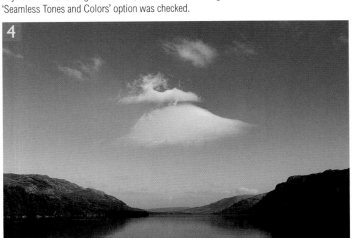

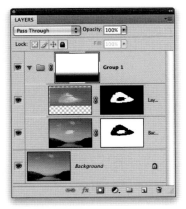

4 This shows the result of the Auto-Blend Layers command, where I also grouped the two layers and applied a group layer mask to fade the opacity at the bottom. The layer mask applied to the cloud layer in Step 3 did have a bearing on the outcome here. If you are trying this out for yourself and don't like the result, you'll need to undo the layer mask and try again. It did take me quite a few attempts and a little tweaking to get the result shown here, but I think you'll agree this is a powerful feature.

Replacing film grain

You may encounter a problem if the photographic original contains noticeable film grain, since even with the selective application of the Dust & Scratches filter you may end up with some softening where you retouch the image. To counteract this it may help to apply a small amount of noise after you have applied the Dust & Scratches filter. Add enough noise to match the grain of the original (usually around 2–3%). This will enable you to better disguise the history brush retouching.

Alternative history brush spotting technique

This spotting method has evolved from a technique that was first described by Russell Brown, Senior Creative Director of the Adobe Photoshop team. It revolves around using the Remove Dust & Scratches filter, which is found in the Filter ⇨ Noise submenu. If this filter is applied globally to the whole image, you can easily end up with a very soft-looking result. So ideally, this filter should be applied selectively to the damaged portions of a picture. The technique shown here has the advantage of applying the filtered information via the history brush such that only the pixels which are considered too dark are painted out. This modified approach to working with the Dust & Scratches filter avoids destroying the tonal values in the rest of the picture.

As you can see, the technique works well when you have a picture that is very badly damaged and where using the clone stamp would be a very tedious process. What is really clever is the way that the Lighten (and Darken) blend modes can be used to target which pixels are repaired from the stored Dust & Scratches history state.

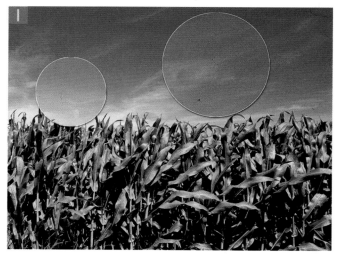

1 This scanned photograph serves as a good example with which to demonstrate the history brush spotting technique, as there are a lot of dust marks clearly visible in the enlarged detail views shown in this picture.

2

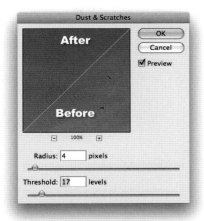

2 I went to the Filter menu and chose Noise ⇨ Dust & Scratches, checked the Filter dialog preview and adjusted the Radius and Threshold settings until I could verify that most of the dust marks would be removed. I then clicked OK to apply this filter to the image.

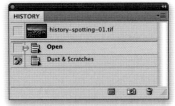

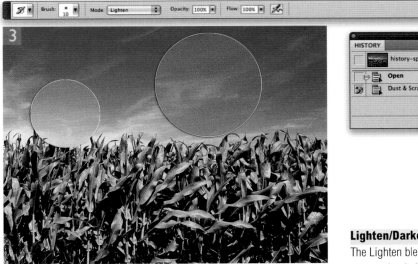

3 I then went to the History panel and clicked on the previous unfiltered image history state, but set the Dust & Scratches filtered version as the history source to paint from. I then selected the history brush and in the tool Options bar changed the history brush blending mode to Lighten. As I painted over the dark spots, the history brush lightened only those pixels that were darker than the sampled history state. All other pixels remained unchanged. I continued using the history brush in this way until I had painted out all the dust spots in the photograph.

Lighten/Darken blend mode

The Lighten blend mode was used to remove the dark marks in the image. Similarly, one can use the Darken blend mode to remove any light blemish marks. For example, if you were to retouch a scanned color negative, the dust spots there would show up as white marks.

Portrait retouching

Here is an example of a restrained approach to retouching, where only a minimal amount of Photoshop editing was used. Of course you can retouch portraits as if they were fashion shots, and some publications may demand this, but I thought I would start off with something more subtle.

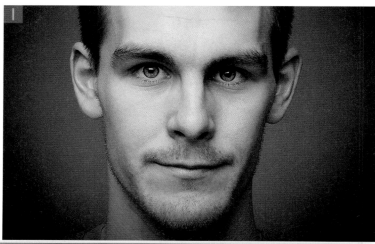

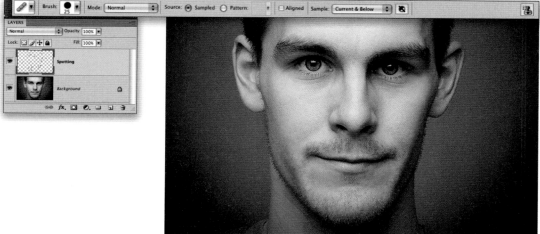

1 The top photograph shows the unretouched before version and the version below this shows the results of the initial retouching in which I mainly used the healing brush to remove some of the skin blemishes. The key thing here was to not overdo the retouching. I regard what I did here as being more like 'tidying and grooming' rather than 'digital surgery'.

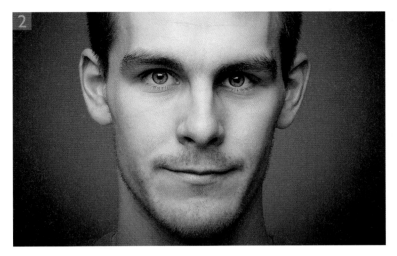

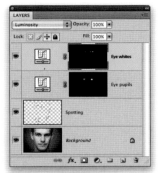

2 For this next step I wanted to lighten the eyes. To do this, I used the lasso tool to define the outline of the pupils. In the Adjustments panel I clicked to add a Curves adjustment and adjusted the curve shape to lighten the selected area. I then selected the whites of the eyes and applied a separate Curves adjustment. My aim here was to add more contrast to the pupils making the eyes slightly lighter overall.

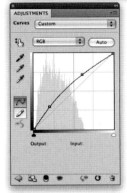

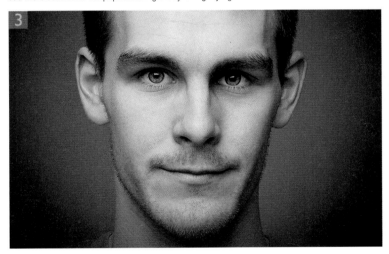

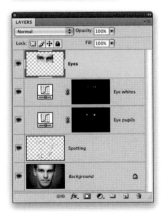

3 Lastly, I wanted to adjust the shapes of the eyes. To do this, I used the ⌘ ⌥ Shift E / ctrl alt Shift E command to create a merged copy layer at the top of the layer stack. I made a marquee selection to include the eyes, inverted the selection and hit Delete (this was done to keep the file size down). I then went to the Filter menu and chose Liquify (described later in this chapter), where I made the left eye smaller, opened up the eye on the right and raised the eyebrow slightly. I then clicked OK to complete the retouching shown here.

Getting the balance right

The main thing I show on these pages is how to use the paint brush to smooth the skin tones on the face and hands. I happen to prefer using the manual painting approach (rather than relying on a blur filter), because the painting method offers more control over the retouching. An important issue here is 'how much to retouch?' This is mostly down to personal taste. My own personal view is that it is better to fade any painting work that's done and let the natural skin texture show through – let there be a few wrinkles and flaws! It is possible to retouch to produce a clean-looking image, but still keep the model looking vaguely human.

Beauty retouching

Beauty photographs require more intense retouching, and the objective is usually to produce an image where the model's features appear to look flawless. This can be done through a combination of healing and painting brush work.

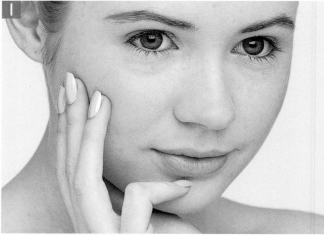

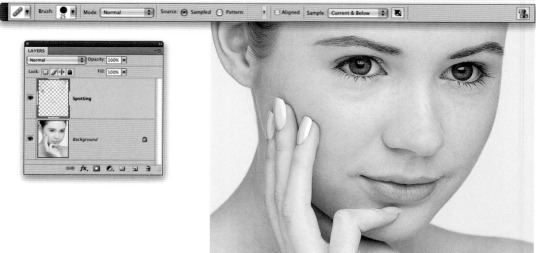

Client: ET Nail Art
Model: Karen Gillan @ Bookings
Makeup: Camilla Pascucci

1 The top photograph here shows the before version and the one below shows how the same image looked after I had added a new empty layer and carried out some basic spotting work (mostly using the healing brush) to clean up the nails, removed some spots and got rid of unwanted stray hairs.

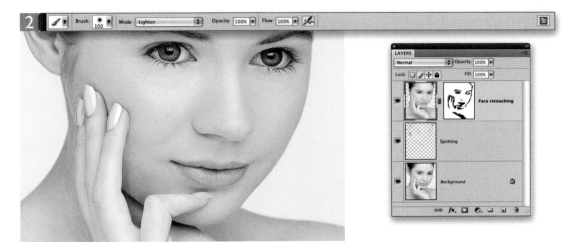

2 After that I used the ⌘ ⌥ Shift E ctrl alt Shift E command to create a merged copy layer at the top of the layer stack and worked with the paint brush on the merged layer. The trick here was to hold down the ⌥ alt key to sample a skin tone color and gently paint using low opacity brush strokes with the blend mode set to 'Lighten'. This meant the paint strokes only affected those colors that were darker than the sample color. Similarly, I switched to Darken mode when I wished to darken only those pixels lighter than the paint sample color. This selective method of painting can produce more controlled results compared to using the Normal blend mode.

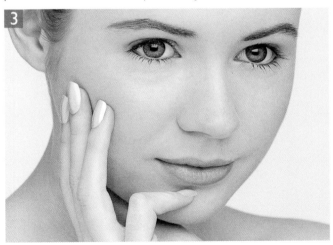

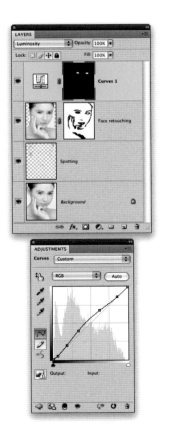

3 This shows the finished retouched version in which I faded the opacity of the painted layer to 60% and added a layer mask so that I could carefully mask the areas where the paint retouching had spilled over. Lastly, I added a Curves adjustment to lighten the eyes slightly.

Liquify tools

Warp tool (W)

Provides a basic warp distortion with which you can stretch the pixels in any direction you wish.

Reconstruct tool (R)

Used to make selective undos and restore the image to its undistorted state.

Twirl clockwise tool (C)

Twist the pixels in a clockwise direction. Hold down the ⌥ alt key to switch tool to twirl in a counterclockwise direction.

Pucker tool (S)

Shrinks pixels and produces an effect similar to the 'Pinch' filter.

Bloat tool (B)

Magnifies pixels and is similar to the 'Bloat' filter.

Push left tool (O)

Shifts the pixels 90° to the left of the direction in which you are dragging.

Mirror tool (M)

Copies pixels from 90° to the direction you are dragging and therefore acts as an inverting lens.

Turbulence tool (T)

Produces random turbulent distortions.

Freeze mask tool (F)

Protects areas of the image. Frozen portions are indicated by a Quick Mask type overlay. These areas are protected from any further liquify distortions.

Thaw mask tool (D)

Selectively or wholly erases the freeze tool area.

Hand tool (H)

For scrolling the preview image.

Zoom tool (Z)

Use to magnify or zoom out.

Liquify

The Liquify filter is designed to let you carry out freeform pixel distortions. When you choose Filter ⇨ Liquify, you are presented with what is called a modal dialog, which basically means you are working in a self-contained dialog with its own set of tools and keyboard shortcuts, etc. It is therefore operating like a program within the Photoshop program. To use Liquify efficiently, I suggest you make a marquee selection first of the area you wish to manipulate before you select the filter and, once the dialog has opened, use the ⌘ 0 ctrl 0 shortcut to enlarge the dialog to fit the screen.

Basically, you select one of the Liquify tools to manipulate the image preview and when you are happy with your liquify work, click *Enter* or *Return* to OK the pixel manipulation. This will then calculate and apply the liquify adjustment to the main image.

The Liquify tools are all explained in the column on the left and the chart shown in Figure 8.10 also summarizes the effect each of these tools will have on an image. The easiest of these to get to grips with is the warp tool, which allows you to simply click and drag to push the pixels in the direction you want them to go in. However, I also like working with the push left tool, because it lets me carry out some quite bold warp adjustments. Note that when you drag with the push left tool it shifts the pixels 90° to the left of the direction you are dragging in and when you ⌥ alt drag with this tool it will shift the pixels 90° to the right.

The pucker tool is sometimes useful for correcting over-distorted areas and squeezing the pixels inwards again. The reflection tool is perhaps the most unwieldy of all, as it copies pixels from 90° to the direction you are dragging and therefore acts like an inverting lens, which if you are not careful will easily rip an image apart! Apparently, retouchers who work on adult magazines are fond of working with the turbulence tool. This is for reasons I have yet to fathom and probably inappropriate for me to enquire about further in this book!

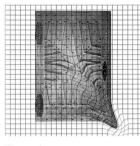

Warp tool

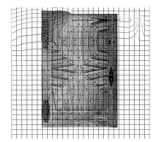

Reconstruct tool

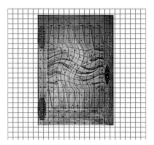

Twirl tool

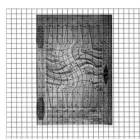

Twirl tool (with ⌥ alt key held down)

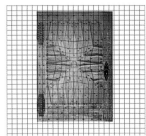

Pucker tool

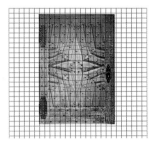

Bloat tool

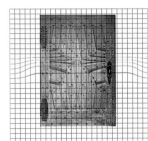

Push left tool

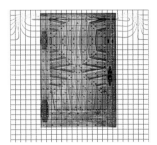

Mirror tool

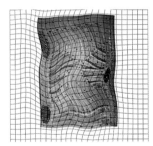

Turbulence tool

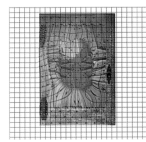

Freeze mask tool

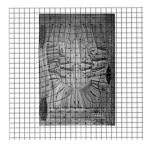

Thaw mask tool

Figure 8.10 These illustrations give you an idea of the range of distortion effects that can be achieved using the Liquify tools described on page 406.

One step at a time

The key to working successfully with the Liquify filter is to use gradual brush movements to build up a distortion. This is why I prefer to set the 'Brush Pressure' at an extremely low setting and use a Wacom pad to apply the liquify brush strokes, with the Stylus Pressure option selected.

Liquify shortcut

Prior to CS4 you could access Liquify using the ⌘ Shift X ctrl Shift X shortcut. This has now been removed in CS4, but you can easily reset this as a custom keyboard shortcut.

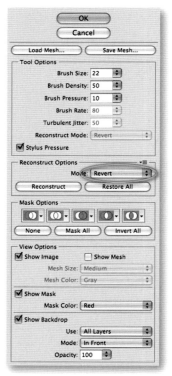

Figure 8.11 The Liquify dialog options. The Reconstruct Options are shown circled here.

Liquify tool controls

Once you have selected a tool you will want to check out the associated tool options, which are shown in Figure 8.11. All the tools (apart from the hand and zoom tool) are displayed as a circular cursor with a crosshair in the middle. The tool options are applied universally to all the tools and these include: Brush Size, Brush Density, Brush Pressure and Brush Rate. If you mouse down on the double-arrow icon next to the field entry box, this will pop a dynamic slider which can be used to adjust the settings. You can also use the square bracket keys [ ] to enlarge or reduce the tool cursor size, and the rate of increase/decrease can be accelerated by holding down the Shift key. I highly recommend that you use a pressure-sensitive pen and pad such as the Wacom system and, if you do so, make sure that the Stylus Pressure option is checked and set the brush pressure to around 10–20%. Note that the Turbulent Jitter control is only active when the turbulence tool is selected. In this context the jitter refers to the amount of randomness that will be introduced in a turbulence distortion applied with this tool.

Reconstructions

Next we have the Reconstruct Options. The standard mode is Revert and if you apply a Liquify distortion and click on the Reconstruct button, the image will be restored to its undistorted state in gradual stages each time you click the button (while preserving any areas that have been frozen with the freeze tool). If you click on the Restore All button the entire image will be restored in one step (ignoring any frozen areas). The default Revert mode produces scaled reversions that return you to the original image state in the preview window. However, there are some alternative options which are more relevant once you have created a frozen area. For example, the Rigid mode provides one-click reconstruction. Stiff, Smooth and Loose provide varying speeds of continual reconstruction, producing smoother transitions between the frozen and unfrozen areas as you revert the image. You can use esc or

⌘ . ctrl . to halt the reconstruction at an intermediate stage (but do avoid applying this shortcut twice, as this will exit the Liquify dialog and you'll lose all your work!) Another way to reconstruct the image is to click on the options triangle in the Reconstruct Options and select one of the options from the list. This will pop a dialog control like the one shown in Figure 8.12, which will allow you to use a slider to determine what percentage of reconstruction you would like. The reconstruction can also be achieved using the reconstruct tool to selectively restore the image.

Mask options

The mask options can utilize an existing selection, layer transparency or a layer mask as the basis of a mask to freeze and constrain the effects of any Liquify adjustments. The first option is 'Replace Selection' and this replaces any existing freeze selection that has been made. The other four options allow you to modify an existing freeze selection by 'adding to', 'subtracting from', 'intersecting' or creating an 'inverted' selection. You can then click on the buttons below. Choosing 'None' clears all freeze selections, choosing 'Mask All' freezes the entire area, and choosing 'Invert All' inverts the current frozen selection.

Multiple undos in Liquify
Don't forget that you also have multiple undos at your disposal while inside the Liquify dialog. Use ⌘ Z ctrl Z to undo or redo the last step; ⌘ ⌥ Z ctrl alt Z to go back in history, and ⌘ Shift Z ctrl Shift Z to go forward in history.

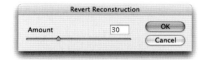

Figure 8.12 You can control the exact amount by which an image is reconstructed to its original state by going to the Reconstruct Options and selecting the desired reconstruction mode.

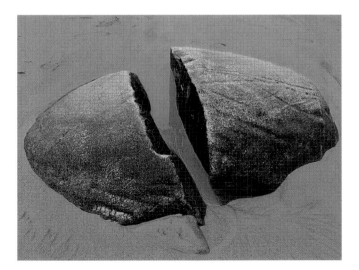

Figure 8.13 Freeze masks can be used to protect areas of a picture before you commence doing any liquify work. In the example shown here a freeze mask was loaded from a layer mask. When you freeze an area in this way it is protected from subsequent distortions so you can concentrate on applying the Liquify tools to just those areas you wish to distort. Frozen mask areas can be unfrozen by using the thaw mask tool.

Liquify and Smart Filters

Note that the Liquify filter cannot be applied to a Smart Object as a Smart Filter.

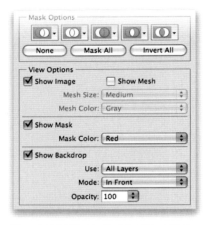

Figure 8.14 The Liquify dialog View options.

View options

The freeze mask can be made visible or hidden using the Show Mask checkbox in the View options, where you can also set the color of the mask (Figure 8.14).

The mesh grid can be displayed at different sizes using different colors. This provides you with an indication of the underlying warp structure and will readily help pinpoint the areas where a distortion has been applied. You can use the checkboxes in this section to view the mesh on its own or have it displayed overlaying the Liquify preview image.

The Show Backdrop option is normally left unchecked. If the Liquify image contents are contained on a layer, then it is possible to check the 'Show Backdrop' option and preview the liquified layer against the Background layer, all layers or specific layers in the image. Here is how this option might be used. Let's say that you want to apply a liquify distortion to a portion of an image and you are starting out with just a flattened image. Make a selection of the area you wish to work on and make a copy layer via the selection contents using ⌘ J ctrl J . As you apply the Liquify filter you can check the Show Backdrop checkbox and set the mode to 'Behind'. At 100% opacity the Liquify layer will cover the Background layer completely, but as you reduce the opacity you can preview the effect of your liquify distortion at different opacity percentages. This technique can prove useful if you wish to compare the effect of a distortion against the original image or a target distortion guide (see Figure 8.16).

Saving the mesh

If you are working on an extremely large image then it may take a long time to carry out a liquify distortion. This is where the 'Save Mesh...' and 'Load Mesh...' buttons can come in useful. If you carry out your Liquify distortions on a scaled-down version of the master image first, you can save the mesh as a separate file. Later, you can open up the master file, load the mesh you saved earlier and apply it to the master image.

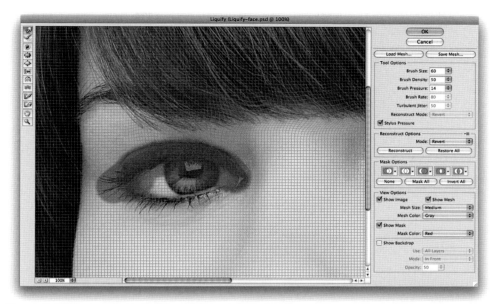

Figure 8.15 This shows the Liquify dialog with the mesh view switched on.

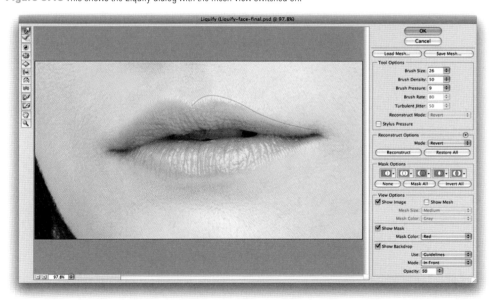

Figure 8.16 If you have a predetermined idea of what the final distortion should look like you can create an empty layer, draw the target distortion shape on this layer and use the 'Show Backdrop' options discussed here to select that specific layer, and have the ability to switch the guide Layer visibility on or off.

Straightening a fringe with Liquify

1 The objective here was to straighten the model's fringe using Liquify. First I used the ⌘ ⌥ Shift E ctrl alt Shift E command to create a merged copy layer at the top of the layer stack, then made a selection of the area of interest, inverted the selection and hit Delete.

2 I then chose Filter ⇨ Liquify and selected the freeze mask tool to protect the eyes from being edited. I then selected the warp tool and with a succession of low pressure brush strokes, gradually moved the fringe line into better shape.

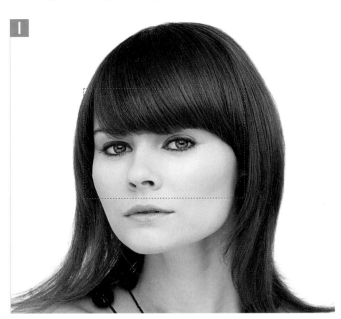

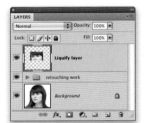

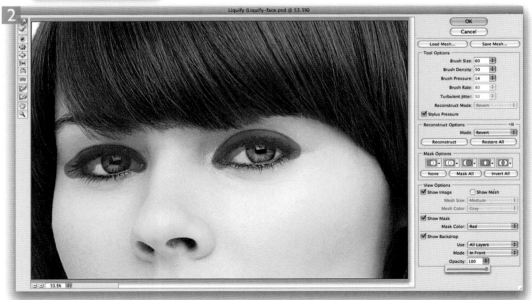

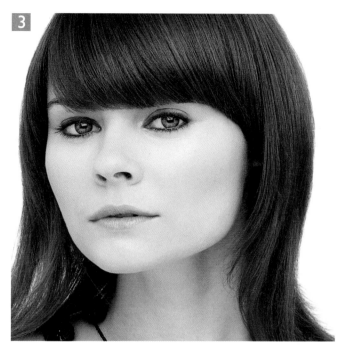

3 When I was happy with the way the fringe looked, I clicked OK. This screen shot shows how the fringe appeared after applying the Liquify filter.

4 Finally, I wanted to even up the eyes and make the left eye bigger. With the layer selection still active, I chose 'Liquify' again. This time there was no need to apply a freeze mask, so I simply selected the warp tool and used more low pressure brush strokes to carefully push the edges of the eye outwards and make the left eye a little bit bigger. When I was done, I clicked OK again to apply the Liquify filter.

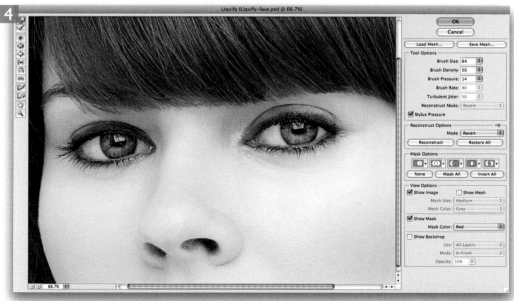

Warp Transforms

The Liquify filter is ideal for applying intricate distortions such as the example shown on the previous two pages. This is because you have a large selection of tools to work with and various options for modifying the liquify distortions. If you need to distort larger areas of a picture and create more continuous distortion shapes, then the warp transform tool is a better tool to use. I'll be discussing this in more detail in Chapter 9, but in Figure 8.17 you can see an example of a transform applied to a copied layer where I was able to smoothly distort the shape of the strap and the necklace.

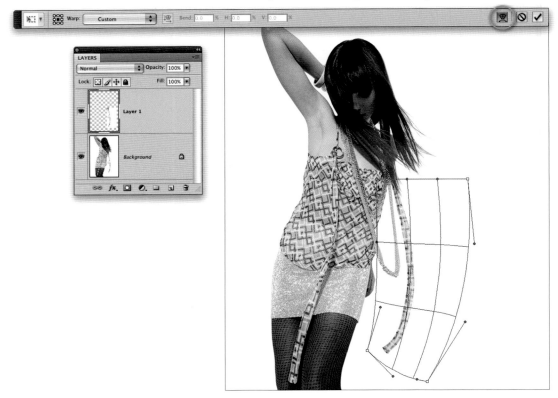

Figure 8.17 The Warp transform command offers an effective way to transform larger objects such as the straps in this picture. What I did here was to make a copy layer of the area of interest. I then went to the Edit menu, chose Free Transform (⌘ T ctrl T) and clicked on the Warp mode button in the Options bar (circled). This allowed me to adjust the Transform handles and segments to achieve the desired warp effect.

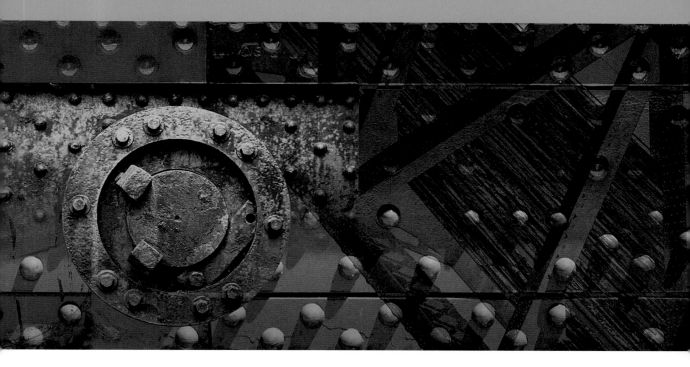

Chapter 9

Layers, Selections and Masking

For a lot of people the real fun starts when you can use Photoshop to swap parts of one photograph with another and make composite photographs using different image elements. This chapter explains the different tools that can be used making composites as well as the intricacies of working with the Layers panel, Channels and the pen tool. But to begin with, let us focus on some of the basic principles of how to make a selection and the interrelationship between selections, alpha channels, masks and the Quick Mask mode.

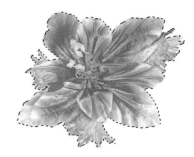

Figure 9.1 A selection is represented in Photoshop using marching ants.

Selections and channels

When you read somewhere about masks, mask channels, image layer mask channels, alpha channels, quick masks and saved selections, these are basically all the same thing: an active, semipermanent or permanently saved selection.

Selections

There are many ways you can create a selection in Photoshop. You can use any of the main selection tools such as the Select ⇨ Color Range command, or convert a channel or path to a selection and, when you use a selection tool to define an area within an image, you will notice that the selection is defined by a border of marching ants (Figure 9.1). Selections are only temporary though, because if you make a selection and accidentally click outside the selected area with the selection tool, it will disappear. Although, you can restore a selection by using the Edit ⇨ Undo command ($\mathcal{H}$ Z *ctrl* Z).

During a typical Photoshop session, you will typically use selections to define the areas of the image where you wish to carry out image edits or copy the pixels, and when you are done, deselect them. If you end up spending any length of time preparing a selection, you will usually want to save such selections by storing them as alpha channels (also referred to as 'mask channels'). To do this, go to the Select menu and choose Save Selection. The Save Selection dialog box (Figure 9.2) will then ask if you want to save

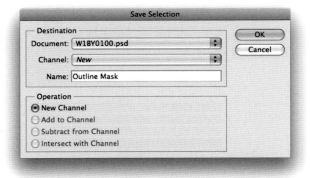

Figure 9.2 To save a selection as a new alpha channel you can choose Select ⇨ Save Selection and select the New Channel button option.

the selection as a new channel. If you select a pre-existing channel from the Channel menu you will have the option to add, subtract or intersect with the selected channel. You can also create new alpha channels by clicking on the 'Save selection as a channel' button at the bottom of the Channels panel, which will convert a selection to a channel. If you look at the Channels panel shown in Figure 9.3, you will notice how a saved selection is added as a new alpha channel (this will be channel #6 in RGB mode, or #7 if in CMYK mode). Also, you can click on the 'Create new channel' button, then fill the empty new channel with a gradient or use the brush tool to paint in the alpha channel using the default black or white colors. New channels are always stored when you save the image.

To load a saved channel as a selection, choose 'Load Selection' from the Select menu and select the appropriate channel number from the submenu. Alternatively, you can ⌘ *ctrl*-click the alpha channel in the Channels panel, or select a channel and click on the 'Load channel as a selection' button.

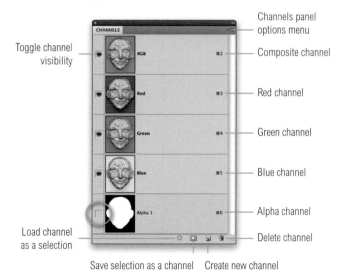

Toggle channel visibility

Load channel as a selection

Channels panel options menu
Composite channel
Red channel
Green channel
Blue channel
Alpha channel
Delete channel

Save selection as a channel   Create new channel

Figure 9.3 When you save a selection it is added as a new alpha channel in the Channels panel. An alpha channel can be viewed by clicking on the channel name. If you keep the composite channels selected and click on the empty space next to the channel (circled), you can preview an alpha channel as if it were a quick mask.

417

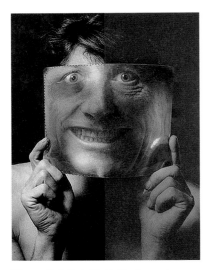

Figure 9.4 The left half of the image shows a feathered selection and the right half shows the Quick Mask mode equivalent display.

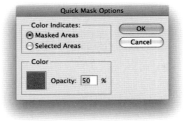

Figure 9.5 The Quick Mask Options.

In marching ants mode, a selection is active and ready for use. Any image modifications you carry out will be applied within the selected area only, but remember, selections are only temporary and can be deselected by clicking outside the selection area with a selection tool or by choosing Select ⇨ Deselect (⌘ D ctrl D). If you simply want to temporarily hide the marching ants, then use ⌘ H ctrl H.

Quick Mask mode

You can also preview and edit a selection in Quick Mask mode where the selection will be represented as a transparent colored mask overlay. To switch to Quick Mask mode from a selection, click the quick mask icon in the Tools panel (Figure 9.6) or use the keyboard shortcut Q to toggle back and forth between the selection and Quick Mask modes. Whether you are working directly on an alpha channel or in quick mask, modifications can be carried out using any of the fill, paint or selection tools even. You can also use any combination of Photoshop paint tools or image adjustments to modify the alpha channel content. If you double-click the quick mask icon, this opens the Quick Mask Options shown in Figure 9.5, where you can alter the masking behavior and choose a different color from the Color Picker (this might be useful if the quick mask color is too similar to the colors in the image you are editing).

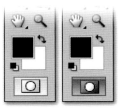

Figure 9.6 The Quick Mask mode button is in the Tools panel just below the foreground/background swatch colors. Shown here are the two modes: Selection mode (left) and Quick Mask mode (right). You can switch between these by clicking on this button. Double-click to adjust the Quick Mask color settings.

Creating an image selection

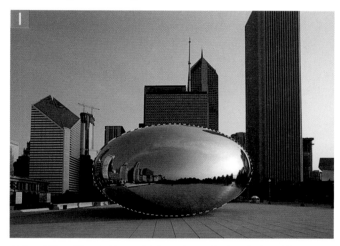

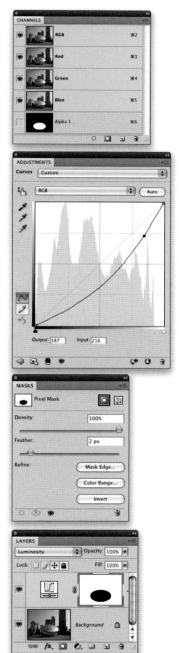

1 I thought I would start with a straightforward example where I selected the elliptical marque tool and dragged it to define the shape of the mirrored sculpture. In order to preserve the selection, I saved it as a new channel, which was then added to the Channels panel list.

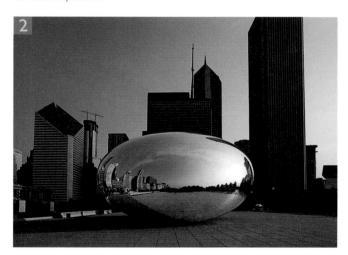

2 It's all very well making a selection, but what do you do with it once you have made it? Well, in this example I used the selection to modify the image. Here, I loaded the selection, went to the Adjustments panel and added a new Curves adjustment using the settings shown here. This applied the adjustment to the selected area only. I then went to the Masks panel and clicked on the Invert button to invert the selection and set the mask Feather to 2 pixels.

Reloading selection shortcuts

To reload a selection from the saved mask channel, go to Select ⇨ Load Selection. ⌘ ctrl-clicking a channel is the other shortcut for loading a selection and, by extension, combining ⌘ ⌥ channel # ctrl alt channel # (where # equals the channel number) does the same thing.

One thing to be aware of here is that in CS4 the usual shortcut numbers have been shifted along by two. I have mentioned this a couple of times already, but it is worth repeating since this is something that is likely to catch people out who are used to working with previous versions of Photoshop. Basically, ⌘ 0 ctrl 0 is used (as before) to zoom the image to fit the screen and ⌘ 1 ctrl 1 is now used to zoom to 100%. Where ⌘ ` ctrl ` was once used to select the composite channel, the new shortcut is now ⌘ 2 ctrl 2. This means that you should use ⌘ 3 ctrl 3 to select the red channel, ⌘ 4 ctrl 4 to select the green channel, ⌘ 5 ctrl 5 to select the blue channel and subsequent numbers to select any additional mask/alpha channels that are stored in an image.

Modifying selections

You can modify the content of a selection using the modifier key methods discussed earlier in Chapter 1 (see pages 34–35). Just to recap, you hold down the *Shift* key to add to a selection, hold down the ⌥ *alt* key to subtract from a selection and hold down the ⌥ *Shift* *alt Shift* keys to intersect a selection as you drag with a selection tool. The magic wand is a selection tool too, but all you have to do is to click (not drag) with the magic wand, holding down the appropriate keys to add or subtract from a selection. Note also that if you select either the lasso or one of the marquee tools, placing the cursor inside the selection and dragging moves the selection boundary position, but not the selection contents.

Alpha channels

An alpha channel is effectively the same thing as a mask channel and if you choose Select ⇨ Save Selection, you can save any selection as a new alpha channel; these are stored by default in numerical sequence below the main color channels. Just like normal color channels, an alpha channel can contain up to 256 shades of gray in 8-bits per channel mode or up to 32,000 shades of gray in 16-bits per channel mode.

You can select channels by going to the Channels panel and clicking on the desired channel. Once selected, it can be viewed on its own as a grayscale mask and manipulated almost any way you like inside Photoshop. An alpha channel can also effectively be viewed in a 'Quick Mask' type mode. To do this, first select an alpha channel and then click on the eyeball icon next to the composite channel, which is the one at the top of the Channels panel list (see Figure 9.3). You will then be able to edit the alpha channel mask with the image visible through the mask overlay. There are several ways to convert an alpha channel back into a selection. You can go to the Select menu, choose Load Selection and then select the name of the channel. A simpler method is to drag the channel down to the Make Selection button at the bottom of the Channels panel, or ⌘ ctrl-click a channel in the Channels panel.

Adding to an image selection

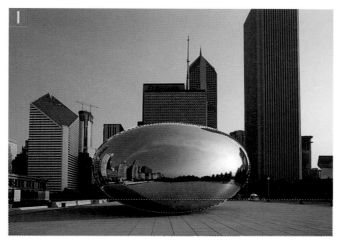

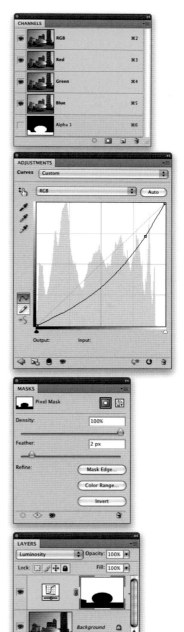

1 Let's add an extra step to the example shown on page 419. Here, I started off with an elliptical selection. I then selected the rectangular marquee tool and dragged across the image with the *Shift* key held down in order to add to the elliptical selection.

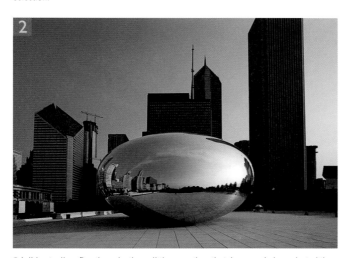

2 I did actually refine the selection a little more than that, because I also selected the polygon lasso tool and again, with the *Shift* key held down, clicked a few more times to add the outline of the building on the left. As with the previous example I added a Curves adjustment and clicked on the Invert button in the Masks panel so that the adjustment darkened the areas outside the selection. I then added a 2 pixel feather to the selection edge to obtain a smoother edge blend.

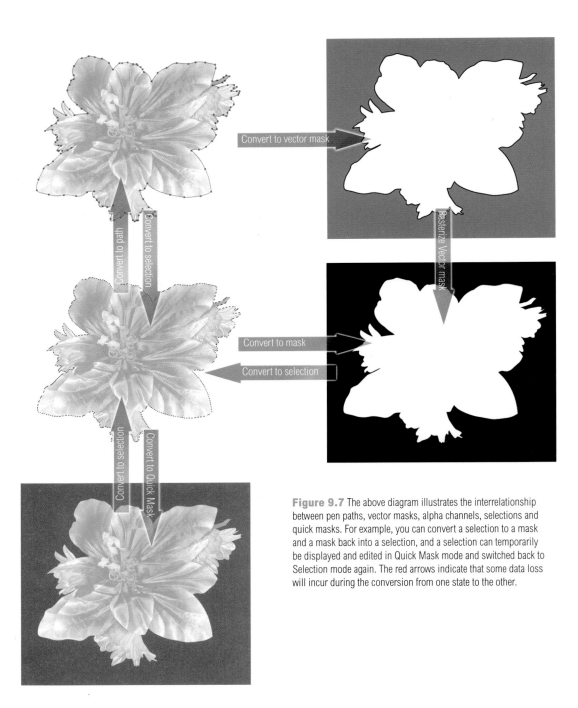

Figure 9.7 The above diagram illustrates the interrelationship between pen paths, vector masks, alpha channels, selections and quick masks. For example, you can convert a selection to a mask and a mask back into a selection, and a selection can temporarily be displayed and edited in Quick Mask mode and switched back to Selection mode again. The red arrows indicate that some data loss will incur during the conversion from one state to the other.

Selections, alpha channels and masks

As was pointed out at the beginning of this chapter, there is always an intertwined relationship between selections, quick masks and alpha channel masks. This interrelationship also extends to the use of vector paths and vector masks (vector paths are discussed towards the end of this chapter). The accompanying diagram in Figure 9.7 illustrates these relationships more clearly.

Starting at the top left corner, we have a path outline that has been created with the pen tool in Photoshop. A pen path outline can be saved as a path and an active path can be used to create a vector mask, which is a layer masked by a pen path mask (see pages 480 and 484–486). A vector mask can also be rasterized to make a layer mask (a layer that is masked by an alpha channel). Meanwhile, a pen path can be converted to a selection and a selection can be converted back into a work path. If we start with an active selection, you can view and edit a selection as a quick mask, and a selection can also be converted into an alpha channel and back into a selection again.

When preparing a mask in Photoshop, most people will start by making a selection to define the area they want to work on and save that selection as an alpha channel mask. This will allow you to convert the saved alpha channel back into a selection again at any time in the future. The other way to prepare a mask is to use the pen tool to define the outline first and then convert the pen path to a selection. If you think you will need to reuse the pen path again, such as to convert to a selection again at a later date, then it is worth remembering to save the work path as a named path via the Paths panel.

The business of using vector masks and layer masks is covered in more detail later on, but basically, a layer mask is an alpha channel applied to a layer which defines what is shown and hidden on the associated layer, and a vector mask is a pen path converted to a vector mask that defines what is shown and hidden on the layer.

Converting vectors to pixels

In Figure 9.7 I mention that some of the conversion processes will incur a loss of data. This is because when you convert vector data to become a pixel-based selection, what you end up with is not truly reversible. Drawing a pen path and converting the path to a selection is a very convenient way of making an accurate selection. However, if you attempt to convert the selection back into a pen path again you will not end up with an identical path to the one that you started with. Basically, converting vectors to pixels is a one-way process.

Converting a vector path into a pixel-based selection is a good thing to do, but you should be aware that converting a pixel-based selection into a vector path will potentially incur some loss of data. More specifically, a selection or mask can contain shades of gray, whereas a pen path merely describes an outline where everything is either selected or not.

Grow and Similar

The Grow and Similar options enlarge the selection using the same criteria as used with the magic wand tool, regardless of whether the original selection was created with the wand or not. To determine the range of color levels you want the selection to expand by, enter a tolerance value in the Options bar for the magic wand tool. A higher tolerance value means that a wider range of color levels will be included in the enlarged selection.

The Select ⇨ Grow option expands the selection, adding contiguous pixels, i.e. those immediately surrounding the original selection of the same color values within the specified tolerance. The Select ⇨ Similar option selects more pixels from anywhere in the image that have the same color values within the specified tolerance.

Expanding and shrinking selections

To expand or shrink a selection choose Select ⇨ Modify ⇨ Expand/Contract, where you can modify the selection size up to a maximum of 100 pixels. Although the most accurate way to expand or contract an active selection is to choose Select ⇨ Transform Selection and use the bounding box handles to scale the selection more accurately.

Smoothing a selection

Other options include Border and Smooth. The border modifications are rather crude, but they can sometimes be improved by feathering the border selection or saving the selection as an alpha channel and then applying the Gaussian Blur filter.

If you create a selection using the magic wand, the chances are that the selection won't be as smooth as you think. You will mostly notice this when you view such a selection in Quick Mask mode. The Smooth option in the Select ⇨ Modify submenu addresses this by letting you adjust the level of tolerance and thereby determine how much to smooth out the pixels that are included in the selection.

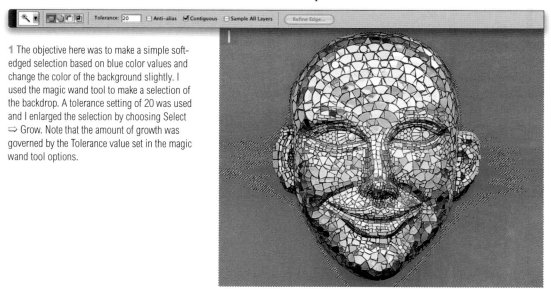

1 The objective here was to make a simple soft-edged selection based on blue color values and change the color of the background slightly. I used the magic wand tool to make a selection of the backdrop. A tolerance setting of 20 was used and I enlarged the selection by choosing Select ⇨ Grow. Note that the amount of growth was governed by the Tolerance value set in the magic wand tool options.

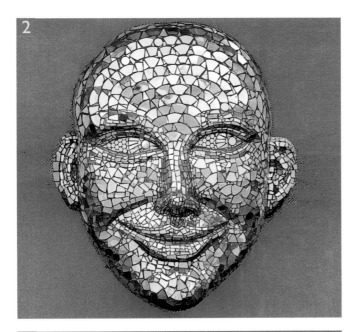

2 The magic wand tool may not select all the desired backdrop pixels, so I chose Select ⇨ Modify ⇨ Smooth, and entered a Radius value of 5 pixels. This made the selection a lot smoother. Smooth works like this: if the Radius chosen is 5, Photoshop will examine all pixels with an 11 x 11 pixel block around each pixel. If more than half are selected, any stray pixels will be selected as well. If less than half are selected, those stray pixels will be deselected.

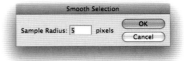

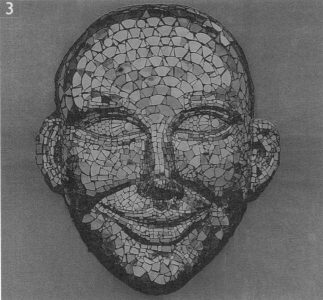

3 To show you the result of the Smooth selection, here is a view of the image with the selection shown in Quick Mask mode.

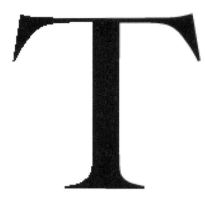

Figure 9.8 The above illustration shows a graphic where the left half is rendered without anti-aliasing and the right half uses anti-aliasing to produce smoother edges.

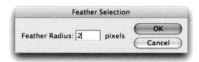

Figure 9.9 If you want to soften the edges of a selection, then use Select ⇨ Feather and enter the desired feather radius.

Anti-aliasing

Bitmapped images consist of a grid of square pixels. Without anti-aliasing, non-straight lines would be represented by a jagged sawtooth of pixels. Photoshop gets round this problem by anti-aliasing the edges, which means filling the gaps with in-between tonal values, so that non-vertical/horizontal sharp edges are rendered smoother by the anti-aliasing process (Figure 9.8). Wherever you encounter anti-aliasing options, these are normally switched on by default and there are only a few occasions when you might wish to turn this off.

If you have an alpha channel where the edges are too sharp and you wish to smooth them, the best way to do this is to apply a Gaussian Blur filter using a Radius of 1 pixel. Or, you can use the blur tool to gently soften the edges.

Feathering

When you are doing any type of photographic retouching it is important to always keep your selections soft. If the edges of a picture element are defined too sharply, it will be more obvious to the viewer that a photograph has been retouched or montaged. The secret of good compositing is to avoid creating hard edges and keep the edges of your picture elements soft so that they merge together more smoothly.

There are two ways to soften the edges of a selection. You can go to the Select menu and choose Modify ⇨ Feather (*Shift* *F6*) and adjust the Feather Radius setting (Figure 9.9). Or, if you have applied the selection as a layer mask, you can use the Feather slider (as shown on pages 419 and 421) to feather the mask 'in situ'. A low Feather Radius of between 1 or 2 pixels is enough to dampen the sharpness of a selection outline, but there are times when it is useful to select a much higher Radius amount. For example, earlier on pages 332–333, I used the elliptical marquee tool to define an elliptical selection, applied this as a Curves adjustment layer mask and feathered the selection by 100 pixels via the Masks panel. This allowed me to create a smooth vignette that darkened the outer edges of the photograph.

Layers

Layers play an essential role in all aspects of Photoshop work. Whether you are designing a web page layout or editing a photograph, working with layers lets you keep various elements in a design separate from each other. Layers also give you the opportunity to construct an image in stages and maintain the flexibility to make any edit changes you want at a later stage. The Photoshop Layers feature has evolved in stages over the years and Photoshop CS2 onwards includes new ways for selecting multiple layers and linking them together, but first let's look at managing layers and the different types of layers you can have in a Photoshop document.

Layer basics

Layers can be copied from one file to another by using the move tool to drag and drop a layer (or a selection of layers) from one image to another. This step can also be assisted by the use of the *Shift* key to ensure the layers are centered with the destination file. To duplicate a layer, drag the layer icon to the New Layer button. To rename a layer in Photoshop, simply double-click the layer name, and to discard a layer drag the layer icon to the Delete button in the Layers panel.

Image layers

The most common type of layers are image layers, which contain pixel information only. New empty image layers can be created by clicking on the New Layer button in the Layers panel (see Figure 9.13). They can also be created by copying the contents of a selection to create a new layer within the same document. To do this, choose Layer ⇨ New ⇨ Layer via Copy, or use the *⌘ J* *ctrl J* keyboard shortcut. This will copy the selection contents, duplicating them so that they become a new layer in register with the image below. Alternatively you can cut and copy the contents from a layer by choosing Layer ⇨ New ⇨ Layer via Cut or use the *⌘ Shift J* *ctrl Shift J* keyboard shortcut.

Layer number limits

You can add as many new layers as you like to a document up to a maximum limit of 8000 layers!

Deleting hidden layers

There is a Delete Hidden Layers command in both the Layers panel submenu and the Layer ⇨ Delete submenu to remove hidden layers.

Deleting multiple layers

To delete multiple layers, use a *Shift*-click or *⌘* *ctrl*-click to select the layers or layer groups you want to remove and then press the Delete layer button at the bottom of the Layers panel.

Application frame windows

Note that when using the Application frame window environment you cannot drag and drop layers from one document to another (or from the Layers panel). You can only do so if the foreground image window is undocked from the Application window.

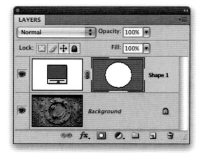

Figure 9.10 The pen tool and shape tools include a Shape layer mode button for creating shape layer objects defined by a vector path.

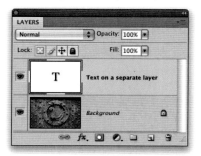

Figure 9.11 Text layers are created whenever you add type to an image. Text layers can be re-edited at any time.

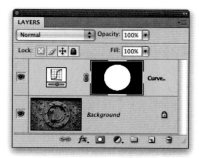

Figure 9.12 Adjustment layers don't contain pixels or vector objects. They are image adjustments that can be placed within an image, and they apply image adjustments to individual or multiple layers. Like other layers, you can mask the contents and adjust the blending mode and layer opacity.

Shape layers

Shape layers is a catch-all term used to describe a non-pixel layer where the layer is filled with a solid color and the outline is defined using either a vector or pixel layer mask. A shape layer is created whenever you add an object to an image using one of the shape tools, or draw a path using the Shape layer mode, or when you add a solid fill layer from the adjustment layer menu. Figure 9.10 shows an example of a shape layer that is basically a solid fill layer masked by a vector mask.

Text layers

Typefaces are essentially made up of vector data, which means that Text layers are basically vector-based shape layers. When you select the type tool in Photoshop and click or drag with the tool and begin to enter text, a new text layer is added to the Layers panel. Text layers are symbolized with a capital 'T', and when you hit _Return_ to confirm a text entry, the layer name will display the initial text for that layer, making it easier for you to identify (see Figure 9.11). Note that double-clicking the text layer icon highlights the text within your image.

Adjustment layers

Adjustment layers are image adjustments in the form of layers. These allow unrestricted opportunities to edit an adjustment, plus you can toggle an adjustment on or off by clicking the layer eyeball icon (Figure 9.12). The chief advantages of working with adjustment layers is that you can re-edit the adjustment settings at any time and you can use the paint, fill or gradient tools to selectively apply the adjustments to an image.

Layers panel controls

Figure 9.13 provides an overview of the Layers panel controls. The blending mode options determine how a selected layer will blend with the layers below, while the Opacity controls the transparency of the layer contents and the Fill opacity controls the opacity of the layer contents independent of any layer style (such as a drop shadow) which might have been applied to the layer. Next to this are the various layer locking options. Most of the essential layer operation commands are conveniently located in the Layer panel fly-out options. At the bottom of the panel are the layer content controls for layer linking, adding layer styles, layer masks, adjustment layers, new groups, new layers as well as a Delete Layer button.

Layer visibility

You can selectively choose which layers are to be viewed by selecting and deselecting the eye icons. If you go to the History panel options and check 'Make Layer Visibility Changes Undoable', you can make switching the Layer visibility on and off an undoable action.

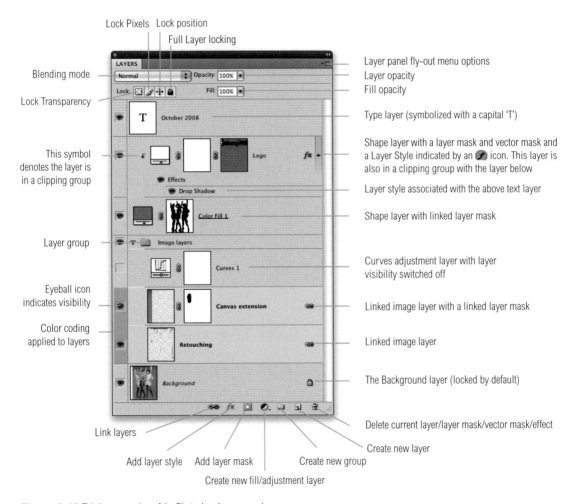

Lock Pixels   Lock position

Full Layer locking

Blending mode

Lock Transparency

This symbol denotes the layer is in a clipping group

Layer group

Eyeball icon indicates visibility

Color coding applied to layers

Link layers

Add layer style   Add layer mask

Create new fill/adjustment layer

Layer panel fly-out menu options

Layer opacity

Fill opacity

Type layer (symbolized with a capital 'T')

Shape layer with a layer mask and vector mask and a Layer Style indicated by an *f* icon. This layer is also in a clipping group with the layer below

Layer style associated with the above text layer

Shape layer with linked layer mask

Curves adjustment layer with layer visibility switched off

Linked image layer with a linked layer mask

Linked image layer

The Background layer (locked by default)

Delete current layer/layer mask/vector mask/effect

Create new layer

Create new group

Figure 9.13 This is an overview of the Photoshop Layers panel.

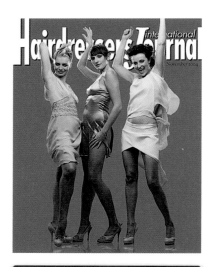

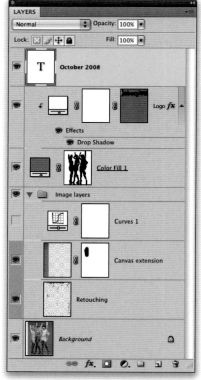

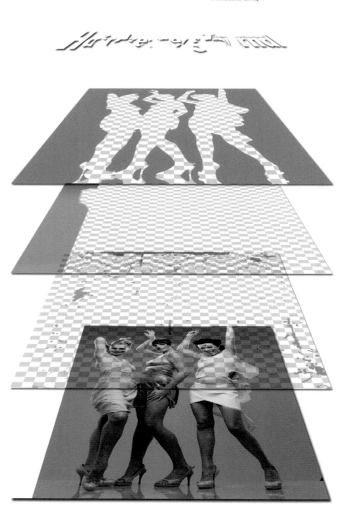

Figure 9.14 Here is an expanded diagram of how the layers in a magazine cover image file were arranged inside Photoshop, one on top of the other. The checkerboard pattern represents transparency and the layers are represented here in the order they appeared in the Layers panel.

Client: Goldwell Professional Haircare.

Masking layers

You can hide the contents of a layer either wholly or partially by adding a layer mask, a vector mask or both. Layer masks are defined using a pixel-based mask, while vector masks are defined using path outlines. Masks can be applied to any type of layer: image layers, adjustment layers, type layers or shape layers. Click once on the Add Layer Mask button to add a layer mask, and click a second time to add a vector mask (in the case of shape layers a vector mask is created first and clicking the button will then add a layer mask). The most important thing to remember about masking in Photoshop is that whenever you apply a mask you are not deleting anything – only hiding the contents. By using a mask to hide rather than to erase unwanted image areas, you can go back and edit the mask at a later date. Or if you make a mistake when editing the layer mask, it is easy enough to correct such mistakes – you are not limited to a single level of undo.

Adding a layer mask

Click once on the Add Layer Mask button to add a layer mask to an image layer, type layer or shape layer (when you add an adjustment layer or fill adjustment layer a layer mask is added automatically). The layer mask icon will appear next to the layer icon and a dashed stroke surrounding the icon tells you which is active.

To show or hide the layer contents, first make sure the layer mask is active. Select the paintbrush tool and paint with black to hide the layer contents and paint with white to reveal.

To add a layer mask based on a selection, highlight the layer, make the selection active and click on the Add Layer Mask button at the bottom of the Layers panel, or choose Layer ➪ Layer Mask ➪ Reveal Selection. To add a layer mask to a layer with the area within the selection hidden, ⌥ *alt*-click the Layer Mask button in the Layers panel, or choose Layer ➪ Layer Mask ➪ Hide Selection.

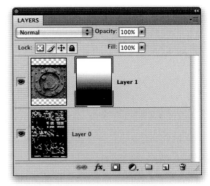

Figure 9.15 The Layers panel view shown here contains two layers, and the selected layer is the one that's highlighted here. The dashed border line around the layer mask icon indicates that the layer mask is active and any editing operations will be carried out on the layer mask only. There is no link icon between the image layer and the layer mask. This means that the image layer or layer mask can be moved independently of each other.

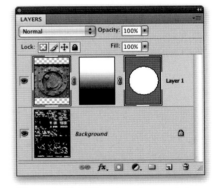

Figure 9.16 In this next panel screen shot, the border surrounding the vector mask indicates that the vector mask is active and that any editing operations will be carried out on the vector mask. In this example, the image layer, layer mask and vector mask are now all linked. This means that if the image layer is targeted and you use the move tool to move it, the image layer and layer masks will move in unison.

Copying a layer mask

You can use the ⌥ *alt* key to drag/ copy a layer mask across to another layer.

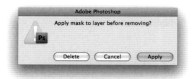

Figure 9.17 The remove layer mask options.

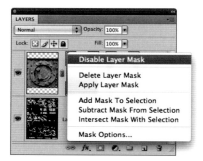

Figure 9.18 The layer mask contextual menu options.

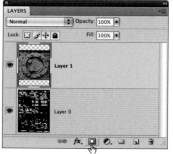

Figure 9.19 Click the Add Layer Mask button to add a layer mask where the contents remain visible. ⌥ *alt*-click to add a layer mask filled with black, where the contents are all hidden.

Viewing in Mask or Rubylith mode

The layer mask icon preview shows you roughly how the mask looks. But if you ⌥ *alt*-click the layer mask icon the image window view will switch to display the mask. If you ⌥ *Shift* *alt* *Shift*-click the layer mask, the layer mask will be displayed as a Quick Mask type transparent overlay. Both of these steps can be toggled.

Removing a layer mask

To remove a layer mask, select the mask in the Layers panel and click on the Layers panel Delete button (or drag the layer mask to the Delete button). A dialog box will appear asking if you want to 'Apply mask to layer before removing (Figure 9.17)?'. There are several options here: if you simply want to delete the layer mask, then select 'Delete'. If you wish to remove the layer mask and at the same time apply the mask to the layer, choose 'Apply'. Or click 'Cancel' to cancel the operation.

To temporarily disable a layer mask, choose Layer ⇨ Layer Mask ⇨ Disable and to reverse this choose Layer ⇨ Layer Mask ⇨ Enable. You can also *Shift*-click a mask icon to temporarily disable the layer mask (when a layer mask is disabled it will be overlaid with a red cross). A simple click will restore the layer mask (but to restore a vector mask you will have to *Shift*-click again). Or alternatively, *ctrl* right mouse-click the mask icon to open the full list of contextual menu options to disable, delete or apply a layer mask (Figure 9.18).

Adding an empty image layer mask

If you create an empty layer mask (one that is filled with white) on a layer, you can hide pixels in a layer using the fill and paint tools. To add a layer mask to a layer with all the layer remaining visible, click the Layer Mask button in the Layers panel. Alternatively, choose Layer ⇨ Add Layer Mask ⇨ Reveal All. To add a layer mask to a layer that hides all the pixels, ⌥ *alt*-click the Add Layer Mask button in the Layers panel. Alternatively, choose Layer ⇨ Add Layer Mask ⇨ Hide All. This will also add a layer mask filled with black (Figure 9.19).

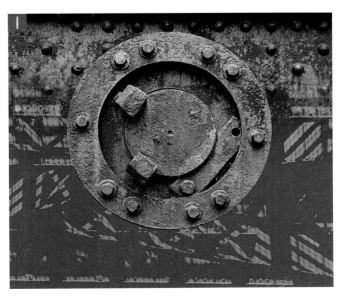

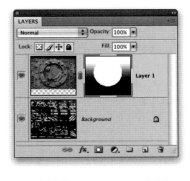

Hide mask shortcut

The backslash key (⬛) can be used to toggle showing the layer mask as a quick mask and returning to normal view mode again.

1 This shows an example of how you can preview a layer mask in Quick Mask mode by ⌥*Shift* *alt* *Shift*-clicking the layer mask icon.

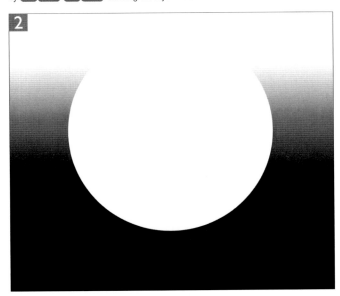

2 If, instead, you ⌥ *alt*-click the layer mask icon, you can preview a layer mask in normal mask mode. The mask can still be edited in either of these preview modes.

Density and mask contrast

The Density slider answers requests to have some kind of control over the mask contrast. A lot of layer masks will originate as black and white masks where the image adjustments or pixel layer contents are either at full opacity or hidden (the same is true of vector masks of course). The Density slider allows you to preserve the mask outline, but fade the contrast of the mask in a way that is completely re-editable.

Masks panel options

Figure 9.20 shows the Masks panel options menu, where you can use the menu options shown here to add, subtract or intersect the current mask with an active selection. Imagine you want to add something to a selection you are working on. You simply choose the 'Add Mask to Selection' menu option to add it to the current selection.

Masks panel

I have already shown a few examples of how the Masks panel can be used to modify pixel or vector layer masks, and the Masks panel controls are identified below in Figure 9.21. The pixel mask/vector mask selection buttons are at the top of the panel and can also be used as 'Add mask' buttons. Below that are the Density and Feather sliders for modifying the mask contrast and softness. Next are the Refine mask buttons, which are only accessible if a pixel mask is selected. The Mask Edge... button opens the Refine Edge dialog (so why not call it Refine Edge?) where, as you can see opposite, you can further modify the edges of a mask. The Color Range button opens the Color Range dialog, where you can use a Color Range selection (as shown on pages 334–335) to edit a mask. The Invert button inverts a pixel mask, but if you want to do the same thing with a vector mask you can do so by selecting a vector path outline and switching the path mode (see page 484). At the bottom of the panel there are buttons for loading a selection from the mask, applying a mask (which deletes the mask and applies it to the pixels) plus a Delete button.

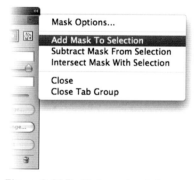

Figure 9.20 The Masks panel controls.

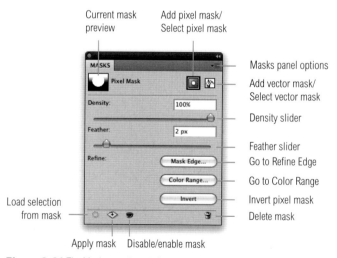

Figure 9.21 The Masks panel controls.

Refine Edge command

The Refine Edge controls include everything you need to modify a layer mask edge. You can of course use Refine Edge via the Select menu or the Options bar (when a selection tool is active), but if you are preparing a selection in order to create a mask it makes more sense to use Refine Edge when you are working on an active layer mask. I should point out this isn't something that's necessarily new to Photoshop CS4, as you could do this before in CS3, but the ability to refine the layer mask edges is now made more obvious in CS4.

When you select Refine Edge, the initial preview shows the layer masked against a white background, which isn't so helpful when editing a layer mask, but you can hide the white background by pressing **X**. The trouble here is that this only offers a temporary 'hide' and the overlay reappears as soon as you modify the Refine Edge adjustments. Alternatively, you can click on the Standard preview button (circled in Figure 9.22) to see the layer mask previewed as a marching ant selection. You can then use the **⌘ H** **ctrl H** shortcut to hide the ants to preview the mask properly. You'll then be able to edit the mask without distractions.

The main Refine Edge controls are mostly summarized on the right. The Radius slider offers a primary means for softening the mask edges and improving the mask transitions over edges that are already slightly blurred or mask soft textures such as fur. The Smooth slider is designed to smooth edges without rounding out the corners, but if you want to achieve a more aggressive smoothing you can use Refine Edge's Feather and Contrast sliders. Simply increase the Feather to blur the mask and then increase the Contrast to get back to the desired edge sharpness. The Contract/Expand slider is like a choke control that you can use to adjust the size of the mask, making it shrink or expand till the mask fits just right around the object you are masking. I usually find that the Radius and Contract/Expand sliders are the main ones to use for adjusting the mask shape, followed by the Feather and Contrast sliders when refining the mask further.

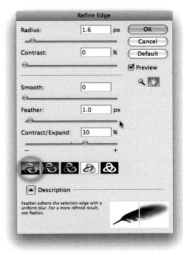

Figure 9.22 There is a Description section at the bottom of the Refine Edge dialog that helps explain what each of the controls do (these are summarized below).

The Refine Edge sliders

Radius

Increasing the Radius improves the edges in areas of soft transitions.

Contrast

This makes soft edges crisper and removes artifacts along the edges of a selection.

Smooth

This helps smooth out jagged selection edges (then use Radius to help restore some of the detail).

Feather

This uniformly softens the edges of the selection and helps produce a soft-edged mask.

Contract/Expand

This is the choke control and works like the Maximum and Minimum filters by shrinking or expanding a mask.

435

Quick selection brush settings

The quick selection brush settings are the same as for the other paint tools, except adjusting the brush hardness and spacing won't really have any impact on the way the quick selection tool works. But if you are using a pressure-sensitive tablet, it is worth checking that the Pen Pressure option is selected since this will offer you a certain degree of control, allowing you to use gentle pressure to make small brush tolerance selections and greater pressure to increase the tolerance (see Figure 9.23).

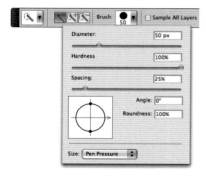

Figure 9.23 This shows the quick selection tool brush settings where the Pen Pressure option has been selected. This links pen pressure to the tolerance of the quick select tool rather than the cursor size.

Working with the quick selection tool

The quick selection tool is grouped with the magic wand in the Tools panel. I don't know about it being quick, but quick selection is certainly a more sophisticated kind of selection tool that has smart processing capabilities. You can use the quick selection tool to make a selection based on tone and color by clicking or dragging with the tool to define the portion of the image that you wish to select. You can then keep clicking or dragging to add to the selection without needing to hold down the *Shift* key as you do so. You can then subtract from a quick selection by holding down the ⌥ *alt* key as you drag. What is clever about quick selection is that it remembers all the successive strokes that you make and this provides stability to the selection as you add more strokes. So as you toggle between adding and subtracting, the quick selection is temporarily storing these stroke instructions to help determine which pixels are to be selected and which are not.

Sometimes you may find it helps if you make an initial selection and then apply a succession of subtractive strokes to define the areas you don't want to be included. You won't see anything happen as you apply these blocking strokes, but when you go on to select the rest of the object with the quick selection tool, you should find that as you add to the selection, the blocking strokes you applied previously help prevent leakage outside of the area you wish to select. This aspect of quick selection behavior can help you select objects more successfully than was ever possible before with the magic wand. However, as you make successive additive strokes to add to a selection and then erase these areas from the selection, you'll have to work a lot harder going back and forth between adding and subtracting with the quick selection tool. In these situations it can be a good idea to clear the quick selection memory by using the 'double Q trick'. If you press the **Q** key twice, this will take you to Quick Mask mode and back to Selection mode again. The stroke constraints will be gone and you can then add to or subtract from the selection more easily since you have cleared the quick selection memory.

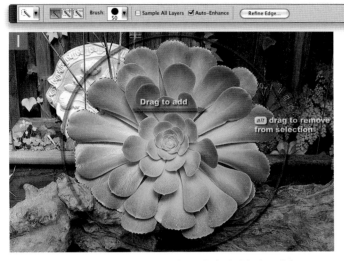

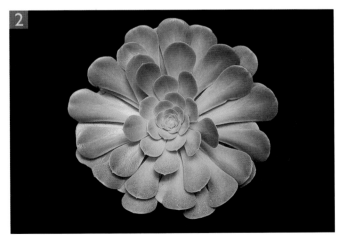

1 In this example, I selected the quick selection tool, checked the Auto-Enhance edge option and dragged to make an initial selection of the plant interior. Then, with the ⌥ *alt* key held down, I dragged around the outer perimeter area to indicate the areas that were not to be included in the selection. I then continued clicking and dragging to select more of the plant leaves (while also ⌥ *alt* dragging outside) to fine-tune the selection edge.

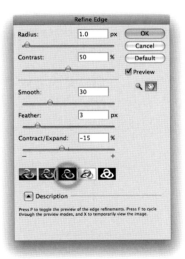

2 I then clicked on the Refine Edge... button and selected the 'on black' mask option (circled), which displayed the cut-out selection against a black background color. I contracted the selection slightly and applied a Smooth amount of 30 to smooth out the jagged edges. I found that by raising the Feather to 3 pixels and increasing the Contrast this was the right combination to get the selection outline I was after.

Combining quick selection with Refine Edge

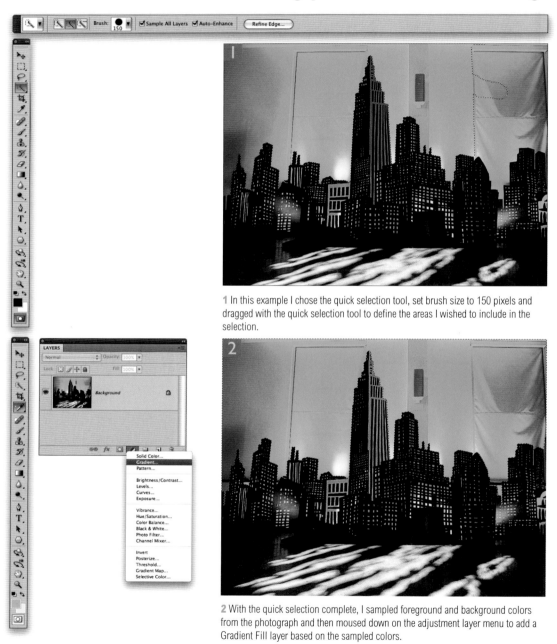

1 In this example I chose the quick selection tool, set brush size to 150 pixels and dragged with the quick selection tool to define the areas I wished to include in the selection.

2 With the quick selection complete, I sampled foreground and background colors from the photograph and then moused down on the adjustment layer menu to add a Gradient Fill layer based on the sampled colors.

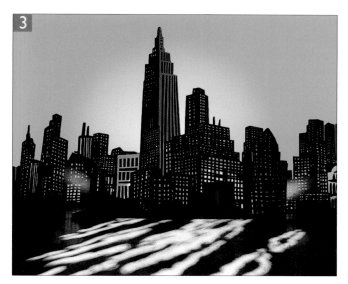

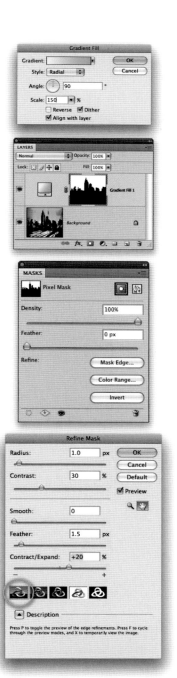

3 This single step automatically converted the quick selection into a layer mask and opened the Gradient Fill dialog shown here, where I chose a Radial gradient and set the Scale to 150%.

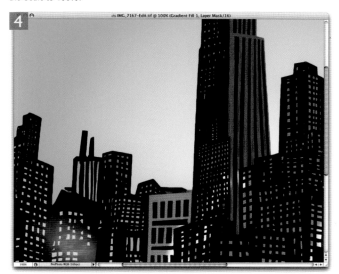

4 As long as the layer mask was selected, I was able to fine-tune the mask by going to the Masks panel and clicking on the Mask Edge... button. In the example shown here, I selected the 'Standard' view mode (circled) and used ⌘ H ctrl H to hide the marching ants. I was then able to preview the Refine Edge adjustments on a layer mask that actively masked the Gradient Fill layer.

Color Range masking

So far I have introduced you to using the quick selection tool combined with Refine Edge to replace a background. Let's now look at how to create a cut-out mask for a more tricky subject where, quite clearly, the quick selection tool would be of little help here. Advanced users might be tempted to use channel calculations to mask a picture like this. That could work, but you know, there is a simpler way. Since the Color Range has been updated, it can now be considered an effective tool for creating mask selections prior to applying controlled image adjustments, or when compositing images together. In fact, I would say that the quick selection and Color Range adjustment are powerful tools that offer relatively speedy (and sophisticated) masking.

1 This shows a photograph taken of a sailing ship mast against a deep blue sky. Obviously, creating a cut-out mask of the complex rigging can be regarded as a tricky task. One approach would be to analyze the individual RGB color channels and see if there was a way to blend them together to create a good cut-out. An easier way was to use the new improved Color Range command. So to start with, I went to the Select menu and chose 'Color Range...'.

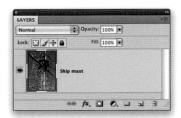

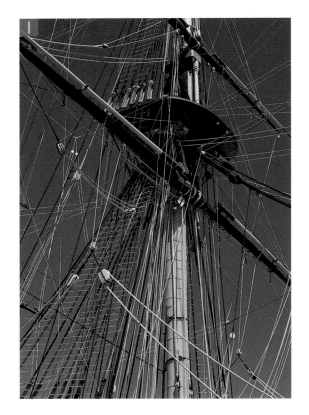

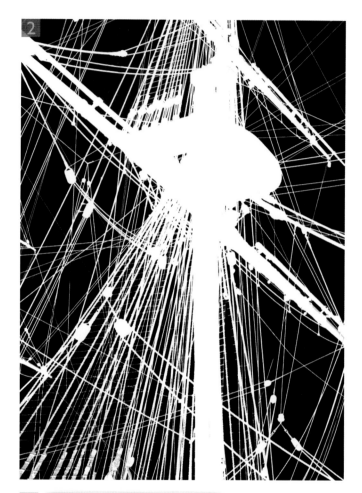

2 This opened the dialog shown below, where the standard eyedropper was selected. You can simply click with the eyedropper anywhere in the image window to sample a color to mask with, but to create a more accurate selection, I checked the 'Localized Color Clusters' box and then used the plus eyedropper (circled) to add to the Color Range selection. You can click or drag inside the image to add more colors to the selection and also use the minus eyedropper (or hold down the ⎇ *alt* key) to subtract from the selection. The Fuzziness slider increases or decreases the number of pixels that are selected based on how similar pixels are in color to the already sampled pixels, while the Range slider determines which pixels are included based on how far in distance they are from the already selected pixels. The Color Range preview is rather tiny, so you may find it helps to do what I did here, which was to select the Grayscale Selection Preview so that I could see the mask big on the screen.

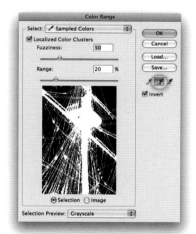

3 You should be able to get a good mask using Color Range on its own, but if not, you can do what I did here and apply a direct Levels adjustment (⌘ *L* *ctrl L*) to boost the mask contrast.

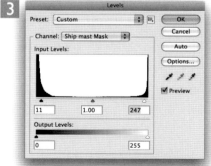

4 Having completed the selection I clicked on the 'Add layer mask' button in the Layers panel to convert the active selection to a layer mask that masked the ship mast layer. I then wanted to blend the masked image with a photograph of a cloudy sky. This could be done by dragging the masked ship mast layer to the sky image or, as I did here, drag the sky as a layer to the ship mast image and place it at the bottom of the layer stack.

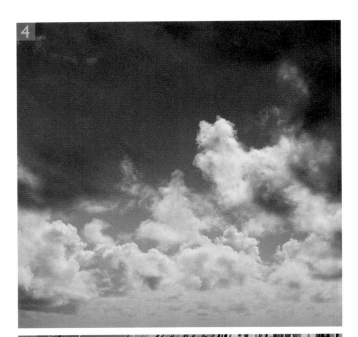

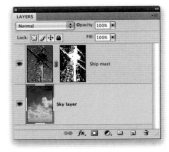

5 This shows a 1:1 close-up view of the masked layer overlaying the sky layer. In the Masks panel there was no need to feather the mask. Instead, I clicked on the Mask Edge... button.

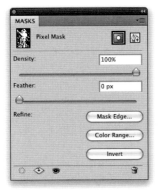

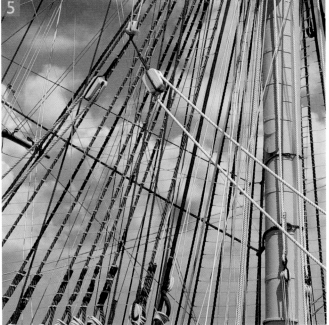

442

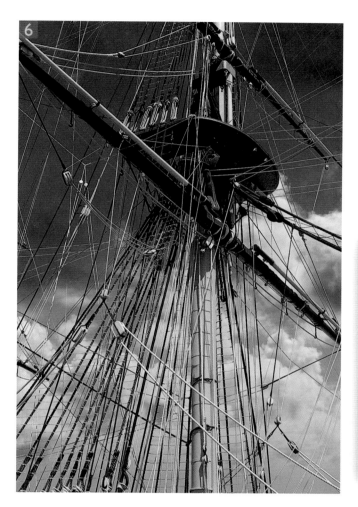

6 This shows the finished composite image, in which I used the Refine Edge controls to fine-tune the mask edges. As in the previous example, I selected the 'Standard' view mode (circled) and used ⌘ H / ctrl H to hide the marching ants. I was then able to preview the Refine Edge adjustments on a layer mask that actively masked the Gradient Fill layer. I didn't have to do too much here. I set the Radius to 0.6 pixels, contracted the mask by −15% and set the Refine Edge Feather to 0.5 pixels.

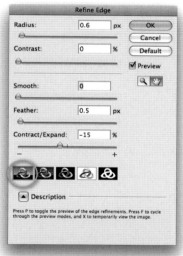

Layer blending modes

The layer blending modes provide a way for controlling how the contents of a layer blend with the layer or layers immediately below it. These same blend modes can also be used to control how the paint and fill tools interact with the pixels they are painting. I have already mentioned a few of the blend modes that I use all the time, such as the Luminosity blend for blending adjustment layers without affecting the color component of an image. To help you learn and understand how the blend modes work, over the next few pages I have provided a summary of all the blend modes currently found in Photoshop CS4.

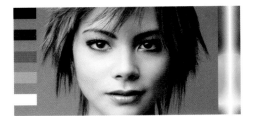
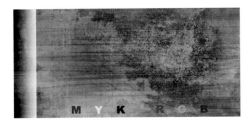

Figure 9.24 The following pages illustrate all the different blending modes in Photoshop. In these examples, the photograph of the model was added as a new layer above the gray textured Background layer and the layer settings recorded in the accompanying panel screen shots.

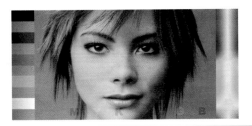

Normal

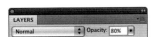

This is the default mode. Changing Opacity simply fades the intensity of overlaying pixels by averaging the color pixels of the blend layer with the values of the composite pixels below (Opacity set here to 80%).

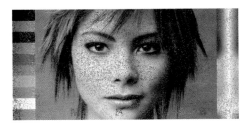

Dissolve

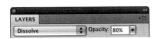

Combines the blend layer with the base using a randomized pattern of pixels. No change occurs when Dissolve is applied at 100% opacity. As the opacity is reduced, the diffusion becomes more apparent (Opacity set here to 80%).

Darken

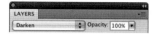

Looks at the base and blending colors and color is only applied if the blend color is darker than the base color.

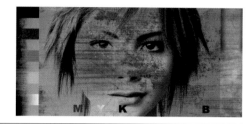

Multiply

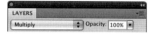

Multiplies the base by the blend pixel values, always producing a darker color, except where the blend color is white. The effect is similar to viewing two transparency slides sandwiched together on a lightbox.

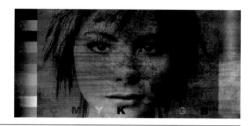

Color Burn

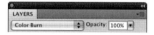

Darkens the image using the blend color. The darker the color, the more pronounced the effect. Blending with white has no effect.

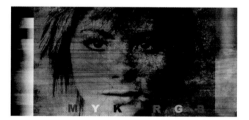

Linear Burn

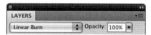

The Linear Burn mode produces an even more pronounced darkening effect than Multiply or Color Burn. Note that the Linear Burn blending mode will clip the darker pixel values and blending with white has no effect.

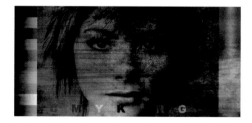

Darker Color

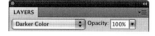

Darker color is similar to the Darken mode, except it works on all channels instead of working on a per-channel basis. When you blend two layers together, only the darker pixels on the blend layer will remain visible.

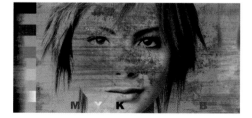

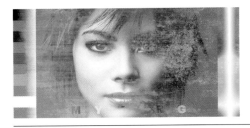

Lighten

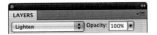

Looks at the base and blending colors and color is only applied if the blend color is lighter than the base color.

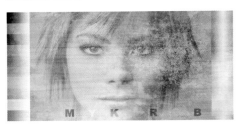

Screen

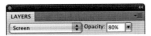

Multiplies the inverse of the blend and base pixel values together, always making a lighter color, except where the blend color is black. The effect is similar to printing with two negatives sandwiched together in the enlarger.

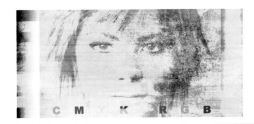

Color Dodge

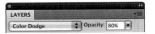

Brightens the image using the blend color. The brighter the color, the more pronounced the result. Blending with black has no effect (Opacity set here to 80%).

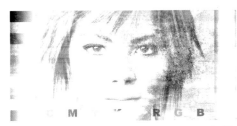

Linear Dodge (Add)

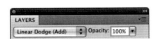

This blending mode does the opposite of the Linear Burn tool. It produces a stronger lightening effect than Screen or Lighten, but clips the lighter pixel values. Blending with black has no effect.

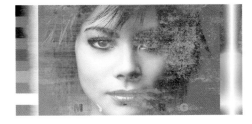

Lighter Color

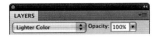

Lighter color is similar to the Lighten mode, except it works on all channels instead of working on a per-channel basis. When you blend two layers together, only the lighter pixels on the blend layer will remain visible.

Overlay

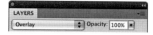

The Overlay blending mode superimposes the blend image on the base (multiplying or screening the colors depending on the base color) whilst preserving the highlights and shadows of the base color. Blending with 50% gray has no effect.

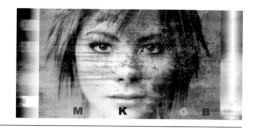

Soft Light

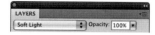

Darkens or lightens the colors depending on the base color. Soft Light produces a more gentle effect than the Overlay mode. Blending with 50% gray has no effect.

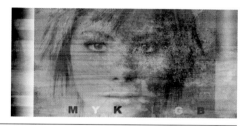

Hard Light

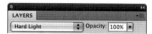

Multiplies or screens the colors depending on the base color. Hard Light produces a more pronounced effect than the Overlay mode. Blending with 50% gray has no effect.

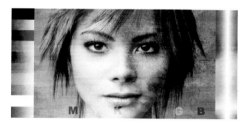

Vivid Light

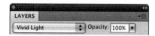

Applies a Color Dodge or Color Burn blending mode, depending on the base color. Vivid Light produces a stronger effect than Hard Light mode. Blending with 50% gray has no effect.

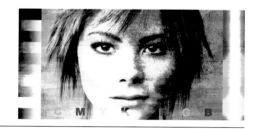

Linear Light

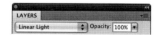

Applies a Linear Dodge or Linear Burn blending mode, depending on the base color. Linear Light produces a slightly stronger effect than the Vivid Light mode. Blending with 50% gray has no effect.

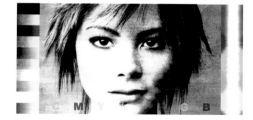

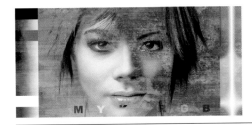

Pin Light

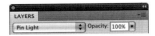

Applies a Lighten blend mode to the lighter colors and a Darken blend mode to the darker colors. Pin Light produces a stronger effect than Soft Light mode. Blending with 50% gray has no effect.

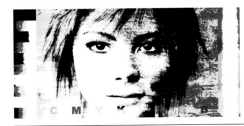

Hard Mix

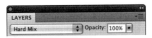

Produces a posterized image consisting of up to eight colors: red, green, blue, cyan, magenta, yellow, black and white. The blend color is a product of the base color and the luminosity of the blend layer.

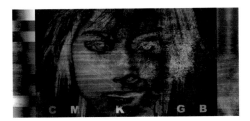

Difference

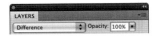

Subtracts either the base color from the blending color or the blending color from the base, depending on whichever has the highest brightness value. In visual terms, a 100% white blend value will invert (i.e. turn negative) the base layer completely, a black value will have no effect, and values in between will partially invert the base layer. Duplicating a Background layer and applying Difference at 100% will produce a black image. Dramatic changes can be gained by experimenting with different opacities. An analytical application of Difference is to do a pin register sandwich of two near identical images to detect any image changes – such as a comparison of two images in different RGB color spaces.

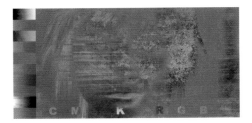

Exclusion

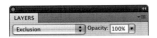

A slightly muted variant of the Difference blending mode. Blending with pure white will invert the base image.

Hue

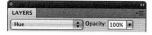

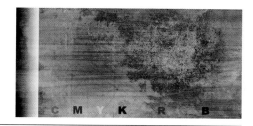

Preserves the luminance and saturation of the base image, replacing with the hue of the blending pixels.

Saturation

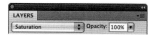

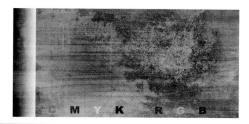

Preserves the luminance and hue of the base image, replacing with the saturation of the blending pixels.

Color

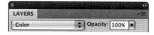

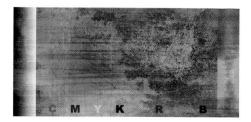

Preserves the luminance values of the base image, replacing the hue and saturation values of the blending pixels. Color mode is particularly suited for hand-coloring photographs.

Luminosity

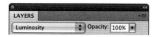

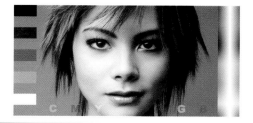

Preserves the hue and saturation of the base image while applying the luminance of the blending pixels.

Client: Taylor Phillipps. Model: Tina at FM.

Advanced Blending options

Layer groups allow you to group a number of layers together such that the layers contained within a layer group behave like a single layer. In Pass Through blending mode the layer blending passes through the set and the interaction is no different than if the individual layers were in a normal layer stack. However, when you select any of the other blending mode options, the layer group blending results are equivalent to what would happen if you chose to merge all the layers in the current group into a single layer and then adjusted the blending mode.

Knockout options

Among the Advance Blending modes, the Knockout blending options (see Step 2 on page 451) allow you to force a layer to punch through some or all of the layers beneath it. A 'Shallow' knockout punches through to the bottom of the layer group only, while a 'Deep' knockout punches through to just above the Background layer (see the example on the page opposite).

Blend Interior effects

Layer styles are normally applied independent of the layer blending mode. However, when you check the Blend Interior Effects as Group box, such effects will take on the blending characteristics of the selected layer.

To put all this into practice, try opening the image shown on page 451 from the DVD and follow the steps outlined here. In particular, observe how the 'Blend Interior Effects as Group' option works on Layer C which is using the Difference blending mode. When you check the Blend Interior Effects as Group option, the result will be the same as if you had first 'fixed' the interior layer style using the Normal blend mode and then changed the blend mode to 'Difference'. Other aspects of the Layer Style blending options dialog box are covered in the Layers Styles section in the *Photoshop CS4 for Photographers Help Guide*, available from the DVD.

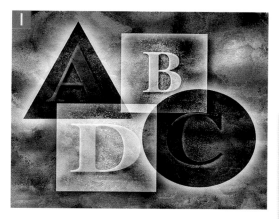

1 The four letter layers shown here are grouped together in a layer group. Layer A is using the Multiply blending mode; B is using Overlay; C is using Difference; and D is using the Screen blending mode. The default blending mode of this layer group is Pass Through. This means that the layers in the layer group blend with the layers below the same as they would if they were in a normal layer stack.

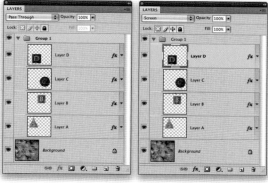

2 If you select Layer D and double-click the layer to open the Layer Style dialog, you can alter the Advanced Blending options. The Knockout options allow you to 'punch through' the layers. A 'Shallow' knockout will punch through the three layers below it to just above the layer or layer group immediately below. A 'Deep' knockout will make the Layer D punch through all layers below it, straight down to the Background layer. Layer D now appears as it would if resting directly above the Background layer.

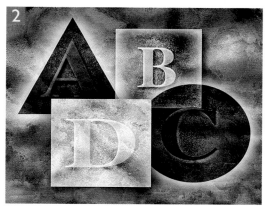

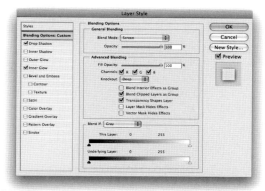

3 The default layer group blend mode is Pass Through. If you change the layer group blending mode to anything else, the layers within the group will blend with each other as before, but will not interact with the layers underneath as they did in Pass Through mode. When the blend mode is 'Normal', the group layers appear as they would if the Background layer visibility were switched off.

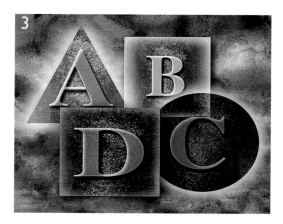

The other layout options

Auto

The Auto layout works best in most cases and I suggest that you use Auto first to see what it does, before considering any of the alternative layout options. Auto tends to flatten the perspective and prevent the corners of a photomerge from shooting outwards.

Perspective

The Perspective layout doesn't inhibit the perspective from becoming exaggerated. It can produce good results when the processed photos are shot using a moderate wide-angle lens or longer, but can otherwise produce very distorted composites.

Cylindrical

The Cylindrical layout aligns photos on the horizontal axis only. This is useful for keeping the horizon line straight when using Photomerge to process a series of photos that make up an elongated panorama.

Spherical

This is new to CS4. It can transform and warp the individual photos in both horizontal and vertical directions. This layout option is more adaptable when it comes to aligning tricky panoramic image sequences.

Collage

This positions the photos in a photomerge layout without transforming the individual layers, but does rotate them to achieve the best fit.

Reposition

The Reposition layout simply repositions the photos in the photomerge layout, without rotating them.

Creating panoramas with Photomerge

The Photomerge feature has been made a lot simpler to work with. Gone is the interactive Photomerge dialog. This is because the recent improvements to Photomerge alignment and blending should be all you need to produce the best photomerged results and, in the majority of cases, the Auto layout option is all you need.

There are two ways to generate a Photomerge. You can go to the File ⇨ Automate menu in Photoshop and choose Photomerge... This will open the dialog shown in Step 2, from where you can choose, say, 'Add Open Files' and add these as the source images. Or, you can use Bridge to navigate to the photos you wish to process and open Photomerge via the Tools ⇨ Photoshop submenu.

To get the best photomerge results, you need to work from photographs where there is a significant overlap between each exposure. You should typically aim for at least a 25% overlap between each exposure and overlap the photos even more if you are using a wide-angle lens. For example, the Photomerge in CS4 is even optimized to work with certain fish eye lenses, but if you do so, you should aim for maybe as much as a 70% overlap between frames. Here are the basic steps you would use.

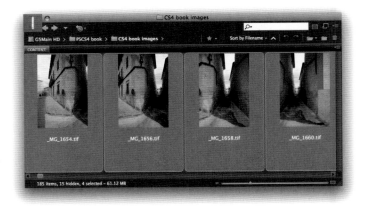

1 To create the photomerge shown here, I started by selecting the four photographs shown here in Bridge. I then went to the Tools menu and chose Photoshop ⇨ Photomerge...

452

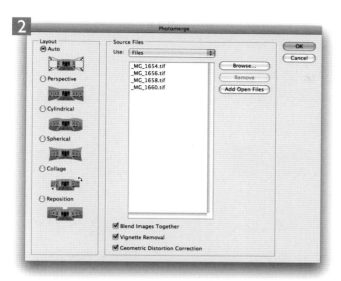

2 This opened the Photomerge dialog, where you'll note that the 'Auto' layout option was selected and the four selected images were automatically added as source files. All I really needed to do here was to check the three options at the bottom and click OK to proceed.

Blending options

The 'Blend Images Together' option completes the Photomerge processing because it adds layer masks to each of the photomerged layers (see the Layers panel view in Step 3). You can choose not to run this option and select the Edit Auto-Blend Layers option later to achieve the same end result (see page 455). 'Vignette Removal' and 'Geometric Distortion Correction' are optional and can help improve the result of the final image blending, especially if you are merging photos that were shot with a wide-angle lens.

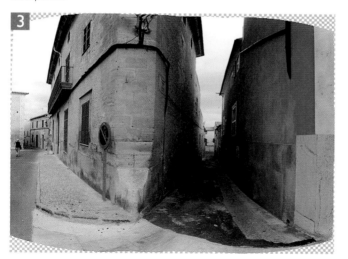

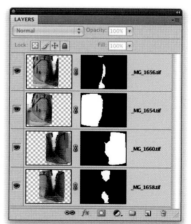

3 In most cases, the Auto option is usually the best one to select and, as you can see here, it aligned the four photos automatically, applied a blend step to blend the tones and colors between the layers, followed by an auto layer mask step in which the individual layers ended up being masked so that each part of the photomerge image consisted of no more than one visible layer.

Depth of field blending

The Edit ⇨ Auto-Blend Layers command now allows you to blend objects that were shot using different points of focus and blend them into a single image.

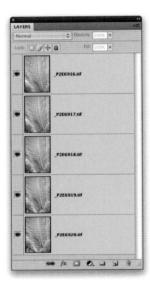

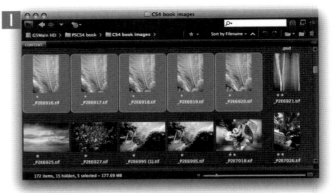

1 I began by going to Bridge to select a group of photographs that had been shot at different points of focus. I then went to the Tools menu and chose Photoshop ⇨ Load Files Into Photoshop Layers. This opened the five selected photos as a multi-layered image in Photoshop.

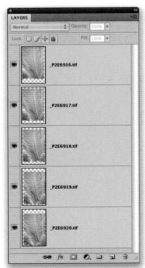

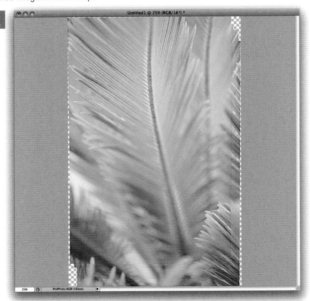

2 With all the layers selected, I then went to the Edit menu, chose 'Auto-Align Layers...' and selected the Auto projection option. This aligned the layers as shown here.

3

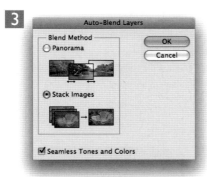

3 The next step was to merge the layered photos together, which I did by going to the Edit menu again and this time selected 'Auto-Blend layers...'. Here, I selected 'Stack Images' and made sure the 'Seamless Tones and Colors' option was checked.

4

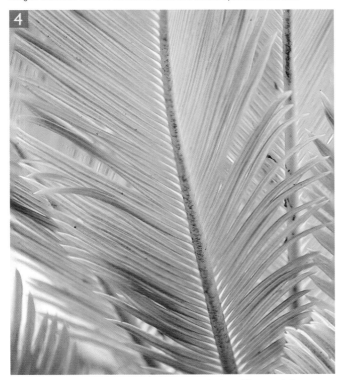

4 To get the best results it is important to carry out the Auto-Align step before you apply the Auto-Blend. As you can see, this last step carried out a pixel blending step on the individual layers and added layer masks to each image based on a calculation of where the sharpest detail was on each layer. The success of this depth of field blending will also be down to the care with which you shoot the original photographs.

Blending retouch tip

Depth of field blending works reasonably well in most instances, but won't always produce perfect results. You will notice in Step 4 there is an out-of-focus edge around the palm leaves in the bottom right corner. One solution is to preserve a duplicate layer group of all the aligned layers (before you carry out the auto-blending), add layer masks filled with black to each of these layers, and place this layer group at the top of the layer stack. You can then retouch the image by carefully painting with white on the layer masks for these layers, filling in the gaps where the auto-blending did not work quite as well as you had hoped.

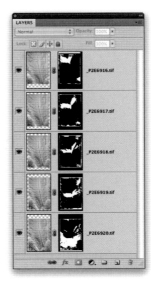

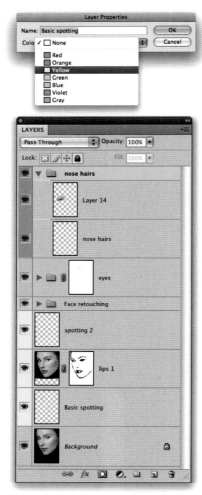

Figure 9.25 Layers can be color coded. Choose 'Layer Properties' from the Layers panel fly-out menu and pick a color. Alternatively, you can ⌥ *alt* double-click a layer to open the Layer Properties dialog shown here.

Working with multiple layers

Layers have become an essential feature in Photoshop because they enable you to do all kinds of complex montage work, but as layer features have evolved there has been an increasing need to manage them more efficiently.

Color coding layers

One way to manage your layers better is to color code them, which can be done by selecting a layer and choosing 'Layer Properties' from the Layers panel fly-out menu. This opens the dialog shown in Figure 9.25, where you can rename a layer and pick a color label. The downside is that you can only adjust the label color coding one layer at a time (unless you are changing the layer properties for a layer group).

Layer group management

Multi-layered images can be unwieldy to navigate, especially when you have lots of layers placed one above the other, but they can be organized more efficiently if you place them into layer groups. Layer groups have a folder icon and the general idea is that you can place related layers together inside a single layer group and the layer group can then be collapsed or expanded. Therefore, if you have lots of layers in an image, layer groups can make it easier to arrange the layers and layer navigation becomes simpler.

If you click on the Create a New Group button in the Layers panel, this will add a new layer group above the current target layer, while ⌘ *ctrl*-clicking on the same button will add a layer group below the target layer and ⌥ *alt*-clicking opens the New Group from Layers dialog (Figure 9.26).

Layers groups can be made visible or invisible by clicking on the layer group eye icon. It is also possible to adjust the opacity and blending mode of a layer group as if it were a single layer, while the subset of layers within the layer group itself can all have individually set opacities and use different blending modes. You can also add a layer mask or vector mask to a layer group and use this to mask the layer group visibility, as you would with individual layers.

To reposition a layer in the Layers panel, click on the layer and drag it up or down within the layer stack. To move a layer into a layer group, drag it to the layer group icon or drag to an expanded layer group. To remove a layer from a layer group, just drag the layer above or below the group in the stack (see page 458).

(see page 458)

Group layer shortcut

Selected layers can be grouped together by choosing Layer ⇨ Group Layers, or by using the ⌘ G ctrl G shortcut. You can also lock all layers inside a layer group via the Layers panel submenu.

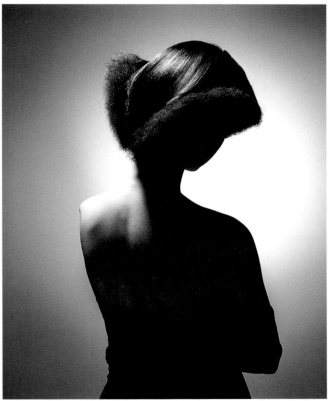

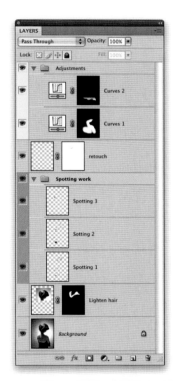

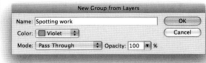

Figure 9.26 When a Photoshop document ends up with this many layers, the layer stack can become difficult to manage, but it is possible to organize layers within layer groups. In this example, I used a *Shift*-click to select the three spotting layers near the bottom of the layer stack. I then went to the Layers panel fly-out menu and chose 'New Group from Layers...'. I entered a name for the new group and selected a violet color to color code the layers within this group.

Once I had done this, the visibility of all layers within this group could be switched on or off via the layer group eyeball icon and the opacity of the group could be adjusted as if all the layers in the group were a single merged layer.

Client: Andrew Collinge Hair & Beauty. Hair by Andrew Collinge artistic team, Make-up: Liz Collinge.

Nested layer groups

You can have a layer group (or groups) nested within a layer group up to three nested layer groups deep.

Managing layers in a group

The following steps help illustrate the workings of the layer group management discussed on the preceding pages.

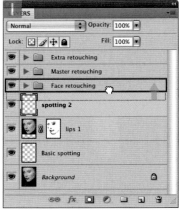

1 Layers can be moved into a layer group by mousing down on a layer and dragging the layer into the desired layer group.

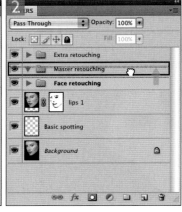

2 The same method can be used when you want to move a layer group within another layer group. Mouse down and drag the group to another layer group.

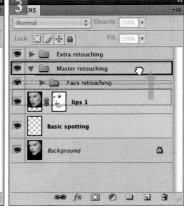

3 You can also move multiple layers at once. Make a *Shift* select or ⌘ *ctrl* layer selection of the layers you want to move and then drag them to the layer group.

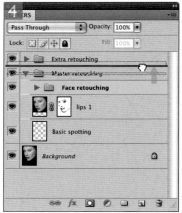

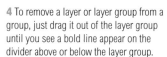

4 To remove a layer or layer group from a group, just drag it out of the layer group until you see a bold line appear on the divider above or below the layer group.

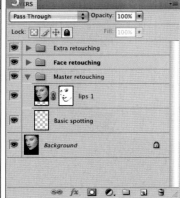

5 Here is a view of the Layers panel with the Face retouching group now outside and above the Master retouching layer group.

Clipping masks

Clipping masks enable you to mask the contents of a layer based on the transparency and opacity of the layer beneath it. So, if you have two or more layers that need to be masked identically, one way to do this is to apply a layer mask to the first layer and then create a clipping mask with the layer or layers above it. Once a clipping mask has been applied, the upper layer or layers will appear indented in the Layers panel (Figure 9.27). You can alter the blending mode and opacity of the individual layers in a clipping group, but it is the transparency and opacity of the lower (masked) layer that will determine the transparency and opacity of all the layers that are in a clipping mask group.

The main advantage of using clipping masks is that whenever you have a number of layers that you require to share the same mask, you only need to apply a mask to the bottom-most layer. Then when you make a clipping mask, the layer (or layers) in the clipping mask group will all share the same mask. So for example, if you edit the master mask, the edit changes you make to it are simultaneously applied to the layer (or layers) above it.

Creating a new clipping mask

To create a clipping mask, select a single layer or make a *Shift* selection of the layers you want to group together and choose Layer ⇨ Clipping Mask ⇨ Create. Alternatively, ⌥ *alt*-click the border line between the layers. This action toggles creating and releasing the layers from a clipping mask group. Plus you can use the ⌘ ⌥ *G* *ctrl* *alt* *G* keyboard shortcut to make the selected layers form a clipping mask with the layer below.

You can also create clipping masks at the same time as you add a new layer. In the example that's shown on the next few pages, you can see how I ⌥ *alt*-clicked the Add New Adjustment Layer button, which opened the New Layer dialog. This allowed me to check the 'Use Previous Layer to Create Clipping Mask' option (the same thing applies when clicking the Add New Layer button).

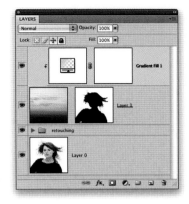

Figure 9.27 This shows an example of a clipping mask, where the Gradient Fill layer forms a clipping mask with the masked image layer beneath it. Note how the layer in the clipping mask group appears indented in the layer stack.

Adjustments panel

Once an adjustment layer has been created, you can create a clipping mask with the layer below by clicking on the Clipping Mask button in the Adjustments panel. This allows you to toggle quickly between a clipping mask and non-clipping state (see Figure 9.28).

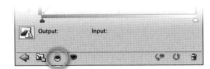

Figure 9.28 This shows the Clipping Mask button in the Adjustments panel that allows you to toggle between enabling and disabling a clipping mask with the layer beneath the adjustment layer.

Masking layers within a group

I use clipping masks quite a lot, but there is also another way that you can achieve the same kind of result and that is to make a selection of two or more layers and convert them into a layer group (choose Layer ⇨ Group Layers). With the layer group selected, click on the Add Layer Mask button in the Layers panel to add a layer mask to the group. If you now edit the layer mask for the layer group, you can simultaneously mask all the layer group contents.

Clipping layers and adjustment layers

The following steps show how clipping masks can be used to group a fill layer with an image layer and how to group two adjustment layers together so that they form a clipping mask.

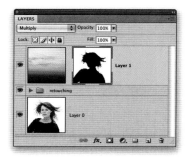

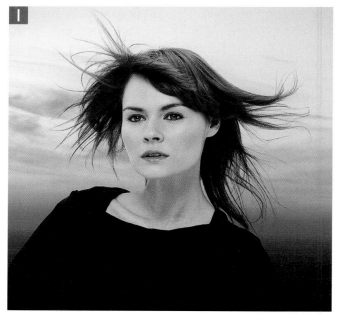

1 This shows a composite image in which I had carried out most of the retouching on the face and added a layer containing a new backdrop image. In this instance, the mask allows the model to show through from the layer below.

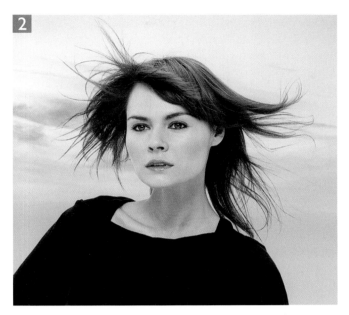

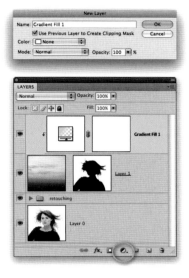

2 In this next step I added a Gradient Fill layer with a solid peach color fading to transparency, using a linear gradient. As you can see, when adding this new fill layer I created a clipping mask with the backdrop image layer. One way to do this was to hold down the ⌥ *alt* key as I clicked on the Add New Adjustment Layer button (circled). This opened the New Layer dialog shown here, where I checked the 'Use Previous Layer to Create Clipping Mask' option.

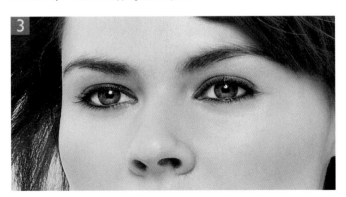

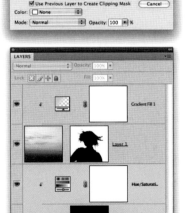

3 Lastly, I made a lasso selection of the model's eyes and added a new Curves adjustment to lighten the eyes. I then did the same thing as in Step 2. I held down the ⌥ *alt* key as I clicked on the Add New Adjustment Layer button and chose a Hue/Saturation adjustment. Again, I checked the 'Use Previous Layer to Create Clipping Mask' option so that when I desaturated the reds, this adjustment was clipped to the same mask as the one used for the Curves adjustment.

Move tool alignment options

The alignment options are also integrated into the move tool Options bar. To find out more about layer alignment and distribution, refer to pages 472–475.

Selecting all layers

You can use the ⌘ ⌥ A ctrl alt A shortcut to select all layers (except a Background layer) and make them active.

Layer linking

When working with two or more layers you can link them together by creating links via the Layers panel. Start by Shift-clicking on the layers to select contiguous layers, or ⌘ ctrl-clicking to select discontiguous layers. At this point you can move, transform or convert the layers to a group. But if you need to make the layer selection linking more permanent, the layers can be formally linked together by clicking on the Link Layers button at the bottom of the Layers panel (Figure 9.29). When two or more layers are linked by layer selection or formal linking, any moves or transform operations are applied to the layers as if they were one. However, they still remain as separate layers, retaining their individual opacity and blending modes. To unlink, select the layer (or layers) and click on the Link button to turn the linking off.

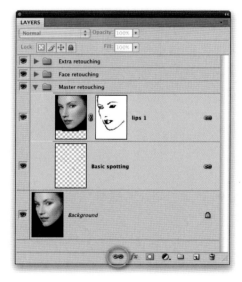

Figure 9.29 To link two or more selected layers, click on the Link button at the bottom of the Layers panel (circled).

Layer selection with the move tool

When the move tool is selected, and the Auto-Select and Layer options are checked in the move tool options, you can auto-select layers by clicking or dragging in the image (Figure 9.30), plus you can also use the contextual menu to auto-select specific layers (Figure 9.31).

Auto-select shortcut

If Auto-Select Layer is unchecked, you can toggle the behavior by holding down the ⌘ *ctrl* key as you click.

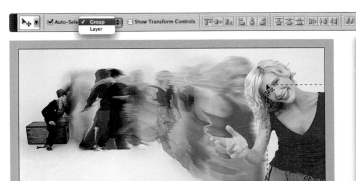

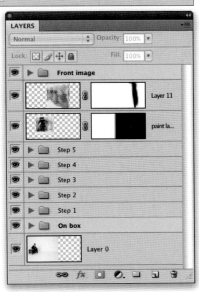

Figure 9.30 When Auto-Select Layer is checked, you can marquee drag with the move tool from outside the document bounds to make a layer selection of all the layers within the marqueed area, but the move tool marquee must start from outside the document bounds, i.e. you must start from the canvas area and drag inwards. In the example shown here, the 'Auto-Select' and 'Group' options were checked and only the layer groups that came within the marquee selection were selected by this action.

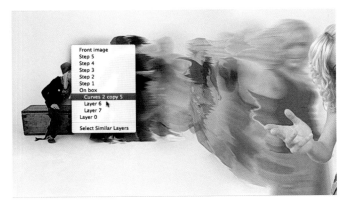

Figure 9.31 When the move tool is selected, you can use the contextual menu to select individual layers. Mouse down on the image using *ctrl* right mouse-click to access the contextual menu shown here and click to select a named layer. The contextual options will list all of the layer groups in the document plus just those layers within the layer group (indented) immediately below the mouse cursor.

Selecting Similar layers

The 'Select Similar Layers' option allows you to select layers that are of a similar kind, i.e. if a type layer is selected, the 'Select Similar Layers' option will select all other type layers in the document.

Client: Hitachi/Ogilvy & Mather Direct.
Model: Lidia @ MOT.

Layer mask linking

Layer masks and vector masks are linked by default to the layer content and, if you move a masked layer or transform the layer content, the mask is adjusted with it (as long as no selection is active). It can sometimes be desirable to disable the link between layer mask/vector mask and the layer it is masking. When you do this, movements or transforms can be applied to the layer or the layer/vector mask separately. You can tell if the layer, layer mask or vector mask are selected, because a thin black dashed border surrounds the layer, layer mask or vector mask icon.

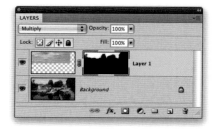
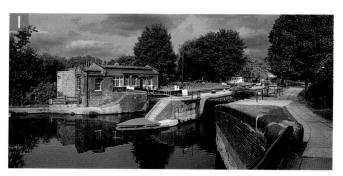

1 This photograph contained a clouds layer that had been masked by the outline of the trees. The layer and layer mask are normally linked and here you can see a dashed border surrounding the layer mask, which meant that the layer mask was currently active.

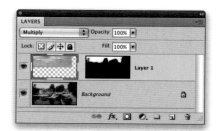
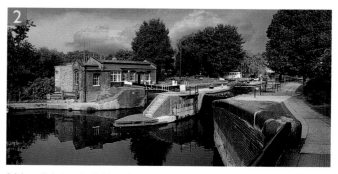

2 I then clicked on the link icon between the layer and the layer mask, which disabled the link between the mask and the layer. Now, when the layer was selected (note the dashed border around the layer thumbnail) I was able to move the sky layer independently of the layer mask.

Layer locking

The layer locking options are to be found at the top of the Layers panel just below the blending mode options. Photoshop layers can be locked in a number of ways and to apply one of the locking criteria listed below, you need to first select a layer and then click on one of the Lock buttons. These have a toggle action, so to remove the locking just click on the button again.

Lock Transparent Pixels

When Lock Transparent Pixels is switched on, any painting or editing you do will be applied to the opaque portions of the layer only. Where the layer is transparent or semi-transparent, the level of layer transparency will be preserved (Figure 9.32).

Lock Image Pixels

The 'Lock Image Pixels' option locks the pixels to prevent them from being edited (with, say, the brush tool or clone stamp). If you attempt to paint or edit a layer that has been locked in this way, you will see a prohibit warning sign (Figure 9.33).

Lock Layer Position

The 'Lock Layer Position' option locks the layer position only. This means that while you can edit the layer contents, you won't be able to accidentally knock the layer position with the move tool or apply a Transform command (Figure 9.34).

Lock All

You can select combinations of Lock Transparent Pixels, Lock Image Pixels, and Lock Layer Position, plus you can also check the 'Lock All' option which will let you lock absolutely everything on a layer (Figure 9.35).

The above options mainly refer to image layers. With non-pixel layers you can only choose to lock the layer position or lock all.

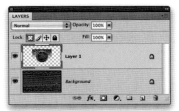

Figure 9.32 This shows the Layers panel with a Layer 1 image layer above the Background layer. Lock Transparent Pixels prevents you accidentally painting in the layer's transparent areas.

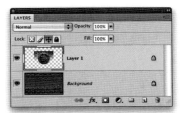

Figure 9.33 Lock Image Pixels prevents you accidentally painting on any part of the image layer, but allows movement of the layer.

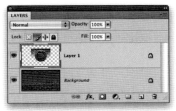

Figure 9.34 Lock Layer Position prevents the layer from being moved when you edit it.

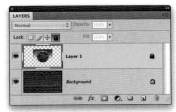

Figure 9.35 The Lock All box locks absolutely everything. The layer position is locked and the contents cannot be edited. The opacity or blend modes cannot be altered, but the layer can still be moved up or down the layer stack.

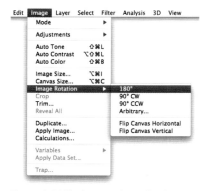

Figure 9.36 The Image ⇨ Image Rotation submenu. This menu is used to rotate or flip the entire image.

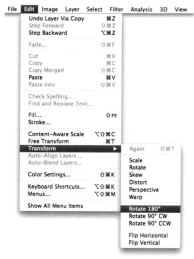

Figure 9.37 The Edit ⇨ Transform submenu. This menu is used for transforming and rotating individual layers, linked groups of layers or image selections.

Transform commands

The Image menu provides a choice of options in the Image Rotation submenu to rotate or flip an image. You can use these commands to flip or rotate the whole image, such as when a photo has been scanned upside down (Figure 9.36).

The Transform commands are all in the Edit ⇨ Transform menu (Figure 9.37) and these allow you to apply transformations to individual or linked groups of layers. Select a layer or make a selection of the pixels that you wish to transform and choose either Edit ⇨ Transform or Edit ⇨ Free Transform, or check the Show Transform Controls box in the move tool Options bar (Figure 9.38). The main Transform commands include: Scale, Rotate, Skew, Distort and Perspective, and these can be applied singly or combined in a sequence before clicking *Enter* or double-clicking within the Transform bounding box to OK the transformation (which is applied using the default interpolation method selected in the Photoshop preferences to calculate the new transform shape).

You can apply any number of tweaking adjustments before applying the actual transform and you can at any time use the Undo command (*⌘Z* *ctrl Z*) to revert to the last defined transform preview setting. You can also adjust the transparency of a layer during mid-transform. This means that you modify the opacity of the layer as you transform it and this can help you align a transformed layer to the layers below.

Of all the options, the Free Transform option is probably the most versatile and the one you will want to use most of the time. Choose Edit ⇨ Free Transform or use the *⌘T* *ctrl T* keyboard shortcut and modify the transformation using the keyboard controls as indicated on the following pages. The Free Transform command is also available via the contextual menu. Just *ctrl* right mouse-click on a layer and select 'Free Transform'.

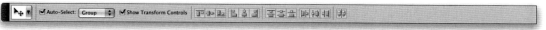

Figure 9.38 The transform options are also available via the move tool Options bar (check 'Show Transform Controls').

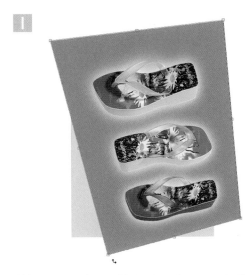

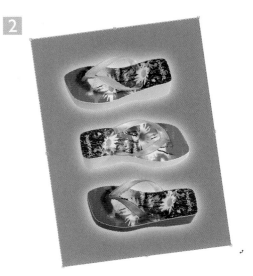

1 You can rotate, skew or distort an image in one go using the Edit ⇨ Free Transform command. The following steps show you some of the modifier key commands to use to constrain a free transform adjustment.

2 Place the cursor outside the bounding border and drag in any direction to rotate the image. If you hold down the *Shift* key as you drag, this constrains the rotation to 15° increments. You can also move the center point to change the center of the rotation.

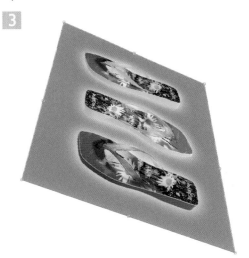

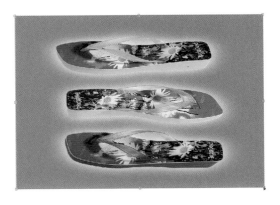

3 If you hold down the ⌘ *ctrl* key as you click any of the handles of the bounding border, this allows you to perform a free distortion.

4 If you want to constrain the distortion symmetrically around the center point of the bounding box, hold down the ⌥ *alt* key as you drag any handle.

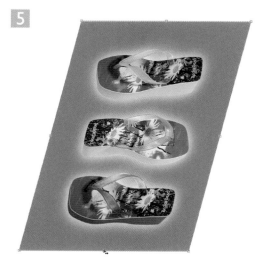

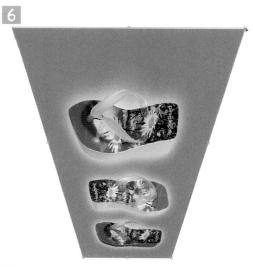

5 To skew an image, hold down the `⌘` `Shift` `ctrl` `Shift` keys and drag one of the side handles.

Photograph by Davis Cairns. Client: Red or Dead.

6 To carry out a perspective distortion, hold down the `⌘` `⌥` `Shift` `ctrl` `alt` `Shift` keys in unison and drag on one of the corner handles. When you are happy with any of the new transform shapes described here, press `Enter` or `Return` or double-click within the Transform envelope to apply the transform. Press `esc` if you wish to cancel.

Repeat Transforms

After you have applied a transform to the image data, you can get Photoshop to repeat the transform by going to the Edit menu and choosing: Transform ⇨ Again (the shortcut here is `⌘` `Shift` `T` `ctrl` `Shift` `T`). This can be done to transform the same layer or a separate layer. I generally find the Transform Again command most useful when I need to repeat a precise transform on two different layers. There is an example coming up on pages 473–475 that shows a creative application of the Free Transform command, where it was used to create a kaleidoscope image effect from a single image.

Numeric Transforms

When you select any of the Transform commands from the Edit menu or check 'Show Bounding Box' in the move tool options, the Options bar displays the Numeric Transform commands shown below in Figure 9.39. The Numeric Transform options enable you to accurately define any transformation as well as choose where to position the centering reference point position. For example, the Numeric Transform is commonly used to change the percentage scale of a selection or layer. You just enter the scale percentages in the Width and Height boxes. If the Constrain Proportions link icon is switched off you can set the width and height independently. You can also change the central axis for the transformation by repositioning the black dot (circled).

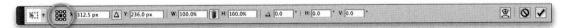

Figure 9.39 This shows the move tool Options bar in Transform mode.

Transforming selections and paths

You can also apply transforms to Photoshop selections and vector paths. For example, to transform a selection, choose Select ⇨ Transform Selection (note: if you choose Edit ⇨ Transform, this will transform the selection contents!). Transform Selection works just like the Edit ⇨ Free Transform command. You can use the exact same modifier key combinations to scale, rotate and distort the selection outline. Or, you can use *ctrl* right mouse-click to call up the contextual menu of transform options. With Transform Selection, you can modify a selection shape quite effortlessly.

Whenever you have a pen path active, the Edit menu switches to Transform Path mode. You can then use the Transform Path commands to manipulate a completed path or a group of selected path points (the path does not have to be closed). But remember, you won't be able to execute a transform on an image on an image layer (or layers) until you have deselected any active paths.

Expand/Contract selections

Earlier on page 424, I mentioned how you could use the Select ⇨ Modify menu to expand or contract a selection. One of the downsides of this approach is that when you enlarge a rectangular selection in this way, you'll end up with rounded corners. If, instead, you use the Transform selection method, you can preserve the sharp corners of a rectangular selection.

Warp transforms for retouching

There was an example earlier on page 414 where I showed how a warp transform could be used on a fashion photograph to change the shape of a portion of the image. As I pointed out, warp transforms are better suited for editing large areas of a picture where the Liquify filter is less able to match the fluid distortion controls of the warp transform. More infamously, warp transforms have been used a lot in fashion retouching to make skinny models look even skinnier.

Warp transforms

The Warp transform provides a perfect solution for all those Photoshop users who have longed for a means to carry out direct, on-canvas image warping. The Warp transform is therefore more like an extension of the Free Transform. All you have to do is to select the Free Transform option from the Edit menu and then click on the Transform/Warp mode button (circled in Figure 9.40) to toggle between the Free Transform and Warp modes. The beauty of this is that you can combine a free transform and warp distortion into a single pixel transformation.

When the Warp option is selected you can control the shape of the warp bounding box using the bezier handles at each corner. The box itself contains a 3×3 mesh and you can click in any of the nine warp sectors and drag with the mouse to fine-tune the warp shape. What is also great about the warp transform is the way that you can make a warp overlap on itself, as shown on the following page.

You can only apply warp transforms to a single layer at a time, but if you combine layers into a Smart Object, you can apply non-destructive distortions to multiple layers at once. For more about working with Smart Objects, go to pages 476–479.

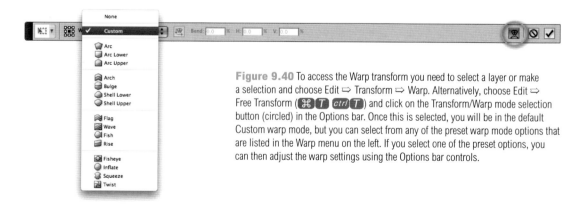

Figure 9.40 To access the Warp transform you need to select a layer or make a selection and choose Edit ⇨ Transform ⇨ Warp. Alternatively, choose Edit ⇨ Free Transform (⌘ T ctrl T) and click on the Transform/Warp mode selection button (circled) in the Options bar. Once this is selected, you will be in the default Custom warp mode, but you can select from any of the preset warp mode options that are listed in the Warp menu on the left. If you select one of the preset options, you can then adjust the warp settings using the Options bar controls.

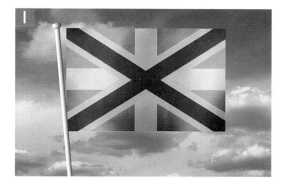

1 The easiest way for me to illustrate the power of the Warp transform is to take a made-up flag layer and use the custom warp controls to distort the flag shape to make it appear as if it were flapping in the wind. In the Layers panel view shown here, you can see that I had the flag layer and a shadow layer above it. I began by selecting both these layers before converting them into a Smart Object.

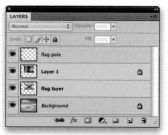

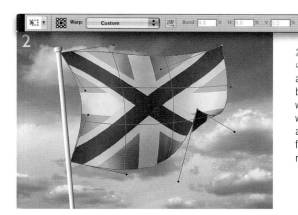

2 I then went to the Edit menu and selected Edit ➪ Transform ➪ Warp. The default option is the Custom mode, where I had access to the bezier control handles at the four corners of the warp bounding box. These could be adjusted in the same way as you would manipulate a pen path to control the outer shape of the warp. Here, I was able to drag the corner handles and click inside any of the nine sectors and drag with the mouse to manipulate the flag Smart Object layer, just as if I were stretching the image on a rubber canvas.

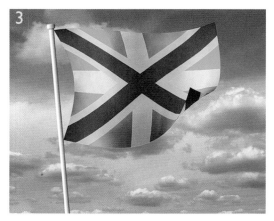

3 I was able to adjust the warp so that the flag was twisted in on itself to reveal the reverse side of the flag. You will notice below how the distorted flag existed as a Smart Object layer, where the two layers that make up the flag design were both warped in unison.

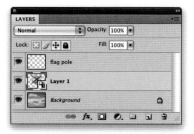

Arrange, Align and Distribute shortcuts

Note here that all the Layer menu and Layers panel shortcuts are listed in a separate appendix which is available on the DVD as a PDF document.

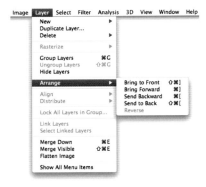

Figure 9.41 The Layer ⇨ Arrange submenu.

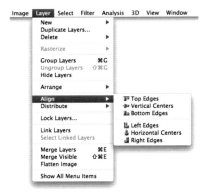

Figure 9.42 The Layer ⇨ Align submenu.

Transforms and alignment

When you have more than one layer in an image, the layer order can be changed via the Layer ⇨ Arrange submenu (Figure 9.41), which you can use to bring a layer forward or send it further back in the layer stacking order (you can also use the keyboard shortcuts shown here).

If two or more layers are linked, these can be aligned in various ways via the Layer ⇨ Align Linked menu (Figure 9.42). To use this feature, first make sure the layers you want to align are selected, are linked together, or are in a layer group. The Align commands can then be used to align the linked layers using the different rules shown in the submenu list. i.e. you can align to the Top, Vertical Centers, Bottom, Left, Horizontal Centers or Right Edges, and the alignment will be based on whichever is the top-most or left-most layer, etc. There is also the Distribute submenu, which contains an identical list of options to the Align menu but is only accessible if you have three or more layers selected, linked, or in a layer group. The Distribute commands allow you to distribute layer elements evenly based on either the Top, Vertical Centers, Bottom, Left, Horizontal Centers or Right axes. So for example, if you had three or more linked layer elements and you wanted them to be evenly spread apart horizontally, and you also wanted the distance between the midpoints of each layer element to be equidistant, you would select all the layers and choose Layer ⇨ Distribute ⇨ Horizontal Centers.

Rather than use the layer menu options you can also click on the Align and Distribute buttons in the move tool Options bar (Figure 9.43). Generally, I would say the Align and Distribute features are perhaps more useful for graphic designers, where they might want to precisely align image or text layer objects in a Photoshop layout.

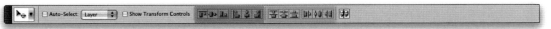

Figure 9.43 This shows the move tool Options bar in alignment/distribution mode. Note that the alignment options (shaded blue) will only become available when two or more layers are selected, and the distribution options (shaded green) are only available when three or more layers are selected.

Using transforms to create a kaleidoscope pattern

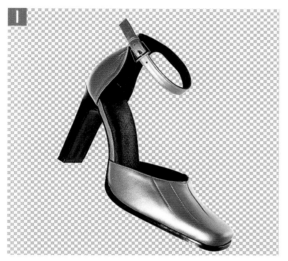

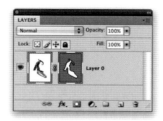

1 The following steps show how I created a kaleidoscope image from a single shoe image that was cut out using a vector mask (see pages: 484–486).

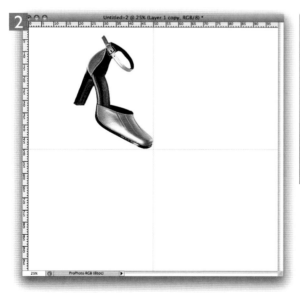

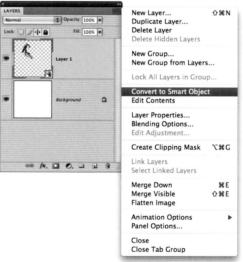

2 I dragged and placed this layer in a new image document, with the layer aligned to the guides shown here. I then converted the layer to a Smart Object (I did this by going to the Layers panel fly-out menu and chose 'Convert to Smart Object').

Photograph by Davis Cairns. Client: Red or Dead.

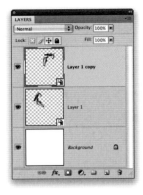

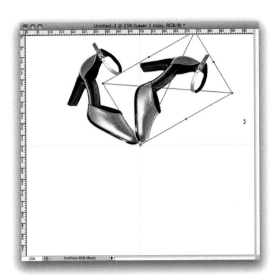

3 I duplicated the Smart Object layer by dragging it to the New Layer button in the Layers panel. I then selected 'Free Transform' from the Edit menu and positioned the central axis point on the point where the two guides cross, and dragged outside the bounding box to rotate the layer. I held down the *Shift* key as I did this, to constrain the rotation to 4 x 15° increments (i.e. rotated it 60°).

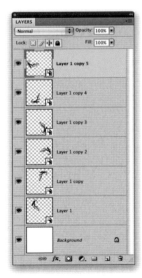

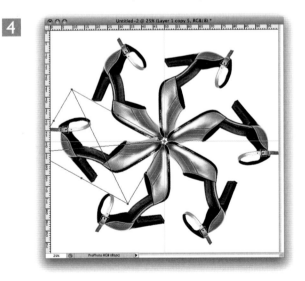

4 I repeated this exercise four more times until I ended up with the kaleidoscope pattern image shown here. You can also apply such Repeat Transforms using the *⌘ Shift T* *ctrl Shift T* keyboard shortcut.

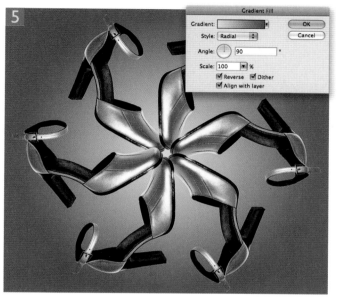

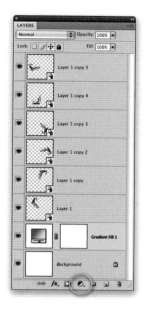

5 I then clicked on the Add New Adjustment/Fill button in the Layers panel (circled) to add a radial Gradient Fill layer just above the Background layer, using the colors shown here.

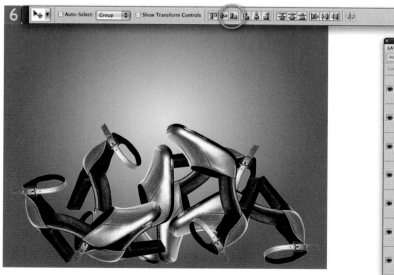

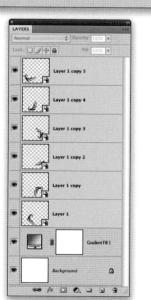

6 Lastly, just for fun, I selected all the shoe layers and clicked on the Align Bottom Edges button in the move tool Options bar. This aligned all the shoe layers to the layer with the bottom-most edge.

Smart Filters

If you go to the Filter menu, there is an option there called 'Convert for Smart Filters'. What this does is to convert a selected layer to a Smart Object, which this is no different from choosing 'Convert to Smart Object from the Layers panel fly-out menu. With Smart Objects you can apply most Photoshop filters (including some third-party filters), but not all. However, you can enable all filters to work with Smart Objects by loading the 'EnableAllPluginsforSmartFilters.jsx' script. I'll be explaining how this is done later in Chapter 10.

Smart Objects

One of the main problems you face when editing pixel images is that every time you scale an image or the contents of an image layer, the pixel information becomes degraded, and if you make cumulative transform adjustments the image quality degrades quite rapidly. If you convert a layer or a group of layers into a Smart Object (Figure 9.44), this stores the layer (or layers) data as a separate image document within the master image. The Smart Object data is therefore 'referenced' by the parent image and edits that are applied to the Smart Object layer (such as a transform adjustment) are applied to the proxy only instead of to the pixels that actually make up the layer.

With Smart Object layers you can use any of the transform adjustments described so far (including warp transforms) plus you can also apply filters to a Smart Object layer (known as Smart Filtering). What you can't do is edit a Smart Object layer directly using, say, the clone stamp tool or paint brush, but you can double-click a Smart Object layer to open it as a separate image document, where you can then apply all the usual edit adjustments before closing it, after which the edit changes are updated in the parent document.

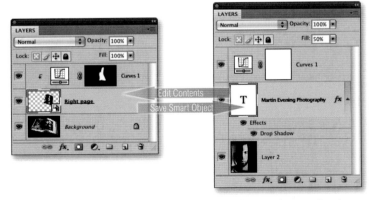

Figure 9.44 You can promote a layer or group of layers to become a Smart Object. A Smart Object becomes a fully editable, separate document within a Photoshop document. The principal advantage is that you can repeatedly scale, transform or warp a Smart Object in the parent image without affecting the integrity of the pixels in the original Smart Object document.

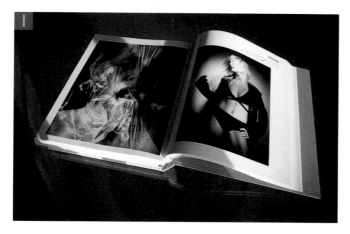

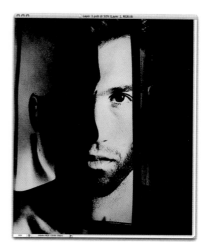

1 We'll now examine in more detail how you would use a Smart Object in Photoshop. Here is a photograph of a book that shows a couple of my promotional photographs, where let's say I wanted to place the male portrait image so that it matched the scale, rotation and warp shape of the photograph on the right-hand page.

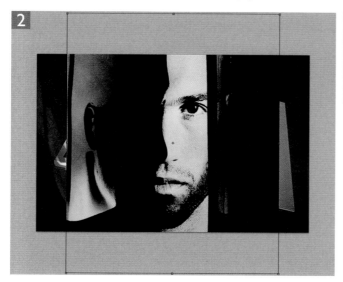

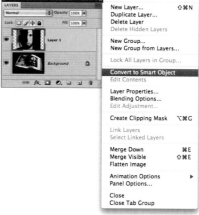

2 I used the move tool to drag the photograph across to add it as a new layer and then went to the Layers panel options and chose 'Convert to Smart Object'. This action preserved all the image data on this layer in its original form. I then went to the Edit menu and chose Free Transform. Because the layer boundary exceeded the size of the Background layer, I had to zoom out in order to access the corner handles of the Transform box.

Quick tip

In these situations it is useful to remember that you can use the ⌘ O ctrl O keyboard shortcut to quickly zoom out just far enough to reveal the transform bounding box handles.

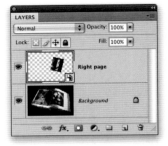

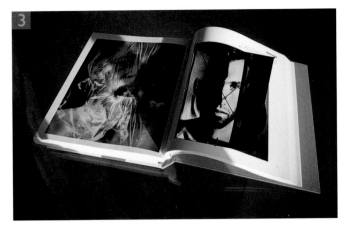

3 I then scaled the Smart Object layer down in size so that it more closely matched the size of the photograph on the page. I also dragged the cursor outside the transform bounding box, in order to rotate the photograph roughly into position.

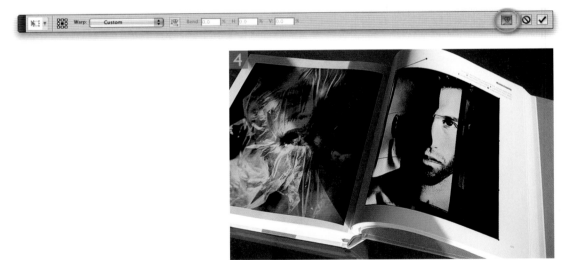

4 After that, I clicked on the Warp button in the Options bar (circled). This allowed me to fine-tune the position of the Smart Object layer, by using the corner curve adjustment handles to modify the outer envelope shape. I then moused down inside some of the inner sections and dragged them so that the inner shape also matched the curvature of the page.

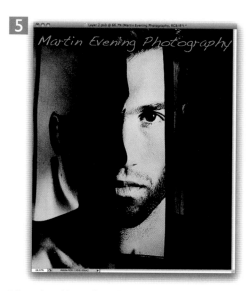

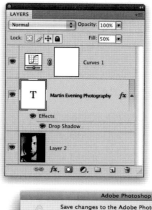

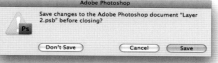

5 I was then able to edit the Smart Object layer any way I liked. To do this, I went to the Layers panel fly-out menu and selected 'Edit Contents'. An alternative option was to simply double-click on the Smart Objects layer in the Layers panel. In the example shown here, I added a Text layer plus a Curves adjustment layer to turn the photograph blue. I then closed the window and as I did so this popped the prompt dialog shown here, reminding me to click 'Save' in order to save and update the master Smart Object layer.

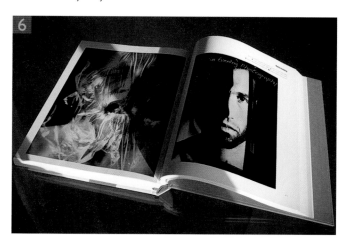

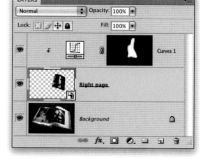

6 Here is the final image in which I added a Curves adjustment layer in a clipping group with the Smart Object layer so that the shading matched that of the original photograph on the page.

Selections to paths

An active selection can also be converted to a path by clicking on the 'Make work path from selection' button at the bottom of the Paths panel. Alternatively, choose the 'Make work path' option from the Paths panel fly-out menu.

Photoshop paths

The selection tools are nice and easy to use and many people will quite happily use Color Range and the quick select tool to make selections of the bits they wish to edit in a photograph. Other times, you might get by painting on a quick mask to define a selection. However, if you are editing anything other than low resolution images there will be times when the standard selection tools just won't give you the precision you are after. It's times like these when you really need a more accurate way to define an outline, and this is where the pen tools and vector paths come in.

Granted, it's not easy to master the pen tool, but if you are planning to work with large files, you will find it quicker to draw a path and convert this to a selection rather than rely on the selection and paint tools alone. Figure 9.45 shows a summary of how a pen path can be converted to a selection or a vector mask that isolates an object.

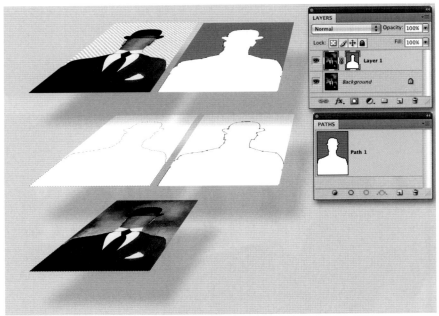

Figure 9.45 An active path can be converted to make a selection. You can also use a path to make a vector mask (from the Layer menu choose Add Vector Mask ⇨ Current Path).

Path modes

The pen tool has three operating modes, of which there are only two modes that we are interested in. If the pen tool is in Shape layers mode (Figure 9.46), when you draw with the pen tool it will create a vector mask path outline that masks a solid fill layer filled with the current foreground color. If you click on the Paths mode button in the pen tool Options bar this will allow you to create a pen path without adding a fill layer to the document. You can of course use any path outline to generate a vector mask, so I usually suggest you switch the pen tool to Paths mode and leave it set like this.

Drawing paths with the pen tool

Unless you have had previous experience working with a vector-based drawing program like Adobe Illustrator, drawing with the pen tool will probably be an unfamiliar concept. It is difficult to get the hang of at first, but I promise you this is a skill that's well worth mastering! It's a bit like learning to ride a bike – once you have acquired the basic techniques, everything will start to fall into place. Paths are useful in several ways: either for applying a stroke with one of the paint tools, for saving as a clipping path, or defining complex shapes, which in turn can be converted to a selection or applied as a vector mask to mask a layer.

Guidelines for drawing pen paths

We shall start with the task of following the simple contours illustrated in Figure 9.47. You will find a copy of this image as a layered Photoshop file on the DVD – this image contains saved path outlines of each of the shapes. The Background layer contains the Figure 9.47 image and above it there is another layer of the same image but with the pen path outlines and all the points and handles showing. Make this layer visible and fade the opacity as necessary so that you can follow the handle positions when trying to match the paths yourself. Start at the basic level with the 'd' shape (Figure 9.48). If you have learnt how to draw with the polygon lasso tool, you will have no problem drawing this path outline. Click on the corner points one

Shape layers   Paths

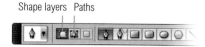

Figure 9.46 The Shape layers mode has in the past been the default setting in the pen tool options. I usually recommend that you click on the Paths mode button and leave this as your new default.

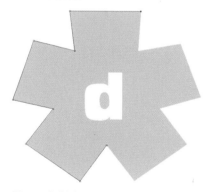

Figure 9.47 The Path tutorial file which can be found on the DVD.

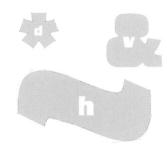

Figure 9.48 Simply click with the pen tool to create straight line segments.

Figure 9.49 To draw a curved segment, instead of clicking, mouse down and drag as you add each point. The direction and length of the handles define the shape of the curve between each path point.

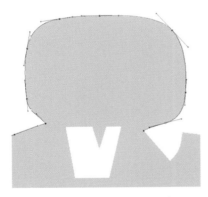

Figure 9.50 When you create a curved segment the next handle will continue to predict a curve, continuing from the last curved segment. To make a break, you need to modify the curve point by converting it to a corner point. To do this, hold down the ⌥ *alt* key, click on the path point and drag to create a new predictor handle going off in a new direction.

after another until you reach the point where you started. As you approach this point you will notice a small circle appears next to the cursor, which indicates you can now click to close the path. Actually this is better than drawing with the polygon lasso, because you can zoom in if required and precisely reposition each and every point. To do this, hold down the ⌘ *ctrl* key to temporarily switch the pen tool to the direct selection tool and drag a point to realign it precisely. After closing the path, hit ⌘ *Enter* *ctrl* *Enter* to convert the path to a selection, or click *Enter* on its own to deselect the path.

Now try to follow the 'h' shape (Figure 9.49). This will allow you to concentrate on the art of drawing curved segments. Note that the beginning of any curved segment starts by you dragging the handle outward in the direction of the intended curve. (To understand the reasoning behind this, imagine you are trying to define a circle by following the imagined edges of a square box that contains the circle). To continue a curved segment, click and hold the mouse down while you drag to complete the shape of the end of the previous curve segment (and predict the initial curve angle of the next segment). This last statement is written assuming that the next curve will be a smooth continuation of the last. If there happens to be a sharp change in direction of the shape you are trying to follow, you will need to add a corner point. You can convert a curved anchor point to a corner point by holding down the ⌥ *alt* key and clicking on it. Click to place another point and this will create a straight line segment between the two points. Now, if you hold down the ⌘ *ctrl* key you can temporarily access the direct selection tool and reposition the points. When you click on a point or a segment with this tool, the handles are displayed and you can use the direct selection tool to adjust these and refine the curve shape.

With the 'v' shape (Figure 9.50) you can further practice making curved segments and adding corner points. These should be placed whenever you intend the next segment to break with the angle of the previous segment. In the niches of the 'v' shape, hold down the ⌥ *alt* key and drag to define the predictor handle for the next curve shape.

Pen tool shortcuts summary

To edit a pen path, you use the ⌘ *ctrl* key to temporarily convert the pen tool to the direct selection tool, which you use to click on or marquee anchor points and reposition them. You use the ⌥ *alt* key to convert a curve anchor point to a corner anchor point and vice versa. If you want to convert a corner point to a curve, ⌥ *alt*+mouse down and drag. To change the direction of one handle only, you ⌥ *alt* drag on a handle. To add a new anchor point to an active path, simply click on a segment with the pen tool, and to remove an anchor point, you click on it again.

Rubber Band mode

There are a number of occasions where I find it necessary to use the pen tool to define an outline and then convert the pen path to a selection. In the end, the pen tool really is the easiest way to define many outlines and create a selection from the path. One way to make the learning process somewhat easier is to switch on the 'Rubber Band' option which is hidden away in the Pen Options on the pen tool Options bar (Figure 9.51). In Rubber Band mode, you will see the segments you are drawing take shape as you move the mouse cursor, and not just when you mouse down again to define the next path point. As I say, this mode of operation can make path drawing easier to learn, but for some people it can become rather distracting once you have got the basic hang of how to follow a complex outline using the various pen tools.

Editing path segments

You can edit a straight line or curved segment by selecting the direct selection tool, clicking on the segment and dragging. With a straight segment the anchor points at either end will move in unison. With a curved segment, the anchor points will remain fixed and you can manipulate the shape of the curve as you drag with the direct selection tool.

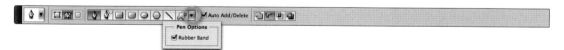

Figure 9.51 The easiest way to get accustomed to working with the pen tool is to go to the Pen Options in the Options bar, mouse down on the Pen Options (circled) and check the 'Rubber Band' option.

Hiding/showing layer/vector masks

You can temporarily hide/show a layer mask by *Shift*-clicking on the layer mask icor. Also, clicking a vector mask's icon in the Layers panel hides the path itself. Once hidden, hover over it with the cursor and it will temporarily become visible. Click it again to restore the visibility.

Vector masks

A vector mask is just like an image layer mask, except the mask is described using a vector path (Figure 9.52). A vector mask is therefore resolution-independent and can be transformed or scaled in size without any loss in quality, and the mask can be edited using the pen path or shape tools. To add a vector mask from an existing path, go to the Paths panel, select a path to make it active, and choose Layer ⇨ Add Vector Mask ⇨ Current Path. Alternatively, you can go to the Masks panel and click on the Add Vector Mask button (see Figure 9.21 on page 434).

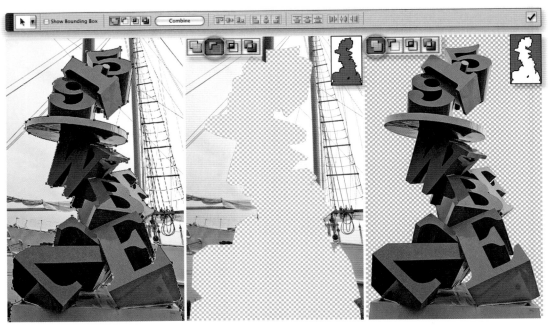

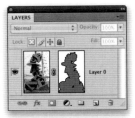

Figure 9.52 A vector mask can be created from a currently active path such as the one displayed here in the image on the left. The path mode influences what is hidden and what is revealed when the path is converted into a vector mask. If a path has been created in the 'Subtract from path area' mode (as in the middle example), the area inside the path outline is hidden. If the path is created in the 'Add to path area' mode (as in the right-hand example) the gray fill in the path icon represents the hidden areas, where everything outside the path outline is hidden. However, it is very easy to alter the path mode. Select the path selection tool (shown above), and click on the path to make all the path points active. You can then click on the path mode buttons in the Options bar to switch between the different path modes.

Isolating an object from the background

Let's now look at a practical example of where you might use a vector path to mask an object in preference to using a pixel layer mask. Remember, one of the benefits of using a vector mask is that you can use the direct path selection tool to manipulate the path points and fine-tune the outline of the vector mask.

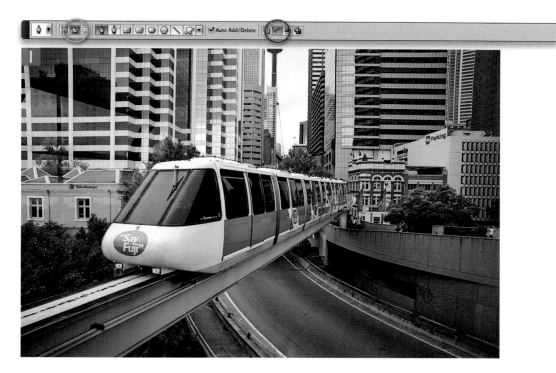

1 I used the pen tool here to define the outline of the train and the mono rail. Note that the pen tool was in the Path mode (circled in green in the Options bar). Also, because I wanted to create a path that selected everything outside of the enclosed path, I checked the Subtract from Path Area button (circled in red) before I began drawing the path. When the path was complete, I went to the Paths panel and dragged the work path down to the Create New Path button, which converted it into a permanent path that could be saved with the image. It is important to remember here that a work path is only temporary and will be overwritten as soon as you deselect the work path and try to create a new work path.

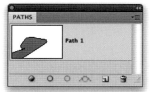

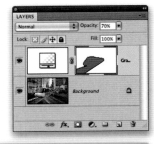

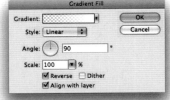

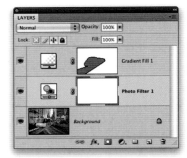

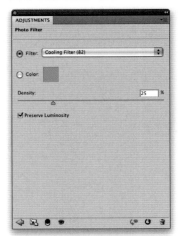

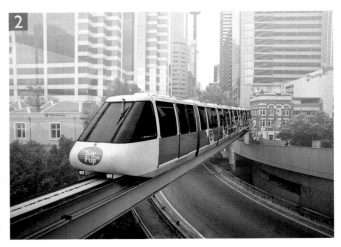

2 With the work path active and white as the foreground color in the tools panel, I clicked on the Add New Adjustment Layer button in the Layers panel and selected the Gradient Fill option. I chose the foreground color (white) to transparency gradient and added this as a linear gradient using the settings shown here. This added a fog effect to the scene and, as you can see, the vector mask prevented the Gradient Fill adjustment from being applied to the train and the mono rail.

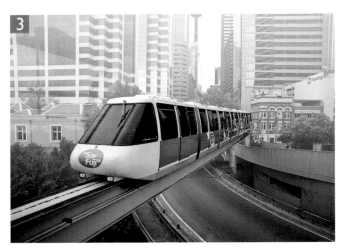

3 To make the scene look a little more like winter, I added a Photo Filter adjustment sandwiched between the Background layer and the Gradient Fill layer, then selected a cooling filter from the Filter menu options.

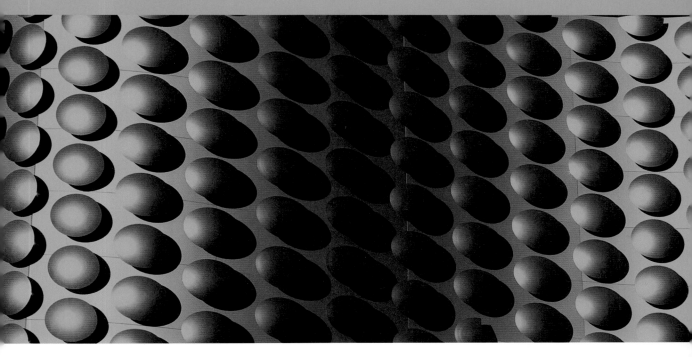

Chapter 10

Essential Filters for Photo Editing

One of the key factors that can be attributed to Photoshop's success has been the program's support for plug-in filters. A huge industry of third-party companies has grown in response to the needs of users wanting extra features within Photoshop. Instead of covering all the hundred or more filters that are in Photoshop, I have concentrated here on just those filters that I believe are useful for photographic work, everyday production jobs and creative output. I will also show you ways you can use the Smart Filters feature to extend your filtering options.

RGB only filters

You will notice that most of the effects filters work in RGB mode only. This is because they can have such a dramatic effect on the pixel values, and would easily send colors way out of the CMYK gamut. To unleash the full creative power of Photoshop plug-ins, you really do need to edit in RGB mode.

16-bit filters

Photoshop supports a limited number of filters in 16-bit. However, most of the essential filters, such as those used to carry out standard production image processing routines, can all run in 16-bit.

Filter essentials

Most Photoshop filters provide a preview dialog with slider settings that you can adjust, while some of the more sophisticated plug-ins (such as the Lens Correction filter) are like applications operating within Photoshop. These have a modal dialog interface, which means that whenever the Filter dialog is open Photoshop is pushed into the background, which can usefully free up already-assigned keyboard shortcuts. With so many effects filters to choose from in Photoshop, there are plenty enough to experiment with. The danger is that you can all too easily get lost endlessly searching through all the different filter settings. There is not enough room to describe every Photoshop filter here, but we shall look at a few of the ways filters can enhance an image, highlighting some of the more useful ones plus a few personal favorites.

Blur filters

There are 11 different blur filters in the Filter ➪ Blursub-menu and each will allow you to blur an image differently. You don't really want to bother with the basic Blur and Blur More filters, but what follows is a brief description of some of the blur filters and why I think you will find them useful.

Adding a Radial Blur or Spin Blur to a photo

The Radial Blur can do a very good job of creating blurred spinning motion effects. For example, the Zoom blur mode, shown in Figure 10.1, can do a neat simulation of a zooming camera lens, while the Spin blur mode, shown in Figure 10.2, can be used to apply a circular spin effect (I also used a Spin Radial Blur to add movement to the car wheels in Step 3 on page 491). The Radial Blur filter may sometimes appear to be sluggish, but it is after all carrying out major distortions of the image. For this reason you are offered a choice of render settings. For top quality results, select the Best mode, but if you just want to see a quick preview of the whole image area select the Draft mode option.

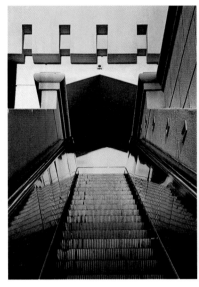 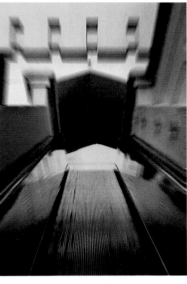 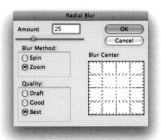

Figure 10.1 When using the Radial Blur filter in Zoom mode, you can create fast zoom lens effects such as in the example shown here on the right. You can also drag the center point in the filter preview dialog to approximately match the center of interest in the image you are about to filter.

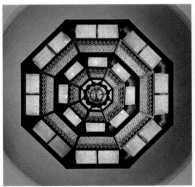 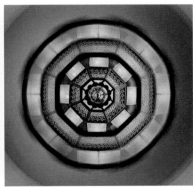 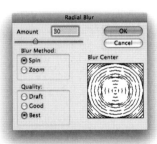

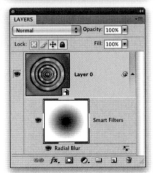

Figure 10.2 When you use the Radial Blur filter in Spin mode, you can apply a circular spin blur effect such as the example shown on the right. Again, you can drag the center point in the Filter dialog to match the center of interest of the image you are about to filter.

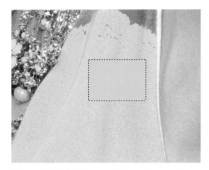

Figure 10.3 The Average Blur can be used to merge the pixels within a selection to create a solid color which can then be used to take a sample color measurement of the average color within that selection area.

Gaussian Blur

The Gaussian Blur is a good general purpose blur filter which can be used for many purposes from blurring areas of an image to softening the edges of a mask.

Average Blur

The Average Blur simply averages the colors in an image or a selection. At first glance it doesn't do a lot, but it is a useful filter to have at your disposal. Let's say you want to analyze the color of some fabric to create a color swatch for a catalog. The Average filter merges all the pixels in a selection to create a solid color and you can then use this to sample with the eyedropper tool to create a new Swatch sample color (see Figure 10.3).

Motion Blur

The Motion Blur filter can be used to create an effective impression of blurred movement. It adds a linear blur that spreads in both directions and you can use the Filter dialog sliders to control the angle of the blur as well as the distance of the blur spread. In the example shown on these pages, I used the Motion Blur filter to add blurred movement to a static photograph of a car.

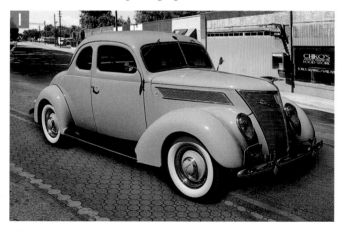

1 This shows a photograph of a car that has been cut out and placed as a new layer against a street scene. While the perspective and shadowing may look correct, we don't get any sense of movement in this picture.

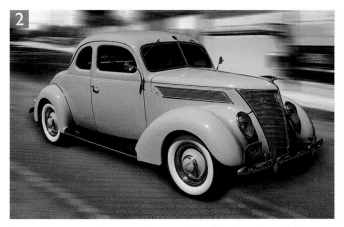

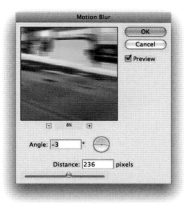

2 Next, I converted the Background layer to a Smart Filter layer (essentially a Smart Object), chose Filter ⇨ Blur ⇨ Motion Blur and applied a 236 pixel blur at an angle of −3°. This blurred the entire backdrop layer and began to give the impression of movement in the picture.

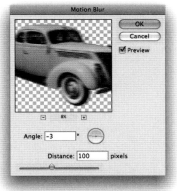

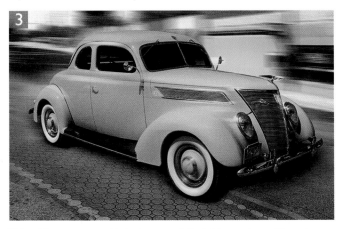

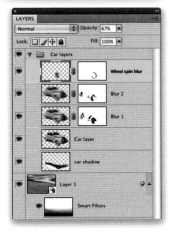

3 To get the car movement to look more realistic, I did several more things. I applied a gradient mask to the background Smart Object layer so that the motion blur appeared strongest in the distance. I then duplicated the car cut-out layer and applied a 100 pixel Motion Blur filter. I also duplicated this layer and applied a 400 pixel Motion Blur filter. I moved both layers slightly so that they trailed behind the car, faded the opacity of the softer blur layer and added a layer mask to each so that I could selectively remove some of the Motion Blur areas. Lastly, I selected each of the wheels, copied each one to a new layer, used a Free Transform to make them circular and then used the Spin Radial Blur filter to add circular movement. I then reversed the transform on each layer so that I ended up with a convincing circular spin on each wheel.

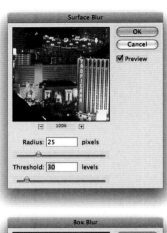

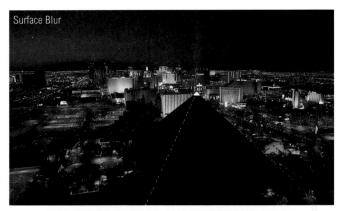

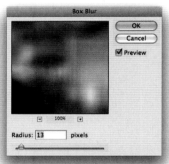

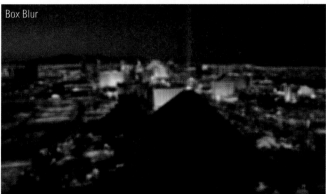

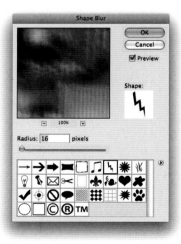

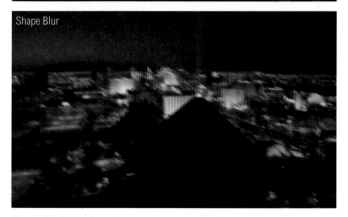

Figure 10.4 This shows, from top to bottom, the Surface Blur, Box Blur and Shape Blur filters.

Surface Blur

This might be considered an edge preserving blur filter. The Radius adjustment is identical to that used in the Gaussian Blur filter; the higher the Radius, the more blurred the image will become. But it is the Threshold slider that determines the weighting given to the neighboring pixels and whether these become blurred or not. Basically, as you increase the Threshold this extends the range of pixels (relative to each other) that become blurred. So as you increase the Threshold, the flatter areas of tone are the first to become blurred and the high contrast edges remain less blurred (until you increase the Threshold more).

Box Blur

The Box Blur uses a simple algorithm to produce a square shape blur. It is a fairly fast filter and could be useful for creating certain special effects.

Shape Blur

The Shape Blur filter allows you to specify any shape you like as a kernel with which to create a blur effect. You can then adjust the blur radius accordingly. In Figure 10.4 (bottom image) I selected a lightning bolt shape and this enabled me to simulate a camera shake effect with this filter. The Shape Blur is no match for the power of the Lens Blur filter, but it is nonetheless a versatile and creative tool.

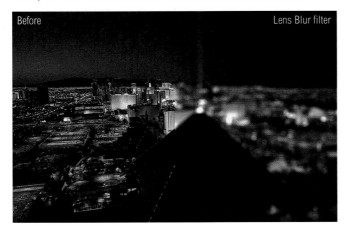

Before   Lens Blur filter

Fade command

Filter effects can be further refined by fading them after you have applied the filter. The Fade command is referred to at various places in the book (you can also fade image adjustments and brush strokes, etc.). Choose Edit ⇨ Fade Filter and experiment with different blending modes. The Fade command is almost like an adjustment layer feature, but without the versatility and ability to undo later. It makes use of the fact that the previous undo version of the image is stored in the undo buffer and allows you to calculate many different blends but without the time-consuming expense of having to duplicate the layer first. Having said all that, history offers an alternative approach whereby if you filter an image, or make several filtrations, you can return to the original state and then paint in the future (filtered) state using the history brush or make a fill using the filtered history state (providing Non-linear History has been enabled in the History panel options).

Figure 10.5 The best way to learn how to use the blur filters discussed here is to experiment with an image like the one shown here (which is available on the DVD). In this night-time scene there are lots of small points of light; you can use this image example to get a clear idea of how the Specular Highlights and Iris controls work, and observe how they affect the appearance of the blur in the photograph.

Smart Filters/Smart Objects

When you go to the Filter menu and choose 'Convert for Smart Filters', you are basically doing the same thing as when you create a Smart Object. So, if a layer or group of layers have already been converted to a Smart Object, there is no need to choose 'Convert for Smart Filters'.

Third-party plug-ins

With third-party plug-ins, you will find that those plug-ins that have been recently updated for CS4 should have an embedded smart filter marker that will automatically make them compatible with Smart Filters in CS4. If that is not the case, then enabling all filters (as described on page 498) will help your get around such restrictions, but with the proviso that any filter you apply as a Smart Filter must be a 'value-based' filter if it is to fit in successfully with a Smart Filter workflow.

Smart Filters

For years now Photoshop users have requested the ability to apply live filters, the same way as you can apply image adjustments as adjustment layers. Now that we have Smart Filters, I do wonder just how many people actually use this feature on a regular basis. Having said that, Smart Filters can be particularly useful when working with the blur filters discussed in this chapter, because you may very often want the ability to re-edit the blur amount. I have already shown a couple of examples of Smart Filters in use with the Spin Blur and Motion Blur filters, plus there is a further example coming up later on pages 500–501 where I show how to apply the Lens Blur filter as a Smart Filter. You can switch Smart Filters on or off, combine two or more filter effects, mask the overall Smart Filter combination as well as adjust the Smart Filter blending options. These allow you to control the opacity and blend modes for individual filters. As I have shown below in Figure 10.6, you can also group one or more layers into a Smart Object and filter the combined layers as a single Smart Object layer.

Double-click to edit a Smart Object

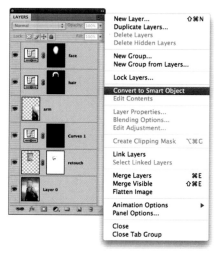

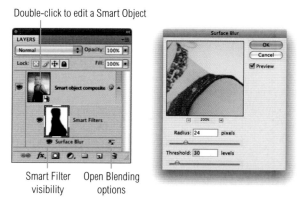

Smart Filter visibility   Open Blending options

Figure 10.6 You can make a selection of more than one layer in a document and convert these into a Smart Object. From there you can add filter effects that will be applied as Smart Filters to a composite version of all the selected layers. The multi-layered image can still be accessed and edited by double-clicking the Smart Object thumbnail.

Applying Smart Filters to pixel layers

Smart Filters are essentially filter effects that are applied to a Smart Object. The process begins with you converting a layer or group of layers to a Smart Object, or selecting a layer and choosing Filter ⇨ Convert for Smart Filters. Smart Filters allow you to apply most types of filter adjustments non-destructively. The following steps provide a brief introduction to working with Smart Filters in which I show how you can also use Smart Filters to apply Shadows/Highlights adjustments non-destructively.

The appeal of Smart Filters is that you can apply any filter non-destructively to an image in Photoshop, but this flexibility comes at the cost of larger file sizes (4 to 5 times bigger), a slower workflow switching between the Smart Object and parent documents, and longer save times. Or at least this has been my experience when working with a fairly fast computer with lots of RAM memory. This is not the first time we have come across speed problems like this: some Photoshop techniques are a little ahead of themselves and we have to wait for the computer hardware to become faster before we can use them comfortably. While Smart Filtering does offer true non-destructive filtering, it is a technique you probably want to use sparingly. In this book I have highlighted a few of the situations where Smart Filters may offer some benefit, like the example shown on pages 500–501 where I blurred the Backdrop layer.

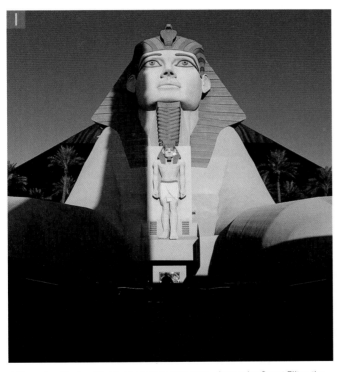

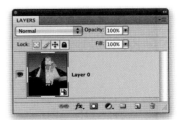

1 To apply a Shadow/Highlight adjustment as a non-destructive Smart Filter, the Background layer (or a group of layers) must first be converted to a Smart Object. To do this I went to the Filter menu and chose 'Convert for Smart Filters'. This converted the Background layer to a normal, Layer 0 layer.

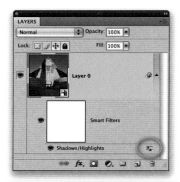

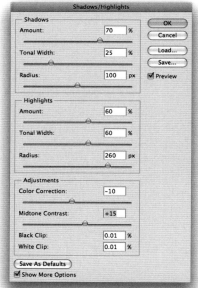

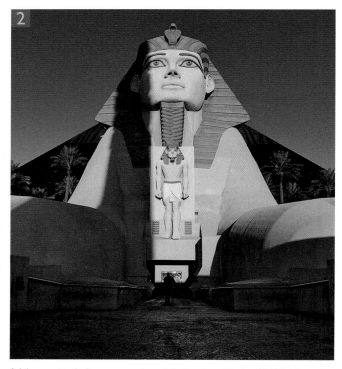

2 I then went to the Image menu, chose Adjustments ⇨ Shadows/Highlights and applied the settings shown here. As you can see, I mostly used the Shadows/Highlights adjustment to bring out more detail in the shadows. If you check the Layers panel you will notice that the Shadows/Highlights adjustment added a Smart Filter layer to the layer stack. I could now click the eye icon to switch the effect on or off, and when I double-clicked on the Smart Filter blend options button (circled), this opened the Blend Options dialog which allowed me to reduce the opacity of the Smart Filter adjustment (plus I could also change the blend mode).

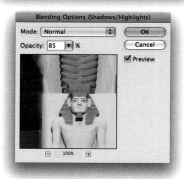

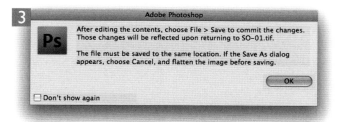

3 I then double-clicked the Smart Object layer to edit the layer contents separately. This opened the dialog shown here, reminding me that I would need to save the edited Smart Object contents for the changes to be reflected in the master document.

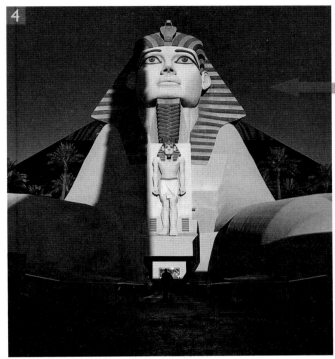

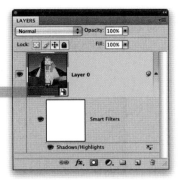

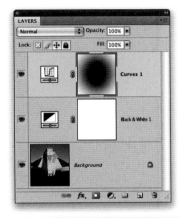

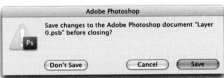

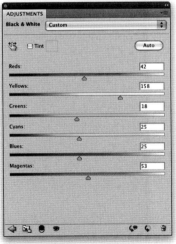

4 This shows the original Smart Object image document, but without the Shadow/Highlight Smart Filter adjustment. I could now edit this document as one would do normally. If you look at the Layer panel for the Smart Object you will notice that I added a Black & White adjustment layer to convert the image to monochrome, plus a Curves adjustment layer to apply a darkening vignette to the edges of the photograph. That pretty much completed all the work I wanted to carry out on the Smart Object. When I closed the document window a dialog box prompted me to choose 'Save'. As was pointed out in Step 3, you must do this each time in order to save the Smart Object adjustments back to the parent document.

Enabling Lens Blur as a Smart Filter

Smart Filters are mainly intended for use with value-based filters only, such as the Add Noise or Unsharp Mask filter. They are not intended for use with filters such as Lens Blur (as shown here) because the Lens Blur can sometimes make calls to an external alpha channel and, if the selected alpha channel were to be deleted at some point, this would prevent the Smart Filter from working.

However, so long as you are aware of this limitation, it is still possible to enable Smart Filters to work with the Lens Blur filter. Go to the File ⇨ Scripts menu in Photoshop CS4 and choose Browse.... This opens a system navigation window and from there you will want to use the following directory path: Adobe Photoshop CS4 folder/Scripting Guide/Sample Scripts/Javascript and select: EnableAllPluginsforSmartFilters.jsx. Once you have located this script, you can click 'Load' or double-click to run it, which will then show the Script Alert dialog shown in Figure 10.7. If you wish to proceed, click 'Yes'. The Lens Blur, as well as all other filters will now be accessible for use as Smart Filters. If you want to turn off this behavior, run through the same above steps and click 'No' when the Script Alert dialog shows.

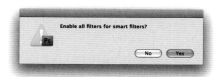

Figure 10.7 The Script Alert dialog.

Lens Blur

If you want to make a photograph appear realistically out of focus, it is not just a matter of making the detail and the image more blurred. Consider for a moment how a lens works. The camera lens focuses an object to form an image that is made up of circular points on the film/sensor surface. When the radius of these points is very small, the image is considered sharp and when the radius is large, the image appears to be out of focus, plus it is particularly noticeable the way bright highlights tend to blow out and how you can see the shape of the camera lens iris in the blurred highlight points. The Lens Blur filter has the potential to mimic the way a camera lens forms an optical image. The best way to understand how it works is to look at the shape of the bright lights in the night-time scene in Figure 10.5, which shows the image before and after I had applied the Lens Blur filter (you will find this image on the DVD).

The dialog looks intimidating, but the main controls to concentrate on are the Radius slider, which controls the amount of blur that is applied to the image, and the Specular Highlights controls that can be used to control the lens flare. If you want to add lens flare, increase the Brightness slightly and carefully lower the Threshold amount by one or two levels and check to see how this looks in the preview area. Usually it is better to have the More Accurate button checked, if you want to predict how the Lens Blur effect will look.

Depth of field effects

With the Lens Blur filter you can also use a mask channel to define the areas where you wish to selectively apply the Lens Blur. This allows you to create shallow depth of field effects, such as in the example shown on the right. Basically, you can use a simple gradient, or a more complex mask, to define the areas that you wish to remain sharp and those that you want to have appear out of focus. You can then load the channel mask as a 'Depth Map' in the Lens Blur dialog and use the Blur Focal Distance slider to determine which areas remain sharpest.

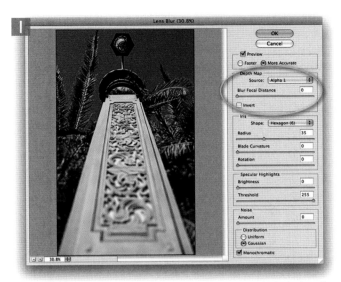

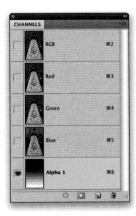

1 In this example, I created a linear gradient mask channel called Alpha 1, where the gradient went from white to black. I then loaded the Alpha 1 channel in the Lens Blur filter dialog to use this as a depth map. With the Alpha 1 channel selected, I could adjust the Blur Focal Distance slider (circled) to determine the point where I wanted the image to remain sharp and not have the Lens Blur affect this portion of the image.

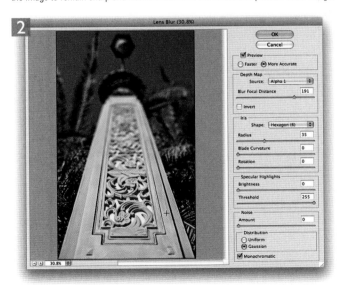

2 Another way to use a depth map is to click in the preview area to set the point where the image should be sharpest. Basically, the degree of Lens Blur is linked to the gray values in the Depth Map source channel.

Iris shape

The Iris shape controls should be regarded as fine-tuning sliders that govern the shape of the out-of-focus points in the picture. You can select from a menu list of different iris shapes and then use the Blade Curvature and Rotation sliders to tweak the iris shape. The results of these adjustments will be most noticeable in the blown-out highlight areas.

Applying Lens Blur to a composite image

To finish off this section on the blur filters and Smart Filters, here is a short step-by-step example showing how I applied the Lens Blur filter as a Smart Object to make the background in this composite image appear out of focus.

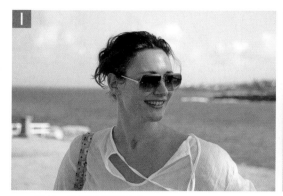

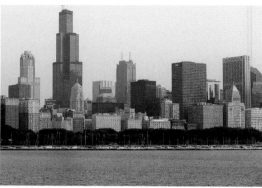

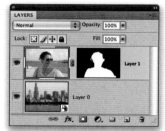

1 For the following steps I took two separate photographs and created a mask for the outline of my wife in the picture on the left, and placed this as a new layer above a photograph of the Chicago skyline.

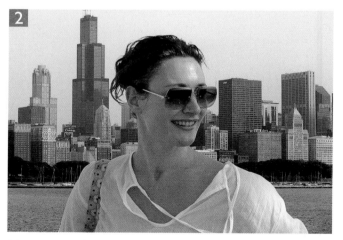

2 As you can see, when the two images were merged, the buildings in the background looked too sharp. So in preparation for applying the Lens Blur filter, I selected the Chicago skyline layer, went to the Filter menu and chose 'Convert for Smart Filters'. This was essentially the same thing as choosing Layer ⇨ Smart Objects ⇨ Convert to Smart Object. Do read the sidebar notes on enabling Smart Objects to work with the Lens Blur filter (on page 498), before proceeding to the next step.

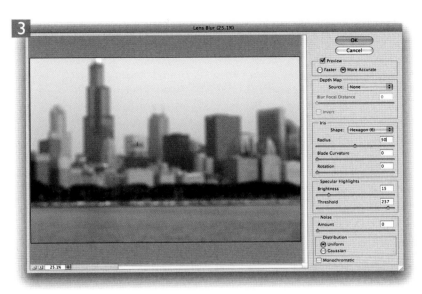

3 To make the background appear out of focus, I selected the Chicago skyline, Smart Filter layer and chose Filter ⇨ Blur ⇨ Lens Blur. Here, I adjusted the Specular Highlights Threshold setting, bringing it down just enough until the highlights started to bloom. I then adjusted the Specular Highlights Brightness setting to create the desired amount of lens flare. The Iris Radius slider was used to control the width of the blur (the effect of this adjustment was particularly noticeable in the specular highlights).

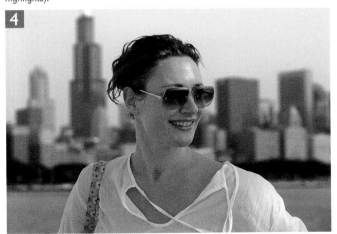

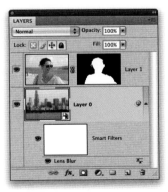

4 This shows the finished result, where you can see the Lens Blur Smart Filter attached to the Smart Object layer. The advantage of this approach is that I retained the ability to re-edit the Lens Blur filter settings and vary the background layer focus.

Other 'Add Noise' options

'Add Noise' options are already included in a lot of Photoshop features such as the Brush options, Gradient Fill layers and the Lens Blur filter (See Figure 10.8).

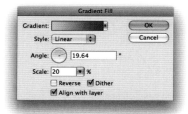

Figure 10.8 A number of Photoshop dialogs contain a Dither option. This shows the Gradient Fill dialog, where you would normally be advised to keep the Dither option checked so that a small amount of noise is added to prevent any banding.

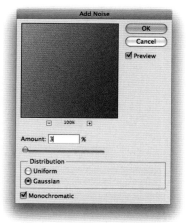

Adding noise to disguise retouching

As well as removing noise you sometimes need to actually add more noise. When you use Photoshop to retouch a photograph you may at times find yourself painting with what might be called 'pure pixels'. If you are cloning pieces from one part of the picture to another then you are probably not going to run into too many problems. But if you use the paint brush tool and apply gradients or blurs to parts of a photograph, there can be a mismatch where the smoothness of the pixels painted using Photoshop does not match the texture in the rest of the image. You should therefore consider selectively adding noise whenever you add a gradient or paint with Photoshop. The Add Noise filter (shown in Figure 10.9) is well worth remembering any time you wish to hide banding or make Photoshop painting work appear to merge better with the grain of a scanned original.

The 'Uniform' option applies a standard, simple noise pattern, while the 'Gaussian' option adds a more pronounced noise effect that appears a lot more random than the 'Uniform' option. The noise effect will normally be random in all color channels, unless you check the Monochromatic box, which removes the random color variation from the noise filter.

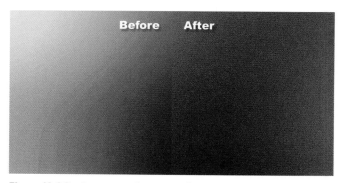

Figure 10.9 Banding can sometimes occur when you draw a gradient or apply a heavy Gaussian Blur filtration. The best way to hide banding is to add a small amount of noise via the Noise ⇨ Add Noise filter. This example shows a close-up of a gradient. The before view on the left has a lot of banding, but the right half shows that the banding was eradicated after using the Add Noise filter settings shown here.

Adding noise to create a grain effect

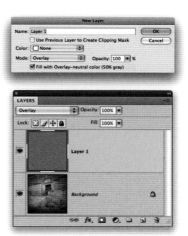

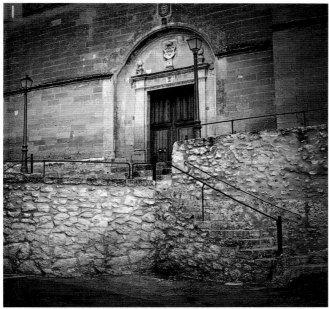

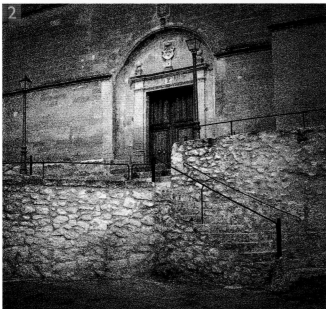

1 To add noise on a separate layer, I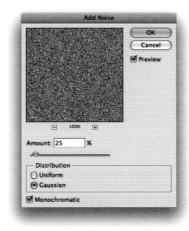
alt-clicked the Add New Layer button in the Layers panel. This popped a New Layer dialog, where I selected 'Overlay' as the blending mode. You will notice that I was now able to check the Fill with Overlay-neutral color (50% gray) box. Choosing this blending mode meant the new layer had no visible impact on the underlying layer.

2 I was then able to create a film grain effect by applying the Add Noise filter to this layer. To keep the noise neutral, I selected the Monochromatic option in the Add Noise dialog.

Chromatic aberration and Vignetting

Some lenses will suffer from other kinds of optical defects, such as chromatic aberration, which can sometimes be noticed along high contrast edges. You can remove these quite easily using the two chromatic slider controls in the Chromatic aberration section of the Lens Correction dialog. You may also sometimes notice a darkening vignette towards the edges of a picture when you are shooting with an ultra wide-angle lens. The Vignette controls allow you to compensate for this as well. Or if you prefer, you can use them to introduce a vignette. These topics are also covered on pages 194–197.

Set Lens Default

If the image you are editing contains EXIF metadata describing the lens, focal length and *f* stop used, you can click on the Set Lens Default button to archive the settings used. These will be available in the future as a 'Lens Default' option in the Settings menu.

Edge pixels

As you apply Lens Correction Transform adjustments, the shape of the image may change. The Scale slider can be used to crop a picture as you apply a correction. If you prefer not to do this (or wish to reduce the scale), there is the problem of how to render the outer pixels. The default setting uses the Edge Extension mode to extend the edge pixels. This may be fine with skies or flat color backdrops, but is otherwise quite ugly and distracting, although extending the pixels may make it easier to apply the healing brush in these areas.

Lens Corrections

Photographers are always striving for optical perfection but sadly not all lenses are capable of delivering the goods. Fortunately, the Lens Correction filter in Photoshop offers several ways that you can correct images that suffer from different types of optical distortion. The most obvious problems are the pin cushion and barrel lens effects, which are all too common when shooting with lower quality lenses. You can use the distort tool to drag toward or away from the center of the image, to adjust the amount of distortion in either direction. Or, you can use the Remove Distortion slider, which I find offers more precise control.

The rotate tool can be used to straighten photographs. Drag with the tool on the preview to define what should be a correct horizontal or vertical line and the image will rotate to align correctly. You can also adjust the rotation in the Transform section of the Filter dialog, but I also recommend you click in the Angle field (circled in Figure 10.10) and use the up and down keyboard arrow keys to nudge the rotation in either direction by small increments.

The grid pattern can prove useful for helping you judge the alignment of the image and you can also use the move grid tool to shift the placement of the grid. The grid controls at the bottom of the Lens Correction filter dialog also enable you to change the grid color and dynamically adjust the grid spacing, plus toggle showing or hiding the grid.

The Transform controls let you adjust the vertical and horizontal perspective. These offer an immense amount of control with which to correct the perspective view of a photograph, such as the vertical keystone effect you get when pointing the camera up to photograph a building, or the horizontal perspective you get when photographing a subject from the side instead of dead center. You should only need to use these controls where you need your subject to appear perfectly square on to the camera, such as in architectural photography (see the before and after examples shown in Figure 10.11).

Lens Correction tools: distort tool; rotate tool; move grid tool; hand tool; zoom tool

Lens Correction preset settings

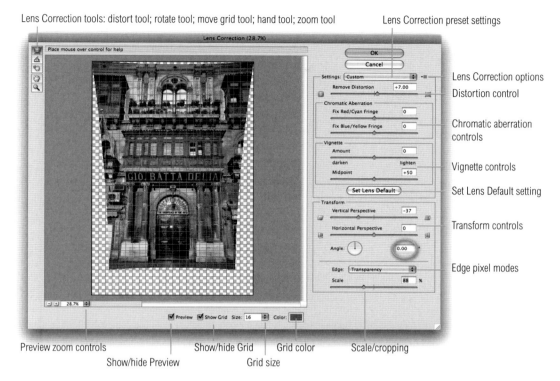

Lens Correction options

Distortion control

Chromatic aberration controls

Vignette controls

Set Lens Default setting

Transform controls

Edge pixel modes

Preview zoom controls

Show/hide Preview

Show/hide Grid

Grid size

Grid color

Scale/cropping

Figure 10.10 The Lens Correction filter dialog

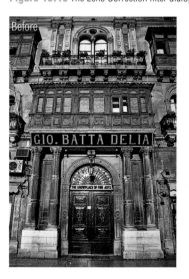

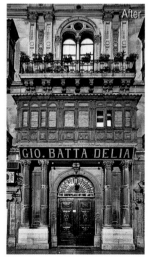

Figure 10.11 The Lens Correction filter was applied to the before image to correct for the barrel lens distortion in the original image. I also aligned the vertical lines of the building to the grid in the dialog shown in Figure 10.10. The combined Lens Correction settings (excepting the Transform settings) can be saved as presets via the Lens Correction options to the designated Settings folder. These presets can be associated with the lenses that you use most often and, if saved to the correct folder, will appear listed in the Lens Correction preset settings menu.

Rapid filter access

There are around 100 filters in the Filter menu. That's a lot of plug-ins to choose from, of which many are used to produce artistic effects. The Filter Gallery makes 47 of these filters accessible from the one dialog. The following filter categories are available: Artistic; Brush Strokes; Distort; Sketch; Stylize; Texture (but note that not all the filters in the above categories are included in the Filter Gallery).

Filter Gallery

To use the Filter Gallery, select an image, choose Filter Gallery from the Filter menu and click on various filter effect icons revealed in the expanded filter folders. The filter icons provide a visual clue as to the outcome of the filter, and as you click on these, the filter effect can be previewed in the preview panel area. This gives you a nice large preview for many of the creative Photoshop filters. As you can see in Figure 10.12, you can combine more than one filter at a time and preview how these will look when applied in sequence. To add a new filter, click on the New Effect Layer button at the bottom. As you click on the effect layers you can edit the individual filter settings. To remove a filter effect layer, click on the Delete button.

Filter Gallery preview

Collapse/expand filter effects   Filter effect settings

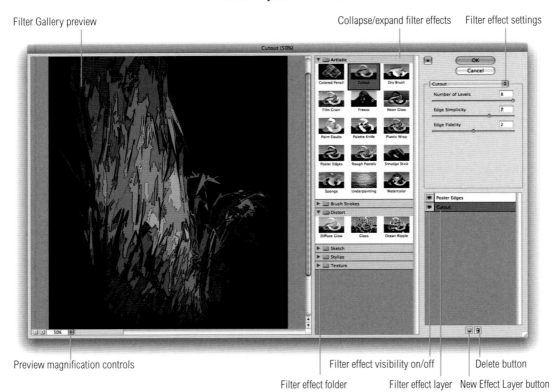

Preview magnification controls

Filter effect visibility on/off   Delete button

Filter effect folder   Filter effect layer   New Effect Layer button

Figure 10.12 The Filter Gallery.

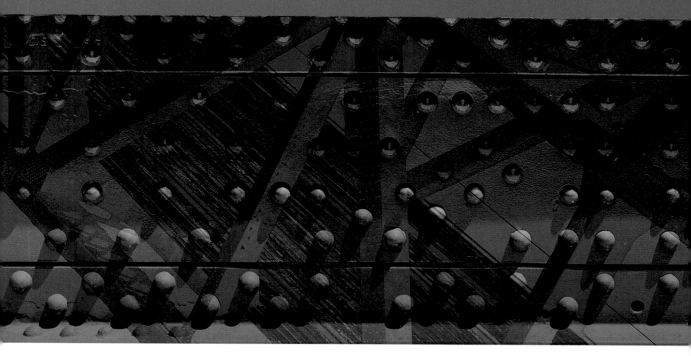

Chapter 11

Image Management

O ne of the consequences of working with digital images in Photoshop is that you will soon find yourself struggling to cope with an ever-growing collection of image files. In order to address this, you'll want something more than the system folder browser to preview the files on your computer system. At a minimum you need some kind of file browser program that will allow you to preview images easily, choose which ones you want to open in Photoshop, and carry out basic file management tasks such as rating the images you like most and adding metadata.

Bridge alternatives

Operating systems may in future offer better image browsing tools and on the PC platform it is interesting to note how the latest Vista operating system contains a photo browser that offers improved image navigation for photographs. With the latest Macintosh 10.5 operating system you can use the spacebar to quickly preview selected images, or use the Cover Flow View folder navigation mode to visually inspect the contents of a folder. In the meantime, there are several dedicated file browser programs on the market that will help you manage your images better such as Extensis Portfolio™ and PhotoMechanic™. There is also Expression Media™, which is more than just a file browser; it is also a sophisticated database cataloging program that will allow you to manage your images efficiently and quickly. More recently, we have seen the emergence of digital photography workflow programs such as Apple's Aperture™ and Adobe Photoshop Lightroom™, which are designed to provide a complete workflow management solution from digital raw processing through to image library management.

The Bridge solution

Bridge is included with Photoshop, as well as being part of the Creative Suite package, and is best described as a dedicated file browser program. Bridge integrates smoothly with the Adobe Camera Raw plug-in to let you work directly with your raw image files within Photoshop (assuming your camera's raw format is supported). It may not be as sophisticated as some of the other programs mentioned in the sidebar, but it does provide you with a direct way to manage your photographs via Photoshop. On the plus side, Bridge comes free, it integrates nicely with Adobe Camera Raw and contains most of the tools you need to import, raw process and manage your images, plus it can work with the automation tools in Photoshop, such as Photomerge and Image Processor. Bridge CS4 does feature some neat and useful improvements over previous versions. The interface is better and offers easy workspace switching, plus we have one-click full screen previews and a revised Collections feature. However, there are a few negatives. Even though Bridge's performance has been improved (especially when working with large numbers of images), it still doesn't seem to perform quite as fast as some other browser and cataloging programs. There are now built-in Web and PDF output features, but these remain as slow as ever, and inputting metadata and keywords is still an awkward process.

Configuring the General preferences

First things first, let's go to the Bridge preferences (which are located in the Edit menu in Windows and the Bridge menu in Mac OS X) and look at the General settings. These govern the Bridge interface appearance and basic behavior. The first section contains the Appearance controls where you can adjust the general user interface brightness and below that the brightness for the image Content and Preview panel areas. These are normally set quite light and my preference is to make both a little darker (the Figure 11.1 settings were used for all the screen shots shown in this chapter). The Accent Color menu offers a range of color options for accentuating the image highlighting and Bridge menu items, and you'll note that the Default color switches between orange and blue colors, depending on the User Interface Brightness setting.

The Behavior section let's you make Adobe Photo Downloader launch by default whenever a new camera card is inserted (or if the camera is connected to the computer directly). The 'Double-click Edits Camera Raw settings in Bridge' option allows you to override the default behavior and forces Bridge to be the program that always hosts the Camera Raw plug-in. The '⌘ ctrl-click Opens the Loupe When Previewing or Reviewing' option applies to the Preview panel and Review modes so that the loupe only shows when the ⌘ ctrl key is held down. Meanwhile, the Bridge program maintains a list of most recently visited folders to enable fast and easy access. The default number is 10, but you can make this any number you want. The Favorites section contains checkboxes that allow you to select which items you want to see appear listed in the Favorites panel (see Figure 11.29) and lastly, the Reset button, which can be used to reset all the alert warning dialogs in Bridge.

Open anything

Most files can be opened via Bridge. Well, almost anything. You can think of Bridge as being like an advanced File Navigation dialog for all the programs in the Adobe Creative Suite, although you are not just limited to opening CS4 Creative Suite documents. For example, you can also open things like Word files in the Word program via Bridge, plus you can drag and drop documents from the Bridge window to an external folder or vice versa.

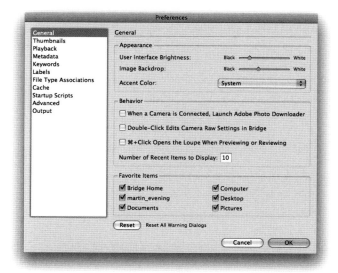

Figure 11.1 The Bridge General preferences.

Adding new folders

New folders can be added by choosing 'New Folder' from the File menu in Bridge [⌘][Shift][N] [ctrl][Shift][N] or [ctrl] right mouse-click in the Content area and choose 'New Folder' from the contextual menu.

Override JPEG Camera Raw settings

You can also edit JPEG and TIFF images via Camera Raw, but be warned that this added capability can also lead to confusion when opening images. Basically, you can use the Camera Raw preferences (page 158) to determine how JPEG and TIFF images are handled. You can disable the ability to open JPEGs and TIFFs via Camera Raw, you can enable automatic opening of all supported JPEGs and TIFFs, and you can enable the automatic opening of only those JPEGs or TIFFs that have previously been processed via Camera Raw. To override these last two preferences, hold down the [Shift] key as you double-click to open the image. If Camera Raw settings have been added to an image previously, these will be applied as you open. If there are no Camera Raw settings associated with an image, it will open directly into Photoshop as normal.

Launching Bridge

There are several ways you can launch Bridge. The most direct method is to click on the Bridge button [⊞] in the Photoshop CS4 Application bar (Figure 11.2). Clicking this button will launch Bridge and open the Bridge window, shown in Figure 11.3, to display the contents of the folder you last visited. You can also launch Bridge by choosing File ⇨ Browse in Bridge... or by using the [⌘][⌥][O] [ctrl][alt][O] or [⌘][Shift][O] [ctrl][Shift][O] shortcuts. Note here that the [⌘][⌥][O] [ctrl][alt][O] command can also be used when you wish to go from Bridge back to Photoshop. To open an image from Bridge, simply double-click a thumbnail and the image will open directly in Photoshop, and if you want the Bridge window to close as you open the image, then simply hold down the [⌥] [alt] key as you double-click. Now, if you refer back to Chapter 3, you will remember how opening Camera Raw files will vary depending on how the preferences have been configured. When you double-click on a raw camera file thumbnail, or multiple thumbnails in Bridge, this normally opens the raw images via the Adobe Camera Raw dialog hosted by Photoshop, and if you go to the File menu in Bridge and choose Open in Camera Raw... ([⌘][R] [ctrl][R]) the images will open via the Camera Raw dialog hosted in Bridge. The subtle distinctions between which application hosts Adobe Camera Raw are elaborated on in Chapter 3 (and also on page 509), but essentially a double-click opens a raw file via Camera Raw in Photoshop, and if you hold down the [Shift] key as you double-click, you can open a raw image bypassing the Camera Raw dialog.

Rotating the thumbnails and preview

You can apply 90° rotations via the Rotate commands in the Bridge Edit menu or use the following keyboard shortcuts: [⌘][[] [ctrl][[] rotates a thumbnail anti-clockwise and [⌘][]] [ctrl][]] rotates a thumbnail clockwise. Alternatively, you can use the Rotate buttons in the top right section of the Bridge window (note that the rotation of the image only takes place when you come to open the actual image).

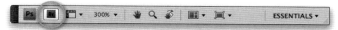

Figure 11.2 The Photoshop Application bar with the Bridge button (circled).

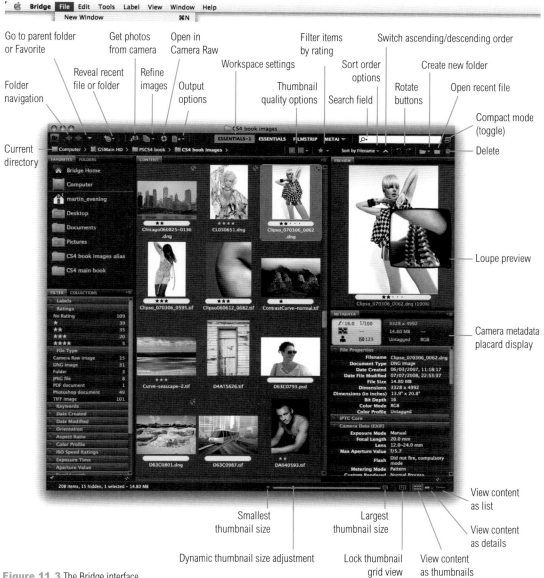

Go to parent folder or Favorite

Get photos from camera

Open in Camera Raw

Filter items by rating

Switch ascending/descending order

Folder navigation

Reveal recent file or folder

Refine images

Workspace settings

Sort order options

Create new folder

Output options

Thumbnail quality options

Search field

Rotate buttons

Open recent file

Compact mode (toggle)

Current directory

Delete

Loupe preview

Camera metadata placard display

View content as list

View content as details

View content as thumbnails

Smallest thumbnail size

Largest thumbnail size

Dynamic thumbnail size adjustment

Lock thumbnail grid view

View content as thumbnails

Figure 11.3 The Bridge interface.

Workspace shortcuts

You can also select workspace settings using the ⌘ F1 ctrl F1 through to ⌘ F6 ctrl F6 shortcuts, where ⌘ F1 ctrl F1 selects the 'Essentials' workspace. Note though that when you create a new workspace setting, this shifts the keyboard shortcut assignment along one in the order the shortcuts appear listed, so the above shortcuts will update each time you save a new workspace setting.

Content panel grid lock

If you click on the 'Lock thumbnail grid view' button (bottom of Figure 11.3) you can lock the thumbnail grid so that as you resize the Content panel area the number of columns always remains locked.

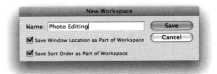

Figure 11.4 To create a new workspace setting, go to the Window menu and choose Workspace ⇨ New Workspace...

Arranging the Bridge contents

You can customize the visibility and order of the various panels and rearrange the Bridge layout to suit your own requirements. For example, you can click on the Workspace settings buttons shown in Figure 11.5, to quickly switch between the different pre-configured Bridge workspaces. These include workspaces that have been designed for different types of Bridge tasks such as Filmstrip viewing or Metadata editing. Or, you can set about creating your own custom workspace layouts. To do this, go to the Window menu where you can highlight a panel item to toggle making it either hidden or visible. Now mouse down on a panel and try dragging it to a new position or grouping arrangement in either of the three main panel areas. The panel sizes can be adjusted in height by dragging the horizontal panel dividers, and you can double-click a Panel tab to quickly collapse the panel contents to show the tab only; double-clicking the Panel tab will expand the panel contents to their former size. If you double-click on a panel divider (as shown in Figure 11.6) you can collapse all the panels in that section plus, if you hit the *Tab* key, you can toggle collapsing or revealing both the side panels. When all this is done, you can save the Bridge layout as a new custom workspace setting. To do this, go to the Window menu and choose Workspace ⇨ New Workspace... This opens the dialog shown in Figure 11.4, where you have the option to include both the window location and sort order setting with the workspace setting. This new workspace setting will now appear first in the list.

You can also rearrange the thumbnails in the Content panel by dragging them to a new position with the mouse. This will change the sort order to 'custom' and the new sort order will remain sticky until such time as you change the sort order again.

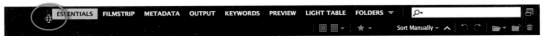

Figure 11.5 This shows an enlarged view of the Workspace settings list. If the list is partially obscured, then mouse down on the divider line circled here and drag out to the left to reveal the full workspace list options.

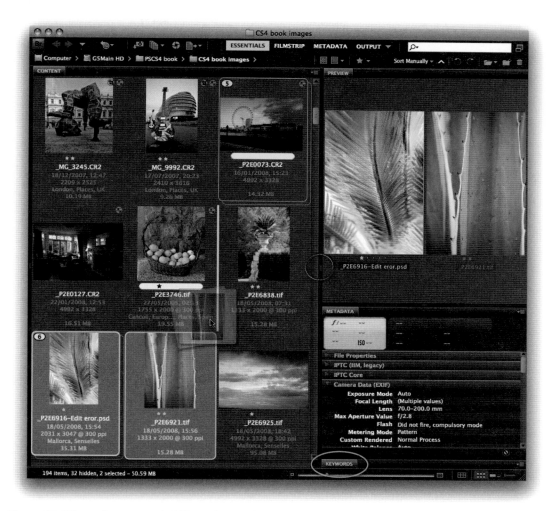

Figure 11.6 The panel arrangements in Bridge can be customized to suit your own preferred way of working, plus the thumbnails can be moved around within the content area, as if you were shuffling photographs on a lightbox. If you double-click on a Panel tab, such as I have done here with the Keywords panel (circled in blue), this collapses the panel to just a tab. The panel sizes can also be adjusted by dragging on the vertical and horizontal dividers, and if you double-click on the divider bar (circled in red) you can toggle showing and hiding the side panel sections. In this example, you can see how some of the images had been grouped into stacks and the Preview panel expanded so that we get to see a large preview of the selected thumbnail (or thumbnails where more than one image is selected in the Content panel).

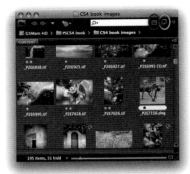

Customizing the panels and content area

Let's now take a look at how the Bridge interface is structured. The Bridge window interface consists of three adjustable sections and these are used to contain the individual Bridge panels, with a main Content panel that is always visible. The individual panels can be adjusted vertically as well as horizontally and placed in any section of the Bridge interface. Meanwhile, the Content panel has Thumbnails, Details and List viewing modes, and you can switch between these by going to the View menu, or by clicking on the buttons in the bottom right section of the Bridge window. By combining different panel layouts with these three Content panel viewing modes, it is possible to achieve a wide variety of workspace layouts. In Figure 11.8 you can see a bare bones layout of the Bridge interface, where the Content panel only is visible in the middle. In Figure 11.9 I show a Bridge layout where the content area remains in the Thumbnails view mode and just the Folders panel is visible, while in Figure 11.10 I added a Metadata panel and switched the content area view to Details mode.

Figure 11.7 To shrink the size of a Bridge window, click on the Switch to Compact Mode button (circled in blue), and click on the button again to restore the window to the original view mode and size. If you click on the button to the left (circled in red), you can compact a window to ultra-compact mode. Note that Compact mode Bridge windows always remain in the foreground, in front of any documents or other programs. To change this behavior, go to the compact Bridge fly-out menu and deselect 'Compact Window Always on Top'.

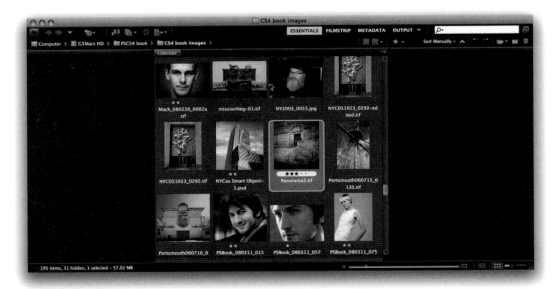

Figure 11.8 Here is a basic view of the three panel sections that make up the Bridge interface, where just the Content panel is visible (you can't hide the Content panel).

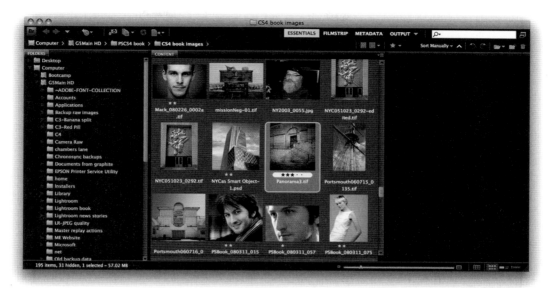

Figure 11.9 One can make more panels visible by going to the Window menu in Bridge and highlighting the ones you wish to add (those panels that are already visible will have a tick mark next to them). Here, I made the Folders panel visible within the left panel section.

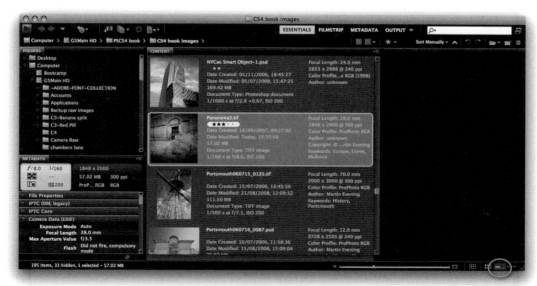

Figure 11.10 Here, I made the Metadata panel visible, adding it to the panel section on the left, plus I switched the content area to the Details mode by clicking on the Details button (circled).

Content panel scrolling

The Content panel has a small menu icon in the top right corner where, if you mouse down, you can select a Horizontal, Vertical or Auto scrolling layout (this is circled in Figure 11.11). You can use this option to force the thumbnails in the Contents panel to scroll vertically (which is the default used for most of the workspace layouts) or scroll horizontally (such as in the Filmstrip workspace layout). If you select Auto, Bridge automatically works out which direction to scroll the thumbnails in.

Bridge workspace examples

Let's now look at just some of the available workspace settings. The Light Table layout shown in Figure 11.11 is useful should you wish to maximize the Content panel size and have it fill the screen. The Filmstrip setting shown in Figure 11.12 (⌘ F2 ctrl F2) is great for editing large photos using a large Preview panel size with a horizontal filmstrip running along the bottom of the window; you can use the left and right keyboard arrow keys to navigate through the filmstrip thumbnails. These two workspaces provide nice simplified Bridge layouts that are ideal for navigating images. If you look closely, you will notice that the Content panel has a fly-out menu for controlling the Content thumbnail layout (see sidebar). This means you can create a Vertical filmstrip layout with a narrow Content panel in the middle set to vertical scrolling and a large Preview panel in the right column. Figure 11.13 shows the Metadata layout where the focus is on the Metadata panel and the Content panel is in Details mode, displaying the main essential image data alongside the thumbnails.

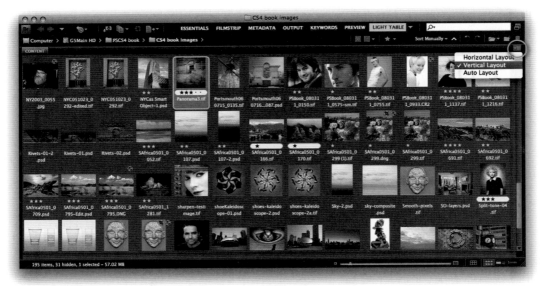

Figure 11.11 Here is a view of a Bridge window configured using the Light Table workspace preset (note the Content panel layout options shown top right).

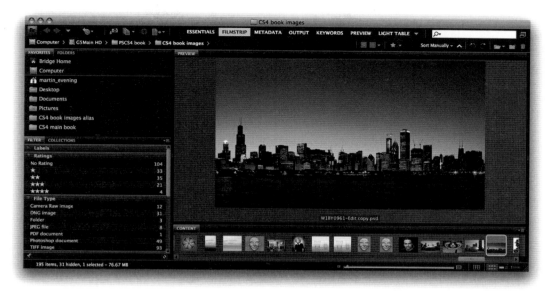

Figure 11.12 The Filmstrip workspace (⌘ F2 ctrl F2) combines a large Preview panel with a narrow Content panel that runs along the bottom using a Horizontal scrolling layout.

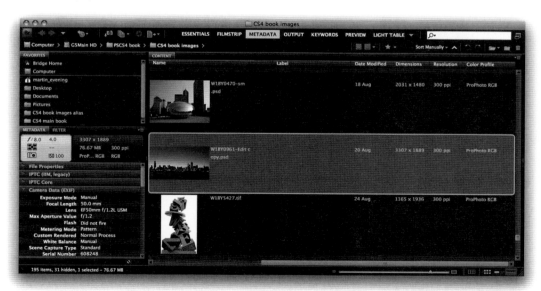

Figure 11.13 The Metadata Focus workspace displays the Content panel in Details view mode with the Favorites, Keywords and Metadata panels on the left.

Synchronized displays

If you choose Window ⇨ New Synchronized Window (⌘ ⌥ N) (ctrl alt N), you can create two synchronized windows. These can be on the same monitor screen, or you can have one on each monitor. For example, you could have one window displaying a Light Table workspace and the other using the Preview workspace.

Working with multiple windows

You can also have multiple Bridge window views open at once. This means you can access more than one folder of images at a time, without having to use the Folders panel or window navigational buttons to navigate back and forth between the different image folders. That's not all though, because multiple windows can also make it easier to make comparative editing decisions when reviewing a collection of images, such as in the Figure 11.14 example shown below.

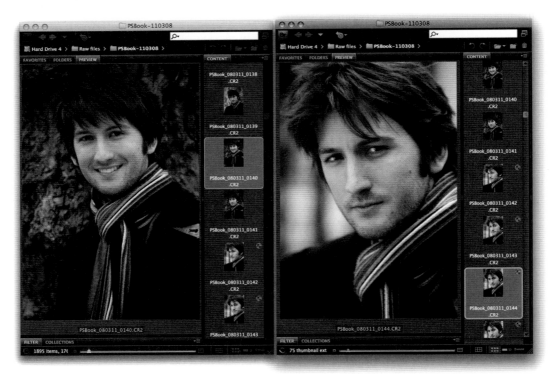

Figure 11.14 In this example I pointed Bridge at a folder of images using a modified Preview workspace layout, where single images could be previewed large in the Preview panel and the Content panel used to display a vertical filmstrip of thumbnails. I then chose File ⇨ New Window to create a duplicate window view and dragged this off to the right. I was then able to navigate through the image thumbnails in the second window and compare alternative shots with the one displayed in the first window.

Slideshow mode

The Bridge Slideshow feature can be considered useful for making quick on-screen presentations, but I think you will find that the Slideshow viewing mode also offers a nice clear interface with which to edit your pictures; one that's devoid of all the clutter of the Bridge window interface. Figure 11.16 shows the Bridge Slideshow in Full screen mode, where you have access to all the usual image rating controls. As you review edit a folder of photos, you can use the 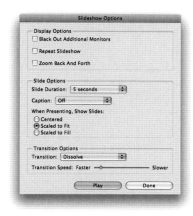 keyboard arrow keys to progress through the shots and you can use the ░ key to increase and the ░ key to decrease the star rating, or a single-click with the apostrophe key to toggle adding or subtracting a rating. To access the Slideshow settings (including the slide transitions and zoom options) go to the View menu and choose Slideshow Options.... (Figure 11.15)

Figure 11.15 This shows the Slideshow Options dialog, which includes a choice of slide transition options.

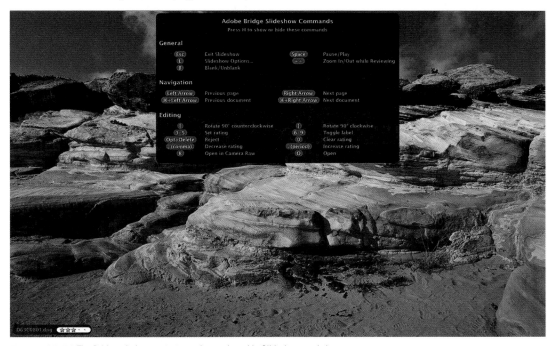

Figure 11.16 The Bridge window contents can be previewed in Slideshow mode by choosing View ➪ Slideshow (⌘ *L* *ctrl* *L*). Press *H* to call up the Slideshow Commands menu shown here, where you'll note that you can also use the ⊕ ⊖ keys to zoom in and out during playback. There is also a triple-click shortcut for zooming into the corners at 100%, but in practice it's rather complicated to use.

Limiting preview generation

It can take a long time for Bridge to generate preview images of large image files. If you have the Maximize PSD Backwards Compatibility preference turned on (see page 99) the layered PSD files will generate a composite image layer when saved. This will certainly reduce the time it takes to build each preview in Bridge. If you limit the file size for rendering previews using 'Do not process file larger than: x MB' this will also help speed up the time it takes to build a cache of previews of very large files.

Thumbnail settings

If you go to the 'Thumbnail quality' options in the Bridge window you can select a policy for the thumbnail generation (Figure 11.17). 'Prefer Embedded' uses whatever previews it finds and makes the browsing of non-cached images faster (you can also click on the button to the left to switch to this mode). The 'High Quality On Demand' option aims to rebuild accurate previews, but only when you actually click to select a thumbnail. Lastly, the 'Always High Quality' option rebuilds the thumbnails for all files it encounters that are not already stored in the Bridge cache.

If you go to the Bridge Thumbnails preferences (Figure 11.19) you can limit the thumbnail generation to files that are of a certain size or lower (setting the limit lower can help speed up the thumbnail generation). In the Details

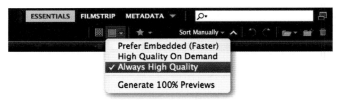

Figure 11.17 The Thumbnail quality options.

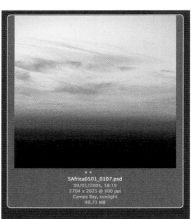

Figure 11.18 Up to four additional lines of metadata can be added beneath the thumbnails in Bridge.

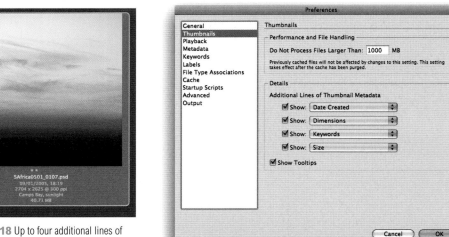

Figure 11.19 The Bridge Thumbnails preferences.

section you can have extra lines of metadata appear beneath the thumbnails in the content area (as shown in Figure 11.18). The 'Show Tooltips' option is useful if you want to learn about each section of the Bridge interface, and does also allow you to read long file names in the Bridge content area more easily.

Cache management

From the moment you open an image folder in Bridge, the program sets to work, building the thumbnails and previews, reading in the image file metadata as it does, taking into account things like: Camera Raw edits, image rotation instructions, file ratings and labeling. This is quite a lot of information that Bridge has to process, and if it is your intention to use Bridge to manage large collections of images (especially large numbers of raw files) you really do need a fast computer, or Bridge will appear frustratingly slow. The information that is built up during this process is stored in the form of 'cache data', which has two components: the image metadata and the thumbnail cache. Every time you open a folder, Bridge checks to see if there is an image cache for that folder located in the Username/ Library/Caches/Adobe/Bridge CS4/Cache folder (you can change this location in the Cache preferences). If a cache is present, the inspected folder will display the archived thumbnails, previews and metadata almost instantaneously. This works fine so long as the folder is being inspected on the computer that created it and the folder name has not changed since the cache was created. If these two conditions are not met, then Bridge has to start all over again and build a fresh cache for that folder.

Proprietary raw files present a particularly problem because the Camera Raw database in the Bridge cache is the only place where the metadata information such as the rotation, image rating and Camera Raw adjustments can be kept, that is unless you go to the Camera Raw preferences (Figure 11.20) and choose to save the image settings to 'Sidecar ".xmp" files'. When you do this, the metadata information is also saved to XMP sidecar files that are

Thumbnails only

You can use the ⌘ T ctrl T keyboard shortcut to toggle hiding and showing the text information that appears below the image thumbnails in the content area.

Cache building routines

When you point Bridge at a folder of images it will speedily generate low res thumbnails and, when that is done, a second pass will add higher resolution data.

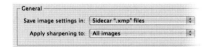

Figure 11.20 The Camera Raw General preferences.

XMP and Sidecar files

File-specific information that can generally be read by other programs, such as the custom IPTC metadata and Camera Raw settings (which only other Adobe programs can read), is normally stored in the file header XMP space. However, because proprietary raw files are an unknown entity it is only safe to store such data within a separate XMP sidecar file that travels with the raw file when it is moved from one folder to another. It will also get renamed if the original master is renamed.

Image_0077.CR2   Image_0077.xmp

Figure 11.21 If the Camera Raw preferences are set to save .xmp files as sidecar files, you will see sidecar files like this appear alongside a raw image file that has been modified via Bridge.

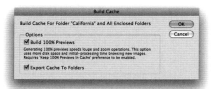

Figure 11.22 If you go to the Tools ⇨ Cache submenu, you can choose 'Build and Export Cache'. This opens the dialog shown here, which will let you force-build a cache for the selected folder and any subfolders. You have additional options to select 'Build 100% Previews' and 'Export Cache to Folders'.

stored alongside each raw image. Obviously, it is very useful to make the cache information accessible, which is why it is also a good idea in the Cache preferences (Figure 11.23) to choose 'Automatically Export Cache To Folders When Possible'. Bridge then automatically updates the cache by adding a couple of cache data files within the same image folder (these will normally be hidden from view). The advantage of doing this is that it does not matter if you move or rename a folder, because the image cache will always be recognized. This is especially important if you are about to share a folder of images that you have edited in Bridge with another Bridge user, or you are about to archive pictures you have edited to a CD or DVD disk, as this ensures the cache data is always preserved. Sometimes a cache may appear out of date and require a forced update. To do this, go to the Tools ⇨ Cache menu and choose the 'Build and Export Cache' option (Figure 11.22). You can use this to force Bridge to prioritize building a cache for not just the current targeted folder, but the subfolders as well. You might find it beneficial to get Bridge to cache large folders of images during idle times, such as at night. The other Cache preference items let you

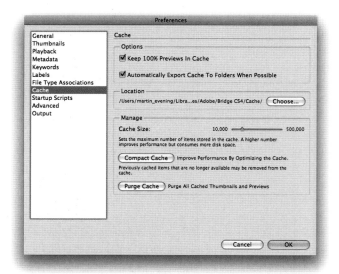

Figure 11.23 The Bridge Cache preferences.

manage the cache. For example, when the 'Keep 100% Previews in Cache' option is selected (Figure 11.23), this will potentially increase the size of the cache, but you'll have faster access to full-sized previews. The cache size itself can be limited in size to a set number of files. As more files are cached, the older cache items get deleted, so increasing the cache size limit means more cache data is preserved, but at the expense of increased disk space usage. The 'Compact Cache' and 'Purge Cache' items can also be used to keep the cache size under control.

Advanced and miscellaneous preferences

Bridge by default uses hardware acceleration to drive the graphics display, but if you are working with an underpowered graphics card you may find it better to check 'Use Software Rendering' and relaunch Bridge (Figure 11.24). The 'Generate Monitor-Size Previews' ensures that the cached previews are big enough to fill the screen, such as when using the Slideshow or Review modes.

The International section allows you to regionalize Bridge for international languages and for use with international keyboard designs. Note that the changes applied here only will come into effect on restart.

Enabling Backward compatibility

It is a good idea to switch on the 'Maximize the PSD and PSB compatibility' option in the Photoshop File Handling preferences. This will force Photoshop to save a flattened version of the image when saving a file using the PSD and PSB formats, and this in turn will speed up the writing of the thumbnail cache file.

Automatic Bridge launch

If you check the 'Start Bridge at Login' option in the Advanced preferences, you can get Bridge to launch automatically each time you start up the computer.

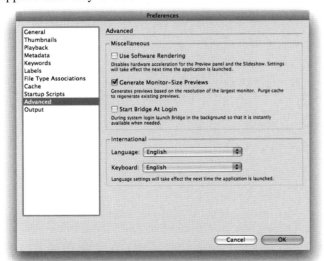

Figure 11.24 The Bridge Advanced preferences.

One-click previews

With Bridge CS4 you can now use the spacebar to quickly preview an image at full size on the screen. Once you are in this Full screen preview mode, you can click with the mouse to enlarge a photo to 100%, click to return to the full screen view again and use the arrow keys to navigate to the next or previous photo. To return to the Bridge window, just hold down the spacebar again and click.

Deleting contents

The *Delete* key can be used to delete selected images. If you click *Delete* or click on the Delete button (🗑) in Bridge, this will pop a dialog asking if you want to send a file to the trash directly. This action removes the thumbnail from the Bridge window and sends the original file to the Trash (Mac) or Recycle bin (PC). Even so, a file won't be permanently deleted until you empty the contents of the Trash (Mac)/Recycle bin (PC) at the operating system level. If you use *⌥ Delete* *alt Delete*, rather than proceed to the delete message, this will 'mark' an image with the word 'Reject' in red. You can then use the Filter panel to select the 'mark as rejected' images only and delete them as required. Note that when it comes to deleting folders via Bridge, you can only do so if they are empty.

Stacking images

You can use the Stack menu in Bridge to group files into stacks. In Figure 11.25 you can see an example where some of the files have been grouped in this way. To use this feature, select two or more files, go to the Stack menu and choose 'Group as Stack' (⌘ *G* *ctrl G*). This groups the images, indicating they are part of a stack with a number showing how many files are included in the stack. To ungroup images from a stack use: ⌘ *Shift G* *ctrl Shift G*. To expand a stack use: ⌘ ➡ *ctrl* ➡ and to collapse a stack again use: ⌘ ⬅ *ctrl* ⬅. If you want to expand all stacks use: ⌘ ⌥ ➡ *ctrl alt* ➡ and if you want to collapse all stacks use: ⌘ ⌥ ⬅ *ctrl alt* ⬅.

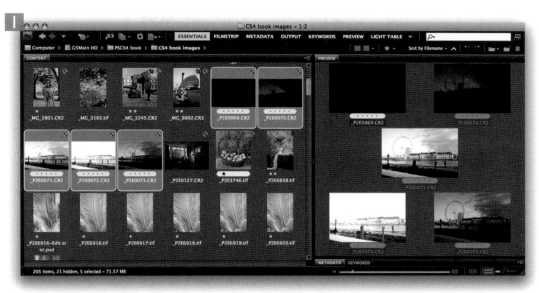

1 This shows five thumbnails selected in the Content panel. To group these images into a stack, I used the ⌘ G *ctrl* G shortcut.

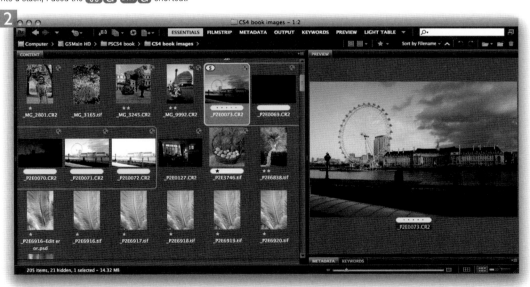

2 Here, you can see how the files were displayed in the Content panel area when the stack was expanded. For this step, I selected the best exposed image (the last in the group shown in Step 1) and chose Stacks ⇨ Promote to Top of Stack. This made the selected file the key image used to identify all the images in the stack.

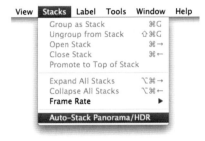

Figure 11.25 This shows the Stacks Auto-Stack Panorama/HDR command.

Auto-stacking

Earlier in Chapter 7 we looked at how to merge bracketed exposure images together, and in Chapter 9 how to use Photomerge to blend overlapping image sequences to build panorama images. In Bridge CS4 you can now use the Stacks ⇨ Auto-Stack Panorama/HDR command (Figure 11.25) to auto-stack such images in a selected folder. The way this works is that Bridge scans the images and, where it finds two or more images that have been shot within an 18-second time-frame, makes these candidate photos for a panorama or Merge to HDR image set. Once it has done this, it further analyzes the images using Photoshop's auto-align technology. Where a sequence of images overlap by no more than 80%, these are assumed to be part of a panorama sequence and where a sequence overlaps by at least 80% (and the EXIF data shows that the exposure values are changing by one or more stops), these are assumed to be part of a Merge to HDR set. Using this logic, Bridge is able to organize photos into stacks and at the same time create and store metadata information that can be used later to auto-process the stacked images as either panoramas or as Merge to HDR sets. You'll note in Figure 11.26 how the auto-stack feature generates an XML file that is added to the folder and stores the 'how-to-process' information. The processing can be done by choosing Tools ⇨ Photoshop ⇨ Process Collections in Photoshop (Figure 11.27). In actual fact, you can carry out this step directly, without applying an auto-stack first. When you apply this command, the images that have been auto-collected into stacks are automatically processed in Photoshop. Now, the plus sides of this feature are that it will benefit large volume panorama or HDR shooters, especially the ability to group photos into stacks. On the downside, there is no interface that can be used to modify, say, the time-frame period from 18 seconds or apply particular settings to the Photomerge composites. When it works well it has the potential to be a powerful tool, when it doesn't, you'll just have to redo the work manually. Overall, it's an interesting innovation that is bound to be improved upon in future Bridge updates.

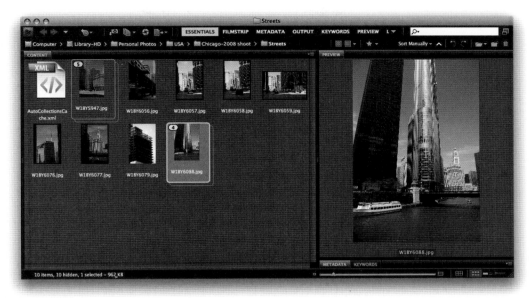

Figure 11.26 Here, you can see a Bridge window view where I had selected the Auto-Stack Panorama/HDR command and the panorama candidate photos were automatically gathered into stacks.

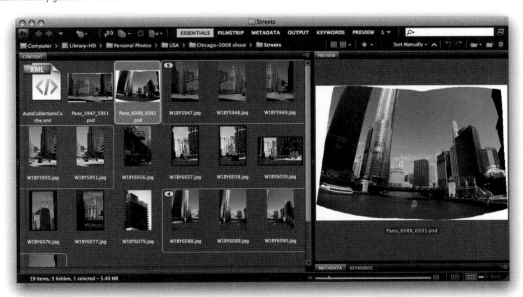

Figure 11.27 Here you can see the same folder after I applied 'Process Collections in Photoshop'. This generated two panoramas and saved them as PSD files.

527

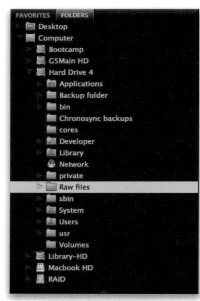

Figure 11.28 The Folders panel displays a complete list view of all the folders on your main hard drive and any mounted disks. Bridge will allow you to drag and drop folders with ease within the content area and folders panel areas, as well as drag directly to external folders.

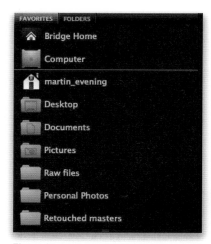

Figure 11.29 The Favorites panel contains a list of commonly-accessed folder locations.

Bridge panels

Let's now take a look at some of the other panels in Bridge and what they do.

Folders panel

The Folders panel (Figure 11.28) displays an expandable list tree view of the folder contents on all the drives that are currently connected to the computer. When you highlight a folder in the Folders panel, all the files in that folder will be displayed as thumbnails in the content area on the right (note that Bridge is only able to create previews of image files it already understands or has a file import plug-in for). While this is happening, Bridge writes a folder cache of all the image thumbnails and previews, which is stored in a central folder location; although, as was pointed out on pages 521–522, you can configure the Bridge preferences so that the cache information is exported locally to the image folder as well. This saved cache should make the thumbnails appear quicker the next time you visit a particular image folder. If a folder contains a cache that was exported from Bridge CS3 or earlier, Bridge CS4 will be able to read it, but earlier versions of Photoshop will not be able to interpret Bridge CS4 cache files. Figure 11.30 shows how you can also use the file path directory to quickly navigate to alternative folder destinations.

Favorites panel

The Favorites panel (Figure 11.29) provides a set of shortcuts to various folder locations, such as the Desktop or Pictures folder. The items that appear in Favorites are determined in the Bridge General preferences (see page 509), but you can also add your own Favorites by dragging a folder from the Content panel across to the Favorites list.

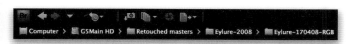

Figure 11.30 You can also use the file path name for folder navigation. If you mouse down on the chevron icons, this will call up a menu list of all the other alternative folders that are available at the same root level.

Preview panel

The Preview panel (Figure 11.31) displays large previews of the selected images and, as you will have seen already (such as in Figure 11.12), the Preview panel can be adjusted to any size to make the preview area as big as you like. When more than one image is selected in the Content panel, the Preview panel will display all the images at once up to a maximum of nine images. If you need to inspect any more than this, you will be better off using the Review mode (see the following page).

If you click anywhere in the Preview panel, this will reveal a loupe magnifying glass adjacent to the point where you clicked, displaying that particular section of the preview image at a 1:1, actual pixels view (but see sidebar on ⌘ *ctrl* key behavior). You can then use the ⊞ ⊟ keys to zoom in (up to 800%) or zoom out again. To close, click inside the loupe. To reposition it, simply click anywhere inside or outside the loupe and drag with the mouse. You can have an active loupe on each image in the Preview panel: just click to add a new loupe and, if you want to synchronize the loupe position so that you can compare close-up details in two or more images at once, hold down the ⌘ *ctrl* key as you drag the loupe.

Rotating loupe

When you work with the loupe tool and drag it to the corner of a preview image you may sometimes see the loupe spin round to reveal the corner details of an image. This is normal behavior.

⌘ *ctrl* key behavior

As was pointed out earlier, if you go to the Bridge general preferences there is an option you can select where a ⌘ *ctrl*-click is required to initiate opening the loupe (instead of just clicking). This preference has no effect on using the ⌘ *ctrl* key to synchronize the loupe scrolling though.

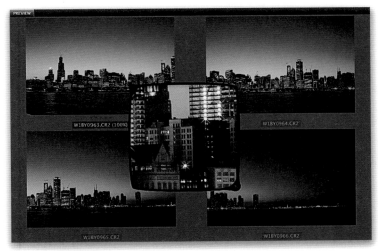

Figure 11.31 The Preview panel, showing a loupe close-up view of an image.

Review mode

Instead of relying on the Preview panel, you can use the Review mode (Figure 11.32) to inspect large numbers of images at once. The Review mode can be accessed from the View menu (⌘ B *ctrl* B) and presents the selected photos in a carousel type display that has more than a passing resemblance to the Quick View folder navigation in Macintosh OS X 10.5. You can cycle through the selected photos using the arrow keys in the bottom left corner, remove photos from a selection with the downward pointing arrow, open a loupe view on the foreground image and create new collections. Overall, I would say that the one-click preview feature offers a great innovation for speedy previewing, and in light of this it is hard to see how the Review feature adds much to the party.

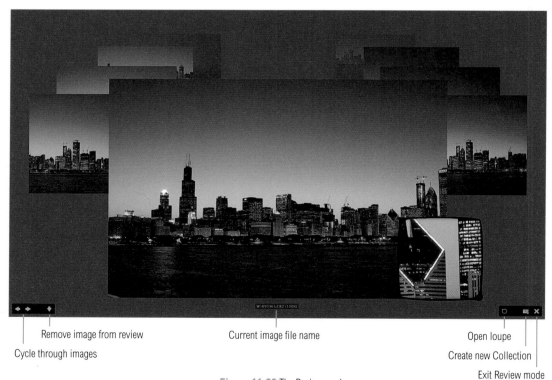

Remove image from review

Cycle through images

Current image file name

Open loupe

Create new Collection

Exit Review mode

Figure 11.32 The Review mode

Managing images in Bridge

As the number of photographs stored on your computer system continues to grow, you'll soon end up becoming frustrated unless you add basic metadata and keyword information to categorize the photographs in your image library. The metadata tools in Bridge are designed to help you get started with the task of cataloging your image files. Do this and you'll soon reap the rewards when you need to conduct filtered file searches.

Let's first consider how metadata information is used to manage other types of files on a computer. A program like iTunes can update its music database automatically. Insert a CD into your computer and iTunes will query an online database, downloading the album title, artist, track listings and genre of music. This is a good example of metadata in action, and how it can be used to help you manage your music collections more easily. When you convert music files to an MP3 format, the cataloging is effortless because it can take place in the background automatically. The big difference with cataloging image files is that you mostly have to input all the metadata manually.

Although Bridge has the potential to be used as an image asset manager, it does lack the sophistication of other fully dedicated asset management programs like Expession Media™ or Lightroom. To be honest, I mainly use Bridge for specific file browsing tasks (such as when working on a book project like this). Otherwise, I find Lightroom is a better program to use for most image asset management and workflow tasks. This is because Lightroom allows me to import camera files exactly the way I want and has a better and more versatile library management interface for editing and managing the metadata. If you are serious about library management and cataloging your images, you may want to try Lightroom out, or else consider some of the other popular products such as Expession Media™ or Apple's Aperture™ program.

Adobe Photoshop Lightroom

A lot of people have been asking: if I have Photoshop and Bridge, why do I need Lightroom? I usually point out that Lightroom is a workflow program that allows you to manage your images efficiently all the way from import through to web or print output. For some people, the combination of Bridge and Camera Raw provides them with all the tools that they ever need to manage their pictures and work in Photoshop. For amateurs and professionals who are looking for a faster and more streamlined approach for their image processing and management, Lightroom will be the answer. I do still use Bridge for some file browsing tasks, but I find that I now mostly use Lightroom because it integrates smoothly with Photoshop and offers some rather nice and unique approaches to image processing that you won't find in any other program. Overall, I find I can work much faster and more efficiently using Lightroom.

Cancelling and turning off labels

The labeling controls have a toggle action. For example, if you select an image and use ⌘6 *ctrl* 6 to label it red, you can use the same keyboard shortcut to cancel the label color. You can also turn off the labeling by selecting No Label from the Label menu.

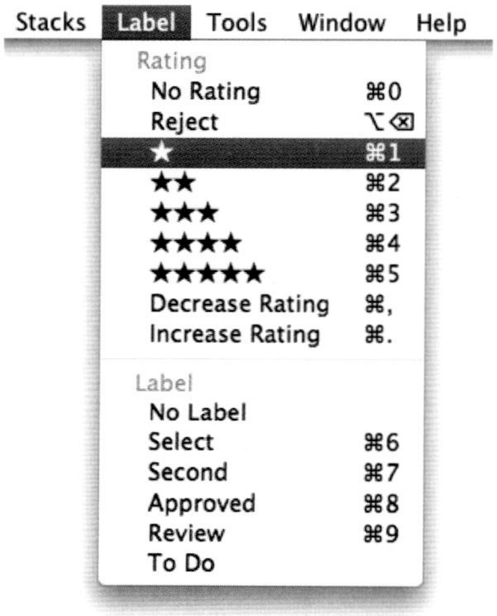

Stacks	**Label**	Tools	Window	Help

Rating	
No Rating	⌘0
Reject	⌥⌫
★	⌘1
★★	⌘2
★★★	⌘3
★★★★	⌘4
★★★★★	⌘5
Decrease Rating	⌘,
Increase Rating	⌘.
Label	
No Label	
Select	⌘6
Second	⌘7
Approved	⌘8
Review	⌘9
To Do	

Figure 11.33 Image ratings and labels can be applied via the Label menu in Bridge, or by using the keyboard shortcuts described in the main text. You can also mark an image as being a reject (see page 524). This is not the same as deleting, you are simply labeling it as a potential delete image.

Image rating and labeling

One of the main tasks you will want to carry out in Bridge is to rate the images, sorting out those that you like best from the rejects and arranging them into groups. The Bridge program provides two main ways to categorize your images. In the Label menu Rating section (Figure 11.33) you can apply ratings to an image in the form of stars, going from one to five. This image rating system allows you to apply cumulative ratings to the images you like and it is therefore useful to familiarize yourself with the keyboard shortcuts that can be used to apply ratings to images. These range from ⌘0 *ctrl* 0 to ⌘5 *ctrl* 5 (to apply 0–5 stars) but you can also use ⌘. *ctrl* . to increase the rating by one star, or ⌘, *ctrl* , to decrease the rating for an image. The above shortcuts can make it easier for you to focus your attention on the images as you use the ← → arrow keys to progress from one picture to the next. In addition to this you can still use the ⌘ *ctrl* +' (apostrophe) keyboard shortcut as a simple binary rating system that will allow you to add or remove a single star rating from an image. How you use the ratings is up to you, but generally speaking it is a good idea to be sparing with your ratings. Unrated images can be the rejects, while one and two stars can be used to mark the images you like best. And three stars upwards should be reserved for those pictures that are really special.

Color labels can be used to signify other things. Author Peter Krogh, suggests in his *DAM book* that labels can be used to apply negative ratings, where a zero star represents an image that has been inspected but rated neutral, a red label means yet to be rated, a yellow label means it's an out-take and a green label means 'trash me'. Meanwhile, a wedding photographer might use color labels to quickly separate out shots according to the location they were shot in. It is a simple matter of selecting the individual or multiple images you would like to label and then choosing a color from the list in the Label menu. Or, you can use the keyboard shortcuts that range from ⌘6 *ctrl* 6 for red, to ⌘9 *ctrl* 9 for blue, plus you can also use *ctrl* right mouse to apply label colors via the contextual menu. If you go to the Labels preferences in Bridge (Figure 11.34), you will note that you can edit the text descriptions given to each label color. You can rename these as you see fit, although this can potentially cause confusion where other programs (such as Lightroom) use different text descriptions for the color labels.

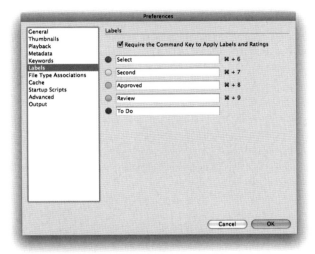

Figure 11.34 The Bridge Labels preferences.

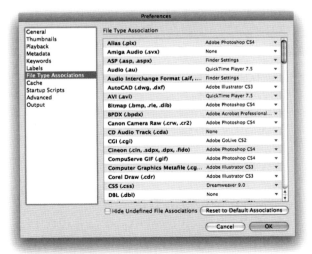

Figure 11.35 The Bridge File Association preferences.

Universal rating methods

You are not limited to using the rating controls just within Bridge. The rating keyboard shortcuts described here work equally well when you are reviewing your images in the Camera Raw dialog or the Slideshow and Review viewing modes. Just to add to the confusion though, in the Slideshow and Review modes you only need to tap in single keyboard numbers to add ratings or labels, where you can use 0–5 to apply a star rating and use 6–9 to apply a red, yellow, green or blue color label.

File Associations

The Bridge File Association preferences (Figure 11.35) list the default programs to use when opening specific files. Most of the time you can leave these as they are, but there are times when you may want to force certain types of files to open in a specific program. For example, some photographers may still use the EPS file format to save press-ready files. Bridge CS4 normally opens these using Adobe Illustrator, therefore you may in this instance want to change the File Association setting to Photoshop CS4.

Refreshing the view

If you alter the contents of a volume or folder at the System level, outside Bridge, then the Bridge Folder panel and Content panel area won't always know to update the revised volume or folder contents. If you ever need to refresh the view in Bridge, use this menu item or the F5 keyboard shortcut.

Sorting images in Bridge

You can change the order the images are displayed in the Content panel by going to the Sort menu shown in Figure 11.36. If you mouse down on the menu here you can choose from a range of different new sort criteria and if you click on the arrow button next to this menu list (circled in Figure 11.36), you can choose whether you want to see the images displayed in an ascending or descending order. Normally this is set to the default 'By Filename' setting, but to give you just one example, if you were to select the 'By Date Modified' option (in ascending order) the files that were edited most recently will appear first in the Content panel.

Earlier, in Figure 11.6, I showed how you can manually drag the thumbnails to rearrange their position in the Content panel. Just be aware that if you do this, the Sort option defaults to 'Manually' and you will have to revisit the Sort menu to restore the previously applied sort order rule (note that you can also access the Sort options by going to the View menu in Bridge). As we come on to looking at methods for filtering the images displayed in the Bridge Content panel, you will see how combining the filtering with the Sort options is perfect for organizing how the thumbnail images are arranged in the Content panel.

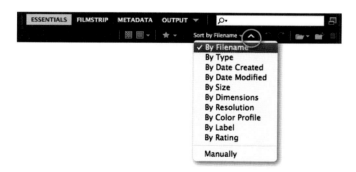

Figure 11.36 The Bridge window Sort menu options allow you to arrange the displayed thumbnail images by ascending or descending order (by clicking on the button circled here). You can use any of the criteria listed in the Sort menu to rearrange the Content panel display.

Filter panel

The Filter panel allows you to see and choose single or cumulative, multiple criteria for filtering images in the Content panel area. The Filter panel options are grouped into sections and as soon as you click on any item listed in the Filter panel, the contents of the Content panel are filtered accordingly.

When managing large folders or hierarchies of folders, these filtering controls can really make it easier to narrow down an image search. For example, in Figure 11.37, you can see how Bridge was pointed at a folder where the image files in that folder were labeled using red and yellow labels and the ratings ranged from no rating to three stars. In this example, I clicked on the Red label plus the one, two and three star filters. This filtered the photos so that only those images with red labels plus one, two or three stars were displayed in the Content panel. Similarly, I could have gone to the Keywords section and clicked on one or more of the keyword tags listed there and made a filtered selection that was based on a combination of specific keywords. But wait, there's more... . In the Filter panel you can filter images by other criteria such as: by file type, date created/modified, image orientation, speed ISO rating, camera serial number or copyright notice. You can also use the keyboard shortcuts shown in the sidebar to filter files by label or rating.

In Bridge CS3 there was a Flatten View button in the Filter panel. This feature is still present in CS4, but you will need to go to the View menu and select 'Show Items from Subfolders'. If you then point Bridge at a folder that contains a nested group of subfolders, you can use this command to get a flattened view of all the subfolders in that particular folder. The only downside is that Bridge temporarily loses track of the master folder in the Folders panel, but this can easily be restored by deselecting 'Show Items from Subfolders' in the View menu. There is also a pin marker button in the Filters panel (circled in Figure 11.37). If you click this, it preserves the filter criteria as you continue browsing. Just click again to cancel this filter.

Filtering shortcuts

The following shortcuts can be used to filter images in the Content panel:

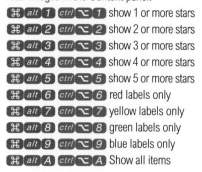

⌘ alt 1 ctrl ⌥ 1 show 1 or more stars
⌘ alt 2 ctrl ⌥ 2 show 2 or more stars
⌘ alt 3 ctrl ⌥ 3 show 3 or more stars
⌘ alt 4 ctrl ⌥ 4 show 4 or more stars
⌘ alt 5 ctrl ⌥ 5 show 5 or more stars
⌘ alt 6 ctrl ⌥ 6 red labels only
⌘ alt 7 ctrl ⌥ 7 yellow labels only
⌘ alt 8 ctrl ⌥ 8 green labels only
⌘ alt 9 ctrl ⌥ 9 blue labels only
⌘ alt A ctrl ⌥ A Show all items

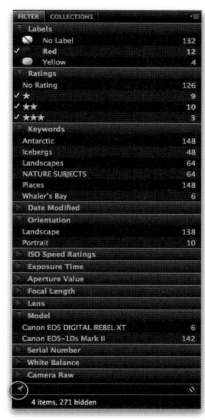

Figure 11.37 The Filter panel.

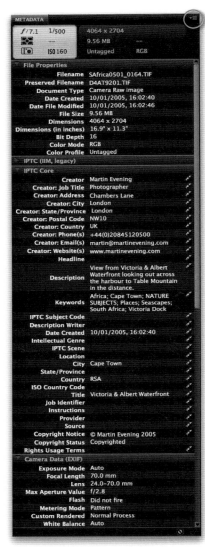

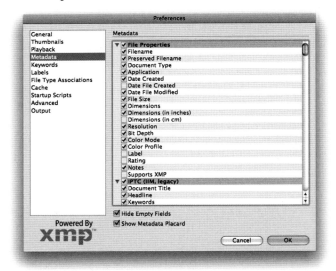

Metadata panel

The Metadata panel information is divided into several sections (Figure 11.38). The File Properties section lists the main file statistics such as file name and size, etc., while the IPTC sections are used to hold the file-specific metadata information. To edit these, click in the field next to the metadata heading and type in the data you wish to enter (the pencil icons indicate where metadata items can be edited). When you are done, click the Tick button at the bottom, or hit *Enter*. How the remaining sections appear listed will depend on how the Metadata preferences have been configured (Figure 11.39). Some of the items you see listed here are specific to other CS4 suite programs, or specialist users. Basically, you can use the Preferences dialog to determine which items you want to see displayed in the Metadata panel.

Figure 11.38 The Metadata panel displays the metadata information contained in a file. The metadata sections can be compacted to make viewing easier and the IPTC fields can all be edited. You can also increase the font size in the Metadata panel via the panel fly-out menu. This will make it easier when adding new metadata and locating existing entries.

Figure 11.39 If you mouse down on the Metadata panel options (circled in Figure 11.38), you can open the Bridge Preferences dialog for the Metadata display content. Each metadata item has a checkbox against it, allowing you to show or hide individual items. Since it is unlikely that you will really want to see or use all the metadata items listed here, you can deselect the items you don't need. If the Hide Empty Fields box is checked, the checked items will only be displayed in the Metadata panel if there is an accompanying data entry. The main ones you will want to use will be the EXIF Camera Data, Camera Raw data, and the Edit History log.

Image metadata

Maybe you are wondering what all the information in the Metadata panel is useful for. Well, quite a lot actually, especially if you are running a photography business or are an amateur who shoots lots of digital photographs. Metadata is usually defined as being 'data about data' and the concept of metadata is one you should already be quite familiar with. Librarians use metadata to classify and catalog books in a library – in the old days they would have used index cards to search by an author's name or by the title of a book. Everything is now computerized of course and it is possible to record much more information about individual files and use this information to carry out sophisticated searches and cross-reference files.

File Info metadata

The File Info dialog (Figure 11.40) has been around since the early days of Photoshop, but it seems that until recently few people had bothered using it. The File Info dialog is designed to let you inspect all the metadata relating to an image document as well as edit the IPTC image metadata that relates to the picture content. Photoshop has

Metadata everywhere

Metadata usage is commonplace on the Internet. Enter a search term into any search engine and within seconds web link suggestions will appear on the screen. Web designers add metadata tags to the header section of websites and this enables search engines to catalog them more effectively. Parents and schools use metadata to filter out the web content that children can safely access. MP3 players use metadata to categorize your music collections. Metadata is used in all sorts of ways and if anything we seem to have too much metadata out there – web search engines will often offer you thousands of possible links, when you would rather have your choice narrowed down to a smaller selection. The trick is for distributors to provide metadata that is useful and for retrieval systems to intelligently sort through the metadata.

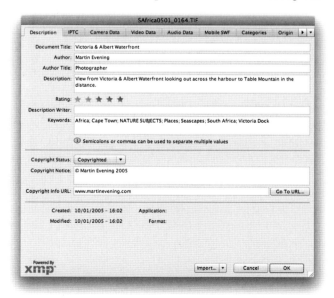

Figure 11.40 Here is an example of the File Info dialog, shown here displaying the Description information. To save you time when filling out the editable sections of File Info dialog, you can mouse down on the little fly-out menu buttons next to each field entry and select from a list of previously entered metadata entries.

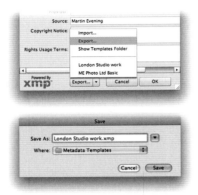

Figure 11.41 You can configure the File Info dialog and create a custom metadata template containing the metadata items you might wish to regularly apply to collections of images. If you mouse down on the Import/Export metadata options (shown above and also circled in Figure 11.43) you can choose 'Export...' which will open the Save dialog, where you can save the current metadata settings as a new metadata template.

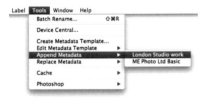

Figure 11.42 Following on from Figure 11.41, once you have done this you can apply the template to other images by going to the Tools ⇨ Replace Metadata/Append Metadata menu. 'Replace Metadata' substitutes all pre-existing metadata with that in the template. 'Append Metadata' is the safer option since it only adds to the metadata that is already embedded in the image file.

always supported the information standard developed by International Press Telecommunications Council (IPTC), which was designed to help classify and label images and text files using metadata. In early versions of Photoshop, you could access the 'File Info' via the File menu and use it to title an image, add the name of the author, add keywords and inspect the camera capture metadata. File Info is still in the Photoshop File menu, but if you highlight an image, or group of images in Bridge, you can access it via the Bridge File menu, or use the ⌘ ⌥ Shift I ctrl alt Shift I keyboard shortcut. In CS4, the File Info dialog now contains 13 sections, some of which are editable, such as the Description section shown in Figure 11.40, while other sections, like the camera EXIF metadata, provide information only. You can use File Info with single or multiple image selections to edit the IPTC metadata, add your name as the author, mark the images as being copyrighted, add a copyright notice, etc. Marking an image as being copyrighted in the 'File Info' has the extra advantage of adding a copyright symbol to the title bar of your image window whenever anyone opens it in Photoshop.

After configuring the File Info settings you can then save these as a metadata template. For example, you can select an image, enter some basic custom metadata such as author name, copyright tag, etc., then follow this by going to the Import/Export options (discussed in Figure 11.41) and save as a new metadata template. Once you have saved a custom metadata template, you can select other images and choose this or any other pre-saved template from the 'Append Metadata' or 'Replace Metadata' menus in the Tools menu (Figure 11.42). When you create a new template it is best to work on a dummy image and enter the exact information that should be saved and nothing else. Don't add any keywords or captions, unless you want these to be included in the saved template. To help guide you, in Figure 11.43 I have completed most of the sections that can be filled in the IPTC section and offered guidance on where to go to find more specific information about news codes, etc.

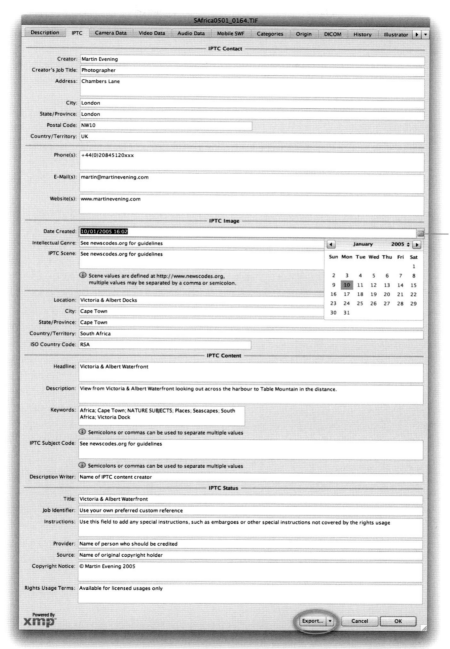

Click on this button to open the calendar shown here, which will enter a calendar date in the correct date format

Figure 11.43 This shows an expanded view of the File Info IPTC section.

Future uses of metadata

It is quite scary to consider the number of freely distributed digital images out there that contain no information about the contact details of the person who created the image. Imagine a scenario in the future where metadata can be used to embed important information about usage rights. Imagine also that a third-party developer could service a website that allowed interested purchasers to instantly discover what specific exclusive usages were currently available for a particular image? You could even embed a self-generating invoice in the image file. If someone tried to strip out the metadata, you could use an encrypted key embedded in the file to reimport the removed metadata, and/or update specific metadata information. I predict that metadata will offer tremendously powerful advantages to individual image creators who wish to distribute their creative work more securely over the Internet and profit from legitimate image rights purchases.

Other types of metadata

Metadata comes in many forms. In the early days of digital camera development, the camera manufacturers jointly came up with the EXIF metadata scheme for cataloging camera information. You may find it interesting to read the EXIF metadata that is contained in your digital camera files, as this will tell you things like what lens setting was used when a photo was taken and the serial number of the camera. This could be useful if you were trying to prove which camera was used to take a photograph when there were a lot of other photographers nearby trying to grab the same shot and also claiming authorship. The EXIF metadata can describe everything about the camera's settings, but the EXIF schema cannot be adapted to describe anything but camera data information. In 2001, Adobe announced XMP (eXtensible Metadata Platform) which, to quote Adobe, 'established a common metadata framework to standardize the creation, processing and interchange of document metadata across publishing work flows'. Adobe has already integrated the XMP framework into Acrobat, InDesign Illustrator and Photoshop. XMP is based on XML (eXtensible Markup Language) that is the basic universal format for using metadata and structuring information on the Web. Adobe has also made XMP available as an open-source license, so it can be integrated into any other system or application. Adobe's enormous influence in this arena means that XMP has now become a common standard in the publishing and imaging industry. Adobe and also third-party companies are now able to exploit the potential of XMP to aid file management on a general level and for specific needs such as scientific and forensic work.

Some of the metadata items that can be listed in the File Info and Metadata panels include things like GPS metadata, where if GPS coordinates happen to be embedded in a file, you can cross-reference these with another application such as Google Earth. Other items have specific uses, such as the DICOM metadata which is used for storing important medical information in medical images.

Edit history log

If the History Log options are enabled in the General preferences (Figure 11.44), an edit history can be recorded in either the file metadata, as a separate text file log, or both. The edit history has many potential uses. An edit history will record how much time was spent working on a photograph and could be used as a means of calculating how much to bill. In the world of forensics, the history log can also be used to verify how much (or how little) work was done to manipulate an image in Photoshop. The same arguments can apply to validating images that are used to present scientific evidence. In the case of images that have been processed via the Adobe Camera Raw plug-in, the Camera Raw metadata section stores a record of the Adobe Camera Raw (or Lightroom) settings used.

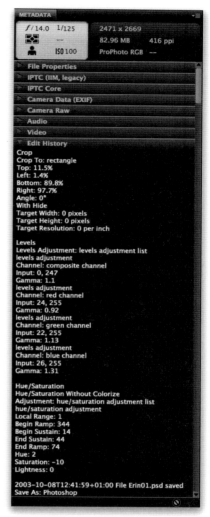

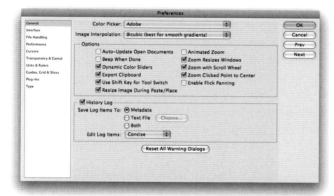

Figure 11.44 To record a history log, the 'History Log' option must first be checked in the Photoshop General preferences. A history log can be saved to the file metadata, as a text log file, or as both, and the 'edit log' items can be recorded as session information only, concise or as a verbose record (see Figure 11.45), of what was done to a file in Photoshop.

Hidden metadata

Lastly, I should mention that there may be hidden metadata that won't show up in any of the Metadata panel sections. This could be things like camera manufacturer EXIF metadata containing proprietary information that only the camera manufacturer's software has access to.

Figure 11.45 If the 'History Log' options have been configured in the Photoshop General preferences, the history log content can record: sessions only (such as the time a file was opened and closed); a concise log listing of what was done in Photoshop; or, as shown here, a detailed log will include a comprehensive list of the settings applied at every step. If you choose to embed the history log in the file metadata, the edit history log can be viewed via the Bridge Metadata panel.

Where keywords are stored

Like other metadata, keyword information (including the keyword hierarchy) is stored directly in the file's XMP space or, in the case of raw files, either to the Camera Raw cache database or as a sidecar file. The Keywords panel displays the accumulated information that it has read from various image files' metadata and can also be used to write keyword metadata back to the files.

Other keywords

As you enter keywords via the File Info panel, any keywords that are unrecognized will appear listed under the category: 'Other Keywords'. You can then use the Keywords panel to rearrange these into a suitable hierarchy and have the option to make them persistent. You will also find that where Bridge is unable to read the hierarchy of keywords that have been entered via another program, these too may appear listed under 'Other keywords'.

Keywording

Keywording provides a way to group and organize images within Photoshop. By using keyword tags to describe the image content, you'll be able to catalog your files more comprehensively.

If you can, it is usually best to add keywords as new images are added. For example, Figure 11.46 shows a detailed view of the Description section of the File Info dialog where you can add keywords to an image. It is important to note here that each keyword must be separated by a semi colon (;). This is important as it ensures the keywords are clearly separated (see how the keywords are entered in Figure 11.46). Such keyword metadata can also be included when you create a metadata template. For example, every time you shoot a particular sporting event you might want to have a template that applies relevant keyword metadata you always need for these types of assignments, such as the name of the stadium location and home team. Unfortunately, you can't create a keyword hierarchy as you enter the keywords (see sidebar on 'Other keywords'). You also need to know the exact keyword phrases to type if they are to match with the keyword data used elsewhere for other images, which is why it is sometimes better to use the Keywords panel to do this.

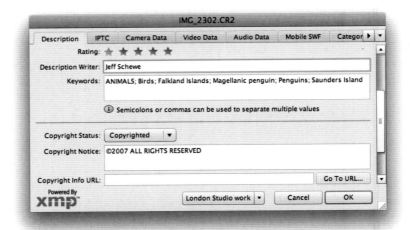

Figure 11.46 The File Info Description section.

Keywords panel

The Keyword panel (Figure 11.47) provides a display of all the keywords that are associated with the images currently selected. The Keywords panel provides a basic level of organization, as it allows you to arrange keywords that you come across into a hierarchy list, plus you can also use the Keywords panel to add new keywords. Click on the Add Keyword button to create a keyword category, such as 'People' or 'Places', type in the name and hit *Enter* to add the keyword (or use *esc* to cancel). You can then highlight the keyword and click on the Add New Sub Keyword button to add more new sub keywords. Once keywords appear listed in the Keywords panel you can make a thumbnail selection within Bridge, go to the Keyword panel and click on the empty square to the left of the desired keyword to apply, or click again to remove. This method allows you to assign one or more keywords to multiple images at once. As long as the 'Automatically Apply Parent Keywords' option is checked in the Bridge Keywords preferences (Figure 11.48), checking a sub keyword automatically selects all the parent keywords too.

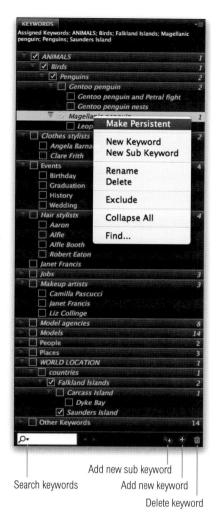

Search keywords
Add new sub keyword
Add new keyword
Delete keyword

Figure 11.47 In this view of the Keywords panel an image was selected and I can see that five keywords were assigned, telling me that this was a photograph taken on Saunders Island in the Falklands islands and that the subject matter was of Magellanic penguins. To make a keyword persistent, use a *ctrl*-click (Mac) or right-mouse click to open the contextual menu shown here and choose 'Make Persistent'.

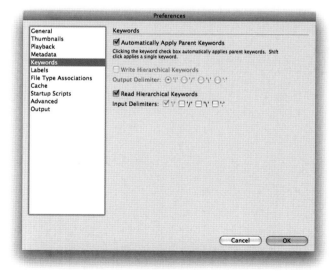

Figure 11.48 The Bridge Keywords preferences.

Search criteria

The search criteria can be almost anything you want. The source folder will default to the folder you are viewing in the front-most Bridge window, but you can select other folders to look in and, in some cases, it will be necessary to select a folder that contains a lot of subfolders, where you'll need to make sure that the 'Include All Subfolders' option is checked. The search criteria can be adapted in many ways. For example, you can include search terms where you ask Bridge to search for files that exclude specific criteria.

The keyword information accumulates as you select further images and you will notice that some of the 'visited image' keywords appear in italics. This indicates that they are only temporary. If you quit Bridge and relaunch, the temporary keywords will all be cleared from the list. To make keywords more permanent use the contextual menu (described in Figure 11.47) to make them persistent.

Image searches

Image searching is now mostly faster in Bridge CS4. The new search field allows you to use a standard Bridge search or use a system-based file search (such as Spotlight on the Mac). All you have to do is select the folder you want to search in, enter the phrase you want to search by and hit Enter or Return. This will carry out an instant search that includes all subfolders. If that fails to produce any results, or you want to expand the search criteria, you can click on the New Search button which will open the Find dialog shown in Step 3. Here, you'll find more search options such as the ability to combine different match criteria and match policies. If Bridge has not had a chance to cache the files in all folders yet, you can select the 'Include Non-Indexed Files' option. This will make for more thorough, but slower searches.

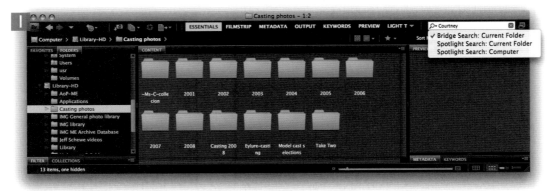

1 This shows a Bridge window view where I was about to carry out a file search of a master Casting photos folder, looking for any images that matched the term 'Courtney'. You'll note that there are three search options available. In this instance I used a Bridge search, which would carry out a search by file name and keywords.

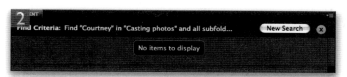

2 The standard Bridge search gave no results, so I clicked on the New Search button.

Skipping the Bridge search field

You can skip the Bridge search field completely and open the Find dialog shown in Step 3 directly. Just go to the Edit menu and choose 'Find', or use the ⌘ F ctrl F keyboard shortcut.

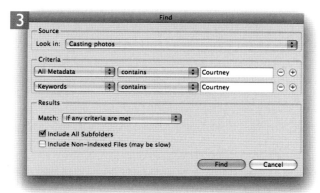

3 This opened the Find dialog, which allowed me to expand the search criteria used. Here, I changed the 'File Name' criteria to 'All Metadata' (note: you'll have to retype the search phrases again when you do this) and clicked 'Find'.

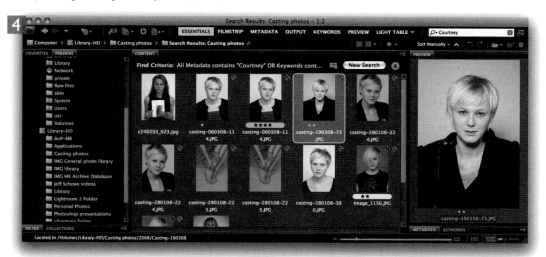

4 This time I was more successful, because Bridge now included all metadata search criteria such as the Caption IPTC metadata that had been edited via Lightroom and the results of the search were now displayed in the Content panel area.

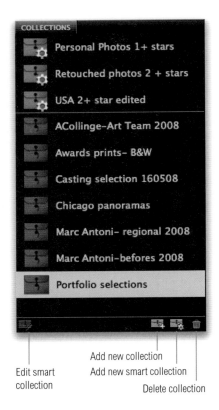

Add new collection
Edit smart   Add new smart collection
collection
                    Delete collection

Figure 11.49 The Collections panel showing
normal and smart collections.

Collections panel

The Collections panel (Figure 11.49) is kind of new to
Bridge CS4. I say 'kind of' because there was previously a
Collections panel in Bridge, which has now made a return
by being better as well as smarter than before.

The ability to create collections is an important feature
in any image management program (such as Lightroom),
but it's even more important for a file browser program
such as Bridge. This is because collections can allow you to
quickly access specific groups of images. To create a new
collection, all you have to do is make a selection of images
in Bridge and then click on the Add New Collection button
in the Collections panel. Or, you can click on the Add New
Collection button first to create a new collection and then
drag files to the collection. You see, with collections you
are not limited to refining the images in single folders;
you can drag image across from other folders in order to
create a group of images. In Figure 11.49 I highlighted the
'Portfolio selections' collection, and as the title suggests,
this collection could be used to store images that have
portfolio potential. To remove photos from a collection,
you need to make a selection of the photos and then click
on the Remove From Collection button (Figure 11.50). To
delete a collection, select the collection in the Collections
panel and then click the Delete button.

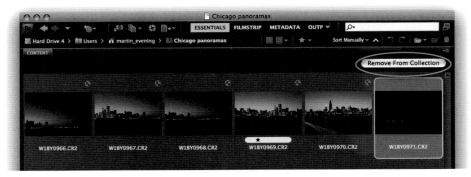

Figure 11.50 To remove a file (or files) from a collection, click on the Remove
From Collection button (circled).

Smart Collections

As well as creating normal collections, you can also click on the Add New Smart collection button to open the Edit Smart Collection dialog shown in Figure 11.51, where you can choose the folder group to look in, followed by the various criteria to filter by. In Figure 11.51 I filtered the images in the Retouched masters folder to create a collection containing PSD files only with a two star rating or higher.

Smart Collection rules

The Criteria section can be used to add one or more file selection criteria and each item will have conditional rules. So for example, when you select 'Document Type', you can choose to filter according to whether files equal or don't equal this criteria. When the 'Rating' option is selected you can choose to filter according to whether files have the exact same rating, or the same and greater, etc. Next comes the Match section. If you select the 'If any criteria are met' option, this acts as an 'AND' sort function, where files are sorted according to whether they meet any one of the individual criteria. If the 'If all criteria are met' option is selected, this acts as an 'OR' sort function, where files are sorted according to whether they meet all of the individual criteria.

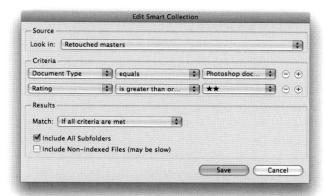

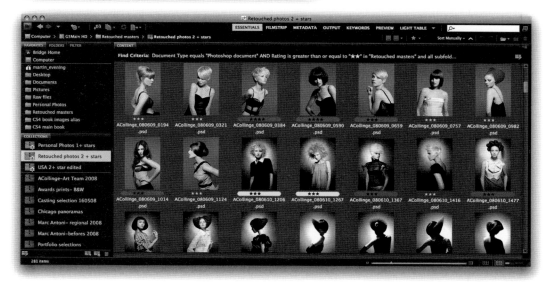

Figure 11.51 This shows the Edit Smart Collection dialog and, below, the results that the Smart Collection settings produced.

Automatic sRGB conversions

Prior to CS4 you had to make sure that all the RGB source files were in the sRGB color space, otherwise the colors could look very different when viewed in a non-color managed web browser (i.e. just about all web browsers). Bridge CS4 now automatically converts everything to sRGB.

Output to Web and PDF

There has been a radical shake-up in the way web galleries and contact sheets are generated in CS4. These are now Bridge output options and both have brand new interfaces. Not too much has been lost in this transition and there are a few small improvements, although in my view the changes in CS4 represent only a tiny step forward and there's been a missed opportunity here to make some really significant improvements to the Web and Contact sheet output.

To put Bridge into output mode, click on the Output workspace. This will reveal the Output Preview and Output panels, where you can choose between the PDF and Web Gallery output options

Web output

We'll start with the Web Gallery output, which can be used to process selected images and automatically generate all the HTML code that's needed to build a website, complete with thumbnail images, individual gallery pages and navigable link buttons. This feature can

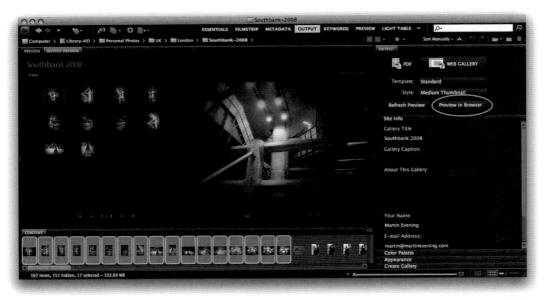

Figure 11.52 This shows an example of a Web Gallery output preview in Bridge.

save you many hours of repetitious work. Imagine you have a set of Photoshop images that need forwarding to a client or colleague. When you build a self-contained web gallery (such as the example shown in Figure 11.52), the processed images and HTML pages can be output to a destination folder or uploaded directly to a designated server address. The source can be any folder of images, regardless of whether they are in RGB or CMYK color mode, because the Web Gallery output process converts all images to sRGB anyway and the image order can be changed by simply dragging the thumbnails in the Bridge window. It is not essential that you resize them to the exact viewing size, as the 'Web Gallery' options allow you to precisely scale the gallery images and thumbnails down in size while they are being processed.

There is a choice of 19 template styles to choose from in Bridge, a few of which are shown in Figures 11.53–11.57. Some of these templates have a simple HTML table design, while others utilize frames and basic JavaScript. All these gallery styles can be customized to varying extents by adjusting the settings shown in Figures 11.58–11.61. Once you have selected a gallery style and adjusted the settings, you can then click on the Preview in Browser button (circled in Figure 11.52) to see an updated preview in the Output Preview panel. This offers a quick overview of the gallery layout using the photos that you are about to process and does so without leaving Bridge. Alternatively, you can use the Preview in Browser button to generate a temporary website on-the-fly that can be previewed in an actual browser program. Now, the thing to be aware of here is that whichever method you choose, the output preview only generates a gallery preview from the first 10 photos that have been selected in the Content panel. The reason for this is because the web gallery has to rebuild from the original source files each time you make the slightest change to a gallery layout (even if its just a simple change to the banner description). For this reason, the Web Gallery previews are restricted to no more than 10 photos.

Web Photo Gallery alternative

If you want to know what happened to the Web Photo Gallery, it has been removed from the default installation of CS4, but it can still be installed into Photoshop (not Bridge). There should be a folder called 'Extras' on the CS4 DVD and you'll need to look out for the WebContactSheetII. plugin and install this in the Photoshop application/Plug-ins/Automate folder. You will also need to copy across the Web Photo Gallery folder and place it in the Photoshop application/Presets folder. Now restart Photoshop. Once you have done this, you will find that the Web Photo Gallery appears listed in the File ⇨ Automate submenu. This will then give you access to all the extra 'old style' gallery templates, which include useful gallery styles such as the Feedback template, where visitors can send you an email that includes their chosen selection of images plus any feedback comments. Unfortunately, you won't be able to generate web galleries from selected photos in Bridge. Your only option will be to output direct from a chosen folder. Or, you could still keep Bridge CS3 installed on your computer for those times when you wish to use the old Web Photo Gallery feature via the Tools menu.

Output gallery styles

This shows you a few examples of the Web Gallery templates in Photoshop CS4. These pages were created using the default Web Gallery settings. As you will read over the page, there is plenty of scope for you to produce your own customized Web Photo Gallery pages.

Output gallery settings

Over the next four pages (550–553) I have provided a rundown of all the Web Gallery output options, and included the alternative panel options where these vary for the different types of gallery styles.

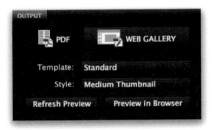

Figure 11.53 The Standard 'Medium Thumbnail' gallery style.

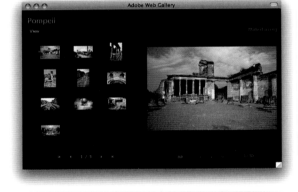

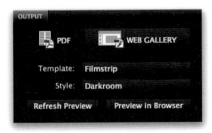

Figure 11.54 The Filmstrip 'Darkroom' gallery style.

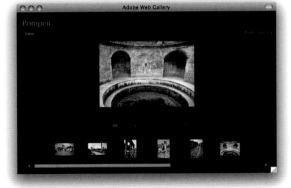

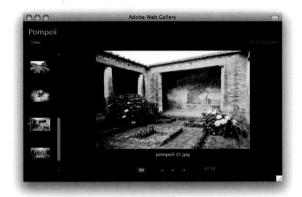

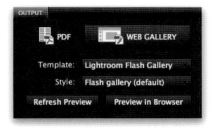

Figure 11.55 The default Lightroom Flash gallery style.

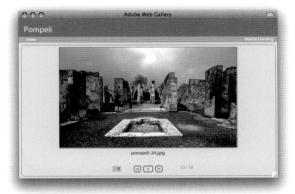

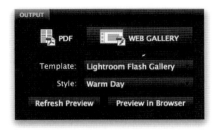

Figure 11.56 The Lightroom Flash Gallery 'Warm Day' gallery style (shown here in Slideshow page mode).

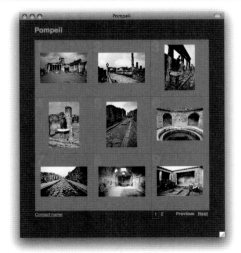

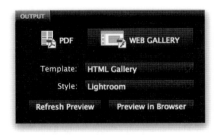

Figure 11.57 The Lightroom HTML gallery style.

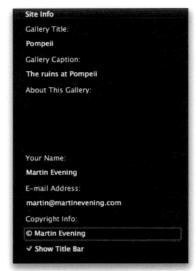

Figure 11.58 The Site Info panel can be used to add extra information such as a title and caption for the gallery pages and contact info. For example, you could type in your name, and the email address you enter below will become a link that is associated with the 'Your Name' section. Visitors to the pages can simply click here to open a new email window (addressed to you) in their mail program. All this is dependent on whether you have the 'Show Title Bar' option checked. If this is switched off, no Site Info will be added to the gallery pages.

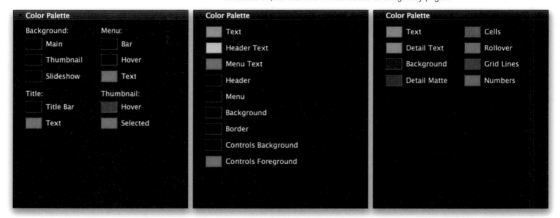

Figure 11.59 The Color Palette panel can be used to customize the appearance of the pages. These screen shots show the default Color Palette settings for (from left to right) the Bridge Standard Flash galleries, Lightroom Flash and Lightroom HTML galleries. As you can see, the options are slightly different for each and there are plenty of opportunities to create different design appearances. For example, check out some of the Lightroom Flash gallery templates to see what is possible.

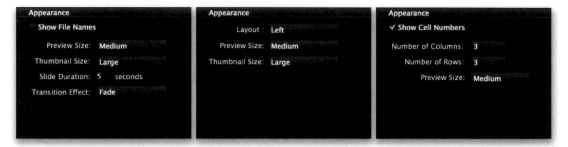

Figure 11.60 The Appearance panel can be used to adjust the gallery layouts. These screen shots show the default Appearance panel settings for (from left to right) the Bridge Standard Flash galleries, Lightroom Flash and Lightroom HTML galleries. So for example, with the main Bridge Flash gallery styles you can adjust things like the size of the thumbnails and preview images, the slide duration time for the Flash gallery styles, and fade effects. Obviously, the smaller the thumbnail size, the faster the gallery pages will load. For the Lightroom Flash galleries you can choose from the Scrolling, Left, Paginated and Slideshow Only styles, and for the Lightroom HTML gallery you can choose the number of columns and rows to use.

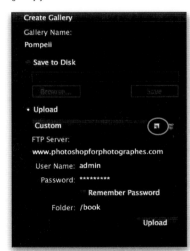

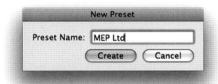

Figure 11.61 The Create Gallery panel can be used when choosing either 'Save to Disk', which saves the gallery pages to a folder on the computer, or when choosing 'Upload', where the gallery pages can be automatically uploaded to a pre-configured server address. Here, you will need to enter the server address, the user name and password, plus a primary folder location. Once you have done this, click on the Upload button to begin uploading directly to the server. You can save server settings by clicking on the document button (circled) and naming them. These settings will then be available as a menu option where it currently says 'Custom'.

Managing folders on the server

It is great that you can upload galleries direct to a server, but you will still need to use an FTP program to manage the folders once they have been uploaded there. For example, you can only use the Create Gallery panel to add folders to the server. You can't use it to remove them.

Output preferences

There are just a few final points to take into consideration when generating output files via Bridge. If you go to the Output preferences (Figure 11.62), you can check the 'Use Solo mode for Output panel behavior' to allow single-panel clicking to expand the selected panel and close all others at the same time. I would suggest that you keep the 'Convert Multi-Byte Filenames to Full ASCII' item checked, as this helps overcome any file naming irregularities that might otherwise trip up a web server and prevent any web output files from being uploaded. The 'Preserve Embedded Color Profile' option is best left unchecked. Normally, in a color managed workflow you would want to preserve embedded profiles. However, in this instance, preserving the embedded profile overrides the built-in 'convert to sRGB' procedure and keeps the images in their current profile spaces. Since very few web browser programs can actually read embedded profiles, you should leave this unchecked and let everything convert to sRGB. In the case of PDF output it gets very confusing, because if you select this option it skips the convert to sRGB step and 'assigns sRGB' instead! Why is unclear, so leave it unchecked.

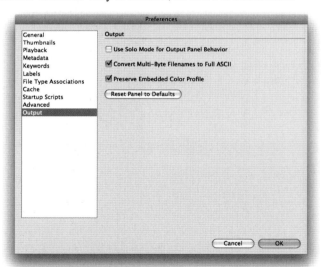

Figure 11.62 The Bridge Output preferences.

PDF Output

The 'PDF Output' option offers a replacement for the previous Contact Sheet II and PDF Presentation automated plug-ins. Conceptually, PDF Output has the potential to offer an improved PDF presentation and contact sheet layout tool. Unfortunately, this new feature is badly compromised by a number of design flaws. As with the Web Gallery output, there is no image cache to store the output preview images and Bridge has to read the image data from the selected images in the Content panel each time you make so much as a small change to the layout settings and click on the Refresh Preview button. If you intend to use PDF Output to print contact sheets, you'll also have to go through the additional step of opening the PDF output via a PDF reader program and print from there, rather than print direct from Bridge. Another problem is that you can't create custom contact sheet layout presets. My advice is if you have Lightroom, you don't need Bridge output. This is because Lightroom does store a cache of the image previews and makes use of this in two ways. It uses the image cache to quickly build a preview of how the contact sheet will look, and it also allows you the option to print directly in 'draft mode' from the preview data. The net result of all this is that Lightroom can generate contact sheet prints roughly 100 times faster than Bridge, which is quite a big difference in performance speed between these two programs!

That said, for the sake of non-Lightroom users I shall continue to run through the remaining options here, but I do suggest you read through the sidebar on how to install the previous Contact Sheet II feature, should you wish to use this as an alternative to PDF Output. One of the benefits of using Contact Sheet is that you can print direct out of Bridge although, as with the PDF Output, Contact Sheet II can only generate contact sheets by reading in all the original print data, rather than make use of an image cache.

Contact Sheet II alternative

The Contact Sheet II feature has also been removed from the default installation of CS4, but can still be installed into Photoshop (not Bridge). There should be a folder called 'Extras' on the CS4 DVD and you'll need to look out for the ContactSheetII.plugin and install this in the Photoshop application/Plug-ins/Automate folder. Then restart Photoshop. Once you have done this, you will find that Contact Sheet II... appears listed in the File ⇨ Automate submenu. This will then allow you to create contact sheets via the old Contact Sheet II interface, where you will find it quicker to preview the grid layout when setting out a cell grid structure for your contact sheets (although you won't be able to see the images previewed of course). Unfortunately, you won't be able to print out from selected photos in Bridge. Your only option will be to print direct from a chosen folder. Or, you could still keep Bridge CS3 installed on your computer for those times when you wish to use Contact Sheet II via the Tools menu.

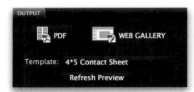

Figure 11.63 The Output panel.

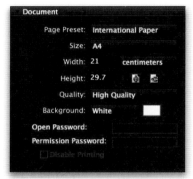

Figure 11.64 The Document panel

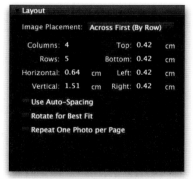

Figure 11.65 The Layout panel

The PDF Output panels

We'll start here with the Output panel (Figure 11.63), where you can choose the PDF Output option which will switch the Output panel into PDF output mode. Here, you will see the 'Template' option, where you'll find a choice of eight output templates which, incidentally, are identical to the ones found in the old Contact Sheet II feature. The Refresh Preview works the same as the Web Gallery. It generates a preview of how the template design will look based on the selected photos, using as many photos as are required to fill a full page template. So for example, if you selected the 4*5 Contact Sheet template, Bridge will use the first 20 images only to generate a contact sheet preview.

The Document panel (Figure 11.64) can be used to set the document size based on International, U.S. Paper, Photo or Web page presets. Depending on the option selected here, this will affect the Size options below. Alternatively, you can enter in a custom page size, in a choice of units. The Background color can be black or white, or you can click on the color swatch next to this to pick a custom color. If you want, you can use the 'Open Password' and 'Permissions Password' options to make the PDF document password protected (including the ability to prevent people from printing the document).

The Layout panel (Figure 11.65) is where you can customize the layout, by editing the number of columns and rows, and set the maximum allowed size for each image plus margin height and width. The margin spacing should be at least as wide as that allowed by your printer. In most instances, the leading page edge (the right margin) will require a wider margin gap than the Top, Bottom or Left margin edges. Bridge doesn't provide any clues here, so unless you know what this margin gap should be, your best bet is to use trial and error to work out the safe margin width. One option is to select the 'Auto-Spacing' option, where Bridge will use its knowledge of the maximum printable page area to auto-adjust the placement of the images. If the 'Rotate for Best Fit' option is selected, Bridge will auto-rotate landscape and portrait images so that each prints as big as possible within the horizontal and vertical size limits. Lastly, the 'Repeat One Photo per page' option can be used to create PDF layouts where each image is repeated multiple times on each page document.

The Overlays panel (Figure 11.66) lets you add the filename below each image. The other options let you decide which font, font size and color can be used.

The Playback panel options (Figure 11.67) apply specifically to the creation of PDF presentations, where you can use the settings here to determine whether the PDF is opened automatically in Full screen mode, how long each image will appear on the screen for and whether to loop the slideshow presentation from the beginning again. The Transition menu provides lots of image transition options from a simple 'Fade dissolve' to more fancy special effects, some of which will provide additional parameter options.

The Watermark panel (Figure 11.68) lets you add a custom text overlay. This would typically be used for adding a copyright message to each image so that when someone is viewing images as a PDF slideshow, they are made aware that they are looking at copyrighted images. The thing to be aware of here is that Bridge places just a single watermark dead center on the page and it is therefore only really useful if you are using it to output single images, although you could use it to apply a © symbol in a large font size in the foreground. Given this limitation, the Watermark panel is not really of much use when it comes to generating multiple image contact sheet outputs.

PDF Output options

Once you have configured everything in the above panels, you'll be ready to click on the Save... button. This pops a dialog asking where you want to save the PDF to (but without offering any further PDF options). The main thing to watch out for here is that you have the 'Preserve Embedded Profile' switched off in the Bridge preferences. It's confusing, I know, because in this instance choosing 'Preserve Embedded Profile' will actually mess up the color management rather than improve it!

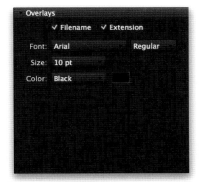

Figure 11.66 The Overlays panel.

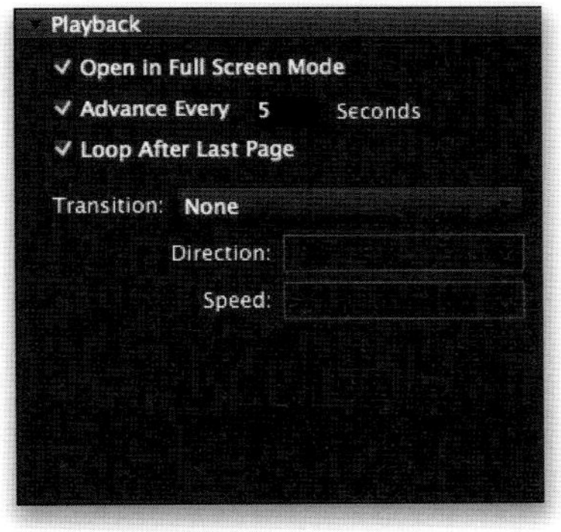

Figure 11.67 The Playback panel.

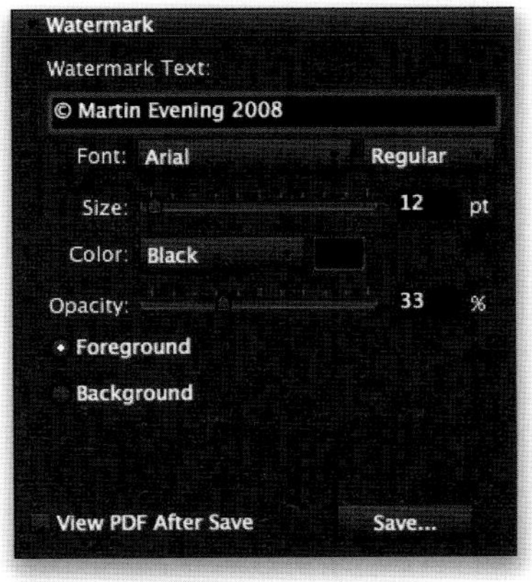

Figure 11.68 The Watermark panel

Photomerge with non-raw images

If you are working from non-raw originals, you might like to consider using the 'Load Files Into Photoshop Layers...' option. This allows you to open all the selected images as layers in a single Photoshop image first. You can then use Image ⇨ Image Size to reduce the pixel dimensions before choosing Edit ⇨ Auto-Align layers followed by Edit ⇨ Auto-Blend images.

Bridge automation

The Photoshop Automate features can all be accessed directly in Bridge by going to the Tools menu and selecting one of the options from the Photoshop submenu (Figure 11.69). For example, to apply a Photoshop action, make a selection of images in Bridge and choose Tools ⇨ Photoshop ⇨ Batch... . You can then configure the Batch dialog to apply an action routine to the selected photos. The Image Processor can be used to batch process images in Photoshop where you typically want to output, say, a set of JPEG versions of an image at a set pixel size and compression setting (see Chapter 15 for more about Batch and Image Processing). The Merge to HDR feature was discussed earlier on in Chapter 7 and Photomerge was discussed in Chapter 8. Using the Tools ⇨ Photoshop menu, you can carry out either of these processes directly from Bridge. The thing to watch out for here is the size of your source images. If you are working from raw originals in Bridge, you may want to open these via the Camera Raw dialog first, go to the workflow options (see page 147) and set the pixel output size to something lower than the full image size, then click on the Done button to apply this setting to the selected images. Then, when you choose Photomerge, Bridge will open all these files at the smaller size that was set in Camera Raw.

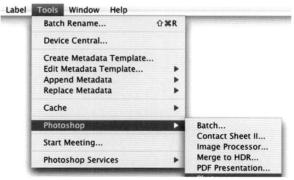

Figure 11.69 The Photoshop Automate menu is available from the Tools menu in Bridge.

Renaming images

To rename an image in Bridge, just click and hold the mouse down on the file name and then type in a new one. To batch rename a selection of images, choose Batch Rename... from the Tools menu (⌘ *Shift* R *ctrl* *Shift* R), which will open the Batch Rename dialog shown in Figure 11.70. You can rename the files in the same folder or rename and move them to a new (specified) folder. In the New Filenames section you can configure the file renaming structure by clicking on the plus buttons to add new components to the file renaming structure. Note that when you mouse down on a renaming component there will often be further options that you can choose from.

In the example shown here, the first field was set as a Text entry, in which I entered the word 'Casting', followed by an underscore. Next, I chose a YYMMDD Date Time setting based on the date the file was created. This was followed by another text underscore and, lastly, a four digit serial number that started with the number '1' (if I had wanted the serial number to begin at a number other than 0001, I could enter a new number to start the sequence from). Note there is no need to enter a file extension at the end, because Bridge does so automatically.

Editing the Batch renaming fields

In the Batch Rename dialog, the default mode settings are configured to do nothing at all but, once you start editing the pop-up menus, you will discover that the renaming options are quite extensive. You can select items such as Text, where you can enter your own text data. You can also incorporate the original file name in parts of the new name, which will make a lot of people I know very happy.

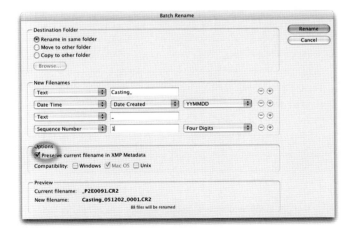

Figure 11.70 The Batch Rename dialog will let you copy the files to another folder as you rename, as well as preserve the current file name in the XMP Metadata (circled).

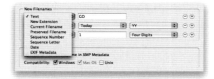

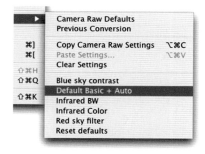

Figure 11.71 Lots of extra options become available as you mouse down on the pop-up menus. Selecting the 'Preserved Filename' option will restore the original file name, providing the option circled in Figure 11.70 is checked.

Figure 11.72 The Bridge Edit ⇨ Develop Settings submenu.

Renaming schemes

The renaming scheme you use can be anything you choose. There are no hard and fast rules. But whatever method you decide to use, it should be done with a view to the future and should avoid the possibility of you creating file names that overlap with other files. I prefer to adopt a naming scheme where a short text description (such as the client name or an abbreviation) is followed by the date shot, using the YYMMDD format, followed by a four digital serial number.

Undoing a Batch Rename

If you inspect the 'Batch Rename' options closely you will notice there is an option to preserve the original file name. So if you do slip up for some reason, Bridge and Photoshop CS4 are able to locate and reassign the original name to the file. But, and it's a big but, this will only be possible if you remember to check the box that says 'Preserve current filename in XMP Metadata'.

Applying Camera Raw settings

You can use the Edit ⇨ Develop Settings menu in Bridge to apply a saved Camera Raw preset setting to selected images or choose 'Previous Conversion' to apply the last used Camera Raw setting. The settings listed here will be like the ones you also see listed in the Camera Raw Preset panel (see page 225–226).

You can also use this menu to copy and paste settings from one file to another, or better still work with the keyboard shortcuts. Use ⌘ ⌥ C ctrl alt C to copy a setting and ⌘ ⌥ V ctrl alt V to paste. The Clear Settings command will remove any applied develop settings and reapply the default Camera Raw settings.

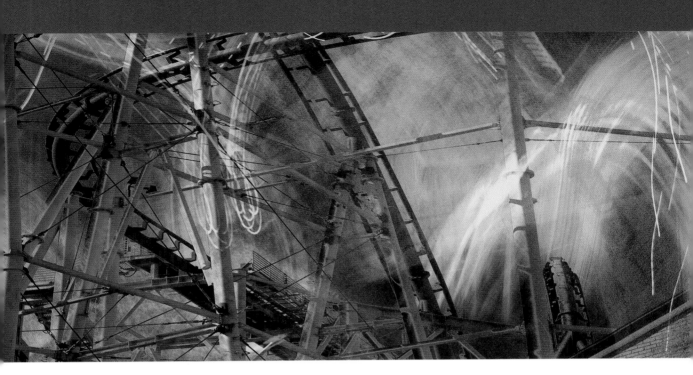

Chapter 12

Color Management

Photoshop 5.0 was justifiably praised as a ground-breaking upgrade when it was released in the summer of 1998, although the changes made to the color management setup were less well received in some quarters. This was because the revised system was perceived to be complex and unnecessary. Bruce Fraser once said of the Photoshop 5.0 color management system 'it's push-button simple, as long as you know which of the 60 or so buttons to push'! Attitudes have changed since then (as has the interface) and it is fair to say that most people working today in the pre-press industry are now using ICC color profile managed workflows. The aim of this chapter is to introduce the basic concepts of color management before looking at the color management interface in Photoshop and the various color management settings.

The need for color management

An advertising agency art buyer was once invited to address a meeting of photographers. The chair, Mike Laye, suggested we could ask him anything we wanted, except 'Would you like to see my book?' And if he had already seen your book, we couldn't ask him why he hadn't called it back in again. And if he had called it in again we were not allowed to ask why we didn't get the job. And finally, if we did get the job we were absolutely forbidden to ask why the color in the printed ad looked nothing like the original photograph!

That in a nutshell is a problem which has bugged many of us throughout our working lives, and it is one which will be familiar to anyone who has ever experienced the difficulty of matching colors on a computer system with the original or a printed output. Figure 12.1 has two versions of the same photograph. One shows how the Photoshop image looks previewed on the monitor and the other is an example of how a printer might interpret and reproduce those same colors if no attempt is made to color manage the image.

So why is there sometimes such a marked difference between what is seen on the screen and the actual printed result? Well, digital images are nothing more than just bunches of numbers, and good color management is all about making sense of those numbers and translating them into meaningful colors at the various stages of the image making process.

The way things were

Fifteen or more years ago, most photographers only used their computers to do basic administration work and there were absolutely no digital imaging devices to be found in a photographer's studio (unless you counted the photocopier). If you needed a color print made from a chrome transparency, you gave the original to the printer at a photographic lab and they matched the print visually to your original. Professional photographers would also supply chrome transparencies or prints to the client and the photographs then went to the printer to be digitized

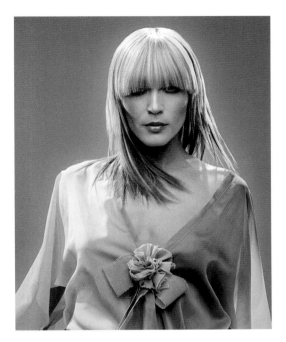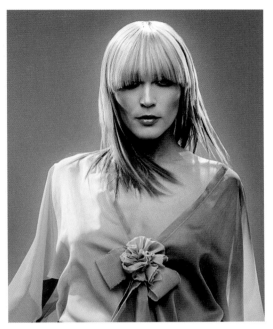

using a high-end drum scanner, which would be configured to produce a CMYK file ready to insert in a specific publication. That was probably about the limit of the photographer's responsibilities, and if color corrections were required the scanner operators would carry this out themselves on the output file.

These days a significant number of photographers, illustrators and artists are now originating their own files from digital cameras, desktop scanners or directly within Photoshop. This has effectively removed the repro expert who previously did all the scanning and matching of the colors on the press. Therefore, there is no getting away from the fact that if you supply digital images to a printer, you will be deemed responsible should any problems occur in the printing. This may seem like a daunting task, but with Photoshop it is not hard to color manage your images with confidence.

Figure 12.1 The picture on the left shows how you might see an image on your screen in Photoshop and the one on the right represents how that same image might print if sent directly to a printer without applying any form of color management. You might think it is merely a matter of making the output color less blue in order to successfully match the original. Yes, that would get the colors closer, but when trying to match color between different digital devices the story is actually a lot more complex than that. The color management system that was first introduced in Photoshop 5.0 will enable you to make use of ICC profiles, which can match these colors from the scanner to the screen and to the printer with extreme accuracy.

Client: Russell Eaton. Model: Lidia @ MOT.

Why not all RGB spaces are the same

Go into any TV showroom and you will probably see rows of televisions all tuned to the same broadcast source but each displaying the picture quite differently (Figure 12.2). This is a known problem that affects all digital imaging devices, be they digital cameras, scanners, monitors or printers. Each digital imaging device has its own unique characteristics, and unless you are able to quantify what those individual device characteristics are, you won't be able to communicate effectively with other device components and programs in your own computer setup, let alone anyone working outside your own system color loop.

Some computer monitors have manual controls that allow you to adjust the brightness and contrast (and in some cases the RGB color as well) and the printer driver will also allow you to make color balance adjustments, but is this really enough? Plus, if you are able to get the monitor and your printer to match, will the colors you see on your screen appear the same on another person's monitor?

RGB devices

Successful color management relies on the use of profiles to describe the characteristics of each device, such as a scanner or a printer, and using a color management system to translate the profile data between each device in the chain. Consider for a moment the scale of such a task. We wish to capture a full color original subject, digitize it with a scanner or digital camera, examine the resulting image via a computer screen and finally reproduce it in print. It is possible with today's technology to simulate the expected print output of a digitized image on the display with remarkable accuracy. Nevertheless, one should not underestimate the huge difference between the mechanics of all the various bits of equipment used in the above production process. Most digital devices are RGB devices and, just like musical instruments, they all possess unique color tonal properties, such that no two devices are always identical or will be able to reproduce color exactly the same way as another device. Nor is it always possible to match in print all the colors which are visible to the human eye, and converting light into electrical signals via a device such as a CCD chip is not the same as projecting pixels onto a computer screen or reproducing a photograph with colored ink on paper.

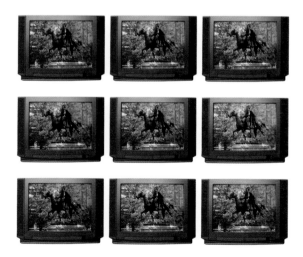

Figure 12.2 While some digital devices may look identical on the outside, they'll all have individual output characteristics. For example, in a TV showroom you may notice how each television screen displays a different colored image.

The versatility of RGB

A major advantage of working in RGB is that you can access all the bells and whistles of Photoshop which would otherwise be hidden or grayed out in CMYK mode, and if you use Adobe RGB or ProPhoto RGB you will have a larger color gamut to work with. These days there is also no telling how a final image may end up being reproduced. A photograph may get used in a variety of ways, with multiple CMYK separations made to suit several types of publications, each requiring a slightly different CMYK conversion (because CMYK is not a 'one size fits all' color space). For example, high-end retouching for advertising usage is usually done in RGB mode and the CMYK conversions and film separations are produced working directly from the digital file to suit the various media usages.

Photographers are mainly involved in the RGB capture end of the business. The proliferation of Photoshop, plus the advent of high quality desktop scanners and digital cameras, means that more images than ever before are starting out in, and staying in, RGB color. This is an important factor that makes color management so necessary and also one of the reasons why I devote so much attention to the managing of RGB color, here and elsewhere in the book. So, if professional photographers are more likely to supply a digital file at the end of a job, how will this fit in with existing repro press workflows that are based on the use of CMYK color? Although digital capture has clearly taken off, the RGB to CMYK issue still has to be resolved. If the work you create is intended for print, the conversion of RGB to CMYK must be addressed at some point and so for this important reason we shall also be looking at CMYK color conversions later on in this chapter.

Color management references

If your main area of business revolves around the preparation of CMYK separations for print, then I do recommend you invest in a training course or book that deals with CMYK repro issues. I highly recommend the following books: *Real World Color Management* by Bruce Fraser, Chris Murphy and Fred Bunting. *Color Management for Photographers* by Andrew Rodney and *Getting Colour Right, The Complete Guide to Digital Colour Correction* by Neil Barstow and Michael Walker.

Color vision trickery

They say that seeing is believing, but nothing could be further from the truth since there are many interesting quirks and surprises in the way we humans perceive vision. There is an interesting book on this subject titled *Why We See What We Do*, by Dale Purves and R. Beau Lotto (Sinauer Associates, Inc). There is also a website at www.purveslab.net where you can have a lot of fun playing with the interactive visual tests, to discover how easily our eyes can be deceived. What you learn from studies like this is that color can never be properly described in absolute mathematical terms. How we perceive a color can also be greatly influenced by the other colors that surround it. This is a factor that designers use when designing a product or a page layout. You do this every time you evaluate a photograph, often without even being aware of it.

Beyond CMYK

There are other types of output to consider, not just CMYK. Hexachrome is a six-color ink printing process that can extend the printing color gamut beyond the conventional limitations of CMYK. This advanced printing process is currently available only through specialist print shops and is suitable for high quality design print jobs. Millions have been invested in the four-color presses currently used to print magazines and brochures, so expect four-color printing to still be around for a long time to come, but Hexachrome will open the way for improved color reproduction from RGB originals. Photoshop supports six-color channel output conversions from RGB, but you will need to buy a separate plug-in utility like HexWrench. Multimedia publishing is able to take advantage of the full depth of the sRGB color range (which is probably about the limit of most LCD screens). If you are working in a screen-based environment for CD, DVD and web publishing, RGB is ideal. And with today's web browsers, color management can sometimes be turned on to take full advantage of the enhanced color control these programs can now offer.

Output-centric color management

Printers who work in the repro industry naturally tend to have an 'output-centric' view of color management. Their main concern is getting the CMYK color to look right on a CMYK press, and printers can color correct a CMYK image 'by the numbers' if they wish. Take a look at the photograph of the young model in Figure 12.3. Her Caucasian flesh tones should contain equal amounts of magenta and yellow ink, with maybe a slightly greater amount of yellow, while the cyan ink should be a quarter to a third of the magenta. This rule will hold true for most CMYK press conditions and the accompanying table compares the CMYK and RGB space measurements of a flesh tone color. However, you will notice there are no similar formulae that can be used to describe the RGB pixel values of a flesh tone. If you were to write down the flesh tone numbers for every RGB device color space, you could in theory build an RGB color space reference table. From this you could feasibly construct a system that would assign meaning to these RGB numbers for any given RGB space. This is basically what an ICC profile does, except an ICC profile may contain several hundred color reference points. These can then be read and interpreted automatically by the Photoshop software and give meaning to the color numbers.

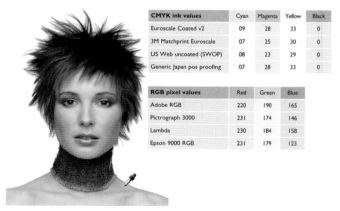

CMYK ink values	Cyan	Magenta	Yellow	Black
Euroscale Coated v2	09	28	33	0
3M Matchprint Euroscale	07	25	30	0
US Web uncoated (SWOP)	08	23	29	0
Generic Japan pos proofing	07	28	33	0

RGB pixel values	Red	Green	Blue
Adobe RGB	220	190	165
Pictrograph 3000	231	174	146
Lambda	230	184	158
Epson 9000 RGB	231	179	123

Figure 12.3 The tables shown here record the color readings in RGB and CMYK color spaces of a typical Caucasian flesh tone. As is explained in the text, while the CMYK readings are all fairly consistent, this is not the case when you try to compare the RGB values.

Profiled color management

The objective of profiled color management is to use the measured characteristics of everything involved in the image editing workflow, from capture through to print, to reliably translate the color at each stage of the process. In a normal Photoshop workflow, the color management begins with reading the profiled RGB color data from the incoming file and if necessary converting it to the current Photoshop RGB workspace. While an RGB image is being edited in Photoshop the workspace image data is converted on-the-fly to the profiled monitor space and sent to the computer display, so that the colors are viewed correctly. When the image is finally output as a print, the RGB workspace data is converted to the profile space of the printer. Or, you might carry out an RGB to CMYK conversion to the CMYK profile of a known proof printer.

A workspace profile is therefore a useful piece of information that can be embedded in an image file. When a profile is read by Photoshop and color management is switched on, Photoshop is automatically able to find out everything it needs to know in order to manage the color correctly from there on. Note that this will also be dependent on you calibrating your monitor, but essentially all you have to do apart from that is to open the Photoshop Color Settings from the Edit menu and select a suitable preset such as the US Prepress Default setting. Do this and you are all set to start working in an ICC color managed workflow.

Think of a profile as being like a postcode (or ZIP code) for images. For example, the address label shown in Figure 12.4 was rather optimistically sent to me at 'Flat 14, London', but thanks to the postcode it arrived safely! Some labs and printers have been known to argue that profiles cause color management problems. This I am afraid is like a courier company explaining that the late delivery of your package was due to you including a ZIP code in the delivery address. A profile can be read or it can be ignored. What is harmful in these circumstances is an operator who refuses to use an ICC workflow. If you feel you are getting the runaround treatment, it may be time to change labs.

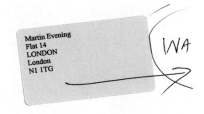

Figure 12.4 Even if you have never been to London before, you know it's a fairly big place and 'Flat 14, London' was not going to help the postman locate my proper address. However, the all-important ZIP code or postcode was able to help identify exactly where the letter should have been delivered. An image profile is just like a ZIP code – it can tell Photoshop everything it needs to know about a file's provenance.

Translating the color data

One way to comprehend the importance of giving meaning to the numbers in a digital file is to make a comparison with what happens when language loses its meaning. There is an excellent book by Lynne Truss called *Eats, Shoots & Leaves: The Zero Tolerance Approach to Punctuation*. It is partly a rant against poor punctuation, but a so stresses the importance of using punctuation to assign exact meaning to the words we read. Remove the punctuation and words will easily lose their true intended meaning. Another good example is the way words can have different meanings in other languages. So a word viewed out of context can be meaningless unless you know the language that it belongs to. For example, the word 'cane' in English means 'dog' in Italian.

Color Management Modules

The International Color Consortium (ICC) is an industry body that represents the leading manufacturers of imaging hardware and software. The ICC grew out of the original Color Consortium that was established in 1993 and has been responsible for extending and developing the original ColorSync architecture to produce the standardized ICC format, which enables profiles created by different vendors to work together. All ICC systems are basically able to translate the color gamut of a source space via a reference space (the Profile Connection Space) and accurately convert these colors to the gamut of the destination space. At the heart of any ICC system is the Color Management Module, or CMM, which carries out all the profile conversion processing. Although the ICC format specification is standardized, this is one area where there are some subtle differences in the way each CMM handles the data. In Photoshop you have a choice of three CMMs: Adobe Color Engine (ACE), Apple ColorSync, or Apple CMM. There are other brands of CMM that you can use as well, but this really need not concern most Photoshop users as I recommend you use the default Adobe (ACE) CMM in Photoshop.

The Profile Connection Space

If the CMM is the engine that drives color management, then the Profile Connection Space (PCS) is at the hub of any color management system. The PCS is the translator that can interpret the colors from a profiled space and define them using either a CIE XYZ or CIE LAB color space. The Profile Connection Space is an interim space. It uses unambiguous numerical values to describe color values using a color model that matches the way we humans observe color (see Figure 12.5). You can think of the PCS as being like the color management equivalent of a multilingual dictionary that can translate one language into any other language.

If an ICC profile is embedded in the file, Photoshop will recognize this and know how to correctly interpret the color data. The same thing applies to profiled CMYK files.

Photoshop uses the monitor display profile information to render a color correct preview on the monitor screen. It helps to understand here that in an ICC color managed workflow in Photoshop, what you see on the monitor is always a color corrected preview and you are not viewing the actual file data. So when the RGB image you are editing is in an RGB workspace, such as Adobe RGB, and color management is switched on, what you see on the screen is an RGB preview that has been converted from Adobe RGB to your profiled monitor RGB via the PCS (see Figure 12.6). The same thing happens when Photoshop previews CMYK data on the screen. The Photoshop color management system calculates a conversion from the file CMYK space to the monitor space. Photoshop therefore carries out all its color calculations in a virtual color space. So in a sense, it does not really matter which RGB workspace you edit with. It does not have to be exactly the same as the workspace set on another user's Photoshop system. If you are both viewing the same file, and your displays are correctly calibrated and profiled, a color image should look near enough the same on both monitors.

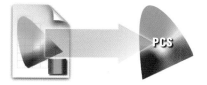

Figure 12.5 A color management system is able to read the profile information from an incoming RGB file and behind the scenes it will build a table that correlates the source RGB information with the Profile Connecting Space values.

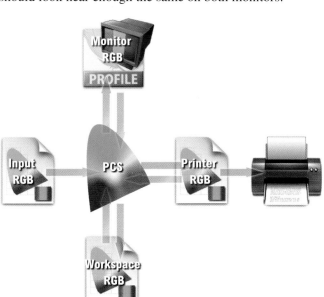

Figure 12.6 Photoshop can read or make use of the profile information of an incoming RGB file and translate the data via the Profile Connecting Space and make an RGB to RGB conversion to the current RGB workspace in Photoshop. As you work in RGB mode, the image data is converted via the PCS and uses the monitor profile to send a profile-corrected signal to the monitor display. When you make a print, the image data is then converted from the workspace RGB to the printer RGB via the PCS.

The ideal RGB working space

If you select an RGB workspace that is the same size as the monitor space, you are not using Photoshop to its full potential and more importantly you are probably clipping parts of the CMYK gamut (see Figure 12.7). For many years I would have advised you to choose Adobe RGB as your workspace, because it appeared to offer the best compromise between encompassing most of the CMYK gamut but without being so large as to be unwieldy. However, a few years ago I was in conversation with the late Bruce Fraser and he convinced me that cautionary warnings against ProPhoto RGB were perhaps a little overstated (even if you are going to end up converting a file from 16-bit to 8-bit RGB). So following Bruce's advice I mostly now use ProPhoto RGB as my principal RGB workspace, although I would still strongly advise making the big tone edits in 16-bit before converting to 8-bit. The only other thing I would caution you about is to never supply clients with ProPhoto RGB master files. If I am sending a file to someone who I believe is ICC color management savvy, I'll send them a profiled Adobe RGB version. If I am sending a file by email, or to someone who may not understand color management, I always play safe and send them an sRGB version.

Choosing an RGB workspace

Although I highly recommended that you switch on the color management settings in Photoshop, you cannot assume everyone else will. There are many other Photoshop users and color labs from the Jurassic era who are running outputs from files with Photoshop color management switched off and are not bothering to calibrate their displays properly.

If you are using Photoshop 6.0 or later it matters less individually which RGB color space you choose in the RGB setup, as long as you stick to using the same space for all your work. RGB to RGB conversions are not as destructive as RGB to CMYK conversions, but the space you plump for does matter. Once chosen you should not really change it. Plus whichever color workspace you select in the RGB color settings, you will have to be conscious of how your profiled Photoshop RGB files may appear on a non-ICC savvy Photoshop system. What follows is a guide to the listed RGB choices.

Apple RGB

This is the old Apple 13" monitor standard. In the early days of Photoshop Apple RGB was used as the default RGB editing space where the editing space was the same as the monitor space. If you have legacy images created in Photoshop on a Macintosh computer using a gamma of 1.8, you can assume Apple RGB to be the missing profile space.

sRGB IEC-61966-2.1

sRGB was conceived as a multipurpose color space standard that consumer digital devices could all standardize to. It is essentially a compromise color space that provides a uniform color space which all digital cameras and inkjet printers and monitors are able to match, since sRGB aims to match the color gamut of a typical 2.2 gamma PC monitor. Therefore if you are opening a file from a consumer digital camera or scanner and there is no profile embedded, you can assume that the missing profile should be sRGB. It is an ideal color space for web design but unsuitable for photography or serious print work. This is mainly because the sRGB space clips the CMYK gamut quite severely and you will never achieve more than 75–85% cyan in your CMYK separations.

ColorMatch RGB

ColorMatch is an open standard monitor RGB space that was implemented by Radius. ColorMatch has a gamma of 1.8 and is favored by some Macintosh users as their preferred RGB working space. Although not much larger than the gamut of a typical monitor space, it is at least a known standard and more compatible with legacy, 1.8 gamma Macintosh files.

ProPhoto RGB

This is a large gamut RGB space that has the advantage of preserving the full gamut of raw capture files when converting the raw data to RGB. It is also suited for image editing that is intended for output to photographic materials such as transparency emulsion or a photo quality inkjet printer. This is because the gamut of ProPhoto RGB extends more into the shadow areas compared with most other RGB spaces, resulting in better tonal separation in the shadow tones.

Adobe RGB (1998)

Adobe RGB (1998) has become established as a recommended RGB editing space for RGB files that are destined to be converted to CMYK. For example, the Photoshop prepress color settings all use Adobe RGB as the RGB working space. Adobe RGB was initially labeled as SMPTE-240M which was a color gamut proposed for HDTV production. As it happens, the coordinates Adobe used did not exactly match the actual SMPTE-240M specification. Nevertheless, it proved popular as an editing space for repro work and soon became known as Adobe RGB (1998). I have in the past used Adobe RGB as my preferred RGB working space, since it is well suited for RGB to CMYK color conversions.

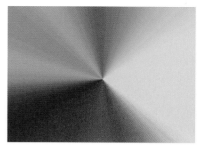

Figure 12.7 A CMYK color space is mostly smaller than the monitor RGB color space, and not all CMYK colors can be displayed accurately due to the physical display limitations of the average computer monitor. This screen shot shows a continuous spectrum going through shades of cyan, magenta and yellow. The image was then deliberately posterized in Photoshop and then captured from the view that was displayed on the monitor. Notice how the posterized steps grow wider in the yellow and cyan portions of the spectrum. This simple exercise helps pinpoint the areas of the CMYK spectrum which fall outside the gamut of a typical monitor.

Eyeball calibration

If you don't have a monitor calibration device, you can always build a profile for your monitor using a visual calibration method. You could, for example, use the Display Calibration Assistant that comes with the Mac OS X system. However, the problem with relying on visual calibration is that because our eyes are so good at adapting to light, our eyes are poor instruments to use when calibrating a device like a monitor display

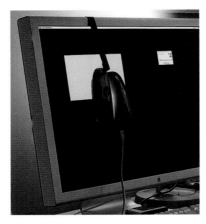

Figure 12.8 Good color management is very much dependent on having your display calibrated and profiled. This should ideally be done using a hardware calibration device such as the X-Rite Eye-One system.

Profiling the display

To get color management to work in Photoshop you have to calibrate and profile the screen display. This is by far the most important and essential first link in the color management chain. You can live without scanner profiling and it is not the end of the world if you can't profile every printer/paper combination. But you simply must have a well-calibrated and profiled display. It is after all the instrument you rely upon most when you make color editing decisions.

In Chapter 3 I mentioned some of the equipment and software options that you can buy these days and showed a quick run through of how to calibrate a computer screen with a calibration device. I would strongly urge you to purchase a proper measuring instrument and use this to calibrate the display on a regular basis. A hardware calibration device combined with a dedicated software utility is the only way that you can guarantee getting good color from your system, as this will enable you to precisely calibrate your display and build an accurate monitor profile. At the time of writing, I have found four basic monitor profiling packages, which include a colorimeter and basic software program, all for under $300. Highly recommended is the basICColor Display and Squid combination. Then there is the X-Rite Eye-One Display 2 that comes with Eye-One Match 2 software, the Monaco Optix XR system and lastly the ColorVision Monitor Spyder and Spyder2 Pro Studio. Of these I would probably recommend the X-Rite Eye-One Display 2, since I am very familiar with the (more expensive) Eye-One spectrophotometer system, which I use to calibrate and profile the display in my office (Figure 12.8). It is also an emissive spectrophotometer so I can use it to build custom printer profiles as well. The other units I have listed here are all colorimeters so these can only be used for building monitor profiles, but they are usually regarded as being equally as good as the more expensive spectrophotometers for this type of task.

Calibration and profiling

Profiling devices can be attached to the screen via rubber suckers to a CRT, or hung over the edge of an LCD display using a counter weight that gently rests the calibrator against the surface. Don't use a calibrating device with suckers on an LCD as this can easily damage the delicate surface.

The software packages used will vary in appearance but they essentially all do the same thing. The first stage is to calibrate the display to optimize the contrast and brightness, where you should end up with a display luminance of around 90–110 cd/m². Most CRT monitors will allow you to manually adjust the individual color guns to help neutralize the screen, but on an LCD display all you can adjust is usually the brightness (note that if you are using a CRT monitor it must be switched on for at least half an hour before you attempt to calibrate and profile it). Once this has been done you will want to lock down the hardware controls so they cannot be accidentally adjusted. This should be done before performing the calibration in which a series of colors are sent to the screen and the measurements used to adjust the video card settings that fine-tune the display to achieve optimum neutralization.

The second part is the profiling process. Once the screen has been calibrated, a longer sequence of color patches is sent to the screen and measured to build a profile describing how the neutralized screen displays these known colors. This data is collected together to build the profile, and at the end you will be asked to name the profile; it should be automatically saved to the correct folder location and assigned as the new default monitor profile.

Some CRT monitor displays such as the Sony Artisan or Barco have built-in internal calibration mechanisms. You literally just switch them on and they self-calibrate to provide optimized performance. This takes a lot of the guesswork out of the calibration process.

Do remember that the performance of the display will fluctuate over time (especially a CRT display), so it is therefore important to check and calibrate the monitor at regular intervals.

Locating the display profile

On the Macintosh, the profile should automatically be saved in the Library/ ColorSync/Profiles/Displays folder. On a PC, save to the Windows/System32/Spool/ Drivers/Color folder.

Monitor profile creation settings

Before you build a profile there are several option settings you have to decide upon. First there is the gamma space, which I recommend should be 2.2 (even if it says somewhere that Macintosh users should use 1.8), although for LCD screens you can use the 'native gamma'. The white point should be set to 6500 K, or with LCD displays you can use the native white point. If given the option, save a small profile size for CRT profiles and large profile size for LCD profiles.

LCD hardware calibration

Some high-end LCD displays are also beginning to feature hardware-level calibration such as Eizo Coloredge and Mitsubishi Spectraview.

Camera Raw profiling

As was explained in Chapter 3, the Camera Raw plug-in uses data accumulated from two sets of profiles which have been produced using daylight balanced and tungsten balanced lighting. This method of profiling works really well with most normal color temperature settings, but the data gathered is based on a small sample of cameras (sometimes just one!) and cannot be regarded as offering absolute accuracy. It may be helpful to follow the calibrate procedure (described in the same chapter) to obtain the most accurate colors.

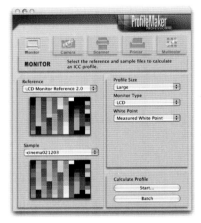

Figure 12.9 The ProfileMaker Pro™ interface.

Profiling the input

Input profiling is possible but it's easier to do with a scanner than it is with a digital camera. To profile a scanner you'll need to scan a film or print target and use profile creation software such as X-Rite's ProfileMaker Pro™ program to read the data and build a custom profile based on readings taken from the scanned target (Figure 12.9). The target measurements are then used to build a profile that describes the characteristics of the scanner. This profile should be saved to the Macintosh Library/ColorSync/Profiles folder or, on a PC, save to the Windows/System32/Spool/Drivers/Color folder. It can then be incorporated into your color managed workflow to describe the image data coming into Photoshop (refer back to Figure 12.6). This can be done by selecting the profile in the scanner software or by assigning the profile in Photoshop as the file is opened.

Camera profiling is a lot trickier to do and few photographers feel this is something worth bothering with. This is because the camera sensor will respond differently under different lighting conditions and you would therefore need to build a new profile every time the light changed. This is not necessarily a problem if you are using a digital camera in a studio setup with a consistent strobe lighting setup. In these circumstances it is probably very desirable that you photograph a color checker chart and take measurements that can be used to create a custom input profile for the camera. For example, the X-Rite Eye-One Photo system offers camera profiling.

Overall, I would not stress too much about input profiles unless it is critical to your workflow that you have absolute color control from start to finish. For example, a museum photographer who is charged with photographing important works of art would absolutely want to profile their camera. But is it always necessary or desirable? In Figure 12.10 I suggest that the correct white balance and input profiling is sometimes irrelevant, as it is more important to trust what you see on your monitor display and obtain good color management between the image displayed on the screen and what you see in the print.

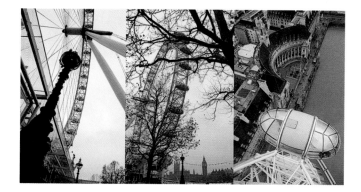

Figure 12.10 Here are three photographs taken on and around the London Eye ferris wheel. These pictures have each been processed using an incorrect white balance setting. In this situation, input color management becomes irrelevant and it matters more how consistent the appearance is between the computer display and the print output.

Profiling the output

Successful color management also relies on having accurate profiles for each type of media paper used with your printer. The printer you buy will come with a driver on a CD (or you can download one) and the installation procedure should install a set of canned profiles that will work when using the proprietary inks designed to be used with the printer and for a limited range of branded papers. The canned profiles that ship with the latest Epson printers for their Epson papers tend to be of a very high quality and all you really need for professional print results. However, it is recommended that you carry out custom profiling to build profiles for other types of print/paper combinations. This can be done by printing out a test target like the one shown in Figure 12.11, without color managing it. Once the test print has been allowed to stabilize, it can be measured the following day with a device like the X-Rite Eye-One spectrophotometer (Figure 12.12). The patch measurement results can then be used to build a color profile for the printer. The other alternative is to take advantage of Neil Barstow's remote profiling service special offer which is available to readers of this book (see the back of the book) and, if using custom printer profiles, you'll need one to be built for each printer/media combination. You can use a profiled printer to achieve good CMYK proofing even from a modestly priced printer, which comes close to matching the quality of a recognized contract proof printer.

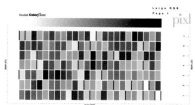

Figure 12.11 This Kodak™ color target can be used to construct a color ICC profile. A profile service company will normally supply you with instructions on how to print it out. When they receive your prints, they can measure these and email the custom ICC profile back to you. For example, Neil Barstow of www.colourmanagement.net is offering a special discount rate to readers of this book (see the back of the book for more details).

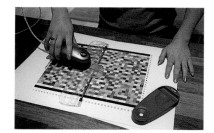

Figure 12.12 Once a print profile has been printed out, the color patches can be read using a spectrophotometer and the measurements used to build an ICC profile.

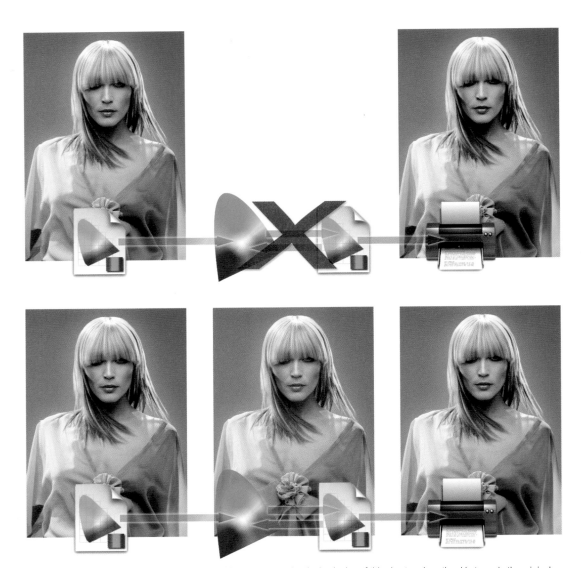

Figure 12.13 This illustration re-examines the problem encountered at the beginning of this chapter where the skin tones in the original image printed too blue. In the upper workflow no printer profile was used and the image data was sent directly to the printer with no adjustment made to the image data. In the lower example I show a profile color managed workflow. The profile created for this particular printer is used to convert the image data to that of the printer's color space before being sent to the printer. The (normally hidden) color shifting which occurs during the profile conversion process compensates by making the skin tone colors more red, but applies less color compensation to other colors. The result is an output that more closely matches the original. This is a simple illustration of the ICC-based color management system at work. All color can be managed this way in Photoshop, from capture source to the monitor display and to the final print.

Photoshop color management interface

By now you should be acquainted with the basic principles of Photoshop ICC color management (see Figure 12.13). It is relatively easy to configure the Photoshop system and at the simplest level all you have to do is calibrate and profile your display, then go to the Photoshop Color Settings (Figure 12.14) and select an appropriate prepress setting (don't use the default). A prepress setting will switch on the Photoshop color management policies and should be enough to get you up and running in a color managed workflow. But if you want to discover more about how color management works, then do read on.

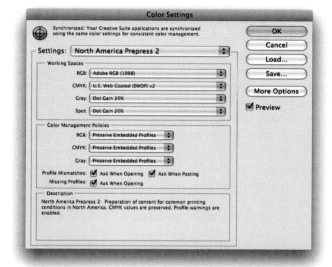

Figure 12.14 All the Photoshop color settings can be managed from within the Photoshop Color Settings dialog. Photoshop conveniently ships with various preset settings that are suited to different Photoshop workflows. Unfortunately, the default setting is not an ideal choice for a color managed workflow, so use the Settings menu shown in Figure 12.15 to switch to a prepress setting such as the one shown here. As you move the cursor pointer around the Color Settings dialog, Help messages are provided in the Description box area below – these provide useful information which will help you learn more about the Photoshop color management settings and the different color space options.

The Color Settings

The Color Settings are located in the Edit menu. The first item you will come across is the Settings pop-up menu (Figure 12.15). Photoshop provides a range of preset configurations for the color management system and these can be edited to meet your own specific requirements. In Basic mode, the default setting will be some sort of General Purpose setting and the exact naming and subsequent settings list will vary depending on the region where you live.

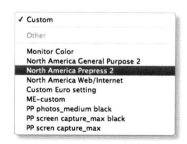

Figure 12.15 The default settings are just defaults. I advise changing the setting to one of the prepress settings as this will configure Photoshop to use Adobe RGB as your RGB workspace and switch on the Profile Mismatch and Missing Profiles alert warnings.

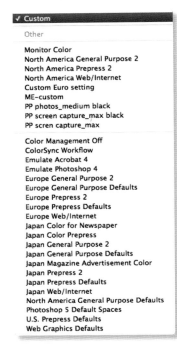

Figure 12.16 Here is a full list of the preset settings (as seen when 'More Options' is selected). The General Purpose presets will preserve RGB profiles, but use sRGB as the RGB workspace instead of Adobe RGB, and CMYK color management will be switched off. This is a little better than the previous Web Graphics default and may help avoid confusion among novice users. In the basic Fewer Options mode, the choice will be restricted so that all you see will be the color settings for your geographical area.

I would recommend that you follow the advice in Figure 12.15 and change this default to one of the prepress settings. So if Photoshop was installed on a European computer, you would select the Europe Prepress Default setting from the list in Figure 12.16. If a preset color setting says 'prepress', this will be the ideal starting point for any type of color managed workflow, especially if you are a photographer. That is all you need to concern yourself with initially, but if you wish to make customized adjustments, then you can make custom changes in the Working Spaces section. For help selecting an ideal RGB workspace, refer back to the section on RGB spaces on pages 570–571 (where I recommend using ProPhoto RGB). The CMYK and Grayscale settings will be covered later.

Color management policies

The first thing Photoshop does when a document is opened is check to see if an ICC profile is present. The default policy is to preserve the embedded profile information. So whether the document has originated in sRGB, Adobe RGB or ColorMatch RGB, it will open in that RGB color space and after editing be saved as such. This means you can have several files open at once and each can be in an entirely different color space. A good tip here is to set the Status box to show 'Document profile' (on the Mac this is at the bottom left of the image window; on a PC it is at the bottom of the system screen). Or, you can configure the Info panel to provide such information. This will allow you to see each individual document's color space profile.

Preserve embedded profiles

The default policy of 'Preserve Embedded Profiles' allows you to use the ICC color management system straight away, without too much difficulty. So long as there is a profile tag embedded in any file you open, Photoshop gives you the option to open that file without converting it. So if you are given an sRGB file to open, the default option is to open it in sRGB and save it using the same sRGB color space. This is despite the fact that your default RGB workspace might be ProPhoto RGB or some other RGB color space. The same policy rules apply to CMYK and grayscale files. Whenever 'Preserve Embedded Profiles' is selected, Photoshop reads the CMYK or Grayscale profile, preserves the numeric data and does not convert the colors, and the image will remain in the tagged color space. This is always going to be the preferred option when editing incoming CMYK files because a CMYK file may already be targeted for a specific press output and you don't really want to alter the numbers for those color values.

Profile mismatches and missing profiles

The default prepress color management policy setting is set to 'Ask When Opening' if there is a profile mismatch (Figure 12.17). This means you will see the warning dialog shown in Figure 12.18 whenever the profile of a file you are opening does not match the current workspace. This will offer you a chance to use the embedded profile (which is recommended), convert the document colors to the current workspace or discard the profile.

A newcomer does not necessarily have to fully understand how Photoshop color management works in order to use it successfully. When 'Preserve Embedded Profiles' is selected this will make the Photoshop color management system quite foolproof and the color management system is adaptable enough to suit the needs of all Photoshop users, regardless of their skill levels. Whichever option you select – convert or don't convert – the saved file will always be correctly tagged.

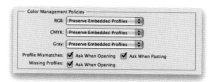

Figure 12.17 The Color Management Policies, with the Profile Mismatches and Missing Profiles checkboxes checked.

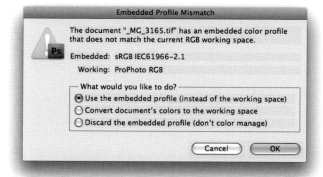

Figure 12.18 If the 'Preserve Embedded Profiles' color management policy is selected and the Ask When Opening box is checked in the Profile Mismatches section (Figure 12.17) you will see the dialog shown here, whenever there is a profile mismatch between the image you are opening and the current working space. You can then open using the embedded profile, override the policy and convert to the working space, or discard the embedded profile. Whatever you do, select one of these options and click OK, because if you click 'Cancel' you'll cancel opening the file completely. I usually prefer to use 'Preserve Embedded Profiles' and deselect 'Ask When Opening', so that I am not constantly shown this dialog.

Include a 'Read Me' file

When you save a profiled RGB file, you might want to enclose a Read Me file on the disk to remind the person who receives the image that they should not ignore the embedded profile information.

Convert to Working space

If you select the 'Convert to Working space' policy, Photoshop automatically converts everything to your current RGB or CMYK workspace. If the incoming profile does not match the workspace, then the default option will be to carry out a profile conversion from the embedded profile space to the current workspace (when the incoming profile matches the current RGB, CMYK or grayscale workspace, there is of course no need to convert the colors). 'Preserve Embedded Profiles' is usually the safer option because you can't go wrong if you just click 'OK' to preserve the embedded profile in Figure 12.18. 'Convert to Working space' can be a useful option for RGB mode because you may wish to convert all RGB images to your working space (but not the CMYK files). For batch processing work I sometimes prefer to temporarily use a Convert to Working space RGB setting because this allows me to apply a batch operation to a mixture of files in which all the images end up in the current RGB workspace.

Figure 12.19 If the Convert to Working RGB color management policy is selected (but without checking 'Ask When Opening' in the Profile Mismatches section), this dialog will appear whenever there is a profile mismatch between the image you are opening and the current working space. When you see this dialog, click 'OK' to convert the document colors to the current color working space. Click 'Don't show again' if you don t wish to be reminded each time this occurs.

Figure 12.20 If the Convert to Working RGB color management policy is selected and the Ask When Opening box is also checked in the Profile Mismatches section you will see the dialog shown here, where you can make a choice on whether to open to convert to the working space, use the embedded profile, or override the policy and discard the embedded profile.

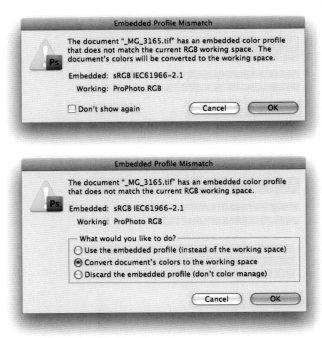

Color Management Off

The other option is to choose 'Color Management: Off'. When this option is selected Photoshop will appear not to color manage incoming documents and it will assume the default RGB or CMYK workspace to be the source. If there is no profile embedded, then the document will stay that way. If there is a profile mismatch between the source and workspace, the profile will be removed (with an alert message pointing out that the embedded profile information is about to be deleted). But if the source profile matches the workspace, there is no need to remove the profile, so in this instance the profile tag will not be removed (even so, you can still remove the ICC profile at the saving stage). So in this instance, Photoshop will still be color managing certain files and strictly speaking is not completely 'off'.

Turning the color management off is not recommended for general Photoshop work, so check the Color Settings to make sure you are not using one of the Web/Internet preset settings that will disable Photoshop's color management.

Sometimes it is desirable to discard a profile. For example, you may be aware that the image you are about to open has an incorrect profile and it is therefore a good thing to discard it and assign the correct profile later in Photoshop. I would not recommend choosing 'Off' as the default setting though. Just make sure you have the Color Management Policies set to 'Ask When Opening' and you can easily intervene and discard the profile when using the 'Preserve Embedded Profiles' or 'Convert to Working RGB' color management policies settings.

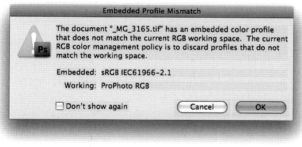

Figure 12.21 If the 'Color Management Off' policy is selected (but without checking 'Ask When Opening' in the Profile Mismatches section), this dialog will appear whenever there is a profile mismatch between the image you are opening and the current working space. When you see this dialog, click 'OK' to discard the embedded profile. Click 'Don't show again' if you don't wish to be reminded each time this occurs.

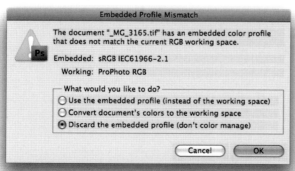

Figure 12.22 If the Ask When Opening box is checked in the Profile Mismatches section, you will see the dialog shown here. You can make a choice on opening to discard the embedded profile, use the embedded profile or convert to the working space.

RGB to RGB conversion warning

A 'Convert to Profile' is just like any other image mode change in Photoshop, such as converting from RGB to Grayscale mode, and it is much safer to use than the old Profile to Profile command in Photoshop 5.0. However, be careful if you use 'Convert to Profile' to produce targeted RGB outputs that overwrite the original RGB master. Any version of Photoshop since version 6.0 will have no problem reading the embedded profiles and displaying the image correctly; and will recognize any profile mismatch (and know how to convert back to the original workspace). As always, customized RGB files such as this may easily confuse other non-ICC savvy Photoshop users. Not everyone is using Photoshop, nor does everyone have their color management configured correctly. Some RGB to RGB conversions can produce RGB images that look fine on a correctly configured system, but look very odd on one that is not (see page 588).

Profile conversions

As you gain more experience you will soon be able to create your own customized color settings. The minimum you need to know is which of these listed color settings will be appropriate for the work you are doing. To help in this decision making, you can read the text descriptions that appear in the Description box at the bottom of the Color Settings dialog. For example, you might want to start by loading one of the presets present in the Color Settings menu and customize the CMYK settings to match those required for a specific CMYK workflow output.

Convert to Profile

Even if you choose to preserve the embedded profile on opening, it can be useful to convert non-workspace files to your current workspace after opening. This is where the Convert to Profile command comes in, because you can use it to carry out a profile conversion at any time, such as at the end of a retouch session, just before saving. Let's suppose we want to open an RGB image that is in Adobe RGB and the current working space is sRGB. If the 'Preserve Embedded Profile' option is selected then the default behavior would be to open the file and keep it in Adobe RGB without converting. We could carry on editing the image in the Adobe RGB color space up until the point where it is desirable to carry out a conversion to another color space. To make a profile conversion, go to the Edit menu and choose 'Convert to Profile...'. The Source space shows the current profile space and in Basic mode, there will be a single Destination Space menu that will most likely default to 'Working RGB' (which in this case would be sRGB). This menu lists all of the available profiles on your computer system (depending on how many profiles you have installed). However, if you click on the Advanced button, you will see the Advanced Convert to Profile dialog (Figure 12.23) where the 'Destination Space' options are broken down into color mode types, such as: Grayscale, RGB, Lab and CMYK, plus other more esoteric options such as Multichannel and Abstract profile modes. Because the color modes are segmented in this way, it will make it easier for you to access specific types of profiles when carrying out a conversion.

The Convert to Profile command is also useful when you wish to create an output file to send to a printer for which you have a custom-built profile but the print driver does not recognize ICC profiles. For example, one of the printers I use is the Fuji Pictrograph. I have built a custom profile for this printer, but unfortunately there is no facility within the File Export driver to utilize the output profile. Therefore, I use the Convert to Profile command to convert the color data to match the space of the output device just prior to sending the image data to the printer.

Whenever you make a profile conversion the image data will end up in a different color space and you might see a slight change in the on-screen color appearance. This is because the profile space you are converting to may have a smaller gamut than the one you are converting from. Whether an image is imported that is not in the working color space, or has been converted to one that is not, Photoshop appends a warning asterisk (*) to the color mode in the title bar (Mac) or status bar (PC).

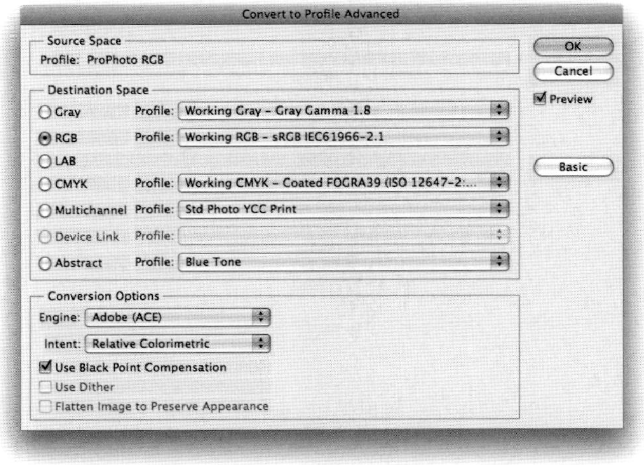

Figure 12.23 'Convert to Profile' (shown here in Advanced mode) is located in the Edit menu and can be used to convert color data from one profile color space to another profiled space, such as when you want to convert a file to the profiled color space of a specific output device.

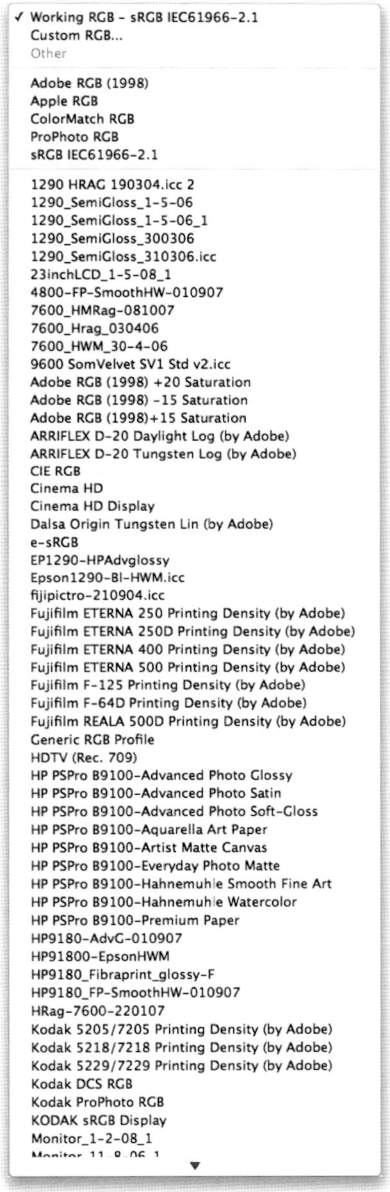

Figure 12.24 The profile list will display all the profiles that are available on your computer.

583

Incorrect sRGB profile tags

Some digital cameras won't embed a profile in the JPEG capture files or worse still embed a wrong profile, yet the EXIF metadata will misleadingly say the file is in sRGB color mode. The danger here is that while you may select Adobe RGB as the RGB space for your camera, when shooting in JPEG mode the camera may inadvertently omit to alter the EXIF tag which stubbornly reads sRGB.

This can be resolved by going to the Photoshop menu and choosing: Preferences ⇨ File Handling... . If you check the 'Ignore EXIF Profile tag' option, Photoshop will always ignore the specified camera profile in the EXIF metadata and only rely on the actual profile (where present) when determining the color space the data should be in.

Assign Profile

When an image is missing its profile, or has the wrong profile information embedded, the color numbers become meaningless. The Assign Profile command (Figure 12.25) can be used to correct mistakes as it allows you to assign correct meaning to what the colors in the image should be. So, for example, if you know the profile of an opened file to be wrong, you can use the Edit ⇨ Assign Profile command to rectify this situation. Let's suppose you have opened an untagged RGB file and for some reason decided not to color manage the file when opening. The colors don't look right and you have reason to believe that the file had originated from the sRGB color space. Yet, it is being edited in your current ProPhoto RGB workspace as if it were a ProPhoto RGB image. By assigning an sRGB profile, we can tell Photoshop that this is not a ProPhoto RGB image and that these colors should be considered as being in the sRGB color space. Most of the time, assigning sRGB will bring the colors back to life and if that doesn't work, then try one of the other commonly used RGB workspaces such as Adobe RGB or Colormatch.

You can also use Assign Profile to remove a profile by clicking on the Don't Color Manage This Document button, which allows you to strip a file of its profile. However, you can also do this by choosing File ⇨ Save As... and deselect the Embed Profile checkbox in the Save options.

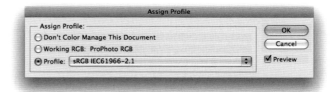

Figure 12.25 The Assign Profile command is available from the Edit menu in Photoshop. Edit ⇨ Assign Profile can be used to assign a new correct profile to an image or remove an existing profile.

Profile mismatches when pasting

One problem with having images in multiple color spaces open at once concerns the copying and pasting of color data from one file to another. Whenever you copy and paste image data, or drag copy an image with the move tool, it is possible that a profile mismatch may occur; although this will very much depend on how you have the Color Management Policies configured in the Color Settings (see Figure 12.26). If the Profile Mismatches: Ask When Pasting box is unchecked in the Color Settings and a profile mismatch happens, you will see the dialog shown in Figure 12.27. This will ask if you wish to convert the color data to preserve the color appearance when it is pasted into the new destination document. If the Profile Mismatches: Ask When Pasting box is checked in the Color Settings, then you will see instead the dialog box shown in Figure 12.28. This dialog offers you the choice to convert or not convert the data. If you select 'Convert', the appearance of the colors will be maintained when you paste the data, and if you choose 'Don't Convert' the color appearance will change but the numbers will be preserved.

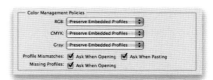

Figure 12.26 The Profile Mismatches settings in the Color Management section of the Color Settings dialog will influence Profile Mismatch behavior.

Paste mismatch warning

If Profile Mismatches: Ask When Pasting is deselected, you will only see the warning dialog shown in Figure 12.27 if the destination space is something other than the current RGB workspace. This is one more reason why it is advisable to keep the 'Ask When Pasting' option checked.

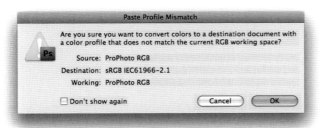

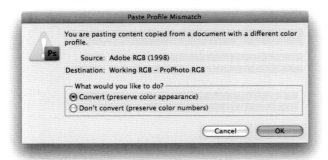

Figure 12.27 If you attempt to paste image data from a document whose color space does not match the destination space (and the Profile Mismatches: Ask When Pasting box is unchecked), this dialog warning will appear, alerting you to a profile mismatch between the source and destination documents. If you click 'OK', Photoshop will convert the data and preserve the color appearance of the image data.

Figure 12.28 If the Profile Mismatches: Ask When Pasting box is checked in the Color Settings dialog and you attempt to paste image data from a document whose color space does not match the destination space, this dialog warning will give you the option to 'Convert' the colors (as in Figure 12.27 above), or 'Don't Convert' and preserve the numbers instead.

Saving a Color Setting

If you have configured the settings to suit a particular workflow, you can click on the Save... button to save these as a custom setting that will appear in the Color Settings menu the next time you open this dialog. When you save a setting you can enter any relevant comments or notes about the setting you are saving in the text box (see Figure 12.29). This information will then appear in the Color Settings dialog text box at the bottom. You might name a setting something like 'Client annual report settings' and might want to write a short descriptive note to accompany it.

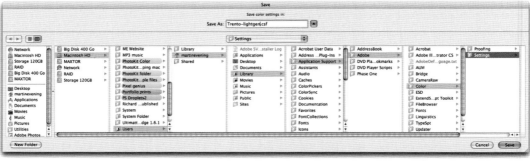

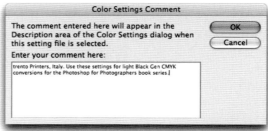

Figure 12.29 Custom color settings can be loaded or saved via the Color Settings dialog. The relevant folder will be located in the username/Library/Application Support/Adobe/Color/Settings folder (Mac OS X) or Program Files/Common Files/ Adobe/Color/Settings folder (PC). When you save a custom setting it must be saved to this location and will automatically be appended with the '.csf' suffix. When you save a color setting you have the opportunity to include a brief text description in the accompanying dialog. A Color Settings file can be shared between some Adobe applications and with other Photoshop users.

Reducing the opportunities for error

When you adopt an RGB space such as ProPhoto RGB as the preferred workspace for all your image editing, you have to take into account that this might cause confusion when exchanging RGB files between your computer, which is operating in a color managed workflow, and that of someone who is using Photoshop with the color management switched off. When sending image files to other Photoshop users, the presence of a profile will help them read the image data correctly, so long as they have the Photoshop color settings configured to preserve embedded profiles (or convert to the working space) and their monitor display is calibrated correctly. They will then see your photographs on their system almost exactly the way you intended them to be seen. The only variables will be the accuracy of their display calibration and profile, the color gamut limitations of the display, and the environment it is being viewed in. Configuring the Color Settings correctly is not difficult to do, but the recipient does have to be as conscientious as you are about ensuring their monitor display is set up correctly. The situation has not been helped either by the way the default color settings have shifted about over the last eight versions of the program. The default settings in Photoshop CS4 use 'Preserve Embedded Profiles', but prior to that we had settings like 'Web Graphics' in which color management was switched off. Consequently, there are a lot of Photoshop users out there who have unwittingly been using sRGB as their default RGB workspace, with color management switched off. Even where people do have the color management switched on, the monitors they are using may not have been profiled in months or are being viewed in a brightly lit room!

It is important to be aware of these potential problems because it is all too easy for the color management to fail once an image file has left your hands and been passed on to another Photoshop user. With this in mind, here are some useful tips to help avoid misunderstandings over color. The most obvious way to communicate what the colors

Playing detective

How you deliver your files will very much depend on who you are supplying them to. I often get emails from readers who have been given the runaround by their color lab. One typically finds that the lab may be using a photo printer, such as the Fuji Frontier, which does not read incoming profiles and is simply calibrated to expect sRGB files. So far so good. As long as you send an sRGB file, you shouldn't have any problems. But if the color lab operator has Photoshop color management switched off, they will not know how to handle anything other than an incoming file that is in sRGB. If you then supply them with an Adobe RGB file they won't read the profile and the colors will end up looking different in the final print, and then they blame the customer!

It helps to do a little detective work to ascertain the skill level of the recipient. The first thing you need to know is what color settings are they using? This will help you determine which RGB space they are using and whether the color management is switched on or off. The other thing to ask is 'do you have your monitor display calibrated and profiled?' And if the answer is yes, then ask how often they calibrate and profile their display. The answers to these questions will tell you quite a bit about the other person's system, how you should supply your files and also how accurate their monitor display is at displaying colors. Basically, if you have any doubts, the safest option is to convert to sRGB at your end before delivering anything.

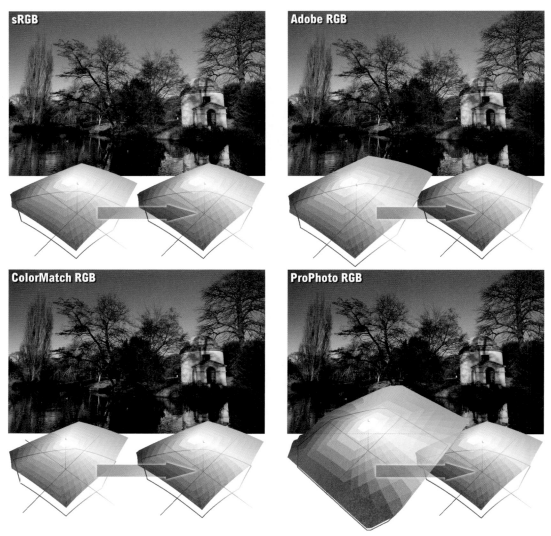

Figure 12.30 The purpose of this illustration is to show what happens if you submit an RGB file to a Photoshop user who has their Photoshop system configured using sRGB as their RGB workspace and with the Color Management Policies set to 'Off' (ignoring incoming profiles). The top left picture is the correct version and shows how the photograph looks if I supply the image converted to the sRGB color space (anticipating that the other user is using this as their default RGB space). The remaining examples show how the picture looks if I supply the same picture using different RGB spaces and the person receiving the file ignores the embedded profile. If the picture is delivered as an Adobe RGB file, the gamma matches, but because Adobe RGB has a larger gamut than sRGB the colors appear slightly desaturated. If I supply a ColorMatch RGB file, sRGB interprets this as a darker image because ColorMatch has a lower gamma of 1.8. And, lastly, ProPhoto RGB has a much larger color gamut than Adobe RGB so the colors appear even more muted when brought into sRGB without any color management.

are supposed to look like is to supply a printed output. In fact this is considered routine when supplying images to a printer. If you are sending a file for CMYK repro printing, then the file should be targeted to the CMYK output. Supplying a print is an unambiguous visual reference, which if done properly can form the basis of a contract between yourself, the client and the printer.

If the person you are supplying the file to is in the same building or you are in regular contact with them, then you probably have a clear idea of how their system is set up. If they have Photoshop color management switched on, they can read any file you send them in any color space and it will be color managed successfully. However, you cannot always make too many assumptions about the people you are sending image files to and so you should sometimes adopt a more cautious approach. I am often asked to supply RGB files as large JPEGs for initial approval by the client before making a finished print. In these situations I find it safer to supply a profiled sRGB image. I do this by choosing Edit ⇨ Convert to Profile... and selecting sRGB as the destination space. If the recipient is color management savvy, then Photoshop will read the sRGB profile and handle the colors correctly. If the recipient has not bothered to configure their color management settings then one can be almost certain that they are using sRGB as their default RGB workspace. So in these instances, targeting the RGB colors to sRGB is probably the safer option. Figure 12.30 shows a comparison of how a single image that was edited using different RGB workspaces would look on a Photoshop system configured using a (non-color managed) Web Graphics, Monitor Color or Color Management Off setting. In this example, the version that is converted to sRGB is the only one that stands a chance of being displayed correctly. I am certainly not advocating you use sRGB as your standard RGB workspace, because it is still a poor space to use for photographic work, but it can be a useful 'dumbed down' space to use when communicating with unknown users.

Grayscale for screen display

If you intend creating grayscale images to be seen on the Internet or in multimedia presentations, choose the Default Web Graphics color setting. The Grayscale workspace will then be set to a 2.2 gamma space, which is the same gamma used by the majority of PC computer screens. The truth is, you can never be 100% sure how anybody who views your work will have their monitor calibrated, but you can at least assume that the majority of Internet users will have a PC monitor set to a 2.2 gamma. The Macintosh 1.8 gamma setting should really be relegated to ancient history. The reason it exists at all s because in the very early days of the Macintosh computer, and before ICC color management, a 1.8 gamma monitor space most closely matched the dot gain of the Apple monochrome laser printer.

Matching grayscale gamma

If you are using the Epson Advanced B&W options to print grayscale images, it is best to make sure that the Gray working space matches the gamma of the RGB working space. If this is the case, use the following Gray gamma settings:
Colormatch RGB: 1.8 gamma
Adobe RGB: 2.2 gamma
sRGB: 2.2 gamma
ProPhoto RGB: 1.8 gamma

Working with Grayscale

Grayscale image files can also be managed via the Color Settings dialog. The color management policy can be set to either 'Preserve Embedded Profiles' or 'Convert to Grayscale' workspace. If the profile of the incoming grayscale file does not match the current Gray workspace (and the Ask When Opening box is checked), you will be asked whether you wish to use the tagged grayscale space profile, or convert to the current grayscale workspace.

If you examine the 'Gray' workspace options, you will see a list of dot gain percentages and monitor gamma values. If you are preparing grayscale images for display on a monitor, such as on a website or in a multimedia presentation, then you will want to select 'Gray Gamma 2.2' (see the sidebar 'Grayscale for screen display'). If you want to know how any existing prepress grayscale image will look like on the Web as a grayscale image, select the View ⇨ Proof Setup and choose Windows RGB or Macintosh RGB. You can then select Image ⇨ Adjust ⇨ Levels and adjust the Gamma slider accordingly to obtain the right brightness for a typical PC or Mac display. If you are using grayscale mode to make prints via the Advanced B&W print options for an Epson printer, you should make sure that the Grayscale workspace uses a gamma setting that matches the gamma of your current RGB workspace. This ensures there is no gamma compensation when you convert from RGB to Grayscale (see sidebar 'Matching grayscale gamma').

For prepress work you should select the dot gain percentage that most closely matches the anticipated dot gain of the press. It is important to note that the Gray workspace setting is independent of the CMYK workspace. If you want the Gray workspace dot gain value to match the black plate of the current CMYK setting, then mouse down on the Gray setting and choose Load Gray... . Now go to the Profiles folder which will be in the Library/Application Support/Adobe/Color/Settings folder on a Mac and in the Program Files/Common Files/Adobe/Color/Settings folder on a PC. Select the same CMYK space as you are using for the CMYK color separations and click the Load button.

Advanced Color Settings

The advanced settings normally remain hidden, but if you click on the More Options button, you'll see the expanded Color Settings dialog shown in Figure 12.31. These advanced settings unleash full control over the Photoshop color management system. But don't attempt to adjust any of these expert settings until you have fully understood the intricacies of customizing the RGB, CMYK, Gray and Spot color spaces. I would suggest that you read through the remaining section of this chapter first before you consider customizing any of these settings.

Custom Gray space settings

Figure 12.38 shows a range of dot gain values that can be used as a guide for different types of press settings. This is a rough guide as to which dot gain setting you should use on any given job. When the Advanced color settings option is checked you can enter a custom gamma value or dot gain curve setting (see 'Dot gain' on pages 597–598).

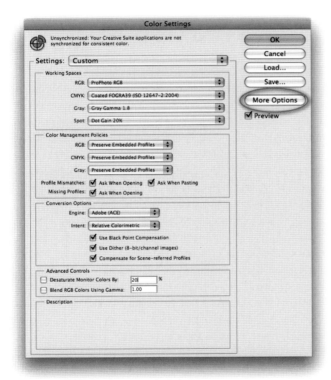

Figure 12.31 This shows the Photoshop Advanced Color Settings dialog. Clicking on the More Options button (circled) will unleash full control over all the Photoshop settings. The following sections of this chapter show how you can customize the color management settings in this advanced mode. Note that the button in this Color Settings dialog view will normally say 'Fewer Options'; I edited the screen shot to say 'More Options', simply to make it more obvious where to click.

Black Point and Proof printing

You will want to use Black Point Compensation when separating an RGB image to a press CMYK color space. However, in the case of a conversion from a CMYK proofing space to an inkjet profile space we must preserve the (grayish) black of the press and not scale the image (because this would improve the blacks). It is for these reasons that the Black Point Compensation is disabled in the Print with Preview dialog when making a proof print to simulate the black ink.

Scene-referred profiles

Photoshop CS4 contains a new advanced preference called 'Compensate for Scene-referred Profiles'. This isn't of any real significance for photographers. It is switched on by default and designed to automatically apply video contrast when converting between scene and output-referred profiles. This basically matches the default color management workflow for After Effects CS4.

Conversion options

You have a choice of three Color Management Modules (CMMs): Adobe Color Engine (ACE), Apple ColorSync or Apple CMM. The Adobe color engine is reckoned to be superior for all RGB to CMYK conversions because the Adobe engine uses 20-bit per channel bit-depth calculations to calculate its color space conversions.

Rendering intents

The rendering intent influences the way the data is translated from the source to the destination space. The rendering intent is like a rule that describes the way the conversion is calculated. We will be looking at rendering intents in more detail on pages 602–605.

Black Point Compensation

This maps the darkest neutral color of the source RGB color space to the darkest neutrals of the destination color space. Black Point Compensation plays a vital role in translating the blacks in your images so that they reproduce as black when printed. As was explained in Chapter 3, there is no need to get hung up on setting the shadow point to anything other than zero RGB. It is not necessary to apply any shadow compensation at the image editing stage, because the color management will automatically take care of this for you and apply a black point compensation obtained from the output profile used in the mode or profile conversion. If you disable Black Point Compensation you may obtain deep blacks, but you will get truer (compensated) blacks if you leave it switched on.

Use Dither (8-bit per channel images)

Banding may occasionally occur when you separate to CMYK, particularly where there is a gentle tonal gradation in bright saturated areas. Any banding which appears on screen won't necessarily always show in print and much will depend on the coarseness of the screen used in the printing process. However, the 'Dither' option can help reduce the risk of banding when converting between color spaces.

Blend RGB colors using gamma

This item allows you to override the default color blending behavior. There used to be an option in Photoshop 2.5 for applying blend color gamma compensation. This allowed you to blend colors with a gamma of 1.0, which some experts argued was a purer way of doing things, because at higher gamma values than this you might see edge darkening occur between contrasting colors. Some users found the phenomenon of these edge artifacts to be a desirable trapping effect. However, many Photoshop users complained that they noticed light halos appearing around objects when blending colors at a gamma of 1.0. Consequently, gamma-compensated blending was removed at the time of the version 2.5.1 update. If you understand the implications of adjusting this particular gamma setting, you can switch it back on if you wish. Figure 12.32 illustrates the difference between blending colors at a gamma of 2.2 and 1.0.

Desaturate monitor colors

The 'Desaturate Monitor Colors' option lets you visualize and make comparisons between color gamut spaces where one or more gamut space is larger than the monitor RGB space. Color spaces such as ProPhoto RGB have a gamut that is much larger than the monitor space is able to show. So turning down the monitor colors saturation allows you to make a comparative evaluation between these two different color spaces. It is in essence a 'hurt me' button, because if you don't understand how to use this feature, you might inadvertently leave it on and end up assuming all your images are desaturated.

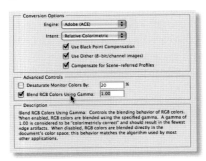
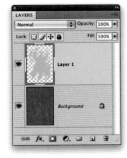
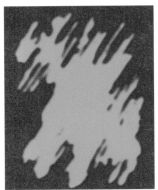
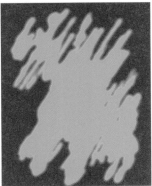

Figure 12.32 In this example we have a pure RGB green soft-edged brush stroke that is on a layer above a pure RGB red Background layer. The version on the left shows the combined layers using the normal default blending where 'Blend RGB Colors using Gamma' is deselected, and the version on the right shows what happens if you check this item and apply a gamma of 1.0. As you can see, the darkening around the edges where the contrasting colors meet will disappear.

Custom RGB and workspace gamma

Expert users may wish to use an alternative custom RGB workspace in place of one of the listed RGB spaces. If you know what you are doing and wish to create a customized RGB color space, you can go to the 'Custom...' option in the pop-up menu and enter the information for the White Point, Gamma and color primaries coordinates (Figure 12.33). My advice is to leave these expert settings well alone. Do avoid falling into the trap of thinking that the RGB workspace gamma should be the same as the monitor gamma setting. The RGB workspace is *not* a monitor space.

Adobe RGB is considered a good choice as an RGB workspace because its 2.2 gamma provides a more balanced, even distribution of tones between the shadows and highlights, while others prefer the 1.8 gamma ProPhoto RGB space for its wide color gamut. Remember, you do not actually 'see' Adobe RGB or ProPhoto RGB, and the RGB workspace gamma has no impact on how the colors are displayed on the screen (so long as Photoshop ICC color management is switched on). In any case, these advanced custom color space settings are safely tucked away in Photoshop and you are less likely to be confused by any apparent discrepancies between the monitor gamma and the RGB workspace gamma.

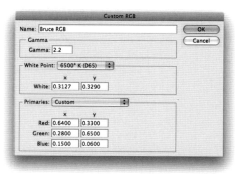

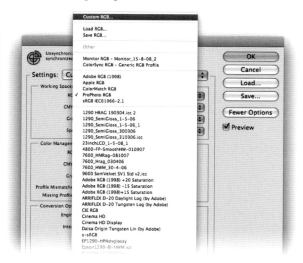

Figure 12.33 You can use the Custom RGB dialog to create custom RGB workspaces. The settings shown here have been named 'Bruce RGB', after Bruce Fraser who once devised this color space as a suggested prepress RGB space for Photoshop.

RGB to CMYK

Digital scans and captures all originate in RGB but professional images are nearly always reproduced in CMYK. Since the conversion from RGB to CMYK has to happen at some stage, the question is: at what point should this take place and who should be responsible for the conversion? If you have decided to take on this responsibility yourself then you need to know something more about the CMYK settings. When it comes to four-color print reproduction, it is important to know as much as possible about the intended press conditions that will be used at the printing stage and use this information to create a customized CMYK setup.

CMYK setup

If you examine the US prepress default setting, the CMYK space says U.S. Web Coated (SWOP). This setting is by no means a precise setting for every US prepress SWOP coated print job, because there can be many flavors of SWOP, but it does at least bring you a little closer to the type of specification a printer in the US might require for printing on coated paper with a web press setup. If you mouse down on the CMYK setup pop-up list, you will see there are also US options for web uncoated and sheetfed press setups. Under the European prepress default setting, there is a choice between coated and uncoated paper stocks, plus the latest ISO coated FOGRA39 setting. Then there is also Custom CMYK... where you can create and save custom CMYK profile settings.

Creating a custom CMYK setting

Figure 12.34 shows the Custom CMYK dialog, which is better known as the familiar 'Classic' Photoshop CMYK setup. Here, you can enter all the relevant CMYK separation information for a specific print job. Ideally you will want to save each purpose-built CMYK configuration as a separate color setting for future use and label it with a description of the print job it was built for.

There are some people who will tell you that in their 'expert opinion', Photoshop does a poor job of separating to CMYK. I bet if you ask them how they know this to be the case, they will be stumped to provide you with a coherent answer. Don't let anyone try to convince you otherwise. Professional quality CMYK separations can be achieved in Photoshop. You can avoid gamut clipping and you can customize a separation to meet the demands of any type of press output. The fact is that Photoshop will make lousy CMYK separations if the Photoshop operator who is carrying out the conversion has a limited knowledge of how to configure the Photoshop CMYK settings. For example, a wider gamut RGB space such as Adobe RGB is better able to encompass the gamut of CMYK and yield CMYK separations that do not suffer from gamut clipping. This is one big strike in favor of the Photoshop color management system. Remember, CMYK is not a one-size-fits-all color space and CMYK conversions do need to be tailor-made for each and every job.

Saving custom CMYK settings

Custom CMYK settings should be saved using the following locations: Library/ColorSync/Profiles/Recommended folder (Mac OS X). Windows/System32/Spool/Drivers/Color folder (PC).

Once you have configured a new CMYK workspace setting, this will become the new default CMYK workspace that is used when you convert an image to CMYK mode. Note that altering the CMYK setup settings will have no effect on the on-screen appearance of an already-converted CMYK file (unless there is no profile embedded) because the CMYK separation setup settings must be established first before you carry out the conversion.

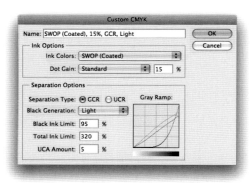

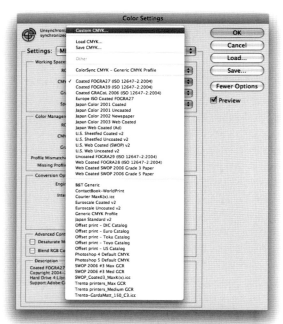

Figure 12.34 When you select the 'Custom CMYK...' option at the top of the pop-up menu list, this opens the dialog box shown above, where you can enter the specific CMYK setup information to build a custom targeted CMYK setting. If you click on the More Options button in the Color Settings, you will have a wider range of pre-loaded CMYK profile settings to choose from.

Ink Colors

If you click on the Ink Colors menu, you can select one of the preset Ink Colors settings that are suggested for different types of printing. For example, European Photoshop users can choose from Eurostandard (coated), (uncoated), or (newsprint). These are just generic ink sets. If your printer can supply you with a custom ink color setting, then select 'Custom...' from the Ink Colors menu. This will open the dialog shown in Figure 12.35.

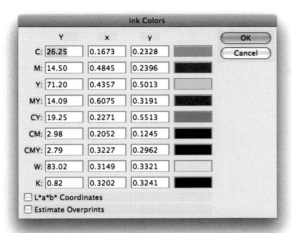

Figure 12.35 Here is a screen shot of the Custom Ink Colors dialog. For special print jobs, such as where non-standard ink sets are used or the printing is being done on colored paper, you can enter the measured readings of the color patches (listed here) taken from a printed sample on the actual stock that is to be used. You could measure these printed patches with a device such as the X-Rite Eye-One and use this information to create a custom Ink Colors setting for an individual CMYK press setup.

Dot gain

Dot gain refers to an accumulation of factors during the repro process that will make a dot printed on the page appear darker than expected. Among other things, dot gain is dependent on the type of press and the paper stock that's being used, and the dot gain value entered in the CMYK setup will determine how light or dark the separation needs to be. If a high dot gain is encountered, the separated CMYK films will need to be less dense so that the plates produced lay down less ink on the paper and produce the correct-sized printed halftone dot for that particular type of press setup. You can see for yourself how this works by converting an image to CMYK using two different dot gain values, inspecting the individual CMYK channels afterwards and comparing their appearance. Although the dot gain value affects the lightness of the individual channels, the composite CMYK channel image will always be displayed correctly on the screen to show how the final printed image should look.

If you select the 'Dot Gain Curves' option, you can enter custom settings for the composite or individual color plates. In the preparation of this book I was provided with precise dot gain information for the 40% and 80% ink values (these are shown in Figure 12.36).

Advanced CMYK settings

There is not a lot you can do with the standard CMYK settings: you can make a choice from a handful of generic CMYK profile settings or choose 'Custom CMYK...'. If you check the More options box and switch to the Advanced Color Settings view, you'll be able to select from a more comprehensive list of CMYK profile settings in the extended menu (depending on what profiles are already in your ColorSync folder).

CMYK previews in Proof Setup

Once the CMYK setup has been configured, you can use View ⇨ Proof Setup ⇨ Working CMYK to see a CMYK preview of what the image will look like after converting, while you are still editing an image in RGB mode.

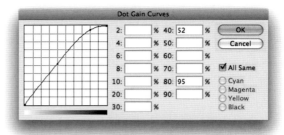

Figure 12.36 If you select 'Dot Gain: Curves...' from the CMYK setup shown in Figure 12.34, this will open the Custom Dot Gain dialog. If your printer is able to provide dot gain values at certain percentages, then you can enter these here. You can make the dot gain curves the same for all channels, but since the dot gain may vary on each ink plate, you can enter dot gain values for each plate individually. Note that when you select 'Custom Dot Gain...' from the Grayscale workspace menu, a similar dialog appears. If you are preparing to save a color setting designed for separating prepress CMYK and grayscale files, you will want to check that the black plate dot gain setting is consistent.

Gray Component Replacement (GCR)

The default Photoshop setting is GCR, Black Generation: Medium, Black Ink Limit 100%, Total Ink Limit 300%, UCA Amount 0%. If you ask your printer what separation settings they use and they quote you these figures, you'll know they are just reading the default settings from an unconfigured Photoshop setup. They either don't know or don't want to give you an answer, and if you are creating a custom CMYK setting it is more likely you will want to refer to the table in Figure 12.38 for guidance. Or if you prefer, don't bother configuring the Custom CMYK settings and just stick to using the prepress CMYK setting that most closely matches the output (such as US Sheetfed/Web Coated/Uncoated, or one of the European FOGRA settings).

Black generation

This determines how much black ink will be used to produce the black and gray tonal information. A light or medium black generation setting will work best for most photographic images. I would therefore advise leaving this set to 'Medium' and only change the black generation if you know what you are doing.

You may be interested to know that I specifically used a maximum black generation setting to separate all the dialog boxes that appear printed in this book. Figure 12.37 shows a view of the Channels panel after I had separated the screen grab shown in Figure 12.35 using a Maximum black generation CMYK separation. With this separation method only the black plate is used to render the neutral gray colors. Consequently, this means that any color shift at the printing stage will have no impact whatsoever on the neutrality of the gray content. I cheekily suggest you inspect other Photoshop books and judge if their panel and dialog box screen shots have reproduced as well as the ones shown in this book!

Undercolor Addition (UCA)

Low key subjects and high quality print jobs are more suited to the use of GCR (Gray Component Replacement) with a small amount of UCA (Undercolor Addition). GCR separations remove more of the cyan, magenta and yellow ink where all three inks are used to produce a color, replacing the overlapping color with black ink. The use of UCA will add a small amount of color back into the shadows and is useful where the shadow detail would otherwise look too flat and lifeless. The percentage of black ink used is determined by the black generation setting. When making conversions, you are usually better off sticking with the default GCR, using a light to medium black generation with 5–10% UCA. This will produce a longer black curve with improved image contrast.

Undercolor Removal (UCR)

The UCR (Undercolor Removal) separation method replaces the cyan, magenta and yellow ink with black ink in just the neutral areas. The UCR setting is also favored as a means of keeping the total ink percentage down on high-speed presses, although it is not necessarily suited for every type of print job.

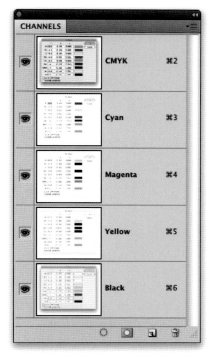

Figure 12.37 Here is a view of the Channels panel showing the four CMYK channels after I had separated the screen grab shown in Figure 12.35 using a Maximum black generation CMYK separation. Notice how all the neutral gray information is contained in the Black channel only. This is a good separation method to use for screen grabs, but not so good for other types of images.

Separation settings	Ink colors	Separation method	Dot gain	Black generation	Black ink limit	Total ink limit	UCA
US printing							
Sheetfed (coated)	SWOP coated	GCR	10–15%	Light/Medium	95%	320–350%	0–10%
Sheetfed (uncoated)	SWOP uncoated	GCR	15–25%	Light/Medium	95%	260–300%	0–10%
Web press (coated)	SWOP coated	GCR	15–20%	Light/Medium	95%	300–320%	0–10%
Web press (uncoated)	SWOP uncoated	GCR	20–30%	Light/Medium	95%	260–300%	0–10%
Web press (newsprint)	SWOP newsprint	GCR	30–40%	Medium	85–95%	260–280%	0–10%
European printing							
Sheetfed (coated)	Eurostandard coated	GCR	9–15%	Light/Medium	95%	320–350%	0–10%
Sheetfed (uncoated)	Eurostandard uncoated	GCR	15–25%	Light/Medium	95%	260–300%	0–10%
Web press (coated)	Eurostandard coated	GCR	15–20%	Light/Medium	95%	300–320%	0–10%
Web press (uncoated)	Eurostandard uncoated	GCR	20–30%	Light/Medium	95%	260–300%	0–10%
Web press (newsprint)	Eurostandard newsprint	GCR	30–40%	Medium	85–95%	260–280%	0–10%
Asian printing							
Sheetfed (coated)	Toyo Inks coated	GCR	8–15%	Light/Medium	95%	320–350%	0–10%
Sheetfed (uncoated)	Toyo Inks uncoated	GCR	15–25%	Light/Medium	95%	260–300%	0–10%
Web press (coated)	Toyo Inks coated web offset	GCR	12–20%	Light/Medium	95%	300–320%	0–10%
Web press (uncoated)	Toyo Inks uncoated	GCR	20–30%	Light/Medium	95%	260–300%	0–10%
Web press (newsprint)	Toyo Inks uncoated	GCR	30–40%	Medium	85–95%	260–280%	0–10%

Figure 12.38 These separation guidelines reflect a typical range of settings one might use for each type of press output. These are guidelines only and reflect the settings you will already find in Photoshop. For more precise settings, consult your printer.

Choosing a suitable RGB workspace

The RGB space you choose to edit with can certainly influence the outcome of your CMYK conversions, which is why you should choose your RGB workspace carefully. The default sRGB color space is widely regarded as an unsuitable space for photographic work because the color gamut of sRGB is in some ways smaller than the color gamut of CMYK (and most inkjet printers). If you choose a color space like Adobe RGB or ProPhoto RGB, you'll be working with a color space that can adequately convert from RGB to CMYK without significantly clipping the CMYK colors. Figure 12.39 highlights the deficiencies of editing in sRGB compared to editing in Adobe RGB.

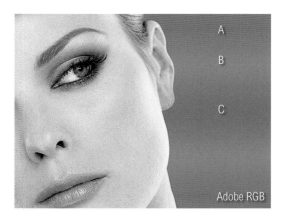

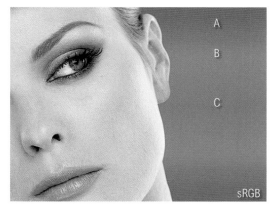

CMYK Info (Adobe RGB)	A	B	C
Cyan	97	75	95
Magenta	10	6	9
Yellow	96	8	5
Black	0	0	0

CMYK Info (sRGB)	A	B	C
Cyan	84	72	75
Magenta	18	7	10
Yellow	80	8	6
Black	1	0	0

Figure 12.39 This example shows what happened to a Lab mode color image that was converted to CMYK once via Adobe RGB and once via sRGB. The green to cyan color gradient was deliberately chosen to highlight the differences between these two RGB color spaces. As you can see, if you compare the separations shown above, the sRGB version is weaker at handling cyans and greens and there is also a slight boost in warmth to the skin tones.

If you are converting photographic images from one color space to another, then you should mostly use the 'Relative Colorimetric' or 'Perceptual' rendering intents. 'Relative Colorimetric' has always been the default Photoshop rendering intent and is still the best choice for most image conversions. However, if you are converting an image where it is important to preserve the shadow colors, then 'Perceptual' will often work better. For these reasons, I recommend that you use the Soft proofing method, described in the following chapter, to preview the outcome of any profile conversion and check to see whether a Relative Colorimetric or Perceptual rendering will produce the best results.

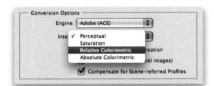

Figure 12.40 The default rendering intent is set by choosing More Options in the Color Settings dialog and mousing down on the Intent menu in the Conversion Options.

Rendering intents

When you make a profile conversion, such as when converting from RGB to CMYK, not all of the colors in the original source space will have a direct equivalent in the destination space. RGB spaces are mostly bigger than CMYK and therefore those RGB colors that are regarded as 'out of gamut' will have to be translated to their nearest equivalent in the destination CMYK space. The way this translation is calculated is determined by the rendering intent. In the Color Settings dialog you can choose which rendering intent you would like to use as the default method for all color mode conversions (Figure 12.40), but you can also override this setting and choose a different rendering intent whenever you use the Edit ⇨ Convert to Profile command (Figure 12.41), or soft proof an image using View ⇨ Proof Setup ⇨ Custom (Figure 12.42).

Perceptual

Perceptual (Images) rendering is an all-round rendering method that is suitable for certain types of images. Perceptual rendering compresses the out-of-gamut colors into the gamut of the target space in a rather generalized way (so that they don't become clipped), while preserving the visual relationship between those colors. More compression occurs with the out-of-gamut colors, smoothly ramping to no compression for the in-gamut colors. Perceptual rendering provides a best guess method for converting out-of-gamut colors where it is important to preserve tonal separation (such as in the shadow detail areas), but it is less suitable for images where there are fewer out-of-gamut colors.

Saturation (Graphics)

The 'Saturation' rendering intent preserves the saturation of the out-of-gamut colors at the expense of hue and lightness. Saturation rendering preserves the saturation of colors making them appear as vivid as possible after the conversion. This rendering intent is best suited to the conversion of business graphic presentations where retaining bright bold colors is of prime importance.

Relative Colorimetric

'Relative Colorimetric' is the default rendering intent
utilized in the Photoshop color settings. Relative
Colorimetric rendering maps the colors that are out of
gamut in the source color space (relative to the target space)
to the nearest 'in-gamut' equivalent in the target space.
When doing an RGB to CMYK conversion, an out-of-
gamut blue will be rendered the same CMYK value as
a 'just-in-gamut' blue and out-of-gamut RGB colors are
therefore clipped (see Figure 12.43). This can be a problem
when attempting to convert the more extreme out-of-gamut
RGB colors to CMYK color, but if you are using View
⇒ Proof Setup ⇒ Custom (Figure 12.42) to call up the
Customize Proof Condition dialog, you can check to see
if this potential gamut clipping will cause the loss of any
important image detail when converting to CMYK with a
Relative Colorimetric conversion.

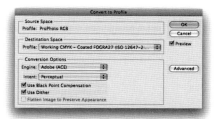

Figure 12.41 The default rendering intent
setting can be overridden when using the Convert
to Profile command.

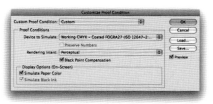

Figure 12.42 You can also change the
rendering intent in the Custom Proof dialog. This
allows you to preview a simulated conversion
without actually converting the RGB data.

Absolute Colorimetric

'Absolute Colorimetric' maps in-gamut colors exactly from
one space to another with no adjustment made to the white
and black points. This rendering intent can be used when
you convert specific 'signature colors' and need to preserve
the exact hue, saturation and brightness (such as the colors
in a commercial logo design). This rendering intent is
seemingly more relevant to the working needs of designers
than photographers. However, you can use the Absolute
Colorimetric rendering intent as a means of simulating a
target CMYK output on a proofing device. Let's say you
make a conversion from RGB to CMYK using either the
Relative Colorimetric or Perceptual CMM, and the target
CMYK output is a newspaper color supplement printed
on uncoated paper. If you use the Absolute Colorimetric
rendering intent to convert these 'targeted' CMYK colors
to the color space of the proofing device, the proof printer
can reproduce a simulation of what the printed output on
that stock will look like. Note that when you select the
'Proof' option in the Photoshop print dialog, the Absolute
Colorimetric rendering is applied automatically to produce
a simulated proof print.

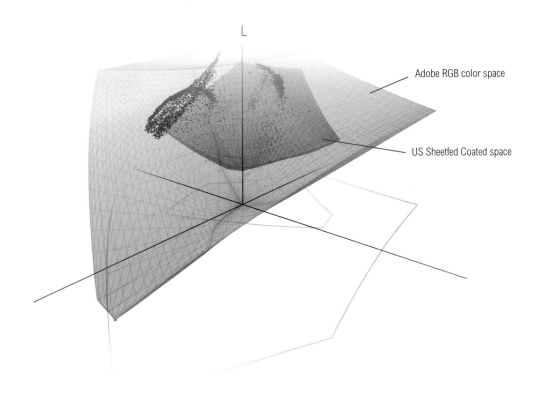

L

Adobe RGB color space

US Sheetfed Coated space

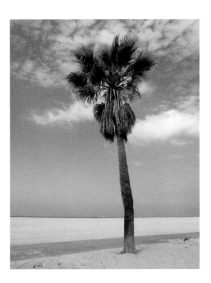

Figure 12.43 To illustrate how the rendering intent can influence the outcome of a color mode or profile conversion I used Chromix ColorThink 2.1.2 to help me create the diagrams shown on these two pages. The above diagram shows the Adobe RGB color space overlaying a US Sheetfed Coated CMYK color space. As you can see, Adobe RGB is able to contain all the colors that may be squeezed into this smaller CMYK space. The photograph opposite has been plotted on this diagram so that the dots represent the distribution of RGB image colors within the Adobe RGB space.

When the colors in this image scene are converted to CMYK, the rendering intent will determine how the RGB colors that are outside the gamut limits of the CMYK space will be assigned a new color value. If you look now at the two diagrams on the opposite page you will notice the subtle differences between a relative colorimetric and a perceptual rendering (I have highlighted a single blue color in each to point out these differences). The upper example shows a relative colorimetric rendering, where you will notice that the out-of-gamut blue colors are all rendered to the nearest in-gamut CMYK equivalent. Compare this with the perceptually rendered diagram below and you will see that these same colors are squeezed in further. This rendering method preserves the relationship between the out-of-gamut colors but at the expense of sometimes (not always) producing a less vibrant separation.

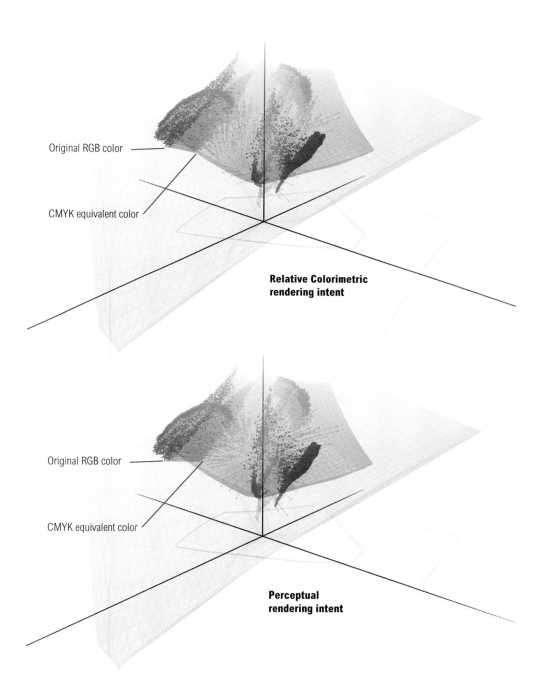

Original RGB color

CMYK equivalent color

**Relative Colorimetric
rendering intent**

Original RGB color

CMYK equivalent color

**Perceptual
rendering intent**

Specular and non-specular highlights

Specular highlights are shiny highlights such as highlight reflections off metal surfaces, while non-specular highlights are highlight areas that contain important detail. Refer to pages 168–171 in Chapter 3 to read more about how to determine where to clip the highlights and shadow areas in a picture.

When levels have to be set manually

You should be aware that some repro companies operate what is known as a closed-loop system where they edit files in CMYK and do not use a profiled workflow. This is something that may only affect high-end repro users of Photoshop and, if this is the case, you may need to target the shadows manually according to the conditions of the printing press. The same is also true if you are editing a grayscale file in Photoshop that is going to print.

Fine-tuning the CMYK endpoints

You can use the black point and white point tools in the Levels or Curves adjustment dialogs to assign specific pixel values to the shadows and the highlights. Normally you can rely on an image mode conversion to adjust the shadow points, but there are certain situations where it may be desirable to fine-tune the endpoints manually, such as when you are working on grayscale images that are destined to be printed in a book, magazine or a newspaper. It may also be necessary if the image is already in CMYK mode, but is missing an embedded profile, and you know what the press output should be. Instead of relying on the profile conversion to assign the end points, you can assign these manually. The eyedropper tools can also be used to color correct an image and remove color casts from the shadows or highlights of an image, plus the gray point tool can be used to assign a target gray color to the midtones (this was covered earlier in Chapter 5).

Let's now run through the basic steps for assigning the end points via the shadow point and highlight point tools. But before you do anything else, select the eyedropper tool in the Tools panel and go to the Eyedropper Options panel and set the Sample Size to 3 × 3 Average (or higher). Now open the Levels or Curves dialog. The default values for the shadow point and highlight point tools are 0% and 100%, but if you want to set the shadows and highlights in a grayscale or CMYK image for repro output, you will need to set these differently. The shadow point should obviously be higher than 0% (in order to take into account the dot gain) and may typically need to be set to 4%, while the highlight point for the non-specular highlights should be slightly darker than 100% (this ensures that the highlight detail will hold on the press) and should be set to around 96% or lower. This method of assigning the end points allows you to decide exactly where the highlight and shadow points should be, but, as I say, this is only really necessary when profiled conversions are not an option. In a normal workflow you should never need to bother with setting the end points in this way.

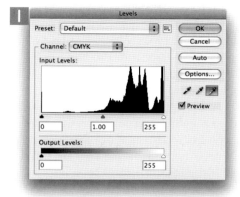

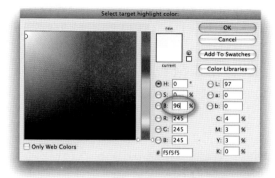

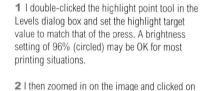

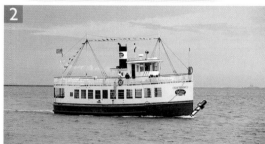

1 I double-clicked the highlight point tool in the Levels dialog box and set the highlight target value to match that of the press. A brightness setting of 96% (circled) may be OK for most printing situations.

2 I then zoomed in on the image and clicked on the area I wanted to assign as the highlight target point (this should be a subject highlight and not a specular highlight such as a reflection or glare).

3 Next, I double-clicked the shadow point tool and set a brightness setting of 4% (circled), or higher, depending on the press.

4 I then zoomed in on the image to identify the darkest shadow point and clicked with the shadow point tool to set the new shadow value (having done this, you may want to use the Levels Gamma slider to adjust the relative image brightness).

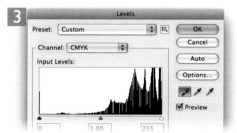

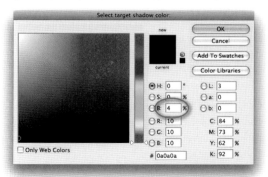

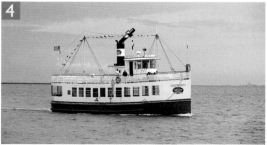

CMYK to CMYK

It is not ideal for CMYK files to be converted to RGB and then converted back to CMYK, as this is a sure-fire way to lose data fast! I always prefer to keep an RGB master of each image and convert to CMYK using a custom conversion to suit each individual print output. Converting from one CMYK space to another is not really recommended either, but in the absence of an RGB master, this will be the only option you have available: just specify the CMYK profile you wish to convert to in the Convert to Profile dialog box. Remember, the Preserve Embedded Profiles policy ensures that tagged incoming CMYK files can always be opened without converting them to your default CMYK space (because that would be a bad thing to do). This means that the color numbers in the incoming CMYK files will always be preserved, while providing you with an accurate display of the colors on the screen.

Lab Color

The Lab Color mode is available as a color mode to convert to via the Image ⇨ Mode menu and the Convert to Profile command, but note that Lab color does not use embedded profiles since it is assumed to be a universally understood color space. It is argued by some that converting to Lab mode is one way of surmounting all the problems of mismatched RGB color spaces. You could make this work, so long as you didn't actually do anything to edit the image while it was in Lab mode, but I would not really advise this. In fact, these days I see less and less reason to use the Lab color mode in Photoshop. Now, a few people have taken me to task over not covering Lab mode image editing in this book, so let me clarify why I don't advocate this. In the early days of Photoshop I would use Lab color to carry out certain tasks in Photoshop, such as sharpening the Lightness channel separately. This was before the introduction of layers and blending modes, where I soon learnt that you could use the Luminosity and Color blend modes to neatly target the luminosity or the color values in an image without having to convert to Lab mode and back to RGB again. While it is true that Luminosity blend mode sharpening is not exactly the same as sharpening the Lightness channel, such arguments have been superseded by the latest improvements to Camera Raw sharpening, where it is now possible to filter the luminance sharpening using the Detail and Masking sliders (see Chapter 4).

Let's just say that there are no right or wrong answers here. If you can produce good looking prints using whatever methods work best for you, and you are happy with the results, well who can argue with that? However, I would hope by now that having learnt about optimizing tones and colors in Camera Raw, followed by what can be achieved using Photoshop, you'll realize that these provide all the tools you'll ever need to process a photograph all the way through to the finished print stage. My response to the Lab color argument is that it is simply adding complexity where none is needed. There are good reasons why in recent years the Adobe engineering teams have devoted considerable effort to enhancing the Camera Raw image editing for Photoshop and Lightroom. Their aim has been to make photographic image editing more versatile, less destructive and, above all, simpler to work with.

Info panel

Given the deficiencies of the color display on a monitor, such as its limited dynamic range and inability to reproduce colors like pure yellow on the screen, color professionals will sometimes rely on the numeric information to assess an image. Certainly when it comes to getting the correct output of neutral tones, it is possible to predict with greater accuracy the neutrality of a gray tone by measuring the color values with the eyedropper tool. If you are editing an image in a standard RGB space such as sRGB, Adobe RGB or ProPhoto RGB and the RGB numbers are all equal, it is unquestionably gray (Figure 12.44). Interpreting the CMYK ink values is not so straightforward. This is because neutral CMYK gray is not made up of an equal amount of cyan, yellow and magenta. If you compare the Color readout values between the RGB and CMYK Info panel

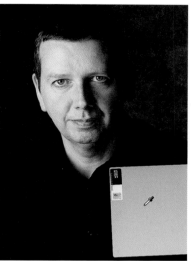

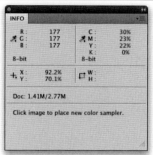

Figure 12.44 When you are editing an RGB image, the Info panel readings can help you determine the neutrality of a color. If the RGB values are all equal, and the RGB color space you are editing in is one of the standard spaces, such as Adobe RGB, sRGB or ProPhoto RGB, etc., then equal values of R, G & B equate to neutral gray.

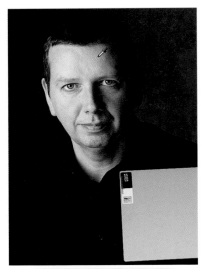

Figure 12.45 You can use the CMYK values in the Info panel to help check if the skin tones are the correct color or not by comparing the percentage of cyan to the magenta and yellow inks

readouts, there will always be more cyan ink used in the neutral tones, compared with the yellow and magenta inks. This is because a greater proportion of cyan ink is required to balance out the magenta and yellow inks to produce a neutral gray color in print (if the CMY values were equal, you would see a color cast). This is due to the fact that the process cyan ink is less able to absorb its complementary color – red – compared with the way magenta and yellow absorb their complementary colors. This also explains why a CMY black will look reddish/brown, without the help of the black plate to add depth and neutrality.

When you are retouching a portrait (such as in Figure 12.45), you can use the Info panel CMYK readout numbers to help judge if the skin tones are the right color. Set the panel options to display RGB and CMYK readouts. Then use the eyedropper to measure the skin tone values. Caucasian skin tones should have roughly a third or a quarter as much cyan as magenta and slightly more yellow than magenta. Black skin tones should be denser, have the same proportion of cyan to magenta, but usually a higher amount of yellow than magenta and also some black.

Keeping it simple

Congratulations on making it through to the end of this chapter! Your head may be reeling from all this information about Photoshop color management. But successful color management doesn't have to be complex. Firstly, you need to set the Color Settings to the prepress setting for your geographic region. This single step will configure the color management system with the best defaults for photographic work. The other thing you must do is to calibrate and profile the monitor of course. As I said before, if you want to do this right, you owe it to yourself to purchase a decent colorimeter device and ensure the monitor display is profiled regularly. Do just these few things and you can achieve a reliable color management workflow.

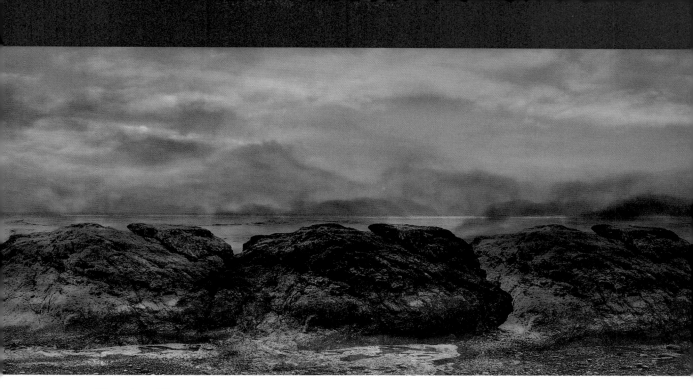

Chapter 13

Print Output

The preceding chapter considered the issues of color management and how to maintain color consistency between digital devices, while this chapter deals with the process of making prints from your images. The print quality that you can get from the latest inkjet printers has improved enormously over the last decade, such that this is now the main form of printing most photographers prefer to use. From contact sheets to fine art to commercial proof print, nearly everyone is using inkjet printers. Although companies like HP and Canon have done a lot to boost their presence in the photographic inkjet market, Epson do continue to dominate as the leading company in this market, which is why I mostly tend to concentrate on describing their printer models and drivers in my books.

Real World Sharpening

If you want to find out more about Bruce Fraser's writing on sharpening and output sharpening, I can again recommend his book: *Real World Sharpening with Adobe Photoshop CS2*. ISBN: 0-321-44991-6. Bruce is sadly no longer with us, but the techniques in his book, although described for Photoshop CS2, are still completely valid when working with Photoshop CS4.

Rather than go into all the details about different print processes, the different ink sets and papers that you can choose from, I have pared this chapter down to concentrate on just the essentials of inkjet printing (these other topics will be elaborated upon in a joint book I am writing with Jeff Schewe called *Adobe Photoshop CS4 for Photographers: the ultimate workshop*). There are two important things you need to do before making a print: you first need to sharpen an image before sending it to the printer and, secondly, you may want to soft proof the image so that you can anticipate as best as possible how the colors will actually be reproduced in the final print. To start with we'll look at the print sharpening

Print sharpening

Earlier in Chapter 4, I outlined how you can use the Detail panel sharpening sliders in Camera Raw to capture sharpen different types of images. This pre-sharpening is something that all images need. The goal in each case is to prepare an image according to its image content so that it ends up in what can be considered an optimized sharpened state. The aim is to essentially sharpen each photograph just enough to compensate for the loss of sharpness that is a natural consequence of the capture process.

Output sharpening is a completely different matter. Any time you output a photograph to be printed – either in a magazine, on a billboard, or when you send it to an inkjet printer – it will always require additional sharpening. Some output processes may incorporate automatic output sharpening, but most don't, so it is therefore essential to always include an output sharpening step just before you make any kind of print output. The question next is: how much should you sharpen? If you bear in mind that the capture sharpening step has already been tailored to the individual characteristics of each image, the output sharpening is a standard process, but is one that is dictated by specific factors, namely: the output process (i.e. inkjet printer or halftone printing), the paper type (glossy or matte) and the output resolution.

Judge the print, not the monitor

It is difficult, if not impossible, to judge how much you should sharpen an image for print output by looking at the monitor. Even if you reduce the viewing size to 50% or 25%, what you see on the screen will bear no resemblance to the final print output.

The ideal print output sharpening can be calculated on the basis that at a normal viewing distance, the human eye resolves detail to around 1/100th of an inch. So if the image you are editing is going to be printed from a file with a resolution of 300 pixels per inch, the edges in the image will need a 3 pixel Radius if they are to register as sharp in print. When an image is viewed on a monitor at 100%, this kind of sharpening will look too sharp and quite ugly (because you are viewing the image much closer up than it will actually be seen in print), but the actual physical print should appear nice and sharp. So, based on the above formula, images printed at lower resolutions will require a smaller pixel radius sharpening and those printed at higher resolutions will require a higher pixel radius sharpening. Now, different print processes and media types will require slight modifications to the above rule, but essentially, output sharpening can be distilled down to a set formula for each print process/resolution/media type. This was the basis for the research carried out by Bruce Fraser and Jeff Schewe when they devised the sharpening routines used for Photokit Sharpener (see sidebar).

High Pass filter edge sharpening technique

The technique described on pages 614–615 shows an example of just one of the formulas used in the Photokit Sharpener product for output sharpening. In this case I have shown Bruce Fraser's formula for sharpening a typical 300 pixel per inch glossy inkjet print output, so make sure you have resized the image to the exact print output dimensions and at a resolution of 300 pixels per inch beforehand. You will notice that it mainly uses the High Pass filter combined with the Unsharp Mask filter to apply the sharpening effect.

A demo version of Photokit Sharpener is available on the DVD and there is also a special discount coupon available at the back of this book which entitles you to a 10% discount. Photokit Sharpener provides Photoshop sharpening routines for capture sharpening, creative sharpening and output sharpening (inkjet, continuous tone, halftone and multimedia/Web). The Camera Raw sharpening sliders are based on the Photokit Sharpener methods of capture sharpening, so if you have the latest version of Photoshop or Lightroom, you won't need Photokit Sharpener for the capture sharpening. If you have Lightroom 2, you will find that the output sharpening for inkjet printing is actually built-in to the Lightroom print module. Therefore, if you don't have Lightroom 2, you'll definitely find the Photokit Sharpener output sharpening routines useful for applying the exact amount of output sharpening that is necessary for different types of print outputs and at different pixel resolutions. Try out the demo to see how the print output compares to using no sharpening or other print sharpening methods.

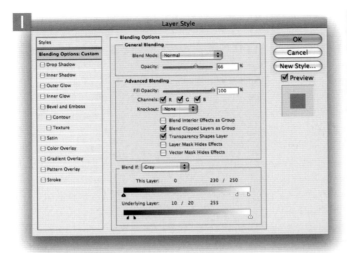

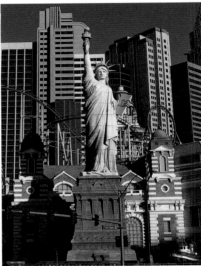

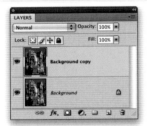

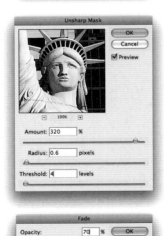

1 The sharpening method described here is designed for sharpening an inkjet print on glossy paper at 300 ppi. To begin with, make a duplicate copy of the Background layer and set the layer opacity to 66%, then double-click on the duplicate layer to open the Layer Style options and get the Blend If sliders to match the settings shown here.

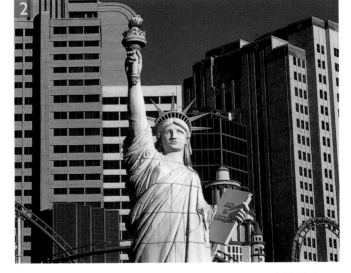

2 Next, apply the Unsharp Mask filter to the layer using an Amount of 320, Radius of 0.6 and Threshold of 4. Then choose Edit ⇨ Fade, change the blend mode to 'Luminosity' and reduce the opacity to 70%.

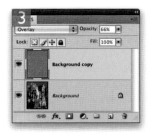

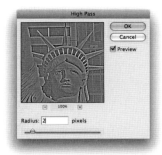

3 Now change the Layer blend mode from 'Normal' to 'Overlay', go to the Filter menu and choose Other ⇨ High Pass filter. Apply a Radius of 2 pixels. Note that the sharpening layer can be increased or decreased in opacity or easily removed so that the underlying Background layer remains unaffected by the sharpening steps.

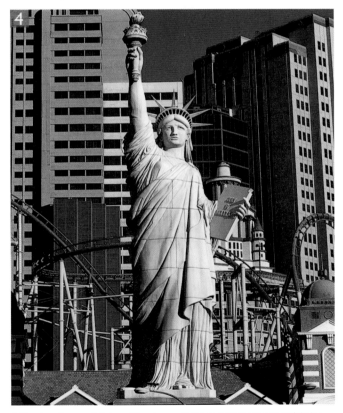

4 Here is a close-up 1:1 view of the sharpened image. Remember, you can't judge the sharpening by looking at the monitor, but you should be able to judge the effectiveness of the technique by how sharp the photograph appears here in print.

Gamut warning

The View menu contains a 'Gamut Warning' option that can be used to highlight colors that are out of gamut. The thing is, you never know if a highlighted color is just a little or a lot out of gamut. Gamut warning is therefore a fairly blunt instrument to work with, which is why I suggest you use the soft proofing method described here.

Print from the proof settings

The Customize Proof condition is also important because when it is active and used to preview an image, the Photoshop Print dialog can be made to reference the soft proofed view as the source space. This means that you can use Customize Proof Condition to select a CMYK output space and the Photoshop print dialog will allow you to make a simulated print using this proof space.

Soft proof before printing

Color management can do a fairly good job of translating the colors from one space to another but, for all the precision of measured targets and profile conversions, it is still essentially a dumb process. When it comes to printing, color management can usually get you close, but it won't be able to interpret every single color or make aesthetic judgements about which colors are important and which are not, plus some colors you see on the screen simply can't be reproduced in print. This is where soft proofing can help. If you use the Custom Proof Condition dialog as described here, you can simulate pretty accurately on screen how the print will look when printed. Soft proofing shows you which colors are going to be clipped and also allows you to see in advance the difference between selecting a 'Perceptual' or 'Relative Colorimetric' rendering intent. All you have to do is to select the correct profile for the printer/ paper combination that you are about to use, choose a rendering intent and make sure 'Black Point Compensation' plus the 'Simulate Paper Color' (and by default simulate black ink) are checked.

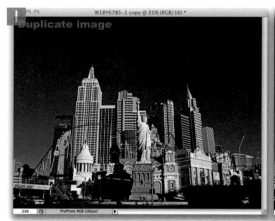 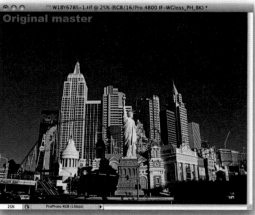

1 To begin with I opened the image shown here, went to the Image menu and chose 'Duplicate...' to create a duplicate copy image, which is shown here on the left next to the original on the right. In this screen shot you can see a slight difference between the color of the sky. This is because I had applied the Customize Proof Condition shown in Step 2 to the original master image.

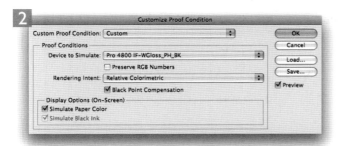

2 To soft proof the master image I went to the View menu and chose Proof Setup ⇨ Custom... . Here I selected a profile of the printer/paper combination that I wished to simulate, using (in this case) the Relative Colorimetric rendering intent and with the 'Simulate Paper Color' option checked in the on-screen display options.

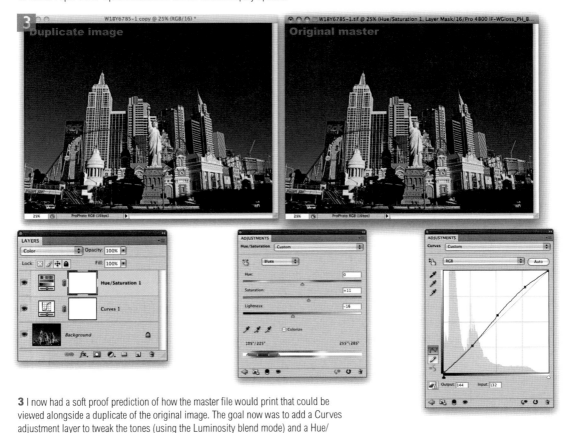

3 I now had a soft proof prediction of how the master file would print that could be viewed alongside a duplicate of the original image. The goal now was to add a Curves adjustment layer to tweak the tones (using the Luminosity blend mode) and a Hue/Saturation adjustment to tweak the colors (using the Color blend mode). A few minor adjustments were enough to get the soft proofed master to match closer to the original.

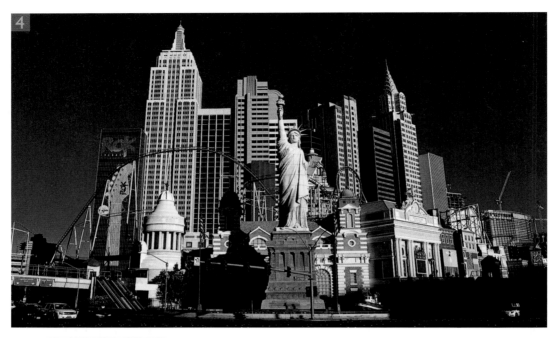

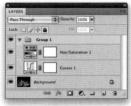

4 In this final version, you see the corrected, soft proofed master image. When this corrected version is sent to the printer, the print output should match very closely to what is seen here on the screen. I recommend the correction adjustment layers be preserved by grouping them into a layer group. Turn the visibility off before saving and only switch it back on again when you need to make further prints.

Saving print presets

To help minimize print setup errors, it is often worth creating print presets. Apply all your page setup and print settings first, then pull down the Print Presets menu (see page 627), choose 'Save As…' from the bottom, and name it appropriately.

Making a print

The print menu items in Photoshop can be accessed via the File menu and are all fairly straightforward. We have a Page Setup… menu (⌘ Shift P / ctrl Shift P) for setting up the printer and paper settings and a Photoshop application Print… menu item (⌘ P / ctrl P) that takes you directly to the Photoshop Print dialog. The Print One Copy command (⌘ ⌥ Shift P / ctrl alt Shift P) is there should you wish to make a print using the current configuration for a particular image, but wish to bypass the print dialogs – but do heed later warnings about print settings not always being sticky! Use this with caution.

Page Setup

Let's start with the Page Setup. The first thing you need to do is go to the Page Setup dialog (see Figures 13.1 and 13.2) and make sure the right printer is selected (you may have to do this each time in Mac OS X). Choose a paper size that matches the paper you are about to print with and select the right orientation: either portrait or landscape.

Scale setting in Page Setup

Although the Mac OS X Page Setup dialog allows you to adjust the print scale size, I don't advise you to do this – either here or in the Photoshop Print dialog – unless you absolutely must. It is always much better to resize the image in Photoshop first and print using a 100% scale size.

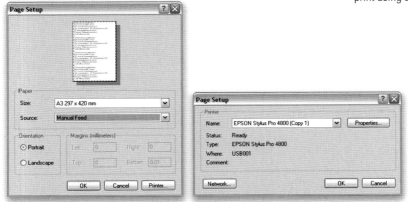

Figure 13.1 If you are using a PC computer, go to the File menu and choose Page Setup... . In the main Page Setup dialog you will want to click on the Printer... button to select which printer model you want to print to. Click 'OK' and this will return you to the Page Setup dialog again where you can select the paper size, print feed method and print orientation: Portrait or Landscape.

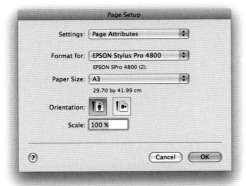

Figure 13.2 If you are using Macintosh OS X, go to the File menu and choose Page Setup... . Where it says 'Format For' select the printer you want to print to and then select the paper size and print orientation: Portrait or Landscape.

Ensuring your prints are centered

We would all love Photoshop printing to be simpler, but unfortunately there are no easy solutions and this is not necessarily all Adobe's fault either. The problem is that you have a multitude of different printer devices out there and, in addition to this, you have two main types of operating systems, each of which has their own protocols as to how the system print dialogs should be organized.

Making sure a print is centered is just one of several problems that require a little user intervention. If you center a print in the Photoshop Print dialog, but it does not print centered, this is probably due to the default margin settings being uneven. The reason for this is that some printers require a trailing edge margin that is wider than all the other margins. But as I have shown below in Figure 13.3, you can overcome this by creating your own custom paper sizes and margin settings.

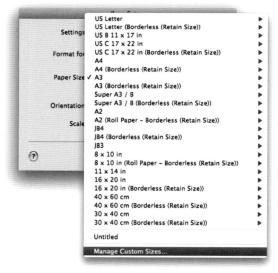

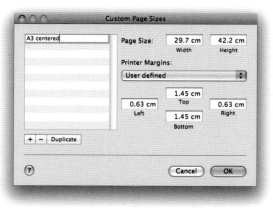

Figure 13.3 On Mac OS X, go to the Page Setup menu and choose 'Manage Custom Sizes...' from the Paper Size menu. In the Custom Page Sizes dialog check the margin width for the bottom trailing edge margin for the selected printer. If you want your prints to always be centered, all you have to do is to adjust the Top margin width so that it matches this bottom measurement. Set a Width and Height for the new paper size and save this as a new paper size setting and add 'centered' so you can easily locate it when using the Page Setup dialog.

Photoshop Print dialog

When you choose 'Print...' from the File menu, Photoshop takes you to what I prefer to describe as the Photoshop Print dialog (Figure 13.6), as opposed to the System Print dialog. This dialog was once known as 'Print with Preview' and since CS3 it has undergone a major overhaul to provide better settings control and a larger color managed print preview. We shall start by looking at the Output settings.

Output settings

To adjust the Output settings, make sure that 'Output' is selected from the top menu. The Printer model you selected in Page Setup should be visible in the Printer menu and below that you will see a Page Setup... button. You could, if you like, bypass going to Page Setup and access everything via this Photoshop Print dialog. Although, if you are using a PC, the Page Setup button takes you directly to the System Print dialog. This is because you have already chosen a printer model and the paper size, and orientation controls will also be available in the System Print dialogs. Oh boy, see my comments on the previous page about the operating systems forcing the print pipelines to be so different and confusing.

When the Center Image box is deselected and the Show Bounding box is enabled, you can position an image anywhere you like, by dragging inside the preview area. Or, you can position the image by entering in measurements for the Top and Left margins. In the Scaled Print Size section, if the image overflows the currently selected page size, you can choose 'Scale to Fit Media', which automatically resizes the pixel resolution to fit the page (the Print resolution PPI will adjust). You can also enter a specific Scale percentage, or Height and Width for the image, but as I pointed out on page 619, it is not really a good idea to resize the image via the Print dialog if you can help it.

On the right, you can select any extra items you wish to see printed outside the image area. The Calibration Bars will print an 11-step grayscale wedge on the left and a smooth gray ramp on the right. If you are printing CMYK

Output options

To apply some of the Output options mentioned here, you must be using a PostScript print driver and you should also allow enough border space surrounding the print area to print these extra items.

For example, when the 'Include Vector Data' option is unchecked, it will rasterize the vector layer information, such as type at the image file resolution. However, if it is checked, it will rasterize the vector information such as type much crisper at the full printer resolution, provided that you are outputting from a PostScript RIP.

Freeform placement on the page

When the bounding box is made visible, you can drag the box and box handles to visually arrange the page position and scale. If a selection is active before you select Print Options, and Print Selected Area is checked, the selected area only will be printed.

16-bit printing

Image data is normally sent to the printer in 8-bit, but some more recent inkjet printers such as the Canon ipf5000 are now enabled for 16-bit printing (providing you are using the correct plug-in and the 16-Bit Output box is checked). There are certain types of images that theoretically may benefit from 16-bit printing and where it can avoid the possibility of banding appearing in print, but I have yet to see this demonstrated. Let's just say, if your printer is enabled for 16-bit printing, Photoshop now allows you to send the data in 16-bit.

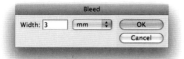

Figure 13.4 The Bleed option will work in conjunction with the 'Corner Crop Marks' option and determine how far to position the crop marks from the edge of the printed image.

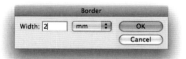

Figure 13.5 The Border option will allow you to add a black border and choose the size.

separations, tint bars can also be printed for each plate color and the Registration Marks will help a printer align the separate plates. The Corner and Center Crop Marks indicate where to trim the image and the Bleed button (Figure 13.4) determines how much the crop marks are indented. Checking the Description box prints any text that was entered in the File ⇨ File Info box Description field and check the Labels box to have the file name printed below the picture. Click on the Background... button to print with a background color other than paper white. For example, when sending the output to a film writer, you would choose black as the background color. Click on the Border... button (Figure 13.5) to set the width for a black border. But be aware that the border width can be unpredictable. If you set too narrow a width, the border may print unevenly on one or more sides of the image.

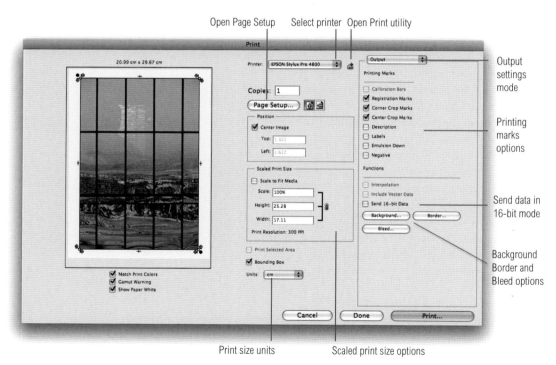

Figure 13.6 The Photoshop Print dialog, showing the Output settings mode options.

Color Management

Now let's look at the Color Management settings for the Photoshop Print dialog (Figure 13.8). The source space can be the document profile (which in this case was ProPhoto RGB) and if you click on the Proof button it will default to using the current CMYK workspace, or can use whatever Custom Proof Condition you might have set (see page 616).

Next we come to the Color Handling section. If printing from an RGB image, there are three options. 'No Color Management' should only be used when printing out a target print to build a print profile. The 'Printer Manages Colors' option can be used if you want to skip to the system Print dialog and let the printer driver manage the color output, but if you want the best print quality, you should really select the 'Photoshop Manages Colors' option (as shown in Figure 13.7). When this option is selected you can use the Photoshop Print dialog to manage the print color pipeline. First of all you will need to mouse down on the Printer Profile menu, where you'll see a long list of profiles. Here you need to select the printer profile that matches the printer/paper you are about to print with. It used to be the case that canned profiles were frowned upon as being inferior, but I would say that with the latest Epson printers at least, the printers they make these days are extremely consistent in print output and the canned profiles they supply work very well, so you would be advised to use their own brand profiles for the papers that their printers support.

The rendering intent can be set to Perceptual, Saturation, Relative Colorimetric or Absolute Colorimetric. For normal RGB printing the choice boils down to the choice of two settings. 'Relative Colorimetric' is the best setting to use for general printing, as it will preserve most of the original colors. 'Perceptual' is a good option to choose when printing an image where it is important to preserve the detail in saturated color areas, when printing an image that has a lot of deep shadows, or when printing to a smaller gamut output space, such as a fine-art matte paper. Whichever option you choose, I advise you to leave Black

Accessing canned printer profiles

A set of canned printer profiles should be installed in your System profiles folder at the same time as you install the print driver for your printer. If you can't find these, try doing a reinstall, or do a search on the manufacturer's website.

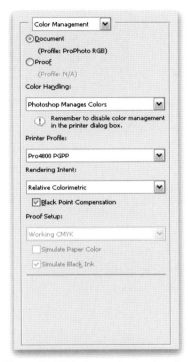

Figure 13.7 This shows a close-up view of the Color Management Photoshop Print dialog options.

Color Management mode

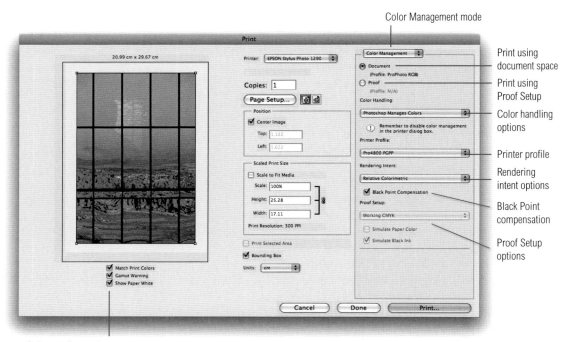

Print using
document space

Print using
Proof Setup

Color handling
options

Printer profile

Rendering
intent options

Black Point
compensation

Proof Setup
options

Color proofing options

Figure 13.8 The Photoshop Print dialog, showing the Color Management options.

Point Compensation switched on, because this maps the darkest colors from the source space to the destination print space. Black Point Compensation preserves the darkest black colors and maximizes the full tonal range of the print output. The Print dialog preview can be color managed by checking the 'Match Print Colors' option. Admittedly, the preview could be made a bit bigger, but it does at least give you some indication of how a photograph will print and you will notice that as you pick a printer profile or adjust the rendering intents, you can preview on screen what the printed colors will look like. When proofing an RGB output in this way you can also check the 'Show Paper White' option to see an even more accurate simulation that takes into account the paper color of the print media. There is also a 'Gamut Warning' option, but as I pointed out on page 616, this isn't as useful as using the soft proofing method described earlier to gauge your print output.

Setting the Proof Setup in the Print dialog

Earlier, in the Soft proof before printing section (see page 616), I described using the soft proof setup to predict how an RGB photograph might actually print via an inkjet or when printed in CMYK. If the soft proofing is active for a document window and you check the Proof button in the Photoshop Print dialog (Figure 13.8), this can become the new source space to print from (providing you also have 'Current Custom Setup' selected in the Proof Setup section below). You can therefore use a custom CMYK setting in the Customize Proof Condition dialog and then use this as the source space when printing to any profiled printer output. Alternatively, you can check the Proof button in the Photoshop Print dialog and select 'Working CMYK' in the Proof Setup menu. 'Simulate Black Ink' is always checked by default, but you can also include 'Simulate Paper Color' when creating a proof print.

Proof print or aim print?

Using the proof setup, you should be able to produce very nice targeted CMYK prints, providing you are printing to a decent paper. You can use high quality photo paper, or you could use papers that are specially designed for proof printing. However, if you carry out what is referred to as 'Photoshop cross-rendered proofing' the prints you produce can only really be described as 'aim prints'. These are not official 'contract proof' prints, but even so, they are accepted by many repro houses as a welcome guide to how you anticipate the final print image should look.

About the print dialogs

The following dialogs include the Mac and PC instructions for the Epson 4800 inkjet printer settings. The Epson interface and main controls will be fairly similar for other makes of inkjet printers, but not identical. Figure 13.8 shows how I would go about making a print from an RGB image in Photoshop using one of the Epson 4800 printer profiles that were automatically loaded when I installed the Epson 4800 printer driver on my computer.

Managing print expectations

When you use soft proofing to simulate a print output your initial response can be 'eek, what happened to the contrast?' This can be especially true when you also include 'Simulate Paper Color' in a soft proof setup. If we assume that you are using a decent monitor and that it has been properly calibrated, the soft proof view should still represent an accurate prediction of the contrast range of an actual print, compared to the high contrast range you have become accustomed to seeing on an LCD monitor. One solution is to look away as you apply the soft proof preview so that you don't notice the sudden shift in the on-screen appearance so much.

Overcoming dull whites

When 'Simulate Paper Color' is selected, the whites may appear duller than expected. This does not mean the proof is wrong, rather it is the presence of a brighter white border that leads to the viewer regarding the result as looking inferior. To get around this try adding a white border to the outside image you are about to print. When the print is done, trim away the outer paper white border so that the eye does not get a chance to compare the dull whites of the print with the brighter white of the printing paper used.

Print quality settings

In the Print settings, a higher print resolution will produce marginally better-looking prints, but take longer to print. The 'High Speed' option enables the print head to print in both directions. Some people prefer to disable this option when making fine quality prints, but with the latest inkjet printers, the 'High Speed' option shouldn't give you inferior results.

System Print dialog settings

Click 'Print...' in the Photoshop Print dialog and you will be taken to either of the System Print dialogs shown here, where you can configure the printer driver settings.

The 'System Print dialog' options will vary a lot from printer to printer. As well as having Mac and PC variations, you might have a lot of other options available to choose from and your printer driver may look quite different. If you are using the Photoshop Print dialog to manage the colors, there are just two key things to watch out for. You need to make sure you select the correct media setting in the print settings and that you have the printer color management turned off. This will mean selecting 'No Color Adjustment' in the Print Settings or Color Management sections (don't pay any attention to any of the other options you might see such as 'EPSON Vivid' or 'Charts and Graphs').

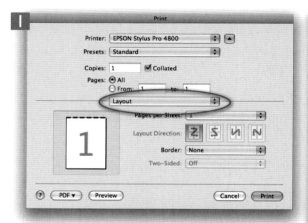
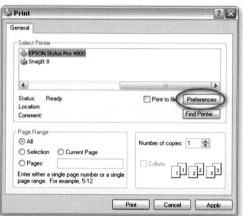

1 When you click the Print button in the Photoshop Print dialog, it will take you to the Mac or PC System Print dialog shown here. How these appear will depend on the printer and print driver you are using, but even though all the settings may be arranged differently, you'll find the following steps show which specific settings you need to configure. If using Mac OS X, mouse down on the main print driver menu (circled, above left) and select 'Print Settings'. If using a PC, click to select the printer and then click on the Preferences... button (circled) to proceed to the next step.

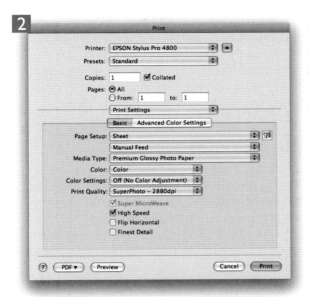

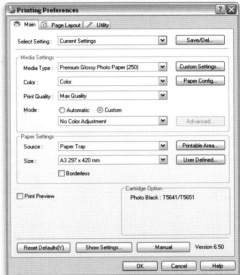

2 You will now need to select a media type that matches the paper you are going to print with. If using Mac OS X, go to the Media Type menu and choose the correct paper. Likewise, do the same if using the PC driver. Next, you will want to select a print quality setting that might say 'Super-duper Photo' or 'Max Quality'. Lastly, look for the Color Settings menu and set this to 'Off' (No Color Adjustment). This is because you do not need to make any further color adjustments. All you have to do now is click on the Print button at the bottom of the Mac dialog, or click 'OK' in the PC Advanced dialog and wait for your image to print.

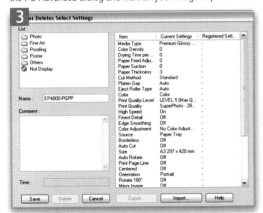

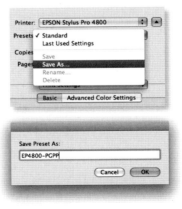

3 Once you have established the print settings shown here for a particular printing setup, it makes sense to save these settings as a preset that can easily be accessed every time you want to make a print using the same printer and paper combination. It is also the only way for the settings to remain 'sticky' when you wish to access them again.

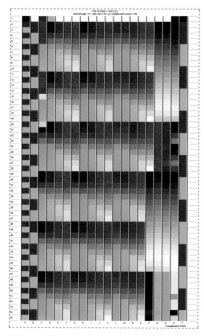

Figure 13.9 Here is an example of an X-Rite colo⁻ target that can be used to build an ICC colo⁻ profile. The target file must be opened in Photoshop without any color conversion and sent directly to the printer without any colo⁻ management; the print dimensions must remain exact. If it is necessary to resize the ppi reso ution make sure that the Nearest Neighbor interpolation mode is selected.

Custom print profiles

As I say, the profiles that are shipped with the latest inkjet printers, and especially the Epson models, can be considered reliable enough for professional print quality work (providing you are using the manufacturer's branded papers). If you want to extend the range of papers you can print with, then you will either have to rely on the profiles supplied by these paper companies or consider having a custom printer profile built for each paper type.

One option is to purchase a complete calibration kit package such as the X-Rite Eye-One Photo with ProfileMaker software. The other alternative is to get an independent color management expert to build a profile for you. There are quite a few individuals who are able to offer these services, such as Andrew Rodney who is based in the USA (go to: www.digitaldog.net). If you refer to the back of this book, you'll see that a company called colourmanagement.net are also offering a special coupon to readers that entitles you to a discount on their remote printer profiling services.

Remote profiling is a simple process. All you have to do is to follow the link to the website, download a test target similar to the one shown in Figure 13.9 (as well as the instructions), and follow these instructions closely when preparing a target print for output. Send the printed target to the address you are given and you'll be sent back an ICC profile via email. The important points to bear in mind are that you must not color manage the target image when printing. The idea is to produce a print in which the pixel values are sent directly to the printer without any color management being applied. The patch readings are then used to build an ICC profile that represents the characteristics of a particular paper type on your individual printer. The Print dialog settings used to produce the target print should be saved so that the exact same print settings are used when you then follow the steps outlined on pages 623–624 and pages 626–627.

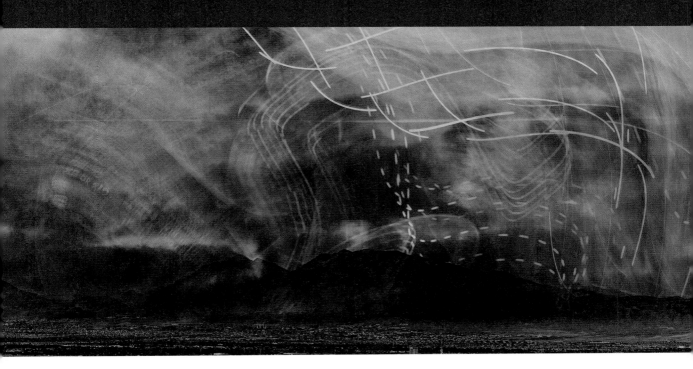

Chapter 14

Output for the Web

There is the well-known saying 'a picture is worth a thousand words', and it is so true – pictures allow us to communicate visually with clients, friends and family, in ways that words alone cannot. The Internet is something most of us use every day and having the means to transmit images has become extremely important to us. The most obvious advantage of sending or displaying images via the Web is its immediacy. Pictures can be sent around the world almost instantly and it is quick and easy to prepare an image to be distributed. The downsides are that, unlike producing a finished print, you have little or no control over the way the image is viewed, plus there are many other pitfalls associated with the limitations of some Internet software. This chapter aims to guide you with suggestions on how best to output your work online.

Sending multiple images by email

Email programs can accept single or multiple attachments of any format, but not as a folder, unless it has been compressed as an archive first. Aladdin™ Software make the ubiquitous Stuffit™ program which is great for compressing files in his way. It's available for Mac or Windows and handles ZIP compression as well as using its own proprietary format, which uses lossless compression. A Stuffit archive will have a .sit extension, which requires expansion by Stuffit (which is incorporated into the Mac OS), but this can also be saved as a self-extracting archive. In this instance, the archive will bear the .sea extension and either WinZip or Stuffit can expand such Mac created archives. If you are using the latest Mac OS X system, you can also use the contextual menu to select the 'Compress File' option to quickly create a ZIP archive on-the-fly. If the pictures in the source folder are JPEGs, then you will probably not notice a big difference in the final file size. But don't worry, this compression will not compromise the quality of the JPEG images any further.

Sending images over the Internet

Let's look at the ways you can distribute images over the Web. With the increasing popularity of Broadband, cable and ADSL connections, you can effectively use any fast connection to the Internet to transmit and receive large files.

Email attachments

The easiest way to send image files is to send them as attachments via email. Email programs may differ, but most should let you simply drag a file from a folder on your computer into the body text area of an email. Click 'Send' and you're done – the attached document will be distributed along with the text message in the email. It's relatively easy to do, but not completely flawless. For example, there is no reliable way of knowing if the recipient's email program can decode an attachment that has been sent from your email program. If you communicate using email this way, it is a good idea to keep the attachments small. As a rule, I tend to keep all attachments under 1 MB (assuming the recipient also has a broadband type connection) and I do like to check first with the recipient, before sending anything bigger, to see if they mind receiving an attachment bigger than this. The Internet suffers quite enough already with bandwidth being consumed by unwanted junk emails. So don't add to the problem by sending large, unsolicited attachments. But if it is OK to send a big file, ask the recipient if there is a limit in place for the size of files they can receive in a single email, because if you exceed this your email will only bounce back.

As long as you are aware of the parameters and restrictions of email programs and the possible limitations of the recipient's server, email can be an effective way to transfer smallish documents. Lots of people use email this way to share photographs. And the advanced email programs are also capable of displaying image file attachments within the body text area. But remember, this is by no means a foolproof way to send all images.

Uploading to a server

With email you are sending a message that has the image embedded in it. Another alternative is to upload the image file to a server. You can then send an email that contains a clickable link that launches the recipient's web browser and this will take them directly to a page from where they can download the file, or simply download the file directly. The advantage of this is that the email you send is small, as it only contains a text link to the server. There is also less risk of the email being rejected and if the person you are sending the email to needs to share the image link with someone else, they only have to forward the message – they don't have to forward the entire image attachment all over again. But first you need to know how to upload to a server. If you connect to the Internet using a subscription service, your Internet Service Provider (ISP) will most likely have provided you with a limited amount of server space that you can use to host your own website and upload files to. If you don't have a subscription service or your ISP doesn't provide enough adequate server space, then you can always rent space from a company that maintains a dedicated server and provides web hosting.

Once you have some server space you'll most likely need a dedicated FTP program to upload and manage the files on the server. Figure 14.1 shows how I would normally go about making an FTP connection to a server using the Fetch™ program for Macintosh OS X. To avoid having to re-enter the information each time you connect, it should be possible to save this information (along with the password if you wish) as a shortcut so that logging on to the server becomes almost as easy as opening a folder on your hard disk. Once the FTP connection window opens, this is like any other hierarchically structured folder. The main connection window displays the website documents and subfolders. In Figure 14.1 you can see how I have created new subfolders with names like 'portraits' and 'Snaps'. I use these specific folders to upload web galleries and images to so that they do not get mixed up with the folder structure of the main website. I can then double-click

FTP software for Mac and PC

You will need File Transfer Protocol (FTP) software to upload documents to the server space. If using a Macintosh, I recommend using Fetch™: www.fetchsoftworks.com If you are working on a PC, try using WS_FTP Pro www.ipswitch.com or Flash FXP™ www.flashfxp.com All FTP software is more or less the same. To establish a connection you need to provide a link address to connect to the server. Next, you need to enter your user ID and finally your password. If you are familiar with the steps required to configure your email account, you should already have the username and password information to hand. You may need to enter a subdirectory folder as well, but if you have trouble configuring the connection, speak to your ISP. They are the best people to help you in these instances.

Macintosh iDisk

Another option available to Macintosh users is iDisk which is part of the now superseded Mac.com package, renamed MobileMe. iDisk is an online server space that you can use for off-site backup storage or as a space to place publicly accessible files and folders.

Yousendit.com

In the last year or so, yousendit.com™ has become extremely popular as an FTP replacement file delivery service. All you have to do is go to the above site address, create a new user account and use the website to upload files that can be sent to recipients. The service is free for single file transfers up to 100 MB.

Download a sample image file

I have uploaded a photograph to my server which you can access by typing in the following URL address in your web browser: www.martinevening.com/portraits/evening.pdf This image document was saved as a Photoshop PDF file. You will probably be asked if you want to save the file to the desktop. Click 'Save' and the file will start to download. The reason I saved this image as a Photoshop PDF was to demonstrate the security features that are available when using this format. To open the PDF file you will need to enter the password 'evening' when prompted.

on a folder such as 'portraits' to reveal the subfolder contents and drag the Internet-ready files or folders across into this window. And that's it. The time this takes to accomplish will depend on the size of your files and Internet connection speed. All you have to do is to supply people with a weblink such as the one in the accompanying sidebar, so that they can access these files. When they click on the link you give them, the file should start to download automatically to their computer.

In the case of Bridge and Lightroom, you can now upload Web Galleries directly to a server, without the need for additional FTP software. When using the Create Gallery panel in the Bridge Output workspace, you'll need to enter the same login information and password as you would to establish an FTP connection, but you'll still probably need FTP software to manage and delete these files and folders.

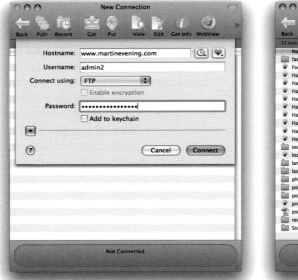
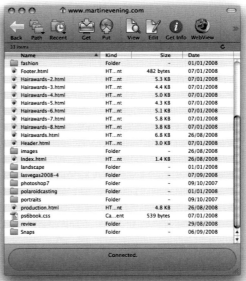

Figure 14.1 The Fetch™ 5.3 FTP software interface, showing how a new server connection can be made.

File formats for the Web

Now that we have covered the fundamentals of how to access a server and administer your allocated server space, let's look at preparing images to be displayed on the Web, some of the different file formats you can use, and which are the best ones to choose in any given situation.

JPEG

The JPEG (Joint Photographic Experts Group) format provides the most dramatic way to compress continuous tone image files. The JPEG format uses what is known as a lossy compression method. The heavier the compression, the more the image becomes irreversibly degraded. If you open a moderately compressed JPEG file and examine the structure of the image at 200%, you will probably notice that the picture contains a discernible pattern of 8 × 8 pixel squares, and this mosaic pattern will easily be visible at a 1:1 pixels view when using the heavier JPEG settings. JPEG compression is usually more effective if the image contains soft tonal gradations, as detailed images do not compress quite so efficiently and the JPEG artifacts will be more apparent (see Figure 14.2). The JPEG format is mostly used for web design work, because a medium to heavy amount of JPEG compression can make most photographs small enough to download quickly over the Internet. Image quality is less of an issue here when the main object is simply to reduce the download times. To be honest, do you really want images that anyone and everyone can access on-line to be of the highest technical quality anyway?

Photoshop compresses images on a scale of 0–12, where a setting of '12' applies the least amount of compression and yields the highest image quality, while a setting of '0' applies the greatest amount of compression and is therefore the most lossy. When you choose to save as a JPEG and have the 'Preview' option checked in the JPEG Options dialog (Figure 14.3), you'll be able to preview the effects of the JPEG compression in the image document window as you adjust the 'Quality' in the Image Options section. This shows how the image will look when it is

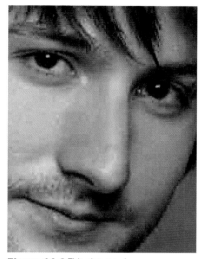

Figure 14.2 This shows a close-up view of a JPEG image that was saved at the '0' Quality setting in Photoshop. This clearly reveals the underlying 8 x 8 pixel mosaic structure, which is how the JPEG compression method breaks down the continuous tone pixel image into large compressed blocks. At the higher quality settings you will have to look very hard to even notice any change to the image.

Keeping files small

Only one thing matters when you publish images on the Web and that is to keep the total file size of your pages as small as possible. The JPEG format is the most effective way to achieve file compression for continuous tone images, but graphics that contain fewer distinct blocks of color should be saved using the GIF format. Some web servers are case sensitive and will not recognize capitalized file names, so go to the Photoshop Preferences menu ➪ File Handling and make sure the Use Lower Case Extensions box is checked.

reopened as a JPEG. The JPEG Options dialog box also indicates the compressed file size in kilobytes.

If you save a master file as a JPEG and then decide the file needs further compression, you can safely overwrite the last saved JPEG using a lower JPEG setting. For as long as the image is open in Photoshop, all data is held in Photoshop's memory and only the version saved on the disk is degraded, so it is possible to repeat saving in the JPEG format this way. However, once an image has been compressed using the JPEG format and reopened, it is not a good idea to repeatedly resave it as a JPEG again, because this will only compound the compression that's already been applied to the image structure. Having said that, unlike other programs, the JPEG compressor used in Photoshop converges, so that after repeated opening and saving using the same JPEG settings (and without modifying the pixels), the data loss diminishes with every save, to the point where there will be little or no further loss.

The JPEG format can primarily be used to send smaller-sized email attachments and ensure that visitors to your website don't have to hang around while the images download. You can also use the JPEG format to archive images for faster electronic distribution, or when you

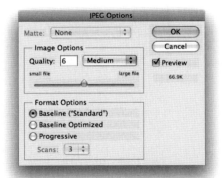

Figure 14.3 This shows the JPEG Options save dialog box. 'Baseline ("Standard")' is the most universally understood JPEG format option and one that most web browsers will be able to recognize. 'Baseline Optimized' will often yield a slightly more compressed sized file than the standard JPEG format and most (but not all) web browsers are able to read this correctly. The 'Progressive' option creates a JPEG file that will download in an interlaced fashion (the same way you can encode a GIF file).

are forced to save a large file to a restricted amount of disk space. For example, a 10" × 8" RGB file at 300 ppi resolution would normally be about 20 MB in size if saved as a TIFF. By saving it as a high quality JPEG this same file can be reduced in size to around 1 MB with hardly any degradation to the image quality. Some purists argue that JPEG compression should never be used under any circumstances when saving a photographic image. It is true that if a TIFF file is saved with JPEG file compression there are some rare instances where this can cause problems when sending the file to some older PostScript devices. Otherwise, the image degradation is barely noticeable at the higher quality compression settings, even when the image is viewed on the screen in close-up at actual pixels viewing, never mind how it will be seen when printed.

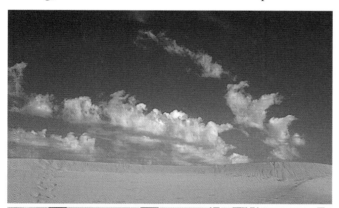

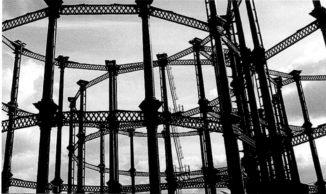

Figure 14.4 Here are two JPEG images: both have the same pixel resolution and both have been saved using the same JPEG quality setting. Yet the Sahara desert image will compress to just 21 kilobytes, while the gas works picture is over three times bigger at 74 kilobytes. This is because it contains lots of extra detail. The more contrasting sharp lines there are in an image, the larger the file size will be after compression. If you are editing an image that is intended to go on a web page, you can deliberately apply blur to some of the less critical portions of an image to remove distracting detail and thereby reduce the JPEG size (this is an option in the Save for Web & Devices dialog, see page 639).

Choosing the right compression type

JPEG compression offers the most effective way to reduce file size, but this is achieved at the expense of throwing away some of the image data (as was demonstrated in Figure 14.2). JPEG is therefore known as a lossy format, so you need to be careful not to apply any more compression than is necessary. If you refer to Figure 14.5 below, you can compare the different file sizes that were obtained when saving a 500 x 600 pixel image with different JPEG settings. As an uncompressed, 8-bit RGB TIFF, this file was 1.8 MB in size. When saved using the highest JPEG quality setting, there was barely any degradation to the image, yet the JPEG file size was just 232 kilobytes, or 12% of its original file size, which is quite a saving! When a medium (8) JPEG quality setting was used, the file size was reduced further to just 72 kilobytes. This is probably about the right amount of compression to use when preparing photographs to go on a website where you wish to strike the right balance between maintaining decent image quality, yet still keep the files compact in size. The lowest compression setting squeezed the image down to just 34 kilobytes, but at this level photographs will appear extremely 'mushy' and the lower quality settings are therefore best avoided.

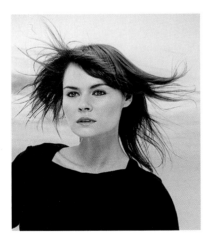

Name	Dat...fied	Size ▼	Kind
Uncompressed-image.tif	Today	1.8 MB	Adobe Photoshop TIFF file
JPEG-12.jpg	Today	232 KB	Adobe Photoshop JPEG file
Compuserve-GIF.gif	Today	140 KB	Adobe Photoshop GIF file
JPEG-8.jpg	Today	72 KB	Adobe Photoshop JPEG file
JPEG-4.jpg	Today	44 KB	Adobe Photoshop JPEG file
JPEG-0.jpg	Today	32 KB	Adobe Photoshop JPEG file

Figure 14.5 Here we have one image saved six different ways and each method producing a different file size. The opened image measures 500 x 600 pixels and the uncompressed TIFF file size is: 1.8 MB. Below that are the JPEG versions which were saved using different quality settings. Lastly, a GIF version was saved, which as you can see, does not offer the most efficient compression method, and is unsuitable anyway for saving most kinds of images.

TIFF compression for FTP transfer

I mention the TIFF format again here because it is the standard file format used for transferring files used for pre-press work. If you save a layered image as a TIFF using no image compression with Run Length Encoding (RLE) layer compression, the uncompressed TIFF format doggedly records every pixel value and will therefore be large in size. If you need to speed up the time it takes to transfer TIFF files via the Internet, such as when sending TIFF files via the yousendit.com FTP service, you might want to employ one of the compression methods described below in Figure 14.6. As you can see, LZW, ZIP or JPEG compression combined with ZIP layer compression can cut the file size down by half or more. The only downside is that the save times will be noticeably slower and not all RIPs accept files in a compressed TIFF format.

Lossless and lossy compression

The LZW and ZIP methods of compression are lossless. They can reduce the file size, but without degrading the image. The JPEG compression is lossy and you can only use it when saving TIFF images that have been converted to 8-bits per channel (although you can preserve the layers).

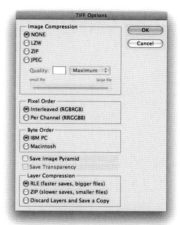

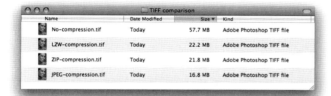

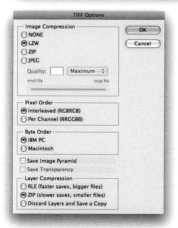
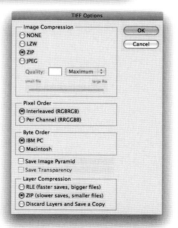
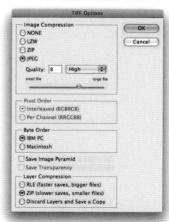

Figure 14.6 Here, I took an 8-bit, layered, RGB TIFF image saved with no compression, which was 57.7 MB in size, and saved it using three different methods of TIFF compression. The lossless LZW and ZIP compression methods efficiently reduced the file size to less than half the original size, while the lossy JPEG compression method had the potential to reduce the TIFF file size even further

You will find that when designing graphic images to be converted to a GIF, those with horizontal detail compress better than those with vertical detail. This is due to the GIF format using Run Length Encoding (RLE) compression.

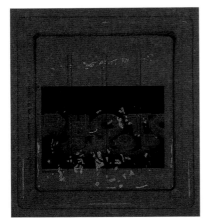

Figure 14.7 The GIF file format is mostly used for saving graphic logos and typography. The picture shown here is one that was used for the cover design of an earlier edition of this book. This is also a good example to illustrate the type of image that would be suitable for saving in the GIF format for use on a web page design. Note that the image contains a large amount of solid red and few other colors. This photograph was reduced in size to around 350 x 300 pixels. I then converted the image to Index Color mode using a palette of 16 colors. When the image was saved as a GIF it measured a mere 19 kilobytes.

GIF

The GIF (Graphics Interchange Format) is normally used for publishing graphic type images such as logos. Some people pronounce GIF with a soft G (as in George) and others use a hard G (as in garage). Neither is right or wrong as both forms of pronunciation are commonly used. Or as Julieanne Kost likes to say: 'it's pronounced, get a life!'

To prepare an image as a GIF, the color mode must be set to 'Indexed Color'. This is an 8-bit color display mode where specific colors are 'indexed' to each of the 256 (or fewer) numeric values. You can select a palette of indexed colors that are saved with the file and choose to save as a CompuServe GIF. The file is then ready to be placed in a web page and viewed by web browsers on all computer platforms. Photoshop contains special features to help web designers improve the quality of their GIF outputs (Figure 14.7), such as the ability to preview Indexed mode colors whilst in the Index Color mode change dialog box, and an option to keep matching colors non-dithered. This feature will help you improve the appearance of GIF images and reduce the risks of banding or posterization. Be aware that when the 'Preview' is switched on and you are editing a large image, it may take a while for the document window preview to take effect, so make sure that you resize the image to the final pixel size first.

PNG (Portable Network Graphics)

This file format can be used for the display and distribution of RGB color files on-line and is also available as a file format option in 'Save for Web'. PNG (pronounced 'ping') features improved image compression and enables alpha mask channels (for creating transparency) to be saved with the image. Other advantages over JPEG and GIF are higher color bit depths, support for channels and limited built-in gamma correction recognition, so you can view an image at the gamma setting intended for your monitor. Mozilla's Firefox and Microsoft's Internet Explorer web browsers support the PNG format, as does Apple's Safari web browser program.

Save for Web & Devices

The 'Save for Web & Devices' option (⌘ ⌥ Shift S ctrl alt Shift S) can be accessed via the File menu. This comprehensive dialog interface (Figure 14.8) gives you complete control over how images can be optimized for web use, offering a choice of JPEG, GIF, PNG-8 or PNG-24 formats. The preview display options include: Original, Optimized, 2-up and 4-up views (Figure 14.8 shows the dialog window in 2-up mode display). With 'Save for Web & Devices' you can preview the original version of the image plus up to three variations using different web format settings. In the annotation area below each preview,

Saving for devices

The saving for devices bit was introduced in CS3 and enables you to preview how a Photoshop image will look when displayed on various types of devices such as mobile phones. The details aren't really so relevant to a book on photography, so they're not covered in this chapter.

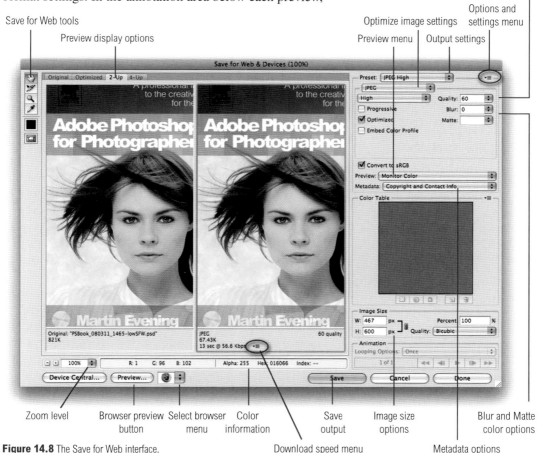

Figure 14.8 The Save for Web interface.

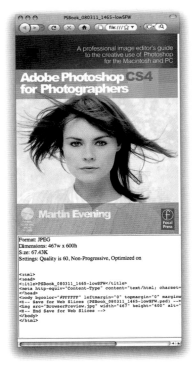

Format: JPEG
Dimensions: 467w x 600h
Size: 67.43K
Settings: Quality is 60, Non-Progressive, Optimized on

```html
<html>
<head>
<title>PSBook_080311_1465-lowSFW</title>
<meta http-equiv="Content-Type" content="text/html; charset=
</head>
<body bgcolor="#FFFFFF" leftmargin="0" topmargin="0" marginw
<!-- Save for Web Slices (PSBook_080311_1465-lowSFW.psd) -->
<img src="BrowserPreview.jpg" width="467" height="600" alt="
<!-- End Save for Web Slices -->
</body>
</html>
```

Figure 14.9 When you click on the browser preview button, a temporary page will be opened, like the one shown here. This allows you to preview the Save for Web processed image as it will appear on the final web page. This is especially useful for checking if the RGB editing space used will be recognized differently by the browser. So if you are relying on embedded ICC profiles to regulate the color appearance on screen, you can check to see if the profile is indeed being recognized by the selected web browser program.

you can make comparative judgements as to which format and compression settings give the best payoff between image quality and file size, and also determine how long it might take to download at a specific modem speed. Use the N-up Download speed menu (circled in purple) to select from a list of modem and Internet connections on which these download times are based.

Web browser previews

The Web browser menu allows you to select which web browser to use when you preview a document that has been optimized for the Web, such as the example shown in Figure 14.9, where I was able to preview the Save for Web & Devices image using the Firefox Web browser.

You can use the Preview menu list to select a preview setting and simulate how the web output will display on either a Macintosh display, a Windows PC display or with Photoshop compensation. Although these days I reckon it is safe to assume that everything will be viewed on a monitor using the PC 2.2 gamma standard.

Optimize image settings

The Optimize image settings section provides an option for Progressive JPEG formatting. Most browsers such as Firefox and Internet Explorer support this enhancement, whereby JPEGs can be made to download progressively interlaced the way GIFs can. If you check the 'Optimized' checkbox this option can be used to apply more efficient compression, but again it is not generally compatible with older web browser programs. The quality setting can be set as Low, Medium, High, Maximum or set more precisely as a value between 1 and 100%. The 'Embed Color Profile' option can be considered useful for those few browsers that do recognize profiles (such as Safari), but many don't and the downside of including an ICC profile is that this will add to the overall web image file size, so I suggest you only use this option in special circumstances. The Blur control allows you to soften an over-sharpened original and obtain further file compression when using the JPEG format. Also new to CS4 is the ability to refine the amount of metadata

saved with the web output images. Limiting the amount
of metadata saved can also help keep the file size small.
Once you have configured these settings, you can go to the
Options and settings menu (circled in red in Figure 14.8) and
choose 'Save Settings...'. You can then name the settings and
be able to access them in future via the Presets menu.

The 'Image Size' options are fairly similar to those
found in the Image ⇨ Image Size dialog box. Just simply
enter the new percentage for scaling the image and check
what impact this will have on the file size (this will change
the file size in all the optimized windows). An alternative
approach is to select 'Optimize To File Size' from the fly-
out menu (see Figure 14.10). You can use this to target the
optimized file to match a specific kilobyte file size output
and, if you wish, have Photoshop automatically determine
whether it is better to save as a GIF or JPEG.

'Save' options

The Save for Web dialog lets you save your output using
'Images Only', 'HTML Only' or 'HTML and Images'
(Figure 14.11). If you select 'Images Only', this simply
saves a web-ready image that you can use to place in a
website design, such as a blog entry, or as an image ready
to email. If you select the 'HTML and Images' option, you
can generate an HTML file with a link to the image, which
will be placed in an accompanying 'images' folder.

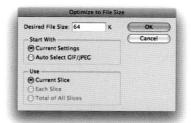

Figure 14.10 If you mouse down on the
Options and settings menu (circled in red in
Figure 14.8) you can choose 'Optimize to File
Size', which will open the dialog shown here,
where you can set a desired file size to optimize
the image to.

Edit Output Settings

The Edit Output Settings lets you
determine the various characteristics of
the Save for Web output files such as: the
default naming structure of the image files
and slices; the HTML coding layout; and
whether you wish to save a background file
to an HTML page output.

Efficient JPEG saving

The Save For Web & Devices dialog may
look intimidating, but once you figure
out which settings need concern you,
simply save these as a custom setting. I
have also recorded the Save for Web &
Devices as an action step, so that I don't
even need to look at this dialog. The main
thing to be aware of here is that Save for
Web & Devices offers the most efficient
way to prepare images for web use, since
it automatically strips out all previews,
and this can make your web images
dramatically smaller compared to using
File ⇨ Save As... to save as a JPEG.

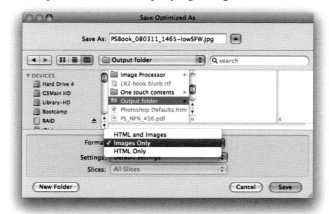

Figure 14.11 The 'Save for Web & Devices' save options.

Web palette colors

The Web palette contains the 216 colors common to both platforms and is therefore a good choice for web publishing if viewers are limited to looking at the image on an 8-bit color monitor display. Now to be honest, restricting your colors to a Web palette should not really be that necessary these days, but the option is still there. However, the Web Snap slider will let you modify the color table by selecting those colors that are close to being 'browser safe' and making them snap to these precise color values. The Web Snap slider determines the amount of tolerance and you can see the composition of the color table being transformed as you make an adjustment.

GIF lossy options

The 'Lossy' option allows you to reduce the GIF file size by introducing file compression. This can be helpful if you have an overlarge GIF file. But too much compression will noticeably degrade the image until it looks like a badly tuned TV screen.

Interlaced GIFs

The 'Interlaced' option will make the image appear to download progressively in slices, but will add slightly to the file size.

GIF Save for Web & Devices

The GIF Save for Web & Devices options (Figure 14.12) are also quite extensive. You have the same control over the image size and you can preview how a resulting GIF will appear on other operating systems and browsers – the remaining options all deal with the compression, transparency and color table settings that are specific to the GIF format. The choice of color reduction algorithms will allow you to select the most suitable 256 maximum color palette to save the GIF in, which includes the 8-bit palettes for the Macintosh and Windows systems. These are fine for platform-specific work, but such GIF files may display differently on the other system's palette. The Perceptual setting produces a customized table with colors to which the eye is more sensitive. The default Selective setting is similar to the Perceptual table, but more orientated to the selection of web safe colors. This is perhaps the best compromise solution to opt for now as every PC setup sold these days is able to display 24-bit color. The Adaptive table palette samples the colors which most commonly recur in the image. In an image with a limited color range, this type of palette can produce the smoothest representation using a limited number of colors.

The Diffusion dithering algorithm is effective at creating the impression of greater color depth and reducing any image banding, and the Dither slider allows you to control the amount of diffusion dithering (the 'Pattern' and 'Noise' options have no dither control). If the image to be saved has a transparent background, the 'Transparency' option can be kept checked in order to preserve the image transparency in the saved GIF. To introduce transparency in an image you can select the color to make transparent using the eyedropper tool and then click inside the image preview area. The color chosen will appear selected in the color table. Select one or more colors and click on the Map Selected Colors to Transparent button in the color table (see Figure 14.13). You can then apply a diffusion, pattern or noise dither to the transparent areas, which can help create a smoother transparent blend in your GIF.

Select dither algorithm   Optimize image settings   Options and settings menu

Color reduction algorithm   Output settings

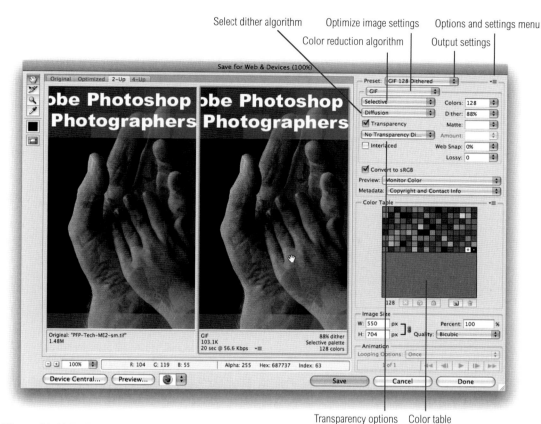

Transparency options   Color table

Figure 14.12 The Save for Web interface showing the GIF settings.

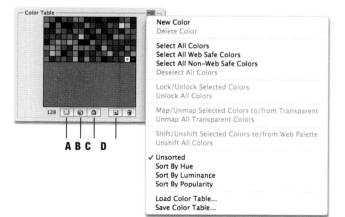

A B C D

Figure 14.13 The color table with the Color palette options menu shown.

A: Maps the selected color to transparency.
B: Shifts/unshifts selected colors to the Web palette.
C: Locks the color to the palette to avoid deletion.
D: Adds an eyedropper-selected color to the palette

Photograph: © Jeff Schewe.

Zoomify™ Export

The 'Zoomify™ Export' option in the File menu allows you to create an output folder containing all the necessary components to produce zoomable image web pages (Figure 14.14). Visitors will be able to view the pages created with the Zoomify export plug-in so long as they have an up-to-date Flash plug-in for their browser. Zoomify pages are ideal for portfolio presentations and commerce websites, where customers can easily view large images in close-up. If you go to the Zoomify website at www.zoomify.com, you can see some examples of customer sites where the export plug-in has been used.

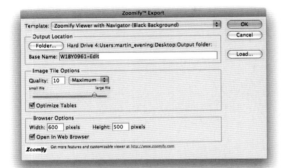

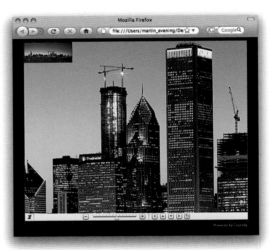

Figure 14.14 Here is the Zoomify™ Export dialog box showing typical settings that might be used to create a zoomable image. The output will be a folder that contains all the necessary components to display a zoomable image. Once created, all you have to do is upload the folder to your website and add /foldername/ basefilename.htm/ to the usual URL weblink (note that the base file name referred to here is based on the image's file name). Visitors to such pages can left mouse-click on an area of interest to zoom in and ⌥ *alt*-click to zoom out. You can mouse down and drag to scroll, or use the navigator preview to select an area of interest to scroll to. According to the current information on the site, there are no usage fees or restrictions on usage of this plug-in.

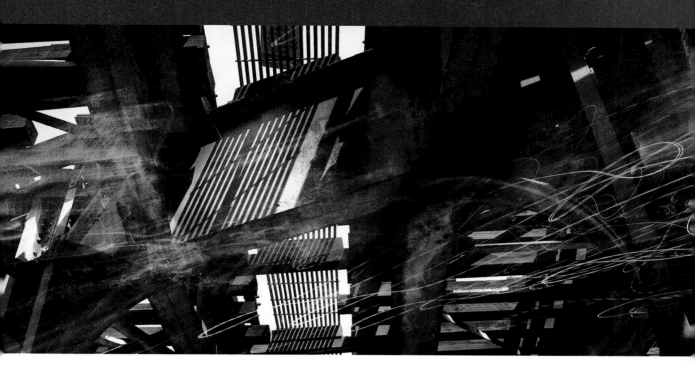

Chapter 15

Automating Photoshop

Getting to know the basics of Photoshop takes a few months, although it will take a little longer to become a fluent Photoshop user. One way you can speed up your Photoshop work is by learning how to use many of the keyboard shortcuts. There are a lot of them in the program and so it is best to learn these shortcuts a few at a time, and not try to absorb everything at once. Throughout this book I have indicated the Mac and PC key combinations for the various shortcuts that are available in Photoshop. While I have probably covered nearly all the keyboard shortcuts one might use on a regular basis, there are even more shortcuts you can learn! Most of these are listed in the Shortcuts table PDF which is on the DVD that comes with the book, which you can also print out. Or, you can go to the Keyboard Shortcuts dialog in the Photoshop Edit menu.

When you first install Photoshop you will find some actions already loaded in the Default Actions Set and you can load more by going to the Actions panel fly-out menu and clicking on one of the action sets in the list (see Figure 15.1). There are also many more Photoshop actions that are freely available on the Internet. A useful starting point is the Adobe Studio Exchange site at: http://www.adobe.com/cfusion/exchange/index.cfm This site contains a comprehensive list of actions, plug-ins and scripts, etc. and offers ready-prepared actions or sets of actions with examples of the types of effects achieved with them for you to freely download for use in Photoshop.

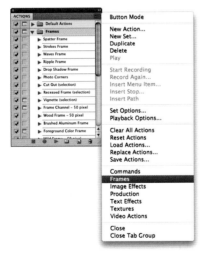

Figure 15.1 Here is the Actions panel showing the panel fly-out menu options. You can add more action sets by selecting them from the list.

Working with actions

You can record a great many operations in Photoshop using what are known as actions. Photoshop actions are application scripts that you can use to record a sequence of events carried out in Photoshop. Actions that you record while working in Photoshop can then be replayed on other images. Actions can therefore save you the bother of laboriously repeating the same steps over and over again on subsequent images, as well as enabling you to batch process several images at once. Actions are always saved within action sets and these can then be shared with other Photoshop users so they can replay the same sequence of Photoshop steps on their computers.

Playing an action

The Actions panel already contains a set of prerecorded actions called Default Actions.atn. If you go to the Actions panel fly-out menu you can load other sets from the menu list such as 'Frames' and 'Image Effects' (Figure 15.1). To test these out, open an image, select an action from the menu and press the Play button. Photoshop will then apply the recorded sequence of commands to the selected image. If the number of steps in a complex action exceeds the number of available histories, there will be no way of completely undoing all the commands when the action has completed. As a precaution, either take a Snapshot via the History panel or save the document before executing an action. If you are not happy with the result of the action, you can go back to the saved snapshot in history or revert to the last saved version. Photoshop actions are normally appended with the *.atn* file extension and saved by default to the Photoshop Actions folder, inside the Photoshop Application Presets folder, but you can store them anywhere you like. If you want to install an action you have downloaded or someone has sent to you, all you have to do is double-click it and Photoshop will automatically load the action into the Actions panel (and launch Photoshop in the process if the program is not already running at the time).

Recording actions

To record an action, open up a test image to work with. You must first create a new action set to contain the new action. Next, click on the Create new action button at the bottom of the Actions panel (Figure 15.2). This adds a new action to the set. Give the action a name and then press the Record button. At this stage you can also assign a custom keystroke using the Function keys (*F1*–*F15*) combined with the *Shift* and/or *⌘* *ctrl* keys. You can then simply use the key combination to initiate running a particular action. Now carry out the Photoshop steps you wish to record and when you are finished click the Stop recording button.

Watch out for recording commands that rely on the use of named layers or channels that may be present in your test file, as these will not be recognized when the action is applied to a new image. Also, try to make sure that your actions will not always be conditional on starting in a specific color mode, or being of a certain size. If you intend recording a complex action, the best approach is to carefully plan in advance the sequence of Photoshop steps you intend to record. A Stop can be inserted in an action and this will always open a message dialog at a certain point during playback (see Figure 15.4). It can include a memo to yourself (or another user replaying the action), reminding you of what needs to be done next at a certain stage. Or, if the action is to be used as a training aid, the message could include a teaching tip or comment.

If you want to save an action, it must be saved within a set. So if you want to separate an action to save on its own, click on the New Set button in the Actions panel to create a new set, drag the action to the new set, name the set and then choose 'Save Actions...' from the Actions panel fly-out menu (the action set must be highlighted, not the action). If you hold down the *⌘* *⌥* *ctrl* *alt* keys as you choose 'Save Actions...' this will save the text descriptions of the action steps for every Photoshop action currently in the Actions panel. The following steps show how to record a basic action.

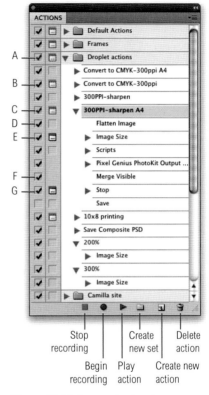

Figure 15.2 Actions panel column icons.

A: The Set contains inactive operations.
B: The action contains inactive operations.
C: Indicates the action step is active and
   contains a Stop.
D: An active operation that has a dialog box.
E: An active operation with a Pause, which will
   open a dialog box.
F: An active operation with no dialog box.
G: A Stop which will open a message dialog.

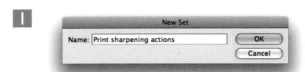

1 I wanted to offer a practical example of how to create an action, by showing how the print sharpening steps shown on pages 614–615 can be recorded as an action. The first step is to create a new action set. To do this, I clicked on the Create new set button (see Figure 15.2), named this 'Print sharpening actions' and clicked 'OK'.

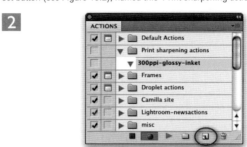

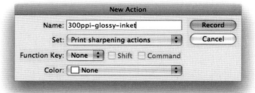

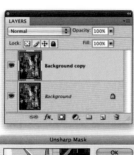

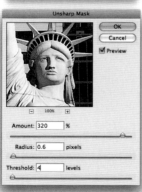

2 I then clicked on the Create new action button (circled) in the Actions panel, named this action '300ppi-glossy-inkjet' and clicked the Record button.

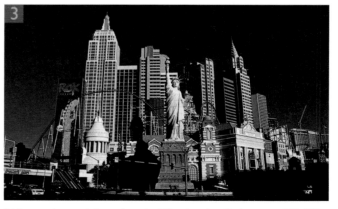

3 I then used a sample image to apply all the steps described on pages 614–615.

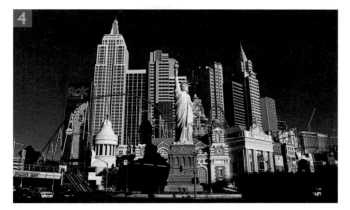

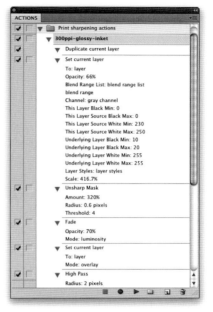

4 When I had finished recording the steps, I clicked the Stop button to complete the recording. In the Actions panel view shown on the right you can see a fully expanded list of all the steps, including the settings used. The action was now ready for testing and, once checked to be OK, could be applied to other images by clicking on the Play button, or applied as a batch action process (which I'll be discussing later).

Troubleshooting actions

Check that the image to be processed is in the correct color mode. Many actions are written to operate in RGB color mode only, so if the starting image is in CMYK, the color adjustment commands will not work properly. Quite often, assumptions may be made about the image data being flattened to a single layer. One way to prevent this from happening is to start each action by using Layer ⇨ Arrange ⇨ Send to Front, followed by a Merge Visible to layer command (⌘ ⌥ Shift E / ctrl alt Shift E). This adds a new flattened merged layer at the top of the layer stack. Some pre-written actions require that the start image fits certain criteria. For example, the Photoshop-supplied 'Text Effect' actions require that you begin with an image that contains layered text and with the text layer selected.

If you have just recorded an action and are having trouble getting it to replay, you can inspect it command by command. Open a test image and expand the Actions panel to display all the items. Hold down the ⌘ / ctrl key and click on the Play button. This will play the action one step at a time. If there is a problem, double-click the command item in the list to re-record it, then hold down the ⌘ / ctrl key again and click on the Play button to continue.

Volatile actions

One thing you have to be aware of is that although actions will remain stored in the Actions panel after you quit Photoshop, a newly installed or created action can easily become lost should you suffer a computer or program crash before you quit. Photoshop Actions will also become lost if you trash the Photoshop preferences or uninstall Photoshop. It is therefore always a good idea to take the precaution of saving any newly created or newly edited action sets so you don't lose them! These can be saved anywhere, but the Photoshop CS4/Actions/Presets folder is where they should be stored if they are to be seen at the bottom of the Actions panel fly-out menu.

Recording ruler units

For actions that involve recording the placement of objects or drawing of marquee selections, it is a good idea to record setting the ruler units as part of the action. For example, if you go to the Photoshop preferences and choose 'Units & Rulers', you can set the rulers to 'Percentage'. By doing this, all positions can be precisely recorded, measured as a percentage of the document's dimensions. When you then replay an action it can work effectively no matter what the size or proportions of an image.

Limitations when recording actions

Most Photoshop operations can be recorded within an action such as image adjustments, History panel steps, filters, and most Photoshop tool operations and tools such as the marquee and gradient fills are recorded based on the currently set ruler unit coordinates (see sidebar on 'Recording ruler units'). Avoid using commands which as yet cannot be recorded with an action. Certain operations such as brush strokes (or any of the other painting tools) cannot be recorded as this goes beyond the scope of what can be scripted in Photoshop.

Actions only record changed settings

One of the problems you commonly face when preparing and recording an action is what to do if certain settings are already as you want them to be. Actions will only record a setting as part of an action if it actually changes. So for example, you are recording an image size adjustment where you want the image resolution to end up at 300 pixels per inch, but the image is already defined in the Image Size dialog as 300 pixels per inch. In these situations, Photoshop does not record anything. To resolve these potential problems, you have to deliberately make the image size something else before you record the step, and then when you change the pixel resolution this will get recorded. In this particular example, you would go to the Image Size dialog and temporarily make the image, say, 200 pixels per inch, then record setting the resolution to 300 pixels per inch and delete the 200 pixels per inch step from the completed action.

Backgrounds and bit depth

The lack of a Background layer can also stop some actions from playing. There is not much you can do about this, other than to convert the current base layer to a Background layer by choosing Layer ⇨ New ⇨ Background from Layer before playing the action. Alternatively, you could make a flattened duplicate of the current image and then run the action. You may also want to check the bit depth of the image you are applying the action to. If the bit depth is 16-bit, not all Photoshop filters will work and you will need to convert the photograph to 8-bit per channel mode first.

Action recording tips

Action recordings should be as unambiguous as possible. For example, if you record a step in which a named layer is brought forward in the layer stack, in playback mode the action will look for a layer with that name. Therefore, when adding a layer include naming the layer as part of the action. Do not use Layer 1, Layer 2, etc. as this can only cause confusion with Photoshop's default layer naming. Also, always use the main Layer menu or Layer key command shortcuts to reorder the layer positioning. Doing this will make your action more universally recognized.

Inserting menu items

There are some things which can be added as part of a Photoshop action that can only be included by forcing the insertion of a menu item. For example, Photoshop will not record zoom tool or View menu zoom instructions. However, if you select 'Insert Menu Item' from the Actions panel fly-out menu, as you record an action, you will see the dialog in Figure 15.3. The Menu Item dialog will initially say 'None Selected', but you can now choose, say, a zoom command from the View menu and the zoom instruction will be recorded as part of the action, although frustratingly the image won't actually zoom in or out until you replay the action! I often use the 'Insert Menu Item' to record opening dialogs that I regularly access, such as the various Automated plug-ins. This saves me always having to navigate the File menu to access these specific items.

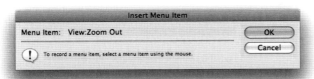

Figure 15.3 The Insert Menu Item dialog will initially say None Selected. You can then select a menu item such as Window ⇨ Arrange ⇨ Tile, and click OK. When the Action is replayed the inserted menu item will be included in the playback.

Stop and pause

When editing an action, you can insert what is known as a Stop, which will allow you to halt the action process to display an alert message. This could be a useful warning like the one shown in Figure 15.4, which could be displayed at a key point during the action playback. If you want to display a dialog setting during playback, you can insert a Pause by clicking in the blank space to the left of the action step (see Figure 15.2).

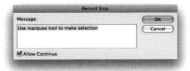

Figure 15.4 The Record Stop dialog.

Override Action 'Open' Commands

If there is a recorded 'Open' item, such as an ACR processing step in an action, checking 'Override Action "Open" Commands' will override popping the ACR dia og for each image and simply apply the ACR processing. However, if you check this and there is no open step recorded in the action, it will prevent such actions from running, so use with caution.

Batch processing actions

One of the great advantages of actions is having the ability to batch process files. The Batch dialog can be accessed via the File ⇨ Automate menu, plus it can also be accessed via the Tools ⇨ Photoshop menu in Bridge. You first need to select an action set and action from the Play section and then you'll need to set the 'Source' and 'Destination'. The 'Source' can be all currently open images, the selected images in the Bridge window, an Import source or a specific folder, in which case, you'll need to click on the Choose... button below and select a folder of images. The following items in the Source section only show if the Folder or Bridge options are selected and these basically decide how to handle files that have to be opened first before applying an action. The 'Override Action "Open" Commands' is a tricky one to understand (see sidebar), but basically, you'll want to leave this unchecked most the time. Check the 'Include All Subfolders' option only if you want to process all the subfolders within the selected folder

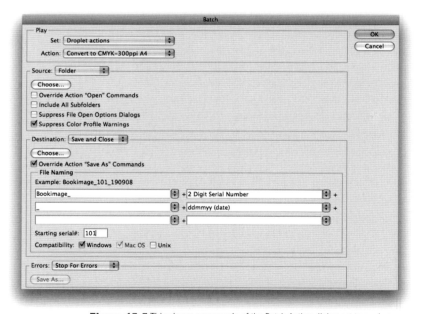

Figure 15.5 This shows an example of the Batch Action dialog set to apply a prerecorded action. The Windows box has been checked here to ensure file naming compatibility with PC systems.

and check 'Suppress File Open Options Dialogs' if you are processing a bunch of raw files and wish to override seeing the ACR dialog. Lastly, check the 'Suppress Color Profile Warnings' option to prevent the Missing Profile and Profile Mismatch dialogs appearing when you batch process images. If there is a profile mismatch, Photoshop checks what you did previously. If you previously chose to keep the image in its own profile space, then this is how the images will be batch processed. If there is no profile present, Photoshop will check to see if your previous preference was set to 'Ignore', 'Assign a profile', or 'Assign and convert to the working space', and act accordingly.

In the Destination section you have three options. If you choose 'None', Photoshop processes the selected files and leaves them open. If you choose 'Save and Close', Photoshop does just that and overwrites the originals, and if you choose 'Folder', you'll need to click on the Choose... button to select a destination folder. The action you are using for the batch process may contain a Save or Save As command that uses a specific file format and format settings, and this action step will also have recorded a Save destination. Now it might so happen that the Save destination is an important part of the action, but if the destination folder no longer exists, the action will fail to work (besides, you can specify a destination folder within the Batch dialog). So in the majority of instances, if the action contains a Save instruction, I recommend you check the Override Action 'Save As' Commands checkbox. And if the action does not contain a Save or Save As command, leave it unchecked.

If a folder is selected as the destination, you have six editable fields at your disposal. You can use any combination you like, but if you select a custom file extension option, this must always go at the end. As you edit the fields, you will see an example of how the naming will work on a nominal image called *MyFile. gif*. The file naming options let you define the precise naming and numbering structure of the batch processed files; Figure 15.6 shows the complete list of naming and numbering options.

Customized file naming

It is easy to customize the File Naming with your own fields. In Figure 15.5, I created a batch process where the images were renamed 'Bookimage_' followed by a two digit serial number, followed by an underscore '_' and the date expressed as: day; month; and year. Note that the numbering was set to start at '101'. So in this example the file name structure would be something like: Bookimage_101_230208.

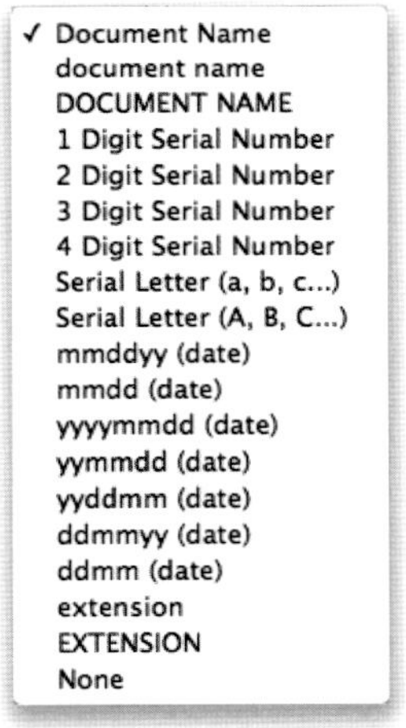

Figure 15.6 The Batch interface naming and numbering options.

Error handling

If 'Stop For Errors' is selected this will halt the batch processing in Photoshop every time an action trips up over a file for whatever reason. You can prevent this by selecting the 'Log Errors to File' option instead. This allows the batch processing to complete, but creates a log report of the files that failed to process.

Cross-platform droplets

You can name a droplet anything you like, but to be PC compatible you should add a .exe extension. If someone sends you a droplet that was created using a PC, it can be made Mac compatible by dragging it over once to the Photoshop application icon.

Creating a droplet

A Photoshop action can also be converted into a self-contained batch processing application, known as a droplet. When you drag a document or a folder on top of a droplet icon it will launch Photoshop (if the program is not already running) and initiate the action sequence contained in the droplet. The beauty of droplets is that you only need to configure the batch processing settings once and they are then locked into the droplet. Droplets can be stored anywhere you like, although it makes sense to have them readily accessible such as via a folder on the desktop (Figure 15.7).

To make a droplet, go to the File ⇨ Automate menu and choose 'Create Droplet...'. Figure 15.8 shows the Create Droplet interface (the 'Create Droplet' options are identical to those found in the Batch Actions dialog). Choose a location to save the droplet to and choose a destination folder for the droplet processed files. When you are done, click 'OK'. Droplets can play a useful role in any production workflow. They are effectively self-contained Photoshop batch processing routines and I have got into the habit of keeping a folder located on the desktop specifically designed to contain Photoshop droplets and their associated destination folders.

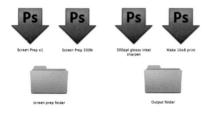

Figure 15.7 When you drag and drop an image file on top of a droplet, this will launch Photoshop and perform a single or batch processing operation within the program. Droplets can perform Save and Close operations or save the processed results to an accompanying folder.

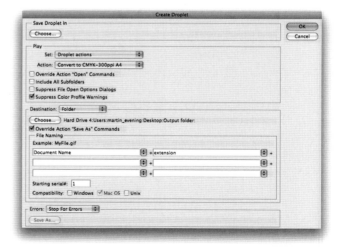

Figure 15.8 The Create Droplet dialog.

Image Processor

The Image Processor is located in the File ⇨ Scripts menu in Photoshop and can also be accessed via the Tools ⇨ Photoshop menu in Bridge. The Image Processor is a fine example of what Scripts can do when they are presented via an easy-to-use interface. The Image Processor basically allows you to select a folder of images (or use all open images) to process and select a location to save the processed files to. The Image Processor can then be configured to run a Photoshop action (if required) and save the processed files using either the JPEG, PSD or TIFF file formats. However, it will also allow you to simultaneously process and save the files to more than one format at a time. This is very handy if you wish to produce, say, a TIFF version at high resolution and a JPEG version ready to place in a web page design.

When you are preparing images that are destined to be shared by email or published via the Web, the Image Processor is a handy tool to use because you can not only resize the images as part of the image processing, but you can instruct the Image Processor to convert the image from its current profile space to sRGB, which is an ideal RGB space for general purpose web viewing.

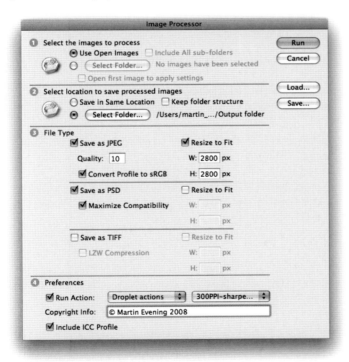

Figure 15.9 The Image Processor (formerly known as Dr. Russell Brown's Image Processor). This Scripting dialog can be configured to process single or multiple images, applying a Photoshop action, with the ability to add copyright info and save the files to a designated folder location in one or more of the following file formats: JPEG, PSD or TIFF. The destination folder will contain the processed images and these will be separated into folders named according to the file format used. Once configured, you can click on the Save... button to save the settings and load them again at a future date.

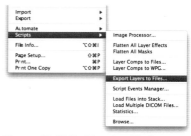

Figure 15.10 The Photoshop CS4 Scripts menu.

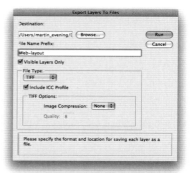

Figure 15.11 An example of the Export Layers to Files... script dialog.

Scripting

One of the most neglected aspects of Photoshop has been the ability to write scripts to automate the program. Scripts can do more than you can with actions alone, although for most of us the prospect of writing scripts is quite scary, and I freely confess I am one of those who has looked at the scripting manuals and simply shuddered at the prospect of learning such computer programming. Steps have been taken though to make this more accessible to the general user. You can start by referring to the Photoshop Scripting Guide and other PDF documents about scripting that can all be found in the Photoshop CS4/Scripting Guide folder. You can also download pre-made scripts from the Adobe Studio Exchange website: http://www.adobe.com/cfusion/exchange/index.cfm

To start with, go to the Scripts menu in the Photoshop File menu (Figure 15.10). There are a few sample Scripts here to experiment with, and among these is a script called 'Export Layers to Files' (Figure 15.11), which can be used to generate separate file documents from a multi-layered image.

Script Event Manager

The Script Event Manager can be configured to trigger a Javascript or an action in Photoshop whenever a particular operation is performed. Figure 15.12 shows a simple example of what can be done using scripting.

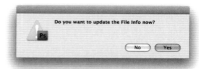

Figure 15.12 The Script Event Manager is located in the File ⇨ Scripts menu. The dialog shown here has been configured to trigger popping the File Info dialog whenever a document is saved.

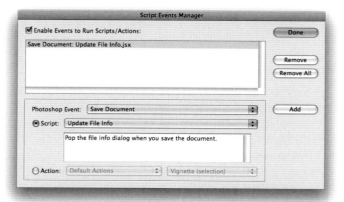

Automated plug-ins

The Automation features described on this page are examples of Automated plug-ins. What distinguishes these from normal plug-ins is that they enable Photoshop to perform a complex set of procedures based on simple user input. Some Automated plug-ins are like 'wizards' that feature a step-by-step interface to guide you through various options and help you produce the desired result. Adobe has made Automated plug-ins 'open source', which means it is possible for third-party developers to have the means to build their own Automated plug-ins for Photoshop. I believe that Pixel Genius (of which I am a co-founder) is so far the only company who has made use of this feature in Photoshop to produce the PhotoKit, PhotoKit Sharpener and PhotoKit Color Automated plug-ins.

Crop and Straighten Photos

This Automated plug-in is very straightforward to use, if you have scanned images that need to be rotated and cropped. Gang up several images on your scanner, scan the pictures in as one image and choose 'Crop and Straighten Photos' from the Automate submenu (note: this option is not available in Bridge). Photoshop then creates a rotated and cropped copy version of each picture (Figure 15.13). It kind of works, but only if the background has an absolutely solid color. 'Crop and Straighten' therefore works best when processing scans of chrome transparencies where the border is a deep black; it sometimes helps if you make a selection around an individual image first.

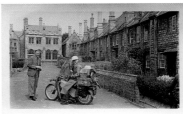

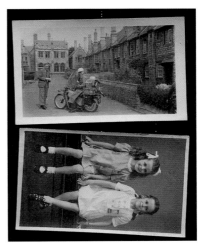

Figure 15.13 The Crop and Straighten Photos plug-in can be used to extract scanned photos that need to be rotated and cropped.

Fit Image

'Fit Image...' is a very simple Automated plug-in that bypasses the Image ⇨ Image Size menu item (Figure 15.14). It is well suited for the preparation of screen-based design work. Enter the pixel dimensions you want the image to fit to, by specifying the maximum pixel width or height. Note that if you enter the same pixel dimensions for the width and height, 'Fit Image' can be used to batch process landscape and portrait format images simultaneously.

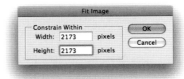

Figure 15.14 The Fit Image dialog.

How To help files

It is all very well having books like mine to help you understand the program, but there are times when you want quick answers and solutions without having to flick through manuals. The Help menu contains a list of 'How To' items and these cover a variety of subjects, from how to fix and enhance photos to working with 3D images.

The 'How To' format can also be adapted and used by anyone who wishes to write and publish their own 'How To' help files. These can be shared or published in the same way actions and other Photoshop settings can be distributed between fellow users. For example, the 'How To' shown in Figure 15.15 below was created by Rod Wynne-Powell, who is the technical editor of this book.

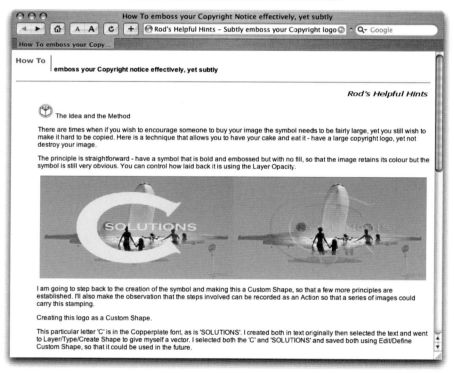

Figure 15.15 This 'How To' shows how to add a copyright symbol to an image, and was created by Rod Wynne-Powell.

Adobe™ Configurator application

This is not something you will find in Photoshop CS4, but is a small application that you will be able to download separately for free via the Adobe Labs website at http://labs.adobe.com (Figure 15.16). This was a pet project of Project manager John Nack, who introduced this as an antidote to all those customers who wished Photoshop could be made less complicated to work with. Basically, you can use the Configurator interface shown in Figure 15.17 to drag and drop select tools and menu commands to the workspace area and design your own panel of favorite tools and commands. Once you are happy with your selection of Configurator components, you can choose File ⇨ Export to export this as a new panel. To load the exported panel, go to the Window menu ⇨ Extensions submenu in Photoshop.

Configurator-1.air

Figure 15.16 The Configurator application can be accessed free via the Adobe Labs website: http://labs.adobe.com/.

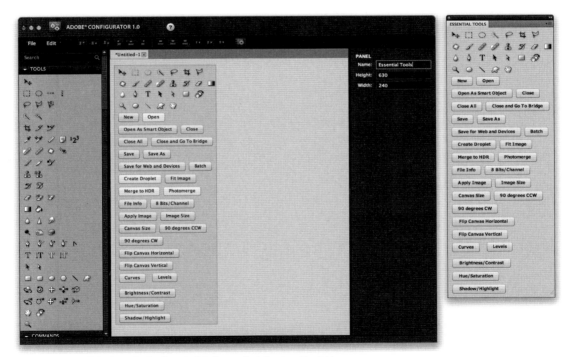

Figure 15.17 This shows the Configurator interface on the left and, on the right, how the exported panel looked when viewed in Photoshop.

Index

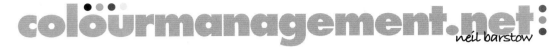

676

Pixel Genius PhotoKit plug-in
www.pixelgenius.com

PhotoKit
Analog Effects for Photoshop

This Photoshop compatible plug-in is designed to provide photographers
with accurate digital replications of common analog photographic effects.
PhotoKit is quick and simple and allows for a greatly enhanced workflow.
Priced at $49.95.

PhotoKit SHARPENER
A complete Sharpening Workflow for Photoshop

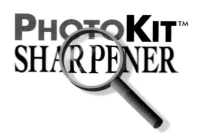

Other products may provide useful sharpening tools, but only PhotoKit
SHARPENER provides a complete image 'Sharpening Workflow'.
From capture to output, PhotoKit SHARPENER intelligently produces
the optimum sharpness on any image, from any source, reproduced on
any output device. But PhotoKit SHARPENER also provides the creative
controls to address the requirements of individual images and the
individual tastes of users. PhotoKit SHARPENER is priced at $99.95.

PhotoKit Color
Creative color effects for Photoshop

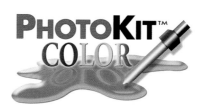

PhotoKit Color applies precise color corrections, automatic color
balancing and creative coloring effects. This plug-in also provides a
comprehensive suite of effects that lets you recreate creative effects like
black and white split toning and cross-processing.
PhotoKit Color is priced at $99.95.

Pixel Genius is offering a 10% discount on any whole order, which must
be placed from the Pixel Genius store at: www.pixelgenius.com. This is
a one-time discount per email address for any order made from Pixel
Genius. This coupon will not work on affiliate sites. Also it cannot be
combined with other discounts or programs except for certain cross-sell
items. Please note that this coupon will expire upon next revision of
Adobe Photoshop for Photographers.

Coupon ID: PSFPCS4ME

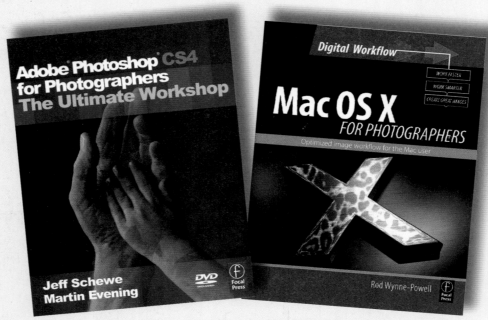

Adobe Photoshop CS4 for Photographers: The Ultimate Workshop

By Martin Evening and Jeff Schewe

- Become a Photoshop master with teaching from the dream team of professional photographers, Martin Evening and Jeff Schewe
- Follow the professional workflow of two Photoshop gurus
- The only Photoshop book for the advanced user who wants to really push the limits of CS4

Professional commercial photographer and digital imager Jeff Schewe has teamed up with best-selling Photoshop author Martin Evening to provide advanced Photoshop users with this goldmine of professional advice and techniques.

Building on Martin Evening's successful Adobe Photoshop for Photographers series of titles, this new guide takes Photoshop users to further depths exploring the power of Photoshop CS4. Highly visual, with clear, step-by-step tutorials, this advanced guide will appeal to Photographers looking for unmatched results in Photoshop.

Mac OSX for Photographers

By Rod Wynne-Powell

If you're a photographer using a Mac – and why wouldn't you be – then you need this book.

Macs are still the hardware of choice for the cream of digital imaging experts – over two million registered Mac users of Adobe Photoshop can't be wrong. Let the expert advice of Rod Wynne-Powell help you to:

- Configure your Mac for a trouble-free life from capture to output
- Speed up your photography workflow using Photoshop, Bridge and the rest of the Adobe Creative Suite
- Optimize your color management system and ensure the highest quality image results
- Save time through effective storage and retrieval of images

Years of experience dealing with digital image makers' queries on a day-to-day basis means he also knows that problems can and do happen – even on a Mac – so this book is also packed full of vital troubleshooting advice and ways to avoid the pitfalls in the first place.

The only Mac OS X book written specifically for photographers, this unique guide to troubleshooting and working with digital images on a Mac is fully updated for the Leopard release of OS X.